Interest and emotion

This book is published as part of the joint publishing agreement established in 1977 between the Fondation de la Maison des Sciences de l'Homme and the Press Syndicate of the University of Cambridge. Titles published under this arrangement may appear in any European language or, in the case of volumes of collected essays, in several languages.

New books will appear either as individual titles or in one of the series which the Maison des Sciences de l'Homme and the Cambridge University Press have jointly agreed to publish. All books published jointly by the Maison des Sciences de l'Homme and the Cambridge University Press will be distributed by the Press throughout the world.

Cet ouvrage est publié dans le cadre de l'accord de co-édition passé en 1977 entre la Fondation de la Maison des Sciences de l'Homme et le Press Syndicate of the University of Cambridge. Toutes les langues européennes sont admises pour les titres couverts par cet accord, et les ouvrages collectifs peuvent paraître en plusieurs langues.

Les ouvrages paraissent soit isolément, soit dans l'une des séries que la Maison des Sciences de l'Homme et Cambridge University Press ont convenu de publier ensemble. La distribution dans le monde entier des titres ainsi publiés conjointement par les deux établissements est assurée par Cambridge University Press.

Interest and emotion

Essays on the study of family and kinship

Edited by
HANS MEDICK
DAVID WARREN SABEAN

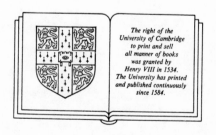

The right of the
University of Cambridge
to print and sell
all manner of books
was granted by
Henry VIII in 1534.
The University has printed
and published continuously
since 1584.

CAMBRIDGE UNIVERSITY PRESS

Cambridge
New York   New Rochelle   Melbourne   Sydney

EDITIONS DE LA MAISON DES SCIENCES DE L'HOMME

Paris

Published by the Press Syndicate of the University of Cambridge
The Pitt Building, Trumpington Street, Cambridge CB2 1RP
32 East 57th Street, New York, NY 10022, USA
10 Stamford Road, Oakleigh, Melbourne 3166, Australia
and Editions de la Maison des Sciences de l'Homme
54 Boulevard Raspail, 75270 Paris Cedex 06

© Maison des Sciences de l'Homme and Cambridge University Press 1984

First published 1984
Reprinted 1986
First paperback edition 1988

Printed in Canada

Library of Congress catalogue card number: 83-14371

British Library Cataloguing in Publication Data

Interest and emotion.

1. Family
I. Medick, Hans   II. Sabean, David Warren
306.8'5   HQ728
ISBN 0 521 24969 4 hard covers
ISBN 2 7351 0063 4 (France only, hard covers)
ISBN 0 521 35763 2 paperback
ISBN 2 7351 0241 6 (France only, paperback)

Contents

Contributors

ALAIN COLLOMP (1936) studied medicine in Paris and wrote his doctoral dissertation in medicine on the poet and playwright, Antonin Artaud, in 1963. Since then he has practised medicine in Paris and Nanterre. Beginning in 1970, he studied history at the Ecole des Hautes Etudes en Sciences Sociales, centring his interests on the history of the family. He has had numerous publications in the *Annales ESC*, *Ethnologie française*, and *L'Homme*. He will soon publish a work of historical anthropology on a group of villages in the Haute-Provence in the seventeenth and eighteenth centuries: *La Maison du Père* (Presses Universitaires de France, 1983).

ESTHER GOODY (1932) received her PhD in Social Anthropology from the University of Cambridge in 1961. She is currently Lecturer in Social Anthropology at Cambridge and Fellow of New Hall. Her books include *Contexts of Kinship* (Cambridge, 1973) and *Parenthood and Social Reproduction* (Cambridge, 1982). She has also edited *Questions and Politeness* (Cambridge, 1978) and *From Craft to Industry* (forthcoming, Cambridge University Press). She is currently interested in the problem of the relationship between systems of production and roles of authority, the relations of production in domestic groups, and the implications of technology for the division of labour.

HERBERT G. GUTMAN (1928) received his PhD from the University of Wisconsin in 1959. He taught at the University of Rochester, the State University of New York at Buffalo, and the City College of New York. He is currently Distinguished Professor at the Graduate School of the City University of New York. His publications include: *The Black Family in Slavery and Freedom 1750–1925* (Oxford, 1976), *Work, Culture and Society in Industrializing America* (New York, 1977), *Slavery and the Numbers Game: A Critique of Time on the Cross* (Champaign, Ill. 1975). During 1982–3 he held a chair in American Civilization at the Ecole des Hautes Etudes en Sciences Sociales in Paris. He is presently engaged in a study of the relationships between class, immigration, and race in nineteenth-century America.

KARIN HAUSEN (1938) received her doctorate from the Freie Universität Berlin in 1969. She has taught at the Freie Universität and is presently Professor of Economic and Social History at the Technische Universität Berlin. Her publications include: *Deutsche Kolonialherrschaft in Afrika. Wirtschaftsinteressen und Kolonialverwaltung in Kamerun vor 1914* (Zürich/Freiburg, 1970), with H.G. Haupt (eds.) *Die Pariser Kommune von 1871* (Frankfurt, 1979), 'Die Polarisierung der "Geschlechtscharaktere" – Eine Spiegelung der Dissoziation von Erwerbs-und Familienleben', in W. Conze (ed.) *Sozialgeschichte der Familie in der Neuzeit Europas. Neue Forschungen* (Stuttgart, 1976), 'Technische Fortschritte und Frauenarbeit. Zur Sozialgeschichte der Nähmaschine', in *Geschichte und Gesellschaft*, 4 (1978). Her current research interests are on the household and family in the nineteenth and twentieth centuries.

VANESSA MAHER (1947) received her PhD from Cambridge in 1973. She is at present Professore Associato in Cultural Anthropology at the University of Turin, Italy. She has published *Women and Property in Morocco: Their Changing Relation to the Process of Social Stratification in the Middle Atlas* (Cambridge, 1974) and several articles on Morocco exploring the ways in which women experiences are constrained by and act upon their social, economic, and political environments. She was co-editor of a volume of *Quaderni storici*, 44, (1980) on child-birth and maternity. At present she is engaged in research on seamstresses and dressmakers in Turin 1930–55. She also has an interest in ritual and symbolism in relation to the 'construction of gender' and the impact of missionary activity on this field.

HANS MEDICK (1939) received his doctorate from the University of Erlangen-Nürnberg in 1971. He is presently a Research Fellow at the Max-Planck-Institut für Geschichte at Göttingen and has held visiting appointments at the Universität Hannover and in the Department of History, The Johns Hopkins University. His publications include: *Naturzustand und Naturgeschichte der bürgerlichen Gesellschaft* (1973, 2nd edn Göttingen, 1981), 'The Proto-Industrial Family Economy: The Structural Function of Household and Family during the Transition from Peasant Society to Industrial Capitalism', *Social History*, 1 (Oct. 1976), together with Peter Kriedte and Jürgen Schlumbohm, *Industrialization before Industrialization: Rural Industry in the Genesis of Capitalism* (Cambridge/Paris, 1981), 'Plebejische Kultur, plebejische Öffentlichkeit, plebejische Ökonomie. Über Erfahrungen und Verhaltensweisen Besitzarmer und Besitzloser in der Ubergangsphase zum Kapitalismus', in R. Berdahl, *et al.* (eds.), *Klassen und Kultur. Sozialanthropologische Perspektiven in der G · schichtsschreibung* (Frankfurt, 1982). He is at present engaged in a study on the economy and culture of everyday life in a South German weavers' village from the seventeenth to nineteenth centuries and is interested in problems of anthropology and history as they relate to plebeian life in the transition towards capitalism.

DAVID WARREN SABEAN (1939) received his PhD from the University of Wisconsin in 1969. He has taught at the University of East Anglia and the University of Pittsburgh. He is presently a Research Fellow of the Max-Planck-Institut für Geschichte. His publications include: *Landbesitz und Gesellschaft am Vorabend des Bauernkriegs* (Stuttgart, 1972), 'Communal Basis of Pre-1800 Peasant Uprisings in Western Europe', *Comparative Politics* 8 (1976), 'Aspects of Kinship Behaviour and Property in Rural Western Europe before 1800', in Jack Goody, *et al.* (eds.), *Family and Inheritance: Rural Society in Western Europe, 1200–1800* (Cambridge, 1976), 'Unehelichkeit: ein Aspekt sozialer Reproduktion kleinbäuerlicher Produzenten', in Robert Berdahl, *et al.* (eds.), *Klassen und Kultur* (Frankfurt, 1982). He is also co-editor of *Political Symbolism in Modern Europe* (New Brunswick, NJ, 1982). He is at present writing a volume on kinship and the family in a German village from 1700 to 1870 and a group of essays on the peasant concept of the person and community in the early modern period.

ROGER SABLONIER (1941) attained the degree Dr phil.habil. in 1977 at the Universität Zürich, where he is presently Professor. His publications include: *Krieg und Kriegertum in der Crònica des Ramòn Mutaner* (Bern/Frankfurt, 1971), *Adel im Wandel: Eine Untersuchung zur sozialen Situation des Ostschweizerischen Adels um 1300* (Göttingen, 1979). His present interests include: rural society in the high and late Middle Ages, family in the Middle Ages, and medieval material culture.

KAREN SACKS (1941) received her PhD from the University of Michigan in 1971. She is currently Director of Research and Information of the Business and Professional Women's Foundation in Washington DC. Her publications include: *Sisters and Wives: The Past and the Future of Sexual Equality* (Westport, Conn., 1979). Her current research is on women workers and family and kinship.

REGINA SCHULTE (1949) received her Dr phil. from the Universität München in 1979. At present she is an Associate of the German Historical Institute in London. Her publications include: *Sperrbezirke. Tugendhaftigkeit und Prostitution in der bürgerlichen Welt* (Frankfurt, 1979), 'Dienstmädchen im herrschaftlichen Haushalt. Zur Genese ihrer Sozialpsychologie', *Zeitschrift für bayerische Landesgeschichte*, 41 (1978), 'Die Kindsmörderin Anna H. Eine Fallgeschichte aus dem bayerischen Dorfalltag im 19.Jahrhundert', *Journal für Geschichte*, 5 (1981). At present her research includes work on female servants and on criminality in nineteenth-century rural Bavaria. She is also engaged in a comparative project dealing with village society in Sussex and Upper Bavaria from 1750 to 1914.

MARTINE SEGALEN (1940) earned the degree doctorat de 3e cycle in sociology at the Sorbonne in 1970. She is presently a director of research at the CNRS, Centre d'Ethnologie Française, Paris. Her publications include: *Mari et femme dans la société paysanne* (Paris, 1980), *Amours et mariages de l'ancienne France* (Paris,

1981), and *Sociologie de la famille* (Paris, 1981). She is presently engaged on research on kinship and marriage in the Pays Bigouden.

GERALD M. SIDER (1938) received the PhD degree in 1971 from the New School for Social Research. He is Associate Professor for Anthropology at the College of Staten Island of the City University of New York. His publications include: 'Christmas Mumming and the New Year in Outport Newfoundland', *Past and Present*, 71 (1976), 'The Ties that Bind: Culture and Agriculture, Property and Propriety in the Newfoundland Village Fishery', *Social History*, 5 (1980), 'Lumbee Indian Cultural Nationalism and Ethnogenesis', *Dialectical Anthropology*, 1 (1976), 'The Qualms of the Heart: The Logic of Archaic Agriculture, the Status of Women, and the Reproduction of Inequality in the Ancient Near East' (forthcoming). His present research interests are: class and culture in North Atlantic maritime communities, Native North America, and state formation.

ANDREW STRATHERN (1939) received his PhD from Cambridge in 1966. He is presently Professor of Anthropology, University College London, and Director of the Institute of Papua New Guinea Studies, Port Moresby. His publications include: *The Rope of Moka* (Cambridge, 1971), *Self-Decoration in Mount Hagen* (with Marilyn Strathern) (Toronto, 1971), *One Father, One Blood* (London, 1972), *Ongka* (London, 1979). Current research interests are: social change, culture and development, and semantic anthropology.

LOUISE A. TILLY (1930) received her PhD from the University of Toronto in 1974. She is presently Professor at the University of Michigan. She has published (with Joan Scott) *Women, Work and Family* (New York, 1978) and 'Paths of Proletarianization: Organization of Production, Sexual Division of Labour, and Women's Collective Action', *Signs: Journal of Women in Culture and Society*, 7 (1981). With Charles Tilly, she has edited *Class Conflict and Collective Action* (Beverly Hills, 1981). She has prepared with Kathryn Tilly an edited version in translation of *Mémé santerre* (forthcoming, Schocken). Her present research interests are: labour force formation and working class politics in Milan, 1880–1900, and a comparative history of the movement for reform and legislation on maternal and infant health in Britain, USA, France, and Italy from 1800 to 1930.

BERNARD VERNIER (1940) earned the degree doctorat de 3e cycle in sociology at the Université Réné Descartes (Sorbonne) in 1977. He was Assistant in sociology at the Université de Dijon from 1969 and Chargé de Conférences Complémentaires at the Ecole des Hautes Etudes en Sciences Sociales from 1979. His publications include: 'Les Paysans de la rive orientale du bas Nestos' (with P.Y. Pechoux), *The Greek Review of Social Research* (1969), 'Emigration et déréglement du marché matrimonial', *Actes de la recherche en sciences sociales*, 15 (1977), 'Représentation mythique du monde et domination masculine', *The Greek Review of Social Research* (1981). A book on Karpathos will appear soon. Current research is centred on ethnology and sociology of the family.

Preface

The papers in this volume were originally discussed at a Round Table between anthropologists and historians in Paris in June 1980. An earlier meeting on the subject of 'working processes' took place in Göttingen in June 1978, and some of those papers have been published in Robert Berdahl, *et al.* (eds.), *Klassen und Kultur. Sozialanthropologische Perspektiven in der Geschichtsschreibung* (Frankfurt, 1982). For both meetings and the production of books, the editors of this volume have cooperated closely with Robert Berdahl, Alf Lüdtke, and Gerald Sider. Our discussions would not have been possible without the institutional base of the Max-Planck-Institut für Geschichte in Göttingen and the active support of its director, Professor Rudolf Vierhaus. Over the years, we have also enjoyed close contacts with the Maison des Sciences de l'Homme in Paris, whose director Clemens Heller has helped establish a fruitful international discourse. Our meeting in Paris was made possible by the joint support of the two institutions. Many of our ideas have been tried out first in discussion with Jack Goody, who has always been a close and helpful friend. During the preparation for the second Round Table, we were able to profit from the advice of Maurice Aymard. Without his help, the meeting could not have gone so smoothly. The essays in this volume by Collomp, Hausen, Sablonier, Segalen, Schulte, and Vernier were translated by J.C. Whitehouse and that by Medick by David Sabean. Stefan Mielke produced the artwork. We wish to thank Maria Pinkert, Brigitte Bartels, and Anita Kulp for the difficult job of typing the manuscripts and revisions over and over in various languages. While this book was in preparation, a version of the essay by Vernier appeared in the *Actes de la recherche en sciences sociales* (Jan. 1980); that by Collomp in the *Annales ESC*, 36 (1981). An earlier version of the joint paper by Medick and Sabean appeared in *Peasant Studies*, 8 (1979).

Göttingen, October 1982

H.M.
D.W.S.

xi

Introduction

HANS MEDICK and DAVID WARREN SABEAN

In recent years, social historians have been calling into question many aspects of their practice. They are no longer sure in what way the story which they relate is part of a larger story of political change, the struggle for power, and the analysis of the forces of domination.[1] There is a tendency on the part of some of the profession to regard structures, especially those amenable to statistical abstraction, as the proper object of investigation, whilst others centre their interest on an analysis of agency.[2] In the debate many assumptions of an earlier tacit synthesis are being put into question, and one of the insights which is most rapidly spreading waves through the discipline is that the 'progress' and institutional growth in Western industrial lands did not happen without enormous cost to those parts of the world which did not 'share' in that progress.[3] Faith in the need and indeed the possibility for others to tread the same path has been shaken. This changed orientation, furthermore, made it possible to see that the *internal* costs might also have been other than one thought. An interest arose in historical 'losers' or in non-establishment views of the processes of change – history from the 'bottom up'.[4] One began to confront the 'other' not just in the primitive but inside our own history. Besides the problem of how this new 'object' was to fit into a social history which was not depoliticized, the debates over structure and agency revealed the problem of whether and how the object of investigation might be reconstituted as a historical subject.[5] Central problems of the old hermeneutical discussion of how to deal with subjective experience and find meaning in texts flooded back, but under a radically altered awareness on the part of historians. The cultural unity and continuity of experience which were assumed in the older hermeneutic tradition as a precondition for understanding could no longer be taken for granted.

The eye of the ethnographer, trained in the participant observation of societies other than his own, often proved to be more helpful for the historian in search of his new subject than the standard procedures of a discipline whose principal goal was believed to be the appropriation (however critical it might be) of an existent tradition, shared by the historian and his object alike. Historians, as a result,

1

have begun to talk to anthropologists with an intensity not found since the turn of the century, when hermeneutic questions were likewise at the centre of the discipline. In more than one way the historian's object has thus become like the anthropologist's subject, and historians have begun to change as well.[6]

Just when historians are turning to anthropology for help, quite ironically the latter are undergoing an internal turmoil of their own, and, if not exactly getting from historians what they need to refashion their craft, they are at many points concerned with developing their own historical practice.[7] To a large extent, attention to new problems has been occasioned by transformations in so-called 'primitive' societies under the impact of world capitalism, state formation, and the new international division of labour. Transformations of this magnitude broke into the atemporal syntheses of structural-functionalism with force. On the one hand, the notion of the 'timeless primitive' itself disappeared as it was discovered that even his society was constituted in the processes which transformed the world over the last several centuries. The traditional 'cult units' of anthropology in the form of cultural and social isolates were radically put into question.[8] Such societies arose and differentiated in the course of the expansion of commerce and capitalism. On the other hand, structure itself has been called into question and within the image of a never-ceasing reconstitution of society, much discussion has come to focus around the categories of 'practice' and 'strategy' as more satisfactory analytical ones for describing action than such notions as 'moral community' or institutionalized value systems embedded in kinship.[9] There is, however, the danger in this approach of dissolving 'strategy' into 'manipulation' and seeing action as grounded in generalized needs which escape being constituted by society. It is here that the hermeneutic problem creeps back in as the acknowledgement of 'otherness' disappears in a model of action based on ideologized assumptions of Western individualism. The problem of the connection between subjective experience and strategy on the one hand and objective structures on the other, between practice and the social consti-tution of values, perceptions and meanings, between individual and institution, has been caught up in issues of class formation, the dialectic of historical change, processes of transformation, and forces of social reproduction. The 'crisis' of anthropology throws its practitioner into historical practice willy-nilly.

In this conjuncture of the new social history and social anthropology, the possibility for a fruitful dialogue between the two disciplines has arisen. For both of them it is time to go beyond a sharp dichotomy opposing objective, material, structural, or institutional factors to subjective, cultural, symbolic, or emotional ones. One can no longer proceed from the hermeneutical concept of the individual as the main agent in the production and attribution of meaning. If 'meaning' takes on new interest, it is meaning publicly assigned – meaning in the interplay of social relations. But that does not imply that the social constitution of the individual is to be seen as prescriptive or static. To argue that the individual is socially constituted is to suggest that this happens inside the contradictions, disjunctions, and conflicts of society. Public understanding is only possible inside class constituted, contradiction-ridden, jarring processes. If the subject comes back to the centre of the stage, he does so within this context of the production of meaning – the complex process of selecting from the shared pool of connotations, values, and symbols available in a culture. This process, however, does not take place on neutral ground nor with equal ability or chances. It is composed of the constant exchange of and struggle for meaning within contexts of reciprocity, dependence, and resistance.[10]

The conference at which the essays in this volume were discussed explored some of the issues arising from this convergence of social history and anthropology by dealing with a limited subject, which it took from the central terrain of both disciplines. The family has long been under discussion by anthropologists, although pushed a bit to the side in the last several years by interest in the new problems, but only brought into discussion by social historians in the process of the renovation of their discipline. Our entry into the issues used as a vehicle a consideration of the way 'emotions' and 'material interests' are treated, and we offered a discussion paper, which appears in this volume in revised form.

Our argument began with the historian's hermeneutic problem. It was suggested that the subjective emotional life of others is not open to the observer for inspection. 'Meaning' is not what we search for but the 'meaning of meaning', or, otherwise put, the expression of emotion as a 'grammar' or symbolic system of social relationships. Emotions are socially constituted and are not only the expression of experience but also the determinants of experience and practice.[11] It often seems as if historians carry around a field bag of emotions – the archeological artifacts of their investigations – from which they can pull out items to tag with stickers, such as 'mother, 1720, Languedoc' or 'male child, handloom weaving family, 1816, Swabian Alp'. To reexamine the issues, it was suggested first that language, itself socially constituted, often misleads the researcher into exchanging the subject's own label for the 'real thing', and second that strategies for analysing family dynamics were necessary to embed the analysis of emotional expression into a set of social practices. Therefore we introduced the historians to anthropological notions of rights and duties, claim and obligation.

One of the most intractable problems in this regard is the tendency to think in terms of 'hard' and 'soft' alternatives, of action and motivation determined by interest on the one hand and emotion or moral value on the other. Historians sometimes string psychological motivations together as a continuum between these two poles. Classes and epochs can be suitably identified along the string, and, what is more, Western history, as far as the family is concerned, has been seen to move along the string from hard to soft. We argued that both emotions and material interests are socially constituted and that they arise from the same matrix. The problem is to embed them in property relations, working processes, and the structures of domination. Property too should not be reified but understood as a relationship structured by and structuring emotions and needs. As a strategy for analysing the social matrix, we offered the notion of 'mediation' and discussed one form of family rituals of mediation – perhaps the central one – namely, food preparation and meals.

As for anthropologists, their problem – assessing meaning and action within ongoing process – sometimes resolves itself into alternatives of 'social reproduction' or 'transformation'. Either the individual is bound by processes of social control, domination, or socialization such that social structures are maintained or are only slowly subject to change, or breaks occur because of exogenous influences, setting the individual free from inherited values, institutions, and structures. However, this way of breaking process up creates serious problems. Anthropologists are discovering that history is not just something imposed on native populations from the outside, solely by their integration into the 'modern world system', but is also an essential feature of native peoples' own creative efforts within the contexts, contradictions, and conflicts of their own cultures and societies. We engaged the anthropologists on issues that arise from dealing with structures and institutions in change and illustrated the problem with a number of strategies for analysing the family as a matrix of class relationships. The problem from one view is to see how, within moving contexts, emotions are constantly mapped onto new terrains, and with the changes of position, reorder and restructure experience and meaning.

Bernard Vernier takes up several of these issues in a case study of inheritance and social reproduction on the Greek island of Karpathos. He shows how the dynamics of property are closely linked to the web of social relations, how family mediates class relations, and how calculation and sentiment grow from the same matrix. He introduces and expands Bourdieu's concept of 'symbolic capital' in an effort to solve the problem of the dichotomy of property and emotion.

The ideology of Western social science has often made a rough division between male and female along the lines of interest and emotion. The bond between mother and child is taken as quintessentially emotional and non-interested, something belonging rather to nature than to culture. (How this integrative, spontaneous tie is symbolized, used, and exploited in family relations and beyond, and – being marketed as a commodity – serves material interests well outside the bonds which it means to affirm, is shown in the essay by Karin Hausen.) Regina Schulte discusses the mother/child nexus in an extreme situation. She shows in her analysis of infanticide among propertyless rural servants in late nineteenth-century Bavaria how sexual relations, birth, and attachment to the new born child were all dependent upon and embedded in work processes and class relationships. Vanessa Maher argues that rural women in Morocco take radically different attitudes towards male and female children and that this in turn is part of a process of alienation rooted in the contradiction opening up between their own access to property and the way in which their bodies and reproductive and productive capacities are subsumed under the property rights of their husbands.

Jack Goody has pointed out that property transmission is not only one way by which the reproduction of the social system takes place, but it is also a way in which interpersonal relations are structured.[12] This is the theme of three of the essays in this volume. Martine Segalen discusses the transmission of property between generations in a partible inheritance system in Brittany. She shows how relations between generations and among adult siblings were structured by transmission as a process over a long time, producing constant and lasting competition among siblings. By contrast Alain Collomp deals with a stem family system, regulated by contract, in early modern Haute-Provence. Interweaving property and personal relations, he discusses the authority structure of older men and takes up the sometimes bitter conflicts between brothers and between mothers and sons-in-law. David Sabean analyses the relations between brothers-in-law among South German peasants in a period of capitalization and intensification of agriculture. With severe shortages of capital, brothers-in-law were forced into mutual cooperation for production, but at the same time into conflict over land and inheritance.

The political activities of family members or their particular position in the polity may also be viewed as part of the 'estate' which stamps the relations of members within a family. Andrew Strathern considers the political strategy of a Papua New Guinea 'big-man' to show how the relations of other family members are structured by the construction and maintenance of his political network. At a time when the nature of the social and economic system is undergoing rapid transformation, political power based on forms of public display and exchange is becoming uncertain. Much of family life centres around the desire on the part of some to reproduce the political network, whilst others are finding new ways to structure relations in the changed situation. Transformation and political structure are also themes handled by Roger Sablonier's analysis of inner-familial relationships in the Aragonese royal family at the turn of the fourteenth century. He examines trends towards centralization of state administration and parallel attempts to centralize the regulation of royal family affairs. Relations among siblings were under the strong impact of the father/king, whose central concern was passing his estate to a single heir.

Just as family sentiment and interpersonal relations can be patterned around an 'estate', whether composed of land or political connection or office, so the wider problems of mere survival or the desire to maximize the chances of offspring can be important for the emotional structuring of relations. Herbert Gutman takes up the problem of the way propertyless American slaves and their descendants created their own culture and class values under severe conditions within an idiom of family and kinship. He shows how enlarged kin networks transmitted ways of structuring interpersonal relations and created a basis for reciprocity and obligation. Esther Goody explores the issue of fostering young children in other homes, a common practice among West Africans, and deals with the patterning of sentimental relationships consonant with this practice. She describes a confrontation in an English court between a West African family and an English foster family, who alleged that the emotional tie with the parents of origin had been severed by giving the child out to be fostered. This situation is only seemingly analogous to the one which Brecht described in his 'Caucasian Chalk Circle'. The drama reaches beyond family and class, since it is not the lack of parental affection versus the proofs of true affection which is put on trial here but fundamentally different ways two societies and cultures have of relating familial affection with the social organization of survival.

Family as a mediator of class and class practice is a theme further examined by Karen Sacks. She deals with the working routines of Black female hospital workers – ward secretaries – to show how the values invoked in confronting authority and status were derived from everyday family experiences. Conflict resolution in family situations provided the experience necessary for political work and the maintenance of social and political networks. Louise Tilly also looks closely at the interrelationships of class and family. By examining family relations of nineteenth-century weavers in Cambrésis in the context of work, she is able to analyse how inner-familial relations at once mediate class values and play a part in the reproduction of the work force.

Not only can family be a matrix for the production of class and class values, but it can also furnish the idiom for relations external to itself and for the symbolic structuring of social reality. In this way family mediations of self-interest and emotion can serve as points for measuring or giving meaning to extra-familial situations. Hans Medick takes up the *Spinnstube* or village 'spinning bee' in early modern Germany, a focal point for winter evening conviviality and work. This institution provided a ritual moment of separation from the family and socialization into adult sexual culture, and at the same time provided a means for the transmission of village culture and the reproduction of the village property system, since it functioned as a marriage market. The ambivalence of custom is also the subject of Gerald Sider's essay on Newfoundland 'scoffs', parties at which stolen food was shared. The elements of the custom mirrored familial and inter-familial relations under the prevalent form of merchant capitalism. He shows that within and among families there was at once mutual aid and intense mistrust, both unity and warmth, exclusion and tension. Karin Hausen analyses the way a modern custom – the German Mother's Day – became established by a conjunction of business interests, modern advertizing, welfare concern, and the peculiar situation of post World War I families. The symbol of 'mother' was embedded in a fanciful image of a completely self-sacrificing woman who provided the natural emotional centre of male fantasies.

Discussion at the Round Table revealed certain differences in the way social historians and anthropologists dealt with problems of the family. In general a central concern of anthropologists was with social transformation and discontinuities in historical development. Situations undergoing radical alteration by modern market forces, capital development, and cash-cropping or wage labour pose serious problems of analysis for anyone dealing with the contemporary third world. Rather than relying on older notions of 'custom' and 'tradition' or centring on enduring structures, anthropologists tended to assume that values were continually being created anew. Such an approach puts a stress on action, practice, and change and radically throws into question the notion of a persistent 'moral community' as a starting place for analysis. But anthropologists were not just interested in problems of recent change. Sharp discontinuities in the West European past also came in for discussion and raised a series of issues about dominating social groups and the range of material forces which brought about historical breaks. In considering the trend towards 'nuclear' family relations in the early Middle Ages, the intrusion of the Church and its interest in land control was crucial. While several contributors pointed to the way forces of production and processes of work were central for family relations, it was also pointed out that other material forces such as the technology of communication and the organization of violence were central to analysing social transformation.

Social historians were also interested in change, but most of their attention was focussed on the interplay between the family and the formation of class. How the emotional nexus centred in the family mediated class values or was the locus for the development of class consciousness was the main issue. Whilst change was not ignored by the historians, they showed a strong interest in questions of structure and the logic of social systems and were apt to organize their thinking around the category of 'reproduction' in contradistinction to that of transformation.

Discussion between the two disciplines came to focus on the problem of 'culture' and the associated concept of 'custom'. It was argued that custom and tradition are often opposed to the category of 'strategy' and that one way this is done is to assign tradition to the generation of grandparents and strategy to the active family heads facing everyday crises. Such an approach in turn rests on a viewpoint which sees emotion as derivative from material interests rather than seeing them both as embedded in the social relations and the cultural practice governing the access to property. By making emotion derivative, one is left with 'strategy' as the connecting link, and this tends to be historically flat. In addition this creates difficulties for understanding the capacity of dominated people to act, for what gives them this capacity is their sense of history. One of the central issues on the agenda of both disciplines is to bring this understanding to the problem of action in the context of historical change. Custom – or in Bourdieu's term, 'habitus', and the meaningful action connected with it – is not just a reflex of inherited relationships but also a source of historical innovation and in certain ways the matrix of multivalent social practice.

NOTES

1 The problem has been announced with a series of trumpet blasts. Some of the works that might be consulted are: Elizabeth Fox-Genovese and Eugene D. Genovese, 'The Political Crisis of Social History: A Marxian Perspective', *Journal of Social History*, 10 (1976–7), 205–19; Tony Judt, 'A Clown in Royal Purple: Social History and the Historians', *History Workshop*, 7 (1979), 66–94; Geoff Eley and Keith Nield, 'Why Does Social History Ignore Politics?', *Social History*, 5 (1980), 249–271. There is also the question of narrative in its relation to these issues: cf. Lawrence Stone's article 'The Revival of Narrative: Reflections on a New Old History', in Lawrence Stone, *The Past and the Present* (London, 1980), originally published in, *Past and Present*, 85 (1979), and the debate which followed it: Eric Hobsbawm, 'The Revival of Narrative: Some Comments', *Past and Present*, 86 (1980), 3–8, and Philip Abrams, 'History, Sociology, Historical Sociology', *Past and Present*, 87 (1980), 3–16.

2 An interesting discussion of the issues is found in E.P. Thompson, *The Poverty of Theory and Other Essays* (London, 1978).

3 See Eric Wolf, *Europe and the People without History* (Berkeley, Los Angeles, 1982), and the debates surrounding the work of Immanuel Wallerstein, *The Modern World System*, vols. 1, 2 (New York, London, 1974, 1980).

4 See the remarks by G. Allardyce, 'The Rise and Fall of the Western Civilization Course', *American Historical Review*, 87 (1982), 704–14.

5 Carlo Ginzburg and Carlo Poni, 'La Micro-historie', *Le Debat*, 17 (1981), 133–6; a similar problem in Malinowski's work is discussed by Marshall Sahlins, *Culture and Practical Reason* (Chicago, 1976), 74–5, 86.

6 See B. Cohen 'History and Anthropology: The State of Play', *Comparative Studies in Society and History*, 22 (1980), 198–221; R. Isaac, 'Ethnographic Method in History: An Action Approach', *Historical Methods*, 13 (1980), 43–61; Natalie Z. Davis, 'Anthropology and the Possibilities of the "Past"', *Journal of Interdisciplinary History*, 12 (1981/2).

7 Renato Rosaldo, *Ilongot Headhunting 1883–1974: A Study in Society and History* (Stanford, 1980); Jack Goody, *Cooking, Cuisine and Class: A Study in Comparative Sociology* (Cambridge, 1982); Jack Goody, *Production and Reproduction* (Cambridge, 1976); Jack Goody, *The Domestication of the Savage Mind* (Cambridge, 1977).

8 See on this the fine article by Eric Wolf, 'Culture and Ideology: An Essay in Honour of Angel Palerm', *Festschrift for Angel Palerm* (forthcoming). Wolf quotes Raoul Narrol on the concept of 'cult-units'.

9 Pierre Bourdieu, *Outline of a Theory of Practice* (Cambridge, 1977).

10 For the preceding remarks we are indebted to our conversation with Rhys Isaac.

11 See the illuminating discussion in Michelle Rosaldo, *Knowledge and Passion: Ilongot Notions of Self and Social Life* (Cambridge, 1980).

12 Jack Goody, 'Introduction', in Jack Goody, *et al.* (eds.), *Family and Inheritance: Rural Society in Europe 1200–1800* (Cambridge, 1976), 3.

Part I. Family and the economy of emotion

1. Interest and emotion in family and kinship studies: a critique of social history and anthropology

HANS MEDICK and DAVID WARREN SABEAN

The history of the family as a branch of social history has begun in the past few years to pose a new range of questions. At the end of the 1960s and the beginning of the 1970s, largely under the influence of Peter Laslett,[1] interest was centred around the structure of inner-familial relationships specific to class, group, and culture. Since the end of the 1970s, there has been a development in two broad directions. First there is a new emphasis on the problem of continuity and change in the social function of the family. Above all research has been centred on the role of the family in processes of social reproduction, socialization, and work, especially since the beginning of industrialization. The social history of the family is no longer caught so firmly in the grip of over-arching sociological theories of modernization and industrialization but undertakes research in concrete, local, and regional situations and seeks to derive theory in tandem with empirical investigation.[2]

A second direction involves the analysis of the reciprocal action of fundamental economic and social processes on inner-familial structure and distribution of roles and an assessment of how these roles were allocated to some extent by the defining power of bureaucrats and professionals. Some of the new themes are the effect of the organization of work on the household and family, the differential profiles of family life among property-holding and non-property-holding groups, the 'domestication' of family life through the policing of the family by the modern state. In this second direction, a new aspect to the family has been brought forward – no longer so much the structural and statistical moments, which might be called 'objective' – but rather the peculiarities of family experience and norms and modes of behaviour at different periods and in different classes and cultures. In this way of viewing the matter, family and household are no longer taken for granted as fixed magnitudes. One looks through and beyond the family to consider changes in sexual relationships, questions of inner and extra-familial sexuality, childhood, youth, old age, and death.[3]

The strong point of these new 'subjective' perspectives in the history of the family – their reference to the immediate context of experience and problems of the researcher and reader – does not always outweigh the disadvantages. The structural and material conditions of family life are not intentionally screened out but are usually introduced only as 'objective' aspects in the context of global change. Consequently, they are considered indirectly and rather superficially to the development of family relationships.

The difficulties in handling the interplay of subjective and objective moments of family life can be seen clearly in the way the relationship between emotional needs and material interest is handled in both the disciplines of social history and anthropology. In analysing the family, anthropologists and social historians have often found difficulties in handling this relationship, and rather than carefully sorting out the nature of rights and duties, claims and counter-claims within families in different social and cultural contexts and delineating the corresponding specific territories in which emotion, trust, and sentiment are structured, emotions and interest are often treated as opposites which cancel each other out. In addition there is an attempt to legitimate such a view by means of evolutionary or ideological perspectives, which contrast much too easily a 'modern' emotional-laden nuclear family to 'traditional' family relations based on a different structure of motives altogether. In a way similar to but more emphasized than Flandrin and Foucault, Edward Shorter describes the pre-history and history of the modern middle class family in Europe of the eighteenth and nineteenth centuries as a progressive 'sentimentalization', for which the analysis of matters such as property relations seems irrelevant. Succinctly, Shorter puts it this way: 'when we encounter young men passing up fat dowries to wed their heart's desire, we shall know we're standing before romance'.[4] As a pendant to this, 'peasant' family relationships are regarded as mediated solely through such interests: marriages are formed without regard to sentiment, and the ruling forces of parent/child relations are direct, tangible items of property. The more play a *sachliches Element* has in shaping family relationships, it is assumed, the less room there is for emotion.[5] Working class family relationships in this view appear to be 'liberated' from accumulated wealth, which allows free play to emotion, but caught in the squalor of direct production and disoriented by disintegrative forces in industrial cities, the family becomes an arena of highly transient relationships, waiting for 'embourgeoisement', the penetration of sentimentalized values first produced in another social milieu, in order to attain stability.[6]

It is important in the first instance not to accept the self-articulation of family experience in different classes and at different times at face value, for in one context family experience can be mediated through a highly articulated form of language, whilst in another it might not be subject to expression in linguistic form at all.[7] For example, it has been noted for 'middle class' school children in London in the 1960s that the discourse which they had learned at home involved abstracting from social context and treating people with whom they were communicating in a context specific only to them, accenting their individuality, and attuned to emotional response.[8] In such form of communication, material interest is hidden in the concern to communicate at the level of the individual and the emotional. Considered as an historical or comparative problem, in families such as the ones these children came from, claims to rights and the demands that obligations be fulfilled, property relations, material production, and instrumentality would be mediated through a language intent on expressing relationships in a context of individuality, in which just such material interests would not directly be expressed. For the historian or anthropologist, these forms of 'coding' would have to be grasped in terms of the total set of relationships – emotional and material – that are mediated through them.[9]

There are two implications in this view to be explored here.

1) Material interest cannot be excluded from consideration in analysing the family in those contexts where it fails to be explicitly articulated.[10] This would mean, for example, that any understanding of various forms of nineteenth-century middle class family experience should involve a thorough-going study of the dynamics of property-holding and not just stop with an historical chronicle of sentiments.[11] In addition, the practical experience of family life does not segregate the emotional and the material into separate spheres but is shaped by both at once, and they have to be grasped in their systematic interconnection.

2) The way family experience is talked about, the modes of exchange on a linguistic level vary from family to family, class to class, and over time. The type of 'code' in which the child learns to communicate is generated within a specific set of family relationships, and it remains for the historian and the anthropologist to specify the range of possible codes and the nature of family dynamics as rooted in specific contexts of production and domination which produce particular codes.

Basil Bernstein provides a starting point for the consideration of this latter problem in his notion of 'elaborated' and 'restricted' codes, which he attaches respectively to contemporary 'middle class' and 'working class' school children. To handle only the 'restricted' codes for the moment, Bernstein seeks to understand the general context in which they arise.

Sapir, Malinowski, Firth, Vygotsky and Luria have all pointed out from different points of view that the closer the identifications of speakers the greater the range of shared interest, the more probable that the speech will take a specific form. The range of syntactic alternatives is likely to be reduced and the lexis to be drawn from a narrow range. Thus, the form of these social relations is acting selectively on the meanings to be verbally realized. In these relationships the intent of the other person can be taken for granted as the speech is played out against a back-drop of common assumptions, common history, common interests. As a result, there is less need to raise meanings to the level of explicitness or elaboration. There is a reduced need to make explicit through syntactic choices the logical structure of the communication. Further, if the speaker wishes to individualize his communication, he is likely to do this by varying the expressive associates of the speech. Under these conditions, the speech is likely to have a strong metaphoric element. In these situations the speaker may be more concerned with how something is said, when it is said; silence takes on a variety of meanings. Often in these encounters the speech cannot be understood apart from the context, and the context cannot be read by those who do not share the history of the relationships. Thus the form of the social relationship acts selectively in the meanings to be verbalized, which in turn affect the syntactic and lexical choices. The unspoken assumptions underlying the relationship are not available to those who are outside the relationship. For these are limited, and restricted to the speakers. The symbolic form of the communication is condensed, yet the specific cultural history of the relationship is alive in its form.[12]

Peasant and plebeian societies fulfil Bernstein's criteria of shared history and face-to-face relationships with common interests and assumptions, and it is in such contexts that one expects to find communication largely reduced to concrete symbols in which a great deal remains unarticulated, and meaning, 'implicit'.[13] 'The community of like interests underlying [such a] code removes the need for subjective intent to be verbally elaborated and made explicit.'[14] In communication, therefore, symbolism is 'descriptive, tangible, concrete, visual'.[15] Whereas peasant and 'working class' forms of communication often implicitly express their meanings and reinforce social categories, middle class 'elaborated' codes are oriented towards the individual and towards qualification; they are suited to expressing subjective meaning and develop a vocabulary oriented to personal relationships.[16] It is just this aspect which is a threat to the user of 'restricted' codes:

tender feelings which are personal and highly individual will not only be difficult to express in this linguistic form, but it is likely that the objects which arouse tender feelings will be given tough terms – particularly those referring to girl-friends, love, death and disappointments . . . To speakers of [such a] language tender feelings are a potential threat, for in this experience is also the experience of isolation – social isolation.[17]

Just as the 'elaborated' code is subject to misinterpretation if taken at face value, so too the 'restricted' code. When the peasant expresses himself in a concrete form ('I love the woman with 40 acres'), analysis should not stop with the notion that here only instrumental values are in play and that emotions and feelings are stunted. Both what we might call the 'language of property' and the 'language of sentiment' mediate social categories, the interplay between family members, and the emotionality of family and sexual life, but they have to be read for what they are: the contexts in which they have arisen and the complex layers of relationships which are mediated in their very structures.

All this is to say more than emotions are structured differently in different family contexts, for as an historical and comparative problem, one has to seek the plane, the territory, on which emotions are patterned and to grasp their articulation in specific contexts of concrete material interest, property relationships, and the dynamics of social reproduction. The problem is to capture in the same analytical moment the interpenetration of various levels of exchange – the social relations created, organized, and shaped by persons holding rights or bound by obligations with respect to other persons or things.

The necessity to analyse family relationships as relationships of a many layered exchange can be seen most clearly with the problem of property. For the peasant family, it is assumed that property forms the centre of its relationships. However, it is not so clearly grasped in what way property as a social 'relational idiom' determines the exchange of interests and emotions within the peasant household.[18] According to Davis, 'when we describe rights of ownership, or of use, or of tenancy, we are talking about relationships between people. Rights imply duties and liabilities, and these must attach to people. A hectare cannot be sued at law, nor is a boundary dispute a quarrel with a boundary.'[19]

Because material interest is more directly expressed for peasant or plebeian culture, the task of the anthropologist and historian is to grasp the manner in which property-holding and transmission shape internal family relationships in their complexity.[20] In analysing property,

we are dealing with rights and duties in relation to material goods, goods whose characteristics – their scarcity and the fact that persons or groups claim relatively exclusive rights over them – signify that they are valued. The definition of property revolves essentially around the problem of exclusion . . . we are not dealing with rights of a person over a material object, but rather with rights between persons in relation to a material object. A man without social relationships is a man without property.[21]

This way of viewing property found in the social anthropological analysis of family and kinship relations, not as a concept of individual material interest but as a socially ordered 'relational idiom', offers perspectives which are generally relevant to the study of emotion and material interest. The problem is to grasp and to analyse both elements reciprocally in order to understand the forces which shape inner-familial relationships, determine the levels upon which exchange takes place, and create conflict and tensions which need to be resolved or which bring about the severance of connections. In all of this it should be understood that emotional needs imply social structure and that they can only be fulfilled within relationships whose structure is shaped by complex material forces.

In order to explore some of these problems, we examined the possibilities offered by four themes: 1) central moments of exchange within the family or household – such as the preparation and distribution of food – which mediate both emotion and material interest; 2) the interconnection between various planes of activity – public and the private, interior and the exterior; 3) specific relationships within the family; 4) the role of kinship in survival strategies.

1) Within the family or between families or among neighbours, perhaps the central ritual which mediates various levels of exchange has to do with meal preparation and the distribution and consumption of food.[22] 'The sharing of cooked food . . . is a public statement of inclusion in a single moral and social community among whose members there is trust. Yet at the same time individual community members remain cautious about the safety of such intimate bonds.'[23] Fear of unavoidable food contamination by family members in certain ritual states or anxieties about intended or unintended poisoning by enemies or the ritually unclean are often tied up with perceptions about the

dangerous areas in kinship and other social relations.[24] Marginal people and marginal states within family life sometimes evoke the most powerful symbolic images.[25] Tensions between husband and wife over integration of one of them into the new household or the new village, over the readiness of one of them to adopt new customs or adapt to change, or over the fulfilment of expectations over work, style, or deference can be mediated through conflict or dispute about meals.[26] In many situations where authority is exercised directly and there is little opportunity for resistance, much dissatisfaction is compressed into complaints about food.[27]

Rights and obligations surrounding the sharing of food are often direct translations of rights in other spheres or symbolize such rights: 'the sharing of cooked food is a relational idiom whose emphasis is on inclusion, on being part of a close and interdependent group'.[28] The specification about who is to cook or who is to eat in any particular order or who is to eat with whom may be structured according to the apportionment of sexual rights.[29] Conflict between mother and daughter-in-law over the son/husband may be mediated through the rights to cook for him. The way property is shared between husband and wife can be symbolized through eating rituals, two relational idioms thus being translations of each other, or alternatively the one sphere might be used to accrue symbolic capital to strengthen the position in the other sphere. In Morocco, for example, the male head of the family expects deference at mealtime to the tune of eating first and best, but he has considerably less power vis-à-vis a fragile marital bond, which reflects the fact that wives retain residual rights to property from their own families and that women control the entire marriage market. The degree to which the separation of food consumption within the Moroccan family reflects the separation of certain rights in property, or that to which the separation reflects the desire to develop power in the one sphere to use in the other, is an open question.[30]

Paying close attention to the way food is shared and consumed can be useful for understanding certain aspects of class relations or for analysing internal aspects of class. One finds, for example, that class relationships were compressed and symbolized at mealtimes on the large Austrian 'peasant' farms earlier in this century where the domination of the peasant owner was symbolized by his leadership in prayer before the meal, by the insistence that all of the farm members take part in the mealtime devotions, by the 'bounty' of the offering of the owner's table, the obligation on the part of the labourers and children to eat heartily (even when followed by nausea), the structured silences, and the distribution of the right to laugh during the meal.[31] Being caught in a situation where direct opposition towards the 'peasant-lord' was impossible, the farm labourer almost always terminated his annual contract over the issue of adequate meals.[32]

Also in the working class household of the nineteenth century, the distribution of nutrition mirrored the unequal distribution of social power, above all between men and women.[33] The privileged position of the man as the 'breadwinner' and 'provider' was strengthened as a consequence of capitalist industrialization processes, especially as the earning capacities of women declined. Undernourishment of children and women in workers' households frequently followed. Of course, this was caused by low levels and irregularity of income but was increased by the unequal 'social distribution of welfare' between man and wife. This inequality forced mothers to provide for the rising expenditures of growing families through the limitation of their own needs rather than by cutting the pocket money of the men. In times of rising prices the household budget of the wife remained relatively constant and inelastic. It was more likely that one would save on the daily nutrition of wives and children than on the money that the husband took for his social needs. His public consumption (drinking and smoking in the working class pubs) was and remained an essential element of male honour, especially in a situation in which this honour was less defendable in the increasingly alienating factory industrial working processes. The contemporary German workers' maxim 'wer verdient wird bedient' (who earns gets) meant more than the unequal organization of the chances of survival of members of the workers' families. It points at the same time indirectly to different centres in the emotional exchanges between men and women. Whilst that of the men was oriented more to the 'proletarian public' outside the family, that of the mothers and women was directed to children, family, and kin, above all to the lines of female descent.

To consider food sharing and meal ritual as a relational idiom is to ask how the various levels of relation – rights, obligations, trust, inclusion, exclusion, hierarchy, differentiation – are expressed, to ask about the nature of the mediation itself, and to ask how this idiom is related to other idioms: 'strictly speaking there are no symbolic objects – there are only symbolic relationships. To speak of food . . . as a symbolic object is often a convenient short-hand term, but it is the conceptualization of the object in a given relation that is significant.'[34]

2) Many of the relationships which family members have with each other are shaped by activities or considerations which are in fact external to the family itself. In those societies, for example, dominated by 'honour and shame', the focus of activity is private, but the household is dependent on the public for its ranking in the hierarchy of honour and for its marriage partners.[35] The activities of any member of the family within the household are sharply modified by outside considerations, both in terms of fulfilling cultural expectations and selecting strategies for the advancement of the reputation of the house and its members.

It is then useful to analyse the behaviour of family members among themselves and the experience of family life in terms of such matters as the cultural values of 'honour and shame' or social/cultural situations in which social reproduction is tied closely to household strategies, but in which the behaviour of each member is assigned value in the prestige ledger by the community.[36] Further, the behaviour of family members and the power relations among them are linked to the resources available to them: property, kinship relations, neighbourhood networks, professional status, symbolic capital, money. What we argue for here is widening of the problem of linkages between the 'outside' and the 'inside' to the consideration not just of power relations between members of the family and the impingement of work relationships outside the family on the authority relations inside it but to the experience of living in specific families in specific social contexts, to the behaviour of parents and children among themselves and with kin and in extra-familial contexts, to the territorialization of emotion, to relationships of exchange between family members. The problem here is to analyse the way in which these matters are given shape by the structure and social character of work, the distribution of property rights, and by the facts of domination.

Too often roles played within the household are analysed simply in terms of a crude power balance, with women at a disadvantage because they are tied to child bearing and raising and because the economically useful jobs are captured by males.[37] Setting aside the questions of who evaluates the roles (until recently most information on the part of ethnographers came from men talking to men) and whether power is to be considered as a set quantum with winners and losers, some discussion needs to be focussed on the details of any particular role and the structure of the bundle of roles in terms of a whole set of rights and obligations, interests and strategies, relationships and conflicts.[38] Furthermore, such analyses might usefully consider that roles in the family are shaped within ongoing histories of each family and society; the member under most control and least valued at one point in time may emerge with the greatest respect, consideration, or power later on.[39] The same problem arises with budget studies of working class families, which fail to note that children frequently give up their earnings to their mothers and are more likely to provide for them than for their fathers later on in the family cycle.[40] Heuristically, advances in the study of, for example, male and female roles might be made by systematic analysis of fields of activity and roles played outside the family in terms of their feed-back for the internal family activities or, to change the metaphor, by considering the dialectic between the public and the private. If as in Morocco women totally control the marriage market through a network of female kin relationships and neighbourhood gossip, and are able to contribute to the fragility of the marriage bond through their activities, then the role within the family or larger kinship network of any particular woman takes on a new light. It would be useful to analyse the complex of female strategies, since at this point a woman is dealing with a most important capital resource (marriageable women). Her position of deference and service within the family must be grasped in a totality in which she articulates goals, chooses strategies to attain them, and is able to call upon various resources, capital and symbolic capital, which depending on the context can be traded for one another and transferred from level to level.[41] One must consider that the rights that a Moroccan woman has in the property of her original family shape the strategies that she pursues within her marriage, one of which is the threat to leave.[42] A similar point is made by Bourdieu when he contrasts the difference between official ideology and actual practice in arranging marriages and shows how the power of women is grasped differently when one makes this distinction.[43]

A great deal of interest has been shown in the sexual division of labour for understanding the relationships between husband and wife. In proto-industry, for example, the productive capacities of man and wife are indispensable to one another, and observers have noted a general equality between them and commented occasionally on a lack of clearly defined tasks specifically linked to one sex or the other.[44] In early industrialization, this 'family mode of production' was often carried over with similar results. In peasant families, husband and wife had clearly defined areas in which work and power were direct reflections of one another. With both the bourgeois family and the working class family in high industrialization, the crucial link between home and work disappears and the wife becomes confined to the home with a consequent loss of status and power.[45]

This last example can be examined to show that while it is apparent that the structure of work helps shape inner-familial relationships, it is also necessary to grasp how particular family configurations within particular modes of production in turn play parts in social reproduction:

the Oedipus complex, which begins with the prohibition of the child's sexual activity, falls within the emotionally charged context of parent–child relations in the privatized, nuclear family. Isolated in the nuclear family, the child's entire emotional life is centred on its parents, on their affection and hostility, on their autonomous power to set the rules of the child, on the depth of the identifications the child makes with them . . . The super-ego . . . assumes that the child will *forever be a member of the family*, will forever carry within the dictates and emotional representations of the father. It assumes that even when the child goes outside the family to seek a mate the emotional meaning of the choice will echo heavily the parent of the opposite sex. It makes certain that the bourgeoisie, a group without strong kinship ties, will be able to transmit property through generations.[46]

A further aspect to be taken into consideration here involves the nature of *Herrschaft* (domination), for family members are differentially subject to extra-familial power, and the constellation of domination within the family is a central aspect of the experience of its various members. The problematical connection between useful work and power, with domination brought in to understand the total situation, is provided by the Mount Hagen, Papua New Guinea, case. There the role of women in production is absolutely essential, for women tend the gardens which in turn nourish the pigs which are traded in the ceremonial arena by men. That a central economic role does not translate itself directly into power is clear, for the men by controlling the entire public sphere extract the labour power of women and dominate them through extra-economic means. This is made clear by considering the division of labour between the sexes and . . . competition over political status. The latter takes place overtly between men, but the conditions are set crucially in relations between men and women, since women provide such a contribution to productive labour, as well as to human production, that political competition is essentially built upon their efforts. This same dependence on women's labour has in fact carried over into the cash-cropping sphere, in which women do much of the work in weeding and harvesting coffee plots and in processing the coffee beans for sale . . . In Hagan society, men are dominant, both in dogma and in fact, though not as dominant, of course, as their own dogma might lead us to believe. Their dominance is founded on two main factors: the control of land as a basic means of production; and the control of ceremonial exchange relations (*moka*) between individual partners and groups, in terms of which political competition and consolidation are expressed . . . The dogma of male control over exchange is . . . rigidly upheld, for it is in this sphere of transactions that social and political prestige are specifically gained. And such control begins at home, in terms of relations between husband and wife.[47]

Roles within the family, then, are not to be analysed out of context in terms of a universal set of judgements. Rather, in fulfilling roles, in carrying on family activities, individuals are carrying on a series of transactions or exchanges, which may involve inequality on one level, with a reversal of inequality at another, with more power or respect or consideration flowing to one member at one time and to another at another time, or with systematic inequality considered by sex, age, or rank. Part of the problem lies in the sociological concept of 'role', which is radically individualizing and deceptively quantifiable, and fails to pose the problem of family roles in their relational context and as ongoing process.

3) Anthropologists have spent much of their energies discussing specific diads within the family, searching for the central emotional moment around which structure is built. Thus among the Tallensi, the key to the analysis of trust and conflict is to be found in the relationship between father and eldest brother.[48] Within matrilineal societies, structure turns around the uncle/nephew relationship.[49] Such analyses have tended to ignore women except as counters in the material and psychological game played by men. Where a radical departure from this interest in men takes place, a new diad of mother and child is often substituted.[50] In any event, most interest has been centred on *intergenerational* trust, piety, joking, or conflict. Historians who have dealt with the matter have also centred their interests on similar factors (inheritance, marital strategy of households) and, like anthropologists, their analyses are directed to the moment of intergenerational succession – when the son succeeds the father in the ancestor cult, when the son inherits the farm, how the nephew claims bridewealth from the uncle. There is a great deal in anthropological discussion useful for the historian, for the former have demonstrated that the territorialization of emotions is structured differently in different societies and is patterned according to the way rights and duties, claims and counter-claims (property) are sorted out. Just what it means, for example, for 'bourgeois' society to restrict the field of emotion to the family calls for comparative analysis.[51]

However much the search for the emotional centre to family experience can be found in a particular diad and in the problem of intergenerational succession, it is perhaps time to explore the interrelationships among siblings. First of all, centring analysis on a particular diad focussed towards a particular structural moment ignores the roles that other individuals play in the whole process of reproduction; it also places the centre of interest on reproduction in the dynamics of family life to the detriment of other aspects: production and reproduction of everyday life. If the central moment of family life in the Tallensi is the father/eldest brother nexus,[52] what do the sisters think of this, to what degree are their emotional and material existences organized around this factor, how do the younger sons relate to the ancestors, how are the relations between them and the eldest brother structured over time? The thrust of the problem is to ask to what degree the central emotional and material moment found in each society is ideology, to what degree the ideology is accepted and plays a role in sorting out material and emotional interests of the participants, to what degree by emphasizing a single diadic centre crucial aspects of inner-familial relations are ignored. In extending the problems, analysis has to take into account such diverse phenomena as that in many societies older children raise younger children, siblings divide themselves into jewelry wearers and non-jewelry wearers, children often develop different personality types depending on their expected share in the patrimony, and siblings are often brought up in different households and yet create stronger ties among themselves than in some societies where they are not divided as children.[53]

Most considerations of sibling relationships centre on marriage strategies of a household, making the central point that each marriage in a series has repercussions on subsequent marriages.[54] There is a great deal more to be done on the analysis of the sibling group during the phase of marrying and setting up new households, but the subsequent relationships of primary kin throughout the rest of their lives demands close analysis as well, not the least because this is the original group whose strategies were developed with regard to rights in the same piece of property.[55] Where the status of an out-marrying woman is expressed by a certain kind and level of dowry, her male kin (father and brothers) have continuing rights over her and duties of protection in which residual rights to the woman/dowry are not to be analysed apart from each other.[56] In Western culture, where the in-marrying woman has the least secure position in the household, her male relatives maintain the strongest hold over her dowry – which can offer her considerable protection.[57] Where children are treated with radical inequality, relations among them may be broken off, or they may be bound to each other under severely hierarchical forms.[58]

One important issue is the way that family mediates social differentiation and class formation. This has been graphically dealt with for impartible inheritance regions in Austria, where siblings brought up together on the same farm faced radically different social relations as adults: farm owners vs. farm labourers.[59] This differentiation can also be seen where illegitimacy came to play a significant role and the labour contribution of adult women was integral to agricultural production.[60] Whether the family is the matrix wherein social opportunity is apportioned or whether adult siblings cooperate socially, economically, and politically, the problem can perhaps best be analysed by a close examination of the adults of the same generation who were raised in the same household or recognize a close genealogical relationship.[61]

4) For the historian, the analysis of kinship has largely been neglected, and a great deal of research remains to be done. It is thought by some that for Europe the wider kinship system was the central focus for the individual until the Industrial Revolution demanded a work force based on the nuclear family.[62] By others, it is thought that strong village institutions obviated the necessity for extensive kinship relationships and that the nuclear family was normal for most of Europe from the early Middle Ages onwards.[63] Few have yet systematically examined historical sources to ask about the nature of individual and family *strategies* in placing family members, in political activity, in economic enterprise, or in emotional support or to ask about the *use* of kin in pursuing such strategies. While the work of anthropologists can be suggestive in the search for structure and system in family strategies and the utilization of kin, their work is not often enough informed by the concept of practice or by a thorough analysis of the larger social and economic conditions in which certain structures have developed.[64] Both disciplines have much to do in the analysis of the use that families and individuals make of kin, the nature of claims that can be exercised, the obligations that are undertaken, the degree to which class is experienced through kin, the role that kin play in reproduction and survival.

Even under conditions where family and kinship bonds have ceased to function as the central 'infrastructure' of the productive and reproductive system of a social formation, and the 'family mode of production' no longer forms the core of its productive, property, and power relationships, these bonds remain of vital importance to the 'way of life' and the reproduction of life of its specific classes.[65] They may in addition even retain or create important new functions relating to class societies as a whole. In channelling and limiting the transmission of socio-cultural as well as material capital through 'inheritance' between generations, they can act for instance as central mechanisms, mediating and stabilizing relationships of domination between different classes.[66]

An important limiting case is the role of family and kinship in the survival strategies of propertyless and property-poor populations in emerging class societies. For highly divergent situations, such as those of Afro-American slave populations and their descendants, for contemporary immigrant town dwellers in Africa, Asia, and South America as well as for marginalized peasant groups and for the proletarian and sub-proletarian populations of Europe under emerging capitalism, the importance of kin relations beyond the nuclear family has been shown.[67] It is to be seen above all in their role of managing an often precarious, unplannable, and endangered subsistence. Under conditions of life and death where the conjugal or nuclear family of husband, wife, and children often could and can hardly be said to exist as a permanent concern, and where community arrangements are weak, kin relations often retain or take on basic functions: they help to maintain an economy of cooperation, mutuality, and help in critical life situations, organized around a kinship system.

The manifold uses to which kin were and are put in these situations, whether in the raising of children, in the provision for old age, in housing and helping a relative from the countryside to overcome the first critical phase of his immigration into the town, have been given relatively extensive attention. Much less research has been done into the nature of the specific structures and networks of kin mobilized for these purposes, and into the foundations of those expectations, obligations, and rights on which this mobilization of resources from kin rested.

An interesting example, however, pointing to the direction in which a discussion might go is provided by the controversial efforts of anthropologists to explain the strategic importance of mother, daughter, and kin in the households and networks of the Afro-American poor.[68] It not only led to an increasing awareness of the dangers of introducing alien concepts like the 'nuclear family' or derivations from this concept like that of a disintegrated, fatherless, 'matrifocal' family, but it also showed the intimate connection which exists between a specific way to mobilize resources through the network of kin and a pattern of normative expectations, evaluations, and experiences in which the mother and the mother/daughter diad occupies a central place. Though it seems questionable whether insights derived from the specific case of the Afro-American family may serve as a 'universal rule' by which to judge the importance of kin and family connections amongst the working class in general, it nevertheless was and may be used as a fruitful point of departure to develop hypotheses for other social, economic, and class specific contexts.

In the earlier days of factory industry, when the mother-centred kinship system served to give working-class woman some security in a life beset by its opposite . . . these bonds, important still today, probably counted even more . . . The insecurity of men was translated into an even greater lack of security for women, who needed it more . . . wives could not rely upon their husbands to stand by them while they reared their children. Death too often removed the prop. Nor were they assured of support from husbands whose lives were spared. In an unstable economy, nearly all men were at some time unemployed and at all times frightened of it; and . . . even when they were at work, they frequently kept their families short of money. So the wife had to cling to the family into which she was born, and in particular to her mother, as the only means of ensuring herself against isolation. One or the other member of her family would, if need be, relieve her distress, lend her money, or share to some degree in the responsibility for her children. The extended family was her trade union, organized in the main by women for women, its solidarity her protection against being alone. It is, to judge by anthropology, almost a universal rule that when married life is insecure, the wife turns for support to her family of origin, so that a weak marriage tie produces a strong blood tie . . . Such defensive action might, ironically, produce the very result it was to guard against. Aware that the wife's overriding attachment was to her family of origin, excluded from the warmth and intimacy of the female circle, resentful husbands were only too likely to react by withdrawing themselves to their own consolations outside the home, in the pub and in *their* families of origin.[69]

Without agreement on specific points there seems to be unanimity that the picture of the bourgeois psyche as described by Freud does not fit the emotional dynamics of the family life of the poor. The emotional lives of children, adolescents and grown-ups of these classes and groups cannot be territorialized and mapped within the confines of the nuclear family to the same extent as may be the case with the middle class family. As to the intensity and quality of specific patterns of emotions and their foundation in concrete ways of life and work, in varying degrees of material well-being or misery, generalizations seem difficult. However, if Michael Anderson – in one of the few historical studies which deal with the issue – comes to the conclusion that kin relations amongst the working class poor of Victorian Lancashire were vital for their survival through networks of mutual help and exchange but that the practice of these kin-relations on the other hand bore witness to a 'rather short term calculative orientation', he reaches this conclusion on the basis of an assumption which in an all too linear fashion (not unlike Edward Shorter and Lawrence Stone) links different levels of material well-being with varying degrees of affectivity. He maintains that 'a really strong affective and non-calculative commitment to the kinship net' is always connected to a relative level of 'working class affluence'.[70] In the light of our introduction a different research perspective seems more appropriate: 'feeling might be *more*, rather than less, tender or intense *because* relations are "economic" and critical to mutual survival'.[71]

It seems more than a coincidence that the first historical investigations in this field which explicitly use approaches from social anthropology arrived at conclusions which vindicate this perspective. In his fascinating study of the Afro-American Black family,[72] Herbert Gutman demonstrates the strong affective and creative power of kinship bonds and kinship symbols in organising the defence and survival of the slave population. The study of naming practices and the use of fictive kinship terminology undertaken in the book seems especially interesting in this respect and a model for similar studies.[73] It demonstrates the genesis of connections and consciousness of solidarity of the slave population stemming from emotional and economic changes, which lay at the basis of the material help and symbolic work which reestablished originally broken kinship bonds. The broad and encompassing function of symbolic kinship as an idiom and creator of sociability is developed by Gutman from the specific subjected class situation of American slaves, which did not allow for voluntary associations and an independent community life.

If it emerges from this study that the anthropology and history of working class life and culture should have as one of its central tenets the anthropological investigation of the working class family, Gutman's results at the same time contain a note of caution and an implicit appeal for careful class and group-specific as well as work-specific analysis. The economic and affective importance of kinship bonds amongst the propertyless and property-poor may be related to a relative weakness of community and associational structures. It may well be strongest in the material 'culture of poverty' of marginalized peasants and immigrant town dwellers in emerging capitalist societies where the family as a permanent institution along middle class lines does not exist but whose culture at the same time has been described as the 'family writ large'.

NOTES

1 Peter Laslett (ed.), *Household and Family in Past Time* (Cambridge, 1972).

2 Neithard Bulst, *et al.* (eds.), *Familie zwischen Tradition und Moderne: Studien zur Geschichte der Familie in Deutschland und Frankreich vom 16. bis zum 20. Jahrhundert* (Göttingen, 1981); Jacques Donzelot, *La Police des familles* (Paris, 1977); Michael Mitterauer, *Grundtypen alteuropäischer Sozialformen: Haus und Gemeinde in vorindustriellen Gesellschaften* (Stuttgart, 1980); Jürgen Kocka, *et al.* (eds.), *Familie und soziale Plazierung: Studien zum Verhältnis von Familie, sozialer Mobilität und Heiratsverhalten an westfälischen Beispielen im späten 18. und 19. Jahrhundert* (Opladen, 1980); Heidi Rosenbaum, *Formen der Familie: Untersuchungen zum Zusammenhang von Familienverhältnissen, Sozialstruktur und sozialem Wandel in der deutschen Gesellschaft des 19. Jahrhunderts* (Frankfurt, 1982).

3 Philippe Ariès, *Centuries of Childhood* (New York, 1962); J. L. Flandrin, *Families in Former Times: Kinship, Household and Sexuality* (Cambridge, 1979); Michel Foucault, *The History of Sexuality*, vol. 1 (Harmondsworth, 1981); Ivan Illich, 'Gender' (New York, 1982); Edward Shorter, *The Making of the Modern Family* (New York, 1975).

4 The leading proponent of this view is Shorter, *Making*, 17.

5 *Ibid.*, 55. An important counter-argument to this view is developed by Bernard Vernier, 'Emigration et déréglement du marché matrimonial', *Actes de la recherche en sciences sociales*, 15 (1977), 50. He shows that in the area in Greece where he worked the traditional marriage system, which was tightly controlled by property considerations, is associated with love, while the new system where personal inclination plays a role and old hierarchies are overthrown, with new forms of wealth, is associated with coldness, with mere cash values.

6 See the material gathered by Rudolf Braun, *Industrialisierung und Volksleben* (Erlenbach-Zürich, 1960), 61–72. Along the same lines see Shorter, *Making*, 258–60. Lawrence Stone, *The Family, Sex and Marriage in England, 1500–1800* (London, 1977), 637, holds a similar view.

7 In part this is to historicize the problem raised by Basil Bernstein in his concept of different forms of communication or codes as related to different classes, *Class, Codes and Control*, vol. 1, *Theoretical Studies Towards a Sociology of Language*, (London, 1971), 76–82, 125–8.

8 Bernstein, *Theoretical Studies*, 147–8: 'restricted codes could be considered status or positional codes whereas elaborated codes are oriented to persons. An elaborated code, in principle, pre-supposes a sharp boundary or gap between self and others which is crossed through the creation of speech which specifically fits a differentiated

24   Hans Medick and David Warren Sabean

"other". In this sense, an elaborated code is oriented towards a person rather than a social category or status.'
9 Pierre Bourdieu argues against viewing family and kinship relations as objects, but rather as *practices* which embody *strategies*. Concrete interests of individuals are not reducible to material interests, but neither are they reducible to emotional satisfactions. Understanding interests involves penetrating the screen of language to the concrete matching of practice with social and economic conditions. *Outline of a Theory of Practice* (Cambridge, 1977), 35–6.
10 A comment on this point is made by Pierre Bourdieu, 'Les Stratégies matrimoniales dans le système de reproduction', *Annales ESC*, 27 (1972), 1123–4. A translation appears in Robert Forster, *et al.* (eds.), *Family and Society* (Baltimore, 1976).
11 On the thorough-going interpenetration of middle class families with material interest, see Theodore Zeldin, *France 1848–1945*, vol. 1 (Oxford, 1973), 285–91.
12 Bernstein, *Theoretical Studies*, 176–7.
13 *Ibid.*, 125–30.
14 *Ibid.*, 109.
15 See n8.
16 Bernstein, *Theoretical Studies*, 48.
17 *Ibid.*
18 The concept of 'relational idiom' is developed by Esther Goody, *Contexts of Kinship* (Cambridge, 1973), 2–3, 41–50, 121–8.
19 J. Davis, *Land and Family in Pisticci* (New York, 1973), 73.
20 See David Sabean, 'Aspects of Kinship Behaviour and Property in Rural Western Europe before 1800', in Jack Goody, *et al.* (eds.), *Family and Inheritance: Rural Society in Western Europe 1200–1800* (Cambridge, 1976), 96–111.
21 Jack Goody, *Death, Property and the Ancestors* (Stanford, 1962), 287.
22 See Norbert Elias, *Über den Prozess der Zivilisation*, vol. 1, (Bern, 1969), 110–74.
23 Goody, *Contexts*, 128.
24 Vanessa Maher, *Women and Property in Morocco: Their Changing Relation to the Process of Social Stratification in the Middle Atlas* (Cambridge, 1974), 102. See Yvonne Verdier, 'Pour une ethnologie culinaire', *L'Homme*, 9 (1969), 49–57. For an interesting discussion of food preparation in a rich ethnographic context, see Goody, *Contexts*, 127, 130.
25 Goody, *Contexts*, 130; also Maher, *Women and Property*, 100. Yvonne Verdier discusses the belief in a contemporary French village that during menstruation, women can spoil certain types of food: 'Les femmes et le Saloir', *Ethnologie française*, 6 (1976), 349–64.
26 See David Sabean, 'Intensivierung der Arbeit und Alltagserfahrung auf dem Lande – ein Beispiel aus Württemberg', *Sozialwissenschaftliche Informationen für Unterricht und Studium*, 6 (Oct 1977), 148–52. The progressive integration of a person into a household can also be symbolized or mediated through meal sharing, see Adrian C. Mayer, *Caste and Kinship in Central India: A village and Its Region* (London, 1960), 220.
27 On the importance of food and food disputes for agricultural labourers in Germany, see Franz Rehbein, *Das Leben eines Landarbeiters* (Jena, 1911), 141–3, 205–8.
28 Goody, *Context*, 127.
29 *Ibid.*, 109, 121.
30 Maher, *Women and Property*, 42, 110f, 124–7, 191f, 217f.
31 Franz Innerhofer, *Schöne Tage* (Frankfurt, 1977), 27, and *passim*.
32 *Ibid.*, 27.
33 L. Oren, 'The Welfare of Women in Labouring Families: England 1860–1950', in

Mary S. Hartman and Lois W. Banner (eds.), *Clio's Consciousness Raised* (New York, 1974), 226–44.
34 Raymond Firth, *Symbol, Myth and Ritual* (Ithaca, 1973), 245. For an important analysis of food-sharing as communication, see Roland Barthes, 'Pour une psycho-sociologie de l'alimentation contemporaine', *Annales ESC*, 16 (1961), 977–86.
35 See J. K. Campbell, *Honour, Family and Patronage: A Study of Institutions and Moral Values in a Greek Mountain Community* (Oxford, 1964), 204: 'unrelated families are only dependent on one another in two significant ways, for marriage partners and social reputation'. For another view along similar lines, Peter Loizos, *The Greek Gift: Politics in a Cypriot Village* (Oxford 1975), 65.
36 See Bourdieu, 'Stratégies'.
37 For a view that female roles are determined by child bearing and raising, see Judith K. Brown, 'A Note on the Division of Labor and Sex', *American Anthropologist*, 72 (1970), 1072–8. A strong challenge to this view and a review of the literature is contained in Susan Carol Rogers, 'Woman's Place: A Critical Review of Anthropological Theory', *Comparative Studies in Society and History*, 20 (1978), 123–62.
38 Paul Veyne offers an interpretation of the change of the role of husband and father in Imperial Rome as a reflection of the change of the power of the father in the wider society: 'La Famille et l'amour sous le haut-empire Romain', *Annales ESC*, 33 (1978), 35–63.
39 Campbell makes this point with regards to the wife/mother; see, *Honour*, 163–6.
40 Oren, 'Welfare of Women'.
41 Maher, *Women and Property*, 42–9. On female marriage strategies see Bourdieu, *Outline*, 32–71.
42 Maher, *Women and Property*, 191–221.
43 Bourdieu, *Outline*, 33–43.
44 See Hans Medick, 'The Proto-Industrial Family Economy: The Structural Function of Household and Family during the Transition from Peasant Society to Industrial Capitalism', *Social History*, 1 (Oct. 1976), 291–315.
45 Cf. Thomas Held, *Soziologie der ehelichen Machtverhältnisse*, (Neuwied, 1978), 52–7.
46 M. Poster, *Critical Theory of the Family* (London, 1978), 100, in describing the positions of Freud and Lacan.
47 Andrew Strathern, 'Work Processes and Social Change in Highland New Guinea', paper presented to the Anthropology and History Round Table I (Göttingen, 1978), 2–3.
48 See Meyer Fortes, 'Pietas in Ancestor Worship', in *Time and Social Structure and Other Essays* (New York, 1970), 164–200.
49 Cf. A. R. Radcliffe-Brown, *Structure and Function in Society* (London, 1952), chaps. 1–4.
50 For example, Raymond T. Smith, *The Negro Family in British Guiana* (London, 1956). For a critical appraisal, M. K. Slater, 'The Rule of Legitimacy and the Caribbean Family: A Case in Martinique', *Ethnic Groups*, 1 (1976), 38–87.
51 In discussing the arguments of Deleuze and Guattari, Poster makes the following observations, which point up the problem of the manner in which the family's emotional life is structured under different modes of production: 'Far from a necessary stage in psycho-sexual maturation, the law of Oedipus ensnares the unconscious into the trap of personified desires. The Oedipus complex is not a simple repression of an existing desire, but a double operation of first structuring a desire and then interdicting it. Without the Oedipus complex and before its appearance, "father and mother exist only in pieces and are never organized into a figure nor into a structure capable at once of representing the unconscious and of representing in it the various agents of the

collectivity, but always break into fragments . . ." The Oedipus complex "translates" the unconscious into Papa, Mama and child, who, far from natural or universal figures, are the specific products of capitalism . . . [Deleuze and Guattari] view Papa-Mama (the emotional configuration that is given to parents and elicited by them in the nuclear family) more as products of capitalism than as autonomous agents. Starting from society as a whole, they see the family and its psychic drama only as a segment of the whole and in relation to the whole. In pre-capitalist societies Oedipus exists only as a potentiality, as a space not filled. After capitalism has deterritorialized or reduced the libidinal value of kinship structures, of relations of alliance and descent, Oedipus emerges as a repressing and potent form . . . the family is constituted under capitalism as the place where the production of desire will be blocked and misshaped and will be coded and marked through the castrations of the Oedipus complex . . . Oedipus is a socially imposed repression against the free flux of the unconscious.' Poster, *Critical Theory*, 106.
52 Fortes, 'Pietas'.
53 For examples, Leonard Kasdan, 'Family Structure, Migration and the Entrepreneur', *Comparative Studies in Society and History*, 7 (1965), 345–57; Goody, *Context*.
54 A good example of such an analysis is Alain Collomp, 'Alliance et filiation en Haute Provence au XVIIIe siècle', *Annales ESC*, 32 (1977), 445–7. See also the brilliant article by Pierre Bourdieu, 'Stratégies'.
55 The fact that property rights shape subsequent relationships among sons is discussed by Campbell, *Honour*, 189. Loizos also develops a similar argument, *Greek Gift*, 67–8. See also Emrys Lloyd Peters, 'Aspects of Affinity in a Lebanese Maronite Village', in J. G. Peristiany (ed.), *Mediterranean Family Structures* (Cambridge, 1976), 157–71.
56 In a south German village in the eighteenth century, for example, conflicts between wife and husband were brought before the village court by the father or brother of the wife. Often the property rights of the woman were at issue.
57 An extreme case of this is discussed by Paul Veyne in 'La famille et l'amour'. See also Collomp, 'Alliance et filiation'.
58 See Sigrid Khera, 'An Austrian Peasant Village Under Rural Industrialization', *Behavior Science Notes*, 7 (1972), 29–36, for an example where the sibling group breaks off relations. Vernier, 'Emigration', provides an extreme case of dependence for younger sisters.
59 Khera, 'Austrian Peasant Village'.
60 David Sabean, 'Unehelichkeit: ein Aspekt sozialer Reproduktion kleinbäuerlicher Produzenten. Zu einer Analyse dörflicher Quellen um 1800', in Robert Berdahl, et al. (eds.), *Klassen und Kultur. Sozialanthropologische Perspektiven in der Geschichtsschreibung* (Frankfurt, 1982), 54–73.
61 Campbell, *Honour*, 176–9. See also N. Abu-Zahra, 'Family and Kinship in a Tunisian Peasant Community', in Peristiany, *Mediterranean Family*, 157–71. Goody, *Context*, 200–24, discusses fostering in terms of the claims and counter-claims that grown siblings make on each other. And finally, Bourdieu, *Outline*, 39–40: 'the closest genealogical relationship, that between brothers, is also the point of greatest tension, and only incessant work can maintain the community of interests. In short, the genealogical relationship is never strong enough on its own to provide a complete determination of the relationship between individuals which it unites, and it has such predictive value only when it goes with the shared interests, produced by the common possession of a material and symbolic patrimony, which entails collective vulnerability as well as collective property.'
62 See Peter Laslett, *The World We have Lost* (New York, 1965), 2–6, 78–9; Neil J. Smelser, *Social Change in the Industrial Revolution* (London, 1959), 2–3, 158–62, 198–9, 211–12.

63 The problem has recently been discussed by Ludolf Kuchenbuch, who finds an accent on the nuclear family *before* village institutions developed: *Bäuerliche Gesellschaft und Klosterherrschaft im 9. Jahrhundert* (Wiesbaden, 1978), 59ff.
64 See the works already cited by Pierre Bourdieu.
65 Cf. Claude Meillassoux, *Femmes, greniers et capitaux* (Paris 1975), part 2; for a specific group in the European transition towards capitalism, cf. Medick, 'Proto-Industrial Family Economy'.
66 An excellent example for this is given in the essay of Vernier, 'Emigration'.
67 P. C. W. Gutkind, 'African Urbanism, Mobility and the Social Network, *International Journal of Comparative Sociology*, 6 (1965), 48–60; for the impoverished peasantry in nineteenth-century Ireland see Michael Anderson, *Family Structure in 19th Century Lancashire* (Cambridge, 1971), 81ff. Cf. the interesting remarks in Meyer Fortes, 'Kinship and the Axiom of Amity', in his *Kinship*; Carol B. Stack, *All Our Kin: Strategies for Survival in a Black Community* (New York, 1974).
68 For an overview of the debate see the introductory remarks in Slater, 'Rule of Legitimacy', 38–43; recent positions: Stack, *All Our Kin* and 'Sex Roles and Survival Strategies in an Urban Black Community', in Michelle Z. Rosaldo and Louise Lamphère (eds.), *Women, Culture and Society* (Stanford, 1974), 113–28; N. Tanner, 'Matrifocality in Indonesia and Africa and Among Black Americans', Rosaldo and Lamphère, *Women*, 129–56.
69 Michael Young and Peter Willmott, *Family and Kinship in East London* [1957] (Harmondsworth, 1972), 189.
70 Anderson, *Family Structure*, 178.
71 E. P. Thompson, 'Happy Families', *New Society* (8 Sept. 1977), 499–501, review of Stone, *The Family*: 'The Highland crofter's family was not the same as the Cornish tinner's nor as the Yorkshire weaver's. And to understand these families, and to detect the signs and gestures which disclose their interior emotional life, we must attend very closely indeed to "economics" – or to that daily occupation (farming, fishing, weaving, begging) which gives us their way of living: a way of living which was not merely a way of surviving but also a way of relating and valuing . . . for the vast majority throughout history, familial relations have been intermeshed with the structures of work. Feeling may be *more*, rather than less, tender or intense *because* relations are "economic" and critical to mutual survival. Anthropologists may know of societies without "sentiment" but they do not often show us societies without norms or value systems. That people did not feel or relate to us does not mean that they did not feel at all nor relate in ways which to them were imbued with the profoundest meaning' (501).
72 Herbert G. Gutman, *The Black Family in Slavery and Freedom 1750–1925* (Oxford, 1976), esp. chap. 5: 'Aunts and Uncles and Swap Dog Kin'.
73 A first effort in this direction for Germany has been undertaken in the study of H. Zwahr, *Zur Konstitutierung des Proletariats als Klasse: Strukturuntersuchung über das Leipziger Proletariat während der industriellen Revolution* (Berlin, 1978), without, however, profiting from the anthropological approach; Zwahr is interested in 'Patenschaft' as a medium of 'proletarian community relations', but his macroanalytic approach makes him miss to a large extent the social and emotional infrastructure of these community relations.

2. Putting kin and kinship to good use : the circulation of goods, labour, and names on Karpathos (Greece)

BERNARD VERNIER

Building mills and chapels, acquiring gold pieces, household utensils, and names, monopolizing priestly and presidential positions, and following certain marriage practices were all strategies used by the *canacares*, both to maintain and increase their economic and symbolic capital, which was based on the private ownership of the best land, and to reproduce the balance of economic and symbolic forces that had made it possible.[1] They were all ultimately strategies by which the social order based on their domination was consolidated and perpetuated. As well, any threats to the unity of a patrimony at the moment of succession had to be eliminated. The primitive stage of development of the forces of production (rudimentary agricultural techniques, non-selected seeds, the inadequate protection of animals and crops from disease, and so on) meant that productivity was low. There were no opportunities for investment in a more profitable sector, and in any case the size of farms, even amongst the *canacares*, was too small for the necessary capital to be available. Conversely, the lack of capital and good land made it difficult to increase the size of farms. In such conditions, any division of the land meant, for each generation, the risk of reducing the chance of economic survival for the lines and, more immediately, of endangering the position of each of them in the social structure, even if only by making it dependent on the number of children involved in the succession.

Primogeniture and the reproduction of the social position of male and female lines

In order to solve the problems of its own survival and those of the survival of lines and of the reproduction of the social structure, this society appears to have completely abandoned equality of rights amongst children, keeping only, for the sake of equity, a positive equality amongst the firstborn of each sex, who alone could inherit, and a negative one amongst the younger male and female offspring, who had no rights at all. Property was transmitted in a bilinear fashion, with the eldest daughter inheriting from the mother and the eldest son from the father.[2]

28

The privileges accorded to the eldest were simply a re-translation of hierarchical relationships to the internal structure of the sibling group in the area of rules governing the transmission of property, and corresponded to the logic of safeguarding the integrity of the patrimony. These hierarchical relationships were based on age and were found throughout the whole of the society in relationships of respect structuring dealings between young and old, and they followed naturally from a society based on subsistence farming characterized by the low level of development of the forces of production. In a society simply aimed at self-reproduction, in which the most important part of the knowledge used in production was a legacy from the past, the old were unquestionably the source of both technical expertise and of knowledge concerning the rules of play, which themselves depended on the mode of production. The lack of ready capital and of any opportunity for investment capable of rapidly increasing personal wealth meant that the individual owed the major part of what he had to his ancestors. And yet, because there were both male and female lines – in contrast to what happened in other societies where primogeniture was the norm – it was the eldest of both sexes within each family that inherited. If, for example, the eldest daughter could be the fourth child in order of age and still inherit, it was because the principle of superiority based on age had to compromise with the necessity of the survival of the female line.

The priority given to the interests of the line, which meant that the younger children were disinherited, also obliged the parents to leave the major part of their property to the eldest as soon as the latter were in a position to continue the line. The father did so at the marriage of the eldest son, the mother at that of the eldest daughter. They only kept the usufruct of some of their fields for the rest of their lives. After their death, they reverted to the eldest children by right. They had to live on this 'old-age portion' (*yerondomiri*) and support the remaining children from it. From the patrimony of the two lines, the parents also took another small amount, called the *xalimika*, which they could share out as they wished between the younger male and female children. In most cases, however, the *xalimika* was of very little value. Its main purpose was to provide the *apoxenosis* for the younger children. This was a symbolic gift, amounting to no more than the value of a strip of land or a few olive trees or sheep and sometimes even of a few cooking-pots. It was, however, compulsory, for without it the succession, the chief function of which was, as its name implies, to exclude the younger children from the inheritance, was invalid. What was important was not the gift itself, but its function, which was to keep the patrimony intact. If the younger child did not marry, that share reverted to the one possessing the inheritance from which it had been taken, thus completely restoring the integrity of the patrimony of the line.

Property bequeathed to eldest children were enumerated in exhaustive detail in the marriage contract (*prikosymphonon*): fields, threshing-floors, animals (with or without the young they were carrying), houses and their contents (sheets, clothes, cushions, pots and pans, ornaments, needles and so on) and, where appropriate, gold pieces, mills (or the right to use them for a certain number of hours per year), chapels (in whole or in part) and special places in church. The marriage contract also described the land that the parents intended to keep as *yerondomiri* either until their death or until they were too old to look after it.[3] Sometimes, as in a contract of 1758, the eldest children signed an undertaking to keep their parents once they had received the *yerondomiri*: 'I, (Costas) promise that whenever my master (children called their fathers *afendis*, or master) shall wish to come to me in his old age, I shall take him in, feed and care for him for as long as he shall live, and shall pray for his soul when he is dead. When he comes to me, I shall have the right to his vines.'[4] When parents bequeathed all their goods while they were still alive, it sometimes happened that their eldest children abandoned them and even ill-treated them. In principle, they were obliged by custom either to feed or to pay a certain sum of money to the parent who had given them his *yerondomiri*, but custom could be more or less restrictively interpreted. To the priest who asked him why he did not take care of his father, one son replied, 'first let him eat the silver knife that he kept and then I will look after him'.[5]

Although in theory the total value of the *yerondomiri* and the *xalimika* was purely a matter for the parents to decide, in reality its absolute value and the proportion of the patrimony it represented depended on the strategies the parents used when trying to reconcile their own material and symbolic interests, those of their younger children, and those of their line. Seen from the point of view of their own material interests and those of the younger children, the part kept back was a guarantee. It had to enable them to live and to maintain the younger children. Moreover, it obliged the eldest children to look after them in their old age since, if they did not do so, the old father, for example, could in theory incur debts which his eldest son would have to pay, both in order to get back the *yerondomiri* and to avoid the disgrace of leaving his father's debts unpaid. On the other hand, however, the need to ensure that the material and symbolic interests of the line were preserved and its social position maintained meant that this share could not be large.

The prime necessity was that the eldest children should be able to make a good marriage. Given the competitive situation on the marriage market, the parents had to reduce the *xalimika* to virtually nothing and to calculate the *yerondomiri* very finely indeed if this essential aim was to be achieved. In addition, if the parents kept back too large a *yerondomiri*, it was immediately seen by the rest of the village as a sign that they distrusted their eldest children. If such distrust was not justified, the parents were dishonouring themselves, since they were acting unfairly towards those who had become the true representatives of the lines. On the other hand, if the parents had good cause to protect themselves from their own eldest children, it was to be assumed that they had not brought them up properly. In either case, the parents, in trying to protect their own economic interest, were seriously undermining the symbolic capital of their lines. The value of the *xalimika* varied according to the number of younger male and female children, but that of the *xalimika* and the *yerondomiri* together rarely exceeded

20% of the two patrimonies. The parents preferred to rent land belonging to the *canacares* or to the Church rather than retain an excessive *yerondomiri*.

The father's house was part of the *yerondomiri*. Once the eldest girl had married and settled with her husband in the house she had received from her mother,[6] the parents retired there with their remaining children. The same rule had operated in the preceding generation, and the house the parents went to was inhabited by the daughter's paternal grandparents. If they were both still alive, they rented a house in the village if possible. Otherwise – and it was not infrequently the case – they ceased to be a couple as such, each going off towards his or her own line and fortune. The paternal grandfather stayed where he was with his son and daughter-in-law, and the paternal grandmother went off to live with her eldest daughter or the latter's eldest daughter. In reality, the grandparents often did not, strictly speaking, live with their children or grandchildren, but in a room built onto their house or very close to it. This room was both kitchen and store-room, and was in most cases without any decoration or comfort. They slept on a rough sofa consisting merely of raised planking, with the space thus created used for old clothes and odds and ends.

If, even as late as the start of the century, elderly spouses were still separating, it was because the lines, whose interests were only in partial and temporary concord, were allied in each couple. Indeed, an analysis of the rules governing the management and transmission of patrimonies shows that one of their functions was to stop one of the lines adversely affecting the interests of the other, and *a fortiori* when the latter was a female one. The wife was not responsible for her husband's debts. Once their possessions had been bequeathed to their eldest children, the parents could incur debts only on their part of the *yerondomiri*. Where there were debts on both estates, the husband was obliged to settle first those on the female one. When managing his wife's possessions, the husband had to pass them on intact to her eldest daughter and to make good any deficiencies in money or in appropriate cases in kind, whether it was a matter of missing handkerchieves or of worn-out pots and pans. For that reason, the wife's goods were called *sigoura* (literally, things which are secure). If the husband invested in the wife's estate – by planting trees or improving the house, for example – it was at his own expense, and he could reap no permanent advantage from it. Hence the sayings, 'If donkeys graze on the wife's field, no man cares' and 'In the wife's field plant only artichokes and garlic'.[7] If husband or wife died and the couple were childless, the survivor could not keep the property of the deceased spouse. It returned whence it came: to the brother or brother's son of the husband, to the sister or daughter of the sister of the wife.[8] When one of the spouses died leaving a minor to inherit, the remaining spouse could keep him and manage his estate. The expenses caused by the child, however, were the responsibility of that spouse. Any investment affecting the child's goods had to be approved by a family council consisting solely of the male relatives on the side from which the estate had originally come. Otherwise, such investments remained the responsibility of the surviving spouse. In addition, the widow or widower could in certain cases ask the lineage from which the minor came for reimbursement of the cost of keeping him. From this exhaustive and exhausting listing of rules it can be seen how important the idea of the line was.[9]

The exploitation of the younger female children: an elementary form of exploitation

What became of the children who had no inheritance? Many of the younger sons emigrated, most often for good.[10] The younger daughters mostly remained single and, once the eldest had married, lived in the paternal house with their parents. They worked on both the *yerondomiri* and the land belonging to their eldest sister and her husband. When their mother went to live with her eldest daughter or always when she died, they went to live with their eldest sister or her eldest daughter, serving them as maids and agricultural labourers. The eldest daughters who were *canacares* looked after their houses and their children. Although the other eldest daughters worked in the fields, it was chiefly at times when there was a lot of work, and the more younger unmarried females – sisters or maternal aunts – there were working for them, the less they did so. The younger female children, who did most of the farm jobs allocated to women in the division of labour, were given the most difficult and dirty ones. Hoeing, replacing mules for heavy loads, and fetching the water when they were in the village fell chiefly on them. Like the shepherds, however, and unlike the eldest daughters, they spent most of their time outside the village, sleeping near the fields in houses that were also used to shelter animals. In families owning only a small amount of land, the parents or elder sister would also send them out to work as labourers for wealthier peasants or as maids in a nearby town such as Pigadia or on another island such as Simi or Chalki.[11] The eldest daughters, however, even if they were not *canacares*, never went to work for strangers. They had enough to do in their houses, and such a thing would have been bad for their prestige and that of their line. Overall, younger daughters only went as labourers for others if their own families could not make rational use of them as full-time workers, and their families only took on outside labour if they had not enough younger daughters for the required labour. These younger daughters, as can be seen, were very useful as farm labourers. They worked for their sisters without pay, however, and although they worked on both the *yerondomiri* and the land jointly owned by their sisters and their husbands, they had to live on what the *yerondomiri* alone produced.

This fact best explains the chief function of the transmission of land separated from the *yerondomiri* when the eldest children married. It was less a case of enabling the parents and younger children to survive – this could have been provided for the transmission of an undivided patrimony not bequeathed until the death of the parents – than of completely separating the budget of the young couple from that of their parents and younger siblings. If the parents' land and that of their heirs had not been separated at the marriage of the latter, it could all have been seen as a common property from which all should benefit. By separating the units of consumption and production and in doing so by reducing the likelihood of anyone contesting the way in which the yields were divided up, the transmission of goods at the time of the marriage (apart from the *yerondomiri*) solved the double problem of maintaining the labour force and reproducing the social order. As the eldest, when they married, became the new representatives of the lines whose vitality and fecundity they were now better placed than their parents to assume, they had to inherit the major part of the patrimony at that time if the symbolic and material interest of the lines, and hence their position in the social structure, were to be maintained. But if they were to be able to maintain that position, their inheritance had paradoxically to be reduced when they married. For this meant that the eldest children were not required to maintain the labour force of younger women and could therefore, by their way of life and consumption, represent their line with the greatest possible brilliance. The smaller the *yerondomiri*, the smaller, inevitably, the consumption of the younger sisters. Keeping them as a work force could therefore be done at the least possible cost. Moreover, when the younger sisters subsequently went to live with the eldest, their needs would be all the smaller as they had been shaped by their earlier way of life and as the women were then so much older.

The eldest children of both sexes owned the means of production and exploited the younger sisters by extorting a labour rent from them. For this to become clear, we need only realize that whereas the eldest children only supplied the younger daughters working for them – even if they came from outside – with a reduced standard of living, the latter enabled the eldest, through their work, to have both their own family and a high social status. The relationship of exploitation between the eldest children and the younger female children was chiefly produced by the system of the transmission of goods which made the younger women economically dependent by separating the *yerondomiri* from the rest of the patrimony and by the rules of residence. All the eldest children enjoyed the same privileges, even if it was only a question of the opportunity of marrying and having children, and although their situation varied as a result of the unequal distribution of land, it was nevertheless totally different from that of the younger females. The eldest also had common interests objectively in contradiction to those of the unmarried younger sisters. Although there were within the families relationships based on domination and economic exploitation, it is nevertheless true that, unlike in class relationships, it was the dominant 'group' of the eldest children who, by reproducing themselves biologically, reproduced the dominated 'group' they needed. Those who try to prove that kinship relationships can also be class relationships – as if exploitation needed to be 'noble' in order to exist – forget that within social organization kinship relationships have a dominant

Table 1. *Average no. of children per family according to order of birth and social category of the spouses**

	Wives	Husbands	No. of children
I	Eldest daughters**	Eldest sons	5.4
	Eldest daughters	Younger sons	4.9
	Younger daughters	Eldest sons	3.8
	Younger daughters	Younger sons	3.5
II	Elder daughters		
	poor peasants, shepherds	shepherds	6.5
	poor peasants, shepherds	poor peasants, shepherds	5.9
	canacares, medium peasants	*canacares*	5.7
	canacares, medium peasants	*canacares*, medium peasants	5.3
	canacares, medium peasants	poor peasants, shepherds	4.5
	poor peasants, shepherds	*canacares*, medium peasants	4.5
	Younger daughters***		
	poor peasants, shepherds		4.1
	canacares, medium peasants		3.4

* We included couples who married before 1945 and in which the wife was aged 45 or over (n = 172).
** Given the system of transmitting possessions, which disinherited, in most cases, the eldest daughter of a younger daughter and sometimes, as will be seen, enabled younger daughters to inherit, the difference between the number of children of elder daughters and younger daughters would have been greater if it had been possible to contrast elder daughters of elder daughters and disinherited younger daughters.
*** As there were not too many married younger daughters, it did not prove possible to compare their social category with that of their husbands (n = 46).

In this society, obsessed by lines and setting great store by female fertility, the eldest daughters had more children than the younger ones, so that the couples having most children were those formed by two eldest children (5.4) and those having fewest were those consisting of two younger children (3.5). As they had inherited from two patrimonies, couples of eldest children, or at least the richest of them, could feed and make rational use of a large family labour force. In addition, having a lot of children meant that they had a better chance of being sure that their eldest daughter, once she was married, would have the labour of a younger sister. For opposite reasons, the younger sisters who managed to marry were forced to limit deliberately the number of children they had. (For women marrying before they were twenty, the number of children after fifteen years of marriage also varied according to the order of birth (3.8 for eldest daughters as against 2.8 for younger ones). The small number of children of younger daughters cannot be explained by the fact that they generally married older than eldest daughters.) Eldest daughters married to younger sons had more children than younger daughters married to elder sons (4.9 as against 3.8).

The wife's order of birth was more important than the husband's because women, unlike men, never worked outside once they were married. This meant that their order of birth was much more influential than the man's in the sphere of their overall resources. In addition, in so far as younger sisters worked for their eldest sister rather than their eldest brother, the labour needs of the couple in question were defined by the order of birth of the mother and not of the father. As part II of the table shows, however, attempting to explain fertility strategies in terms of the total resources available and labour needs would be to take a naively materialistic view. It would only offer a partial explanation, and would not account for the fact that the couples with most children were those in which the spouses belonged to the lowest social categories. This paradox can only be understood if we assume that the couples in the highest social categories wanted to ensure the standard of living called for by their social position. It then becomes clearer why the eldest daughters with fewest children were those who married a man from a different social category (the number of social categories has been reduced to two for statistical purposes). It looks as if the husband or wife in the highest social position, in desiring to protect his or her social rank, imposed a limit on the number of children. It was also this same desire to preserve social status that induced younger sisters in the highest social groups to be most rigorous in keeping down the number of children. On average, they had three children fewer than the eldest daughters of poor peasants and shepherds married to shepherds (3.4 as against 6.5). In addition, the difference between eldest and youngest sister tended to disappear, in parallel with the increasing fall in value of the land. If women married before 1935 are separated from those married between 1935 and 1960, it appears that after fifteen years of marriage eldest daughters in both periods had 3.8 children whereas younger sisters had 2.6 for the first period and 3.2 for the second.

position and are quite compatible with exploitation of labour. Rejecting that would mean accepting the indigenous ideology which raised the family, or more exactly the line, to the level of a quasi-sacred institution, the very ideology that in this society made exploitation possible.

In this society, which was so poor that it had to exclude a large number of its members and condemn an equally large number to celibacy, relationships of production could not be exclusively economic ones. The fact that farms were extremely small (the biggest ones being of up to 10 hectares in size, but most being of less than 3 hectares) and that productivity was low because of the primitive level of development of the forces of production meant that there were serious obstacles to the creation of the surplus necessary to pay agricultural labourers' wages. No exploited group outside the dominant group, having its own mode of biological reproduction, could appear. Indeed, the large increase in population which would have followed from this would have been incompatible with the potentiality for subsistence provided by the economy. It could well have brought about a situation in which the whole social order was no longer certain, and the low wages of the local work force would have brought in its wake a massive and, more significantly, uncontrolled wave of emigration,[12] threatening the ability of those owning the means of production to find the necessary agricultural workers. In short, the workers could not be free workers. In other words, they somehow had to be forced both to stay where they were and to work under conditions of exploitation which prevented them from marrying. If other types of constraint, such as the feudal *corvée*, had been logically conceivable, kinship links were there and predisposed to offer the necessary compulsion, since they afforded a complete domination of those exploited. Indeed, it was because they were subject to parental authority that the younger daughters were forced to stay where they were and work for their eldest sisters all their lives. It was also all the easier for parents to command obedience, as, in addition to the 'natural' authority of any parents over their offspring, they had the moral authority of the example of their own self-denial in giving up their possessions when their eldest child married. The chief function of choosing to transmit property at that time was certainly to stop very young children resisting being disinherited, but it also indirectly prepared them for self-sacrifice. Parents could also more easily impose obedience when they wanted their younger daughters to work for their eldest sister and her husband if they themselves derived no economic benefit from such work and could not be suspected of seeking their own ends. It was chiefly the eldest daughter who gained from it, both economically and symbolically. Her prestige was increased by the extra labour that she could direct without dirtying her hands. It also meant that she could withdraw from some of the work. Thus, each younger daughter, by working for her eldest sister, both strengthened the latter's prestige and helped to perpetuate the exploitation of younger sisters as a whole. When the parents died and were no longer there to exert their whole authority on behalf of the eldest daughter, the economic interest of the younger ones alone was enough to make them live with her and work for her. It will be recalled that at that point the *yerondomiri* was divided up between the eldest son and the eldest daughter. The younger daughters, old and no longer able to emigrate, had no other way of staying alive.

The concealment of relationships of exploitation

The chief reason for the effectiveness of the system, however, was the ability of the family as an institution to legitimize and conceal relationships which were in reality purely ones of domination and exploitation. What happened was that the family as an institution transformed, by its own logic, the economic benefits within it into signs of devotion, respect, or affection and helped prevent any realization of their objectively economic nature. For the exploitation of work to become a sacrifice to the maternal line and the economic benefits of the younger daughters to become a gift, all that was needed was that exploitation should be achieved through kinship links. Or rather, the totally free nature of the economic benefits of younger sisters was the vital factor which made it seem to be something other than an economic benefit. A payment, however small, in kind or *a fortiori* in cash, could only have brought with it an awareness of the economic truth of the relationship and a resultant calculating attitude and awareness of exploitation. The fact that younger sisters were not paid had the further objective function of keeping them dependent and thus of forcing them to work ceaselessly for the eldest in the hope that they would be taken in by her and well treated when they were old. Conversely, the material aid sometimes given by the eldest daughter to members of her family when the *yerondomiri* was not enough to keep them could thus seem to be a gift rather than a payment for services received, and she could reap all its symbolic benefits. It could be argued that the younger sisters received wages in that they often shared the food of the eldest daughters or her husband when they worked in the fields. To do so would be to miss the symbolic value of this shared meal. The loss of earnings that it entailed for the eldest daughter and her husband was insignificant compared with their total profits from that implicit reaffirmation of the links of kinship and affection, a renewal of assent which ensured mutual understanding and meant that the younger daughters would accept their place within the relationship of exploitation. But if they were incapable of perceiving that they were dependent, it was also due in part to the very fact of their celibacy, which was a product of the fact that they were disinherited and unpaid. Their celibacy reduced their needs to the minimum [13] and made them see their eldest sister's family as their own. They consequently shared in the joys of family life by proxy, and this in return ruled out the question of wages. What is more, when they were able to amass any personal savings from outside work, they left them to the children of their eldest sister, being condemned, so to speak, to invest all their affections in them. Thus the circle of exploitation was completed.

If exploitation by parents can only exist in societies which give the family a central place, it is because the family as an institution is most successful in protecting relationships of exploitation when it has greatest value in the eyes of those who are sacrificed, and thus manages better to legitimize the sacrifices it expects. Even if the younger daughters had been able, as individuals, to become conscious of the fact that they were exploited, the mode of production, by enclosing them in separate families to which they had ties, meant that they had no chance of becoming conscious of their interest as a group. The extremely high value set upon the line, which implied an intense rivalry with every other line and a state of perpetual competitiveness, worked in the same direction. By involving the younger daughters in the quarrels of the lines, any realization of their common interests was prevented and an effective means of excluding any questioning of the social order was provided.

Although the work of younger daughters was unpaid, it would nevertheless be wrong to conclude that it was totally disinterested. Not only did it enable them to maintain good relations with an elder sister who, in theory, was supposed to house them when their parents died, but also it gave them symbolic advantages. That was their real payment. By working for the eldest sister, they were helping to strengthen the economic and symbolic capital of the line she represented, and they benefited from this indirectly themselves, at least with regard to the symbolic capital. Above all, by devoting and even sacrificing themselves for their eldest sister, they were behaving in the most socially demanded and respect-compelling way, the way most likely to incur general approval. To minimize such advantages is to forget that since younger sisters were totally without material capital, they themselves were all the more likely to value them, since any symbolic capital they might have was their only wealth.

In the final analysis, the fact that they had absolutely no share in the ownership or the means of production was the necessary economic condition which made the exploitation of younger sisters possible. The interaction of parental pressures and their own economic and symbolic interests helped to make them go on working for their eldest sisters. All these conditions together, however, would not have kept them in their native locality. If they were to remain in their villages, living in such conditions that they could not even marry, they had to be induced to accept the fact that they were disinherited as a natural and inevitable fate. This was the basic task of family upbringing as a systematic process of ideological inculcation aimed at making them internalize the overriding importance of the interests of the lines as opposed to those of individuals and of the superiority of the eldest over the younger children (seen from this angle, this cult of lines was the keystone, in ideological terms, of the whole system of exploitation). As a systematic undertaking this upbringing was aimed at developing in them a suitable disposition, that is, a permanent inclination (*habitus*) to sacrifice themselves for their eldest sisters, which would subsequently rule out any awareness of being exploited by creating in them the illusion that their sacrifice was a voluntary one. Amongst the strategies employed to that end, one in particular, that of sending them, when they were very young indeed, to work as maids or labourers for other people, was particularly effective. The effort of training them to accept domestic service – a *habitus* which could later be transferred back to the family – was passed on to another family which could do the job better because it was composed of strangers. One of the advantages – and not the least – of such a strategy was that the younger sister would be all the more likely to accept her situation within her own family if she had something to compare it with and could see herself as being happy that she was no longer an outsider but back among her own kin.

It was in any case the way of life that they were offered and the systematically different way of treating the eldest and the younger daughters rather than what was said that made sure that the latter were properly fitted into the relationships of exploitation. At mealtimes, the eldest girls were given the best food, and the younger ones usually dressed in clothes handed down from the eldest; in quarrels, the eldest, who was her mother's particular favourite, was usually the one in the right. In the case of the younger girls, reprimands were often accompanied by corporal punishments (in the form of slaps across the face), whereas the eldest was usually only scolded, because, as was said, she must not be spoiled. The younger ones had more work to do than the eldest, and were trained to serve her. She, on the other hand, was given a taste for ordering others and being served.

The eldest would embroider her own trousseau, but all the embroidery that the others did was also for her. Yet the most important factor here was not so much the value of what they made for her, the immediate result of their work, as the fact that they were trained in a *habitus* whose true function, that of inducing them to put their labour at her disposal, would only emerge later. In addition, the fact that they were removed from all social life would have been enough to convince them that they were inferior. The younger daughters were kept away from the dances and assemblies to which the eldest were allowed to go as soon as they could walk. Nor did they ever accompany their mothers when they went to a wedding or a christening. That was the privilege of the eldest, and while she went out, the younger daughters worked at home or in the fields. It can thus be seen that the strategies employed with regard both to upbringing and to matters of inheritance made it possible to keep the patrimony undivided and valuable, and therefore contributed to reproducing the place of the lines in the social structure and in so doing to the reproduction of the social order itself.

The circumstances of a village crime of around 1926 give some idea of how effective that upbringing was. An unmarried younger sister had spread the rumour that an eldest sister had aborted an illegitimate child while her husband, who had emigrated, was out of the country. The eldest sister decided to kill her. She went to her house with her own younger sister. The latter cut the woman's throat herself.

The effects of that upbringing became evident too in the new context created by widespread emigration when the work of younger sisters was becoming less and less necessary. We have seen how increased competition amongst girls on a matrimonial market where men had a rarity value meant that the latter were in a privileged position in the bargaining arising from marriages. During a transitional period, when a younger sister had an unusual dowry that was bigger than her sister's, the man who married the elder sister often also obtained it. The younger sisters who sacrificed themselves almost naturally for their eldest sisters in that way found in the public approval of their act by the members of their family and the other villagers a symbolic compensation for their economic loss. Thus, a younger sister, urged by her mother who benefited from her husband's death, renounced her title to her father's estate in order to enable her eldest sister to marry. At the wedding, the guests sang *mandinades*, short poems improvised for the occasion, in praise of the younger girl. At fifty, she still liked to recite them frequently, as if she needed to persuade herself that she had done right to agree:

> Thou who giv'st us to drink
> With all thy beauty,
> Thou hast given thy whole share,
> Thy eldest's marriage was thy duty.
> Our praises we are singing
> For thy fine, fine upbringing,
> Because thou gavest of thy free will
> As if thy father were with us still.

But it was their whole experience – both direct and indirect, and however limited it was – of social life that served to reinforce the effect of their upbringing. In the society they lived in, everything was dominated by the eldest sons and daughters. Out of the ten presidents of Olymbos between 1900 and 1923, there were eight *canacares*, a merchant and an artisan (the latter elected by the shepherds' votes), but they were all eldest sons.[14] Nine married eldest daughters from amongst the *canacares*, the tenth an elementary-school teacher. When people talked of 'eldest' (children or brothers and sisters) to outsiders, *-mas* (meaning 'our') was added to their Christian names – 'our Caliopi'.[15] The eldest had the place of honour at all feasts, and the importance accorded to the celebration of the birth of a child depended not only on the family's social position, but also on its order of birth. Thus it was only the left ears of eldest males that were pierced to receive the single gold ring (*vergeta*), and the celebrations on the seventh day after the birth of a child were of a particular kind when they were for eldest children of either sex. They were more splendid and more guests were invited. As can be seen, all such celebrations discriminated between eldest and younger children and by doing so had the function, amongst others, of reminding younger children of their lowlier social existence and their inferiority. They made such children accept their subordinate position and added to the symbolic capital of their eldest brothers and sisters.

The cult of the lines, the ideology of *anastassi*, and naming strategies

Strategies related to inheritance and upbringing, as we have seen, were aimed at perpetuating the position of the lines in the social structure in each generation. To them were closely related their naming strategies, the function of which was to make clear to all, and thus socially real, the existence and continuity of the lines, which could only be defined in social terms, since, as we shall see, brothers and sisters and even brothers themselves and sisters themselves belonged to different lines although biologically they had the same parent. This aim was achieved by systematically using the ancestral Christian name of the male and female lines. In addition, by giving eldest sons the name of their paternal grandfather, and eldest daughters that of their maternal grandmother, parents were carrying out the sacred duty of *anastassi*, or bringing ancestors back to life. It was said that the souls of the ancestors, who had passed on the material and symbolic patrimony of their line, entered into the body of the persons bearing their names. By giving eldest children the Christian names of venerated ancestors, the naming system added these symbolic goods to the patrimony they had received. Given the ideology underlying it and 'identifying' the eldest children with the ancestors whose names they bore, the chief function of the naming system was, however, to legitimize in the eyes of all, but more especially in those of younger brothers and sisters, the exclusive rights of the eldest to the inheritance.[16] The latter were made the representatives of the lines.[17] The ideology of *anastassi* was one which a society driven, if it was to survive, to legitimizing the inordinate rights of a minority, could not avoid creating. The cult of the lines, the ideology of *anastassi*, and the system of transmitting Christian names were all key pieces in a system of exploitation. In terms of its own logic, each of them contributed to the maintenance of the social order by preventing the development of claims by younger children on the patrimony of the parental lines.

In addition, however, the lines had to neutralize the various threats to their physical reproduction arising in particular from the quirks of demography. If the eldest child died before the birth of a sibling of the same sex, the latter took both his Christian name and his rights to the inheritance. If he died after it, it was the third child of the same sex who replaced him, since the second did not bear his Christian name and therefore owned nothing. It can be seen that the order of birth was of less importance than the possession of the Christian name, which was the social expression of the continuity of the line. The second child was, so to speak, the victim of a system of legitimization which, if it were to benefit the eldest effectively and unopposedly, could permit very few exceptions indeed. If the eldest died after the others had already been given names, the inheritance went to the younger child with a Christian name from the same maternal or paternal line, who then had to give his eldest sibling' of the same sex as himself the Christian name of the ancestor from whom the inheritance came.

The fertility of the couple or the sex of the firstborn might raise snags and necessitate fresh solutions to the problem of reproducing both male and female lines. An only child normally took the Christian name from the appropriate line, but received the possessions of both parental lines. If both parents were *canacares*, the child was said to be a 'double *canacare*'. Such a child only enjoyed the patrimony of the parent of the opposite sex by personal right, however, and had to ensure the continuity of both lines. In the case of a daughter, the patrimony had to be transmitted intact to one of the two younger sons (in principle to the second of them) who received the Christian name and possessions of his mother's paternal grandfather. It can be seen that any accidental irregularity in one generation was removed in the next. The only child temporarily took over the line of his parent of the opposite sex. Estates remained in their respective male and female lines. Similarly, if all the children of a given couple were of the same sex, male for example, the second boy would inherit the female estate,[18] transmitting it on his marriage to his second daughter, who would inherit the estate and Christian name of her father's maternal grandmother.

The consequences of this system can be seen. It was not enough to be the eldest child of an inheritor in order to be able to inherit. In this case, Nicos in generation I did not do so, as his father only enjoyed a patrimony because he was used in the strategy for reproducing the line of his mother, Maria.

There was another complication. When the marriage of two eldest children was childless, the husband often adopted one of the children of one of his brothers, who then became his *parayios*. The wife too could adopt the eldest daughter of one of her sisters, who also became her *paracori* and inherited her possessions. The girl would have to take her maternal grandmother's name, the

42   Bernard Vernier

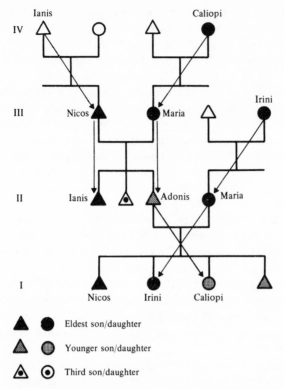

	Eldest son/daughter
	Younger son/daughter
	Third son/daughter

This genealogy and those following are not complete. Only individuals involved in the transmission of possessions or needing to be shown for an immediate understanding of the diagram appear in it. The arrows indicate the direction in which the possessions were transmitted.

boy his paternal grandfather's. The aunt or uncle providing the inheritance took the child into his or her house and the child became to all intents and purposes a son or daughter, respecting and loving them more than his own parents and taking care of them when they were old. Similarly, it was the aunt and not the mother who took the *paracori* to dances, and it was said of her that *eivai yia to cosmos* ('she is there for social life'). It was the aunt's younger sisters who worked in the *paracori*'s fields. When, as sometimes happened, the mother's brother became the adoptive uncle and his family name was a prestigious one, he transmitted it along with his possessions to his sister's son who abandoned his father's.

What was most important, however, was not so much the individual as the preservation of the interests of the lines. In that scheme of things the sex and Christian name of a child were not enough to confer any rights to an inheritance, for the person had to be able to carry out his social function. Hence any eldest child was disinherited if for any reason he emigrated, went to live in another part of Greece or even in another village on Karpathos, even if it was only a few kilometres away from his own. Accepting such eldest children as inheritors would have been equivalent to terminating the line at once and leaving its survival to chance or at least beyond control. In particular, disinheriting an eldest child who emigrated meant avoiding the risk that he might sell the material basis of the existence of the line to outsiders.[19] Similarly, any eldest children who were mad or deformed (such as dwarfs) or infirm (blind, and so on) or even ugly, especially in the case of girls, since it would prevent marriage and threaten the reproduction of the line, were debarred from inheriting.

With younger children, the naming system followed a principle of alternation which functioned separately for both sexes. We have seen that the eldest son took his paternal grandfather's Christian name. The second son took his maternal grandfather's and the third a Christian name from his father's side, more often than not from his father's line, but sometimes from that of his father's maternal grandfather, the fourth took one from his mother's side, and so on. Similarly, the second daughter took her paternal grandmother's Christian name, the third one from her mother's side, most frequently from her mother's own line, but sometimes from her mother's sister or her maternal grandmother's sister, the fourth one from her father's side, and so on.

Keeping and breaking the rules

Giving a father or a mother a new lease of life through their eldest child meant both giving the latter the right to inherit and, more importantly perhaps, carrying out a sacred duty and proving love for parents. Implicit in the fulfilment of an obligation, however, were not only the economic interests of the line but also its symbolic ones. Both legitimization and honour were involved. If a mother's Christian name was given to her eldest daughter, the person giving it was honouring both the mother and himself, since that action affirmed both that the mother was worthy of the honour and that the person conferring it was worthy to do so. No-one dishonoured would ever dare bestow a parent's Christian name. Thus, no illegitimate daughter was ever given her maternal grandmother's Christian name. At the same time as the continuity of the line was ensured, there was a public declaration of pride in belonging to it and of the value of its members. This meant ultimately that there was a participation in reproducing its symbolic capital and, in a society in which the value of each individual was closely dependent on that of his line, in reproducing the conditions in which those individuals would retain their value. Similarly, resuscitating through younger children the members of lines linked to one's own (for a man, his mother's or paternal grandmother's, or a line allied to his wife's) was at once fulfilling one's obligations, honouring them and honouring oneself, reproducing the symbolic capital of the allied lines and hence of one's own, in short, reproducing the conditions of one's own value. Not to do these things, on the other hand, meant shaming oneself, insulting the allied lines and helping devalue both them and that of oneself and one's children. The greater the prestige of a line, the greater its success in maintaining the Christian names that symbolized it and hence in reproducing its symbolic capital. Renewing Christian names was both the cause and the effect of that prestige. It is one of the factors which explain the importance of the part played by grandparents in the choice of Christian names for their grandchildren. Operating through the choice of Christian names and the order in which they were conferred (to the second boy rather than to the third, for example) were the prestige of their line and their own symbolic interests. The point of the principle of alternation was precisely to preserve the interest of all the lines concerned. What was taking place behind the transmission of Christian names was ultimately, at village level, a full and continuous circulation of symbolic capital. The interests involved, however, were not merely symbolic. By means of the circulation of Christian names, younger children were used by the lines in a strategy to reproduce themselves physically, to enable them to perpetuate themselves when the circumstances for doing so had not been provided in the normal way for the preceding generation, because the couple was childless, or had only one child, or children of the same sex, and so on. Thus, one couple might sometimes be responsible for the survival of three or four different lines.

Although it seems that the principle of alternation worked automatically, it can be seen that it would be mistaken to believe that the Christian names of the firstborn of an actual family could be explained by an adhesion of the rules. If we did not speak of 'interest' where the society preferred to talk of 'rules', we should understand nothing of its practices. The explanation of both obedience to rules and rejecting them lies in the play of material and/or symbolic interests. As is shown by the case of a woman who refused to give her eldest daughter the Christian name of her mother who had left her husband, who was a priest, there was a refusal to give a child the Christian name of a dishonoured parent. Similarly, it was easier to accept ensuring the continuity of another line through a younger child if, when giving him the appropriate Christian name, the person doing so attracted the estate that went with it. A daughter adopted by her childless maternal aunt gave her first daughter her aunt's, and not her mother's, Christian name, since the former had provided for her. If her mother was a younger daughter from whom nothing could be expected, and even if the aunt had not adopted her, a girl could transmit the name of the childless aunt with the aim of inheriting from her. She was more likely to achieve that aim if her own sister had not used the same strategy. Particularly when she had not many children, it was rare for her to observe *anastassi* for her mother. Similarly, a man who believed that he might inherit from a childless paternal aunt without a sister would give his second daughter her Christian name rather than his mother's. However, he used that strategy if he only had brothers, for sisters would have been in a better position than he himself was to obtain a female patrimony of such a kind. Even more often it happened that younger sisters gave the name of their eldest sisters directly to one of their daughters and that younger brothers similarly observed *anastassi* for their eldest brothers. The child involved might even be an eldest son. In both cases, the younger brothers or sisters would act with greater willingness if it became clear that the eldest was finding it difficult to have children. The aim of that strategy was in fact to induce the eldest son or daughter to provide for, or even to adopt, the child named after him or her. For younger children finding themselves in such a situation of direct competition, the problem was that of not giving the eldest's name too soon, and thus upsetting him and appearing too interested, or too late, and thus being at a disadvantage compared with the others. There were also cases of the opposite happening, of the eldest giving his younger brother's name to one of his sons. That frequently happened when the mother of both brothers was a younger daughter of a family with no sons and had inherited a male estate that had subsequently passed on to the younger son concerned. In that way, the eldest son could have his son adopted by his younger brother if the latter had no children. By the mere fact of being the eldest, he found himself in a better position than any of his brothers to obtain the inheritance, even if they used the same strategy.

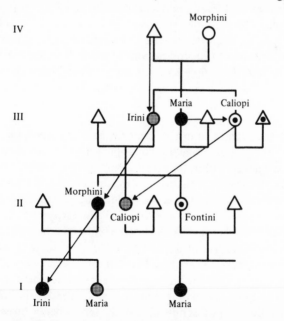

An example will show the complexity of the strategies used. Irini III had not given one of her daughters the Christian name of her childless elder sister, as the latter had gone to live with Caliopi III and had given her her estate. However, she observed *anastassi* in favour of her mother, Morphini IV, and then gave her second daughter the name of her younger sister Caliopi, who had inherited from the eldest. The husband of Caliopi III had gone abroad with his only son and was presumed dead. Caliopi II, however, had several miscarriages. Her sisters Morphini and Fontini II, speculating on her remaining childless and hoping to obtain the inheritance, gave one of their daughters the name of Maria III (their mother's eldest sister) from whom the estate came. In competing with Morphini II, Fontini II came off best although she was younger. Morphini II had given her eldest daughter her mother's Christian name, both because she received an inheritance from that side and because she thought Fontini II could not marry. Against that, Fontini, who had no inheritance to hope for, had given her eldest daughter the name of Maria, which was a greater honour for Maria III.

If we analyse the reasons favouring the resuscitation of one person rather than another, the frequent arguments in families when Christian names were being attributed and the numerous breaches of the rule of alternation show that in each case the choice of a Christian name was a calculated one and that in the last analysis it had to do, whenever the interests of the lines concerned were in conflict, with the relationship of forces within them. Thus a younger (second) daughter called her eldest son after her father while her husband was away. She wanted to observe *anastassi* for her father not only because her own Christian name was one from her side, but also because her eldest daughter had died after the others were born and she had not until then been able to transmit her mother's Christian name in any lasting way. In certain cases, however, disputes about the Christian names of eldest daughters arose almost compulsorily. That was what happened when, for example, the husband was a younger son from a family without daughters (or the wife was the younger daughter from a family without sons). Such people had to ensure the continuity of the maternal line the inheritance came from, and the couple had to continue two female lines. Since each spouse wanted to give the eldest daughter the name of his or her own mother, a conflict inevitably arose, and this would also involve both mothers-in-law. The dispute was all the more violent if the wife, as most frequently happened, was an eldest daughter, in other words the accredited defender of her maternal line. One reason why everyone tried to appropriate the eldest daughter was that the couple was never certain that they would have a second daughter, and there was thus always the threat that one of the female lines would die out. The main reason was, however, that a line continued through a younger daughter suffered a humiliation which could only undermine the integrity of its symbolic patrimony. The husband's mother was likely to come off best in the quarrel if her line had already had to make use of a younger male child to take over the succession. Such disputes, in which every member of the line directly or indirectly concerned took sides, started from the birth of the child and in most cases were only settled after a bid for power within the church itself, on the day the baby was being baptized, the final event in a series of dramas, tables being turned, and peacemakers intervening, with the congregation shouting out its opinions and the disadvantaged line making its protests heard.[20] A further indication of the importance of symbolic capital in that society is the local saying, which still persists, that 'people can be killed there when it is a question of names'. Such events left a lasting mark on relationships between lines whose members had been insulted and often had permanent ill-effects on those between the wife and her mother-in-law. What made it particularly hard to settle the conflict amicably was the lack of agreement between husband and wife. The husband was more likely to consider the symbolic interest of his mother's line, since that was what had saved him from the common fate of younger sons. What finally decided what the choice would be was the greater or lesser attachment of each of the spouses to his or her own line, the skill of those concerned in manipulating events right up to the last moment, the number of people each side could enlist in its support and, above all, the relationships of economic and symbolic forces between the two lines. If the husband won, the eldest daughter took the Christian name of her father's maternal grandmother (whom her daughter had been unable to 'resuscitate') or sometimes, directly, that of her father's mother. She never took that of her mother's mother. If he lost, the second born daughter later took that name.

But husbands without sisters or wives without brothers were not the only ones to try to force their mother's Christian name onto their eldest daughter. It frequently happened that those with an only sister who was finding it difficult to marry, or who had married and had several miscarriages, would speculate on her possible spinsterhood or sterility and use the same strategy. By particularly honouring their mother, they would be in the best position to recuperate her estate in the ensuing competition amongst brothers, if the latter had followed the usual practice and given their eldest daughter the name of their mother-in-law. If there was no brother, they enabled their maternal line to continue by acting thus. They were more inclined to behave in such a way if they were younger sons, married and living locally (which was very infrequent) and bearing a name from their mother's side.

Strategies of dissimulation and clarification

The choice of a Christian name was a calculated one even when it appeared merely to follow from the application of the rule. This was evident in the case of eldest sons, but also true of younger ones whose Christian names, as we have seen, more closely followed the rule that the second son should take the name of his mother's father if there was still a chance of an inheritance from his side. If a woman had no brother or if he died or was disinherited for some reason or other (e.g. emigration), she could thus obtain possession of his inheritance for her younger son. The situation was even better if the brother married but had no children. He could then adopt his sister's son. Conversely, a man whose only sister had no children could give her name to his second daughter. He could not do this directly, as a simplistic understanding of his interests would have dictated, but merely by giving her his mother's name, in accordance with custom. In that way he could at one and the same time retain the chance of obtaining his sister's estate for his daughter (the younger daughter bore the Christian name from which the patrimony came) and give himself the greatest opportunity of achieving his aims vis-à-vis any of his brothers who might have directly resuscitated their sister's name and upset her by behaving in what was obviously a self-seeking way. If his strategy was successful, he gained from both points of view, since he had not only obtained the estate but also achieved an increase in prestige, in that he could claim that he had done nothing to obtain the inheritance.

In the above example we have what Pierre Bourdieu calls 'second-order strategies', that is strategies involving 'the symbolic manipulation of the objective meaning of a practice'. Of these, he says that they are aimed at producing practices within rules, but are part of a class of strategies of officialization, the end of which is to change selfish motives and interest into disinterested, publicly admissible and legitimate ones. It can be seen that although the naming strategies seemed not quite to follow the strict order of material interests, they were really aimed at increasing advantages to the greatest possible degree by making it possible to preserve both material and symbolic interests (apparently disinterested behaviour). Following the same logic, if younger sons who managed to marry also gave (although they had been disinherited) their father's name to their eldest son, it was often because behind the ostensible respect for their father lurked the wish not to let slip any chance of inheriting should their eldest brother happen to die, remain a bachelor, or be disinherited. Similarly, by rapidly reviving the Christian name of a wife's father or a husband's mother, it was possible to protect oneself against the accusation of not reviving them and also to avoid a source of disputes within the marriage that could have led to arguments about the utility of the network of useful relationships on one side and the other. Sometimes the eldest child's Christian name would, although conforming to custom, be the result of a deal in which economic capital was exchanged for symbolic capital. It sometimes happened that a mother (or father) was faced with the threat of no *anastassi* if she (or he) refused to surrender her (or his) estate. Blackmail of this kind was more likely to succeed if the person concerned had few chances of reviving his Christian name or continuing his line in another way.

Maritsa II, although a younger daughter, was to inherit from her mother, Rigo III, as she had the Christian name of her maternal grandmother, Maritsa IV. She was disinherited, however, for on the day of her marriage to a doctor, who had been chosen by her mother, she had eloped with and subsequently married a schoolmaster. When her first daughter was born, she wanted to revenge herself on her mother by giving the child the name of her mother-in-law, Caliopi III, rather than her mother's. All the baby's things had that name embroidered on them. On the day of the baptism, Maritsa's mother, who had not been able to induce her daughter to change her mind, went and created a scene in church, hoping to have the child christened after her. Maritsa's younger brother, Nicos II, having a surname from his mother's side, was predisposed to support her to get his sister to listen to him. He decided to act as peacemaker. He brought the two parties together by means of an agreement that Maritsa should give the baby

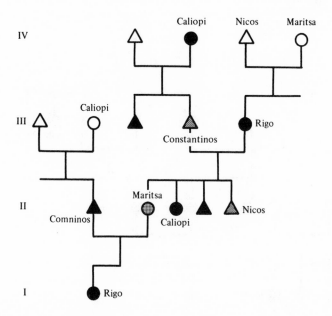

her mother's name, Rigo, in return for which the mother would change her mind about disinheriting the young woman. The arrangement was advantageous to Maritsa II, as she both regained the inheritance and conformed to tradition. Rigo III submitted to the blackmail as she had already been cruelly humiliated. Her husband, who was a younger son of a family without daughters and had inherited the female estate, had made her give their eldest daughter his mother's Christian name. But Rigo III had no other daughter to continue her line. Furthermore, when the baby was born, she had only managed to transmit her own name once, despite having had four children, and then only through the younger daughter of her younger son. Here too, a mere description of the system of rules omits the essential point, which is an analysis of those interests which lie at the heart of both the application and the non-application of the rules.

Sometimes, however, the strategies of hiding interests were better served by the way Christian names happened to be distributed in parental lines, for this left the real origin of a child's Christian name ambiguous if it appeared in both the lines in question. Such confusion was more likely if the total number of Christian names used in the village was restricted. Thus, there was always an opportunity for playing a double game aimed at making the material and symbolic advantages as great as possible.

Nicos III, the younger son of a family with no daughters, had inherited from his mother and was to continue her line. Ignoring the protests of his wife and his mother-in-law, Eugenia IV, he had given his eldest daughter the Christian name of his own mother, Caliopi IV. The dispute left lasting traces between the two allied lines. Maria V had a chapel which went as part of her estate to Caliopi IV and then to Nicos III.

50   Bernard Vernier

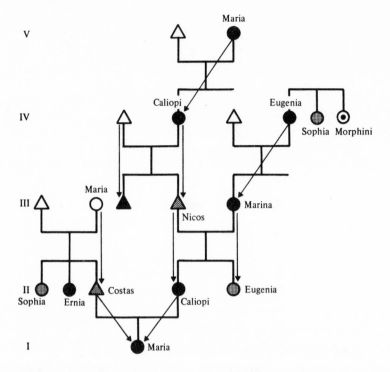

Marina III and her mother's sisters (Sophia and Morphini IV) were helping Nicos III to look after the chapel and the olive trees planted in the small field that went with it. When the latter managed to call his eldest daughter Caliopi, his wife's mother's sisters took everything in the chapel (ornaments, plate, small table) and left it completely empty. Nor would they go on working in the field round it. Nicos had only his mother to help him cultivate it. In addition, Caliopi II, using the opportunity of her mother's absence, called her eldest daughter Maria to continue the line of her father's mother, whence her estate came. The youngest, Maria, was thus Maria V, bearing the name of the maternal grandmother of her mother's father. Caliopi II, who was still alive, was on very good terms with her paternal grandmother, but had fallen out with both her own mother and her maternal grandmother. Of interest here is the attitude of Costas II, who vigorously supported his wife in her quarrel with her mother. What made him also want to call his daughter Maria was the fact that it was also his own mother's name. He had only two sisters. One was still unmarried, and the other, who had only sons, had left the village. By calling his daughter Maria, Costas could hope to obtain two estates for her, i.e. those of Maria V and Maria III. In fact, he always maintained later in public that he had called her after his mother. He thus benefited from the possible confusion created by the existence of the same Christian names in the two lines and of the shorter distance in time between Maria III and Maria I, which meant that everyone in the village knew Maria III, whereas only the old remembered Maria V. In addition, as the youngest Maria bore her father's surname, all the appearances were in his favour. There was also the fact that Maria III was well aware that her son, whose Christian name came from her side, was insisting so much on calling his daughter Maria because, though appearing to take the part of his wife and his father-in-law against his mother-in-law, he wanted to revive her Christian name. She was indeed all the more inclined to believe it as she was afraid that she would not be able to revive it through her own daughters. By this double game, Costas managed to maximize the material and symbolic advantages by subsequently declaring that he had succeeded in giving his daughter his mother's Christian name. The fact that the same Christian name existed in two different lines meant that he could use this strategy, but it only succeeded because the important thing was not so much the truth, i.e. the real origin of the name, as the image of it that he had managed to communicate in the village. It was by utilizing a confusion of the same type that someone had been able to boast publicly that he had revived the names of the three sons of his paternal grandfather.

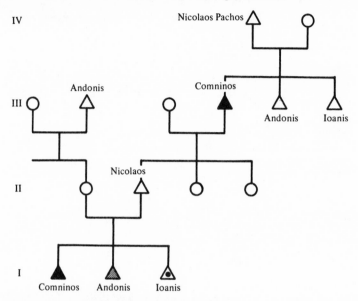

In a *mandinade*, Nicolaos II had this to say:

> Despite my frequent misfortunes
> And my many sighs,
> I have revived three sons
> Of my grandfather Pachos.

In reality, Andonis was the Christian name of his wife's father, but the happy chance that the names were similar two generations apart meant that Nicolaos could draw prestige from them. He had best managed to take the exact place of his paternal grandfather. To do so, he had made use of chance once again: Andonis III (his paternal uncle) had had only daughters and Ioanis III had had no children. This meant that the only people to bear the Christian names of Ioanis and Andonis Pachos were indeed his children. All the appearances were thus in his favour.

The importance of the symbolic interests at work in the choice of a Christian name is shown by the use made of clarification strategies aimed at thwarting the effects of strategies used to divert symbolic capital. By means of these latter strategies, some people profitably exploited the possibilities of confusion.

Maria II was a younger daughter. As, however, her eldest sister had no children, her daughter was to inherit from the female estate of Caliopi III.

Normally, this daughter would have been called Caliopi, but this would have caused confusion, since the two mothers-in-law already had that name. Costas II and his mother were determined that it should be called Caliopi, in order to maintain the confusion. Maria II and her mother, however, would benefit from everyone knowing where the estate came from and whose line the baby was continuing. Once again, the question was settled by a last minute drama. The mother of Maria II, who had come as far as the church to protest insisted on the name of Xatzidena, that of her maternal grandmother.

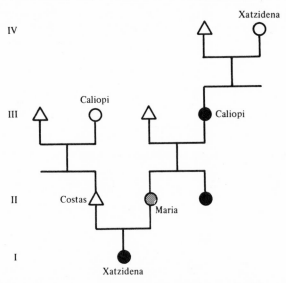

All in all, whether or not Christian names followed the rule of alternation, they always went towards those lines in which estates were potentially available or where there were other types of material interests. The order in which a given person was resuscitated before another expressed the order of importance of the material and symbolic interests that could be preserved by the choice of a Christian name. In other words, a given Christian name cannot be fully explained until the complete table, covering several generations, of the lines of the mother and father, showing their composition by sex in each generation, the fate of each individual (died young, emigrated, disinherited, unmarried, childless, etc.), and the mutual exchanges of economic services between lines, has been established. In addition, if the order of Christian names given does not correspond to the apparent order of interests, or if the choice of a particular name seems random, it is necessary to continue to seek the interests at work rather than assume a disinterested choice.

This was the case with a younger son, the second boy, who was called after the father of his maternal grandmother. This choice of names would have been meaningless without a table of the lines and a history of the transmission of goods. The maternal grandmother was a younger daughter. Her oldest sister had had no children and had adopted the oldest daughter of her younger sister. She could have chosen the daughter of another sister or another daughter of the same sister. In return for her preferential choice, she had therefore stipulated that the female inheritor should revive her father's Christian name through one of her younger sons. If the inheritor had not met that obligation, she would have been dishonoured. The choice of Christian name therefore coincided with the preservation of her symbolic interests.

Similarly, if there were no longer any prospects of an inheritance and the youngest children of large families were given the apparently disinterested names of saints (e.g. Maria) or those of very distant relatives ('just to please them') such a choice was not infrequently part of a strategy for hiding interests.[21] Apart from the fact that by giving a saint's name the person concerned was shown to be both disinterested and pious and thus strengthened his symbolic capital, it often became clear on analysis that the saint's name was also that of a distant relative. The latter was not infrequently an 'American' uncle or aunt, in other words someone who had emigrated, was likely to acquire wealth and might return, and who, it was hoped, would feel some obligation to the person called after him.

Custom also decreed that as a sign of gratitude, a mother should call her daughters after her own younger unmarried sisters or, as appropriate, after her mother's, since they worked in her fields. It was said that for single people the supreme joy was to know that their soul would pass into the body of a young child. By following the custom, the mother preserved her symbolic interests (by showing her gratitude) and also, at little cost to herself, her material ones. The importance of 'resuscitating' in another person was so great that unmarried women were inclined to work for their eldest sister or her eldest daughter in the hope of passing on their name to them. They were also likely to work harder and compete in devotion if they were in competition with each other. Normally, they could not all be 'resuscitated', since their names were only given when all the possibilities of attracting inheritances into the family had been exhausted. The unmarried women for whom *anastassi* had been observed was even more than others devoted body and, so to speak, soul to the inheritor. Thus, the eldest daughters retained the labour of their younger sisters whilst paying them in counterfeit coin, or more exactly in coin which was doubly illusory. This was because the prospect of surviving in someone else was a symbolic reward for a real exploitation and also because the eldest only gave their names to younger daughters, that is to those who had little chance of marriage and hence were unlikely to be able to pass on their name. It can be seen that the ideology of *anastassi*, which offered a justification, legitimized the privileges of eldest sisters and the exploitation of younger ones, also helped in this particular way to maintain relationships of exploitation and ultimately to reproduce the social order.

In addition, just as in our societies social mobility, to however small a degree it may exist, helps to maintain the social order since it offers to the underprivileged

Table 2. *Percentage of cases in which the Christian name conformed to custom, by sex and social category*

	Before 1945	After 1945
Eldest men		
Canacares, medium peasants (n = 224)	73.4	79.2
Poor peasants, shepherds (n = 189)	71.5	92.4
Eldest women		
Canacares, medium peasants (n = 128)	72.2	70.2
Poor peasants, shepherds (n = 127)	68.0	76.2
Younger men		
Canacares, medium peasants (n = 138)	58.2	61.0
Poor peasants, shepherds (n = 129)	42.8	56.2
Younger women		
Canacares, medium peasants (n = 61)	55.0	60.9
Poor peasants, shepherds (n = 65)	38.8	53.1

the possibility of individual escape, so the exceptions to the practice of disinheriting younger children which have been examined above helped to encourage the latter to accept their subordinate (and, in the case of younger sisters, exploited) position in society, encouraging them in other words to behave in accordance with the imperatives of a social order in which certain of them could, exceptionally, have a real stake. This in particular explains how the prospect of perhaps being able to obtain the inheritance of a childless eldest sister could sustain competition amongst younger ones who, as a result of it, were likely to compete in devotion, submission in respect, and even in flattery with regard to the eldest.

Since the real meaning of obedience to the rules is seen most clearly when they were broken, we have attempted to establish the statistical extent of exceptions to the system of naming and, in particular, to the rule of alteration. Searches in the civil records made it possible to trace the origin of the Christian name of a large number of eldest and second children of both sexes. It was materially not possible to obtain precise information concerning other younger children. Table 2 shows that between 68% and 73% of eldest children, depending on sex and social origin, born before 1945, were given a Christian name in the customary way: that of the paternal grandfather for boys and maternal grandmother for girls. A large proportion of the exceptions is satisfactorily explained by the logic of the naming system, which dictates that the name should come from the same source as the estate. Given the possibility of demographic accidents in a single generation (an only child, for example), such a Christian name could come from three or four preceding generations. There are, however, too many exceptions (between 26% and 32%) for that hypothesis to offer a total explanation. If we are to understand them, we must also take into account the fact that in certain cases the choice of Christian name for the eldest was the result of the balance of forces between the parental lines and that in addition not every eldest child was a natural inheritor. As Table 3 shows, the rule was followed most

Table 3. *Origin of the Christian name by order of birth of the child, that of his relative of the same sex, and the social category of the parents, before 1955 (in %)*

Child	Relative of same sex	1	2	3
Eldest	Eldest (n = 225)	82.7	7.0	10.3
(male and	Younger of soc. categ. > that of spouse (n = 42)	64.2	11.6	24.2
female)	Younger of soc. cat. < that of spouse (n = 92)	58.6	17.2	24.2
Younger	Eldest (n = 169)	56.4	11.8	31.8
(male and	Younger (n = 64)	34.3	26.5	39.0
female)				

1 = Christian name conforming to custom.
2 = Inversion of Christian name between eldest and younger child.
3 = Other.

closely in the case of eldest children whose relative of the same sex was also an eldest child (82%). In such cases, the relationship of forces within the couple was so well-balanced that it was rare (7%) for the eldest to take what would normally be the name given to the second child of the same sex, obeying the rule having no doubt generally been the practice in the case of eldest children of eldest children for many generations. As against this, when eldest children were not natural inheritors (i.e. if their relative of the same sex was a younger child) they did not take the appropriate Christian name so frequently. This trend was even more marked in the case of eldest children whose relative of the same sex was a younger child from a family in a social category equal to or lower than that of his or her spouse. The eldest child in such cases was 2.4 times more likely than the eldest child of an eldest child to take the Christian name, which would be insisted on by a socially stronger spouse, normally given to the second born of his sex. If, generally speaking, eldest children with relatives of the same sex who were younger children were two or three times more likely to take a name which was neither appropriate nor the one usually given to the second born of their sex than the eldest children of eldest children, it was because it was through the former that attempts were made to obtain lateral inheritances, as in the case of the eldest son of a younger son who was called after his father's eldest brother.

What shows, however, that the rule was more closely followed if it was profitable to do so and less closely if it could bring no advantage is the fact that the gap between the rule and the practice of it was even greater in the case of younger children. The rule was followed in the case of eldest children because it often coincided with advantages. However, if (as in Table 2, first period) between 38% and 58% of younger children did not receive the name entailed by the rule of alternation, it was that unlike eldest children such younger ones were not potential inheritors. It is certain that some of the exceptions were simply a result of an overriding decision to give the eldest the name that should have gone to a younger brother or sister.[22] As Table 3 shows, however, in a third of the cases, the younger brother or sister was given neither the appropriate name nor the one that was normally given to the eldest. Overall, younger children took three times more frequently than eldest children a Christian name explicitly linked to an attempt to procure lateral inheritances.

Confirmation of these hypotheses can be found in the way naming practices developed. Later (Table 2, second period) they seemed to follow custom more closely. There is an explanation for this paradox if we remember that the material factors involved in naming practices became less important as the value of land declined. The rules were better obeyed because in doing so it was possible, since there was a smaller proportion of conflicting economic interests involved, to obtain all the symbolic benefits which went with a respect for tradition. The fall in the economic value of land brought with it a decrease in the number of bids for power, a less frequent recourse to strategies aimed at procuring lateral inheritances, and an increasing trend towards giving children the useful names of living grandparents instead of, as custom insisted in certain cases, names from several generations back. As the table shows, conformity to the rule increased most markedly amongst poor peasants and shepherds, whose land lost its value all the more quickly, as they had little and it was of poor quality. There was virtually no change amongst the eldest daughters of *canacares* and medium peasants, because these categories turned such children into the last guardians of the land. What is most striking, however, given the massive emigration in the most recent years, is the time-lag between changes in naming practices and emigration practices, i.e. the persistence of a calculating attitude when one was no longer as necessary as it had been. The high rate of infringement of the rules indicates this. It was as if everyone wanted to suggest, by persisting in being calculating where land was concerned, that his attachment to it was still strong, thus neutralizing the opprobrium associated with emigration. It also seemed that a kind of collective hypocrisy was at work, creating the illusion that emigration was only a temporary phenomenon. However, to the extent that naming strategies were also parental strategies, it may be that in trying to secure an inheritance for their children, parents (at least the most traditional ones) hoped to tie their children to the land, even if only emotionally, and thus increase the likelihood that they would stay in the village or at least come back to it. This also meant that parents were taking the best steps to stop themselves being uprooted. Indeed, they were also providing themselves with the greatest chance of support in their old age from those (and their naming strategy bore witness to this) for whom they had done everything.[23]

Kinship terminology and relations between kin

It is more difficult on Karpathos than anywhere else to deduce kinship from kinship terms, which seem to radiate almost infinitely outwards from the conjugal nucleus.[24] This is because relations between kin, even within the conjugal family, were primarily structured by the origin of Christian names, which was in turn linked to the order of birth of each parent.

Let us take as an example a couple consisting of two eldest children, assuming for simplicity's sake that they too were the offspring of eldest children. Which relatives, for them, would be important because of their respective Christian names, even if only from the point of view of dutiful sympathy? To avoid repetition, a + or − sign will be used here to indicate the importance of the relationship at each level of kinship.
On the husband's side there would be:

  paternal grandfather (+) whose Christian name he has, and his brothers (−)
  father (+)
  mother (−)
  paternal uncles (+) having a particular affection for their eldest brother's eldest son, since he bears their father's name
  paternal aunts (−) including particularly the second born, whose Christian name would come from the same side
  paternal cousins (+) particularly the eldest sons of paternal uncles with the same Christian name

younger brothers (+) who venerate their eldest brother
sisters (−) particularly the second born, with a Christian name from the same side
brothers' eldest sons (+) with his father's Christian name
sisters' eldest daughters (−) with his mother's Christian name.

On the wife's:
maternal grandmother[25] (+) and her sister (−)
mother (+)
father (−)
maternal aunts (+)
maternal uncles (−) including particularly the second born, with a Christian name
    from the same side
maternal cousins (+) particularly the eldest daughters of maternal aunts
younger sisters (+)
brothers (−) more particularly the second born, with a Christian name from the same
    side
sisters' eldest daughters (+) with the same Christian name as her mother
brothers' eldest sons (−) with her father's Christian name.

In contrast to this highly structured and extended network there was a less structured and differently orientated one which included younger children. In particular, as no-one was really concerned with them,[26] the younger children's network of relatives to whom they were linked by the origin of their Christian names had a much lower economic and social value for them.

The example of a couple consisting of two younger children, the husband a second son and the wife a second daughter, illustrates this sufficiently. On the husband's side the most important relative would be his maternal grandfather, whose Christian name he would bear (but who would regard him in turn as fairly unimportant, for after all the younger son would continue his father's and wife's father's lines through his sons). The grandfather would give most of his affection and help to his own eldest son's eldest son, who would have his Christian and surnames and continue his line. The husband's mother and father would have little time to worry about his fate, as they would be preoccupied with that of their eldest son. His mother would of course tend to prefer him to her other sons, as he had a Christian name from her side, but since he did not belong to her line, her relationship with him would not be as close as that between father and eldest son. His uncles and aunts would not be as important to him as they would to his eldest brother, and despite a slight predominance of relationships with his maternal uncles and aunts, there would be almost no difference between his relationships with the maternal and paternal sides. The eldest of his maternal uncles would prefer him to his sister's other children, as both would have Christian names from the same line, but would be chiefly concerned with the eldest sons of his younger brothers. The husband would also have more dealings with his brothers than his sisters and particularly with his eldest brother (+) and his eldest sister (−). At the level of nephews and nieces, he would be most sympathetic towards his brothers' eldest sons, especially his eldest brother's eldest son,[27] and his sisters' eldest daughters, especially the eldest daughter of his eldest sister. On the wife's side the most important relatives (if we take into account the same limiting factors as those operative in the case of the husband) would be her paternal grandmother, her father (+), her mother (−), her paternal uncles and aunts (amongst the latter, her eldest paternal aunt in particular, because of her Christian name), her sisters (+) and brothers (−), especially her eldest sister and eldest brother, whose Christian name would come from the same side, and finally her sisters' eldest daughters and brothers' eldest sons, in particular the eldest children of her eldest brothers and sisters.

The origin of the Christian name played a large part in determining the network of relatives with whom the individual had the closest ties, but that network was of benefit only to those who would inherit, which means those who had a useful role to play in the reproduction strategies of the various lines. Thus, the network of important relatives for younger children only took on a clear structure and real importance if, because of a demographic accident, a line needed to make use of them. For example, if a younger (second) daughter inherited from her paternal grandmother because her father was an only son, she would have close relationships with her father, her paternal relatives and, in particular, her paternal grandmother. It was as if the network had been sketched in as a potentiality by the origin of the Christian name and had suddenly taken on a real form.

The relationships between families related by marriage followed the same principles as those already described. Despite what might be assumed from the fact that there was only one term for kinship (*simpethere*), a married couple would mainly have dealings with the families-in-law of their two eldest children. More precisely, the father would have them with his eldest son's relatives-in-law and the mother with those of her eldest daughter. Where the couple were an eldest son and an eldest daughter, the closest in-law relationships would be those between the husband's father and the wife's mother, since they would be the persons of authority in matters of marriage and problems connected with the transmission of patrimonies and Christian names to the couple's children. However, as we have seen, the greatest risk of conflict was between parents-in-law. Their joint interest lay in helping the young couple and hence strengthening the social position of their respective lines. Their interests could clash, however, as would happen if the wife was barren, one of the spouses behaved dishonourably, or, in more general terms, every time that for one of the reasons given above the transmission of patrimonies and Christian names raised problems and depended on the forces in play between the two lines in question. In addition, even when there appears to have been a high degree of understanding in the relationship between the wife's mother and the husband's father, it may have been the result of a strategy used by one or the other in attempting to serve the interests of his own line as well as possible. Thus, the wife's mother might make sure that she remained on the best of terms with the husband's father before the marriage to induce him to give his future daughter-in-law an uncommonly good present and might also keep the relationship on the same footing after the marriage in order to encourage him to give his eldest son not only the patrimony of his line but also to break with tradition and make over the major part of his personal fortune to him. If such a strategy succeeded, in spite of the opposition of his son-in-law's mother, the increase in the young couple's personal fortune would enrich the female line and subsequently improve the chances of their eldest daughter in the marriage market, especially if she had benefitted from the wealth thus inherited by her father. Conflicts linked to the transmission of goods and

Christian names put the husband and his father in one camp and the wife and her mother in another, dividing relatives whose relationships were particularly close. When wealth acquired by the husband became increasingly important as a result of emigration to far places and the devaluation of land, conflicts between husband and wife on the one hand and between husband and mother-in-law on the other became increasingly frequent. The husband would often want to hand over his wealth to his eldest son or his second daughter, whilst the others would want him to favour his eldest daughter. In such cases, the conflict was even more acute if there was severe competition on the marriage market and the latter might well remain a spinster.

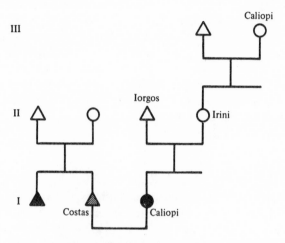

If both spouses were particularly close to the eldest on their own side, there were many conflicts between father and eldest daughter and mother and eldest son.

Caliopi I lived with her husband Costas, as he was the second son of a family with no daughter and had inherited his father's goods. He was also richer than his wife. Iorgos II had gold pieces which his daughter wore as a necklace on feast days before she was married. Shortly after her marriage, Caliopi I asked her mother, during her father's absence, if she could wear the necklace to go to a mass. She readily obtained permission. When she came back from church, she did not return the gold pieces, but hid them. Iorgos tried in vain to recover his goods, and in the end took his son-in-law to court. He, however, came to an agreement with Caliopi III, who testified that she herself had given the gold pieces to her grand-daughter. She later went to live with the young couple and Iorgos never regained possession of his gold.

The most frequent conflicts, however, were those between mother and eldest son, to whom she often preferred her eldest daughter's husband, as is illustrated in the saying: 'a mother would rather see her son lose his sight than that the prick of her eldest daughter's husband should suffer a fleabite'. The mother often urged her husband to give his eldest daughter the wealth that he had personally acquired and would try, as often as she could, to favour the eldest daughter to the disadvantage of the eldest son. Sometimes, when an eldest son was giving his

eldest daughter in marriage and going to live in the parental home with his own
father and mother, the latter would take everything from the house that she could
with her to her daughter's. Indeed she might well steal flour from her son's mill,
or cereals and vegetables from his fields or garden to benefit her eldest daughter,
something which often happened during the last war. In so far as her son would
hesitate to complain, it was less dangerous for her than to steal from strangers.
She had little hesitation in doing so, since she herself had raised the son, who was
after all no part of her line. She would also oppose her son if he did not give a
large share of his acquired wealth to his eldest daughter.[28]

On the whole, the relationship of an individual with his kin were those defined
by the origin of his Christian name, which in its turn was linked to his order of
birth. This network, however, also depended from the point of view of both its
extent and its structure, on the order of birth of his parents, his grandparents, his
spouse, and his spouse's parents and grandparents. Thus, a husband whose wife
was the eldest daughter of a younger daughter would have less binding
relationships with his mother-in-law than he would have done had she been an
eldest daughter. The network, as we have seen, also depended on demographic
accidents in the various lines in question and the solutions to problems of
survival adopted by threatened lines.[29]

Theoretical and real kinship

It would nevertheless be as wrong to deduce mechanically the real kinship
networks from the origin of the Christian name of each official relative as to
deduce them from the terminology of kinship. Belonging to a line was not the
only important factor. Because the interests involved were so considerable, the
canacares had a more extensive and better structured network than others and
more particularly than the poorest peasants and shepherds. If a large proportion
of younger sons emigrated, it could eliminate a fairly considerable part of the
network of kinship of the members of that group, and when a younger son, for
example, married in his home village, he often only had relations with his eldest
brother, who had stayed in the village, and the latter's children. When a younger
daughter married, her relationship with her parents underwent a profound
transformation, and the daily life of a child with its mother created emotional
links that could conflict with belonging to a line. In particular, couples in which
the wife was an eldest daughter had much closer relationships with the wife's than
with the husband's family, given the rules of residence and the custom insisting
that younger sisters should work for their eldest sister and her daughter. This was
even more the case when the husband was a younger son and hence not very
closely linked to his own family.

Theoretically, younger sisters should have worked for the side their Christian
name came from ('We suffer for the wealth that gives us our name'),[30] but in fact
the lines were most important for those in a position to continue them: the eldest

children of both sexes. When they were young, all that younger daughters would get when a member of their line visited the family was only a few sweets more than their brothers. When they were older, it was not where their Christian name came from that decided in advance where they were to work, but the fact that over the years the idea that they had to work for their eldest sisters had been fostered in them. In addition, when they worked for them and helped them in the house, they were in well-known and consequently home-like surroundings. Things would have been different if they had been living with their brothers and a strange wife whose orders they were not prepared to accept. In addition, since outside the families of the *canacares* eldest brothers went away for seasonal work, they would have been under the direct command of their sisters-in-law if they had worked for them. In certain cases, however, the second daughter would go and live with her eldest brother if she did not get on well with her eldest sister or if her brother was richer. In such cases, she would invoke official kinship, which linked her more closely with her brother than with her sister, since his Christian name came from the same side as her own.

The female house, as the couple spent the most active part of their social life there, and dances, baptisms, and so on took place there, was better equipped and decorated than the male house to which the parental couple retired.[31] In the latter, there were only a few plates and dishes on the walls, and the way it was furnished, without much in the way of embroidery or cushions, often gave an impression of austerity or even poverty. It was as if the basic elements of wealth were concentrated in the female house, to make it quite clear that the young woman and her husband were the legitimate representatives of the lines and as if, too, an attempt was being made to increase the chances of the following generation of making a good marriage. Immediately after the last war, it was also in the female house that the cult of the lines was celebrated as splendidly as possible with photographs hanging on the walls and, more recently, standing on tables. At that time, there would not be more than ten or so of them, and they would be almost exclusively of members of the female line. Subsequently, their number has increased several fold. The number increases sharply as one goes up the social scale from shepherds and peasants to *canacares* (sixty were counted in one *canacare* house), not so much because of their economic cost as of their differential symbolic yield according to the lowly or prestigious status of the line. The more symbolic advantages accruing from a line, the greater the splendour of the way in which it is celebrated. Despite recent developments towards a greater number of photographs and a wider circle of people portrayed, a rapid analysis in 1975 of the distribution of photographs by number, size, framing (like a picture, or otherwise), their sitting (more or less centrally placed and readily visible on the walls) still showed a predominance of the female line.

Although it covers a recent period, Table 4 shows certain effects of the rules of residence on the structure of households. In 1938, a quarter of the households were still complex in structure.[32] Three-quarters of the 'outsiders' living with relatives were relatives of the

Table 4. *Relatives living with the couple, by kinship link with the wife or husband (%)*

| | Wife | | Husband | |
	1938 (n = 108)	1972 (n = 44)	1938 (n = 108)	1972 (n = 44)
Mothers	29.6	41.0	12.1	9.1
Fathers	1.8	2.2	1.8	2.2
Sisters	22.2	20.5	6.5	4.5
Aunts	19.5	9.1	—	—
Grandparents	2.8	11.4	—	—
Others	1.9	—	1.8	—
Total	77.8	84.2	22.2	15.8

Source: D. Philippides, *The Vernacular Design Setting of Elymbos* (London, University Microfilms, 1973).

1938 Italian survey: 25.2% of households were complex in structure.
1972 Investigation by D. Philippides: 24% of the households in a sample covering 73% of households were complex in structure.

wife. The proportion of households of complex structure remained unchanged in 1972 as a result of long-distance emigration. The effects of this were already very marked in 1938. The fathers were sometimes away from the village for several years. During these times, the wives like to have their mother or grandparents living with them for company and to help with the house and children. In 1938, parents and grandparents accounted for 48.1% of those outside the nuclear family, whereas the figure for 1972 was 65.9%. The almost complete absence of men amongst relatives living in the house was also a direct effect of emigration. As emigration was permanent, it left houses empty, and as it was to faraway places, it meant that old couples could afford to live in their own house. Women only went to live with their daughters or granddaughters when their husbands died.[33]

Kinship relationships may not have been predetermined by the origin of everyone's Christian name, but it also happened that by speculating on the possibility of procuring lateral inheritances or strengthening the devotion of younger sisters it was possible to use naming strategies to manipulate kinship, that is, to strengthen the most useful kinship links.

Baptism strategies

A final example can be given of the systematic and interested way in which kinship as described here was used in connection with the exploitation of younger daughters and with naming strategies. Peasants, and particularly the wealthier peasants of the middle rank and the *canacares*, did not, as we have seen, marry shepherds, and yet perhaps surprisingly at first glance, peasants acted as godfathers for the children of shepherds and vice versa. The practice of cross-baptisms is initially all the more astonishing as there were sharp clashes of interest between those who owned the land and those who needed large open spaces for their flocks. There were also frequent quarrels between peasants and shepherds over the damage caused by sheep and goats.[34] If this godparent relationship is to be explained, it must first be described. It was never the parents of a child who sought out a godfather (*nonos*) or a godmother (*nona*). It was said that by taking the initiative they would have made people think that no-one wanted the honour of baptizing their child and would have needlessly run the ever-present risk of choosing badly and suffering a humiliating refusal which would also have meant an inauspicious future for the child. In particular, such a course of action would mean running the risk of forcing those who would not dare refuse a request to be a godparent, which entailed certain obligations, to give presents against their wishes. The gift, such as a gold piece or a coat, given by the godparent at the baptism was in fact merely the first of a whole series of gifts between the two families, an exchange which could go on for many years at major occasions such as marriages in the two families and religious feasts such as the Assumption and Christmas. It reached its climax at Easter, however. On Good Friday, a woman from the peasant family would bring a large, round loaf, decorated in relief with an egg in the centre to the shepherd family. The next day, the compliment would be returned in the form of a gift of one or more sheep and various cheeses, cream, and milk. The process would be continued by the women of the peasant family giving the products they had available, such as raisins, beans, broad beans, wheat or barley flour, rolls, cakes, or honey. If there were frequent relationships of this kind between peasant and peasant or shepherd and shepherd, the exchange of gifts was more limited, from the point of view of both lavishness and frequency. There was no point, for example, in exchanging gifts of wheat. It was better to give things that were in short supply on the other side (honey, for example, in the case of peasants) or that the village did not produce (rice, pasta, and so on) or that it was difficult to obtain because of the lack of ready money.

Thus, unlike the exchange of small gifts that was a feature of ordinary relationships of this kind within the same social group, the sequence of giving and returning presents set off by cross-baptisms entailed a real economic exchange which covered a basic part of the necessary trading between shepherds and peasants. Since, however, the fact that what the two groups produced was complementary enough to form the basis of a system of barter, the question arises as to why such a system should happen within a system of spiritual relationships and thus take the form of gifts and counter-gifts. The advantage of a system of kinship over that of pure barter was that it created a link between peasants and shepherds greater than that created by the complementarity of their products, and thus was a better guarantor of their economic interests. What a shepherd hoped for when he established such a relationship with a peasant was that if the latter was his kinsman he would allow his sheep to graze on his fields when the harvest was in and would take his side in quarrels with other peasants if his flocks caused damage, for which assessment was always very high. Similarly, the peasant expected the shepherd to be careful of his growing crops, to make sure that other shepherds did the same, and to take his side in quarrels with other shepherds. Thus, unlike barter, which only takes place within the framework of an already known production, the godparent relationship meant both that it was possible for the two families to obtain both the products they needed and an increased security with regard to those external social conditions which could influence the level of production itself, and hence of consumption by the family. By providing the necessary minimum of protection and economic security, establishing relationships of this kind served to complement the ordinary kinship pattern when the latter was necessary but nevertheless impossible because of the difference in social status separating families.

It is not enough, however, simply to see in this exchange of gifts a system of barter in which each party tried to gain what he needed. Not only did the interests in operation greatly exceed the value of the things exchanged, they were also not of an exclusively economic nature. Behind the exchange of gifts, there was also an important and continual circulation of symbolic capital which was largely due precisely to the social distance between the two groups and the fact that their products were complementary. By establishing a godparent relationship with a peasant, a shepherd was seeking to further his symbolic interests. He was speculating on the honour that kinship with a peasant family must necessarily bring him. In addition, peasants and shepherds linked by spiritual kinship would also automatically invite each other to their major family occasions. When the peasant went to the shepherd's house, he brought him an increase in his symbolic capital not only by his mere presence but also by singing *mandinades*, or improvised poems, which heightened the prestige of the person to whom they were addressed by praising his good qualities such as hospitality, honesty, good looks, and so on and the value of which, i.e. their symbolic yield, was all the greater because they came from a social superior. Also, since a daughter's value on the marriage market depended not only on her beauty and the economic patrimony she might inherit but also on her symbolic capital, and since it was incumbent on the godfather to sing *mandinades* in public to his god-daughter at dances and assemblies, it can be seen that by carrying out his social obligations the peasant, and *a fortiori* the *canacare*, godfather was giving the girl an increase in her symbolic capital that would improve her chances of a good marriage, that is of eventually converting this symbolic capital into economic advantages. For his part, the shepherd, by giving presents of sheep, was removing from the peasant the shameful obligation of having to buy the meat and cream that everyone had to have on his table on feast days.[35] If this had not been the case, people would have been able to say of him, 'he has no friends and is not a great master of a house, since no-one honours him'. It is now easier to see why peasants always thought it lucky to act as godparent for a shepherd's child.

Overall, although the godparent relationship did what mere barter could not do, and thus better served the economic interests of peasants and shepherds, the circulation of economic and symbolic wealth between the two groups tended to strengthen kinship links which were all the more fragile for being only spiritual and linking groups of differing social status, even if only by constantly updating them and, in essence, by keeping them in constant working order. That meant that kinship links were in a better position to carry out one of their basic tasks, that of providing the best possible social protection for the level of production of both groups.

It also seems, however, that the functions of the godparent relationship are to be found in the area of the circulation of products. By initiating a system of regular gifts of great value, this relationship enclosed them, so to speak, within village society. More precisely, it provided both groups with a guarantee that neither would trade to outside groups an essential part of the products the other needed, as if the fact that the products were complementary was not in itself sufficient to guarantee an exchange constantly threatened by the existence of divergent interests, particularly where the ownership of land was concerned. It was also as if village society feared that if it were freed from links of spiritual kinship, goods would be traded in terms of laws which it would no longer be able to control. Indeed, left to its own devices and reduced to a purely economic function, trade, even in the form of barter, would have followed only the laws and logic of private gain and the external market. Enclosing it within the system of kin relationships was aimed not only at ensuring the economic autonomy of the village but also at forcing it to obey certain rules defined by the society of the village and in conformity with its own needs. Or rather, if barter always immediately shows the relative values of the goods exchanged, godparent relationships were aimed at preventing any questioning of the conditions of trade by transforming barter into a system of gifts and counter-gifts. This was achieved by eliminating purely economic considerations. The peasants may have chiefly stressed the essentially economic value of the presents they received ('we had meat until harvest-time'), the shepherds the fact that, economically, the system tended to favour the peasants, and most of the villagers may have thought that it was more or less fair and that, in any case, one did not calculate about such matters ('we didn't tot it all up. The main thing was that we paid each other a compliment'), but the truth is probably that the mixture of economic and symbolic interests involved made any precise calculation impossible, and that the shepherds gained in symbolic advantages what they lost from an economic point of view, whereas the peasants converted the surplus symbolic capital they gave into material advantages. Perhaps one of the functions of godparent relationships was to form the basis for the illusion that allowed an unfair economic exchange to appear equitable.

But even if there was no 'totting up', it did not mean that a calculating mind was not behind these links of spiritual kinship. Another proof of the use made of godparent relationships within a real family strategy aimed at increasing symbolic and economic advantages to the full can be seen in the fact that the *canacares* tried to establish them with the one or two merchant families (thus obtaining goods which the village did not possess) and also that peasants and shepherds who embarked upon such relationships were opposite numbers in their respective groups, for the *canacares* allied themselves with shepherds who had the largest flocks in the village.[36]

Spiritual kinship and the maintenance of the social order

We should, however, be missing the main point if we did not see the significant way in which godparent relationships supported the social order. Exchanges between relatives put a large proportion of the surpluses into circulation in the form of presents that it would be shameful to think about in strictly economic terms. This meant that for a long time the economy of the village was not a money economy and did not depend on fluctuations in prices on an external market. Making the village market part of a wider external market would have implicitly threatened the social order by ultimately creating a distribution of wealth and a social hierarchy no longer necessarily linked to inequalities based on the ownership of land. Restricting trade to a network of kin relationships meant that the social order was protected from outside disturbances. In addition, cross-baptisms certainly did not eliminate the social gap between peasants and shepherds. Paradoxically, they helped in a certain way to maintain it precisely when the peasants had to create the illusion that it was narrowing. Spiritual kinship, which ultimately meant a 'false' kinship,[37] was the closest form of kinship permitted by the social distance between the two groups. That distance was also so real that it found an expression even in the means by which exchanges were conducted. In the case of exchanges brought about by baptism relationships between two peasant families, it was always the godfather or godmother who made the first move. In cases of cross-baptism, however, it was always (apart from the actual ceremony itself) the peasant family, whether it was that of the godparent or of the real parent, which took the initiative, sending a special loaf to the shepherd family at Easter. It was said that this had a force of a *proidopitico*, which was the word used to designate a court order for payment. By sending the loaf, the peasant was telling the shepherd that he was accepting the continuation of the exchange. Even though the shepherd never dared refuse the gift and the concomitant withdrawal from the exchange, the opposite was not the case, and it sometimes happened that one year the peasant would not send the loaf, indicating that he no longer wished to exchange gifts. We can see both that the relationship was dissymmetrical and that ultimately the exchange of gifts would only continue as long as it was in accordance with the interests of the peasant. It would seem that one of the functions of the gift of bread was to reaffirm the social gap between the two families just when they were renewing an alliance which could have created the illusion of an equality of social status. Godparent relationships helped to perpetuate the relative strength of the economic forces operating between peasants and shepherds, and did so by guaranteeing that the terms of the exchange were in accordance with the former's interests, but they also helped to maintain the relative balance of symbolic forces. What the shepherd who had a spiritual kinship with a peasant gained in terms of symbolic capital gave him an advantage over other shepherds without such a privilege, but in no way changed his position in the balance of symbolic forces between the two groups. It would be truer to say that since the peasant's symbolic capital was in no way diminished by the share of it that he gave to the shepherd, the latter, by showing himself desirous of committing himself for reasons of prestige to a kin relationship with an owner of land, was implicitly admitting that he would only be able to increase his symbolic capital by sharing in that *de facto* possessed by any peasant family. If shepherds themselves helped to reproduce the symbolic forces operating between themselves and peasants, it was, therefore, because a perception of the social superiority of the latter underlay their practices.

On the other hand, godparent relationships between peasants and shepherds tended by their very logic to forge a sense of interdependence between families belonging to groups whose basic interests were nevertheless very distinct. Solidarity between members of one group could not but be lessened by them, and there was always the risk that conflicting interests with regard to the distribution of land might lead to violent quarrels. Similarly, such relationships offered a shepherd family the chance of individually obtaining a surplus of prestige by sharing in that of a peasant family, and consequently kept shepherds in a relationship of dependency, thus creating a basic ideological obstacle to any collective struggle to question the inferior social status of their group or the unequal distribution of land on which it was based. The many conflicts of past times clearly illustrate both how real the ever-latent antagonism between the two groups was and the fact that it was so structurally inevitable that godparent relationships alone could not hide it. Indeed, the example of a *canacare*, the president of the village, who was lured into a trap by his godfather, who was a shepherd, and subsequently died, shows that such conflicts were frequently so violent that when they occurred godparent relationships certainly did not diminish them, but were themselves used by one of the families as the best means of wreaking vengeance. It can be seen that apart from such exceptional cases, these relationships strengthened the cohesion of village life and in doing so a social order, the maintenance of which was primarily in the interest of the peasants, who owned the land, and, amongst them, principally those of the *canacares*. Embarking on spiritual kinship with a social group that they despised was to some extent the price the peasants had to pay for the maintenance of a social order which gave them a privileged position.

There was, however, another way in which such links helped maintain the social order. If the exchange of gifts is the only way in which the circulation of goods can be fully recognized in societies which deny the real basis of their lives because they cannot see economic reality for what it is, and if the time elapsing between gift and counter-gift is a necessary interval for them to see as irreversible an exchange structure which constantly threatens to seem interested,[38] then on Karpathos the economic reality of the exchange was all the more thoroughly concealed as goods circulated largely between relatives. Kinship in itself tended to create the illusion of a disinterested exchange. It was as if by hindering the awareness of the economic factor as such, society was indirectly attempting to prevent younger daughters from becoming conscious of the fact that they were exploited. On the whole, as we have seen, ordinary kinship links (in the field of production) and spiritual ones (in the field of circulation) were systematically used to maintain the social order. By acting in this way, the society of Karpathos produced the social conditions for survival which would have been threatened by a questioning of the unequal distribution of land and goods by 'women agricultural labourers' and shepherds.

NOTES

1 This paper, based on research carried out on the Greek island of Karpathos in 1967, 1975, and 1978, is a continuation of the author's earlier article. 'Emigration et déréglement du marché matrimonial', *Actes de la recherche en sciences sociales*, 15 (1977), and takes up the analysis of the kinship system developed in a doctoral thesis defended in June 1977.

2 The right of bilateral primogeniture, which in principle covered only family goods (*ta gonika*) and not those acquired by the parents in their lifetime, was known on Karpathos as *canacariki*. In the sense of 'someone who is spoilt', the term *canacaris* is widespread in Greece. In the Karpathos dialect, *canakizo* means 'I caress'. The eldest son and daughter were called, if they were to inherit, *canacaris* and *canacara* respectively. (The feminine form is used less frequently in the rest of the country.) For them to be heirs, their direct ancestors of the same sex had theoretically to be the firstborn of their own sex themselves right back to the most distant past. The word *canacare*, however (*canacarides* for men and *canacares* for women), had a more restricted meaning when it referred to the socially dominant group. On Karpathos, where more people gained their livelihood from seasonal work away from the island than from the products of their own land, the term referred principally to the richest, and in principle 'eldest child', peasants.

   Not all eldest children were *canacares*, but they did all enjoy the prestigious epithet *protoios* (the firstborn son) or *protokori* (the firstborn daughter). Nowadays, *canacaris* and *canacara* are currently used as mocking terms for people who act selfishly and thoughtlessly. A fisherman shouting at a girl who was amusing herself by climbing into his boat which was moored in the harbour might call out 'E! canacara!'

3 For samples of old marriage contracts, see M. Nouaros, *Nomika Ethima tis Karpathou* (Athens, 1926).

4 E. Manolakakis, *Karpathiaka* (Athens, 1896), 109.

5 N. Consolas, 'Laographika Olymbou Karpathou', *Laographia*, 21 (1964), 246.

6 When a father was giving away his daughter in marriage, his friends would jokingly say to him, 'Your box is out of the *sofa* now.' (The *sofa* was the upper part of the house where the family slept.) This meant that he could start packing his bags.

7 As distinct from olive trees in particular, which only bear fruit after a certain number of years. It sometimes happened that a husband, if he was in a favourable position in the domestic interplay of forces, would make his wife sign an agreement to reimburse her husband's expenditure. Apart from these unusual cases, it seems that the custom described above acted in the past as a not insignificant brake on agricultural investment and even on proper maintenance and improvements to houses.

8 The father's brother or the mother's sister, however, had to be a child of the same mother as the deceased spouse. Half-brothers and half-sisters had no claim on the family inheritance. When the husband died, his heir had to look after the widow for a year, receiving in exchange the harvest for himself. If, however, the widow kept her mourning for less than a year, she was looked after only as long as she wore it. She received, so to speak, economic aid for the symbolic service she gave to her husband's line by wearing mourning.

9 The legal customs of Karpathos were not put into a written code until 1864. According to Nouaros, apart from on the island of Olymbos, which was still very traditional, many family quarrels between younger and elder children and parents in particular, were transformed into endless lawsuits. Mayors, judges, and the clergy did not agree on how to interpret former customs, and the practice of giving bribes became common. What perhaps also induced the authorities to put custom into a written form, however, was that the disappearance of a consensus could eventually endanger the right of bilateral primogeniture. It is certain that every effort was made to preserve the privileges of eldest sons and daughters in the new situation brought about by the development of a money economy and the creation of fortunes outside family patrimonies as a result of greatly increased emigration. Thus the written law allowed the eldest son to choose, if there was no will and if his father's personal fortune was greater than the patrimony of the line, between taking the patrimony or two shares of the patrimony and the personal fortune combined and divided by the number of children plus one. The text of 1864 was signed by six mayors and six notables of the island. With the exception of a school teacher and a linguist, all the signatories were from *canacare* families as is demonstrated by the ecclesiastical origin of their patronyms. It can be seen that the island, just like Olymbos, was still dominated by the *canacares*. Two signatories, one of whom could not write, had to have witnesses to their agreement. According to Nouaros (*Nomika Ethima*), the right of bilateral primogeniture also existed on the islands of Kassos, Tilos, Nissiros, and probably Halki, Andros, and Amorgos. On Nissiros, Tilos, and Halki, heirs (the eldest child of each sex) were called respectively *nikokyris* or *nikokyra* (master or mistress of the house), *protoios* or *protokori* (firstborn son or daughter) and *protonikokyris* or *protonikokyra* (master or mistress of a first-class house). On Kassos, the dominant social group at the end of the century consisted of twenty-four *canacares* (twelve of each sex). As was also the case on Karpathos, they were distinguished by the fact that they alone wore certain kinds of clothes. Only female *canacares* wore the *colaina*, a piece of woven material embroidered with gold thread and covered with gold pieces, which was worn round the neck and over the breast. Other women who had gold pieces had no right to wear them around their necks. On many of the islands in the Aegean Sea, female and male fortunes were also kept separate. On Kos, Skyros, Skiathos, Skopelos, Santorini, and Mykonos in particular, the eldest daughter inherited the mother's fortune, and on Symi, Tilos, Ikaria, Patmos, Andros, Amorgos, Kea, Astypalea, and Ios sons inherited from their fathers and daughters from their mothers. On most of the Aegean islands, too, but also on a part of the Greek mainland, a widow or widower could not keep the fortune of a deceased spouse if there were no children. The fortune returned whence it came: *ta gonika sta gonika*. In his

article 'Ethimikon dikaion Astypaleas', *Laographia* (1950), 124–34, Nouaros gives the text of the legal customs of Astypalea and points out that they appeared in writing for the first time in 1876 in the form of an ecclesiastical code. As was the case throughout the Dodecanese, parents had to transmit intact to children legitimately inheriting it the ancestral wealth that they had received as a dowry, and could dispose as they wished only of their personal wealth. If one spouse died and the couple were childless, the surviving partner had to put the movable and immovable estate into good order and return it whence it came. Almost the whole of the code is devoted to attempting to solve the problems which could arise from the existence of separate male and female lines, each tending to take account only of its own interests. In order to prevent a surviving parent from harming the interests of a child, a family council consisting of the nearest relatives of the child was set up. It was empowered to remove the child from the custody of the surviving parent and put him or her into that of another relative and also to deprive the parent of the power to hold the inheritance. If the council allowed the parent to keep the child, he had to manage the inheritance without benefiting from it. If it was managed so as to produce a surplus after the expenses connected with it had been deducted, it was paid into an ecclesiastical fund, which managed it in the best interests of the child. The Patmos code was drawn up in 1732 in the monastery on the island, and its contents were similar to those of the Astypalea code. It made provision for a sum of 1,000 *grossia* (Turkish money) to be paid to the ecclesiastical court on Kos if custom was not observed, and was signed 'beneath the icon of the great Theologos, for the sake of security' by the abbot and four priests. The text mentioned an earlier code of undetermined date. In 1843 a new, shorter version of the 1732 text was signed by thirty priests, as if custom now needed a more spectacular form of legitimation if it was to survive. On the whole it certainly seems that the Dodecanese islands and perhaps a great part of the Aegean area had an unusual kinship system which had nevertheless been practically unknown to or neglected by ethnologists. As was shown by a reading of Nouaros's work, the village that the author had the chance to observe from 1967 was only the tip of a rather large iceberg. It is not unreasonable to suppose that this kinship system be partly characterized by the existence of clearly separated male and female lines with a material basis of a patrimony transmitted from woman to woman and from man to man.

10 See Vernier, 'Emigration'.
11 The younger daughters of the *canacares* did not work for outsiders.
12 As opposed to that emigration which was the traditional fate of younger sons.
13 This corresponded closely to the interests of the *canacares* who used 'foreign' younger daughters.
14 The first president who was a younger son was elected in 1923. He had acquired his wealth in the United States.
15 Until recently, different terms of reference and address were used for younger and eldest children. The same was true of the feminine Christian name Maroucla. In the case of an eldest daughter, particularly if she was a *canacare*, the unmodified Christian name Maroucla was always used. It was known as *psilo-onoma*, 'the name with the greatest value'. For 'second category' women, as the local phrase has it, the associated familiar feminine form Marou was used. Younger daughters doomed to spinsterhood and poverty were most often called, from their earliest years, by the masculine pejorative Marouclos. Similarly, feminine Christian names such as Magafoula, Vastarcoula, Thetecoula were modified to Magafou, Vastarcou, Thetecou (the familiar forms) or Magafos, Astarcas, Thetecos (the pejorative form).

Certain masculine (and feminine) Christian names had no intermediate familiar form, but merely the formal version (Ianis, Manolis, Costas, Iorgos, Vasilis) and the pejorative form (Anas, Manias, Costaras, Orkas, Asis). In moments of anger, parents would sometimes use the latter form for their eldest sons. Its implicit threat of disinheritance reduced them for a time to the humiliating status of younger sons. Conversely, they would also add the prefix *mou* (my) to the Christian name of their eldest son or daughter to stress the link of special affection between them and those who would continue their line.

The demeaning terms *pissokori* and *pissoios* would also be applied to the youngest daughter and son respectively of large families. *Troutso*, signifying someone deprived of everything, was used for younger children and at least in recent times for youngest daughters, and the very offensive *doula* and particularly *doulara*, meaning a slave, for all unmarried younger daughters. *Troutso* and *doula*, when used in reference, were preceded by the article and followed by the Christian name of the person to whom the younger child belonged: *i doulara tis Ernias*, meaning 'the slave of Ernias', for example.

Since some younger children could in fact inherit, there was no collective pejorative term for all younger children as there was for women in other societies. The dominant ideology as it concerned eldest sons and daughters could only be expressed by means of terms indicating the youngest child of each sex (*pissokori*), who would almost certainly never inherit if the family was a large one, or terms of reference and/or address used for an individual child (e.g. *doula*, a modified Christian name, and so on), in other words, ultimately in interpersonal relationships rather than in inter-group ones.

16 In a society based on primogeniture, the unenviable position of parents once their eldest children had married might seem paradoxical. The logical solution to this problem, however, is provided by the fact that the system of transmitting Christian names gave eldest children those of their grandparents.

17 Religion also gave its powerful sanction to the eldest. Arguments concerning inheritance were submitted to the representative of the bishop, who most frequently decided in favour of the eldest. The *prikosymphonon* transferring a dowry to an eldest son began with the formula: 'In the name of the Father, and of the Son, and of the Holy Spirit.' The obligation of transferring the patrimony intact to the person with the appropriate Christian name was of a religious nature to the extent that if it were not done the soul of the ancestor, it was said, would be tortured by the injustice and unable to enjoy eternal rest. It can be seen that religion, by the device of patronymics justified the domination of the *canacares* over the other villagers. It legitimated that of all of the eldest over the younger children.

18 It was always the younger son bearing his mother's father's Christian name irrespective of the order of birth, normally the second son. The fact of having a Christian name from his mother's side made him closer to her and marked him out as the person to continue the maternal line. In one or two cases, it was an eldest son in the position of a younger son as a child of his father's second marriage.

19 Sales of land were in fact very infrequent and always seen as rather sacrilegious, as making the seller unworthy, since it was said that the eternal rest of the ancestor was at stake. Anyone selling land had always decided to do so because he was emigrating permanently and always waited until the parent from whom he had inherited it had died. In order to give as little scandal as possible, he would always attempt to find a buyer amongst those relatives most closely connected with the estate. Buying back land that had fallen into strange hands by a sale or a mortgage was seen as a sacred duty, and custom insisted that relatives, even distant ones, should have the first option to purchase. According to Nouaros, 'Ethimikon', the price in such cases was always the original one and outsiders would thus inevitably hesitate. Before a local cemetery

was built in 1910, the sacred and non-transferable character of land was, it would seem, strengthened by the practice of burying the dead on their own property.

20 When there was disagreement about the Christian name, the child was often simply called *babi* (baby) until the baptism. This meant that no-one's feelings were hurt and, in particular, ensured the advantage of surprise at the critical moment. If it was in some way advantageous, the child would still be called *babi* in the presence of members of the losing line after the baptism and until emotions had subsided enough for it to be called by its normal Christian name again.

21 Couples who could not have children would sometimes make a vow. If their wish was granted, they would give the child, even if it was a firstborn son, the name of an angel such as Gabriel, who was naturally associated with fertility as it was he who had brought the tidings to Mary. There again one could say that the choice of a Christian name was disinterested. In addition, a child whose father was mad was also called *angelos* (angel). By doing so and avoiding the name from his father's line, people were acting as if he was the child of no-one and to some extent protecting him from madness.

22 The inversion rate was, however, greater for younger children than for the eldest, and this is even more the case if the eldest children of younger children and the younger children of the latter are compared. Parents who themselves were younger children tended, both for economic reasons and reasons connected with the age of marriage, to have fewer children than those who were themselves eldest children. When, however, as a result of some unfavourable balance of forces within the couple, they were unable to give their eldest child the appropriate Christian name, they tended to have more children so that they would be able to give one of the younger ones the name that the eldest should have had. This meant that the proportion of younger children in the group of younger children as a whole taking the Christian name of the eldest was greater than that of eldest children in their group as a whole taking the Christian name of a younger child. If this is less marked amongst the children of eldest children, it is because the latter had more children than younger siblings did. This is a further indication of the importance attached to symbolic capital in the society we are examining.

23 Some of these transgressions, however, are explained by the fact that former strategies had been carried over into the new context in which money had replaced land as the dominant economic symbol. Thus, giving the child the name of someone who had emigrated expressed the hope that he would help it or even its parents. Some of the transgressions that poor peasants had always been guilty of can probably be explained in the same way.

24 On Karpathos as in our own society, we encounter a terminology which takes account of collaterality but not of branching. There is for example a single term for a father's and a mother's brother, but it is not the same as the one for a father. The class of uncles and aunts (*callas* and *calla*) only includes blood relatives of forebears in the direct line of ancestry (parents, grandparents, and great-grandparents). It does not include a sub-class of the great-uncle type allowing a distinction to be made amongst uncles and aunts on the basis of their genealogical distance. The area covered by this class and the way it includes the various genealogical levels are related to the structure of the corresponding social relationships. Uncles and aunts are all those – and this is what also distinguishes them from cousins – who in certain circumstances could give a particular individual their Christian names, bequeath their goods to him, and, in the case of aunts, help him in his home and his fields. The class of cousins also includes several genealogical levels and degrees of collaterality, all collaterals in fact who are not included in the class of uncles and aunts. It does however also include sub-classes which enable very fine distinctions to be drawn, as the table shows.

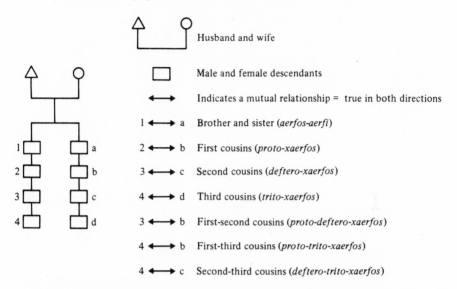

Husband and wife

Male and female descendants

Indicates a mutual relationship = true in both directions

1 ←→ a   Brother and sister (*aerfos-aerfi*)

2 ←→ b   First cousins (*proto-xaerfos*)

3 ←→ c   Second cousins (*deftero-xaerfos*)

4 ←→ d   Third cousins (*trito-xaerfos*)

3 ←→ b   First-second cousins (*proto-deftero-xaerfos*)

4 ←→ b   First-third cousins (*proto-trito-xaerfos*)

4 ←→ c   Second-third cousins (*deftero-trito-xaerfos*)

25 A grandmother would never treat all her grandchildren in the same way. She would give all the help she could to the eldest daughter with her own Christian name, but would not be asked to help pay for a younger daughter's education. If she were, she would reply – and the author has frequently heard such retorts – that she would never help a stranger.

26 Unlike eldest children, younger ones, given the origin of their Christian names, could not continue 'pure' lines which were clearly separate.

27 Younger sons almost always had a photograph of their eldest brother and his eldest son in their homes. The opposite was not the case.

28 Other kinds of conflicts arose between members of the same family. There were, for example, those between an eldest son and his younger brothers if he made use of this position to take from them the goods forming part of the *apoxenosis* or, more recently, if he claimed an inheritance from his father when there were younger sisters to be married off. Recently too, when a father wanted to increase the value of his *yerondomiri* by planting olive trees on it, the younger daughters would do nothing to keep the animals away from the young trees, since such trees take a long time to fruit and they knew that their eldest brother would therefore be the only one to benefit from them.

29 On Karpathos there are, therefore, different types of kinship groups with distinct social functions. On one side there are the male and female lines, each based on an ancestor and most frequently running from the mother to the firstborn daughter and from the father to the firstborn son. These are stable groups, strictly based on sexual unifiliation, and restrictive. The material basis of their existence is indivisible patrimonies and they consist of eldest children of the same sex always with the same two alternating Christian names. By the device of the naming system, they also recruit the younger children they might need in order to ensure their own reproduction. On the other side there are parentela, that is bilateral groups of temporary kinship defined by their relationship to ego who can be called on if necessary for such tasks as building a house, and so on, and for all family festive occasions. It would not, however, be correct simply to speak of the coexistence of these two groups. The existence of the lines partly helps to give the parentela the specific characteristics just described, and in

particular a discrimination between patrilateral and matrilateral kin at least in the case of eldest children. To these two groups must be added the semi-official kinship groups defined by nicknames. To say of someone that he is X or is descended from X is to say that he is of the group X. It is, for example, possible to belong to, *inter alia*, one of the following groups: glass eyes, stutterers, idiots, evil tongues, bad lot, crude lot, little fools, dogs, donkeys, fish (of various kinds), dregs, shit-eaters, beggars, sheep-stealers, grain-stealers, hear-nothings, crop-ears (an actual punishment for certain crimes). These nicknames, although negative, can be considered as symbolic goods, but unlike scarce goods, such as land and buildings, they were passed on indiscriminately to all the descendants of the person to whom they were first given, whether they were eldest or younger children or descendants on the male or the female side. It will have become clear that individuals with different surnames can have the same nickname showing that they are all members of the same group of descendants. In addition, an individual could belong to several kinship groups indicated by nicknames, which certainly could not happen with regard to membership of a line or a parentela. As the principle of inheritance in this way from both father and mother was operative in every generation, it follows that on the one hand the great majority of villagers would have at least one nickname and that on the other many of them would have several, sometimes in fact more than a dozen, as the author himself has observed on the island. Anyone wishing to insult them has a quiverful of barbs at his disposal. He can shade his retort or his aggression according to how he feels at the moment or what the situation calls for by using one nickname or another and either more or less condemnatory. Over a period of time, only the most harmless ones are discarded, those gradually forgotten by villagers only interested in using the most effective ones. On the other hand, the most derogatory ones can, as the author can prove, be handed on for six generations or more. Ultimately, the nickname or nicknames a person has are a collection of light or heavy weapons that others can use against him. Given that the most insulting ones last the longest – and it is said on the island that they never disappear – all the weapons available for this verbal guerilla warfare tend at the village level to become increasingly redoubtable, as if the interconnected play of memory and forgetfulness were producing there the same sort of escalation that one sees elsewhere in the armaments field. There have been unforeseen consequences, for it seems that the gradual modification of the make-up of the stock of nicknames and the cultural changes due to emigration have both helped reduce their use of terms of address, at least in the case of hereditary ones. The villagers are so afraid of the reprisals that a 'leak' could bring that most of them were unwilling to give the interviewer any examples of nicknames. Indeed, their very existence has sometimes been very vigorously denied in public, as an act of allegiance to a community whose most closely kept secrets and hence whose cohesion was being ostentatiously defended, so that it would not make public those of the people defending it. All this explains why marriage strategies paid such great attention to the allocation of nicknames within the social space. When a spouse was being chosen, they were more important than the surname, even if the latter was ecclesiastic in origin and in some ways even more important than possessions. This was because the main concern was to spare any children of the match, and particularly the eldest of each sex, a stigma expressly intended to sully each descendant. Thus, if they were to be successful, the marriage strategies adopted by the lines not only had to obey the rules of class endogamy and order of birth, but also that of what one could call nickname endogamy. This was all the more important as there was no more irreparable form of misalliance than one of such a kind. Infringements of the rules of class endogamy and in certain cases the limitation of the number of possible partners cannot be understood without a consideration of this factor. On the whole, although it was usually the lowest social classes who had the most degrading nicknames, those soubriquets nevertheless helped to define symbolic relationship patterns which were quite independent of the official social hierarchy based on the ownership of land.

30 Given the system of transmitting Christian names, it was possible for younger daughters to have one from the same side (either the father's or the mother's) as their eldest brother, but not for them to belong to the same line.

31 In a society obsessed by the problem of the survival of lines, uxorilocality (the movement of men between female houses) was perhaps both an indication and the effect of the predominance of female lines, at least while the woman was still young and valuable because of her procreative power. This was so for both lines. The existence of female lines, uxorilocality, and the custom that the woman's family should ask for a man in marriage rather than vice versa all suggest the particularly high status of female heirs on Karpathos and, it would seem, on some of the Aegean islands. In attempting to explain the kinship system proper to the region, it can be noted that it accords with the features of the local economy and the sexual division of labour which follows from them. In any economy characterized by a shortage of land suitable for cultivation, which meant that some of the villagers, including eldest sons of non-*canacare* families, had to leave the island for seasonal work, it was the man who emigrated. The woman had to stay at home to produce and raise children, and the seasonal emigration of unmarried younger daughters also seems to illustrate that situation by its opposite. Women were also always more numerous than men, since younger sons emigrated permanently, and were thus, with a few male *canacares*, the only people left to look after the village for many months at a time. The frequent absence of husbands, fathers, and fathers-in-law could not but encourage an increase in their autonomy and power. It could also only help to strengthen the ties of emotion and mutual help existing between mother and daughter in the tasks they both knew – housework, childbirth, bringing up children – and weaken even further those between father and daughter and the much less close ones between daughter-in-law and mother-in-law. At the same time, emigration was also likely to strengthen the links between father and eldest son, who led a very different life from that of the women in the house. Overall, the particular autonomy of women and the fact that with it there went a network of relationships that, as there were no men there to introduce other relationships, tied a woman to her mother, her sisters, and her nearest kin in the female line, her maternal aunts, perhaps encouraged the emergence and/or persistence of female lines and the uxorilocal rule of residence. That rule, in its turn, was bound to facilitate relationships between mother, daughter, sisters and maternal aunts, even if only because it provided a familiar framework for them. It is perhaps also worth noting that a change of residence on marriage would have been costlier for a woman than for a man. The men had already been, so to speak, prepared for living in a different place by seasonal emigration, whereas the women, who had stayed in the village and had closer links with their neighbours and were more tied to their homes, were more dependent on neighbours for the mutual help needed as part of everyday life or on special occasions such as family festivities.

32 Only a part of the household, however, could be complex in structure. Given the rules of residence, young couples often lived alone, with their children, for a certain number of years after their marriage. There may thus be an occasional flavour of the arbitrary in any attempt to work out crudely the extent to which an extended family was present or not from statistics relating to the average number of persons per household or the proportion of households complex in structure.

33 An attempt was made to find out where unmarried younger daughters aged over thirty were living in 1975 (n = 103). Most of those under fifty-one were still with their parents

(73.8%). Of those above fifty, fewer than 10% still lived with them. Younger daughters still living with a married couple other than their parents were, in 82.5% of cases, relations of the wife. A fairly small percentage (34%) of those not living with their parents lived with their eldest sister or her eldest daughter. Those living with either a younger unmarried sister or a younger married one amounted to 11% in each case. 10% lived with an eldest brother or nephew and 31% lived alone. Where they were living either alone or with another younger sister, 51% still had either an eldest sister or the eldest daughter of an eldest sister living in the village. It can be seen that in the new context arising as a result of widespread emigration, where the younger sister lived was now more than previously based on a calculation by her than by her eldest sister. The latter might not want, for example, to share with the former money sent by her husband, or the younger sister might prefer to live with another younger sister richer or less demanding than the eldest. However that may be, emigration to distant parts on the whole encouraged individualism and emancipation amongst younger daughters and at the same time made their help less necessary. It would seem that this is reflected in the development of households with a complex structure (Table 4). In 1938, younger daughters (sisters and aunts) totalled 48% of persons outside the conjugal family, but only 34% in 1972.

34 National and local tax returns show that hardly a day passed without a shepherd being assessed for damage caused by his sheep.

35 The richest peasants would own one or two beasts looked after by shepherds. These would not however meet their needs.

36 The fact that a child could have two or even three godparents and above all that one person could act as godparent for many children made baptism strategies more effective. Thus, apart from the *canacares*, the one or two shopkeepers acted as godparents for a large number of children in the hope of having more customers. Indeed, such godparent relationships are still common all over Greece in both rural and urban areas and transcend class barriers. A rich Athenian woman might act as godmother to a fisherman's child so that the father would deliver his freshest fish to her home. Another one might do the same for her maid's child. Industrialists are godfathers for their workers' children, and just as on Karpathos the *canacares* perform the role many times to build up a political following, members of parliament in the rest of Greece often oblige dozens of their constituents.

37 This kinship was only 'false' in contradistinction to kinship by the alliance of families. Those who had the same godparent could not marry. In order not to reduce the number of possible spouses, which had already fallen due to strict village endogamy, people acted as godparents for children of the same sex, whereas normally men acted as godfathers for girls and women as godmothers for boys.

38 Pierre Bourdieu, *Esquisse d'une théorie de la pratique* (Paris and Geneva, 1972).

Part II. *Materna in extremis*: the clash of interests between mother and child

3. Infanticide in rural Bavaria in the nineteenth century

REGINA SCHULTE

In 1894, thirty women appeared before the Bavarian court of assizes for killing their newborn illegitimate children. Using the fragments of the 'criminal biographies' of female infanticides contained in sixty dossiers from the state prosecutor's office covering the period 1878–1910, I should like to cast light on a social and psychic milieu which made child-killing possible. In civil law, it is considered an offence under para. 216 of the penal code, which proceeds from a natural idea of the mother/child relationship. The code consequently views material and psychological circumstances merely as factors mitigating or aggravating the seriousness of the act. Infanticide appears as an individual, psychiatric, or mystical slip-up of nature, which needs no explanation beyond itself.

By contrast, I wanted to describe it as an event occurring within the everyday circumstances of life and work. The statements and perceptions of police and judicial officials found in the dossiers of the Munich assizes were a starting point for a reconstruction of the subjective, emotional, and material meaning of sexual relationships, maternity, and maternal love in the context of the social fabric and everyday work. When these are considered, the criminal and legal aspect of infanticide disappears almost completely. It remains external to the social biographies of the women and only becomes a reality when they are accused and start their sentences.

I

With a single exception, the women in the Munich dossiers were born and grew up in the country and were children from the lowest stratum of rural society. Amongst the personal details of the accused, the dossiers give either the profession of their parents or their social rank within the range of peasant proprietors. Only one, the daughter of a peasant proprietor, came from a wealthy background. Amongst the parents of the rest were fourteen smallholders, four day labourers, one woodworker, one miner, one quarryman, thirteen artisans and petty tradesmen: cobblers, joiners, tinsmiths, millers, masons, tailors, innkeepers, and so on. In seven cases, the name of the unmarried mother was given, and for two women that of the foster parents. In sixteen cases, no information about parents was given, but the places of birth and residence were indicated. Smallholders, day labourers, and artisans evolved from the peasant population engaged in small and medium-sized undertakings in the second half of the nineteenth century. They normally had a smallholding of not more than 10 hectares of land, a garden and a small, poor house, and often a cow or two. Income from the land was supplemented by day labouring for bigger farmers, who needed extra hands, particularly at haymaking and corn harvesting. In Upper Bavaria, particularly in winter, there were opportunities for woodworking, and in other areas labour was required for reclaiming moorland and in quarries. The material circumstances even of artisans and petty tradesmen were very closely linked to the possession of land. In a primarily agrarian society, only very few could live from earnings from artisanal occupations alone.[1]

The way of life of this stratum of the rural population ranged, depending on the size of the holding, the fertility of the soil, and the profitability of supplementary work, from one of poverty to one of destitution. They were tied by their land and not mobile enough to look for work in the newly developing industries. Their small plot of land was nevertheless what kept them off the very bottom rung of the social ladder, that of the propertyless rural labourers and farm servants, who were struggling to acquire land and eventually to found a family. The life and work of cottagers, like those of peasants, were subject to weather conditions, the change of seasons, and calamities such as hail, cattle epidemics, and sickness in the family, which affected the viability of their smallholding. Housing conditions were for the most part rather primitive and the dwellings miserable and dilapidated.[2] In extreme cases, men and beasts occupied the same space.[3] As was almost always the case in the organization of rural labour, children had to work if the family livelihood was to be secure:

in all families, those of both the smallest and the largest proprietors, the children have to join in the work as far as they can and as soon as they can. At first they are set to work in out-of-school hours and in school holidays looking after the cattle and with small, easy jobs in the house. The elder brothers and sisters look after the youngest ones and are busy in the kitchen and in the cowsheds. As soon as they are strong enough, however, children have to take part in all the tasks involved in the undertaking. Many a large family earns a not inconsiderable supplementary income by picking blueberries and bilberries and gathering fir cones and the like.[4]

Like all other workers, the children worked in the fields, particularly at harvest-times, or replaced the women in the house. In some districts, it was chiefly the children who were used to harvest the potato crop.

By the time they left school, such children had long been accustomed to work. The children of smallholders were usually obliged to seek employment outside the family. Those from medium-sized and larger farms, if they did not inherit, mostly stayed to work on the parental farm until they married or died. They cost less than outside workers, and because they had an interest in the farm, identified with it, and belonged to the family, they were also more serviceable than outside workers. On a smallholding, however, there was no use for their labour once they had grown up, and if they did not seek paid employment elsewhere, they remained a liability.[5] Some children (particularly sons, it would appear from the Munich dossiers) went off as wage labourers together with their parents. They would go turf-cutting on the moors with their other brothers and fathers on a daily basis and also became wood and quarry workers. In the second half of the nineteenth century, there was also emigration to towns and industrial regions, but even up to the end of the century, Bavaria remained chiefly agrarian in structure, and this was evident even in the few towns. In 1882, 50.9% of the working population was employed in agriculture.[6] At this period, a large proportion of the young people from the lowest village stratum still went to a nearby village and hired themselves out as farm labourers or maids. In Schöffau in Upper Bavaria, such workers still amounted to a quarter of the total population in 1895.[7] A large proportion of rural young people over the age of fourteen belonged to this group, which wandered from village to village and farm to farm, moving on each year on 2 February (Candlemas), when labourers and maids started and finished their period of hire.[8]

Of the sixty female infanticides, forty-one worked in agriculture, and thirty-three (55%) of these were servant girls. Their place of work was for the most part in the immediate vicinity of their place of origin, a matter of one to three hours' walk away. Five of the women were still living at home, working on their parents' land and intermittently as day labourers, one as a seamstress on a farm where she sometimes ate and slept. Servant girls, female day labourers, the seamstress, and a waitress lived in a village and peasant environment. To some extent these servant girls also worked occasionally as day labourers or waitresses in inns. The world of work in these peasant communities did not encourage job-specialization. People were dependent on whatever work was available, and their place of work was also where they lived and ate. The seamstress, the day labourers and the servant girl ate at their employer's table and were for the time being members of his household. A farmer's daughter with some property and the widow of a smallholder, neither of whom worked away from home, were the exceptions in this group of infanticides. Of the sixty women, nineteen finished up in service in Munich. They had all worked to some extent in the country before 'going into service for the gentlefolk in the city'. For servants, the town meant social advancement, which is also shown by the fact that five of these servant girls progressed to become cooks.[9] At fourteen and sometimes even younger, the girls left the parental home to take employment with some peasant at the very bottom of the servant hierarchy as goose-girl, undermaid or 'little maid' (the names varied from region to region) or as a day labourer. Only a few moved directly into a town.

Only unmarried maids and farm labourers were found in Bavaria at this time. Domestic service was incompatible with marriage and children in the form in which these were occasionally possible in ecclesiastical and manorial domestic service before secularization. The economy of the simple farms, whether small or large, meant that the children of domestic servants were of no interest as a future source of labour. Although the restrictions on marriage for domestic servants were raised in the second half of the nineteenth century, the economic situation and the fact that the ability to work was dependent on being single necessitated late marriages. As was the case with the farmers, where it was due to matters connected with the laws of inheritance, the age of marriage was around thirty, and sometimes later.[10]

Intermarriage between the lower stratum and the land-owning farmers was unthinkable to the latter, and the social hierarchy of the village remained inviolable. The constant recurrence of this division as a theme in the literature and popular stories of the time helped to perpetuate and mythologize it rather than to call it into question. It was conveyed in a symbolism which directly expressed property relations. Ludwig Thoma, who at the end of the nineteenth century represented villagers in court and as a solicitor in their quarrels and economic struggles, describes this situation as revealed in the churchyard where both the totality and the divisions of the village became visible:

On All Souls' Day one could tell who had money in Erlbach. The graves of the wealthier people were prettily decorated with artificial straw flowers hanging with glass beads. Large red and blue lanterns cast a striking light on the stone angels, the crosses and anchors . . . Nearby, the graves of lesser people looked so poor. The wooden crosses were weathered and the inscriptions on them so illegible that the dear Lord must have found it very difficult not to confuse the small cottagers and servants. There were no artificial flowers or wreaths with glass beads there, only sprigs of pine and holly. Here and there a stable lantern had been put up awry, with a small light burning in it as wretched and mean as the life of the person lying there waiting for the Resurrection.[11]

The daughter of cottagers or the servant girl who wanted to marry a farmer would not be in a position to observe one of the most important of the rituals connected with marriage – the journey of the *Kuchelwagen* (the laden bridal cart) from the bride's to the groom's house two days before the wedding. In the style of its outfitting and what it signified, this cart was a public declaration to the whole village of the wealth and portion of the bride and at the same time the expression of a 'just' claim to marriage. The journey of the *Kuchelwagen* was a ritual that cost the farmer, and with particularly grand weddings several other people from the participating village as well, a day's work:

three or four days before the wedding the *Kuchelwagen* comes, if possible with a team of four horses, with the guide-rope, the whip, and the harness decorated with ribbons of red silk. It brings the wedding goods, consisting of a bedstead, a mattress, a clothes chest, and, if it comes from the bride's house, also a cradle and a distaff. The latter is decorated in a particularly beautiful fashion and must be held by the bride. At her side sits the seamstress and behind them, by the newly-made wooden articles, the joiner. In many villages, the bride's chief attendant, called the *Nächstin*, or person closest to her, takes the former's place in the cart, behind which a nice cow or a magnificent ox is always tied, following it.[12]

For the lower classes a *Kuchelwagen* like this must have been 'a disheartening sight, since it represented more wealth than anyone from the lower stratum could ever hope to amass'.[13] For the servant girls, it was a question of gathering together a dowry and the basic equipment for married life during the fifteen to twenty years they were in service, using savings from their wages and the traditional gift of up to 20 ells of linen and spun flax at Christmas. At the end of the century, however, the latter was increasingly of less account in the additional bonuses given to domestic servants.[14] The dossiers show that servant girls earning 80–150 marks a year with free board and lodging could save between 400 and 500 marks in ten years. An anonymous letter about a servant girl, written by one of the infanticides to the former's suitor, shows how significant such savings were as an attribute of a woman's eligibility: 'do you not know that Klara has not a penny to her name. Do you not know that she has been in service for 13 years and has saved nothing. Do you not think that if you marry her you will soon have the bailiffs on you and you will have saved for nothing.'[15] Like the infanticides, the fathers of the illegitimate children also came from the lower stratum. When the dossiers give no clear information about the identity of the child's father, sometimes because the accused was having several affairs at the same time and it was impossible to establish paternity beyond doubt and sometimes because the criminal records were incomplete, the lists of witnesses at least suggest the milieu in which he was to be found. In the case of Maria M., an unmarried servant girl in Jachenau, all that is known about the father is that he was willing to pay maintenance.[16] The list of witnesses, however, presents the following people: Katharina F., 20, unmarried servant girl in Riedern; Katharina H., 36, unmarried servant girl in Weißach; Maria F., 25, unmarried servant girl in Geißach; Michael L., 30, unmarried servant in Petern; Martin S., 25, unmarried servant in Jachenau; Otto S., unmarried servant in Sachenbach; the midwife and constable from Jachenau; and the regional assize-court doctor. The places mentioned are all near Jachenau where Maria M. was working. The servant girls and labourers appeared in court to testify about the love affairs, pregnancy, and crime of the girl and about her character. They were therefore all from the immediate neighbourhood of the accused, had worked with her, and met her in other ways. In the case of Maria M., it can be assumed that the father was one of the labourers present in court, and a comparison with other dossiers suggests this conclusion. Another woman, Maria N., 23, an unmarried servant girl from Eisenhofen, had simultaneous relationships with three labourers from various villages around Schwabhausen, her most recent place of work.[17] Very many of the fathers of the murdered infants were servants. The rest were day labourers, artisans' assistants, the sons of cottagers, one married farmer, and one married miner. They also came from the same place as the accused.[18]

With servant girls and labourers, in particular, relationships were often begun at the place of work. During the day they worked together and at night slept under the same roof. 'Last year Corbinian G. was working near me. He often had his way with me in the house of my master. He is now at Maier's in Reichersbeuern.' Another one had this to say:

since St James's day last year I have been at Strasser's, the brewer's, as a servant. All day long I work in the cowsheds and sleep at night in a room over a staircase. Theres K., a waitress at Strasser's shares it with me . . . The father of my child is Georg N., a labourer in the brewery. He came into service at Strasser's in October last year, but left on 1 December . . . when I found out that I was pregnant. I often let Jakob S., also a brewery labourer with Strasser in Tittmoning, share my bed.[19]

The description of their relationships shows that there were very rapid contacts between male servants and female servants. The structure of their place of work made this possible. The farmhouse took on servants and maids as members of the family, and the common table describes at once the community of work and of reproduction. With some exceptions, the old patriarchal structure was maintained in Bavaria until the end of the century; 'in this respect, things go on in the quiet traditional manner'.[20] In the village of Schöffau in Upper Bavaria servants lived 'with their masters in the large community of the house and on the whole were treated as members of the family'.[21] In that village, there were in all seventy-five servants, forty-three labourers, and thirty-two maids living on twenty-two farms. On the biggest farm alone there were twelve persons in service. The grades (goose-girl, kitchen maid, dairy maid, head maid) possible on large farms indicate not only the division of labour but also the hierarchies amongst servants. At work there was no rigid division between male servants and maids. Both men and women worked in the stalls and in the fields, and all the jobs were coordinated and complementary. In the working day of a single maid, work in the house, the cowshed, and the fields could all intermingle smoothly and – chiefly at harvest-time – the excess of work and the weather determined when a given number of workers, including the children and the cook, were needed in the fields.[22]

Although domestics were necessary as farm labour, their sex lives and pregnancies could disturb the even flow of work. A farmer had an interest in preventing a maid getting pregnant, as he needed her to be fully able to work. A farmer, Corbinian R., 'noticed that he [the labourer] developed a more intimate relationship with the servant girl and dismissed him after 6–8 weeks. He is now working for Maier'.[23] There were probably no really effective threats or means of control to stop love affairs amongst servants. Labourers and servants were bound neither by the demands of their parents nor the obligations of inheritance. Particularly at a time when labour was in notoriously short supply, they could not be seriously threatened for any really considerable length of time with punishments from either farmers or the police, as they had scarcely anything to lose. In the final analysis, they could make their own decisions about their sex lives. Their material interests being the same and differences in wealth not very great, their choice of lover was more strongly committed to feeling and chance than could have been possible for a farmer's daughter with her obligations to her rank and property. In addition, male servants and maids spent up to twenty years in service, moving around between various farms, villages, and households. This long 'transitional phase' took up the whole of youth and finally left it exhausted:[24]

everything that was not concerned with work was done in secret. Things were so arranged that the workers could communicate with each other simply by means of glances, allusions, and handclasps. If a maid took a labourer's pocketknife at break-time, the others could be certain that he would be in bed with her that evening. There were of course women who would immediately unbutton a man's fly and move their hand around inside. The domestics tried to keep at least the nights to themselves.[25]

The dossiers also show that the servant girls were active in sexual pursuit. Agathe S. invited Michael B., who was working on the farm of farmer P. at Sprittelsberg with her, so openly and urgently to her bed that she clearly embarrassed him. He 'further deposed that S. had often told him to sleep with her . . . but B., who was a harmless and stupid lad in these matters, did not do so'.[26] Police descriptions of the labourer as a 'bumpkin' show clearly that the girl's demands were seen as completely normal. The closeness and uninhibited nature of the relationships is also shown by what one labourer had to say about Theres Z.: 'he had to bring grass to her every morning for the cattle, and once saw her washing her body, which was very bloody'.[27] Anna H., who was pregnant, was talking in the field with the labourers about her condition. She wanted to hide it but had to be open about it, as she was strikingly big. She therefore presumed that the men she was working with had noticed her pregnancy and were interested and also that they would expect her to declare it.[28] The threshold of shame was very low. The signs and events of pregnancy were known to the men and were not tacitly and shamefacedly ignored but discussed throughout the whole household. Living under the same roof or together in a highland pasturehut was, in the eyes of both the police and people in general, as is indicated by the statements of witnesses, constantly taken as circumstantial proof that a given labourer was the father. Shared work in the fields or on the moor as day labourers, amorous behaviour at a dance, walking together after business in the village, from a fair, from market, after some heavy drinking in the inn, or on a Sunday afternoon, all these were a sure sign to the inhabitants of the village and the constable that a child had been conceived on one of these occasions. This was confirmed by the parties concerned.

It is clear and striking in the dossiers that these sexual relationships were short-lived. In the main labourers and servant girls remained at the same place of work only for a year or two. Although movement in the case of those women who did not go on to Munich was limited to villages within a region extending no more than 20 kilometres from the parental home, contact was often broken off when one left a place of work. Thus Theres Z. 'heard nothing more of Georg N. since then. All I can say about him is that he is thought to be from Würtemberg'.[29] Anna H. declared that the father of her fifth child, which died during a premature birth or was aborted, was 'Josef R., from the Tirol . . . but I do not know exactly where . . . Twelve years ago he was a labourer with M. in Waakirchen, where I got to know him'.[30] Typically, and to the same effect, Franz P., one of the fathers, declared: 'at Candlemas this year B. left Baldham and since then I have had no dealings with her at all', although it was not far from Ismaning, where he was then working.[31] The external factor governing the length of a relationship was thus primarily the same place of work. Internal bonds which could bring about problems of separation or plans for a continued relationship in many cases do not seem to have existed. On the other hand, it is true that many of the women concerned hoped that marriage would follow from such relationships and kept them up after a separation, particularly if they had an illegitimate child. If they then entered into a late marriage, the family often had two or three children already.[32]

In nineteenth-century Bavaria, pregnancy outside marriage was not in itself seen as a disgrace.[33] The illegitimacy rate was lower than in the middle of the century but between 1876 and 1895 was nevertheless 12.3% in Bavaria as a whole and 15.7% in Upper Bavaria.[34] In this part of Germany, illegitimacy was integrated into the social pattern of peasant society and did not conflict with the demands and norms of the family as the basic element of the agrarian world. In the Thalhausen *Hofmark*, for example, even illegitimate children could inherit family property, although in Roman law they were outside the institution of family. Unmarried sisters or daughters of the farmer frequently lived on the parental farm with their illegitimate children until they married or died.[35]

In the Munich dossiers there is only one farmer's daughter who had sufficient means to feed her child and whose motive for killing it was the censure 'that she could expect from those who knew her, particularly where she lived'.[36] As was apparently the case here, the position of such a woman seems to have been particularly bad when the father of the child did not correspond to the demands which made possible a suitable marriage. Disgrace meant having visibly sold oneself for the wrong price and having become a laughing-stock, since the illegitimate children were not an economic problem for the farmer, and a wealthy farmer's daughter with a child was still a desirable match. The decisive factor was that the economic safeguards that farmers had built up should not be breached, and certainly not downwards. Those who had slithered down to a lower rung on the scale of property were the ones in disgrace. They were considered losers in the general struggle for 'the thing'. Amongst the farmers, who right until the end of the century gave their children in marriage as a means of protecting and increasing property, any emotion that moved outside the preordained circle of eligible spouses had to be proscribed as a threat. It was shameful, and, as the accused asserted, it was apparent in the behaviour of 'those who knew her where she lived': by which she meant the youth of the landholders.[37]

Apparently the problem of disgrace and the loss of honour did not arise for servant girls. Many of them already had illegitimate children,[38] who lived with the parents of the unmarried mother or were fostered. The foster parents also came from the lower end of the social scale and were day labourers, cottagers, and married artisans, for whom the payment for fostering was a form of additional income often amounting to half a servant girl's wage. The maintenance that the father had to pay was also of an equivalent sum. The father of the first child of Agathe S. paid, after occasional pressure, 80 marks a year to her parents, who had taken the child in. They thought that this was not enough. Although he was a labourer, he was considered to have some means, as he had expectations from his parents.[39] However, none of the women was able to keep her child even for a relatively short time. Anna N., who herself was the illegitimate child of an unmarried servant girl and grew up with her grandparents, said that her mother had never been able to stand her, put her own illegitimate child out to foster parents, where it died before its first birthday. 'I never had the child myself', she said.[40] Most servant girls normally left their place of work for a few days for the confinement, went home to the midwife or foster mother, and handed the child over immediately after the birth. Until the mother married or became self-supporting, the children stayed with their grandparents or in another house that often became their home.

On a farm or in a household, pregnancy, and more particularly the birth of a child, were not provided for. The servant girl was seen and employed simply from the point of view of her ability to work:

when servants are hired it is like buying cattle. If you do not want to be cheated, you look closely and think hard. And if there's something wrong at the start, then it's better to say no right away. With cattle, only legal defects count, whilst others do not allow you to back out of a deal; still they ruin your stable and empty your purse needlessly just the same. Can anyone say that servants aren't like that?[41]

The character-references taken by the court from farmers, burgomasters, and reliable witnesses are only concerned with the work of the women. Sexual affairs and illegitimate children are of no interest. Even in cases where the person concerned was described as 'dissolute' in this connection, statements about her work simply indicate that she 'is a fine, assiduous, and industrious person, with nothing disadvantageous to her good name', that she 'is praised as a worker', that she 'is a very useful, hard-working person'; 'at work, B. was hard-working and steady'.[42] Even arrests for infanticide had no adverse effects on these statements.[43]

If the employer suspected that the girl was pregnant, her job was in danger within a few weeks, as happened with Anna H., who has been mentioned already:

for quite a long time it had looked as if H. must be pregnant . . . It is about 8 weeks since I told her that she was not to bring any trouble into the house and that she was to leave work in good time. I said that I would like to keep her on as long as possible, but she answered 'I'm all right, I'm not pregnant. I've got an abcess and I've got to have an operation.' But she got bigger and bigger, and I was continually urging my wife to get her out of the house.[44]

II

Like sexual relationships, both pregnancy and birth were closely bound up with the course of work, which in accord with the changing seasons brought varying demands on the strength of the servant girls. Some of them described birth simply as work. It was something experienced and undergone in an unspectacular way. As they gave birth alone and in secret, they had to manage without a midwife. The secret pregnancy and, in the case of almost every infanticide, the birth endured alone, meant great demands on their strength and a total rejection of questions and offers of help from others. The replies of one girl to police questioning indicate this: 'I went on to ask her why she had killed the child. To this she replied "I thought, I'm very healthy and I can manage it alone." I do not know what she meant by that, but I assume that she meant that she felt strong enough to conceal the birth.'[45] Those servants who concealed their pregnancy and did not, as was expected of them, leave their place of work at the right time were a threat to the rhythm of work on the farm, where the absence of such a girl, particularly at harvest-time, when labour was scarce and already spoken for everywhere, could not be permitted. The girls knew this and worked all the harder. They carried out all their allotted tasks right up to the birth and then continued with their work as if nothing had happened. The case given below shows this in the statements of the servant girl, a labourer working near her, and the farmer's wife:

I admit that yesterday morning, early on the 20th of the month as we were going to the fields, I was overcome with labour pains and gave birth to a child at the side of a footpath by the arable land. I bent down because of the pains and suddenly saw that the child was coming out. It was straightaway lying on the ground. The cord had come away. I did not tear it. The child did not move, and I thought it was dead. I put earth and perhaps some grass too into its mouth, wrapped it up in an apron, and laid it in the wheat field. I was going to go back to fetch it at midday. I was working near the arable land. I put the earth and grass in the child's mouth to stop it crying if it came back to life. I did not take it back to the house with me at midday because there were too many people around me . . . I do not know how long it took me to go from where it was born to where it was found, but I think it was quite a long time. Perhaps it took twenty minutes. I worked all day and did not notice anything and went to bed without washing. I did not clean myself until after I was arrested in Ismaning . . . I threw the afterbirth into a field near the red cross.[46]

The labourer merely noticed that the rhythm of work had been disturbed:

I worked for D. along with B. On the 20th of this month I went to the fields with the latter about 6.30 a.m. I was walking ahead and B. was following. She stopped by the red cross. I do not know what she was doing there. I had already been working for a long time when she came back. She was there for perhaps half an hour. When I asked her what she had been doing there, she said that her nose had been bleeding. She worked with me in the field during the morning and at midday we went back to the house. It is true that there were several people there. B. still denied that she was pregnant. She looked a bit thinner, it seemed to us. She said to the farmer's wife 'If you had bet that I was pregnant you would have lost 10 marks.' In the afternoon we worked somewhere else. When we went back, she went straight to bed after supper.

The farmer's wife too said in her statement that the working day had gone as usual:

B. was in her fifth month of service with me. I suggested to her that she was pregnant, which she always denied. She even wanted to bet me 10 marks that she wasn't. On the 20th of this month, she went to work as usual and came back at midday. She acted as if nothing had happened, and that is why I too did not notice that she was thinner. She even said to me, 'You would have lost 10 marks if you had taken the bet.' In the evening she finished all her work and went to bed. The same evening the police and Dr U. came. At work B. was hard-working and steady.

Theres Z. attended as usual to her work as a waitress in the evening. During the night she gave birth to a child and killed it and carried on with her work next morning. She took care to carry out all her duties before going to give birth in her bedroom. In the police documents, the description of the sequence work/birth/work follows the train of events without interruption.

On Friday the 17th of last month in the evening after 9 p.m. while I was still attending to my duties as waitress in my place of work and serving customers, I suddenly felt labour pains, but I just carried on with my work. After the customers had gone, the pains were getting worse and worse and I stayed in the tap room opposite the guest room, walking up and down. I suddenly lost blood and water. I sat down on the steps in that room and thought that I would stay there as long as it lasted. I could have called for help, as the maids slept on the ground floor, but I did not want to wake them. I had already locked up, and I went up to my bedroom on the first floor, where the cook was asleep in another bed.
I had no light, but undressed completely and lay down on my outer clothes that I had spread on the bed as quietly as I could so as not to wake the cook. I had very strong labour pains again and about a quarter of an hour later I had a child. It did not cry, but I thought that it had moved a little. On Saturday the 18th of last month, early, about half past six, I cleaned the tap room and then attended to my work as usual. That day I was very hungry so I ate a lot, and it was not until Sunday the 19th of last month that I felt very ill.[47]

Since a servant girl giving birth to a child was something for which no preparation was made and no desire felt on a farm or in a household, every place of birth was also a place of work. Only a few of the servants had their babies in their bedroom and even at night they left the place, which in most cases they shared with others, in the interests of secrecy. Most of them had their babies in the privy, and treated the birth as an evacuation, an everyday event, and as such something which did not appear to affect the daily round and the common task. Many gave birth in a barn: in the horse boxes, on the pile of hay, in the cowshed amongst the cows, that is in their place of work, where they were most at home and spent most time. In extreme cases they immediately carried on with their work. From watching animals give birth there they acquired some of the knowledge that gave them a measure of independence when their own time came.

It is striking that in autobiographical literature of peasant origin in Bavaria at the end of the nineteenth century, birth among animals and humans is an interwoven experience. The birth of an animal is described as tenderly as that of a child, especially so because it lies at the basis of the economic conditions of all that is hoped for. The connection implies no devaluation of the child, not even *a priori* in the case of these servant girls. It is simply that a woman who gave birth in a stable was never the farmer's wife, whose children were expected and for whom a proper lying-in had been prepared. She was enclosed in rituals which were there to frame and protect the soul, the life, the fertility, and the possessions of farmers.[48]

The behaviour of these women during pregnancy and confinement offers certain grounds for believing that they never had any intention of allowing the child to achieve social existence. Most of them made no preparations for the birth or for caring for the child. They denied that they were pregnant, and many subsequently told the judge that they had not known that they were pregnant. They had certainly 'lost something', they admitted, but had not known that it was a child. Even women who had already given birth several times used arguments like these to maintain that they could not wittingly have killed a child if they had known nothing about it. Several cases provide examples of such secretive behaviour and denials. The women seem to have had a common strategy rooted not in mutual acquaintance or arrangements but in the similarity of living conditions in which they had children.[49] In spite of the sharp-eyed observation by people around them which pregnancy almost always entails, they persisted in their denials or in some cases at least managed to create uncertainty about their condition by means of their insistence and explanations. Along with the practical reason of ensuring that they kept their jobs, concealment and denial seem to have had a deeper explanation, one which is not immediately evident from the believability of their assurances. Their denials are a means of refusing to admit to themselves as well as to the world in general that the child had an identity. It was nothing more than a piece of non-human nature without a history, of which they mostly rid themselves in the privy, and in doing so devalued it even more.

I didn't think I was expecting. I was stronger then than I had been since my first confinement. At 6 a.m. on 23 December, after I had not noticed anything all night, I had to go to the lavatory urgently. I saw that whole pieces were coming out – I didn't see what it was – and that my period had started. The traces of blood in front of my bed and between there and the privy are because my period had started again.[50]

I worked in the cowshed all afternoon, and about 6 o'clock the farmer's wife gave the calves a drink, then I said to her 'I can't wait, I've got terrible . . . [document illegible], I'll have to go to the lavatory.' While the farmer's wife was still there I went to the lavatory in the cowshed. Then the farmer's wife and the labourers went to eat, but my stomachache was so bad that I couldn't leave the privy . . . it was as if the waters were breaking when a child comes, everything was over in two minutes. I didn't know that I'd had a baby; I didn't feel it coming out. I didn't pull out the cord and I didn't cut it and afterwards I didn't feel anything between my feet . . . I didn't know until the child was found by the constable that I had given birth. I thought that I had just lost blood clots.[51]

Giving birth in the privy expresses in an extreme form the relationship to the child adopted by the woman. It is experienced and described as faeces or frequently as clotted blood, as something unclean and sick which is rejected. When the women maintain that they 'did not know' that they had had a child, they were perhaps not telling an untruth, even when, like the above-mentioned Anna H., who had already had five children, they were in a position to recognize the physical indications of pregnancy and birth. They reduced those experiences to purely physical phenomena, and in spite of knowledge of their pregnancy, they denied and hindered any knowledge about the child and refused their own maternity. The unborn child produced no picture, no projection, no fantasy about its existence after its birth or its presence in the life of its mother or in the future of a family. It remained in an ambiguous indeterminateness, a marginal state, whose dissolution in birth apparently aroused anxiety in many women confronting the reality of a child.[52]

A birth which was staged and experienced as a bowel movement made it possible for the women not to have to look at the newborn child. Apparently, the fiction of indeterminateness and formlessness of that which 'departed' from them could only be maintained if they did not identify the child as a small human, not to say as a girl or boy. Women who did not deliver in the privy avoided any differentiated notice of the child. They let it lie between their legs, where it remained 'something moving' without form or face. Katharina S. covered the child with an apron 'in order not to have to touch it because I was afraid to'. Theres Z., who gave birth in the hay mow, could not testify to the sex of the child 'because I did not trust myself to look'. They avoided any contact with the child.[53] Even the anxiety that the child might cry was two-fold: discovery and confrontation with the needs of the helpless child, to experience it as alive. Some of the women killed their children in a very crude way, by smashing their heads. Infanticide carried out in this manner demands great strength and resembles the way in which animals, especially poultry and small animals, were despatched. This method seems to express a strong defence against incipient feelings of anxiety and helplessness in connection with the newborn child.[54]

If they were killed immediately after birth, the children remained unclean and soulless in another way, for they were not baptized. Their souls were not cleansed, and they were not accepted into the Christian community. In nineteenth-century Bavaria, a child was normally baptized as soon as possible after birth, at most within the following twenty-four hours, so that it would go straight to heaven if it died.[55]

It does not seem possible to deduce from the reasons given for infanticide by these women any extreme conditions driving them, as distinct from others, into 'desperation' or 'profound spiritual and material need'. The explicit reason often given was that the father would not pay, meaning that he also would not marry the mother. Sometimes paternity was denied and various men claimed to have had sexual relations with the woman. Many women assumed that the father would avoid paying maintenance. Barbara T. had decided to kill her child 'because Josef P., my lover, often told me he would not admit to being the father of the child I was expecting'. Maria N. insisted that she did not know that the father had any wealth. Maria G. was afraid of the father because 'he threatened me, in case I told anyone he had got me pregnant'. Another woman killed her child because 'there was no definite father', as was often the case when there had been sexual relations with several men.[56] More often than not there was no prospect of marriage, although the woman tried hard to bring it about. The children were not then 'conceived before marriage' but outside any family framework, even if initially and for a fairly long time that institution was a fantasy and a projection into the future. A fatherless child was to a certain extent outside the life they were saving for and was a threat to it. Katharina S. thought 'I have already a child to feed, and the burden of keeping the newborn child is mine alone. That meant that I should have less and less and so it would be better for me not to have this child and so I decided to kill it.'[57]

It is not, however, very often that a really unambiguous indication of the reason for what they did emerges. It is usually described as 'material need'. In other cases, what the accused's statement has to say on this matter contradicts what the witnesses say. Agathe Z., for example, had claimed that her parents, who were already bringing up two illegitimate children for her, were too poor to be asked to take on a third. The parents, however, insisted that they had never exerted any pressure on their daughter on account of the two children, nor had they abused her. 'Even if she had kept coming back with a child . . . it would have been brought up just like the other two, and Agathe Z. would have had nothing at all to fear from parents. So she would not, as she claims, have got into want.'[58] Often, as in this case, there was 'no material need', there was 'no particular motive for the deed', the accused 'need have expected no particular disadvantages for herself', was in 'no particular state of excitement' or mentally disturbed.[59] Theres Z. – who had already put a child out to foster parents, was working as a stable maid, and had some means, as she had inherited her parents' smallholding – expressed the ambivalence apparent in many of the women: 'really I did not want to kill the child. I thought I would leave it lying, and if it died that would be all right and if it didn't die that would be all right too . . . I didn't need to kill it because I was poor and worried about keeping it; I would have reared it even if nobody had paid me anything'.[60]

When the accused was being questioned, no 'particular' motives for the deed appeared and certainly none that could be legally relevant. The notion of a lack of motivation of this kind does not, however, correspond to the suppositions of civil law concepts, which see a maternal love deeply rooted in nature in conflict with the desire to rescue virtue. Consequently, the only motives ascribable to infanticide are those of a desire to save honour, those of 'particular' circumstances, or those of psychiatrically significant forms or states of illness.[61] Here the question arises of whether the killing of the children by the servant girls was seen by them as really infanticide as the civil law would see it. There was nothing 'particular' about the situation, no 'particular' motives, and most women had not enough interest in the child to want it to live despite their circumstances. Their decision was taken early, and the children were killed in a kind of late abortion before they had seen them and consequently before even the most rudimentary relationship between mother and child, which might have prevented infanticide, had begun. The accused showed scarcely any feelings of sorrow or guilt. Their reactions after the deed were determined by outside factors, those of the fear of discovery and of imprisonment.

Their behaviour was not outside the prevalent attitudes towards children in Bavaria at the time. There was a specific attitude towards the life and death of children which was rooted in the conditions of peasant life and pre-bourgeois socialization processes. It was spectacularly evident in infanticide, which according to criminal statistics was almost entirely restricted to country areas, but in such areas it was an almost everyday experience.[62] With children, there was no need to 'get excited. One is born every year. If it dies, it's a pity, if it lives, that's all right.'[63]

Children are a blessing from God. If a lot of them come, the blessing can easily be too great. It's well known that the poor are visited with it more often than the rich. Many a wealthy farmer cries out in vain for a son and heir while at his nearest neighbour's – a small cottager's hovel – the little hungry mouths are everywhere. But by and large, a lot of children are begotten; you can reckon on a full dozen in every marriage. The parents are glad to see the first and second children, especially if there's a boy amongst them. But all that come after aren't as heartily welcome. Anyway, not many of these children live. Four out of a dozen at most, I suppose. The others very soon get to heaven. When little children die, it's not often that you have a lot of grief. They're little angels in heaven; we've enough of the rest. If an older child dies, who would soon be able to go off to work with you, everybody is upset – it's already cost so much work and trouble, now it's all been for nothing. It would have been better if one of the little ones had died . . . That comes neither from cruelty nor from a lack of love for them in their parents. If a man has to earn his daily bread himself, he has no other choice, particularly in summer. He can't wait for his children like the rich man does. But the love inside him is just the same.[64]

The women who were accused in Munich had grown up in circumstances like these and had presumably, on the early deaths of their own small brothers and sisters, not only experienced the ambivalence in love for little children (like Anna S., of whose fourteen brothers and sisters three were still alive, or Lorenz K., of whose eleven brothers and sisters six had died before being weaned[65]), but also learnt that to a certain extent the survival of those children was linked to the will of their parents. The high mortality rate for children and babies was a result of wrong or insufficient feeding – only very few women breast-fed their babies – and poor medical care.[66] It was especially after the birth of the fourth and fifth child that parental provision and care for their children slackened. The ubiquitous practice in Bavaria of 'live and let die' (*himmeln lassen*), a kind of 'post-natal family planning',[67] the result of more or less conscious child neglect, was the background to the chances that a child could survive. The religious idea that superfluous children were better taken up to heaven as angels may have been a justification and a consolation. The position of illegitimate children handed over to strangers was, despite social tolerance, even less favourable than that of children growing up within their family. The active interest of foster mothers in their charges seems not to have been very great.[68] The extent to which family planning was attempted by contraceptive means and abortions is not under examination here, but abortive methods and practices were known, and it seems that in some cases of infanticide, abortion had been tried earlier.[69]

The infanticide dossiers offer no approach to the feelings accompanying the death of the babies. They appear not to have existed. Most of the statements are full of indifference, coldness, and callousness, but not perplexity. Even the statements of witnesses give the same impression. From the degree of ability to express feelings, it is extremely difficult to draw conclusions about whether they are present or not. The language used by the women during questioning, which was certainly that normally used by them in talking to the village police, has neither the scope nor the vocabulary for expressing individual feelings, and a seeming emotional muteness consequently gives the impression of a general impoverishment of feeling. The specific nature of the general situation – one in which they were being questioned – must also be taken into consideration. As well, taking down the statements in High German excludes the nuances proper to the dialect and the gestures accompanying it.

From the specific attitude to the life and death of small children, and from the expressionlessness, it cannot at the same time be concluded that children were not loved. The case of Agathe Z. shows that tender relationships between parents and children and the idea that a child could be killed could coexist. In a letter to her parents she showed that she loved her two children living at home and was concerned for their fate. At the same time, while she was in prison, she decided to kill her next illegitimate child. Her mother had a suspicion, later telling the police that:

her daughter had told her last year, when she came home from prison in Sulzach, that there had been so many women there who had killed their children of whom she was afraid and thanked God that she had never had such an idea when she had her last illegitimate child, although she had had a bad time . . . Since then . . . her parents think that she has been going around with the idea that if she had another child, she would do the same and take its life.[70]

We also learn from a former lover of Theres B. that she had often told him 'that she loved her child very much, never that she was upset about its existence'.[71]

III

The decisive moment for the discovery of an infanticide – the crime or the person – was in many cases the 'talk' that had arisen, the 'rumour' that was circulating, or 'what people in general were saying'. The bearer of this talk was an anonymous informant representing in a certain way the whole village:

as is my duty, I hereby bring to the attention of the royal court that in the villages of Piesenkam and Sachsenkam there has been a rumour for some days that the unmarried Anna H. of Waakirchen, presently employed servant girl by the farmer Josef S. in Stumbach, District Miesbach, has aborted her foetus. Consequently I came to Stumbach this morning and requested an official enquiry in connection with the rumour.[72]

That is how the officer at Waakirchen police station in the Miesbach district reported the matter. The constable at Salzburghofen learnt 'by chance that what must have happened was that S., the waitress, gave birth to a child', and followed up the rumour, observing the girl in the inn in question.[73] We read in the first official report by a police officer in Tittmoning, whose investigation was triggered by the discovery of a child's body in the Altwasser, a tributary of the Salzach: 'it is popularly voiced that the servant girl Theres Z. from Tittmoning, employed here at the Krieger brewery, born 1 October 1859, is the mother of the dead child'.[74] The country constabulary, following up 'rumours' and 'talk' were making use of knowledge accumulated independently of any criminal concern. The policeman himself was a member of the village community or of that of the market town. The indications he acquired from talk were consequently as valid for him as for any other member of the community. Police reports included 'talk', described as the popular voice, as a source of information with its own momentum. The bearers of such talk or those who first informed the police of it remained anonymous. Even in statements by witnesses, the origin of a 'rumour' or of 'talk' is untraceable.

In the police files which contain details of investigations, the 'talk' or 'rumour' finally leading to an accusation is decoded as discourse about the girl arising both within the village and at her work. The 'people' taking part in this discourse emerge in the files as villagers and personal acquaintances called as witnesses. In the case of Anna D., the unmarried daughter of cottagers in the moorland hamlet of Kolbermoor, there were in all thirty-two witnesses directly or indirectly included in the proceedings. These include:

9 women: cottagers' wives from the neighbourhood, women day labourers, servant girls
7 men: cottagers, servants, day labourers, the employer – amongst these was the accused's lover.

There were also the midwife, a quack, the doctor, the policeman, the clergyman.[75]

As a member of the village community, the constable was a participant in the discourse and initially only passed on what he heard. To that extent he acted not only as an official but also as a participant in events by virtue of his knowledge. He was an official dealing with criminal matters and also the first witness.

Concealing a pregnancy and the birth of the child became, as police enquiries progressed, a reason for questioning the people connected with the accused, especially the women. The object of the enquiries was to establish whether the infanticide had been planned and whether the pregnancy had been concealed for that purpose. During questioning, the immediate circle of people around the women was revealed, both in towns and in the country, as a collection of observing, surveying, and judging members of the community, and it is clear that in that world of life and work any try at secrecy, although there were always new attempts, was doomed to failure. Knowledge defeated denial. For example, a police officer declared that 'Rubrikatin B. had been pregnant for a long time, but persistently denied it . . . General opinion has it that she committed the crime.'[76] In the case of Theres Z., the 'rumour that she was pregnant . . . had built up because she grew strikingly fat, as happens when a woman is carrying a child'. Her 'unusual birth' had been observed by:

Anna H., married cottager from Kai, Maria H., washerwoman from Tittmoning, Helena L. and Anna St., both day labourers from Tittmoning, who had been told by Z. some weeks ago, that she had such bad stomach pains that she could not manage all her stable work, and that for that reason she had wanted to fetch St. to help out, but that she had not managed to catch her . . . The rumour was also current amongst her fellow-employees.[77]

It was chiefly the women who noted immediate physical changes in the pregnant girls. It was almost impossible, under their knowing and inquisitive eyes, and more particularly those of the official midwife in the village, to conceal a pregnancy. When they were questioned, they described the details of work being carried out and the moments in the days when they first became suspicious, because of small irregularities in her physical state and her behaviour, that the servant girl could be expecting a child. Sometimes she would leave the field while work was going on and disappear into a wood without an explanation. Sometimes during the summer she clothed herself so bulkily that it could be that she was trying to hide her stomach. She gained weight, her eating habits suddenly changed, or she went to the quack. The observation was closest amongst those fellow-domestics who shared a bedroom with the pregnant woman. In the court records, an endless discourse among the women is described. It got started off because the servant girl had not had a period for months, and they wanted to know whom she had last been with. The women apparently claimed a right 'to be informed'. If the pregnant girl denied her condition, speculation did not cease. Uncertainty gave rise to rumour. It also appears that the pregnant girls accepted the demands for an explanation. They fought the rumour continually, anticipating the expected questions. They would talk about their health semi-publicly, report on illnesses that mistakenly gave an appearance of pregnancy and doctors they had seen who had told them that this or that was wrong with them.

The discourse about the servant girl would spread to the village and become 'talk'. The court's establishment of paternity illustrates this extended level of observation, which covered all the woman's life and work in her job and in the household. It was not restricted to everyday events, but spread out to cover occasions at which the village population noted love affairs and pregnancies: holidays, festive occasions, marriages, fairs, markets, dances, and so on. Knowledge about the girl became an open secret, and news about the pregnancy was immediately linked to speculations about the father. In the case of Anna H. from Waakirchen, gossip was fed by her affair with a married cottager. This, as described by some witnesses, is reproduced here:

both G., the midwife, and Anna B., the housekeeper of farmer S., said that from what she had looked like earlier Anna H. was pregnant and that it was no longer a secret in Sachsenkam and Stumbach that she had been intimate with G. a married farmer from Piesenkam.

The housekeeper, who is unmarried . . . declared that in summer last year at a dance in Sachsenkam, Anna H. showed publicly that Sebastian S. . . . a smallholder in Piesenkam, was her lover. When she came onto the dance floor, she whispered in his ear. They were both laughing together as if they were in love and they danced together all the time. Everybody was struck by that.

The midwife said, 'I saw Anna H. at the end of May or early in June – it was summer quarter-day – in Sachsenkam at a dance. She was certainly well on in pregnancy at that time. Everybody was saying "look at the size of her, and she's still dancing".'

Her mother had heard from other people that she was pregnant 'and was also told that . . . the daughter had . . . the Piesenkam cottager . . . she denied both . . . the mother of the accused also stated that at the last market in Tölz her daughter had been in Tölz with S. and that they had both gone home alone together'.

A farmer from Piesenkam said, 'there was only talk now and again that G. wanted to get rid of his old lady'!

The farmer from Piesenkam said that the relationship they had was no secret and that 'nobody could blame G. for it in the circumstances, because his wife no longer treated him as her husband. She didn't cook or do anything for him, so he had to be both the maid and the farm lad for his wife.'[78]

The maid concerned and her alleged lover disputed the relationship, but the statements of other people, as happened in the following case, assumed the nature of an arbitration if paternity was not clear.

The farmer's wife who employed S., 'Anne F.', and many of the inhabitants of Steigerain and Sprittelsberg said that they thought that S. had more likely been made pregnant by Josef D., the farmer's son, who had made her pregnant before, as he often came to see her at his parents' house on Sunday afternoons last autumn. When he was leaving she always used to accompany him part of the way. According to local opinion, this happened very often. S. also boasted, whenever she met her employer, that her sweetheart D. was there again.[79]

From such talk it is clear that people in the village – and, in the case of Munich, particularly the milieu of tradesmen, shopkeepers, small dealers, and employees in the immediate neighbourhood – knew everything that was happening. From that we can conclude that they observed the pregnancy, knew who the father was, and knew how and where the child had probably been conceived. It was in this milieu, and not at the place of work, that the reputation for 'dissoluteness' arose.

The farm formed judgements on the qualities of the woman as a worker but was interested in nothing else. Thus, a woman could be described as 'loyal, hard-working and industrious' from one quarter and as 'dissolute' from another. The latter description has nothing to do with the woman's employment prospects. It concerns her chances of marriage. It appears from the dossiers that women who merited the latter epithet were chiefly those who had relationships with married men or had several lovers, particularly if they had given themselves to 'lads from another area', who had already had a number of children and who, above all, had children of unknown fathers. However, a woman who was also known to be a thief also came close to being 'dissolute'. All such women violated norms of behaviour which in the final analysis even in the lower social strata were oriented towards marriage and property and which were overthrown by premarital sexual relationships. We can tell from a letter from Andreas D. to the servant girl Agathe S., a known thief and the mistress of several men, how afraid he was that he might possibly have to pay maintenance for another man's child, something that apparently often happened.

I no longer believe anything you say . . . just agree that she's taken me for a fool and someone else as well, and makes just me out the father like most of them. Your father will have told you, he knows the circumstances of the Thomas market, that the other one was always running after G., I hadn't been with her for some time then, and think I can protect myself from it . . . I do not wish you any misfortune, or perhaps you will call it good fortune, that you will get beer from Christl or perhaps more if you're short and perhaps nothing at all from Sepl. But I've thought how sorry I am that it has turned out in this way as you wanted it, we've wept and enjoyed the best times, there's nothing else, what's over is over . . . Your idea of going somewhere else where you aren't known is a good one but I don't advise you . . . What would your father say if you were to come down to me? You had the nicest lodgings with Stammerl all for yourself, but your mother hadn't to know that you were with me and I had to know if you were coming.[80]

If the woman had affairs with various men, they were not the only ones to determine her reputation. (In the dossiers the adjective 'dissolute' is applied to her by men who had an interest in not having to pay maintenance.) In such circumstances, she became 'fair game'. In the fact that young men came to an understanding about the sexual relationships of a woman and that on a farm flirtations between labourers and servant girls were clearly scrutinized and discussed amongst the employees, we can see below the level of legal ordinances and prohibitions a control situation which is transmitted via observation and talk. In one case a labourer argued that his fear of being observed by those working with him kept him from accepting an invitation from a servant girl to go to her bedroom because:

he did not love S. very much and he was very hesitant, as he believed that his workmates would watch him and betray him . . . however the people say that it is a sin when a vagabond brat is served at the altar of the Lord. 'Who knows', they say, 'from whom he comes, and what kind of a godless trade his parents might have carried on.' And some peasants say: 'we have our own kids; we don't need any thrown in'. I never could do so when the other two were always watching me go up or you go down. I heard it as soon as they said it.[81]

But this fear also shows that the labourer who went to a servant girl while the others had their eyes on him accepted responsibility before them. If they had known what was going on, he would have had to have paid maintenance if things got serious.

The dossiers show that secrecy was what sparked off this controlling, judging observation. It was also an offence against the 'right to know' that the village demanded of a pregnant woman not just because she wanted to live as member of the locality or the community. If she removed herself from their control, she abandoned the fundamental, common notions of order. Putting these into question, she threatened the established economic structure which had to be maintained. The resources of a village, for example, could not be arbitrarily allocated. Children of unknown fathers fed by the parish poorhouse were unwanted parasites. When unmarried mothers or unemployed pregnant servant girls were expelled from villages, a typical explanation was that they might become a burden on the village poor law funds. This was often tied up with the argument that they were a danger to morality.[82]

Bavarian tales and village stories which were hawked around over many years and eventually recorded provide abundant examples of the fate of children whose origin was not clear. In an autobiographical novel by Lena Christ, a 'foreign bastard' is excluded from Church rituals because no one can exclude the possibility that the intruder is a gypsy child. His unknown origin clings to him, containing menacing demoniac powers that might harm the long-settled, economically and socially totally ranked local population.[83]

In certain circumstances, even local people were subjected to the same strategies as those used for oppressing outsiders. In village life, one of the most powerful means of creating these 'outsiders' was the word, which in village talk described a woman as 'dissolute' and in doing so declared her respectable existence at an end. The material power of a word that could confer a role on someone and the speed by which an economic existence could be destroyed is shown by a typical Bavarian story about a seamstress with four fatherless children who was said to be a *Trud*, a kind of witch:

the farmer's wife had forbidden a seamstress to enter her house and so the latter made her ill. For she was a wild and wicked creature and as everyone thereabouts knew she already had four fatherless children and she was suspected of being a *Trud*. And it happened that at the farmhouse where she had sewn the marriage quilt, that from that hour no-one could sleep. When they opened the quilt they found a packet containing bones, hairs, and burnt sticks. They burnt all this, and all was well once more.

There was a lad, a right fellow, and she had fallen in love with him and wanted him to sleep with her. But he wanted nothing to do with her and had a horror of the creature. But from then on he was oppressed every night by a *Trud* . . . He called several other lads from the village and ran with them to the seamstress's house and they beat her to a pulp, and if she had not had such a hard life she would certainly have died. Thereafter no good came to her either in the village or in the neighbourhood.[84]

As the sequence of declarations in the dossiers indicates, the village, chiefly in its talk, seems to have had a voice as to whether a woman should appear before a judge charged with infanticide. There was a pre-trial judgement in the village, in which it appears that it was not primarily the infanticide itself that was the deciding factor, but chiefly her previous reputation, her conduct, and her position within the village community. The dossiers also include cases of solidarity with the accused woman. She was protected by silence or actively by means of appropriate evidence. No moral judgement of the crime of infanticide itself emerges from the dossiers, and the acts of judgement and sentencing in talk and in the statements of witnesses are principally concerned with the reputation and way of life of the accused. Thus, in the case of Theres Z., for example, who was respected, no-one would have reported the crime if the child's body had not been found by chance a few days later. Although everyone had assumed that she was pregnant, the servant girl who shared a room with her and the village midwife had publicly declared that she could not have given birth to a child, thus countering the chatter of one or two neighbours.[85]

Nor did a conviction for infanticide necessarily mean that the woman was excluded from the village community. Once she had completed her sentence, which in the cases discussed here was between two and (as a maximum) seven years in prison, the village often accepted the woman again. In the case of Anna H., who was released from Würzburg gaol after completing three-quarters of her sentence, an enquiry was sent to her home village about her subsequent fate. The parish replied that Anna H. was an excellent agricultural worker who always found good employment, as such workers were always scarce and greatly in demand.[86]

NOTES

This chapter arose from a research project supported by the Deutsche Forschungsgemeinschaft.
1 On the situation of the lower strata of rural society, see Axel Schnorbus, 'Die ländlichen Unterschichten in der bayerischen Gesellschaft am Ausgang des 19. Jahrhunderts', Zeitschrift für bayerische Landesgeschichte (ZBLG), 30 (1967), 824–52; Hermann Grees, Ländliche Unterschichten und ländliche Siedlung in Ostschwaben, Tübinger Geographische Studien, vol. 58 (Tübingen, 1975), 10ff; John Knodel, 'Two and a Half Centuries of Demographic History in a Bavarian Village', Population Studies, 24 (London, 1970), 353–76, here 362; Alan Mayhew, Rural Settlement and Farming in Germany (London, 1973), 124ff.
2 Untersuchung der wirtschaftlichen Verhältnisse in 24 Gemeinden des Königreiches Bayern (Munich, 1895), 453ff.
3 Ibid., 231ff.

4 *Ibid.*, 231, cf. 169, 200, 260.
5 See Michael Mitterauer, 'Auswirkungen von Urbanisierung und Frühindustrialisierung auf die Familienverfassung an Beispielen des österreichischen Raums', in Werner Conze (ed.), *Sozialgeschichte der Familie in der Neuzeit Europas* (Stuttgart, 1976), 8; cf. Franz Schweyer, *Schöffau. Eine oberbayerische Landgemeinde. Eine wirtschaftliche und soziale Studie* (Stuttgart, 1896), 124ff.
6 Schnorbus, 'Unterschichten', 832.
7 Schweyer, *Schöffau*, 124; cf. *Untersuchung in 24 Gemeinden*, 421, 488, 511ff.
8 Cf. Joseph Schlicht, *Bayerisch Land und bayerisch Volk* (Munich, 1875), 56; *Untersuchung in 24 Gemeinden*, 511ff.
9 'Die Kriminalstatistik für das Jahr 1895–1900', *Statistik des Deutschen Reichs*, new series, vols. 89–139, published by the Reichsjustizamt and the Kaiserliches Statistisches Amt (Berlin, 1897–1902), indicates a similar division among the personal circumstances of the accused. It also indicates that in the second half of the nineteenth century, infanticide was concentrated in rural areas. Of ninety-two infanticides in Prussia, only one took place in Berlin, whereas sixty-one out of 191 abortions were performed there.
10 Cf. Walter Hartinger, 'Bayerisches Dienstbotenleben auf dem Land vom 16.–18. Jahrhundert', *ZBLG*, 38 (1975), 598–638, here 623ff; Antje Kraus, '"Antizipierter Ehesegen" im 19. Jahrhundert. Zur Beurteilung der Illegitimität unter sozialgeschichtlichen Aspekten', *Vierteljahresschrift für Sozial- und Wirtschaftsgeschichte*, 66 (1979), 188; Knodel, 'Bavarian Village', 361. In both the Munich dossiers and the *Kriminalstatistik*, the average age of the female infanticides was approximately twenty-five. Of the sixty women, eleven were aged over thirty, the oldest being thirty-eight.
11 Ludwig Thoma, *Andreas Vöst* (1906), Jubilee edition, vol. 3 (Munich, 1975), 218. On the hierarchical structure of rural societies, see also Grees, *Ländliche Unterschichten*, 48ff.
12 Karl v. Leoprechting, *Bauernbrauch und Volksglaube in Oberbayern* (1855) (Munich, 1975), 218. See also the autobiographical novel by Lena Christ, *Mathias Bichler* (1914), in *Werke* (Munich, 1970), 237ff.
13 Fintan Michael Phayer, *Religion und das Gewöhnliche Volk in Bayern in der Zeit von 1750–1850* (Munich, 1970), 162f.
14 *Untersuchung in 24 Gemeinden*, 337.
15 *Staatsarchiv München* (Munich State Records) *Staatsanwaltschaftsakte* (State Prosecutor's Office) 1177 (hereafter referred to as StAM StAnw).
16 StAM StAnw 1235, cf. 1264. The abbreviations of the surnames of the accused in the text and the quotations are the author's.
17 StAM StAnw 1482.
18 Of the thirty-two known fathers, fourteen were labourers, and of the rest eighteen were day labourers, artisans' assistants, the sons of cottagers, one married farmer and one married miner.
19 StAM StAnw 185, 682.
20 *Untersuchung in 24 Gemeinden*, 231f.
21 Schweyer, *Schöffau*, 126.
22 Cf. StAM StAnw 185, 682, 693, 1177; cf. also Barbara Duden and Karin Hausen, 'Gesellschaftliche Arbeit – geschlechtsspezifische Arbeitsteilung', in A. Kuhn and G. Schneider (eds.), *Frauen in der Geschichte* (Düsseldorf, 1979), 19ff.
23 StAM StAnw 185.
24 *Ibid.* Anna H., who was thirty-eight at the time of the offence, was, according to medical testimony, prematurely aged.
25 Franz Innerhofer, *Schöne Tage* (Salzburg, 1974), p. 26. The novel contains the

author's autobiography. As an illegitimate child of a servant girl on his father's farm, he was raised as a 'bondsman' amongst the labourers, maids, and day labourers.

26 StAM StAnw 1177.
27 *Ibid.* 682.
28 *Ibid.* 185
29 *Ibid.* 616.
30 *Ibid.* 185, 682.
31 *Ibid.* 693.
32 Cf. *Ibid.* 194, 700, 1177, 1668.
33 On the development of illegitimacy in Bavaria in the nineteenth century see the following: W. R. Lee, 'Bastardy and the Socioeconomic Structure of South Germany', *Journal of Interdisciplinary History*, 7 (1977), 403–25; Edward Shorter, 'Illegitimacy, Sexual Revolution, and Social Change in Modern Europe', *Journal of Interdisciplinary History*, 2 (1971), and his ' "La vie intime" '. Beiträge zu seiner Geschichte am Beispiel des kulturellen Wandels in den bayerischen Unterschichten im 19. Jahrhundert', in P. C. Ludz (ed.), *Soziologie und Sozialgeschichte, Kölner Zeitschrift für Soziologie und Sozialpsychologie*, Sonderheft 16 (Opladen, 1973), 530–49. See also Michael Mitterauer, 'Familienformen und Illegitimität in ländlichen Gebieten Österreichs', *Archiv für Sozialgeschichte*, 19 (1979), 123–88; Friedrich Lindner, *Die unehelichen Geburten als Sozialphänomen. Ein Beitrag zur Statistik der Bevölkerungsbewegung im Königreich Bayern*, Wirtschafts- und Verwaltungsstudien mit besonderer Berücksichtigung Bayerns, vol. 7 (Leipzig, 1900).
34 Lee, 'Bastardy', 410; Schweyer, *Schöffau*, 38.
35 Lee, 'Bastardy', 416ff; cf. Rainer Beck, 'Das Dorf Unterfinning. Im ehemaligen Landgericht Landsberg. Eine historische Demographie vom Ende des 17. bis zum Beginn des 19. Jahrhunderts', unpublished master's thesis (Munich, 1978), 47.
36 StAM StAnw 1595.
37 Cf. Oskar Maria Graf, *Das Leben meiner Mutter* (Munich, Vienna and Basle, 1975), 128; Christ, *Madam Bäurin*, in *Werke*, 673–807, *Die Freier*, in *Werke*, 809–20, where the theme is that of the struggle for 'property' which was the dominant factor in peasant love stories.
38 Of these twenty-six illegitimate children, seventeen were still alive at the time of the trials. The sixty women, if the infanticides are included, had a total of eighty-six pregnancies, on average 1.43 for each woman. It should be pointed out, however, that illegitimate children were not systematically indicated in the dossiers. They do not appear amongst the personal details of the accused but are often given in connection with an increase of sentence, details of the birth, and in character references from the home area.
39 StAM StAnw 1177. Cf. also 179, 185, 194, 616, 672, 682, 693.
40 *Ibid.* 1854a; cf. also Innerhofer, *Schöne Tage*, 189; and also the autobiography of Christ, *Erinnerungen einer Überflüssigen*, in *Werke*, 7–246. As the illegitimate child of a servant girl at the end of the nineteenth century, she grew up with her grandparents, amongst other foster parents.
41 Christ, *Rumpelhanni*, in *Werke*, p. 612.
42 StAM StAnw 185, 682, 693.
43 Cf. StAM StAnw 185 (after her release from prison).
44 *Ibid.*
45 *Ibid.* 179.
46 *Ibid.* 693.
47 *Ibid.* 682.
48 Cf. Graf, *Leben meiner Mutter*, 12.
49 Cf. R. W. Malcolmson, 'Infanticide in the Eighteenth Century', *Crime in England*

1550–1800, J. S. Cockburn (ed.), (Princeton, New Jersey, 1977), 194ff, describes similar tactics of denial and secrecy in cases of infanticide in England.

50 StAM StAnw 736.

51 StAM StAnw 185.

52 Representations and fantasies about the unborn child are culturally very varied. See Mary Douglas, *Purity and Danger: An Analysis of the Concepts of Pollution and Taboo* (London, 1966), 95: 'Take, for example, the unborn child. Its present position is ambiguous, its future equally. For no one can say what sex it will have or whether it will survive the hazards of infancy. It is often treated as both vulnerable and dangerous.' Miles Newton compares varying cultural concepts and behaviour patterns vis-à-vis the unborn child. Margaret Mead, Miles Newton, 'Cultural Patternings of Perinatal Behaviour', in Stephen A. Richardson and Alan F. Guttmacher (eds.), *Childbearing: Its Social and Psychological Aspects* (Baltimore, 1967), 152ff. According to M. Höfler, *Volksmedizin und Aberglaube in Ostbayerns Gegenwart und Vergangenheit* (Munich, 1893), 26, the child had, in popular belief, no soul until it was six weeks old.

53 StAM StAnw 179, 682, 1446, 1623. On the meaning of 'ways of seeing', cf. Annie Oakley, *Housewife* (London, 1974), 200ff, and also Maria W. Piers, 'Kindermord – ein historischer Rückblick', *Psyche Zeitschrift für Psychoanalyse und ihre Anwendungen*, 30 (1976), 425: 'Child welfare institutions looking after the adoption of illegitimate children in the twentieth century have found that it is easier for the mothers if they have not seen their children. "There is no active contact, such as the movement or weeping of the child could create."'

54 Cf., for example, StAM StAnw 388, 1482, 1628.

55 Cf. Knodel, 'Bavarian Village', 359.

56 StAM StAnw 529, 542, 974, 1482. In fifteen cases it was obvious that the father would not pay; five fathers were willing to pay, and in two cases a marriage was planned.

57 StAM StAnw 179.

58 StAM StAnw 1177.

59 In all, fifteen cases were described in this way, either by the accused or by the court.

60 StAM StAnw 682.

61 Cf. Wilhelm Wächtershäuser, *Das Verbrechen des Kindesmordes im Zeitalter der Aufklärung. Eine rechtsgeschichtliche Untersuchung der dogmatischen, prozessualen und rechtssoziologischen Aspekte*, Quellen und Forschungen zur Strafrechtsgeschichte, vol. 3 (Berlin, 1973), 146; Gunnar Heinsohn, Rolf Knieper, and Otto Steiger, *Menschenproduktion. Allgemeine Bevölkerungslehre der Neuzeit* (Frankfurt, 1979), 59ff.

62 Cf. Keith Wrightson, 'Infanticide in Earlier Seventeenth-Century England', *Local Population Studies*, 15 (1975), 11: 'The discussion of infanticide thus uncovers a perplexing relativity in popular attitudes towards the value of infant life which contrasts markedly with the clear prescriptions of contemporary morality.' In anthropological literature, the problem of systematic infanticide is chiefly relevant in hunter-gatherer societies, particularly those of the Eskimos, the Australian aborigines, and the Bushmen of South Africa. Infanticide is mainly discussed from the point of view of population policy, strategies of adaptation and survival in extreme environmental conditions, and the special social claims in the lives of hunters, gatherers, and nomads. In the discussion, particularly in the case of Eskimo societies, the infanticide of girl babies is seen predominantly as a means of ensuring a certain balance of the sexes within a population in which men are exposed to greater risk of death while hunting, and in which girls not involved in obtaining food are to a certain extent seen as unproductive. The need to ensure male domination within families also seems to play some part in this. The decision to kill the baby is taken immediately after

birth, either by the family or by the mother. Cf. here: Milton M. R. Freemann, 'A Social and Ecological Analysis of Systematic Female Infanticide among the Netsilik Eskimo', *American Anthropologist*, 73 (1971), 1011–18; Asen Balikci, 'Female Infanticide on the Arctic Coast', *Man*, 2 (1967), 615–25; Carmel Schrire and William Lee Steiger, 'A Matter of Life and Death: An Investigation into the Practice of Female Infanticide in the Arctic', *Man*, 9 (1974), 161–84; Joseph B. Birdsell, 'Some Predictions for the Pleistocene Based on Equilibrium Systems among Recent Hunter-Gatherers', in Richard B. Lee and Irven DeVore (eds.), *Man the Hunter* (Chicago, 1968), 236ff; Claude Meillassoux, *Die wilden Früchte der Frau. Über häusliche Produktion und kapitalistische Wirtschaft* (Frankfurt, 1976), 42.

63 Graf, *Leben meiner Mutter*, 12.

64 Leoprechting, *Bauernbrauch*, 213, 216.

65 StAM StAnw 1828a, 1879a.

66 Cf. Schweyer, *Schöffau*, 33; Knodel, 'Bavarian Village', 359; Lee, 'Bastardy', 417, 422. Between 1879 and 1888, 35.5% of all children born in Bavaria were either stillborn or died within a year of birth. For the years 1850–99, Knodel gives an average of 2.9% stillbirths and 37.7% deaths in the first year of life, of which 45% were in the first tenth of that year. In 1888–9, only 7% of the children dying from debility, emaciation, or intestinal infection had received medical attention.

67 Hermann Hörger, 'Familienformen einer ländlichen Industriesiedlung im Verlauf des 19. Jahrhunderts', *ZBLG*, 41 (1978), 779. See also Utz Jeggle, *Kiebingen – eine Heimatgeschichte* (Tübingen, 1977), 167; and Malcolmsen, 'Infanticide', 9, on 'infanticidal nursing'.

68 Lee, 'Bastardy', 417ff. Cf. StAM StAnw 1854, 'it is difficult to determine how far the persons fostering are to blame here. There need not always be an evil intention, simply a lack of cleanliness, zeal, and a gift for feeding children often to be found in women to whom children are boarded out are the causes of this unhappy phenomenon.' Cf. also StAM StAnw 194, 682. Between 1815 and 1869, the mortality rate for illegitimate children in Bavaria was between 38.9% and 42.0%.

69 Cf., for example, Höfler, *Volksmedizin und Aberglaube*, 115ff, 197, who gives abortifacients known in popular medicine. In the case of Anna N., StAM StAnw 185, a search had been made in her room for abortifacients after a previous examination for abortion. She had consulted 'quacks', amongst them a local farmer. In addition, her mother, who was a midwife, was also assumed to be a quack. Cf. also Leoprechting, *Bauernbrauch*, 100.

70 StAM StAnw 1177.

71 *Ibid* 194.

72 *Ibid*. 185.

73 *Ibid*. 179.

74 *Ibid*. 682.

75 *Ibid*. 672.

76 *Ibid*. 693.

77 *Ibid*. 682.

78 *Ibid*. 185.

79 *Ibid*. 1177.

80 *Ibid*.

81 *Ibid*.

82 Cf. StAM LRA (Landratsakten) 78101, 78105, 78106.

83 Christ, *Mathias Bichler*, in *Werke*, 254.

84 Leoprechting, *Bauernbrauch*, 52.

85 StAM StAnw 682.

86 *Ibid*. 185.

4. Possession and dispossession : maternity and mortality in Morocco

VANESSA MAHER

I intend to explore some contradictions implicit in female roles within a male-dominated society and the attitudes and behaviour to which they give rise in women. I will present fables, rituals, and other behaviour which address themselves to one or another of the paradoxes implicit in the social definition of maternity. Although Moroccan women as individuals display considerable ambivalence towards the maternal role, which entails a high rate of mortality for both mothers and children, it is the women themselves who are particularly concerned with bringing each other back into conformity with it.

In this paper I consider a cluster of Berber-speaking hamlets in relation to the countryside and to the small Arabic-speaking town to which they are commercially and administratively attached. The population of the town, some 11,000 souls, consists to a large extent of people born outside the province. Administrators and teachers from the northern cities, traders from the South, and two battalions of soldiers of various origin come from some distance away. Of more local derivation are the artisans and technicians, small-time shopkeepers, and hospital and post-office employees. Townsmen tend to marry women from the hamlets, and more women than men living in the town are of local descent.

About two-thirds of the hamlet population are engaged in agriculture either on their own fields or as sharecroppers. Few are able to supply all the factors of production, and most plots are cultivated in association, with implements, animals, land, and labour being contributed by two, three, or even four different people. Townsmen may be drawn in to supply funds for seed and fertilizer.

As with one hamlet, where two-thirds of the cultivating households owned less than 5 hectares, holdings are small, and the majority of peasants are able to provide for only 25–30% of their needs from the land.[1] Still, they regard their agricultural endeavours as the most important part of getting a living, although they are forced to find other (wage) work to enable them to live on the land. Thus the agricultural product, comprising wheat, maize, lucerne, hay, pulses, root-vegetables, occasionally milk and eggs, and, in fortunate cases, fruit and nuts, is supplemented by sporadic wage-labour on the part of the household head or his

103

adult sons. They might work as masons, road-builders, or in some more regular capacity as miners or mechanics. Behind this is a national (male) unemployment rate of 20%, which reaches 45% in the countryside.[2] The emphasis which Moroccans give to the land is reasonable enough, since it is their main source of economic and social security.

In the hamlets and rural areas women are responsible for a large part of the agricultural work in addition to their domestic activities. About half of the hamlet women are also involved in spinning wool and weaving carpets or *dgellabas*. Only those whose husbands have no access to land work for wages. Most are *hartaniyin*, the descendants of West African slaves, whose low status finds ritual expression in many contexts. In the town, a few of the poorer women and girls sew in small sweatshops under female overseers; others knit, sew, or embroider for clients on a strictly casual and private basis. Some weave carpets at home for the cooperative of the Union Nationale des Femmes Marocaines. Finally a few educated women work as teachers, lawyers, and nurses. Ideally women should restrict themselves to domestic matters, leaving the 'public sphere' of market transactions and political relations to men. In the town, where women are more strictly secluded, if they do leave the house they wear a *dgellaba* and veil. The children run errands around the town for their mothers, sisters, and aunts.

Both town and countryside are economically and socially stratified. Economic activities are marked by a strong sexual division of labour, and women's activities are subject to considerable ideological constraint. Many households have precarious sources of income, a circumstance which not only restricts the access of all household members to consumption goods of all kinds but is experienced differentially by men, women, and children. For the very poor the role of credit with hamlet and town patrons and shopkeepers in making good the permanent cash deficit is crucial. It is considered shameful for women to work for wages, but the return on credit and patronage often takes the form of domestic services performed by poor women for their patrons' households, often within a framework of fictive kinship and common regional origin.

Property rights and management

The distribution of property rights both reflects the male role of mediator between the domestic and the public sphere and renders it inevitable. Although both men and women inherit, male heirs by Islamic law inherit double the portion transmitted to female heirs. This rule holds both in rural areas where inheritance consists largely in land, animals, and fruit trees essential to the agricultural enterprise and in the town where other kinds of property may be transmitted (houses, shares, cash). The difference between city and country property is that while the former is looked upon as saleable, the latter is not. This is not to say that land is never sold but that sales are inhibited by the claims of kin and/or other members of the community. Since the management of property involves contacts with the public sphere of male activity, women retain only marginal control over their own property. At most they can veto the proposals of their male guardians. The male management of female property has different consequences in the countryside and in the town. Land should not be dispersed. When a woman marries far away (infrequently), she leaves her inheritance in the hands of her brothers, who send her a token share of the harvest.

A lawyer from Nifaddn working in Akhdar explained how most women field-owners regarded their natal village as their real home. He cited his own case somewhat bitterly.

His wife's father had died when she was a baby, leaving considerable property in the form of date plantations in a Saharan oasis. The father's only kinsman had cunningly married the widow, whom he then divorced so that he remained sole trustee of the daughter's property, which he exploited for many years, continuing to do so even after she got married. The income she derived from the property usually amounted to less than 200 drahem (£20) a year. Her indignant husband tried to persuade her to sell it and realise 10,000 drahem (nearly £1,000), but she was appalled. She said that it was ancestral property and interpreted his proposal as an attempt to appropriate it for himself.

Town families can more easily divide an inheritance by translating it into cash or movable goods. Thus a female heir may add her portion to the conjugal fund managed by her husband. In both urban and rural circumstances women remain economically dependent, but the main responsibility for the woman's person is invested in different relationships. The locus of this responsibility, and the authority it confers, is indicated by the passage of bridewealth.

I have argued that in the Middle Atlas of Morocco, bridewealth represents the woman's inheritance right in her family of origin.[3] It generally consists of two parts. One of these, composed of clothes and cash and various symbolic objects, is paid to the bride on marriage by her husband and his family. The other (*sdaq*), usually cash, is paid to her on divorce. The payment of bridewealth confers on the husband the right of bride-removal and the interruption of the wife's contacts with her kin. However, the property (carpets and household effects) which she buys with the bridewealth is considered to belong to the wife, and she takes it away with her on divorce unless she is adjudged by the Koranic court to have been at fault. By accepting the bridewealth, she gives up her right to the protection of her male kin and to an equivalent portion of her inheritance. To pay bridewealth is a sign of 'Arabness' and is characteristic of town dwellers who have a cash income. In the countryside bridewealth in cash can rarely be paid by the small landowner or sharecropper, even if a hypothetical one figures in the marriage contract. This means that the responsibility for the bride and authority over her remain divided between her husband and her male kin. Wives in this situation are rarely secluded and visit their kin frequently. It is understood that female kin may call upon their married relatives to come and help them in times of labour shortage. There is a continuous exchange of gifts between their households. Just as rights in land are pooled and ill-defined within groups of agnates, so are rights in people.

A town bride exhibits in all her behaviour the notion that her husband enjoys exclusive rights in her person. Her movements outside the house are extremely limited, and she always goes out veiled. She is likely to adopt her husband's name and to devote all her labour-power to his household. In terms of exclusive rights in a person or thing the town bride can be regarded as the property of her husband.[4] A Berber mother upbraiding her daughter for complaining about her teacher husband said: 'well, you sold yourself to him, didn't you?'. She implied that a woman who receives bridewealth has no further claim on her husband but only duties.

Similar in theory, the rural bride's position is in practice derived from her rights in her family of origin, which makes divorce an easy and attractive alternative to deprivation in her husband's household. In 1970 the divorce rate in a Middle Atlas semi-urban population (largely of rural origins) was 52% compared with 38% in the town. Among those in the town who were not migrants from the Tafilalet area to the south where bridewealth is seldom paid the divorce rate was 28%.[5]

Rural and semi-urban women then are not secluded, they maintain active relationships with their own and especially their maternal kin, and they are more likely to initiate divorce than their urban counterparts for whom bridewealth has been paid. They do not veil themselves unless they leave the village. They distribute their services between their husband's and their mother's households and do not behave like property to the extent that the townswomen do. They also keep their father's name. There seems to be a greater tolerance of sexual freedom between marriages, which, since the hamlet is conceived of in terms of classificatory kinship (they are patrilateral cousins, *imlahlin*), might be said to be one way of spreading of rights in people among agnates.

A woman's body is property

Playing kin and husband against each other could give rural women a vital sphere of manoeuvre, but their bodies like those of their urban sisters are considered the property of their husbands. I say 'body' and not 'reproductive faculty' or 'sexuality', because their labour-power is vital to the family enterprise. A woman who is too ill to work is liable to be divorced. A woman is also liable to be divorced if she does not bear children or even if she bears all girls. Of course this is practice, not law, but there are no restrictions on the right of a husband to repudiate his wife if he is unsatisfied with her. The Moroccan Code of 1957, however far it is from actual practice, is stated in terms which give the husband rights over the woman's body, while she has none over his. Besides owing him obedience and fidelity, she must breastfeed his children if possible.[6]

Her children derive their social identity from their father. Otherwise, their birth, sustenance, and even sex is her responsibility. Crapanzano affirms:

according to the Moroccan Arabs, women do not contribute at all to the hereditary background of the child. They are only the receptacle which receives the male seed. This seed is molded into the infant by angels who descend into the womb in early pregnancy.

Women and not men are nevertheless responsible for barren marriages and must take measures to ensure their fertility. A woman may affect a child during pregnancy.[7]

In particular pregnant women should not look at animals or ugly or deformed people lest the child be born in their likeness. Recently the cinema, whose ugly images are liable to influence the child, has been added to pregnancy taboos. If the mother is refused a delicacy she fancies, a blemish appears on the child in a place congruent with the spot the mother next touches on her own body. Therefore the mother must experience her senses as a function of the child's welfare, or, rather, she must limit her sense-perceptions to those which favour the child.

A husband also owns the 'belly' of his wife. If she is divorced or widowed, she must wait three months before remarrying. If she proves to be pregnant during this time, she cannot marry until after the birth. The paternity of the child is thus clear to all. Theoretically, the father should pay alimony to the mother until she has borne the child, but many fathers default. The father may also claim all children after they have been weaned (at two years), but again most fathers claim the boys and leave the girls, which frequently leaves mothers with children to rear with the aid of kin. Upon remarriage, a woman cannot take children by a previous husband with her into the new marriage. Being forced to place them with kin forges a further bond with uterine relatives. In the case below the unemployed father considered that if he did not contribute to the upkeep of his divorced and pregnant wife, he was liable to 'lose' the child to her female kin.

Itto was an eighteen-year-old Berber girl from the hamlet Aghzim. She had been twice married and divorced. Her third husband was from a nearby hamlet and had occasional jobs as a housepainter. However, during the winter, he was not employed at all and spent much of the day sleeping. Itto claimed that he was not looking for work, that she had no wood to burn for heating and cooking, and that he had sold the precious wardrobe which had been the pride of the household. Finally she ran away, but his kin and hers persuaded her to go back, his kin providing the couple with grain to tide them over the winter. She ran away again to her mother, and then persuaded the husband to divorce her which he did reluctantly. It then became clear that she was pregnant, and her husband started to send her curdled milk, which he obtained on credit from a friendly shopkeeper. Itto's mother commented, 'He wants the belly' – a remark which may have been part of her campaign to get her daughter to reconsider, since she herself, a widow, could not support the daughter and a baby. She protested that she already supported her old mother. Finally Itto remarried her former husband, an outcome not unconnected with the reluctance of her mother to support the baby and the clear intention of her husband to claim it.

A husband has the legal right to demand that his wife breastfeed his children. That is, he 'owns' her milk. The husband must give permission for a woman to nurse someone else's child. In fact all the cases of milk-kinship I came across (that is, kinship which derives from the fact of breastfeeding rather than that of birth) obtained between a woman and relatives of her husband.

Soraya Altorki, writing on milk-kinship (*rida'a*) in Saudi Arabia, remarks on the 'doctrine' 'that the fluids of both the lactating woman and her husband generate the milk',[8] and that 'in folk theory this situation is simply described as "the milk is from the man" (genitor)'.[9] Further, 'it follows that a boy and a girl each nursed by a different wife of the same man become milk-siblings of each other'.[10] Since the introduction in Morocco of milk powder and bottlefeeding, the issue of the man's 'ownership of the milk' has become a bone of contention. Women are aware that the prolonged breastfeeding without food supplements ruins their health.

Fadma, a woman from Aghzim, had married a primary-school teacher. She was exceptionally well-educated for a woman of the village, having attended primary school and some years' secondary school. In the last month of pregnancy she had an argument with her husband over breastfeeding. Her mother supported her in her project to bottlefeed. Her husband forbade her, saying that it would make the baby ill. In the end she breastfed her son, becoming thereby the shadow of her former self.

Most husbands consider that the difficulties of pregnancy do not concern them, and many disappear in the later stages or become 'ill' to the extent that they are 'unable to make even a cup of tea' (a woman in her fourth pregnancy), so that they require extra service from the woman. This phenomenon, in some ways resembling the 'couvade', prevents the reversal of sexual roles implicit in the womanservant being served by her husband. Women whose husbands have fields to cultivate are expected to work as far as possible into their pregnancies and are admired for doing so whatever the risks to the mother and baby. The claim of the husband to the wife's body as property thus takes the form of rights to her physical prestations without a corresponding duty to safeguard her physical welfare. Although such a relationship has legal endorsement, it appears ultimately to derive from the woman's lack of independent economic means. The husband's power is less absolute where the woman can call upon her kin for economic resources, but this does not necessarily affect his attitudes.

The wife and resources

Yamna was married to Haddou when she was barely fourteen. He was her second husband and had paid a token bridewealth for her in the form of *henna*, almonds, sugar, part of an animal, and some cloths. They were distant kin, and both came from Aghzim. He was about fifteen years older than his wife, who was thirty-nine in 1970. He had a salaried job, which entailed frequent absences, and several fields, which his wife and children worked when he was not there. Haddou had a married brother in the village, and Yamna, her mother, grandmother, and married sister. Yamna had had thirteen children of which nine had survived. She suffered from severe attacks of asthma and was clearly overworked and exhausted. The last birth had been difficult, but her husband said he was too ill to get her a taxi to go to hospital and had arrived (as a patient) soon after her! The episode I wish to present occurred when Haddou ordered his wife to leave the house because she refused to sleep with him. (Her mother told me that she had asked him to buy her contraceptives, but he refused to do so.) Yamna took refuge with her mother, where her eldest son was already living. Bedda, the mother, said she must receive her but recalled episodes of Yamna's mean behaviour to her kin. 'Once when her son was working, he used to bring home sacks of corn. Do you think she thought, I'll just put aside ten kilos for my mother who has none. No. One day I was planning to go to ask the miller to sell me some grain, Yamna said she had some, measured out 6 kilos and charged me 4 drahem. I had to borrow 1 dirham from my other daughter to pay her. When a third sister's husband was out of work and she pregnant, she asked Yamna if she could dip her finger in the dish of honey. Yamna said, "go and buy it for yourself". My other three daughters are all generous. You should share what you have. Your husband doesn't know what's in the kitchen. If you have a good husband, he won't mind. If you have a bad one, he won't notice that a few kilos of grain have gone. Fadma (daughter in the village) says "everything in my kitchen is my mother's if she wants it".'

The son and resources

Bedda then considered whether Yamna's son could help his mother in her dilemma. He was nearly seventeen and out of work. His father wanted him to stay and cultivate the fields, but he said, 'should I, young as I am, become a *fellah* and stay here for the rest of my life?'. Bedda sympathized with the father's position. 'He can't cultivate the fields; he's working and hasn't time', but she considered that he should hire a labourer to work instead of his wife.

When the son was employed, he gave everything he earned to his father. Bedda said he was a fool to do so. When his mother was forced to leave the house, her son went to the mason who usually lent money to Haddou and asked him to give him 50 drahem on behalf of his father. Bedda was scathing: 'he should have asked for 150 and that would have kept him and his mother here. Now Yamna doesn't even send for a cone of sugar from her own house, but I can scarcely support myself let alone two extra.' (Yamna had also brought her youngest baby with her.)

Bedda discussed with me and her other daughter and son-in-law whether to take Yamna to the *cadi*, or judge. Her daughter was optimistic: 'yes, go, and the *cadi* will make Haddou give Yamna a house and an allowance for her and her children. You'll see, a woman and children aren't easy to beat.' At this remark her own husband took offence, thinking she meant that they weren't easy to shake off. He said, 'a woman thinks she can make a man stay with her by having his children, but it's not so'.

In the end, Yamna went back to her husband, although Bedda was prepared to sell a field in order to send her to have her asthma cured and to tide her over the time which she would need to come to a decision or an agreement with her husband.

The relation of the distribution of resources to infant and maternal mortality

First there is the distribution of resources within the household, which tends to follow the hierarchy of statuses. Thus we have seen that Haddou's son was bound to give his entire income to his father. On the other hand, as a near adult male, he had enough credit to borrow money, which would never have been lent to Yamna. As far as food goes, the structural scarcity in peasant households tends to be passed on to women and children, while the portion of adult males is guaranteed.

Such a practice tends to give rise to an unstated 'code' of consumption, which Moroccans from earliest infancy are taught to observe. Mothers are supposed to sacrifice their own share, rather than requiring a special share of resources for their children. True to this principle, no food supplements are available for pregnant or lactating mothers, although women need approximately 350 extra calories per day during pregnancy and 550 extra during lactation, besides treble the normal intake of calcium and double that of Vitamin A.[11]

The result is that in a national economy in which there appears to be enough food for everyone,[12] 49.58% of children under four and 46% of children under twelve suffer from moderate protein calorie malnutrition. Vitamin deficiencies are the rule, and 20% of children have rickets and anaemia.[13] Ferro-Luzzi, in 1962, remarked that malnutrition was particularly common in Morocco among nursing babies and those just weaned, among school-age children (age five to twelve) and pregnant and nursing women. Most pregnant and nursing mothers suffered from severe anaemia often accompanied by the compulsion to eat earth for minerals. The men were better nourished than the women and children.[14] Several authors have remarked on the relationship between malnutrition and illness in pregnant women and the low weight of babies at birth.[15] In turn low birth weight makes infants more vulnerable to infection.[16] Finally, the milk of undernourished mothers is not apparently of poorer quality than that of well-nourished ones, which suggests that the nutrients are taken from reserves which the mother needs for her own health.[17] Jamal Kram Harfouche comments, 'the way in which the nursing mother compensates for an inferior diet remains to be explored'.[18] Indeed, since lactation is prolonged in many societies, both for lack of other foods to feed the child and as a contraceptive measure, we may concur with the Palestinian woman who said, 'every child throws down a pillar of the mother'.[19]

Vallin, in a study of mortality in Algeria, attributes the higher rate of female mortality (at all ages 0–35) to different nutritional standards and parental care during the first fifteen years of life and then to the risks of pregnancy and child-birth, to which we might add lactation for accuracy's sake.[20]

Hildred Geertz, analysing the interview sheets for the 1960 official census of Sefrou, a Moroccan town to the north of the area which I shall be discussing, makes the following remarks:

there is a higher proportion of women to men up until age thirty-nine, when the ratios reverse, and there are increasingly more men than women as age goes up. The differences among Sefrou's social groups lie mainly in the age point at which this reversal occurs. The rural-born groups show the shift occurring at a much earlier age, and the ratio reaching a much greater imbalance in the ages above forty: the Sefrou-born people make the shift later and do not reach so great an imbalance . . . These changes in sex ratios probably reflect differential health conditions for men and women, with the high loss of life in maternity accounting for most of the differences.[21]

Although rural women, as we have noted above, are less subordinate because they maintain active links with their kin, they are often worse off materially, and it is often sheer poverty and starvation which drives them to leave their husbands, as we have seen in the case of Itto. However, once a woman has borne several children, she is less liable to initiate divorce. This is partly for 'sentimental reasons' in that she stands to lose the children to her husband. However, Yamna's case throws light on another mechanism, material indeed, which aligns a woman ever more closely with her conjugal household. The struggle which a woman must face to feed a growing number of children makes her less inclined to divert household resources to her own female kin. The 'meanness' for which Yamna's female kin reproached her so bitterly had certainly estranged her from them, although they still felt obliged to help her in difficulty, in spite of the lack of reciprocity. From the woman's point of view, it is paradoxical to align herself with her conjugal household, since it is she who carries all the costs of child-bearing and rearing, while the social benefits accrue chiefly to the man. In fact, a woman is enjoined to 'sacrifice' herself to her children. One mother, taking off her clothes to exchange them with the worn, thin ones of her adult daughter who was cold, said to me, 'you see what it is to be a mother; she is my daughter, so I give her everything'. Child mortality is attributed to the greed and neglect of mothers, yet it is more likely to be due, as we have seen, to the neglect of the mother's physiological needs.

Daisy Dwyer, in her discussion of fables from the Taroudant area of Morocco reports the belief that women's greed for food, clothes, and extramarital sexuality is a serious threat to their children whom they neglect in order to follow their selfish desires.

Mothers exhibit their frailty in the tales; they endanger their children by perpetuating ignorance and yielding to temptation. Initially caring, they turn away from even their caretaking chores. Only 7 of the maternal characterizations in the 95 tales collected by this anthropologist involve positive deeds by mothers, while 2 are neutral and 22 are negative. The 22 negative delineations depict betrayal in process, betrayal which is petty in origin and brutal in its result. Mothers do not reject their children in response to inescapable dilemmas in which child neglect becomes one of several unhappy life options. Instead maternal disloyalty is triggered by less laudable drives. In the tales, food, wealth, and sexual satisfaction are the benefits which the mother most often seeks when she turns her back on her child.[22]

In other words she seeks those things which are proper to men and not to women. Perhaps these tales represent an unconscious recognition of woman's material deprivation.

Once it is recognized that the physical costs of child-bearing and rearing are so high for women, it is easy to understand the recent trend towards bottlefeeding. A recent 'War on Want' publication has called this the 'Baby-Killer'. Yet it notes that mothers in Third World countries are giving up breastfeeding in increasing numbers, despite the fact that where sanitation is poor, the mortality rate of bottlefed babies is three times that of those which are breastfed.[23] In such countries the immunity to infection conferred by the first breast-milk is probably an essential factor in infant survival. Given the already high infant mortality rate obtaining in Morocco (186/1000 in the mountain areas) and the benign image enjoyed by the companies which produce dried milk for babies, it is unlikely that mothers who turn to bottlefeeding realize that they are killing off their babies. Rather it is a heaven-sent opportunity to break out of the vicious circle whereby every child 'throws down a pillar of the mother'. They also pass on some of the cost of child-bearing to the father of the child, who must pay for the milk. Unfortunately it is likely that without breastfeeding, which provides some immunity to conception, and with high infant mortality, the birth interval is reduced, putting women back where they started.

Women and children as allies

The birth of male children gives women a stake in their conjugal household. A woman who has borne a son may stay on in her husband's house after his death. Ideally sons and brothers are looked upon as a woman's support in difficulty and old age. In reality, however, in old age, women are cared for by their daughters. They are emotionally most close to their daughters and rely on them to help with domestic tasks, agricultural work, and the care of younger children.[24] Mothers often pine for months when their daughters get married.

Although daughters provide a woman with material help, only sons can improve her bargaining power vis-à-vis her husband and his kin. Thus Yamna's sister told me that she would reprove her husband for wasting resources, now that she had borne him a son. It is in this context that his warning to her about a woman thinking she can keep a man by having his children should be understood. On the other hand a woman who bears boys is often rewarded by her husband and his kin with gifts of gold, jewellery, and money, which may be the only possessions of value she ever acquires and which are seen by others as a sign of her husband's trust and appreciation.

The failure to bear sons may lead to divorce or cause a husband to take another wife. In this society the jealousy of co-wives is legend. The following tale, told to me by a woman, illustrates aptly the dangers of barrenness (and consequently the dangers of fertility, which provokes the envy of childless women) and the joys of the ideal relationship between mother and son.

The bad co-wives and the good son

The young wife of a rich man gave birth to a son. Her three barren co-wives, overcome with jealousy, cut off his finger (penis?) and put it in the young mother's mouth, so that her husband, deceived into thinking that she had bitten it off, fell into a fury and banished her to look after the sheep and live in the shepherd's hut in miserable conditions. Her son grew up regarding one of his father's other wives as mother, but one day he was taunted at school by the other children who told him that the woman who looked after him was not his real mother, whom he set out immediately to find. When he found her in the hut on the mountainside, he refused to eat unless she did too, to sit in comfort unless she did too.

The barren woman's position is an extremely stressful one, and her vain desire for children may cause her to become the butt of ridicule. One of the most cutting satirical songs (*Tamdiast*: Berber) which I heard in Aghzim concerned three named childless women of the hamlet who had decided to cook and eat a cat in secret, since the meat of the cat is supposed to confer fertility. However, since women, according to Muslim rules, are not qualified to kill animals, they had asked a man to come and kill it for them. The cat, moved by some dire premonition, scratched the man and ran away. This song was sung by a man to his family and a couple of visitors, and everyone thought it hugely funny. He asked me not to play the tape recording I made of it in the hamlet where the three women lived. Women try to hide their pregnancies until they are well advanced 'into the fifth month', in case something should go wrong, and they should be 'shamed' by their vain desire for pregnancy. The Moroccan description of sexuality is one in which barrenness, monstrous births, child mortality, and female children are the fault of women, while the creation and genetic constitution of the child and the milk to feed it with are the man's achievement. That Moroccan women understand this to be the metaphor of a power relationship rather than a description of reality is indicated by their private scepticism, for example, over the woman's responsibility for barrenness. It is not difficult to discover which partner to a childless marriage was sterile, since his or her fate can be traced in subsequent ones. Women mentioned to me sotto voce their private opinion that men could be sterile as well as women, even if such a view is not noised abroad.

The attitude of Bedda and Yamna's sisters to her plight also reveals a critical attitude to the power relationship which separates men from responsibility in the field of sexuality and turns women into objects which must function well in the service of male interests in order to be housed and fed. Thus Yamna's kin considered that her husband should buy her contraceptives. However, when she withdrew from her appointed role as 'property', her husband's sanction was to deprive her of sustenance and to separate her from the children. In spite of the fact that her mother, due to a rare combination of circumstances, was able to offer a temporary alternative, Yamna returned to her husband after a week.

In the tale which follows, it is the metaphorical rather than the material aspects of the male–female relationship which are transposed. The terms are merely reversed, permitting a temporary identification of the female narrator and her audience with the powerful term of the metaphor. Scepticism about the appropriateness to female experience of current beliefs about reproduction does not seem to intrude. In poetic and structural terms the relationship between men and women remains the same except that the roles are reversed. The tale has cathartic and compensatory value rather than an alternative analysis of reality.

The magic apple or be-done-by-as-you-did

A married woman who had no children went to see a wise woman about a cure for her barrenness. She was given an apple which she hid in the wall, since she had made the visit without her husband's knowledge, and waited for evening to come so that she could eat it. In the evening, her husband came home hungry and coming across the apple hidden in the wall, he ate it himself.

The man became pregnant in the calf of his leg, and the woman, realizing what had happened, upbraided him for his greed and foolishness and the shame of it.

When the time came for him to give birth, she sent him out alone into the woods, saying that he would give birth to a monster, and she was not having it in the house. In the woods the husband gave birth to a little girl, but then a lion appeared and the father/mother fled, leaving the child to be eaten, as he thought, by the lion. The lion did not eat the baby but looked after her until she had grown into a beautiful girl.

One day the king was riding through the woods, saw her, and decided to marry her. And so it happened. However, the king's first wife and his mother were jealous. Inviting the new bride to come and have her hair combed, they pricked her head with the comb so that she turned into a dove. (A new bride is always symbolically welcomed by the women of her husband's household, who undo her long hair and comb it out.)

Every day the dove would go and perch on a wall that the king was having built, and every day the wall would fall down. Finally the king, who had realized that this was no ordinary dove, had the wall painted with tar, so that the dove was caught, whereupon she turned back into a girl. When she told the king what had happened, he punished the other two women, and everyone lived happily ever after.

This story was told me in Moroccan Arabic by an adolescent girl living in the town Akhdar. She had heard it from her grandmother who lived in the Tafilalet in the south of Morocco.

It is interesting that the reversal of roles refers only to the problem of maternity and reproduction, the focus of female anxiety and helplessness vis-à-vis her husband. In fact the first part of the tale contains the themes of barrenness, the fear of a monstrous birth, and finally the birth of a girl (instead of the desirable son), whom its parent abandons. All these faults are attributed to the husband, whereas it is usually the wife who is held responsible for such eventualities. The wife is powerful and contemptuous, forcing her husband to face his fate alone.

In the second part of the story, the girl acquires power, first by enchanting the king with her beauty, and then because the king confers on her the position of chief woman in the household. Thus two dilemmas for women – the problem of maternity and the problem of rivalry and the envy of other women – are resolved by a man acting in an untypical way. Relief does not derive from her actions but from those of the man on whom she depends. All she can do is wait and perhaps, like the patient dove, will win out in the end. Hardly a message of liberation.

The struggle for power

Women are supposed to become more deceitful and greedy as they grow older and gain in sexual experience, while men are supposed to turn away from the unwise ways of youth to become less dependent on women and more concerned with spiritual development. Here again we are faced with paradoxical expectations. The only woman who has real virtue and understanding is the virgin,[25] yet marriage and child-bearing is the path enjoined on all women.

Perhaps it is to this paradox that Palestinian women referred when they attributed child-bearing to a meanness of character. 'Women's work is so hard that it is almost unbelievable that they should wish to be constantly bearing children . . . When it is said, "if there was a noble woman she would not give birth to children at all", it is of course a paradox. The explanation given of this curious expression is two thirds of pregnancy is jealousy.'[26] That is, women have children, not because they desire the children themselves but out of envy of those who already have them. As in Moroccan culture, women are supposed also to cause the illness and death of other women's children through envy.

What causes this envy? Even without children, a woman who is divorced has the right to alimony for a short period (generally three months), and the repayment of her *sdaq*, or bridewealth. If she is widowed, she may inherit an eighth of her husband's property. However, this property is likely to be inaccessible to some degree unless she remains in his village, and, as we have remarked above, the condition for remaining in her husband's house after his death is that she has borne him a son. Thus she becomes a kinswoman to his heirs, his sons and daughters, from whom she can even inherit if they die before her. But, most important, it is these relatives who are considered to have a duty to safeguard her rights and well-being.

Aqshou Said had been married in another hamlet before coming with her son Lhou to marry a man in Aghzim. She had two girls and a boy by her second husband. Both her sons live in Rabat, and her daughters have married, one in the nearby town Akhdar, the other in a village about 30 kilometres away. When their father died, Aqshou's children decided not to split up the inheritance but to leave the usufruct of the fields to their mother until her death. They hired a sharecropper to work the fields and give their mother her share.

Women are often in close and affectionate relations with their brothers and sons. A woman's minimal guarantee of security lies in her bearing sons, but also in her mother having done so and thus providing her with a brother. Even though sons are generally more neglectful than daughters, women continually think about them and remind others of their existence. An old Berber woman I knew would sing laments for her son who never came to see her nor sent news. It seems to me that this is because women's material rights rest on their having borne sons and being, at least nominally, under their protection. It is rare that daughters are lost to sight in this way. This is partly because the mother herself feels freer to visit her daughter than her daughter-in-law and has more pretexts for doing so. A mother, for example, is expected to help her daughter in the last weeks of her confinement and to be present at the birth.[27] The help which mothers, sisters, and daughters give each other, particularly evident in the case of Bedda, cited above, is not to be underestimated, but as Bedda herself noted, it is often of a clandestine nature and depends on deceiving a gullible husband or obtaining the goodwill of an alert one.

It could be said that women look on husbands and fathers as potential enemies and on sons and brothers as potential allies in the struggle they engage in to mitigate the power of the former over the conditions of their existence. A virgin, who does not have to carve herself a sphere of influence by deceit or manipulation or bearing children, appears more honest than a married woman who is engaged in a clandestine struggle to mitigate the power of her husband and his female kin. A married woman must incur her husband's favour, entering into competition with any other woman dependants in the household, whether these are his other wives or his mother and sisters. Since it is a woman's beauty and the bearing of male children which will ingratiate her with him, these are the elements which are considered most vulnerable to the attacks of the other women's 'evil eye'. Both women and children are always protected with prophylactic amulets. Male children are heavily disguised at birth by a sort of mask of *kohl* round the eyes, lipstick, and girl's clothes. This is to deceive the *jnun* or spirits but also envious eyes. In this case, envy does not come only from the women of the household whose privileged relation with its head is threatened by the new birth, but also from visiting women who are low in the social hierarchy because they have not yet borne sons.

Marriage is seen by a woman as the moment when she must confront the hostile female members of the husband's family, who will place obstacles in her path to domestic and social esteem and influence.[28] Yet a wife rarely has to live with such women. Only about 3% of Moroccan men are polygamous, so that the prospect of having a co-wife is more often feared than experienced. Again few women live with their mother-in-law, again about 3% of both my town and hamlet samples and 30% of Belghiti's rural Taroudant sample. Belghiti's sample does not present a uniformly negative view of the relationship, and some women are glad to have another one to share a considerable burden of fieldwork. Some women think the mother-in-law no longer has the power she formerly had. 'Le temps des belle-mères est passée'.[29] Yet, a wife in Akhdar who caused her husband to expel his mother from the household was said to have bewitched him, as was another whose husband when ill did not recognize his sisters. Where the mother and sisters lose the influence they expect to have, they try to show that the wife harms the husband. The problem does not lie so much in the discomforts of cohabitation with female in-laws, as in the potential influence of the latter in the issue of divorce. The sword that hangs over every woman's head is that of divorce, and only the birth of male children can be pointed to as an objective merit by which she acquires rights to the protection of the agnatic kin-group.

Many women said that they preferred daughters because they remain lifelong companions and help-mates. It is the link between uterine siblings (*ulid mma*) which is considered to be closer and more 'protective' than any agnatic relationship. This is only one of the many paradoxes which cause women to regard the dominant characterization of 'good' maternity with ambivalence. Another is the injunction to sacrifice themselves for their children but to react to their death with equanimity. They are not supposed to reveal a desire for maternity, although barrenness is considered a grave failing. A final paradox is the knowledge that in giving life to children women shorten their own. These paradoxes lie behind the rituals I discuss below, which I regard as 'rituals of ambivalence' in a particularly emphatic sense. They are never talked about or officially recognized, unlike the major rites in whose shadow they are performed. Like Audrey Richards I suggest that symbolism itself is ambivalent.

Single explanations of ritual behaviour, however satisfying to the observer, seem to me to deny the nature of symbolism itself and its use in society to express the accepted and approved as well as the hidden and denied, the rules of society and the occasional revolt against them, the common interests of the community and the conflicting interests of parts of it.[30]

Three rituals

The three rituals I will discuss were all enacted by and among women only. For men to catch a glimpse of the goings-on was considered 'shameful'. I present these rites together, not because they are similar but because, in so doing, it is possible to throw into relief the characteristic elements of each and so gain a more rounded picture of women's complex and contradictory attitudes to the material, ideological, and metaphorical relations between the sexes.

The rites consist of a women's *hedra* or spirit possession ritual, a grotesque dance (*tadmaght*: Berber) performed during the feasting at the birth or circumcision of a son, and lastly an 'improvised' ritual which took place when a woman's new-born son died.

I am conscious of having only a glimmer of understanding of these rituals, having witnessed the women's *hedra* only once, the *tadmaght* twice, and been present at the death of a child only once. Further, the readiness with which people would offer interpretations or comments on other rituals such as the Aissaouia *hedra* or marriage or circumcision ritual was in contrast with their monosyllabic, embarrassed, and even disapproving reaction to questions posed about the rituals I discuss below.

In the rituals under discussion, it seems to me that there is a complex collaboration between the person who is the focus of the rite and the spectators/participants. Not only do the latter provide a controlling cultural context in which roles can be transgressed under the stimulus of intense emotion, but they are also the ones who experience the catharsis, in some cases (as in *tadmaght*) while the main actor is merely the focus of the projected emotions of the onlookers.[31] The spectators both identify with the chief actor and control her, but these functions are assumed by different categories of women. In general the older women dominate the proceedings, and the younger, unmarried ones are mere spectators, serving tea and providing the music. It is those in the middle range, most tried by the drama of marriage and maternity, who tend to find the impulses portrayed most 'acceptable' or are at least most affected by the life-experiences to which they relate. Rather than finding the impulses expressed 'socially unacceptable', Berber women seemed to think that they were unacceptable to *men*, from whom they should be hidden. However, on the periphery of all women's rituals are to be found adolescent boys, who usually stand in a group outside the door. They are occasionally chased away, but in general they are tolerated as 'sons', as males who are not yet in an antagonistic or proprietary relationship to women and who hover between the world of women and that of men, curious as adult men would never allow themselves to be.

Women's hedra

Crapanzano, in his description of the Hamadsha brotherhood, points out that new adepts frequently join the cult as a result of mental or physical illness thought to be caused by saints or spirits. They require the patient to follow certain rules in order to be cured.

This interpretation permits during the curing ceremonies the symbolic expression of incapacitating conflicts and the consequent discharge of tensions which may impede social behaviour. This discharge of tensions is not merely an emotional outburst, which may be of little therapeutic import, but a highly structured process which involves the symbolic resolution of such tension producing conflicts.[32]

The main conflict, suggests Crapanzano, concerns sexual identity, whose boundaries are subject to stresses inherent in Moroccan society. He considers mainly men, but his hypothesis is a helpful one for women too. In the area where I worked the main brotherhood is that of the Aissaouia. On the feast of Aid-l Kbir, which marks the end of Ramadan, there is a great assembly of the Aissaouia at the local patron saint's tomb. There do not seem to be female 'brothers', although women are often moved to dance *hedra* in the arena alongside the men.[33]

On the night before the public Aissaouia ritual, the women of the village of Aghzim gathered in a disused mosque, usually inhabited by a story-telling beggar/holy man. Around the entrance some adolescent boys were joking round a fire. Inside the mosque, when I arrived, were seated about twenty women, some very old but most around thirty-five, distributed round three walls. On the fourth were seated about twenty unmarried girls, whom the others addressed as *tishiratin* (Berber: 'little girls'). (A place was made for me among them!) They were much less earnest than the older women who rebuked them for playing about.

Near the door presided a woman – whom we will call Zohar – about thirty, with a baby slung from her back. Every now and then, she got up to chase away the boys from the entrance. They scattered, terrified, shouting, 'Witches!' Next to Zohar, was an older woman in charge of the tea-pot and tray of glasses which the *tishiratin* handed round. They also beat out the rhythm of the repetitive *hedra* songs on a skin tambourine (*tara*: Berber). The other women clapped and sang the verses of praise to Allah and his Prophet, over and over, occasionally changing words and melody. Some beat time with a bucket handle. The noise was deafening and after a few hours disorienting.

A *hartaniya*, about thirty-five, was dancing, shaking her head from side to side and throwing her arms out and back across her chest. Zohar handed her burning twists of paper which she would hold under her chin or put in her mouth, showing the indifference to pain typical of the possessed person. Finally she collapsed with her head in the lap of one of the other women. Then Zohar got up to dance, handing her baby to her neighbour, until she too collapsed and was covered with a white cloth, so that she should not be attacked by spirits while she was in an absent and vulnerable state. Both these women were strong independent characters. The second was known to rule her husband, to cook what she pleased rather than what he asked for, and was feared because she was well-informed and a gossip.

The next dancer was an adolescent with deformed feet and other defects. She seemed in danger of hurting herself, and two women got up to hold her hands, but she went on jerking. When she recovered, she laughed and returned to her place where she had been beating *tara* with the girls. Finally Bedda (mentioned p. 109 and p. 113) danced. She was a widow of nearly sixty, but she danced so long that the other women began to get worried and to hold her, telling the singers to stop their chant. But as soon as the music began again Bedda began to dance. Finally, the women appealed to her youngest daughter, Itto, a divorcee, to sing the song which would 'cool' her mother but she refused to intervene. Itto then went to fetch another older sister, who had stayed at home because she disliked the *hedra*. This daughter, another divorcee, at first merely watched her mother, then took a corner of her mother's cardigan and guided her away from people's feet when she looked as though she might trip up. At one point the daughter herself began to clap and when her mother finally collapsed, she covered her with a white head-veil and left her. The widow, when she came to, went back to her place and started chatting with her neighbour as if nothing had happened.

In the terms of Ioan Lewis, the form of spirit possession we have described is 'peripheral' in that both the practitioners and the spirits are 'peripheral' to the official, social, and moral order in which men and Islam are dominant. Possibly the women who dance are moved by 'deprivation, frustration, and dissatisfaction', and for them possession is a way to 'get attention' and goods first within the domestic sphere ('primary possession') and then in the assembly of women ('secondary possession').[34]

However, the situation seems more complicated. Certainly I do not know the history of possession of the dancers, but their current situation does not strictly correspond to that described by Lewis. First of all, Lewis implies that 'primary possession' derives from the conjugal situation, and it is this which is given value in the assembly where 'secondary possession' takes place. However, none of the four women fulfil fully the female roles defined by the dominant value system. The *hartaniya* is not sought in marriage except by her own kind, and however beautiful she is will always socially be defined 'ugly' and a bad marriage bargain. The deformed adolescent may not marry, this in a society in which all women by definition marry. The widow had borne five girls and a son who never helped her and lived far away, and as we have seen was forced to take upon herself all the responsibilities of the family head, thus usurping male roles. Zohar was criticized for her activity, dominance, and concern with other people's affairs.

Their independence from male determination of their day-to-day lives, their negative value as property, is both ransomed as a fault and presented to the other women as a reason to command their respect. Not by chance do the women attribute possession to the agency of angels, central and positive elements of the religious cosmos, while men say the women are possessed by *jnun*, ambiguous and peripheral spirits. Moreover, the women do not seem to derive either new roles (e.g. of curer) or material benefits from possession.[35] They do aquire a more authoritative voice in informal situations. But this is merely a confirmation of a role they already assume for reasons of personality or because of a practice of 'self-possession' or non-conformity. It is perhaps this non-conformity, claimed as a value, which is evoked whenever *hedra* songs or movements are hinted at or deliberately evoked in other rituals.

However, there is nothing antagonistic to men in these performances. Rather the possessed women offer to the others evidence of a higher passivity. Perhaps they are not property of men, but they obey the higher authority, to whom they belong, just as ordinary women obey their husbands. Thus, at the sensual pole, the possessed women lay claim to their own persons, but at the ideological pole they are said to be 'possessed' by a supernatural agent.

Circumcision and tadmaght

I will describe in some detail the circumcision of three male babies, all under three years old, the sons of two daughters and a daughter-in-law of a Berber-speaking, fairly wealthy *hartani* of Bentaleb hamlet. The daughters lived elsewhere but had returned to their father's house to circumcise the children, a circumstance which gave the ritual a particularly female-dominated tone. (Generally circumcisions take place from the father's house.)

The circumcision proper occurred only on the third day of the festivities and was carried out by a male expert in the presence of men only. Officially the women gathered on the evening of the second day to carry out rituals preparatory to the circumcision, but this was also the occasion for specifically women's rituals which appeared to have a satirical, cathartic, or compensatory significance for the women themselves and did not apparently contribute to the *rite de passage*. In fact the whole evening was broken by explosions of *hedra* and other apparently anomalous evocations.

There were about 150 guests, all of them from the host's hamlet and many of them *hartaniyin*. Compared with those at a marriage ritual I had recently attended, the number of old women was striking. They took a prominent role and were again more serious and attentive than the unmarried girls.

After a certain amount of tea-drinking, chatting, and singing, some *hartani* women began to sing *hedra* songs, at which another woman expressed her disapproval and appealed to a *sherifa* (descendant of the Prophet and so endowed with ritual authority) to forbid them. However the *sherifa* said nothing. The *hartaniyin* began to urge an old woman, respected in the village but apparently well known for her talents as a clown, to get up and dance *tadmaght*. She refused for a while but was finally persuaded to heave all her seventy years and several hundredweight to her feet. First she mimed a vain woman with a mirror in her hand making up. As she became more engrossed in her dance, she occasionally called out a line of a new *hedra* song, which provided the cue for the singing, *tara*-beating, and clapping guests to change melody. Then she gathered her skirt between her legs for trousers and waving her arm in front of her for an enormous penis, began to mime male sexual attitudes in a grotesque manner. At this point the pious verses of the *hedra* had given way to 'Ijik, ijik, ijik' (he/it is coming to you) chanted by the dancer and some of the onlookers, while old and young alike, screamed with laughter, the tears running down their cheeks, begging the old lady to turn her back to them.

Later in the evening, the professional musicians arrived (paid by the household head). They stood discreetly on the threshold with their backs to the women, who had veiled themselves at their arrival. The adolescent boys were as usual gathered around the threshold too. The women got up in ones and twos to dance to the oboes of the musicians, but their style was no longer that of the *hedra* or *tadmaght* but controlled and seductive with a clear sexual reference. One adolescent danced with a divorcee who 'went with men', and who had arrived halfway through the evening mildly drunk, as everyone remarked. The singing and dancing went on until after midnight when plates of stew were brought in. The kinswomen of the boys had spent most of the evening in another room, preparing the meals and the *henna*. *Henna* is a red dye which is generally applied by women to women for decorative and protective purposes, to express hospitality and confer blessing and increase, and to restore health. However, the bridegroom as well as the bride may have his hands painted with *henna* during the marriage rites as do male babies when they are circumcised. On other occasions, I have heard women say that it is dangerous to paint more than one foot of a male child (except at circumcision), and girls do not generally wear *henna* before puberty. It is as if the dangers of the contact between male and female spheres, which occurs both during the marriage rites and when the child leaves the female world to join the male community, must be neutralized by this sign of female concern and blessing. There is no *henna* at the *hedra* for example.

In fact the rest of the ritual has numerous symbolic references to the marriage ritual. The high point of the evening, was 'the *hennaing*' of the children, said by all to be 'the most beautiful' part of the ritual. The two mothers and the grandmother entered in procession, each carrying a boy on her back wrapped in a white cloth, again to protect him from evil spirits in this 'liminal' moment. They were followed by six kinswomen singing the same chant as is sung when the bride is '*hennaed*'. One of the women brought in a silver tray with the spinach-like *henna* paste and a smoking incense-burner. She sat down opposite the women who had carried in the boys, who were dressed in *djellabas* of soft white cotton with the hoods up. The grandmother *hennaed* the boy's hands and feet, and their mothers got up to dance joyfully with the other women of the house. Finally there was a chorus of praise to God and the King, a woman went round the room sprinkling the guests with rose-water, and the music and dancing began again.

The next day the boys were circumcised in the early afternoon, and at four the women gathered to 'take them to the river'. The boys were hoisted on to the backs of three old women, one of whom was the grandmother. Each old woman carried a young bamboo staff (*aghnim*), to which were attached two women's headscarves and a Berber silver bracelet. One staff had a berber shoulder brooch (*msask*) – a typically female object. A fourth old woman carried a bamboo to which was attached the Moroccan flag. (Carrying flags is also a feature of Berber wedding processions in the south but is no longer practised in Akhdar.) The babies were enveloped completely in large white blankets. They were said to be 'ill'. It is a 'dangerous situation for them'.

Many young women both from Bentaleb and from Aghzim joined the procession (none of the previous day's guests had been from hamlets other than Bentaleb), which proceeded to the stream, musicians playing, women dancing, old women thumping their sticks up and down. The old women went to dip their staffs in the stream saying, 'we have cut it that it may not get wet'. This is supposed to 'cool' the wound. Sometimes the boy's leg is dipped in the water. Then the procession returned, making a long tour of the hamlet, singing at first a ritual song, which one woman translated as 'Let us go up to the house. We have taken them to the river that we may enter peacefully and eat.' Then *hedra* songs were sung. At home the boys are given eggs 'to make them stop crying'. Many reasons for this were given by different people. Townspeople tended to 'rational' explanations such as that eggs were a rarity, so that it was a treat for the boys. Some Berber women tended to phallic explanations, saying that the egg resembled the circumcised penis. (Other women said this wasn't true.) The same women considered that the circumcision was intended to enable men to have erections, while the townspeople said it was to admit the boys into the Muslim community. (Circumcision is not, however, a doctrinally necessary Muslim practice.) It seems legitimate to regard the *aghnim* as a phallic symbol, since it actually substitutes for the penis when it is dipped into the water, and its association with female symbols suggests both the separation of the boy from his mother and his future union with his bride.

I will not dwell on the circumcision rite, except to point out the analogy with the marriage rites. What is done for the boy here is done for the bride there. The elements of eating, dancing, perfuming, and flag-bearing are all common to both and dense with sexual reference. Similarly the shedding of blood (deflowering of the bride, circumcision of the boy) is in each case followed by a visit to the river to 'cool' the central actor, and link him/her with the source of natural fertility. Finally the application of *henna* protects the passage from one status to another, and it is a typically female protection. Both bride and child are enveloped in a veil/blanket to protect them from evil spirits. Finally, the 'rebirth' of both actors to a new status is attended by the mother, who plays a conspicuous role and dances more than other women.[36]

All these elements are absent from the *hedra*, in which there are no external symbols which can safeguard the actor, since she is in the hands of the supernatural. In ethnocentric terms, we might say that in the *hedra* there is a recognition of the 'subjectivity' of the actor, so that it is only if the other women sing a melody to which she has a particular relation that she is 'made hot' and 'made cool'. In the wedding and circumcision, bride and boy are made 'hot' by the *henna* and made 'cool' by the water, and their own sentiments are not relevant. It is possible that *hedra* appears wherever female 'subjectivity' appears, providing a cover of 'irresponsibility' and spiritual distance to the expression, however non-explicit, of illegitimate sentiment.[37]

But how is it that the *hedra*, with its total lack of reference to maternity or fertility, with its ambiguous sexual connotation, comes to penetrate a ritual such as that of circumcision, intended to create sexual and reproductive order? What does the *tadmaght* refer to and effect in the onlookers, beside themselves with laughter? Take first the dancer. She is an old woman, beyond the age of child-bearing and to some extent sexually neutral. She is also a *hartaniya*, therefore of low status. She takes upon herself the representation of a part, which is more dangerous for other women than for her, allowing them to distance themselves from the 'responsibility' it involves. She mimes first a woman whom the participants both identify with and find absurd, and then a man, permitting them to identify with male sexual aggressivity. The producers of male children (who are degraded by the circumcision festivities in which they celebrate the opposite sex and are again reminded of their own insignificance) participate in the power represented by the male sexual role and are temporarily released from the position of objects. This is also why they express 'shame', begging the dancer to turn the other way and fearful lest some man should see. 'Shame' (*hashuma*) always attends behaviour which involves the transgression of social roles and particularly that which partakes of the sexual identity of men. The ambiguity of *hedra* is absent because here the nature of male and female roles is precisely indicated by the dancer, although they are made momentarily equally available to the participants.

A ritual of grief

I would like now to consider the way in which the configuration of actors and symbols brought to bear when a mother loses her child helps us to understand more about *hedra* and *tadmaght* and about the way in which women experience sexual roles.

It could be said that the death of a child, especially a son, represents the apex of alienation for a woman, since she is urged to act as if nothing had happened, after having been conditioned to sacrifice her own needs and resources for her child.

It seems to me that the following account of the reaction of a lonely young woman to the death of her only son shows how women are policed into expressing and therefore ritualizing some sentiments and repressing others. It is possible that the scene I witnessed was dense with conflict because of the 'indiscipline' of the woman, a novice in masochistic motherhood.

Zineb was a twenty-two-year-old woman from a northern city. The daughter of a widowed mother, she had married a technician from her own city in government employment and had come with him to Aghzim. Like all city women of her class, she was strictly secluded by her husband, and, as she was also Arabic-speaking, she was extremely lonely in the Berber hamlet where she had come to live. She was also ostracized to some extent because she quarrelled frequently and audibly with her husband. At home, she had helped her mother and sister to weave carpets, and her family was well off because both sons were employed in stable occupations. In Aghzim, Zineb's only occupation was the upkeep of the small house, and although her husband was well-paid he was also heavily in debt and tended to economize on the invisibles, such as the comfort of his wife. Zineb spent the long and bitter winter when she was pregnant without heating. Her family did not intervene in this situation until it was time for her confinement, when her sister came to stay. Zineb's husband quarrelled with her and her sister before the birth and left home, in classical fashion, returning only when the baby was already two weeks old. The two secluded women were helped throughout this period by a Berber woman from the hamlet, who exercised her tongue on the stupidity of townspeople.

Zineb was overjoyed when her son was born, but he was undersize, did not develop a sucking reflex, and after she had fed him on diluted powdered milk for a few weeks, he developed gastroenteritis and died. She was overcome with grief and began a wild desolate chant which could be heard all over the two hamlets, occasionally breaking into an abandoned dance, very similar to *hedra*. 'My son, my son, what shall I do in a house without you.' Her husband brought her into my house, while he went to look for someone who would bury the child, and she immediately stopped wailing and dancing and spoke to me gently. Clearly the anthropologist did not provide the controlling influence which would channel her grief into 'socially acceptable' channels. We went back to her house, where some Berber women had gathered in the courtyard. They crouched silently at first, watching her dance and chant, occasionally getting up to dip her hands in a bowl of water 'to cool her' and to smooth her hair. An adolescent boy stood guard to keep away curious children, and another brought her a mug of water, clearly a ritual gesture since there was plenty of water in the house. Everyone kept offering it to her. Newcomers suggested water as soon as they arrived.

The women were for the most part strangers to Zineb, and they would occasionally stop speaking Arabic to her in order to make comments in Berber which she couldn't understand. Among these women were several of high prestige, wives of rich men in the village, many of them past child-bearing. The others were married women with children, and one was a woman who had had one baby and lost it. The others called Zineb's attention to this fact.

One of the women's main preoccupations (as in the *hedra*) was that Zineb should not hurt herself physically. But after a couple of hours, they began to get impatient. Asking scornfully whether she were crazy, they held her arms to stop her from beating her chest and threw water in her face to stop her from crying. Her husband, too, was gentle to begin with, then began to shout at her and moralize in a way the women endorsed and evidently approved. When he had left the house again in his vain search for someone who would bury the baby, the women began to reproach Zineb bitterly.

'Are you the mother of all the babies that die in the medina, that you cry like that. For shame. You are still young, you will have more. This one was Satan come to plague you. You should be glad he's gone.' In this way they interpret her grief almost in terms of a possession by an evil, supernatural agent. At other times they said, 'Allah took him away just as he brought him. What can you do about it? If he'd been walking or talking there'd be more to cry about. You'd think it was your father who had died.' (The death of a father, the household head, was cited as the ultimate catastrophe, although as we have seen women do not have a particularly close relationship with their fathers.)

They prevented Zineb from seeing her baby before it was finally taken away by her husband and another man for burial. In the early evening, Berber women helped her to prepare a huge *sadaga* or feast of propitiation and almsgiving, to which all the poor women and children of the community were invited to come and eat their fill. Two *fuqaha* (Muslim scholars) came to chant the Koran for two hours in another room of the house, taking tea-breaks at intervals.

Zineb, sat apart from the other women, who forbade her to serve them. The serving was therefore done by a *hartaniya* friend of Zineb's. She occasionally talked about the baby's illness and what had happened at the hospital. The women discussed births in the hamlet and spoke in admiration of a woman whose baby had died and 'she just buried it, without shedding a tear'. When Zineb began to cry again, an old woman told her that she shouldn't cry, she must learn to bear it, everyone must die; and the others spoke harshly saying, 'for shame, the men can hear you'. They offered to take her to sleep in their houses, saying they would leave her only if she promised not to cry.[38]

We have described above women's reactions to what they considered to be an emergency situation. To call them 'ritual' is to stretch a definition if we adopt that of Victor Turner: 'By ritual I mean prescribed formal behaviour for occasions not given over to technological routine, having reference to beliefs in mystical beings. The symbol is the smallest unit of ritual which still retains the properties of ritual behaviour.' He also says, 'I found that I could not analyse ritual symbols without studying them in a time series in relation to other "events", for symbols are essentially involved in social process. . . . From this standpoint the ritual symbol becomes a factor in social action, a positive force in an activity field.'[39] In this sense, it would seem that what we have described above is part of 'social process' by which women bring the mother's 'illegitimate sentiments' (a woman's own desire for a child, rather than that of her husband, at its most subjective and most paradoxical) within the strait-jacket of customary ritual. This ritual is comprised of the religious offices of the *fuqaha*, the summary burial of the child, indicating his unimportance as a social being, and the offering of *sadaqa*.

All of these rites require formal behaviour which distances the mother from her child and reminds her of her duties to the community. Among these is her duty to reserve grief, like the meat in the stew, for the adult males whose property she is. Her attachment to the baby, an insignificant being without social rights, must be interpreted as the work of an evil power. This is an explicit formulation of the boundaries of the female role. The women minimize the death of children and present in positive terms Zineb's future as a mother. They have achieved their high status within the female hierarchy by their conformity to these dictates. However, they use their authority to provide a context of support and control, including an interpretation of reality designed to neutralize Zineb's pain.

Conclusions

Pamela Constantinides considers possession in sex-segregated Sudanese society to be associated with 'same sex support, conflict and competition, and the de-emphasis of cross-sex hostility'.[40] This observation is extremely pertinent to the symbolic exchanges among Moroccan women, in which the absence of hostility to men in ritual contexts contrasts strangely with the conflict and hostility which characterize many individual women's attitudes to men within marriage.

To a certain extent, women are ranked among themselves as they are ranked by men, according to the degree of subordination they exhibit, their value as sexual objects, and as sources of sons and labour-power. However, among women, women may acquire authority for qualities which men value negatively, such as age, intelligence, personality, loyalty to uterine kin, and 'emancipation' from male dictates. Their alienation is not perfect.

In these rituals, women provide a certain space for the expression of sentiments which are not compatible with adherence to the first set of (male-dominated) values. That is, they are a response to an oppressive social role. There is no attempt to trace the material causes of these sentiments; rather, a symbolic version of reality is proffered in which the sentiments themselves are shown to be absurd, inappropriate, or caused by the intervention of a supernatural agent.

Among women, these sentiments are redirected or repressed in such a way as to restore to their owner her self-esteem and to assure her of the esteem of other women. Women show one another how to react to intolerable subjective dilemmas without damaging themselves or expressing antagonism to the men whose control of resources lies at the root of their ills. I am not qualified to say what Moroccan women's sentiments really are. Whatever they may be, the three situations described suggest that they should not be expressed in the presence of men and that there is no unambiguous language for them. 'Illegitimate sentiments' are dealt with in different ways: in the *hedra*, by physical and mental seizure; in the *tadmaght*, through their enactment and *reductio ad absurdum* by an appointed proxy. The most explicit and conscious mother's sentiment is dealt with by the anger of authority and the assurance of support only if the sentiment is repressed, that is, by blackmail.

In all these situations new links of interdependence are created among the participants, because of the experiences of catharsis, projection, identification, support, and deference, which characterize their interaction. By these means, women become the agency by which their own sentiments, or those of recalcitrant sisters, are periodically purged, and the material interest of which such sentiments are a symptom is removed from consciousness.

NOTES

This chapter owes much to years of discussions with my Italian friends and colleagues of the research group of childbirth and maternity, which in 1981 published the volume, 'Parto e maternità: momenti della biografia femminite', *Quaderni storici* 44 (1981). I also derived considerable stimuli from the meetings of historians and anthropologists organized by the Max-Planck-Institut für Geschichte and the Maison des Sciences de l'Homme. In particular I would like to thank Louisa Accati and David Sabean for their invaluable comments and suggestions.

1 According to Villeneuve, 48% of Moroccan households sow less than 2 hectares per household, and a further 24.3% sow between 2 and 8 hectares, M. Villeneuve, *La Situation de l'agriculture et son avenir dans l'économie marocaine* (Paris, 1971), 70.

2 Ministère du Plan, Division Statistique, *Resultats de l'enquête à objectifs multiples (1961–1963)* (Rabat, 1964), 102.

3 See V. Maher, *Women and Property in Morocco: Their Changing Relation to the Process of Social Stratification in the Middle Atlas* (Cambridge, 1974), 163–90.

4 See the definition of 'property' in the *Oxford English Dictionary*. However, there is a sense in which the woman is not outright property, but rights in her are held as in the English 'leasehold'. Her husband has rights of usufruct for the length of the lease, whereupon they revert to her father or agnatic kinsmen. That is, until her marriage she is her father's or agnatic kinsmen's property (hence the right of her father's brother's son either to marry her or cede his right in favour of someone else). They exploit her labour and provide for her subsistence. On her marriage her husband assumes these rights and duties, but if he does not pay bridewealth, her kinsmen retain them in part. The bridewealth corresponds to a payment on the lease. Since the woman receives this payment in lieu of her father, she renounces in due proportion her rights in inheritance and to their product. If her husband interrupts the marriage contract, he must restore to the wife any payment outstanding on the 'lease'.

If he does not interrupt the contract she is his until she expires! I am grateful to M. Ambrosoli for this suggestion.

5 Maher, *Women and Property*, 191–221.

6 F. Mernissi, *Beyond the Veil: Male–Female Dynamics in a Modern Muslim Society* (Cambridge, Mass., 1975), 60.

7 V. Crapanzano, *The Hamadsha: A Study in Moroccan Ethnopsychiatry* (Berkeley, 1973), 48 n9. See also H. Granqvist, *Birth and Childhood among the Arabs (Palestine)* (Helsingfors, 1947), 48–9: 'Nobody scolds if it is the husband to cause miscarriage because he is dealing with his own'.

8 S. Altorki, 'Milk-Kinship in Arab Society: An Unexplored Problem in the Ethnography of Marriage', *Ethnology*, 14 (1980), 233–44, here 233.

9 *Ibid.*, 243, n3.

10 *Ibid.*, 234. On 'owning the milk' and wet-nursing, there are interesting parallels in C. Klapisch, 'Genitori naturali e genitori di latte nella Firenze del Quattrocento', *Quaderni storici*, 44 (1980), 543–63.

11 M. Cameron and Y. Hofvander, *Manual on Feeding Infants and Young Children*, Protein-Calorie Advisory Group of the UN (New York, 1976), 21.

12 J. Laure, M. B. Essatara, and M. T. Jaouadi, *Besoins et apports en nutriments au Maroc*, Institut Agronomique et Veterinaire Hassan II (cyclostyle report) (Rabat, 1977), 3.

13 *Ibid.*, 25–6.

14 G. Ferro-Luzzi, *La situazione alimentare e nutrizionale nel Marocco* (Rome, 1962), 13–17.

15 A. Lechtig, P. Rosso, *et al.*, 'The Effect of Moderate Maternal Malnutrition on the Levels of Alkaline Ribo-Nuclease Activity in the Human Placenta', *Ecology of Food and Nutrition*, 6 (1977), 84–90.

16 I. Rosenberg, N. W. Solomon, and D. M. Levin, 'The Interaction of Infection and Nutrition: Some Practical Concerns', *Ecology of Food and Nutrition*, 4 (1976), 203–6, here 205. See also A. Lechtig, *et al.*, 'The Effect of Morbidity During Pregnancy of Birth-Weight in a Rural Guatemalan Population', *Ecology of Food and Nutrition*, 5 (1976), 225–33.

17 A. Chavez, C. Martinez, and H. Bourges, 'The Role of Lactation in the Nutrition of Low Socio-Economic Groups', *Ecology of Food and Nutrition*, 4 (1975), 159–69.

18 J. K. Harfouche, *Infant Health in Lebanon: Customs and Taboos* (Beirut, 1965), 47–8.

19 H. Granqvist, *Child Problems among the Arabs* (Helsingfors, 1950), 62.

20 J. Vallin, 'La Mortalité en Algérie', *Population*, 30 (1975), 1023–46.

21 C. Geertz, H. Geertz, and L. Rosen, *Meaning and Order in Moroccan Society* (Cambridge, 1979), 401–2.

22 D. Dwyer, *Images and Self-Images: Male and Female in Morocco* (New York, 1978), 117.

23 M. Muller, *The Baby-Killer: A War on Want Investigation into the Promotion and Sale of Powdered Milk in the Third World* (London, 1975), 3. See also S. A. Taha, *Ecology of Food and Nutrition*, 7 (1979), 193–201, here 199: 'The advent of a new pregnancy used to be the commonest cause for stopping breast-feeding; but now more and more children are deliberately weaned at a younger age. Several reasons have been given to explain this trend (*Who Chronicle* 1972), mainly industrialisation with increasing employment of mothers. This does not apply to the Gezira rural community where no mother goes out to work. The natural security of the breast has been now seriously threatened by the introduction of bottle-feeding with highly dilute and invariably contaminated fluids, often milk formulae.'

24 See Maher, *Women and Property*, 121–32; and Dwyer, *Images*, 82–5.

25 Dwyer, *Images*, 65–73.

26 Granqvist, *Child Problems*, 79. For an interesting presentation of psychoanalytical

and sociological speculations on the 'desire for maternity', see L. Baruffi (ed.), *Desiderio di maternità* (Turin, 1980).

27 Cf. the behaviour of Indian Rajput mothers towards their sons and daughters. 'Though desiring sons for their own prestige and that of their husband's family, they do report a preference for daughters in terms of their own emotional reaction. There is some evidence that the women see this preference as a male-imposed value. Women commented that they wished for sons when pregnant because their husbands said they should. It seems probable that a culturally sanctioned preference for boys requires of women a kind of self-degradation which they resent. Many of the stories told by women concern the unfair treatment of a faithful wife by a misguided or inconsiderate husband. Since a good wife is never hostile to her husband, these resentments cannot be expressed directly to the men. It may be that they are expressed in the coldness with which these women treat their sons.' (This includes 'frequent and intense' physical punishment meted out to boys rather than girls.) L. Minturn and W. W. Lambert, *Mothers of Six Cultures* (New York, 1964), 232–5.

28 Cf. F. Zanolla, 'Suocere, nuore e cognate nel primo '900 a P. nel friuli', *Quaderni storici*, 44 (1980), 429–50.

29 Malika Belghiti, 'La condition des femmes dans trois villages du Tessaout', in A. Khatibi (ed.), *Essais de sociologie sur le Maroc* (Rabat, 1971), 333.

30 A. I. Richards, *Cisungu: A Girls' Nubility Rite* (1956), 169.

31 G. Obeyesekere, 'Psycho-Cultural Exegesis of a Case of Spirit Possession in Sri Lanka', in Crapanzano and Garrison (eds.), *Studies in Spirit Possession* (New York, 1977), 235–89, here 236.

32 Crapanzano, *Hamadsha*, 6.

33 In this sense the Berber women's relation to the Aissaouia religious order seemed much less organized than in the situation which Daisy Dwyer described in the Taroudant area of Morocco. She points out that in the Taroudant, not only do many women belong (generally in separately organized but affiliated groups) to Sufi religious orders in which men are formally the chief actors, but it is women who choose the orders to which their sons and daughters will be affiliated. D. Dwyer, 'Women, Sufism and Decision-Making in Moroccan Islam', in N. Keddie and L. Beck (eds.), *Women in the Muslim World* (Cambridge, Mass., 1978), 585–98.

34 I. Lewis, 'A Structural Approach to Witchcraft and Spirit Possession', in M. Douglas (ed.), *Witchcraft in Confession and Accusation* (London, 1970).

35 Contrast Dwyer, 'Women, Sufism, Decision-Making'.

36 It is tempting to cite Freud (a male child as a substitute for a penis), but the sentiment expressed appears not so univocal.

37 The idea of 'legitimate' and 'illegitimate' sentiment was suggested to me by the article of E. Goody, 'Legitimate and Illegitimate Aggression in a West African State', in Douglas, *Witchcraft*, 207–44. Although E. Goody's article deals with behaviour rather than sentiment, it seems to be the attribution of aggressive sentiments to a woman which leads to her being accused of witchcraft.

38 Cf. C. Lefebure who writes of the Ait Atta, 'les larmes ne sont guère admises en pays berbère, même d'une femme: celles d'une mère au moment du départ de son fils que je ramenais en France me valurent les excuses genées de cet ami . . . La poésie feminine beraber comme mode de participation sociale', *Litterature orale Arabo-Berbère*, 8 (1977), 109–42, here 131.

39 V. Turner, *A Forest of Symbols: Aspects of Ndembu Ritual* (Ithaca, London, 1967), 19–20.

40 P. Constantinides, 'Ill at Ease and Sick at Heart: Symbolic Behaviour in a Sudanese Healing Cult', in I. Lewis (ed.), *Symbols and Sentiments* (London, 1977), 61–84, here 82.

Part III. Property in the mediation of family relations

5. 'Avoir sa part': sibling relations in partible inheritance Brittany

MARTINE SEGALEN

As Jack Goody has shown,[1] any system for the transmission of goods is closely linked to the mode of agricultural exploitation and the demographic regime. The impartible inheritance system is generally linked to acquisition of land. From amongst the whole group of children it produces a single heir who receives gifts which are both material (houses, buildings, land, rights to common lands) and symbolic (name, status, and prestige), whilst the remaining children are excluded from inheritance by a modest dowry. Such is the model described by Pierre Lamaison for the Gévaudan; by Alain Collomp for Haute-Provence in the seventeenth and eighteenth centuries; and by Pierre Bourdieu for twentieth-century Béarn.[2] It favours attachment to the home, a long family memory, and the stability of families patterned into something resembling lines. It is easier to study than the partible system of the devolution of goods and with regard to France, at least, better known.

Egalitarian partition seems to be in immediate contradiction to a regime of landowning peasants, for the continued division of farms would take only a few generations to reach a threshold which would make it impossible for a family-based agricultural economy to work. An egalitarian system is profoundly disturbing by virtue of the fact that it tends to undermine family and village holdings. In addition, its destructive effect is increased in periods of population growth. One might assume from that, that society sets up a mechanism to fight against this phenomenon of general impoverishment, which leads in addition to a technical dead-end. And indeed in certain areas of northern France which are assumed to be egalitarian each generation can be seen to be patiently working to consolidate around one-heir holdings which have been dismantled by inheritance. In such activity, marriage strategies have an important part to play. Despite an egalitarian ideology, there is also a non-egalitarian practice which succeeds in introducing differences into a line along which the patrimony is consolidated in every generation, as at Nussey, in the Jura.[3]

An egalitarian system of the transmission of goods goes better with a system of tenant farming, where the farmer has nothing to transmit other than movable

129

goods and a right to a lease which cannot be divided. This precarious mode of tenure gives rise to a fairly considerable mobility of households, which is much harder, of course, to follow over a long period. It is uncommon to find any of the family continuity like the lines observed in central and southern France. This means that it is not easy to include them in the monograph, the normal modus operandi of the historian and the ethnologist.

Non-egalitarian systems are certainly sensitive to demographic constraints but to a lesser degree than egalitarian ones. Thus, Normandy at a very early date experienced a system of limiting births that made regulating the transmission of goods a relatively simple matter. Children are few there, and if there is only a son and a daughter, the girl only receives movable goods, which means that the estate can be kept whole.[4] One can see why the local saying speaks of 'the king's choice' when the sibling group is limited to one son and one daughter.

With Brittany, and Basse–Bigoudennie in particular, we come to an egalitarian region with high fertility where tenant farming predominates. The aim of this article is to study the ideology of the system and how the system works and thus to make a contribution to the study of family relationships in an egalitarian system. Does the competitive situation in which the children find themselves in relation to each other perhaps create special tensions within the sibling group with regard to a patrimony to which any of them may make a claim? The impartible inheritance system socializes the younger son to accept his un-favourable situation and from the very earliest age makes a distinction, by means of a special term, between the 'heir' and the younger son. Breton children, however, who are all *heritourien*, may perhaps not accept a fate which they may see as unjust. What are the relationships between close kin before and after the transmission of the patrimony?

In the southern part of the *pays bigouden*, tenant farming and an egalitarian system of transmitting goods have gone together for a long time. Peasant ownership of land goes back no further than the late nineteenth and early twentieth centuries. In Revolutionary times, the property of émigrés was repurchased within the same families, and landed property remained in the hands of bourgeois families living in towns or families of the old Breton nobility who owned scores of farms within the same area. This explains why the ideology and practice of an egalitarian transmission have been so long-lasting and why the small number of peasant proprietors have had to come to terms with this.

This study is chiefly based on direct interviews with old farmers. In discussing with them their family trees, we have been concerned with how different branches scattered over the region or the particular stability of one line all helped to illustrate the practice of the system of transmitting goods. With regard to the nineteenth century, it was necessary to analyse documents relating in one way or another to the patrimony. This was complicated in so far as drawing up documents before the notary was not a regular practice. There was nothing to say that an old man had to make a will, or that a father had to draw up a marriage contract for his daughter, and indeed such things were not common. Consequently, we have at our disposal none of the beautiful runs of documents that ethnological historians of regions where there was a written law have available for analysis. This study relies on an analysis of documents from the Enregistrement (Legal Registration Department), those concerning changes in an estate upon decease of an individual, which were established in all cases of succession and used for tax purposes. For the population of a village of some 900 inhabitants in the nineteenth century, only 500 such documents were traced. In other words, a significant proportion of the population died without leaving anything that would justify taxation. In addition, a large number of households moved around the region, and the registration was carried out where they were residing when the death occurred.

These documents show the total goods left at death and the name, place of residence, and profession of all the heirs: vital information in an area of such high mobility, which enabled us to follow the movements of sons and daughters across the area and retrace the geography of matrimonial and social relationships. The documents also mention a possible notarized document later extracted from the notarial records. Sometimes it is a matter of a marriage contract, more often of an inventory after a death. These will be used here to illustrate certain points of our account.

The practice of a strict egalitarian system

Right from the start, day labourers, some 40% of the population in the nineteenth century with nothing to transmit to their children, must be excluded from this description. They were not covered by documents dealing with changes in an estate after a death, since there was nothing for the tax authorities to take. They died possessing no material or social capital, and on the decennial registration lists their name is sometimes followed by the word 'pauper'.

Most peasants were tenant farmers and their sole right was a renewal of their lease, renegotiated at Michaelmas every nine years, and to their movable personal goods: furniture, linen, livestock, ploughing implements, standing crops. Tenant farms were more or less stable, depending on current economic circumstances. Landlords did not hesitate to get rid of a tenant who found it difficult to pay his rent at times of bad harvest, and, on their side, tenants often sought to take on larger farms when the number of children they had increased. A rented farm was their only mode of existence, and they held on to it for as long as possible.

What the tenant farmer could transmit, but only to one of his children, was the right to a lease. There are indeed cases of a family succession of tenants. Sometimes, but only fairly rarely, it was possible to get the landlord to divide up the farm into two holdings, so that two children could be settled. Farms were usually quite large, of between 25 and 30 hectares, and could be divided in two and still remain economic, given the level of agricultural technology in the nineteenth century.

The area of Brittany also had a mixed system combining tenant farming and ownership. This was the archaic system of the *domaine congéable* in which a distinction was made between two types of ownership: that of the land and that of the buildings. The land belonged to the outside landlord, a bourgeois or a noble, but the house, outbuildings, the layer of arable land, the slopes were the property of the farmer. The lease was nevertheless uncertain, and the landlord could expel the farmer as if he were a tenant, provided he bought back from him his 'buildings, surfaces and compensatory rights', as the notaries expressed it. To take up a lease, one had to be an owner: if a son succeeded his father, with the landlord's permission, he first had to buy back the compensatory rights from him.

A landowner farming his own land was, in terms of the law, quite within his rights to dispose of his property as he wished, either by really dividing up his land or by giving payments in lieu to his children. According to Jean Yver, 'it was strictly forbidden, by the Most Ancient Custom [of Brittany] to favour any heir more than any other. Most characteristic of the code was the principle of forced restitution'. He goes on to say that 'the institution of favouring an heir, as formulated in the Most Ancient Custom, was to be preserved in articles 230 of the custom of 1539 and 217 of that of 1530'.[5] Breton practice, however, as we can see from the few studies on the subject, wavered between a certain preference for an heir and for a strict egalitarian division of property. Thus, Delroeux has shown that in the Cap area the village of Goulien favoured a single child, had heirs appointed as minors, and created a large pool of bachelors available for second marriages, in a system quite close to that in the Gévaudan mentioned above, whilst in the neighbouring village of Plogoff, goods were divided equally amongst all the children.[6] The general framework was egalitarian, therefore, with each region – perhaps even each village – having its own strategy, and that strategy was closely linked to the socio-economic factors. Goulien is a farming village, and Plogoff a village where both farming and sea-faring are important.

Another open alternative in the system was that either an eldest or a younger son could be chosen as heir. From that point of view, too, there were radical differences between nearby villages. Thus, in the *bigouden* region, which is seen nevertheless as culturally homogeneous, two radically different solutions were adopted. In the north of the area, the eldest son inherited from his parents when he married, the parents retiring to their own house with their reservation,[7] whilst in the south it was rather the youngest, or one from among the younger children, who replaced his father as tenant of the farm or property. In the first case, the succession was settled when the eldest child married. In the second, this happened when the youngest one married.

One of the features peculiar to the Breton egalitarian practice that went beyond the Civil Code and linked that practice with Celtic traditions was the equality of the sexes, which was respected. Property or rented farms were transmitted to both son and daughter – provided in the latter case that there was a son-in-law – without any distinction with regard to the movable or immovable goods, as has been seen in Normandy. A bride's dowry was not directly taken by her father-in-law, as was the case in impartible inheritance systems. It remained her own property and never became part of the joint property, except in cases of mutual gifts between spouses. It was one way of protecting property that came from the mother and of protecting the patrimony of her children as distinct from those from a second marriage.

Relationships amongst siblings and the cycle of family life

Problems related to the succession did not arise immediately after children were born, as in the region we are studying it was the younger ones who inherited. Parents continued to work the farm long after the eldest were married. An age gap of fifteen or twenty years was not unusual in such families with large numbers of children. Although children were closely linked to the farm, they knew that they had little chance of spending all their adult lives on it. There was thus no 'natural' or implicitly designated heir enjoying a particular kind of upbringing or psychological preparation. On the other hand, the children all wanted to be peasants. Massive emigration to the towns did not begin until around 1920. Remaining in the country without owning one's own land was the future that most of these children envisaged.

As we have seen, there was no term within the sibling group to designate an heir, but there were words to describe the position of the first and last born. The eldest was called *ar houz* (the old one) and the youngest *vidohick* (the runt). These were affectionate and mocking nicknames used by the children for each other, with particular enjoyment if the youngest was a sturdy lad. Relationships in these families, where until 1920 there would, on average, be between eight to twelve children, were shaped by the position in the sibling group, individual per-sonalities, mutual affinities, and the responsibilities that each one gradually had to take in relation to the others. Thus, a sister who was a close comrade would be called a true sister, *c'hoar*, whereas a domineering one would be called *ar vestrez*, the mistress, since she already behaved like a grown woman. These childhood nicknames would stick for the rest of their lives. Nicknames were the sign of the affective forces at play amongst siblings. Parent/child relationships were rather cold and characterized by the respect produced by distance, but nonetheless not without a certain chaste tenderness. From childhood on, it was between siblings that arguments and the quest for affection were manifest. Within such large sibling groups it was indeed possible for elective affectivity to occur. Parents could not be chosen, but it was possible to express a preference for such and such a brother or sister. Children formed couples, usually of the same sex, and while they were young founded affective relationships of a deep nature which were strengthened by their home life. No particular area was set aside for intimate relationships, and parents and children slept in the same room that all shared. There were several children to a bed, but from the age of ten the sexes were separated, with all the girls at one side and all the boys at the other. These factors explain the mutual and lifelong affinities that grew up between couples from these large sibling groups.

The process of socialization made a fundamental distinction between the children of day labourers and those of farmers owning or renting their farms. In the latter two groups, children stayed on the parental farm until they married. They therefore had the advantage of a precise identification with a specific area of land, which showed that they were rooted in a hamlet whose very name was a social reference: they belonged to such and such a farm on fertile land or such and such another, near the shore and much more arid. The children of day labourers on the other hand were placed as servants on farms once they were ten or twelve years old. The sibling group was broken up very rapidly, and children were given important responsibilities. Even if a young farm-lad or servant-girl managed to set up a relationship with one of the farm children of his or her own age, whose daily life, fate, and bed he shared, he was essentially socialized outside his own family and cut off from the affective bonds of the sibling group.

The children of day labourers also received much less education than those of landowning or tenant farmers. The latter were at school for longer, the period being more or less identical for all children. Normally, however, boys remained at school longer to learn French better, as they could expect to do military service in some region outside Brittany. Once they were adult (that is when the boys had completed their military service and the girls were seventeen or eighteen years of age), they were expected to 'leave the farm' to 'find a place', to get a husband or wife and some prospect of the lease of a farm. Thus, the eldest gradually left and went to a farm either directly after their marriage or after spending some years living with their parents or parents-in-law and receiving a wage for the work they did on the farm. Later, the younger ones would marry and when the *last to marry* was settled the problem of the inheritance was made final. In systems of this kind, it was at the end of the cycle of family life that goods were transmitted. The most comfortably-off families were able to give their daughters dowries, but there was never a total settlement. That only happened when the parents were old and psychologically and physically ready to retire.

Amongst tenant farmers it was often the youngest son or daughter and her husband who took over the lease. The parents would live with the new head of the household as, typically, they would not be able to afford to build a separate house, given the precarious economic situation of these peasants. The young farmer would then buy the movable goods from his father-in-law, and the parents would share out the proceeds equally amongst the remaining children, now scattered throughout the local area, where they might have moved onto a farm as a result of marriage.[8] In the 1850s the value of such goods ranged on average between 1,000 and 4,000 francs.

Farmers holding their land under the *domaine congéable* system would sell back to the son or son-in-law succeeding them the compensatory rights and compensate their other children. Here, however, unlike the tenant farmer, who had no room for manoeuvre, they could make use of a strategy of a paternal kind, since if they undervalued them, they favoured the one remaining in his place and penalized those who had left, their share being correspondingly smaller.

This paternal strategy and power increased in relation to the value of the goods to be transmitted. Even in an egalitarian system, and despite the appearance of family democracy, the father's wishes played an important part. Amongst those owning the land they farmed, the problems of inheritance would be discussed at family meetings, and the father would come to a decision after something like a family council. The conversations we have had with farmers indicate a practice fairly close to that shown in fiction in the regional novel *Thumette Bigoudène*:

In order to avoid paying death duties to the State, or to pay as little as possible, the older generation in Brittany have adopted the habit of sharing out their possessions while they are still alive.

Nonna and Augustine Le Rhun [the heroes of the novel] knew that their active life was over. They had to make way for the young ones. There was a certain melancholy in that, but Nonna Le Rhun had never tried to go against necessity. His wife, who always thought as he did, was also resigned to being the mistress of Kernével no longer – Kernével, the fine and beautiful farm whither she had come as a bride of seventeen, where she had brought up six sons and her little Thumette, all fine and healthy, except Henry, who had died for his country.

In silence and alone, Nonna reflected, ruminated, planned. He was well aware that no one would raise his voice against his decision. His authority was still whole and absolute, despite the slackness due to the war and the attempts of young people to gain independence. He was still *ar tad*, the father, the master. It was always he who allotted tasks, directed the work, set the rhythm for planting, sowing, and reaping, and he alone who held the money, made investments, did the buying and selling.

And so one Sunday he called together all his children. Henry was represented by his widow and his two little daughters. He told them of his plan. Kernével was to be farmed by Louis and Noël, since there was enough work for two households. One field was to go to Roland, to extend the rather meagre land of the *domaine*. The others were to have money or deeds. Louis and Noël were to pay the profits from their share in cash. Nonna, Augustine, and Thumette, until she married, were to go and live elsewhere from next Michaelmas.[9]

Inheritance strategies covered a whole range of attitudes which could, depending on circumstances, extend from maintaining the integrity of the patrimony to dividing up the land farmed. The former gave an advantage to the eldest child. Like the farmer holding his land under the *domaine congéable* system, the tenant farmer could sell his farm to his successor and undervalue it, so that the brothers and sisters who had left home were less generously treated than the one who had stayed on family land.

The following is an example of a family strategy for keeping the farm together, observed over three generations. The Steud farm, of some 20 hectares, was inherited by André Coïc in 1859, when his father died. His four other brothers and sisters were farmers working their own land elsewhere. When he died in 1888, four daughters from the seven children born to him could claim to inherit. The three eldest were living on farms that their husbands owned. The youngest daughter and her husband received le Steud in 1888 and the others sums of money. Jean D. and Marie-Louise Coïc had seven children. The three sons became elementary-school teachers, two of the sisters became nuns, and the eldest daughter and her husband lived with her parents and farmed le Steud. The latter settled the matter of the succession in 1920. Considering that he had given his children equal shares – his sons an education, two daughters a dowry so that they could enter a convent, and the eldest daughter the farm to live on – Jean D. sold the farm in his old age to his grandson much below its market price leaving the young man to compensate his uncles and aunts, who had left the district, with sums of money well below the value of the farm.

This is a rather exceptional example of a model of family transmission which gives the households something of the shape akin to that of the stem family. It shows that oversimplification should be avoided when studying the practice of succession.

With those owning their land, the commonest solution was to divide the farm not amongst all the children but only amongst two or three of them in order to ensure that, given the technical means of production available at the time, a viable undertaking should be handed on. The following is the will of Joseph Danyel, of the hamlet of Rupape, dated 18 August 1847:

to avoid too great a division of my real estate amongst my [seven] heirs, I wish and intend that my properties consisting of firstly, half the hamlet of Rupape, where I reside, premises, land, and rights, secondly the similar half of the windmill, also premises, land, and rights, and situated at the exit of the aforesaid village, thirdly also the half of the four-fifths of the land, premises, and rights known as Douar Troanon, should belong exclusively and in perpetuity, but after my death and that of my wife, to my aforesaid four children Corentin, Jean-Marie, Jacques Danyel, and Anne Danyel married to Le Page in equal fourth parts.

And to compensate my three other heirs for having no share in the division of my immovable property, I charge my aforesaid four legatees to pay to each one of them a sum of 900 francs to be paid in the following manner: Jeanne Danyel, married to Le Palud, shall receive hers one month after the death of my wife and myself; the two minors, Marie-Jeanne Danyel and Marie Le Queneudec [a little girl whose mother was dead] shall only receive their share when they attain their majority, always in the case of the earlier decease of their parents, with interest at 5% from the date of the two aforesaid deaths until all has been paid.

My four children who are legatees must also pay, themselves, and without recourse to the other heirs, the 180 francs owed by me to Marie-Jeanne and Marie Le Loch and to the minor Struillou to complete the payment of the sale document. This is my firm and constant wish. I desire all my heirs to find it acceptable and if any will not accept these conditions I hereby declare that I declare him deprived of the greatest available portion of my legacies of both movable and immovable goods.

The same strategy was used in the case of the farm acquired by the P. parents around 1900. They farmed 21 hectares at Gorré-Beuzec. Seven of their children survived to adulthood, there being a difference of twenty years between the oldest and youngest. This was at a time of peak demand for land as a result of demographic pressure. The first three children were married to tenant farmers or farmers owning their own farms, all of which were of a similar size. Of the remaining four, two more married and the two who were left lived on their parents' farm. They arranged that the transmission should operate as follows: their farm was divided up into three small ones of 7 hectares each, two for the married children and one for the unmarried ones. The other children received a sum of money strictly equivalent to the value of the farms.

Thus we have an example from the other extreme of a scale of which one pole is the single heir, the other of a division of property carried out in terms of a desire for total equality for each heir. This model occurred in the mid-nineteenth and the early twentieth centuries.

The following is the division operated on 12 March 1848 by Anne Le Berre, the widow of Louis Le Palud, who had four daughters:

the aforesaid Marie Anne Le Berre, advancing in years and wishing to avoid the arguments that could arise amongst her children and grandchildren with regard to inheritance, has decided to divide amongst her children and grandchildren all the goods which would go to them on her death, which goods consist of the place Keryoret bihan, premises, lands, and compensatory rights included situated in the said parish of . . . belonging entirely to the aforesaid Marie Anne Le Berre and giving an annual net income of 90 francs and valued at a capital of 2,000 francs.

Four pieces of land are described in detail in the document, and it is specifically stated that:

the principal house is and shall remain included in the fourth lot and that for that reason the aforesaid fourth lot is of greater value than the first and third lots which have no messuage upon them, thus the legatee receiving the aforesaid fourth lot shall be obliged to pay to the legatees receiving the aforesaid first and third lots half each of a sum of 600 francs as a compensatory payment, which sum shall be payable without interest one month after the death of the said Marie Anne Le Berre.

Auguste C. owned four farms of 60 hectares in all. He had eight children, of whom only four – three sons and a daughter – were still alive when he made his will in 1920 or thereabouts. Two of the sons received farms of 18 and 16 hectares respectively, two others farms of only 13 hectares. To make the division strictly equal, the father stipulated that 2 and 3 hectares of the bigger farms should go to the heirs receiving the smaller ones, with the express condition that they should sell them back to the brothers inheriting the farms they belonged to. This case illustrates the reconciliation of the desire not to favour any particular legatee and at the same time not to break up the farm, this being achieved by means of a compensatory payment between brothers.

When a father had made a decision, it seems never to have been questioned. Succession was arranged once all the children were more or less launched, and the parents tried to ensure that each child benefitted more or less equally. Even if occasionally one or another was in fact favoured by this practice, the prevailing ideology was a deeply egalitarian one. The integrity of the estate could not be defended at the cost of penalizing one of the children, and this way of looking at things seems to have created a feeling of rebellion amongst some of the peasants it was possible to discuss the matter with. It was the parents' responsibility to give each of their children the opportunity of going into farming, of giving them the means of working in the only way they knew, on the land. Marriage and inheritance strategies were thus not directed towards accumulating and maintaining a family material and symbolic capital in the person of a single child but rather towards settling each of them in a way compatible with the family status. As Louise P., aged eighty, said: 'you knew that not everybody would stay on the farm . . . If there was a young man free on a farm (people would say), you will be all right . . . you'll have a farm, you'll know where to go, you'll have land to farm.'

Children married according to their rank, very often with the mediation of a go-between, the *coritache*, and in due course the parents arranged the inheritance, transmitting the farm or the lease, compensating those who did not get them: 'they gave me a bit of money as my share'. Once the family arrangements had been made, there was a visit to the notary to have them set out in due legal form. But the notary did not make decisions; he simply recorded those made within the family.

Monetary compensation and dowries were important matters, particularly at the end of the nineteenth century, when farmers were in a position to buy their farms. They circulated horizontally as a means of compensating siblings. In the diagram, a man buys a farm from his parents and compensates his brothers and sisters by means of the sum of money his wife brought as her dowry, which she had obtained on the division of goods with her brother who had inherited the family farm. In their turn, these sums enabled those who had not inherited to acquire a farm put up for sale by the owner and thus, even if they remained the personal property of each spouse, dowries and compensatory payments – which often were the same thing and were made in a single payment – played a vital part when the system of appropriation was changed at the end of the nineteenth century.

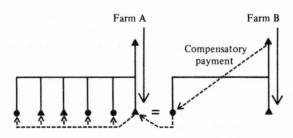

The systems of transmission described here and the relationships between siblings that they gave rise to were complicated by the fact that the mortality rate meant that there were widows and widowers, second marriages, and children of several marriages. Half-brothers and sisters were usually considered to be full ones, and notarial provisions attempted to protect their rights. If a spouse who was still the head of the farm died while he still had children who were minors, an inventory was taken which gave the value of all the movable goods of the community, from the furniture, utensils, linen, personal effects, and livestock to the ploughing implements, standing crops, and assets and debts. If the surviving spouse was still young, he or she would remain on the farm and often remarry very quickly. He or she would then be the guardian of the minor children, and a surrogate guardian would be appointed to examine their accounts. The children were in fact the direct heirs of the property of the deceased unless there had been a gift *inter vivos*.

There were many young fatherless and motherless children under the guardianship of an elder brother or sister, a brother-in-law, or an uncle. Accounts were very strictly checked, as the following document, dated 23 June 1872, indicates: 'Account from guardian to guardian', between a man who was the guardian of his younger brothers-in-law who were minors and another brother-in-law, a major, who was surrogate guardian. Amongst the expenses there appears the total of a public auction after their father's death and the 'total of their rights to movable goods in the estate of Corentin Coïc, their father, and of Louise Coïc, their full sister [which] amounts to 4048.75 francs'. Costs were deducted, mainly for fees for the appointment of the guardian, transfer documents, registration fees, etc.

The network of kinship links was thus mingled with that of monies due and debts, and accounts were often long and complicated. For example, on 25 October 1835 Anne Le Lay, whose father was dead, accepted as a dowry her expectations under his will:

Anne Le Lay says that she possesses some 11,000 or 12,000 francs due to her from the aforesaid Jean Bargain and his wife as her share of her father's estate. Although this account has not yet been settled, she nevertheless intends to immobilize for her benefit and to exclude from the future community the whole amount of the guardianship account, whatever it may be, once it has been audited.

When settling the succession jumped a generation, the inheritance was not, given the high birth-rate, worth a great deal. It certainly did not involve any kind of moral right to a farm and meant at most a sum of ready money decreasing with each generation that passed. There were children inheriting from their grandparents a sixth or an eighth of a half of the compensatory rights on a given holding. Sometimes child mortality had the opposite effect and meant that the share of one of the siblings was increased when the share due to the dead child was added to it.

Fusion and fission: forces at work amongst siblings after their marriage

When siblings left home and married, that coincided with the moment of fission in the sibling group. Brothers rarely set up home close to each other but spread all over the area. And yet there was a real desire to maintain family links between married brothers and sisters, and the habit of choosing brothers and sisters or their wives or husbands as godfathers or godmothers is a sign of this. The godparent link was a major one. It was spiritual, ritual, and also material since, as we have seen, the uncle–godfather was often the guardian if his nephew's parents died. Another indication of the desire to keep sibling links was the practice of mutual help with farming. Even if they lived several kilometres apart, two brothers would not hesitate to help each other out with the moving of the harvest. Brothers and sisters lent each other money temporarily so that each one could buy his farm (around 1900).

Even if it was not a matter of a special occasion, the links between these sibling groups were still marked, despite the distance between households. One informant said that once a week, or more frequently, she would walk for two hours in the evening to visit her sister, of whom she was very fond.

These sibling links were also often strengthened by marriage practices, as the group and those related to it by marriage formed a pool of possible marriage partners. These were not, properly speaking, marriages between blood relations but unions between two family branches in the wider sense, i.e. which had already seen marriages between them. The group of relatives belonging to each set of siblings thus raised the possibility of further fusion as a result of marriages which might take place.

This solidarity was not usually affected by the illness or incapacity of one of the siblings. In such cases, too, it was the responsibility of the one seen to be implicitly the most favoured, as he had inherited the family farm, to take in a brother who could not manage alone. There was sometimes an agreement drawn up before a notary, as in the case of a gift made on 23 May 1836 by Jean Louis Lagadic to René Lagadic and his wife. The donor, who was fifty-two at the time, was a bachelor living with his brother and sister-in-law who:

desiring to show his gratitude for all the goodness shown to him by his brother and sister-in-law and being moreover unable to support himself does this day by the present document hand over to the aforesaid René Lagadic and his wife, who accept it all, his movable and immovable goods on the following conditions, firstly, that the legatees undertake to provide board and lodging both in sickness and in health for their aforesaid brother, Jean Louis Lagadic, and to show the same regard for him as in the past. In addition they shall provide clothing for him in cloth and linen as for the other persons in their household and shall provide him each week with the quantity of smoking tobacco he may need, secondly, on the death of the legator the funeral expenses of the same shall be paid in full by the legatees.

There was the same sort of family solidarity in the case of four married brothers and sisters living on four different farms who settled the future of their mentally-handicapped brother in an 'agreement to feed and treaty between Alain Le Bihan and others' dated 7 August 1870. The document declared that:

their respective brother and brother-in-law, François Le Bihan, aged thirty-seven and residing in the village of Kernivily (with his brother Alain Le Bihan) is an idiot and cannot make his wishes known nor in the opinion of doctors who have been consulted is he capable of undertaking any work now or in the future. All those present agree that it is their duty to help their aforesaid respective brother and brother-in-law whose sole worldly possession is a debt due to him of eleven hundred francs and fifty centimes . . . have agreed to the following arrangement: from this day on Alain Le Bihan formally accepts the obligation to feed, clothe, and care for, both in sickness and in health, his idiot brother, François Le Bihan; secondly, from this day and during the whole lifetime of François Le Bihan, his brother Alain will be solely responsible for what is necessary for him without recourse to his other brothers and sisters; thirdly, to reimburse Alain Le Bihan for the responsibility which he assumes all those present with good will towards their idiot brother and brother-in-law grant and cede to the aforesaid Alain Le Bihan the sum of 11,000 francs and 50 centimes.

This family closeness was also apparent when parents grew old. The child who had inherited the farm had a kind of moral responsibility for them. The wealthier parents would leave and set up home in a local town – as did Nonna and Augustine Le Rhun – or would have a house built on the plot of land they had kept for themselves. Those less well-off would, as we have seen, stay on the farm with their son or son-in-law. But whichever course they took, they were the responsibility of the family who had inherited the farm and stayed on it.

Does that mean that relationships amongst these kinfolk were always as harmonious as these examples would seem to show or as the passage from *Thumette Bigoudène* quoted above would have us believe? Here, we must distinguish between norm and practice and between official and semi-official discourse. The notarial documents quoted or referred to could well bear witness to the solidarity of the sibling group, but they could equally well show that the relatives studied here had been unable to come to an amicable agreement and had had to have recourse to official documents. The solution adopted could well hide a conflict.

People are never proud of rivalry among siblings, and interviews were sometimes difficult. As the work progressed, it was clear that to a great extent family quarrels are the most personal part of what is revealed, and in such cases, that was as little as possible, even to an interviewer with whom good relations had been established. After giving me rather hesitantly a certain amount of information about the fate of plots of land bequeathed to his brothers and sisters now living in town – and nothing was known about those plots more than twenty-five years after the father's death – a farmer with whom I had nevertheless been on good terms for over eight years suddenly told me to leave. Actions of this kind show all the tensions latent in sibling relationships.

It seems that in this area of Lower Brittany most of the tensions occurred within the sibling group and were all the more likely to assume a violent form as the major affective relationships were in fact those within the band of brothers and sisters. Rivalry with regard to the patrimony was strengthened by these strong emotions.

Relationships between parents and children, we have said, were marked by a certain coldness and a great respect for paternal authority. Sometimes the relationship between a father and his children was almost one of fear. During the lifetime of the father, his decisions were accepted even if a sense of unfairness led to an inner questioning. Relations between husband and wife were also marked by a certain reticence and modesty. The system of transmitting goods generally protected the autonomy of women and made them more independent within their immediate family. In the practices of married life, questions relating to the patrimony do not seem to have caused disagreement between husbands and wives, who after all shared the same aim of making the family farm work. (However, there is the case of one old peasant woman who did not hesitate to divorce her second husband because he had failed to give her the house he had promised her before they were married!)

Deep feelings, then, only came to the surface amongst siblings and not between parents and children or between husband and wife. Affective relationships between siblings, whether of love or of hatred, were rooted in earliest childhood and were brought into the open by the competitiveness that the partible inheritance system imposed. That was when quarrels multiplied. In the words of one informant, 'family stories like that . . . they're all over the place'.

The reasons for such quarrels were many, but special mention could be made of the problems arising in connection with the sale of one brother's share of the inheritance to another and the care of aged parents.

In the case of Auguste C., quoted above, the plot of land separated from the main holding had to be sold to enable each child to have an equal share of the inheritance. The obligation, however, was only a moral and verbal one. After the father's death, the heir could refuse to sell back to his brother the plot of land cut off from his holding. There are examples of enduring quarrels when the small plot was sold to an outsider. The other cause of serious annoyance was when the child who remained on the parental farm did not honour his moral obligation to keep his father and mother with him.

Thus Sebastien T. kept the parental farm as a result of what his four brothers and sisters saw as a sale at a remarkably low price. He did not, however, look after his declining father. His sister Marguerite, who had married the blacksmith in the neighbouring village, had to fetch her father in her cart, take him in to live with her, and look after him until his death. Her brother refused any financial help towards his keep. The quarrel was serious enough to lead to a permanent break between brother and sister. They did not speak to each other or invite each other to their house again and their one further meeting was the last: the obligation to attend a parent's funeral took precedence over all quarrels. Reconciliation was all the more difficult as the sibling group had long ago split up into groups of two or three. Quarrels fed upon themselves and became part of the family heritage, assuming a hereditary or quasilegendary quality. Thus a quarrel between two branches of the same line is still alive today, carried on by their children. Tudyne C. prefers to walk 800 metres for her bread to going to the bakery 20 metres from her house because it is kept by her cousin, whose father had provoked her mother's anger sixty years ago.

Bitterness between brothers and sisters can be long-lasting, but was sometimes even more permanent between half-brothers and half-sisters, of whom there were so many in the nineteenth century. The case of a second wife misappropriating property left by the first and using it, with her husband's connivance, for the benefit of her own children was a frequent occurrence. Again, in such situations, the children silently put up with the injustice done to them while their father was alive, but after his death their heart-break came out into the open.

Conclusions

The egalitarian system of transmitting goods thus produced constant and lasting competition between siblings. Goods were never transmitted on one single occasion, when a marriage took place. The elder children had received a share in ready cash and then perhaps had to wait twenty years for the final settlement of the estate, when they themselves had gone a fair way through their own cycle of family life. This meant that children had to live in hopes of receiving a given plot of land and then, if it went to one of their brothers or sisters, to transfer their hopes to the possibility of buying it back. In such a system, nothing was ever finally settled, and it was common to hear a peasant say 'I've still got my share over there', referring to such and such a plot of land that he owns but which is worked, on a kind of verbal lease, by the brother still on the farm.

Tensions, rivalries, and speculation on the future still go on shaping year after year relationships within sibling groups in which the children are still anxious to increase the size of their farms. In our own day, the flight from the land has considerably reduced the number of farms, but rivalry within sibling groups has not always decreased.

As more tenants became owners of their farms, holdings were increasingly broken up into smaller units during the 1950s. At that time, maintaining a strictly egalitarian practice led to a total impasse. There was no way of turning a holding of 14, 10, or 7 hectares into eight farms. One might have expected to see, as in other regions of France, the return of a non-egalitarian practice favouring the child who stayed on the land. The prevailing egalitarian ideology would not have taken kindly to such a system, and farms continued to be divided up. There are now two kinds of situation.

Where a farm is still actively worked, siblings keep their own share, renting it to whichever of them is running the farm. The causes of tension, which are the same as those prevailing in the past, are kept alive by the cultural and social distance between those who stay behind and those who leave. There are, however, also examples of amicable arrangements. When the opposite situation arises and there is no heir resolved to continue farming, the parents divide their property into as many parts as there are children. Each one receives a plot of land on which he has a house – often a second home – built, where he spends weekends or holidays. There are no longer any reasons for tension, as each has his own house and little garden. Thus affective relationships characterized by mutual help and the exchange of services can develop. Young cousins live together during the holidays, and the age of 'family histories' is over.

NOTES

1 Jack Goody, 'Introduction' in Jack Goody, *et. al.* (eds.), *Family and Inheritance: Rural Society in Western Europe, 1200–1800* (Cambridge, 1976), 3.
2 Pierre Lamaison, 'Les Stratégies matrimoniales dans un système complexe de parenté: Ribennes en Gévaudan (1650–1890)', *Annales ESC.*, 34 (1979), 721–43. Alain Collomp, 'Famille nucléaire et famille élargie en Haute-Provence au 18e siècle', *Annales ESC,* 27 (1972), 969–76. Pierre Bourdieu, 'Célibat et condition paysanne', *Etudes rurales*, 5–6 (1962), 32–136.
3 Michèle Dion-Salitot, *La Crise d'une société villageoise. Les survivanciers. Les paysans du Jura français (1800–1970)* (Paris, 1972), 53.
4 Jack Goody, 'Inheritance, Property and Women', in Goody, *Family and Inheritance*, 18.
5 Jean Yver, *Essai de géographie coutumière* (Paris, 1966).
6 Jacques Delroeux, 'Etude d'anthropologie sociale de trois sociétés rurales occidentales, Goulien, Plogoff et Lescoff (sud finistère de 1800 à 1970), recherche du principe de réciprocité', Thése de doctorat d'Etat (University of Paris V, 1979).
7 André Burguière, *Bretons de Plozevet* (Paris, 1975).
8 Martine Segalen, 'L'Espace matrimonial dans le sud du pays bigouden', *Gwechall*, 1 (1978), 109–22.
9 Anne Selle, *Thumette Bigoudène* (Paris, 1935), 32.

6. Tensions, dissensions, and ruptures inside the family in seventeenth- and eighteenth-century Haute-Provence[1]

ALAIN COLLOMP

My study of the society of several villages in Haute-Provence in the seventeenth and eighteenth centuries is based on the results of a micro-analysis and makes observations, as it were, through the strong magnification of a lens. There is an accumulation of details in order to define as completely as possible a village society in all its aspects. The details sketch a model of a complex family residence group in the sense in which Peter Laslett uses the term, with an inheritance strategy of the stem family type, where one of the sons is chosen to succeed his father in the household.[2]

The first pitfall would be to see the model I have described as peculiar to the particular small area of Haute-Provence, and the mass of biographical data on individuals might suggest that the facts are quite particular and specific. However, recent studies have shown that a stem family society was (and is) widespread in many areas of France, particularly in the centre and south (Languedoc, the Pyrenean area of the south-west, Lozère, Aveyron, Limousin), as well as in Spain or Italy (in Tuscany in particular) and indeed in certain parts of Austria.[3] The family structure described here is thus not peculiar to Haute-Provence.

But it would be just as dangerous to lump together every family situation with complex residence structures. The same demographic structures of households may underlie or derive from very different social, economic, and affective situations. If we ignore the nuances and the context which a micro-analysis of society alone can provide, we run the risk of merely producing a schematic and unfruitful historical comparison. For example, an analysis of agrarian structures in Haute-Provence highlights the predominance of the small family farm.[4] It would, however, be rash and hasty to try to link family structure to a small family concern of this kind, since the Haute-Provence family model is more rigorously applied to bourgeois or noble families with large-scale holdings of land worked by farmers. It applies just as well to the families of merchants or artisans for whom the ownership of land and more particularly its profitability are only secondary sources of income.

In earlier studies I viewed family life from the viewpoint of the father engaged in establishing and settling inheritances on his children.[5] I described the successful (and perhaps over-successful) working of a model of a 'patriarchal' society, dominated by the father, derived perhaps too closely from the legal rules found in written sources. My aims here are to check whether this model is only an ideal rule or corresponds to a widespread practice, and to evaluate, using other sources and other viewpoints, the lived reality of family life.

Using legal proceedings, I have now tried to describe not the successful or idealized working of the system but its failures, which means that I have had to make choices. The need to ensure continuity in my investigations has led me to stress the parent/children relationship, just as it had been the major one in real life.[6] As we shall see later, it was the presence or absence of the father, the fact that he was alive or dead, that created the fact that there were two ways of classifying family conflicts. This, I maintain, reflects reality and not just a historian's way of seeing things.

Little attention will be paid here to the normal, and it could be said successful, operation of the residence group or of the division of family property. In the sense meant by David Sabean and Hans Medick in their essay, it is not a case of giving undue weight to an, as it were, 'affective pole' concerned with emotions at the expense of material interests. In reality, as the language of the legal proceedings shows, there is a great deal of 'material interest' in family psychological dramas. And, as Jack Goody has said, 'the linking of patterns of inheritance with patterns of domestic organization is a matter not simply of numbers and formations but of attitudes and emotions'.[7] The division of goods amongst children means that feelings which are often acute will come into play, and the ways in which parents and married children live together have a large affective component.

The material developed here, which is often based on legal sources, might well distort the view one should have of relationships between members of the family. On the one hand, legal documents, especially those of the seventeenth and eighteenth centuries, can easily make the dramas seem more important than they really were, even if only as a result of their high-flown and exaggerated style, or make it seem that family relationships had a certain violent quality, when in fact this was a characteristic of all human relationships at the time, whether within or outside the family. On the other hand, these same legal documents sin by omission. They do not bring out into the open family dramas not leading to legal action, dramas which lasted a lifetime, never emerging from the house or achieving the end that legal action achieves, that of bringing the conflict, and hence the shame of the family concerned, out into the open.[8]

Before we begin to study family conflicts, it seems to me essential to spend a little time putting this investigation into its context, at the eco-demographic and social levels, and then to review the legal conditions in Provence which enabled the family residence group to function at the different stages of its cycle of development.

Family conflicts have been grouped into two major parts. The first contains those in which there are disagreements between members of different generations (parent/children) while the father is still alive, the second conflicts between collaterals of the same generation and also tensions between the widow and her descendants, thus including problems arising after the death of the father. The death of the father seems to me to be the real turning-point, the revolution within the family group in Haute-Provence which makes it possible to establish this dual grouping. It is not simply a stylistic device to enable us to classify family conflicts and law-suits. The death of the father is a deep break between minor and more often than not reversible procedures or conflicts occurring before it and more acute or irremediable family dramas occurring after it, which sometimes fall under criminal jurisdiction.

I

All my ethnological and historical research in Provence has exact spatial and temporal boundaries. It involves some ten or so villages grouped around Saint-André-les-Alpes in the present *département* of the Alpes-de-Haute-Provence in the years between 1640 and 1793. During that century and a half, family law in Provence changed little. The final date, 1793, is that of the promulgation of the first Revolutionary laws of inheritiance, which upset existing practices and for a time at least thwarted the father's existing right to divide his inheritance in an inegalitarian way.

In the mid-eighteenth century, this collection of human beings comprised between 2000 and 2500 individuals, divided up amongst Saint-André, the largest village, with some 600 inhabitants, and other communities which included villages of between 200 and 400 inhabitants. Saint-André lies in the upper Verdon valley in a medium mountain region where snow does not lie long and the stone houses have gently sloping pantile roofs, as in the rest of Provence. Castellane, 20 kilometres to the south, was the capital of the bailiwick and provostship. The nearest fairs were held at Barrème, Colmars, Annot, and Castellane. Yet from certain points of view, Saint-André can be seen as a *bourg*, a tiny 'Mediterranean agro-town',[9] since it had a large number of clergy (four priests), more artisans and merchants than farmers, including in particular a large group of muleteers who both carried and sold goods, and above all it was a place where the liberal professions were well represented, having an advocate, a surgeon and, significantly, three (later two) notaries. The existence of this tertiary sector meant that close links were forged between Saint-André and the surrounding villages. In particular, the extent of the clientele using the services of the two notaries' practices in the village dictated the geographical boundaries of the area studied.

The Saint-André district was part of Provence. Cases going before the Parlement had their first hearing in Aix, the administrative capital of lower western Provence, which was far away from Saint-André but close to Marseilles, the large port absorbing most of the permanent emigrants from Haute-Provence.

The climate of the upper Verdon valley eliminated the last two of the three basic elements of Provençal agriculture: wheat, vines, and olives. Wine and olives were imported into Haute-Provence, but as against that there was normally a surplus of wheat. There was a great deal of pastoral farming, which led to exchange, with inverse transhumance, as the flocks of mountain sheep were wintered in lower Provence.

The settlement pattern was such that each parish consisted of houses grouped as either a single nucleus or as several nuclei, but both small hamlets and big villages were made up of juxtaposed tall houses, each with two storeys for human habitation jammed in between the animal quarters at street level, and storage lofts, particularly for hay, above them. The fields belonging to each farm were widely scattered, ranging from the garden and irrigated meadows near the house to the stony fields on the first slopes of the *saltus*.

The artisans and farmers almost always owned their own house and an area of land varying in size according to their 'condition': the small landowners owned farms which enabled them to sell a part of what they produced. Those 'working their own land', the largest group, found it difficult to tide themselves over to the harvest nearly each year. Even the *manouvriers* (agricultural day labourers) owned their own house, or at least part of a house, a patch of irrigable land for gardening (the Provençaux being great salad-eaters) and some poor land yielding mediocre crops. Only the bourgeois, the members of the liberal professions and one or two successful merchants, owned land concentrated into a small estate with a house for the farmer (the *rentier*). This was called the *bastide*, and was the only type of isolated house and the only example of indirect exploitation.

The power of the lord varied enormously from community to community. It was almost non-existent at Saint-André, where it was represented by a low annual rent paid to a noble lord from Aix who never visited his isolated estates in Haute-Provence, but quite considerable in certain neighbouring villages, where for at least part of the year the lord was in residence and owned considerable estates.

From 1720, there was a clear excess of births over deaths, due to a more balanced diet than in the cereal-producing plains, with mortality crises that seem to have been less deadly than in other climatic areas. The system of small farms run by their owners meant that a household could not feed too many mouths and the fact that without a minimum holding of land it was impossible to eat explains the regular phenomenon of double emigration, seasonal in some cases and permanent in others, but always towards lower Provence and particularly Marseilles and Toulon. This eco-demographic surplus chiefly affected agricultural labourers, but also, for different reasons, certain members of the other extreme of the social scale, bourgeois seeking to satisfy in the towns other aspirations which could not come to anything in the villages.

II

The major part of sources from the seventeenth and eighteenth centuries consists of documents drawn up by notaries. All the registers from notaries' offices in Saint-André are complete without a break from 1640 to the Revolution. These 60,000 or so pages have made it possible to record how the family as an institution worked, what its material needs and some of its tensions were. Amongst these documents one, the marriage contract, is indispensable. It is a totally reliable serial document, never missing even in the case of marriages between the very poorest people, which provides information about the portions of children, the conditions of cohabitation involving two generations, and on the ways and means of a possible dissolution of the community in question. Fifteen hundred marriage contracts, the total involved in both notarial offices in Saint-André between 1640 and 1793, were examined. They furnish names, which makes it possible to reconstruct vertical and horizontal genealogies, and can be compared with other documents concerning the same persons and families. Wills are no doubt less eloquent documents, since provisions regarding inheritance are more frequent and more detailed in marriage contracts. The receipt for goods promised by parents and to be handed over immediately if the parents/children community broke up, which was made by the parents to a son leaving them, is a particularly rich source of information. The fact that it is relatively rare seems to indicate that it was fairly uncommon for the parents/married children community to break up.

All legal documents from pre-Revolutionary times are stored in departmental records under the B series, and with regard to this research, under 'série B, Alpes-de-Haute-Provence'. Here, I made use of two series of documents. The first were those of the lord's court of Saint-André,[10] a collection which fortunately was quite considerable in the eighteenth century, dealing with civil and criminal cases, but also containing the *cahier matricule du greffe*, or the records of the clerk of the court, in which the lieutenant of the lord's judge made a daily note of statements made by villagers concerning their disputes or grievances, which make it possible to grasp the event or the mood as they arose. The second was a published summary inventory,[11] and I was able to select some family law-suits from the multitude of cases in the legal documents of the Castellane bailiwick, of which Saint-André was a dependency.

All the legal texts quoted here express to varying degrees something which is very obvious. They were all occasioned or produced to bear public witness to family dissensions, to take the tensions between the members of the residence group outside the houses where they lived together. Even certain notarial documents quoted above, such as the receipts made out from the father or the widowed mother to a son leaving them, which need the presence of witnesses and the minimal degree of publicity required by notarial documents, exist to show to the village community that the conflict had left the house and that it was not an irreparable one, that agreement followed disagreement as a result of 'the good offices of mutual friends' or even by the mediation of the bishop.

The recourse to the language of legal proceedings from the drawing up of a petition with the help of the village legal practitioner or the local advocate, who mixed the currently conventional florid expression of worthy feelings and innuendoes and barbed remarks about those nearest to them who had become their enemies, to the meeting of witnesses giving their testimony as relations or neighbours, expresses an unbearable tension which could no longer be contained or released in a battle of words or a fight between those concerned. Sometimes family tensions were too much at fever pitch for the subtleties of legal language to suffice and were resolved by recourse, either premeditated or on impulse, to the gun, the bayonet, or poison.

III

Each unit of production, whether peasant or artisanal, was under the authority of the head of the family, who ruled over the members of the residence group as head of the house. Even if the children were majors (over twenty-five years of age), they had no legal power and could not negotiate, sell, deal, or make wills, being 'sons of the family', as long as they lived in the house of the father. Only emancipation gave them the status of 'free men'. On this point, Provençal law stipulated that the following conditions had to be met for the only form of 'tacit' emancipation (i.e. if the father did not give his consent): the son had to have been separated from his father for at least ten consecutive years and the father had to have 'suffered that separation'. Emancipation with the father's consent, which is still described in notarial documents to well into the eighteenth century, had to take the following form. A consul (a municipal officer) and the judge's lieutenant had to be present, with at least two witnesses. The son had to kneel, bare-headed. The father opened his hands to his son (as in the Roman act of manumission) and had to say, 'Go, my son, I make you a free man', often adding 'apart from the respect due to a father', and the son had to thank him humbly. Emancipation often coincided with the son's departure from the family home and served as a gift *inter vivos* corresponding to the share of the inheritance given by parents to a son on condition that he be 'satisfied with that gift' and 'give up any other claim on his parent's estate', or such at least was the legal precautionary measure.

The son had two alternatives. He could remain entirely subject to his father's authority, entirely dependent on him socially, economically and legally as long as he remained in the family house. Or, through emancipation and a gift from his parents, he could set up his own household and become master of his actions.[12]

In reality, the question rarely arose as a choice made by the children. It was generally the father who decided to keep a child, usually the eldest boy, beneath his roof. But the strategies for establishing children by the father were more complicated and had to take into account several factors, principally of a demographic nature, such as the total number of children, their division by sex, the age-gaps between them, unexpected deaths, the age of the father and mother, or the death of the mother and the father's remarriage. There was, however, also the question of the children's health and possible incompatibilities of temperament. These strategies of establishment were also matrimonial strategies.[13]

From the point of view of the boy's parents, there was one major principle at the basis of all domestic strategies, which was the father's desire to keep authority in his house until his old age for as long as possible, most often until his death. He was afraid of ending his days in solitude and of no longer being able to cultivate his land ('if God does not see fit to allow him to continue working', as the formularies expressed it) or to carry on his craft. These reasons seem to have been behind the provisions of family law in Provence, as was the case in most regions having a system of law based on the notion of *préciput*, or preferential legacy. Parents chose one of their children, invariably a son if there was at least one male inheritor, and most frequently the eldest, and made him 'the inheritor of the house'. He would marry and stay with his wife and children under the parental roof. The text of the contract specifies the legal and economic conditions of the common life of the two couples. The young married couple lived totally subject to the authority of the husband's father, who pocketed his daughter-in-law's dowry and supported his married children and his grandchildren, and in fact held the purse-strings. He did not emancipate his son who was to inherit, who assumed the role, well known in the villages of Provence, of the 'son of the family'. The one or two examples of the emancipation of such sons concern men in their fifties, when presumably an octogenarian father, weakened by his years, was happy to give up his power. The son who was to inherit enjoyed no degree of financial independence, as he had received no immediate gift when he married, for the *préciput* was a gift made if the parents died and simply a promise of inheritance. If the father lived to an old age, the son often had to wait a long time to take his place as head of the family. In household censuses it is not uncommon to find a father, head of the family at the age of seventy-eight, having in his house a married son who will inherit and is aged fifty, a daughter-in-law of forty-five, and several grandchildren, amongst them an eldest son aged twenty-five able to marry at the earliest on the death of his grandfather and thus become in his turn the 'son of the family'.

In order to prevent the married children living with the parents from feeling too absolutely subject to them, the marriage contracts always contained a clause making provision for the break-up of the community. It was only when this occurred that a part of the preferential gift became effective and immediate. 'In cases where the parties find each other intolerable', 'when there is mutual antagonism', as the notaries said, the marriage contract specified the total amount of the immediate gift. It was very varied with regard to the sums involved and the quality of the goods given. It is easy to guess, given the details of the gift in the text, that it had been very carefully negotiated both between father and son and between the latter's family and that of the woman going to live in her father-in-law's house. In principle, it had to be big enough to enable the young couple, if they decided to live apart from the parents, to have a house and sufficient land for an economic unit. To this would be added the wife's dowry, which the father had taken and which he would pay back to his son when they went their separate ways.

The father, however, would not want to be over-generous with the immediate gift, since if it was too advantageous for the children it would make it too easy for them to set up their own household and would encourage them to move away from their parents at the first sign of any difficulty in the relationship. Giving too large a share of his patrimony to a son leaving his house would make the father's economic position difficult. In particular, he might not be able to make another try at living with another of his children if he had given away too large a share of his means of production.

All these considerations explain why the totals involved in immediate gifts in case of a break were in practice relatively low in the contracts, often being the same as, or slightly higher than, that of the daughter-in-law's dowry. Not infrequently details were given of how the young couple were to be rehoused. This was either done by dividing up the house or by a gift of the house next door which the father had taken the precaution of buying.[14]

When there was a break-up, the notarial records generally include a document containing, under the heading of 'agreement between X the father and Y the son' (in such language, agreement nearly always implies agreement reached after disagreement), the son's receipt for goods received from his father. Unfortunately, these documents never give the reasons for the rupture.

An analysis of the structure of the extended family residence group gives some suggestion of the tensions which might arise between its members. The group consisted of the father, who was head of the family, sometimes his old mother (who could relinquish her authority more easily than a man), his wife, the mother of the young married son who would inherit, the daughter-in-law who had come with her husband to live with them. The latter was not always an outsider, and might be related to her husband, or, more frequently, come from a family related by marriage with which regular links were usually made. The lines of force of authority within the household can be shown as in the diagram.

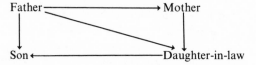

The father was invested with authority over his wife, his son, and his daughter-in-law. A seventeenth-century Provençal jurisconsult calculated the relative authority of each of them as follows: 'as it appears in the example of the son of the family, over whom his father has much more authority than the husband has over his wife'.[15] It seems likely that the son's mother would be all the more keen to exert her authority or weight over her daughter-in-law, as she might well have been in the same difficult position as the latter twenty-five years earlier. Disputes between mother-in-law and daughter-in-law have been a rich source of inspiration for a whole folk-lore, and the rules of cohabitation certainly had much to do with them. 'The wife is obliged to reside with her husband, the antipathy of the mother-in-law notwithstanding', wrote the same jurisconsult, Scipion du Perier.[16] Areas of friction were certainly encouraged by sharing out the same female roles within a house, and this cannot have made the daughter-in-law's position any easier. Given the father's authority, however, these tensions did not very often lead to a break-up. The economic importance of the daughter-in-law, who was worth a certain consideration, has to be taken into account, for the dowry she brought with her was considerable, often in ready money, and could be used to provide a dowry for two or three of the sisters of the young husband. Paying it all back would be a real catastrophe for the head of the family. A girl marrying a son who was to inherit often came from a better-off family than that of her husband. The daughter-in-law also represented the means of reproduction in the family group she had entered, and she alone could produce the third generation which would continue the line and carry the name of the father and the grandfather.[17]

In reality, this schematic way of looking at things is too simple. Often when an inheritor married, even if he married late, some of the other children were not yet established. Given the mother's long period of fertility, there might well be several younger sisters still too young for marriage or younger brothers still working at home with their parents. That was the case with well-to-do small landowners who kept all their children together both because they needed their labour and because it seemed feckless to let others feed them when they could well afford to do so themselves. All this meant that within the household the daughter-in-law had to be able to adjust to her brothers- and sisters-in-law, which was not always easy. The inheritor's sisters, for example, might well begrudge her privileged status, since she had taken a female place in their parent's house, when they were going to be obliged to leave it. The younger brothers might take offence at the preferential gift promised to their eldest brother and treat the couple badly as a result. The daughter-in-law might be worried about having to live not only with her parents-in-law but also with her husband's brothers and sisters, as was the case with a daughter of the local nobility:

Messire Pol de Chailan, seigneur of Moriez, having already foreseen that the seigneur Pierre de Chailan, his son, and the Demoiselle de Demandoulx, his daughter-in-law, that in view of the large number of children he has might find it difficult to live in his house and since the demoiselle has informed him that she had not resolved to enter his household

. . ., the father, to maintain peace amongst his children, 'emancipates his son, lets him leave the paternal château and gives him the 2400 livres promised in his marriage contract if the parties should find each other intolerable'.

Despite all these possibilities of tensions within the extended family living together, there are few cases of a break-up between parents and married children. Out of almost 500 community contracts between 1640 and 1793, there are only about forty such cases. There may be some sins of omission, and one or two documents of agreement and receipt may have slipped through amongst the notarial records, but it is clear that this kind of rupture was rare – around one case in ten – at least while the father was still alive. This does not mean that there were no tensions between father and son or disputes between mother-in-law and daughter-in-law. In the great majority of cases, however, it can be stated that the institution of family community worked well in spite of tensions that were kept from the sight of outsiders.

The notarial documents concerned with break-ups do not provide as much detailed information as one might wish. They have nothing to say about the reasons for the dissensions leading to the break-up and simply note the fact that it had occurred. 'The parties' (with no indication of whether the son or the daughter-in-law, the father or the mother are involved) 'have reached a stage of mutual antagonism', 'an intolerable situation has arisen'. The document then establishes that the goods given by the parents to the children have been receipted and that the daughter-in-law's dowry has been repaid. Nowhere in the legal records are there instances of a son not obtaining the promised goods and taking legal action against his father. In only one of the notarial documents is there a reference to the beginning of a legal action with which the son must have threatened his father in order to obtain the goods promised in his marriage contract should the community break up: 'the son wanted to take legal action to be awarded all the benefits of the gift, and such being the case the parties who would incur costs, to obviate this by the mediation of their common friends have adopted the solution of the following agreement'. The agreement was between Balthazard Chailan, a small landowner of Castelot-de-la-Robine, a little hamlet near Moriez, and his eldest son, Jean Chailan. The agreement was signed in the chateau of the lord of Moriez, who was present with the prior and parish priest of Moriez. The mediation of religious and aristocratic authority, as well as of 'common friends' was thus necessary in this case.

In the absence of other information, it is interesting to note the interval between the son's marriage and his break with his parents. The document quoted above is dated 24 August 1688. Jean Chailan had married Catherine Béraud, who came from a village a dozen kilometres away from Moriez, on 22 September 1687, less than a year before the break-up. A year later, on 12 September 1689, Balthazard Chailan married his second son, Joseph, to a girl from the same hamlet with the same name (Jeanne Chailan) although there was no near relationship. Joseph replaced Jean in the house, became the 'son of the family' who was to inherit, remained under the family roof and was fed by his parents. As he had already done two years earlier for his eldest son, the father promised an immediate gift of 300 livres if they should break up. For both material and emotional reasons, he could not resolve to live and grow old without children in the house. After the failure with his eldest son, he managed to keep his second one with him, and also, it would appear, to effect a reconciliation of his eldest with the house, for Jean Chailan was present at his younger brother's wedding in 1689.

In most cases less than two years lapsed between the date of the marriage contract, which was always drawn up and signed the day before the wedding or on the wedding day itself, and the date of the receipt marking the break-up. Sometimes it was much shorter. Bernardin Chailan, master hatter, of Saint-André, married his son Laurent, who was also a hatter, to Marianne Daumas, the daughter of a small landowner from a village a considerable distance away, on 17 July 1741. As a dowry, she brought with her 600 livres in cash and personal effects. The father promised Laurent that he would make him his heir. He fed him at home and was to give him, if they went their own ways, 600 livres, which would be less than the total value of his wife's dowry. The rupture occurred only two months later. ('After which marriage, the said Chailans, father and son, lived together in common until today, when they can no longer bear with each other and have resolved to part.') The father gave the son the promised 600 livres in personal effects and land.

In that family of artisans from Saint-André, an analysis of certain details of the structure of the residence group makes it possible to speculate on some of the reasons for the break-up. When his son married, Bernardin Chailan was a widower (he had lost his first wife, Isabeau Simon) who many years earlier had taken a second wife, Marguérite Silvestre. Marianne Daumas's mother-in-law was also her husband's stepmother. The daughter of Bernardin Chailan and Marguérite Silvestre, Geneviève Chailan, Laurent's half-sister, also lived in the house. Perhaps the presence of the stepmother and her daughter was the cause of the conflict. In addition, Laurent was Bernardin's younger son. Bernardin, the eldest son, a hatter like his father, had married, five years earlier, in 1736 at Saint-André and had set up home outside the paternal house, being able to do so as he had married an independent heiress whose parents were dead. For reasons which we do not know, Laurent left the Saint-André area after he had separated from his parents (we learn that in 1748 he had been 'absent from the kingdom for at least six years') whilst his wife remained in Saint-André. Meanwhile, the father, Bernardin Chailan, had married his daughter by his second marriage, Geneviève, to a muleteer from Saint-André in 1744. This young man was a younger son whom his mother was happy to establish in return for a gift of 1000 livres, paid in mules, silver, personal effects, and horses. Bernardin Chailan took in the young man as his son and prudently only promised his daughter 300 livres if the arrangement broke down. This is the only example encountered in Haute-Provence of a father with two living sons obliged by circumstances to take a son-in-law into his house.

As was the case in the first two examples, the break between the Honnoré Ferauds, father and son, also occurred less than two years after the marriage. The younger Honnoré Feraud had married Anne Barbaroux, of Colmars, on 3 January 1714. The father had lost his first wife, Anne Pascal. His Christian name was also Honnoré, and on the same day as his son's wedding, he married Marie Barbaroux the (elder?) sister of Anne Barbaroux. In this remarkably structured household, there is no trace of any mother-in-law/daughter-in-law tension, since the two women were sisters, and yet the household broke up on 20 December 1713, less than two years after it was set up.

These descriptions of the rupture between parents and married children should not obscure the more general rule, which was that the heir remained in the family home and subject to his father's authority until the latter died. The family community worked without the tensions arising between members of the group becoming acute enough to become public.

In pre-Revolutionary Provence the cultural model of the family was solidly based on the legal institution which protected fathers and encouraged their strategies for settling their children. The father was the head of the household and quite free to favour one child at the expense of the others by means of his will and by gifts *inter vivos*. All the skill of the father's strategies lay in his way of granting his favours (or of appearing to grant them), especially to the sons, so that everyone was happy with his decisions. As we have seen, the preferential gift to the heir, which was simply a matter of promises (since the immediate gift only came into effect when there was a separation), was a way of appearing to favour the son who was to inherit but in fact of tying him to the family house and patrimony by teaching him to wait. When a father had several sons to marry off, he had to try to strike a balance between these promises to the heir, who in compensation for them remained subject to his parents, and immediate but less considerable gifts, which nevertheless had the attraction of immediate freedom, to his other sons.

In well-to-do families one of the strategies used in settling sons, particularly if there were a lot of them, was to persuade one or more to 'embrace the ecclesiastical estate' as it was expressed at the time. When Alexandre Ravel, a muleteer of Moriez with five sons to see settled, married off his eldest in 1743, he kept him at home and promised to make him an equal heir with the second son. Of the other three, the third had already become a priest, and from the terms of the marriage contract of the eldest, it can be seen that the father was encouraging the two youngest to follow in his footsteps: 'he reserves 1200 livres each for Jean-Paul and Joseph, and if they should wish to take Holy Orders, their father will establish an ecclesiastical fund for them'. They preferred to marry. In other cases parental persuasion was more effective. In the Engelfred family, who were bourgeois of Beauvezer, four of the six sons became priests.

IV

Reconstructing horizontal genealogies makes it possible to analyse how all the children in a group of brothers were settled. This gives the impression that the father, at least as far as his sons were concerned, used the powers conferred on him by the law with moderation so as to favour the eldest. An analysis of the practices of fathers in this matter suggests a concern for fairness on their part with regard to all their sons. Eighteenth-century Haute-Provence was unlike other preferential legacy regions at the time[18] in which the eldest son kept the bulk of his parents' estate and the younger one (and even his sisters) was sacrificed, being condemned to celibacy and working for his father and then for his eldest brother. In Haute-Provence, there were no bachelors, at least until the end of the eighteenth century, the only exceptions being those unable to marry because of some physical or mental defect, and even deaf-mutes married. For young men, the only form of celibacy was that of the priesthood. (A slightly lower proportion of young women married.)

Many of the younger sons of artisan families in Saint-André particularly those with a trade, remained in their home villages and established themselves there. In the poorest families – if indeed the whole family was not forced to emigrate – younger sons had to move into the towns of lower Provence to make a living. And these young mountain people living as immigrants in Marseilles or Toulon found someone to marry. Such a one was Marguerite Blanche from Thorame-Haute in the upper Verdon valley. Working as a servant in Marseilles at the house of 'Mr Chaussefoin, merchant jeweller, of the Cannebière', she wrote to her uncle, a merchant in Thorame: 'I will tell you, my dear Uncle, that there is a good party to settle with, who is a handsome young man who is a shoemaker; begging you to send me my baptismal certificate and the death certificates of my father and mother.' The young – or perhaps no longer young – girl from the mountains managed to settle herself by means of marriage in Marseilles and, by good fortune, with 'a handsome young man'.

If we take the trouble to compare the total of the gifts made to each of his sons by the head of a family, whether it be a bourgeois of Saint-André, a shoemaker's widow of the same town, or a not very well-off small landowner from the nearby village of Courchon, all with three or four sons to see settled, it is rather surprising to find that the heir's advantage is never more than a quarter, that in the case of the Courchon small landowner the heir changed as time went on, and that the shoemaker's widow settled her two eldest sons at Saint-André in their own houses, while she lived with the third with a patrimony probably much reduced by the gifts she had made. The advantage of one quarter was later to be allowed in the Napoleonic Civil Code.

Right up to their deaths, fathers seemed anxious to treat younger sons who had left home with consideration and not to upset them. On their deathbed, in their last will, they would add a little more land or a few more beasts or sacks of grain or debts due to them to the gift that they had made long ago when their sons had left home. Such actions indicate the affection they felt for each of their sons. This anxiety to divide their goods out fairly amongst all their sons was perhaps not unconnected with the fear of the dissensions that might arise between them once the father was no longer there. 'So that there shall be neither lawsuits nor arguments, . . . has made his last will and testament', as the head of the household expressed it on his deathbed.

An analysis of the gifts would indicate that the fathers in question showed the same affection towards each of their sons, and here Provençal law worked to the same end. In an intestate inheritance, parental goods were divided up equally amongst all the sons and there was no provision for any advantage for the eldest.

V

The situation of daughters was very different. If they had a brother, they were excluded from an intestate inheritance. Daughters had to be content with the inconsiderable share of their parent's estate that the law provided for in their case. (If there were two children, a son and a daughter, the son received five-sixths and the daughter one sixth; if there were two sons and one daughter, each son received four-ninths and the daughter only one ninth.) This meagre legal provision was enough to exclude daughters from the rest of the parental estate. In practice, it was not this that excluded them, but the dowry they received when they married. It must be admitted that bearing in mind the number of children the dowry normally amounted to much more than the legal provision. A daughter who married and was 'paid' by her dowry gave up all rights to her parents' estate and had to be content with receiving a much larger sum than the law stipulated. At the same time, the son-in-law receiving the dowry also had to find it acceptable, as this would lessen the risk of a possible lawsuit to increase the legal portion. There were one or two cases where a husband made such claims on his brother-in-law during the months following his inheritance upon his father's death. These were amicably settled, to the heir's advantage, since he had no difficulty in proving that in law the sums paid to his sister as a dowry were much greater than her legal share of the estate.

Gifts to daughters, however, were less than those to younger brothers. In particular, we should not be misled by the total amount of the dowry they received. It was standard practice to give them goods of rather low value, and the gifts were described in this way in their father's wills so that what they intended for their daughters should be clear. Often a third or a quarter of the dowry consisted of 'clothes and personal effects', another third would be money paid over twenty years in 'annual instalments' and, in the best cases, a quarter or a third of the sum in ready cash. (There was a lack of ready cash amongst farmers in particular.)

As we have seen, younger sons were often treated liberally by their fathers even if they had renounced all claims to the inheritance as they had received the gift from their parents. A daughter, married and with a dowry, had been more definitively 'paid'. ('He is a careful householder with just this one son and three daughters, two of whom are married and paid and the third soon will be', as a merchant wrote in connection with marriage plans.[19]) For daughters, exclusion by means of the dowry was final. The father, in his will, simply added nothing other for his daughters than the 'five *sols*', included merely for form's sake and to avoid the risk of paralipsis (the omission of a necessary heir which would make the will invalid). As well as being excluded from inheriting from their parents, daughters were also excluded from the family house (virilocality) once they married.

Having 'only daughters' seems to have been considered by fathers as something which could be openly called a misfortune. If that happened, the father would resolve, in order to be able to continue to work his land and to avoid a lonely old age, to 'take as a son', as it was expressed, the husband of one of his daughters and to take his son-in-law, who bore another name, into his own house.

On 7 August 1748 Honnoré Reboul, who worked his own land at Courchon and was the father of three daughters, married one of them, Jeanne, to Jacques Noé, who worked his land at Moriez. He made Jeanne his sole heir, took his son-in-law into his house as his own son, to be subject to him. He did, however, take the precaution of adding to the marriage contract a codicil to the effect that 'should the said Reboul and his wife have a male child, the said heirship of the aforementioned Jeanne Reboul shall be null and void'. Aging parents marrying off their daughters still kept the fanciful hope that there would be a child, and a male one at that, who would enable them to reject their son-in-law and to exclude their daughter from inheriting the house and land. Such tactics would not make the lot of the son-in-law an easy one. He was subject to a man who was not his father, a father-in-law who was sometimes not much older than he was himself. (It should be remembered that the parents would not have made the daughter their heir until they were fairly sure that they would not have any more children, and neither the younger son who became their son-in-law nor his wife would be young any more.) In such cases, the balance between members of the community was more unstable than it was when it was the son who was the heir. The authority of the father-in-law over the son-in-law, as we have seen, was probably difficult to tolerate, and the two women involved were mother and daughter. The daughter, who had the status of an heiress, could score over her husband by virtue of that fact.

In practice, examples of communities in which the son-in-law was subject to the father-in-law were infrequent. It appears that such a situation was not attractive to unmarried younger brothers, who preferred to wait for an heiress whose father was dead. In such cases, it was easier to be a son-in-law, as the mother-in-law readily abandoned her authority, and the young man was thus head of the family. If this did not happen, living together presented too many problems. That is what happened in the Reboul–Noé community. On 7 July 1750, less than two years after the marriage, the situation was declared intolerable in the usual way. Honnoré Reboul gave back to his son-in-law and daughter, who were leaving him, the 300 livres promised to her and the personal effects that Jacques Noé had brought to his father-in-law's house.

There are not enough community contracts between father-in-law and son-in-law for us to be able to say how well this type of union worked, on the basis of the very few receipts and agreements signed before notaries. There are cases of sons-in-law waiting patiently for ten or twenty years for a father-in-law to die so that they could take over as head of the family, as respectful 'sons of the family' did, without any external sign of dissension appearing. To find signs of disagreement in such cases, it is no longer enough to consult notarial documents. We need to examine judicial sources, for such disagreements often had something of real dramas about them and traces of them are to be found in criminal proceedings. Here are three of these serious matters.

The first took place at Saint-André. On 27 November 1760 Pierre Rolland, a master mason of Saint-André, married Brigitte Dol, the only daughter and sole heir of Pierre Dol, who had died much earlier. Pierre Rolland had been a younger brother, whose eldest brother, Antoine, had stayed on in the parental home, subject to his widowed mother. Pierre Rolland was installed as son-in-law in his wife's house in the *Careironne*, or little street, which she had inherited from her father. At the time the marriage took place, however, it was occupied by Brigitte's mother, Marie Guiou, and her second husband, Grégoire Gibert, a master tailor. It was unusual for a widowed mother to remarry before her dependent children had been settled. Marie Guiou had done so, however, twelve years earlier in June 1749, fifteen years after her first marriage with Pierre Dol in 1734. It may be that as she was a busy midwife in the town she enjoyed both economic and statutory independence. Like Pierre Rolland, Grégoire Gibert was a younger son seeking an establishment outside the paternal home. His brother Antoine had stayed there as 'son of the family', marrying, remarkably, Geneviève Guiou, Marie's sister, ten years before Grégoire's marriage. Another brother, Jean-Baptiste Gibert, a muleteer like his father and eldest brother, was living as son-in-law in the house of another Rolland, a cousin of Pierre, who was a mason.

When Grégoire Gibert's stepdaughter married he was therefore the head of the household, but in a house that belonged neither to him nor to the mother. The bridegroom entered as a son-in-law, but subject to a younger brother who was not his inheriting wife's father but her stepfather. Perhaps Marie Guiou, as the official leading lady of the little town, had a large share of the authority in the house with these two younger sons. A daughter, Marie-Rosalie Rolland, was born in October 1761 and died, aged eighteen months, in April 1763.

On 29 July 1763, Grégoire Gibert was murdered. He was shot in the lower abdomen at 7 a.m. on the main road from Saint-André to the nearby village of La

Mure. Statements from witnesses confirmed that Pierre Rolland, the son-in-law, was the murderer. A neighbour, Joseph Dol, who lived next door to Brigitte Dol, stated that he had met:

at dawn, Marie Guiou and Brigitte Dol, the mother-in-law and wife of the said Rolland; the two women had begged him not to let Pierre Rolland go out. They had left him locked in the room at the side of the hall, and he was trying to get out. He broke the latch and escaped from the room.[20]

Another witness to the drama, a seventeen-year-old girl, said that 'Gibert and Rolland were enemies'. Pierre Rolland managed to escape from Saint-André. Less than a month later, his wife Brigitte Dol had a son christened Pierre-Jacques Rolland. The priest noted discreetly on the birth certificate that 'the father has been unable to sign because of his absence'.

The second affair was very different. Here we no longer have the dispassionate observation of an impulsive shooting but a lengthy legal proceeding by a husband against his wife, charging her with attempting to kill him. The sources are different too: the plaintiff's petition and calling of his witnesses and the legal judgement. They must therefore be read in a different way, with interpretations, as in discourse analysis, taking greater place than observed facts. Analogies in the structure of the network of relations by marriage and in the make-up of the residence group, however, provide a link between the two cases, for in both the husband had married an heiress.

Joseph Reboul, who worked his land at Courchon, married Marguerite Brun, also of Courchon, on 20 November 1738. He had two elder brothers also living in the village. Antoine, the eldest, who had married about 1727, remained at home living with his parents as their heir. The community broke up in October 1730: 'the father, Jean Reboul, desiring to leave his son Antoine in peace with his other children and prevent all the possibilities of interest causing discord amongst brothers, as must be the chief desire of a father towards his children . . . pays to him the 600 livres promised should the community break up'. As Balthazar Chailan had done (see above, p. 154), Jean Reboul married off his second son the year after the break-up and kept him under his authority to replace the eldest. He promised that he would have half the inheritance to share with the third son, Joseph. Marguerite Brun was seventeen when she married Joseph Reboul. She was the only child of Alexandre Brun and Marguerite Ravel. Her parents had only been married for eighteen years (1721), but when their daughter married in 1738, it seems to have been impossible for her mother to have more children, since the girl was described in her marriage contract as the 'only daughter and sole heir'. It should be noted that the mother, Marguerite Ravel, the daughter of a well-to-do small landowner of Courchon, was herself the only daughter and heir of her parents, and that her husband, Alexandre Brun, the younger son of a small landowner of a neighbouring village, went to live as son-in-law with his wife's parents at Courchon, as his own son-in-law was to do in the next generation.

As an heiress and the daughter of an heiress, Marguerite Brun was likely to appear a good match to a younger son in Courchon. She had expectations of an inheritance of 2000 livres in land which would go to her husband and their children. The household which Joseph Reboul entered as a son-in-law was exceptional in that the mother and daughter were (or had been) heirs, whilst the men, the sons-in-law, had only brought into the community possessions representing a quarter or a third of those of their respective wives. This would almost certainly lead to some distortion of the relative forces in operation.

It was, not until 1749, eleven years after the marriage, that Joseph Reboul instituted proceedings against his wife. It would appear from the wording of the first petition that marital differences had begun much earlier. The marriage contract had provided for a two-generation community life in the house of the Brun parents. A document ending this could have been drawn up after two years, the normal period in such cases, if the young couple had wished to leave amiably, given the reluctance of parents-in-law to sign it. The petition notes that the young woman had fled her husband and returned to her parent's house:

the first three or four years the petitioner [the husband] spent living as best he could, bearing with his wife with the greatest possible difficulty. But, after those first years, Marguerite Brun, being unable any longer to hide her ill-feelings towards the petitioner, decided to leave him and to withdraw to her father's house, where she found rather too easy an asylum instead of a good father who would have corrected his daughter appropriately. For some 6 or 7 years that woman has been living as she pleases, separated from her husband and hence in breach of her duty.[21]

Joseph Reboul was thus living either alone or with one of his married brothers (the father having died shortly before the trial took place) in the same quarter as the Brun house, where Marguerite was living.

Joseph Reboul later told in his petition how his wife had tried to do away with him. With a cousin on her father's side, a man named Brun from Vergons who was in their domestic service providing male labour in place of that of the husband, she surprised her husband in his own house and wounded him herself twice with a bayonet. She later persuaded a local surgeon to obtain poison for her. (This was later confirmed in the surgeon's deposition.) The petition finished as follows: 'so that the petitioner was maliciously exposed to the risk of death at the hands of that woman, either by cold steel, by fire, or by poison, and there is no doubt that her father and mother are filled with such a desire'.

There was a remarkable inversion of roles shown in the trial (such as in carnival). In most cases of marital disputes it was the wife, beaten and injured by a drunken husband, who was the victim. Here, amongst those heiresses, it was the man who was weak and abused. Joseph Reboul was perhaps a weakling 'living as best he could'. According to Alexandre Ravel, aged thirty-two, the first cousin of both the husband and the wife, Marguerite seemed to accuse her husband of a lack of virility: 'you are a dead thing. If you had been a man, you would have shown it. Come here, I am not suffering from the plague.' At the time of the trial, the couple was childless, although it is not possible to say categorically that none had been born and subsequently died.

As was normal, but without it being in the foreground of the quarrel, the question of the heiress's possessions was brought forward. Marguerite Brun had been heard saying to her husband, 'You thought that you would have the possessions, but they are for him', pointing to her cousin, Jacques Brun, who was in service with her parents.

A study of the statements made by witnesses and of their identity is interesting for two reasons. In the first place, discourse analysis enables us to see how the inhabitants of a small village saw domestic arguments of this kind. Secondly, and in particular, the identity of the witnesses produced by the petitioner, Joseph Reboul, offers the opportunity of reconstituting a network of kinship and relations by marriage between them, the plaintiff, and the defendant. It is also a neighbourhood network, since in Haute-Provence related families – those originating from a common ancestor – tend to live in the same area.

As a result of the interplay of alliances by marriage one of the witnesses, Pierre Ravel, a small landowner aged seventy, was a first cousin of the mother of Marguerite Brun, Marguerite Ravel, whilst his wife, Marguerite Reboul, was the aunt of her husband, Joseph Reboul. This no doubt placed this witness, called by his wife's nephew as a prosecution witness against his own niece, in a very difficult position. He resolved his dilemma by insisting primarily on his role as a peacemaker. After the incident of the bayonet wounds, 'he summoned his niece and rebuked her soundly and severely for the terrible thing she had done', and later added that Jean-Baptiste Reboul, the husband's brother, 'had ill used his sister-in-law, Marguerite, who came to see her husband'. But no testimony directly contradicted the husband.

The judge decreed that the two women should be arrested, and despite Marguerite Ravel's infirmities they were imprisoned in Castellane. (With regard to the mother, the court proceedings noted that 'this woman is so crippled and unsteady on her legs that she can scarcely move'.) Thus the appropriate male order was reestablished in Courchon in 1750 by the imprisonment of the two women.

In the third family affair in which the husband took up residence as a son-in-law to be reported here it was the wife who accused her husband and submitted a petition. On 26 September 1710, Jean-Baptiste Reboul,[22] aged thirty, bourgeois of Castellane, the small town which was the capital of the bailiwick of which Saint-André and Courchon were dependencies, married Marie Martiny, only daughter and heiress of the seigneur Joseph Martiny, also a bourgeois of Castellane, and the Demoiselle Catherine Arnaud. The notarial contract stipulated that J. B. Reboul was to enter the house as a son-in-law and that the parents-in-law were to feed him. He brought into the community certain personal possessions, notably some lands given by his mother, Marguerite de Villeneuve, the illegitimate daughter of a great Provençal nobleman, the widow of Jean-Baptiste's father who had later married another bourgeois of Castellane. The Martiny parents promised, should the arrangement come to an end, to give their daughter some of their lands as a dowry as well as a floor of their house in Castellane. Within two years of the marriage, Marie Martiny had instituted criminal proceedings against her husband. In her petition she accused him of ill-treating her, even while she was pregnant. A daughter was born in 1711.

When she was questioned, the husband denied the charges and declared:

that the charge had only been brought on the instigation of Joseph Martiny and the Demoiselle Arnaud, the mother, because the said Reboul had often requested them to lease him an apartment in their house, as they had promised to do, to live there with his wife and family, and to be able to attend to his affairs and the maintenance of the goods which they had promised him in his marriage contract.

A desire for independence on the part of the young son-in-law wishing to set up his own household, disagreement between husband and wife, and a reluctance on the part of the parents-in-law to meet this no doubt harsh demand, their reluctance was no doubt increasing by the circumstances: 'even if only in connection with the infirmity of Marie Martigny, who is afflicted with loss of sight'. Joseph Martiny's heiress was blind.

Jean-Baptiste Reboul was perhaps not a very praiseworthy man. He had been to some extent abandoned by his father, the son of a notary, who became an advocate and settled at Castellane. He was ambitious, and had married the illegitimate daughter of the Marquis de Villeneuve. He later regretted this and took proceedings against his wife for 'the premature birth of a boy child' who was none other than Jean-Baptiste Reboul, the husband of Marie Martiny. The sources do not say what the verdict was in this case.

These serious dissensions were special matters involving violence or crimes and setting the son-in-law and his relations by marriage against each other. It is the only household structure in Haute-Provence in which one can point to an open, public conflict dividing two generations of the community family with the father, in his lifetime, supported by his daughter and heiress against a son-in-law and husband. In the legal records of the area in the eighteenth century, there is, on the other hand, no trace of proceedings between a father and his sons. While the father was still alive, these conflicts seemed to stay within the family, contained within the calming limits of agreements drawn up before a notary after a friendly decision to break up the residential and economic commonality in which parents and children lived.

VI

What happened after the death of the father? It seems that his presence, even when he was very old, and the respect due to him sufficiently and effectively contained the passions in play and kept the conflicts within the recognized bounds of friendly agreements, however violent they were. An analysis of certain expressions used in the language of lawyers or notaries supports this. In their documents, the father appears as the guarantor of proper understanding between the members of the family group of brothers and sisters and brothers-in-law and sisters-in-law and the moral warranty of respectful and reasonable behaviour on the part of his sons.

In a case heard in 1749, in which the wife, Marie Berneaud, asked for the separation of her property from that of her husband, J. B. Sigaud, one witness declared: 'since the death of his father, Jean Sigaud, J. B. Sigaud has grown lax in his affairs. At that time he began to frequent the inn and to neglect his property.'[23] The father's death sometimes led to debauchery, or more frequently to the unbridled play of high feelings between collaterals, between brothers in particular, but even between husband and wife. Such feelings had previously often been held in check merely by the presence of the father. On 15 July 1719 Claude Simon, a notary, of Saint-André, whose old father Bernardin Simon, the former lieutenant of the judge, was still alive, had the following declaration taken down by the other notary in the town: 'I, the undersigned, declare that I hereby abandon the petition and proceedings taken out by me against my brother, Jean-Baptiste Simon, for the sake of the love, fear, and respect I bear my father and my brother.' The quarrel must have been a serious one, since a few years later J. B. Simon left Saint-André for good, having sold up all the property coming to him from his parents, but that was after his father had died.

Quarrels between collaterals also broke out after the father's death because when parents died questions of inheritance, division, and hence of material reasons for dissension were opened up. Certain individuals did not feel the same respect for their parents as Claude Simon.

Anne Mandine, the daughter of Jean Mandine, a notary of Le Fugeret and the widow of a notary in a neighbouring village, returned to her father's village where she owned some land. In 1707 she started proceedings against her brother, Louis Mandine, who had succeeded her father: 'for a long time she has been driven beyond endurance, beaten, insulted, and ill-treated by her brother . . . all this she had been resolved to tolerate from respect for him as her brother and out of consideration for their father, Maître Jean Mandine, who is still living'.[24]

The language of dissension between brother and sister is full of the same violence as that only too common between husband and wife. In 1759 Jacques Martel, a mason, of Saint-André, and a cousin of Pierre Rolland, who had murdered his father-in-law,

taking advantage of the absence of his sister's husband, Jacques Martel entered her house, accused her of material wrongs ['she had changed his linen'], called her 'bougresse' and 'garce', threatened to kill her, said that he wanted to quarter her in public, then gave her several blows on the head and face and made all her face bleed . . . hatred of brother for sister, held in check for many years and finally erupting in the man of over forty whose parents had been dead for many years.[25]

More frequently, conflicts between collaterals broke out immediately after the father's death. Joseph and Jean-Jacques Fabre, two of the six sons of Jean Fabre, a wealthy merchant draper of Saint-André, were the only ones to remain in the paternal home, sole joint heirs when the father died in 1752. ('The house of Jean-Jacques Fabre wherein lived Joseph Fabre in community, as in the paternal home.') As the elder of the two, and a married man, Jean-Jacques was the real head of the family, the younger one, Joseph, still being a bachelor. Some months after the death of the father, their communal life was prey to many difficulties. 'One or two differences of opinion on the division of property in connection with their inheritance from their father' led them to exchange blows, and here Jean-Jacques's wife had a part to play. Proceedings were started by both, each accused the other of bodily harm and of intent to kill ('the devil possessed me', said Joseph). But, as a result of the mediation of mutual friends and the intervention of the bishop (two of Marie Bernard's brothers were priests), drama was avoided. In July 1753, the two brothers signed before a notary an agreement on the division of property from their parents. The notary was instructed to write that 'the two brothers wishing to live in peace no longer wish to proceed with all the information they have laid against each other, even Marie Bernard, the wife of the said Jean-Jacques'.

This example taken from amongst others illustrates how hard it was for several collaterals to go on living together in the father's house once he was dead. With or without a quarrel, brothers separated after the father's death (as had more often than not been provided for in the father's will) often dividing up the possessions, particularly the dwelling-house. Just as vertical communities were the rule in Haute-Provence, brothers living together (*frèrèches*) were exceptional and short-lived occurrences.

The division of property between brothers was not always successful in avoiding quarrels between them, particularly if it meant dividing a single but shared possession such as a house (most often divided vertically) or a farmhouse with lands worked by a single holder. This was the case with the Bérard family, who were merchants in Castellane. The Sieurs Honnoré and Mathieu Bérard, who were father and son,[26] instituted proceedings against a different Sieur Mathieu Bérard, who was the brother of Honnoré and the uncle of Mathieu. Father and son declared their petition:

'since sharing a farmhouse and its dependencies with Sieur Mathieu Bérard left to them by their joint father, Sieur André Bérard, near Castellane, his brother has continually provoked him and his family. One of the two brothers is sixty-five years of age, the other seventy-four.' Their hatred was passed on to their descendants, two generations later. 'It would be hard to imagine that a brother could be capable of such views and of passing them on to his children.' They were even passed on to his grandchildren; second cousins would meet in the inn and exchange insults.

Examples of hatred exist between first cousins in the same village, between uncle and nephew both amongst the Saint-André artisans and the noble lords of the village of Moriez, when the estate had been shared out amongst brothers or cousins. There were arguments or fights between cousins on the male side and also between their wives and children when they came out of church.

The father, as head of the family, often made his wife his sole heir or at least the guardian of his children while they were still dependents, on one express condition: that she should remain a widow and not remarry. That was the only phase in the family cycle in which the wife had important responsibilities and carried out the functions of the omnipotent head of the family. But of several, chiefly cultural, reasons – such as the reluctance of men to deal with women, the fact that the latter were rarely literate, in short, largely from 'male chauvinism' – when a mother emancipated her son, the notary ascribed her ability to do so to her '*paternal*' power. The authority her widowhood conferred on her could only be used with difficulty, and a study of the community contracts between a widowed mother and a son who inherited and remained in the paternal house shows clearly that the former was glad to give up that authority when her son married, whilst fathers, as we have seen, never did so. A mother with daughters but no sons wanting to have a man in the house did not hesitate to hand over her authority to her son-in-law, even if it meant regretting it later. Criminal proceedings in which mother and daughter complain of the ill-treatment accorded to them by such a son-in-law are by no means unusual. Marguerite Bourgarel[27] declared in the town clerk's office at Castellane in May 1773 that:

Marguerite Bourgarel, widow of Jean Bourgarel, labourer of La Garde, declares that having married her only daughter, Anne Bourgarel, to Joseph Mistral, a tailor of Vergons, they lived together for a year, during which time the aforesaid Mistral, the petitioner's son-in-law, never let slip a chance of ill-treating her, either by offensive words or by blows, so that she has been obliged to leave her daughter and son-in-law.

Four years later, the daughter, Anne Bourgarel, obtained a separation of property[28] from her husband ('he uses debauched practices and ill-treatment towards his wife').

The widowed mother sometimes even had to endure violence from her own children, something which the father had never suffered. Bearing in mind that the total number of contracts was low, it seems that relatively speaking mutual intolerance was more frequent in the case of widowed mothers and their married sons than was the case while the father was alive. Sometimes, a mother would have to start proceedings against one of her own sons.

This is shown in the petition of the Demoiselle Honorade de Périer, the widow of Sieur Antoine de Bon, lord of Allons, which is dated 1686.[29] In it she declared:

that her son, Jean-Baptiste de Bon, lord of Allons, had lost the respect that was properly due to her after the death of his aforesaid father and had conceived such a hatred of her that he sought all kinds of opportunities to insult her and treat her harshly, which manner of behaviour had convinced the petitioner that her son wished her to make a gift of the property she held.

The gift did not put the rebel son in any better frame of mind. He gathered up the whole band, his children and their tutor, and set fire to the stores of hay on his mother's farm. This mother/son conflict was admittedly not without an admixture of jealousy of his brother, Pierre de Bon, who stayed at his mother's side.

VII

The balance in the relative forces at work in households in Haute-Provence had little room for male subjection to women, whether it was a case of a son and a mother, a husband and wife, or a son-in-law and a mother-in-law. There was sometimes very serious tension between men, as the hatred between brothers that we have seen clearly shows. The relationship of forces between men needed, if it was to remain in equilibrium, the authority conferred by age and the hierarchical dependence of the younger generation on the older, and authority was all the more easily recognized when it was exerted by an older person. In the villages of Haute-Provence there was a kind of love of gerontocracy and a cult of older men, who were generically called 'uncle', as if the cult had to have a genealogical basis.

The basis of the authority of fathers, grandfathers, or uncles in the seventeenth and eighteenth centuries was legal, institutional, and cultural. It was supported by the Church, whose priests led their flocks 'like good fathers', by the nobility, where the lord was said to be the 'father' of his 'vassals', the people under his jurisdiction, and by the state, where the king was seen as a father to all his subjects.

In the Revolutionary period, the reform of the family as a legal institution aimed at achieving universal liberty, and in particular liberty between men and women, and at breaking up larger holdings of land. It tried to shake paternal authority where it was strongest, namely in those provinces where a 'preferential legacy' law was in force. In particular, the law of 17 nivose of year 2 (6 January 1794) made gifts illegal and applied retrospectively to past gifts connected with an inheritance.

What was the effect of these laws in Haute-Provence? A search through the notarial registers of Revolutionary times in Saint-André clearly shows that, as in most other provinces of the kind, peasants and notaries adapted their practices to them very rapidly in order to safeguard their ancestral habits. There were no more marriage contracts, no more wills, and no more gifts. The division of patrimonies between brothers and sisters was rare, and the latter gave up with great ease any claim to their share of the land in return for a cash settlement. They waited patiently, and a few years later the rigour of the Revolutionary laws was softened by amendments. The result was that from 1798 the form of the old documents was in use once more, including gifts and the institution of the son and heir living in the paternal household.

The institution of having a 'son of the family' as heir was too ancient and too essential to the traditional economy of small peasant landowners to yield to a change in the law, and practices were stronger than legal innovations. The peasants of Haute-Provence resisted pressure from the family provisions of the Civil Code which, it is true, were weaker than those of the Revolutionary laws. Henri Baudrillart, studying the contemporary agricultural population of France[30] at the end of the nineteenth century wrote as follows about inheritance practices in the *département* of the Basses-Alpes now that of the Alpes-de-Haute-Provence:

in the *arrondissement* of Castellane and the upper parts of those of Digne and Sisteron, the father joins with one of his sons and heirs and disposes in his favour all the parts of the estate that he can dispose of at will, increased if need be by pretence and low valuations. Such an heir is commonly called 'the support of the family'.

Paternal authority managed to absorb changes in the law, just as it had managed to resist tensions within the community family group.

NOTES

1 I should particularly like to thank David Sabean for his kindness in re-reading this text in such a friendly and perspicacious way.

2 Peter Laslett, 'Introduction', in Peter Laslett (ed.), *Household and Family in Past Time* (Cambridge, 1972).

3 Lutz K. Berkner, 'The Stem Family and the Development Cycle of the Peasant Household: An Eighteenth Century Austrian Example', *American Historical Review*, 77 (1972), 398–417.

4 Alain Collomp, 'Famille nucléaire et famille élargie en Haute-Provence au 18e siècle', *Annales ESC*, 27 (1972), 969–76.

5 Alain Collomp, 'Alliance et filiation en Haute-Provence au 18e siècle', *Annales ESC*, 32 (1977), 445–77.

6 Alain Collomp, 'Maison, manières d'habiter et famille en Haute-Provence aux XVIIe et XVIIIe siècles', *Ethnologie française*, 8 (1978), 301–20.

7 Jack Goody, 'Introduction', in Jack Goody, *et al.* (eds.), *Family and Inheritance: Rural Society in Western Europe, 1200–1800* (Cambridge, 1976), 3.

8 On these matters see, Nicole Castan, 'La Criminalité familiale dans le ressort du Parlement de Toulouse (1690–1730)', in *Crime et criminalité en France, 17e–18e siècles*, Cahier des Annales, vol. 33 (Paris, 1971), 91–107; Yves Castan, *Honnêteté et relations sociales en Languedoc, 1715–1780* (Paris, 1974); Arlette Farge et André Zysberg, 'Les Théâtres de la violence à Paris au 18e siècle', *Annales ESC*, 34 (1979), 984–1015; Elisabeth Claverie, 'L'Honneur en Gévaudan: une société de défis au 19e siècle', *Annales ESC*, 34 (1979), 744–59.

9 Julian Pitt-Rivers, *People of the Sierra* (Chicago, 1961).

10 Archives Départementales Alpes-de-Haute-Provence (abbr. ADAHP), B 1426–B 1434.

11 Marie Zépherin Isnard, *Inventaire sommaire, archives civiles*, series B, vol. 1 (Digne, 1892).

12 Cf. Collomp, 'Alliance et filiation'; Pierre Lamaison, 'Les Stratégies matrimoniales dans un système complexe de parenté', *Annales ESC*, 34 (1979), 744–59.

13 I have been unable to find any household censuses for the Saint-André area. There is, however, a major series in the departmental archives of the Alpes-Maritimes for the neighbouring valley of the Var.

14 See Collomp, 'Maison, manières d'habiter'.
15 Scipion du Perier, *Oeuvres* (1701), vol. 1.
16 *Ibid.*
17 On the problem of names, see my forthcoming article in *L'Homme*, 'Les Noms gardés, la dénomination personelle (nom, prénom, sobriquet) en Haute-Provence aux 17e et 18e siècles'.
18 Castan, *Honnêteté*.
19 ADAHP, 1 E Supp. Boyer.
20 ADAHP, B 1427
21 ADAHP, B 1221. It is possible to make a comparison, at least from the point of view, in both cases, of the wife's refusal to live in the husband's home, with the famous case, *I, Pierre Revière, Having Slaughtered My Mother, My Sister, and My Brother . . . A case of Parricide in the 19th Century*, edited by Michel Foucault (New York, 1975). See p. 58: 'after the marriage my mother stayed on with her parents at Courvaudon'; also p. 60: after the birth of the two children, 'my mother too said she wanted to return to her place and that she would live at Aunay no longer . . . She then returned to her parents, and my father took her back her furniture, he took some of it by night because people laughed at him.'
22 ADAHP, B 1186.
23 ADAHP, B 1107, Séparation de Biens.
24 ADAHP, B 1340.
25 ADAHP, B 1433.
26 ADAHP, B 1218.
27 ADAHP, B 2893.
28 ADAHP, B 1107.
29 ADAHP, B 1162.
30 Henri Baudrillart, *Les Populations agricoles de la France*, vol. 3 (Paris, 1893), 193.

7. Young bees in an empty hive: relations between brothers-in-law in a South German village around 1800

DAVID WARREN SABEAN

I

It is a commonplace that family relationships in peasant society are dominated by considerations of property. The theme of struggle between father and son over the farm is central to the peasant novel, and middle-class observers have shaken their heads for generations over the crassness with which the sons of farm owners and farm tenants have matched field with field and acre with acre in courting their neighbors' daughters. Property as the dominant category for peasant society explains, however, at once too much and too little. It is too large a concept because it crowds out of consideration all the other needs which were and are fulfilled in daily rural life, and it reduces relationships to only one aspect of one element of those relationships. Property in this way tends to be regarded as an inert thing, as a measure which expresses everything else in terms of its essential objectivity – as interest, manipulation, calculation, at once devoid of love, joy, and sensuality. On the other hand, the concept of property explains too little because of an analytical poverty in its use, a failure to grasp the complex character of its role in the mediation of relations between people.[1] To recover a notion of property as mediation, it is necessary to grasp it within a system of claims and rights exercised between people over things. Just as there is no such thing as a pure unmediated emotional attachment between individuals, so there is no system of obligations and duties which is not mediated through a structured set of things – namely property. The way that property is held gives shape to feelings between family members, territorializes emotion, establishes goals and ambitions, and gives to each a sense of dependence and independence.[2]

The initial problem for the historian is to delineate how property gives shape to the range of relationships: to find out where conflict is endemic, to establish where help is forthcoming for the individual, to understand the forces which throw people together, to locate the limits of attachment between people. One must be careful here not to reintroduce a reified notion of property, where all relationships are derived from fundamental ones of property. Rather, we are looking for the rules of exchange, the patterns of negotiation, the areas of disagreement – the way people bend and shape and redefine relationships between each other in common activity regarding things. The problem is to see how, for example, in a society where a married woman receives food from her husband but medical care from her brother, the set of exchanges is ordered in contrast to a society where the husband is expected to provide both.

There are five aspects of property relations that act as guiding principles in the analysis which follows. 1) Property has a durable quality, giving a time dimension to relations patterned upon it. Not just the moment in time is important, but expectations and claims based on future performances also structure present relationships. The constant discussion that often goes on in peasant society about future inheritance is one example of this principle. 2) Property often involves multiple claims, a complex overlayering of rights. One must carefully distinguish power from claims here. A father may for example have the power to disinherit a child, but until that step is taken the claims, obligations, demands, and threats that father and child make vis-à-vis each other define the situation in which they act. A large part of the rights around property are subject to constant negotiation and consequent readjustment of the context of family relations. Claims are divisible and the same object can be subject to different and sometimes conflicting rights. 3) Exchanges between family members and within the larger kinship group make up a much larger system of exchange, of which property relationships form only a part. The fact of rights joining people in a family estate will pattern exchanges on quite different levels – visiting, gift-giving, borrowing, lending, mutual aid in work, sharing meals. Claims met on one level may be reinforced by exchanges on another. 4) Property holding establishes demarcations in a society. Through various strategies regarding property, favoritism is exercised, lines of fission established, certain claimants or potential claimants excluded. The differences established with regard to property between family members, within the kinship group, or between families may be bridged or not according to certain rules – through the exchange of women, through the exercise of domination, through competition or systematic conflict, or through active avoidance. 5) The nature of the property in question – its material basis – also has implications for the patterning of family relations. The inheritance of land means something quite different from the claim to an education. An analysis of the different forms of property would take the argument here in a radically different direction, but in this chapter the concern has largely to do with rights in land where the dynamics of family relations are not yet shaped by the modern form of property, namely commodities.

II

In the following discussion, the relationships between brothers-in-law in a South German village at the turn of the nineteenth century will be examined.[3] During the period *c.* 1760 to 1820, this connection was a central one for the interplay between families and played a central role both for mutual aid and for the sorting out of conflicting claims in the transmission of wealth and resources between generations. That the relationship between brothers-in-law became the focal point of much family emotion is closely related to the facts of intensive, small peasant production and to the system of partible inheritance which made sisters and brothers equal in the inheritance of movable and immovable property. To a large extent, access to land was through family politics, and the issue for many villagers was to get their hands on any land whatsoever, however heavily laden with debts. The interplay between property and family relationships in the village under consideration here (Neckarhausen, District Nürtingen) is best examined by looking at the detail of several cases. To some degree the material provides a distorting lens because most of what is available has to do with disputed rights rather than with mutual aid and cooperation. Nonetheless, if the center of interest lies in the nature of what is negotiable, of claim and counter-claim, of obligations fulfilled or neglected, then the sources offer a balanced account of everyday family relations.

1) The first case involves Johann Georg Riempp, senior, who was married to the widow of Caspar Hentzler, Anna Maria née Falter. Upon her death in January 1808, an inventory of the family property was made, setting out a description of various claims to the inheritance. As usual, the inventory detailed the nature and amount of property which each spouse brought to the marriage or inherited while married to each other, with the increase or decrease (*Errung-enschaft*) split in half and apportioned to each partner. The property of the deceased was then given to the heirs according to the rules of intestate inheritance. In this case, the claimants were the children of Anna Maria by her first husband, Caspar Hentzler, senior, her second husband, Johann Georg Riempp, and the children of her second marriage. The peculiar fascination of this inventory lies in the fact that the couple had managed to go through a property of 5000 fl. (Gulden) (one of the largest fortunes I have yet discovered in the village), ending up with a deficit of *c.* 30 fl. In the document itself, there is no explanation as to how this feat was accomplished, but because of a disputed claim to 200 fl., an exchange of comments by officials was appended, which begins to throw light on a number of family struggles. The wife, Anna Maria Riempp, had had four children in her first marriage who survived to adulthood. A son, Caspar Hentzler, junior, however, died a bachelor, leaving an inheritance for his three sisters (Margaretha, Anna Maria, and Anna Catharina) and his mother. This inheritance was taken over by the mother in usufruct for her lifetime, establishing and maintaining a common interest among the three daughters and their respective spouses in how the property was to be used. As usual, the struggle around the property involved men, even though the transmission rights were through women. Men, who otherwise might have had nothing to do with each other, were brought together over a more or less long period of time by common interest exercised by claims over the same property. In

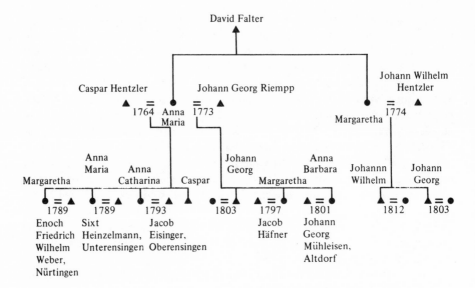

this case the three brothers-in-law came from different localities and exercised different professions, their only connection being through their wives.

The story begins a little earlier. A letter from *Schultheiss* (the village mayor) Hiller in 1807 described the marriage between Johann Georg Riempp and Anna Maria as one of conflict from the beginning. Because of 'troubles at home', he began to drink heavily and follow a 'life of dissipation'. Fearing for a fall in the family estate, and to protect the children of the earlier marriage, his wife went to court to have the property inventoried. The children were put under a guardian and Riempp himself came under the power of an 'administrator'. As each of the daughters married, they received their share of their father's inheritance. In addition, when Caspar Hentzler, junior, died unmarried, he left among other things a quarter of a house to be inherited by his three sisters and mother. Because the house and other property remained in the hands of parents – in usufruct – this inheritance seemed very insecure to the three brothers-in-law (Wilhelm Weber, Sixt Heinzelmann, Jacob Eisinger), and in any event, it was not available at the time for them to use. Since none of them lived in Neckarhausen, it was even harder for them to watch out for their own interests. Wilhelm Weber, married to Margaretha, took the lead in bringing suit before the village court to prevent the mismanagement of the property by Riempp. When subsequently Riempp quite illegally sold some of the land, Weber in vain marshalled the two other brothers-in-law to have the court sell the remaining property and distribute the proceeds to the heirs. Weber then hatched the scheme that eventually got him into trouble. He convinced Heinzelmann and Eisinger to go with him secretly to the *Schultheiss* in Neckarhausen and have the remaining house mortgaged without obtaining the consent of the other heir, namely the mother-in-law. With the mortgage money, Weber then purchased a house for himself and his wife in Nürtingen. This illegal transaction was discovered a few years later when the mortgage records were administratively revised, which led to the financial failure of Weber and the forced sale of his house in Nürtingen. The common interest then of three men from three different localities in the expectation of a single property was maintained over the period *c.* 1789 to 1808. The high point of combined action was 1798 when the illegal mortgage took place with the restructuring of obligation to Weber vis-à-vis Heinzelmann and Eisinger. The crumbling of concerted action against the father-in-law began with the discovery of the illegal transaction during the revision of the mortgage records. In this affair, the role of the mother seems to have shifted somewhat. Earlier in the marriage, in conflict with her husband, she took steps to insure the rights of the children from her previous marriage. The illegal transaction of 1798 in one version gives her as acting in concert with the three brothers-in-law, and in another as not knowing what was taking place – the two versions symbolizing perhaps the turning point of her loyalties, for her children themselves had divided interests. About this time, the Riempp children began marrying and their interests were somewhat opposed to those of the children of the earlier marriage, and that opposition reached a high point with claims of one group for marriage portions and of the other for security of property in the hands of the father.

The theme of brothers-in-law bound together in mutual interest and conflict is illustrated in the earlier relationships between Johann Georg Riempp himself and his wife's sister's husband, Johann Wilhelm Hentzler. Riempp had married into Neckarhausen from another village in 1773, bringing with him a substantial marriage portion. Although an outsider, he was a wealthy landowner, closely allied through marriage to several office holders in the village – notably his brother-in-law, Johann Wilhelm Hentzler, who sat on the village court and council and was in turn son of the *Bürgermeister* (village financial officer). There are indications that the common link through sisters was continually reinforced during the first years after Riempp's arrival. Between 1778 and 1784, the latter was godfather to all of Hentzler's children, while Hentzler acted as godfather in turn for Riempp until the birth of the last child in 1781. (From 1776 to 1785 Riempp was godfather to the children of Johannes Kraushaar, while Kraushaar's wife was godmother to the children of Hentzler.)

Exactly when Riempp came into conflict with his wife is unclear – *Schultheiss* Hiller looking back from 1807 said it was from the beginning. However, Riempp first came into the records for regular drinking and scolding his neighbors and the magistrates on 21 December 1783 (ten years after the marriage). Brought before the church consistory, he was warned about his unpeaceful life with his wife and children. By April 1784, he was before the consistory again. This time he had sent his wife on Maundy Thursday to announce that he would attend communion, but the pastor sent for him to come in person. Riempp refused to go and see the pastor in his house. On Good Friday, he ordered his wife to fetch him more to drink, which she refused to do, whereupon he threw a mug at her head. When he began a drunken fight on Easter Sunday, his family was forced to flee to the *Schultheiss* for protection. Riempp also refused to go to the *Schultheiss* and shouted into the village that the pastor had taken up with a couple of red-headed women. When summoned again, he drank so much that he could no longer walk. Subsequently he went off to the village of Neuhausen (Catholic, belonging to the Habsburgs) and joined the army. Upon sobering up, he purchased his freedom for 28 fl.

The conflict with his wife during the period 1783–4 occurred a few years before his wife's children started to marry. It may well be that claims on the property he held in usufruct brought about the tensions that prompted his behaviour. However, well-documented conflict broke open between him and his brother-in-law over the inheritance of their respective wives (the sisters Anna Maria and Margaretha, daughters of David Falter). After February 1784, Riempp was no longer invited to stand as godparent for Hentzler's children. In July, Riempp was summoned before the village court for slandering Hentzler, claiming that the latter had cheated in the inheritance of their wives' mother. He had also spread the rumour that Hentzler had stolen stores (*Vorrat*) from the Rathaus when his father was *Bürgermeister* and sold them outside the village. Again in 1786, Riempp was before the court for slandering Hentzler in another inheritance matter. It was reported that Riempp lived in rebellion and drunkenness, scolding and swearing against the magistrates. He publicly maintained that his brother-in-law was not fit to be in the village council nor to act as judge in the village court. At home he lived in 'hatred and envy' with his wife and children, who often had to flee to the neighbors for safety. There are no more entries in the village protocols, but it seems that relations between the two brothers-in-law remained poor until Hentzler's death in 1789. Despite their conflicts, Riempp was appointed by the council as guardian of the children and administrator of the estate – a recognition of the responsibilities and priviliges of kinship, an affirmation that tensions and ties go together.

Riempp was apparently under two kinds of pressures at the same time: he was faced with the problem of giving over part of the resources he controlled to his stepchildren and at the same time was in conflict with village authorities. This latter dispute was mediated through conflict over inheritance with his brother-in-law. The fact that he flirted with the possibility of joining a foreign army – and Catholic at that (Neckarhausen was 100% Protestant) – is to be seen as a symbolic gesture of escape from an authority which he was powerless to control. That such conflict could have a direct influence on the accumulation of wealth and strategies of inheritance can be seen by examining some of the land transactions in which Riempp was involved.

Table 1. *Land sales involving Johann Georg Riempp (JGR)*

Seller	Buyer	Type	Date
Georg Fried. Hahn	JGR	Acker (arable)	1778
Michael Friess	JGR	Acker	1780
Michael Friess	JGR	Garten (garden)	1780
Wilhelm Hentzler	JGR	Acker	1780
Johann Zeug	JGR	Acker	1780
Nicolaus Vogler	JGR	Acker	1781
Johann Georg Hess	JGR	Acker	1782
Salomon Brodbeck	JGR	Acker	1782
JGR	Johann Sterr	Acker	1783
Wilhelm Hentzler	JGR	Land (flaxland) (cancelled)	1784 (Jan.)
JGR	Fried. Hentzler	Acker	1787
JGR	Adam Falter	Acker	1789
JGR	David Bauknecht	Acker	1789
JGR	Joh. G. Rieth	Land	1789
JGR	Joh. G. Bauknecht	Acker	1789
JGR	Mathes Sterr	Acker	1789
JGR	Joh. Kühfuss	Acker	1789
JGR	Joh. Kühfuss	Acker	1789
JGR	Joh. Kühfuss	Land	1789
JGR	Jacob Hentzler	Land	1789
JGR (redeemed, so cancelled)	Adam Falter	Acker	1789
JGR	Jacob Hentzler	Acker	1789
JGR (redeemed, so cancelled)	David Bauknecht	Acker	1789
JGR	Nicolaus Vogler	Acker	1790
JGR	Michael Schach	Acker	1794
JGR	Matth. Sterr	Acker	1797
JGR	JGR jun.	Haus	1804
JGR	Michael Hentzler	Wiesen (meadow)	1804
JGR	Jacob Häfner	Acker	1805
JGR	JGR jun.	Acker	1806
JGR	JGR jun.	Acker	1806
JGR	JGR jun.	Acker	1806
JGR	JGR jun.	Acker	1806
JGR	JGR jun.	Acker	1806
JGR	JGR jun.	Wiesen	1806
JGR	Jacob Häfner	Acker	1806
JGR	Jacob Häfner	Acker	1806
JGR	Jacob Häfner	Land	1806
JGR	Wilhelm Hentzler	Wiesen	1807
JGR	Gottlieb Hentzler	Acker	1807
JGR	Jacob Häfner	Häuser (houses)	1807
Jacob Häfner	JGR	Garten	1808
Riempp *Erbmasse*	JGR	Weingarten (vinery)	1808
JGR jun.	JGR	Acker	1809

Table 2. *Selected other transactions*

Seller	Buyer	Type	Date
Sixt Heinzelmann	Wilh. Hentzler	Acker	1789
Sixt Heinzelmann	Wilh. Hentzler	Garten	1789
Sixt Heinzelmann	Wilh. Hentzler	Acker	1789
Sixt Heinzelmann	Jacob Zeug	Weingarten	1790
Sixt Heinzelmann	Joh. Georg Bauknecht	Garten, Wiesen	1791
Jacob Eisinger	Joh. Feldmaier	Wiesen	1794
Jacob Häfner	JGR jun.	Acker	1805
Jacob Häfner	JGR jun.	Weingarten	1806
JGR jun.	Gottlieb Hentzler	Acker	1807
JGR jun.	Joh. Grauer	Acker	1807
JGR jun.	J.G. Hentzler (Wilhelm's Son)	Weinberg (vineyard)	1807
JGR jun.	Joh Bosch	Land	1807
JGR jun.	Conr. Hiller	Acker	1807
JGR jun.	Conr. Hiller	Acker	1807
JGR jun.	Salomon Bauer	Acker	1808

Table 3. *Transactions involving the Erbmassen* (estates) *of Riempp and Caspar Hentzler*

Seller	Buyer	Type	Date
Jac. Eisinger and Riempp heirs	J. G. Hentzler's widow	½ Haus	1808
Riempp *Erbmasse*	Jacob Eisinger	Acker	1808
Riempp *Erbmasse*	Jacob Häfner	Acker	1808
Riempp *Erbmasse*	Jacob Eisinger	Acker	1808
Riempp *Erbmasse*	Jacob Häfner	Garten	1808
Riempp *Erbmasse*	Caspar Kuhn	Land	1808
Casp. Hentzler *Erbmasse*	Sixt Heinzelmann	Acker	1808
Casp. Hentzler *Erbmasse*	Jacob Eisinger	Acker	1808
Riempp *Erbmasse*	Michael Feldmaier	Acker	1808
Riempp *Erbmasse*	Conr. Hiller	Acker	1808

The tables offer a number of observations about the dynamics of family relations. During the time when the break between Riempp and Hentzler took place in 1784, the latter sold a flaxland (*Land*) to Riempp but then cancelled the transaction. In 1789 when Riempp was selling so much land, he put in a clause in many of the transactions which cancelled the sale if a redemption was forthcoming. That is, if someone from the family exercised his right to redeem a plot, Riempp had the right to take it back – which he did on two occasions. The history of his land sales fall into several distinct periods. During the early 1780s he accumulated land from a number of people, whose connection to him cannot yet be shown. Among the sellers of land to him was his brother-in-law. The purchasing of land came to an end in 1784, and at the end of the decade he sold off many plots so long as family members were not forthcoming to redeem them. The conflict and perhaps his isolation caused him to exclude relatives, notably Hentzler, from access to these resources. From 1804 to 1807, he again sold off a great deal of property and at the same time ran up a great number of debts. The effect of this activity was to divest himself and his wife of assets, which at first glance would seem to have effectively disinherited all of his children. Since he was already in conflict with his stepchildren, they tried to arrest the process. Weber complained before the court of Riempp's prodigality. However, not all of the children were negatively affected by the latter's actions. What he was doing was selling as much as possible to his own son, Johann Georg Riempp, junior, and his son-in-law, Jacob Häfner. This gave them as much land as he could provide and loaded the remainder with debts. In selling land, Riempp also made available several plots for the sons of his dead brother-in-law, for whom he had acted as guardian. After Riempp's bankruptcy and semi-retirement, his son and son-in-law in return sold him a few plots to work in his old age.

At the inventory of Riempp's deceased spouse in 1808, since the debts totalled more than the assets, there was danger of a forced sale. Four of the brothers-in-law now saw it in their interest to cooperate to forestall this move. They successfully petitioned to allow themselves to proceed with the sale of the property, settling the debts with the sales. The four involved were Johann Georg Riempp, junior, Jacob Häfner, Jacob Eisinger, and Sixt Heinzelmann. This brought together two parties from each of the two sets of children of the deceased Anna Maria (Hentzler) Riempp. Why were the other two excluded? My suggestion is that Weber's attempt to manipulate the situation with the illegal mortgage, having failed, alienated the other two with whom he had cooperated. At least it ruined him, and he could not profit by the situation of the sale of property heavily laden with debts. On the other side, Johann Georg Mühleisen had angered his brother-in-law, Riempp, junior, by selling one of the pieces of land his wife had received at her marriage for too much money. As a family member, Riempp had the right to redeem the property but at that price could not. Mühleisen came from a village too far away from Neckarhausen to be able to work land there. He probably had no interest in maintaining close connections with family members in the village. Thus the four who had an interest in an accommodation worked together to their own advantage. They sold most of the land to themselves, with part of the house going to one of Riempp senior's wards. Since part of the problem for villagers was getting their hands on any property at all, heavy debts were taken in stride. A buyer would simply pay off the mortgage holder by taking out a fresh mortgage. To a large extent, access to land was through family politics, shaped by the rules of redemption. When in insolvable conflict, it was possible to exclude family members from resources as Riempp did in the late 1780s. Yet connections, however bent and battered, could be repaired as can be seen by his repeated transactions with the sons of his brother-in-law. Failure to fulfill a claim or an expectation could begin a process of fission as in the case of the brothers-in-law Mühleisen and Riempp, junior. However, reinforcement built ever stronger lines of connection and certain connections could be maintained for future use. For example, in 1800 during the time when the three brothers-in-law were in conflict with Riempp, senior, Anna Catharina Eisinger was godmother to her half-sister's child (the son of Jacob Häfner and his wife Margaretha). This may well have aided in the later cooperation to rescue the debt-laden property of Riempp, senior.

2) The family transactions of Friedrich Ludwig Zeug provide the second set of examples of relationships between brothers-in-law. Here again, the decease of a wife offered the occasion for bringing conflict out into the open. At the inventory (18 January 1815) of Zeug's second wife, Catharina, the two sons-in-law, Georg Salomon Bauer and Johannes Ischinger, brought suit to straighten out the property relationships between them and Zeug. They maintained that he held property in usufruct which would fall to them at his death, but because of his many debts the property was not secure. Furthermore, he was selling land that did not rightfully belong to him. The dispute centered around property that had come from three sources: Zeug's deceased first wife, her father, and her brother, who had died unmarried. One problem was to reckon what share of the property held by Zeug came to him via his first wife and what share via her father (Hans Jerg Bosch, senior). The reckoning was complicated by a change in the status of the wife's dowry. Customarily, a dowry (*Heiratsgut*) was provided by the parents at the marriage of a daughter. It was held inviolate until the death of one of the parents. If the daughter wished to share in the inheritance of the deceased parent, she had to return her dowry, a practical move only if a profit could be expected. In this case, Elisabetha Margaretha died ten years before her father, and in the intervening period her dowry remained in the hands of her husband, Ludwig

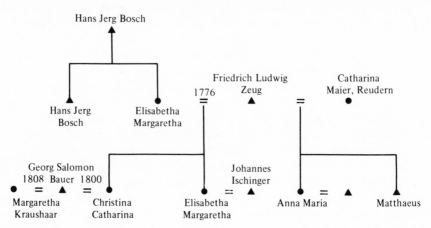

Zeug. When old Bosch died, the dowry was returned so that the heirs could share in the inheritance. This, however, changed the nature of the claims to the property, giving the grandchildren a right to the direct apportioning of the legacy, for so long as the property had been considered as dowry, it remained in Zeug's hands, but as inheritance from the grandfather, it could fall directly to the grandchildren.

The second point of disagreement between the two brothers-in-law and their father-in-law had to do with the manner in which part of the inheritance from Hans Jerg Bosch, senior, was passed on. It was a frequent practice for a man to begin transmitting his property to the next generation as he began to get old, notably in the form of dowries, marriage portions, and gifts. However, one important method was to *sell* many properties to the next generation – often to sons or to sons-in-law. Thus, in 1796, before his death, Bosch was prepared to sell much of his land to his son-in-law, Zeug, but regional officials (*Oberamt*) refused to let the latter buy the land because he had so many unpaid taxes. By 1799, Zeug found the solution to the problem in having Bosch sell the land to Zeug's children, whereupon he took possession of the property. He obviously considered the whole matter a clever maneuver to get around the law and simply treated the property as his own. The two brothers-in-law disputed this right and were supported by the authorities, who expressly considered the trick as cheating.

Both sides were dissatisfied with the reckoning that the authorities undertook. Zeug wrote a moving plea to the *Oberamt* to settle matters in his favor. As an 'old decrepit' man he feared falling into the hands of his two sons-in-law. He considered their attempt to raise themselves at his expense contemptuous. As far as he was concerned, they were only after what he had worked hard to earn (*sein Runges und Gewonnes*). Here again is an example of brothers-in-law cooperating in the issue of an estate involving two sisters. But the pickings were small. In the years following the dispute with Zeug both fell into extreme poverty, were cited for drinking and laziness, and caught for stealing. Ischinger blamed his condition on the dispute with his father-in-law. It does not appear that relations between the two brothers-in-law went much beyond the attempt to pry loose some endebted portions from their wives' expectations. Bauer complained in 1823 of Ischinger borrowing wood from his wife without getting his permission. With little property cementing them together, there seems to have been no basis for creating a relationship of mutual aid. Ischinger's relationships with his other in-laws were also not particularly good. In 1818, Zeug's son and daughter by his second marriage beat Ischinger up with a club and threw rocks at him – the culmination of a running battle over disappointed expectations.

Salomon Bauer seems to have had better relations with his other brothers-in-law, at least as far as land transactions are concerned.[4] He sold land to Anton Waldner twice, to Johannes Grauer three times, and to Johannes Kraushaar twice (and bought from him once) – all brothers-in-law. Transactions were often

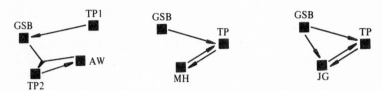

GSB = Georg Salomon Bauer   MH = Michael Hentzler, brother-in-law
TP = Third party   JG = Johannes Grauer, brother-in-law
AW = Anton Waldner, brother-in-law

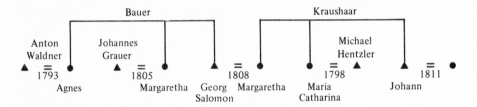

much more complex, involving the putting together of a more advantageous set of properties. For this a group of men had to cooperate together, relying on contacts between brothers-in-law or the willingness of one to follow the lead of the other. Above are examples of complex land sales which took place on three different occasions.

III

The role of women in these transactions is difficult to see, since the husband was the public representative of the married couple. In all of the cases of buying and selling of property or in disputes before legal authorities, the husband appeared as the responsible agent. There were guarantees for women when it came to selling or mortgaging property which they brought into marriage, but, apart from releasing their husbands to act for them, they do not come into the records. Informally, however active they may have been, formally they appeared only through their husbands. There is then a sense that the conflicts which have been described were sibling conflicts – between sisters and between sisters and brothers – although because wives were represented by their husbands they appear as conflicts between brothers-in-law. However, there are good reasons to see the tensions as essentially ones between brothers-in-law. Men had to cooperate closely in agriculture, which brought brothers and brothers-in-law directly together in agricultural production. The claims and obligations which an in-marrying spouse exercised were mediated through his wife and involved all of the tensions that go with the progressive integration of an outsider. Whatever rivalries existed between siblings could be hidden or subsumed under rivalries between brothers-in-law, allowing brothers to act as protector of sisters, and sisters to maintain solidarity among themselves. Because of the tension between the necessity to cooperate and the potential for irreparable break, the relationship between brothers-in-law seems to be one of the central axes around which family and kinship relationships were organized in Neckarhausen. The importance of the man as substitute figure for his wife is recognized in a number of ways. When, for example, a father sells property to his children, he sells to his sons and his sons-in-law, but not directly to his daughters. Men adopt a vocabulary in referring to kin which places them in the position of their wives; for example, one man referred to his wife's brother in contradistinction to her step-brother as 'my real (*echt*) brother'. Thus the position of the brother-in-law is characterized by various different moments. He is the public representative of his own family and as such exercises authority over property and property claims transmitted through his wife. He is in competition over inheritance with the wife's brothers and brothers-in-law and at the same time may well have to cooperate with them over against the wife's father, the law courts, or the village authorities. The brother-in-law is also pulled in the direction of his own family of origin, where solidarity between siblings can play a role. In any event much of his future is determined by property relations established at marriage and which do not end with the death of his wife. The property relations are seldom fixed at one point for all time, but involve negotiation over a more or less extended period. The essential connection in transmission between generations is not seen as one between fathers and daughters but as one between fathers-in-law and sons-in-law (and fathers and sons).

A second fact that determined relationships among brothers-in-law had to do with the nature of peasant production. At marriage, a young couple seldom received enough land or movables to be independent (a Swabian proverb: 'Don't put young bees in a full hive'). Or, even if the couple had considerable land, more resources were available to them than they themselves owned. In the marriage contracts and post mortem inventories, there are many indications that parents informally gave children pieces of land to work. At marriage some strips were formally handed over, although only with full legal force when the marriage contract was drawn up – often up to a year after the marriage took place. In this way children could receive the full legal title over some land or hold it only in usufruct, but it is clear from the sources that the children often had very little land of any kind in their hands. Thus, even after marriage they were still integrated into the productive activities of their parents. It is difficult from scattered evidence to see through this informal, rather make-shift system, but there seems to have been no sharp break in property ownership with marriage. Only the first steps of transmission were taken then, and independence developed only over time. This threw brothers-in-law informally together with the parents and parents-in-law in a series of productive relationships which ranged from occasional help with plowing, hoeing, carting, and the like to independent working of a strip of land. There were many occasions to demonstrate favoritism or impartiality, goodwill or obstinacy, fondness or hatred.

There were other grounds as well for cooperation. Even with land, the marriage contracts demonstrate that many peasants were never supplied with the necessary tools for carrying on agriculture. Very few had horses, and many young couples had no cow. It was therefore necessary to be able to borrow plow animals. Plows and harrows were usually lacking, and few young couples had both. In the post mortem inventories and retirement contracts, there are many examples where one heir received the back part of a wagon and another the front. Thus cooperation in the form of borrowing tools and animals was integral to the system – especially in the early years of family formation. Finally, as the elderly parents retired or as they passed on strips of land, conditions were often set whereby they received regular support from the heirs. This threw brothers-in-law together as mutually responsible for the retired person(s). Friedrich Ludwig Zeug in the second case analysed above refused to accept the retirement agreement of his father-in-law until he was satisfied that the quality of the land he received was equal to that of the latter's son. The evidence shows that brothers-in-law often cooperated together in production, house and building repairs, and drinking.

A third aspect of the relations described here has to do with the fact that there was no sharp break between the generations. In areas of Central Europe where single son inheritance was the rule, the marriage of the heir and the retirement of the parents often coincided. In areas of partible inheritance such as Neckarhausen, the process of transition was protracted, with many tentative moves and reversals, and a complex intertwining of use-rights and obligations. With land often lent for a period, given in usufruct, sold piecemeal, or subject to future expectation there was considerable room for negotiation, development of moral claims, and proof of intent. Such a system was full of tension, subject to continual review and comment, and always for the individual combined with uncertainty. Parents demanded demonstration of capacity, respect, and seriousness. Children expected proof that real exchange would take place.

The cooperation of brothers-in-law in production, their common interest in the same property, their competition for favor from the parents, their mutual responsiblity to care for the latter – all this made the relationship between brothers-in-law a central axis in familial relationships. Indeed, because of inheritance and the extremely crowded conditions of the village, they often were thrown together in the same house sharing use of the kitchen, living room, or farm buildings. Given the rules of redeemability of family property, the failure of one could mean the profit of the other. While on the one hand the relationship was filled with open-ended possibilities and offered the possibility of cooperation, mutual aid, and political support, on the other, the importance of the connection made it also grounds for mutual hostility, conflict, and hatred.

A few suggestions should be offered at this point about the limitations in time and class of the structure of brother-in-law relationships described here. A great deal more needs to be learned about the structure· of economic and social relationships, so what is offered remains highly tentative. My guess is that the double-edged, emotion-filled connection took form in the period 1740 to 1760 and began to break up between 1840 to 1860. It was a connection that was above all crucial for the property holding peasantry and artisanry, but played much less of a role for farm laborers and the marginal small holders.

a) Between 1740 and 1760 the population of the village began to rise, perhaps in response to the first tentative steps in agricultural intensification and market demand for crops based on labor intensive production. There was room for some development of village handicrafts – carpenters, smiths, shoemakers, and the like – but for all village inhabitants access to land was crucial for survival. Greater demand led to higher prices for land, but even with the proper cash, land was not necessarily available without family connection. An interest in being able to purchase land under the market price insured a common family policy. But very important was the law of redeemability, whereby a family member had the right within a year to purchase any alienated family property at the given price. The end to such legal restrictions on property would have destroyed a crucial prop to the system. The extreme inflation of property values might well have brought market calculation into family relationships.

b) The lack of alternative employment made the accumulation of land a necessity. By the 1820s considerable employment for men was offered in road construction and canal building. This was followed soon by opportunities in the enormous drainage projects undertaken in rural areas and in railroad construction. By the 1850s and 1860s factory employment was available even for non-emigrants from the village. Progressively as well, men pulled out of agriculture, leaving women to do the stock-raising and hoeing of root crops. The nature of intensive agriculture limited the size of the unit of production. With land available at an inflated market price and the unit of production limited in size by the limits to the self-exploitation of women, the competition of brothers-in-law for land as well as mutual cooperation in agriculture might well have lessened.

c) In the early phase of the agricultural revolution, the small producer was faced with high capitalization costs. Large debts were run up and bankruptcy was common – especially for the period after 1815. It was perhaps necessary to be able to borrow tools and double up on houses and agricultural buildings to keep the costs of production down. There are signs of increased house building in the 1830s, and reports later on in the century refer to the heavy over-capitalization of the small peasant enterprise. It would appear then that a development in capital equipment took place. This could be explained as an investment policy in the wake of increasing market relationships as far as land is concerned. Each peasant producer tried to become as independent as possible once he no longer expected to gain access to land through family politics. As well, with men only available part-time in agriculture, investment in equipment to make male labor more efficient took place.

NOTES

1 My thinking on the subject of property has been heavily influenced over the years in talks with Esther and Jack Goody. An essential text is the latter's *Death, Property and the Ancestors* (Stanford, 1962).
2 It is not a question here only of property held within the family, but also, of course, of the structure of property rights in the society. The particular form of domination (*Herrschaft*) that a family is subject to affects internal family relations directly. Domination is an essential aspect of property relations. For a rich introduction to the problem of property as external to the family and as a complex nexus of conflicting claims, see E. P. Thompson, 'The Grid of Inheritance: A Comment', in Jack Goody, *et al.* (eds.), *Family and Inheritance: Rural Society in Western Europe, 1200–1800* (Cambridge, 1976). For a view on property relations as crucial for bourgeois psychological development, see Gilles Deleuze and Félix Guattari, *Anti-oedipe* (Paris, 1972).
3 Research on the village of Neckarhausen is described in rather programmatic fashion in David Sabean, 'Verwandtschaft und Familie in einem württembergischen Dorf 1500 bis 1870: einige methodische Überlegungen', in Werner Conze (ed.), *Sozialgeschichte der Familie in der Neuzeit Europas* (Stuttgart, 1976). See also 'Aspects of Kinship Behaviour and Property in Rural Western Europe before 1800', in Goody, *Family and Inheritance*. Most of the sources for this study are found in the village. They are described broadly in the article, 'Verwandtschaft', and will be given in detail in a forthcoming book on family and kinship in the village.
4 As usual cooperation does not exclude conflict. Bauer lived in the same house with his brother-in-law, Kraushaar, and their wives could not get along at all. The women accused each other of stealing from time to time, and both families engaged in a running battle over the obligation to heat the common living room properly.

Part IV. Obligation and power: kinship in the transformation of politics

8. 'A brother is a creative thing' : change and conflict in a Melpa family (Papua New Guinea)

ANDREW STRATHERN

I

In Chapter 1 on material interest and emotion in kinship relations, David Sabean and Hans Medick point out that in certain kinds of society emotions both centre on land as a focus of interest and are expressed in terms of land as a type of material property. Often, the strength of such emotions may be shown only at times of crisis or transition, particularly when inheritance is at issue. Inheritance usually turns on a single crucial relationship, such as that of father/eldest son, and anthropological accounts have accordingly paid close attention to inter-generational ties of this sort. But, the same authors continue, there is a need to consider sibling relationships as a whole, particularly as they develop over time. In what follows, I attempt to explore a segment of sibling relationships in a small social group belonging to the Melpa society of Mount Hagen in Papua New Guinea, keeping this theme of family development in mind.

New Guinea societies in general exemplify well the close interdependence between interests and emotions, since within them obligations of exchange are strongly marked, and much time and effort are expended on producing items which can be fed into exchange networks. In the Highland region, to which Melpa society belongs, these items are food crops, pigs, and shell valuables, the last category now commonly replaced with money. Both sexes contribute to production, but men generally claim superior control over exchange, and certain men seek pre-eminence through their prowess in ceremonial exchange activities. The central values of the society are expressed in the contrast between what is *nyim* (i.e. characteristic of high performance in exchange) and what is *korpa* (that which is 'rubbish', reflecting or causing low performance). The language of praise and insult, affection and dislike, again reflects this same contrast. It constitutes the dimension against which people are evaluated by their kinsfolk as well as by others.

These Highlands societies developed for several thousand years largely on their own, with minimal direct influence from other areas, until the 1930s, when Europeans first penetrated into their region with the aid of light planes. Since 1945, they have experienced rapid political and economic change as a result of pacification, colonization, and from 1975 onwards political independence from the colonial power, Australia. Notably, they have taken up the cultivation of coffee as a means of earning cash. While the stimulus to do so originally came during the 1950s from government agricultural officers and Australian plantation farmers, the Melpa have used their money not only to pay taxes and buy consumer goods, as the colonialists intended them to do, but also as a new kind of valuable in their exchanges, displacing shells. This has had two results. First, the form of the main exchange system, the *moka*, has tended to reproduce itself even though patterns of land use and labour have altered. Second, the conditions of competition for status in the *moka* now include access to cash, while at the same time access to cash gives the opportunity to people also to opt out of the *moka* altogether.

Clearly, in looking at sibling relations in this context, one must be able to take into account the probable differences which cash-cropping has brought with it. The process of accumulation of assets through cash has not, however, been going on for long enough to produce definite changes in inheritance practices. The potential for such changes is present, since coffee is a long-term asset and money earned from it can also be banked or transformed into other durable assets and investments. The likelihood of a class of 'rich peasants' emerging over time is rather high, but one must note also certain factors which slow down the rate of emergence: restrictions on access to land, since most land remains under the control of clan groups, the lack of any indigenous pattern of primogeniture or ultimogeniture, and the lively claims on wealth exercised by exchange partners in the *moka*.

The situation today is, therefore, mixed: capitalism has penetrated and affected deeply the social relations of production, yet it is equally obvious that transformation is far from complete. The complicated texture of relationships in this phase of historical change can be seen through an examination of issues among the family of a particular leader or 'big-man', since 1964. The big-man, called Ndamba, has over the last few years been attempting to arrange a final round of *moka* exchanges in which his own sons would be prominent and which would enable one of them, or all of them together, to retain at least part of the convincing hegemony he has dedicated his own life to establishing. As with inheritance, the most notable point here is the absence of any definite rule of succession, a fact which over the years since 1964, when I first came to know the family through fieldwork, has moved more and more into counterpoint with Ndamba's obvious desire in practice to pass on his mantle within the family. Has his aim affected relations among the siblings themselves, and if so, in what way? Can we argue that with the prospect of *de facto* 'succession' to their father's position they have become more rivalrous and more inclined to grasp at material resources which may help them in competition? The presentation and discussion of data will show that no such simple conclusion can be drawn, but that material and emotional issues are certainly very closely intermeshed.

What is important, however, is to realize that if there is conflict, or *per contra* solidarity between siblings, it is not something which manifests itself only at the point of their father's death, although it may be crucially influenced by the prospect and later the fact of that death. Leadership depends on a gradual building up of influence in exchange, speech-making, and, nowadays, business enterprise as well. There is nothing absolutely to stop several brothers in one family all becoming 'big-men'. One may gradually achieve ascendancy. All may simply remain 'ordinary men'. As brothers grow into early middle age, people do comment on their relative achievements, and gradually a sense of rivalry may spring up between them. There is an ethic that brothers should be mutually supportive in exchanges, but if they are also rivals, they may compromise by simply doing things separately rather than together. Concentration on their respective affinal networks often enables them to do this, since marriage rules require brothers to marry into separate sub-clans. But this separation can also lead to conflict if one brother refuses to 'help' another by contributing, at least, to an exchange in which the latter is prominently involved.[1]

II

In this section I consider, in the main, Ndamba himself and some of his kinsfolk, and set the discussion into the context of the ethnographic situation in 1964–5. The third section considers more recent events in the late 1970s.

Ndamba was already an established, senior leader in 1964. He fought as a youth in battles up to 1945, when the first effective Australian patrols and pacification of the area began. He was jailed after one particular fracas, and he remembers the discomfort of the event vividly. Perhaps partly because of this experience, Ndamba never sought office in the introduced system of political control which the Australians brought; in this, his career contrasts sharply with that of Ongka, his ally and son-in-law, who from early on made friends with government officers and policemen and held a position later as Councillor for the whole Kawelka tribe, to which both Ndamba and he belong.[2] Ndamba concentrated entirely on building up his family base and moving into exchanges, at the head of a small sub-group within the Kawelka Kundmbo clan.

Ndamba was the middle son of three. His father's first wife was a divorced woman from a distant clan, and by her he had Wamb, the eldest son. The second wife was from the Tipuka Kengeke clan, minor enemies in the past of the Kundmbo, but exchange partners now. She bore first a daughter, who married into a clan of the Kombukla tribe, then Ndamba, then a second daughter who married into the same clan as the first (the mother of Owa, a regular friend and ally of Ndamba's sons at least since 1964), then finally Moka. The fortunes of the three brothers have been quite different. Wamb is dubbed a rubbish-man by Ndamba's sons. He keeps to himself, does not speak on public occasions, and is always to be seen carrying a shovel or axe, tools for gardening. Living separately from Ndamba, he has always gardened alone also. Nikint, one of Ndamba's sons, says that Wamb hides away in the bushes and cooks pigs secretly to eat by himself; rather than coming to public meetings and giving pigs away in *moka* exchange, he implies. In this regard, Nikint has fully assimilated his father's ideals: *moka* is good and the only way to demonstrate genuine status. The evaluation is interesting because Wamb in fact displays one characteristic which Ndamba himself judges indispensable, that is, a capacity for work. Yet this capacity is pointless, according to Ndamba, unless one plans for public prominence through *moka* activity. Nikint, by contrast with Wamb, subscribes to the exchange ideology, but is not very keen on work: hence his particular scorn is reserved for Wamb's way of life. Rather predictably, Wamb has turned to other options. He and his children are all baptized converts of the Lutheran Church, and his eldest son takes the lead in making prayers, in communal work for the mission, and in collecting money for the construction of a permanent-materials place of worship at Möi Manga, where the Christians have built their own small village for the converted, just beside the site of the Female Spirit Cult which Ndamba imported and performed in 1973. Wamb and his sons naturally did not take part in this cult performance: mission rules forbid this. Much later, in April 1979, when Ndamba consecrated a new ceremonial ground with a sacrificial killing of pigs to Kundmbo ancestral ghosts, Wamb was struck with a severe headache as he approached the sacred end of the ground. Ndamba greeted him kindly and asked him not to feel upset, later presenting him with a generously large leg of pork. Subsequently, in September 1979, Wamb's sons began to build a new house very close to the ceremonial ground, and Ndamba explained that he had 'drawn them back in'. And in August 1980, Wamb duly contributed money to Ndamba's *moka* gift presented to the Kengeke clansmen.

The youngest brother, Moka, is much closer to Ndamba in every way, including, as one might expect, physical resemblance. He too, however, has specialized and has become a ritual expert (*mön wuö*). His account of how he obtained this craft is interesting, because he attributes his skills partly to the special support of his dead father's spirit. Ndamba, by contrast, stresses his own, self-made character.

There have been times when Ndamba and Moka have come into conflict. As the most forceful of the three brothers and Moka's elder by some ten years, Ndamba was always prominent in dividing out areas of garden land, and Moka on his marriage went to make a separate small settlement nearby. The second sister, married to a Kombukla man, gave Ndamba some pigs, without sparing any for Moka, and he was so angered by this that he went to his house and cursed his sister, saying that his own dead father and mother could come and kill her daughter, Koka. Moka's own wife, who was also from a Kombukla group, quietly told the people of Ndamba's settlement about the curse, and when Koka did in fact fall ill, the sister, her husband, and son, Owa, all arrived and called out to Moka at his own place to settle the talk, but he refused and the girl died. Moka's comment was of the 'I told you so' type, and Ndamba was furious, because if the girl had lived, he could have received a share in the bridewealth for her. At that time he forbade the sister ever to visit Moka again and was angry when Moka gave her a gift of £5.00 at the occasion of Nikint's marriage (1964).

One can see from this example how Moka takes his stand on the relationship with his dead father's spirit, Ndamba on his own efforts. This is not to say that the two refuse to cooperate. Moka was a major supporter of the Female Spirit Cult project, which Ndamba brought to a successful end in November 1973. He contributes also to activities of money – *moka*, which Ndamba organizes, though it is noticeable that he prefers to club in with others of the 'mens' house group' in doing so, rather than directly with Ndamba, explaining himself by saying, 'oh, we are all brothers or the sons of brothers, and we just like to make a show of it by linking up differently and putting on some competition between ourselves' (1977). In this instance, he was referring to money raised for the purchase of a pig to be given as a special gift in a money-*moka*.[3]

He had chosen to associate with his lineage cousin (FFBS), Wöyö, Wöyö's son Puklum, and with Ndat, a man of a different lineage set, in order to put some K 300[4] together for this purpose, while Ndamba and his sons obtained a separate pig for about twice as much. On another occasion (1978), Ndamba was putting together a sum of *c.* K 200 as a minor *moka* repayment to a pair of visiting in-laws. Moka rather reluctantly joined in, exclaiming that he simply had no money, was K 2 short on what he had said he would find, and after this would have none left to help pay for repairs to their collectively purchased four-wheel-drive truck, of which Nikint was the driver and manager. As often as feasible, he goes away to his wife's place, where he has been permitted to plant a grove of coffee trees, and there he stays for many days on end. Nevertheless, if someone in Ndamba's family is sick, he will perform his healing magic for no charge: he did this for a daughter in October 1964, when her leg swelled up badly and it was thought that either her grandparents (FF and FM) were angry because the family was giving away pigs in bridewealth that should have been sacrificed to themselves, or else that a 'wild spirit' (not ancestral) had attacked her. In case it were the latter, Moka made his spell to drive out such spirits. Similarly, in December 1977, Nikint was seriously ill with pneumonia and malaria, and the ministrations of two female ritual experts had no effect. Moka was then called in to make his menstrual pollution ritual, giving Nikint bespelled water to drink. From unrelated people he would have certainly asked for a pig in payment for such services as these. Finally, when one of his sub-clansmen became prominent in the 'red box' money cult of 1970, Moka also went into it as an enthusiastic partner, though he told me much later (1978) that he has always suspected the cult operator of lying and hence had never given his whole-hearted commitment. The operator was one of Ndamba's stepsons by his third wife, and the involvement of the sub-clansmen in this cult has to be interpreted as a part of their wider effort to secure and maintain a kind of financial and political hegemony within the clan. Ndamba gave it his qualified blessing for a few months, although he was always doubtful and never actually went to the seances held. Moka, as a ritual expert himself, did so, but had a professional's scepticism, and when he pulled out, most of the other supporters did as well.[5]

Looking at this generation in the family, we can see that Ndamba dominates the networks of exchange partnerships. His elder half-brother, Wamb, has sought refuge in mission affiliation, from which Ndamba has recently been enticing Wamb's sons, encouraging them to build a house near to his own new ceremonial ground. Moka has similarly looked for, and found, a niche as a traditional-style ritual expert, which enables him now to support and help Ndamba, now to oppose him, and sometimes simply to act independently, though without Ndamba's overall influence on group affairs.

Unlike Moka, then, Ndamba does not speak spontaneously of his father, and he has not attempted to preserve the father's identity by reminiscences of his exploits in warfare. Instead, Ndamba talks of those who have helped his own work: Wöyö, his second cousin, now dead, whom he refers to as a 'little man' (*wuö kel*, i.e. unimportant); Onombe, his 'worker' (*kintmant wüo*), distantly related through his mother's marriage into a related sub-clan, who joined Ndamba instead of his own big-man nephew, Roltinga, with whom he was dissatisfied; then there is Nema, a deaf-mute of Eltimbo sub-clan (now dead), in his time a tenacious worker. Ndamba has also always made a point of doing a large amount of physical labour himself, and it is one of his complaints against the generation of his sons that they do not work consistently as he has done. In 1965, his eldest son Pangk told me that Ndamba's rule in the family was that only those who worked in the gardens should receive food to eat, but both Onombe and Nikint sometimes broke this rule, taking food and then going off elsewhere. Nikint already at this time had a reputation for being disinclined to buckle down and make gardens, and Pangk added that in custom a difference is made between everyday matters and festivals. At feasts, it is necessary to divide out pork and vegetables scrupulously to everyone, whatever one thinks of them: all must have a share. But for ordinary occasions, if a family member does not work and take on responsibility for sections of a particular garden, people may not bother to give him or her food – in which case they must wander off to others, eating *röng pund*, scraps of food, left-overs from a different family's meals.

Pangk himself was at this time already well-established. He had two wives, and children already by each of them. He was to be seen often cutting down swathes of cane-grass in fallow land, preparing for new plantings of sweet potato. His only problem was that his first wife, Kopil, a strong-minded woman, had also a habit of making visits on her own account to kin, leaving him to mind the pigs and sometimes the children. On the occasion of Nikint's first marriage, Ndamba gave one of the pigs returned by the bride's kinsfolk to Kopil, as a replacement for Pangk's contributions to the bridewealth, but she left it in the care of one of Ndamba's co-wives (not her immediate mother-in-law) and went off with Pangk's elder sister to the sister's husband's place. Kopil's co-wife at once complained to Ndamba, and he commented: 'does she want to eat pork or not? If so, let her look after pigs and I will make *moka* with them and bring in food for us.' Here, he meant that even if at pork distributions no-one is completely left out, much more is likely to be distributed to those who are themselves vigorous agents in the family enterprise.

Despite his formal emphasis on meritocratic rules, it seems clear that Ndamba has favoured the senior part of his extensive family of procreation and sees his three sons by his first wife as the spearhead for the future success of their sub-clan in general, the Kiklpuklimbo 'mens' house group' within the Kundmbo clan. There are, as well as the sons, three daughters by this wife: Rangkel (the eldest of the family), Koka and Kwipö. Pepa, the third son, is the second youngest, Kwipö the youngest. Exchange partnerships are pursued with all the in-laws linked through marriage to the sisters and also with their mother's clanspeople, the Minembi Kimbo, and with Ndamba's sister's husband's people of Kombukla. In 1965, only Pangk and Nikint were grown up and married. The others have mostly been married since 1970. The period 1970–80 has thus been one of great expansion of exchange partnerships, under the management of Ndamba, who is now finding it increasingly difficult to hold everyone together. In addition to this 'senior' family section, Ndamba also has two other wives, one whom he himself obtained as a girl (she is the mother of a boy and girl, both now grown up), and one whom he secured through widow-inheritance within the sub-clan: her children by the first husband are Kowa, Rumbukl, Kaka and Ketan, and by Ndamba, a son, Ronom, all now married (see Figure 1, Sect. 1). Rumbukl is the youngest wife of Ongka, another Kawelka big-man. Ndamba is thus Ongka's father-in-law and they have a long-standing alliance, built out of initial child-payments made for Ongka's eldest son by Rumbukl. Predictably enough, Ketan and Ronom, at least partly out of loyalty to their elder sister, are nowadays much more conspicuous in helping Ongka than are the children of Ndamba's senior wife, Woi, who are more concerned to establish partnerships on their own terms now. In particular, definite animosity has grown up between Ongka and Nikint, each making disparaging comments about the other. In this, it appears that one reason is Ongka's preference for the third son, Pepa, both as a partner for himself and as a possible successor to Ndamba in the role of major big-man. This is in turn because Pepa is more of a 'traditionalist' in his ways than Nikint, while entertaining fewer pretensions as to his capabilities for offices such as local government councillor or provincial politician, both of which Nikint has thought about rather seriously. (In May 1980 Nikint stood unsuccessfully for election as a member of a new Provincial Assembly.)

None of Ndamba's children has attended school, though all his grandchildren do. A nearby primary school was set up first in 1970 and has suffered many vicissitudes but is now run by a local headmaster from a nearby clan. Nikint was for two years the President of the school's parents' association, and it was during this time that he began to talk of further political office; but he has now resigned and the Presidency has returned to Wömndi, a man in his forties, who belongs to the same lineage as Nikint himself. With Wömndi, we come to the real locus of tension among the Kiklpuklimbo at present, a locus which shows itself in terms of an effective split in the group itself, and that over the issue of joint participation in exchange arrangements and the claims of Ndamba's children to hegemony in the clan. The next section traces the outlines of the new situation.

III

The father of Wömndi, old Kondi, died on 1 December 1975. His sons, and others of the lineage, as well as many visiting kin, mourned for him loudly. Ndamba and Wömndi together made invocations over the coffin at night, while small pigs were killed, asking Kondi's spirit and those of others recently dead to accept this inadequate offering without anger. Nikint helped to collect money for the coffin and to cook the pigs for sacrifice; he also contributed a pig of his own. Ndamba sat by the coffin in the evening and wept over it. Next day, when more remote kin brought the coffin out and prepared to transport it to the cemetery, the two sons, Wömndi and Parle, threw themselves on it and for a time prevented the bearers from removing it, tears coursing freely down their cheeks.

It was an occasion much more traumatic than the death, a decade earlier, of old Kuperi, Ndamba's uncle (FB) and father of Rongnda. That had been marked only by the expectable quarrel over a pig, Kuperi claiming Rongnda had used it in *moka* against his will and wanting one killed for him in return: such upsets are a prelude to subsequent events, when sicknesses are attributed to the anger of ghosts, and living kin must find pigs to kill in sacrifice. Yet Kuperi had in his time been superior in status to Kondi: he knew some specialist ritual, and he counted himself the proper brother of Kongna, Ndamba's father. It was Kuperi who told me, in August 1964, that Kondi had been taken into the group as a suckling child. Earlier that year Wömndi had told me that his father Kondi and Kuperi were brothers by the same father, Kakla. Kuperi said that Kondi's father was actually a Kiklpukla man, whose sister was married to Kakla. His mother, a Kope woman, had died while Kondi was still suckling at the breast and Kuperi's own mother (Kondi's paternal aunt) took him on. Kuperi said that he saw the new child's faeces and was afraid, and so himself desisted from breast-feeding. Kondi was an only child, and his father died before he grew up, so he belonged to the Kundmbo. There is no doubt that he was fully accepted as a group member, having been 'adopted' at an early age, and no issue regarding his status or that of his sons has ever been made public, to my knowledge. Nevertheless, it is hard not to correlate some features of developing rivalry within the Kiklpuklimbo (a sub-group name actually given on the basis of Kuperi's mother's affiliation, at a time when her sons were grown up) with this initial fact of differential circumstances of birth.

The passage of time since 1964 has brought with it a process of diversification in the interests of the generation junior to Ndamba. While his own networks of influence have expanded in step with the marriages of sons and daughters in his sub-group, it is equally clear that these juniors have also been developing their own networks. When Kuperi and Kondi were alive, Ndamba ran the affairs of their sons as well as his own in virtue of the dominance he exerted over the two men themselves. Since Kuperi's death, Rongnda his son has remained a staunch supporter of Ndamba, but Wömndi, following Kondi's decease, has begun to dissociate himself, albeit quietly, from Ndamba's encompassing influence. Concomitantly, Ndamba himself has begun to feel his age, and his most recent bout of exchanges and plans for exchanges is clearly designed as a last strategy to consolidate his own family and if possible to mark out an informal successor. As he has moved nearer to doing this, so Wömndi has moved psychologically away without actually precipitating a split or making a direct challenge, perhaps because it is quite unclear what kind of support group he could himself command. I interpret his actions more as a refusal to recognize any form of 'succession', however implicit, to Ndamba's hitherto undisputed leadership, than as a clear bid for such leadership himself.

On 25 April 1976, the Kiklpuklimbo held a pig-killing to finish a long period of mourning for Kondi and also as a sacrifice for other recent dead kin. All was harmonious between Ndamba and Wömndi. On the 29th, Wömndi re-cooked parts of a large pig, which he had kept for the occasion on his father's instructions, given just before death. Wömndi divided pork to close kin after consultations with his wife and elder sister. Then he took from the father's old house a small barkcloth bag of his possessions, and sifted through these, removing ones he wished to keep (a handkerchief, some native salt, rope-making bark, a hat). He took the rest and threw it into some bushes, declaring that as his father had died at morning-time, so he must throw away his things at this time too, for otherwise the ghost would be angry. Later, on 18 September having put together a bridewealth in the intervening months, and again with Ndamba's help, he obtained a new wife from the neighbouring Minembi Yelipi clan. The pigs for the bridewealth were all his own, except for one which Parle, his younger brother, supplied; the money was collected widely from within the sub-clan.

In a previous year, Wömndi had lost his first wife and children, who left him and returned to the wife's natal place (where she subsequently remarried in secrecy). Her departure was precipitated not least by the hostility of the second wife, married in 1972. Now the second wife was herself faced with a younger rival. Wömndi argued that they needed another wife to help with the expanding work on coffee-picking and pig-rearing, especially since the older wife had a tendency to get sick and return to her own kin for long periods of time. The established wife accepted his choice but with no real approval, and in the following year she began to make preparations for receiving Christian baptism, a move designed to force Wömndi to discard the younger woman, since if he were baptized also he could not remain a polygamist. The younger wife herself appeared loath to work much, and spent more time picking coffee at her natal home than for Wömndi. He did not, therefore, gain much from the new marriage; his words, however, make it clear that he intended through it to increase his income and standing and to recoup the loss he had suffered when his first wife left (she had, for instance, three children, including an eldest girl who would in a few years be marriageable and in the meantime was at high-school). It was not until 24 December 1977 that he finally obtained a small compensation of K 200 and two pigs for the loss of his first wife and children. Meanwhile, his new wife became more and more errant, and the marriage collapsed. After protracted efforts, he secured an official divorce and part return of bridewealth in September 1980.

Such actions and outcomes are typical of social processes in Hagen society. Men attempt to increase their status but are dependent on family assistance to do so, and they may fail. If they succeed, gradually they may become the centre of a smaller set of male supporters, and their name may eventually attach to a new 'lineage'. There does not need to be sharp rivalry between persons for the pattern to emerge, although rivalries are certainly present. There is also much criticism of those in the lineage who do not pull their weight when a drive to raise money or pigs is on, and this can lead to internal splits.

At the time of my initial fieldwork, 1964–5, the Kiklpuklimbo consisted essentially of two sets of 'father–son units' (which I call lineages, although they should not be thought of as strictly unilineal in recruitment). These were: Wapkang kangemal, 'the sons of Wapkang', and Konda–Kakla kangemal, 'the sons of Konda and Kakla'. Even then, the second set were also known as Kongna (or Pana) kangemal, after Ndamba's father, despite the fact that Kongna was in no way apical to the set. In fact, it was evident that they were so called, not because of Kongna himself, but because of Ndamba's predominant influence. The accompanying genealogies (Figure 1) show the chief relationships between men in the two lineage sets. It is evident that the 'sons of Konda and Kakla' have been the more numerous since 1964, and that the big-man, Ndamba, has probably benefited from this fact. Correspondingly, however, after his death, they are less likely to retain their unity.

In December 1975, I interviewed Nikint on the current composition of kangemal sets in the sub-clan.

Ah yes, now inside Wapkang's sons we broke them up; it was just a device so that we could 'eat things' [i.e. receive more in moka]. We made a boundary at the Kiltpana stream and called those across it 'the men of Rimbri hill', that is Kuri, Kowa, Ndat, and also some Eltimbo sub-clans, men such as Ant and his sons who lived there. Those living on this side

Figure 1
Sect. (1) *Wapkang Kangemal – 'the sons of Wapkang'*

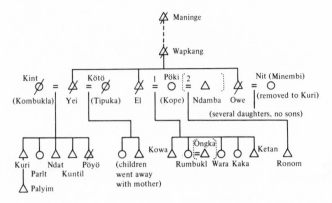

The lineage set had only four co-resident adult men in 1964–5. Kuri's eldest son is now (1980) married with children, but Ronom and Ketan, also married, are associated as much with set (2) as set (1). The daughters are all married and living elsewhere with their husbands. By late 1980 Ndat had also left and was living with Kombukla affines; Kowa had no prestige, and Kuri defaulted entirely on his *moka* debts.

of the Kiltpana and Poklkane streams, we called 'the *kilt* dwellers'. And those across the Kiltpana in the other direction, we named 'the men of Mina settlement'. As for the Rimbri ones, we were tired of them because they did not repay their debts properly, and so we decided they should in future take on their own responsibilities, so we separated them off, hoping they would be ashamed and so start to contribute properly. At Mina are Ndamba's people, himself, Pangk, and Pepa, Moka and Wöyö. At Kiltpana there are Rongnda, Kuntil, Wömndi and Parle, and I help both the Mina and the Kiltpana men. Wamb and his children are in Kongna's sons, with Ndamba, but they don't do anything to help, they're rubbish.

Here, Nikint gave a kind of locality basis to the new (and very fluid) subdivisions, putting together sets across the earlier *kangemal* divisions. The overall effect was rather definitely to isolate the rump of Wapkang's sons more than before, while making a division within the expanded other set. Nikint also saw himself as uncertainly attached, or rather as participating in both sub-sets within Konda–Kakla's sons. The sub-sets can hardly be said to have crystallized into recognized groups, however. The actual situation is more complicated. What is operative is the continuing separation of Kuri, Ndat, and Kowa from the others; a support-group based on Ndamba and Rongnda; and the emergence of Wömndi as a 'loner'. Nikint has continued to cross the 'lines'. Currently (1980), he is closely allied with Parle, Wömndi's younger brother, who has begun to oppose Wömndi on issues to do with modern business activity. Ndamba, much as he would like to, is unable either to hold all of the younger men together under his leadership or to mediate in their disagreements.

Sect. (2) *Konda–Kakla Kangemal – 'the sons of Konda and Kakla'*

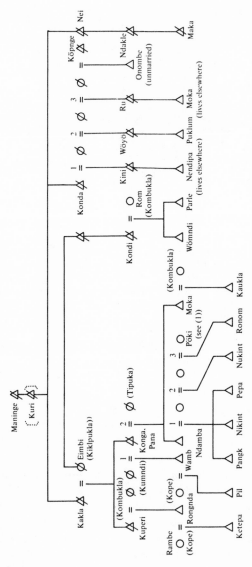

The lineage set had fifteen co-resident adult men in 1980 (thirteen in 1964–5). The ancestral figure Kuri did not appear in genealogies given to me until 1980, when Wömndi introduced him. Wömndi also again presented his father Kondi as an immediate brother of Kuperi rather than a cross-cousin.

IV

Another look back at the situation in 1964 will show some of the roots of the current alignments. Many of the feelings between lineage kinsmen are influenced by their marital histories. This is particularly true in the case of Nikint and his marriages.

On 8 September 1965, eleven months after his first marriage, Nikint told me that the new wife had decided to leave him. Parle, Wömndi's younger brother, had apparently overheard her in conversation with his own wife, who had been married at about the same time and was of a related clan among the Kombukla, planning their joint flight. On the day they named, the two husbands waited secretly for them beside the road, then stepped out and asked where they were going. Wömndi, who was a local government 'Komiti' (councillor's assistant) then made a switch of stinging nettles and said he would beat the girls, asking them who among their kin had persuaded them to run away and why. Parle's wife was beaten rather fiercely, in fact, and her kinsfolk duly came and demanded compensation, knowing that another in-law had recently brought a large cassowary as part of a bridewealth for Mberem, the sister of Wömndi and Parle. They therefore used the occasion to demand this cassowary for themselves. Nikint's wife, Mepil, was not beaten, since Wömndi said she did sometimes stay with her husband and look after him, though he himself claimed she was always visiting other people and chattering to them, rather than staying at home to feed the pigs as she should. He had therefore asked Wömndi to include her in the beating, but Wömndi declined. She took her netbags and left too, and her kin also demanded a cassowary and £20 as well. Nikint gave them £5 and said there was no reason he should give more, since he had already paid the bridewealth. He refused to share with them a further £15 he won in gambling and told them he didn't care if his 'rubbish wife' went with them; he would remove his bridewealth and get another wife. Ndamba wanted to find a cassowary to give her father, but Nikint stopped him. So Mepil did leave, but she still came back occasionally, and over the next ten years they had three children. Parle's wife, however, after bearing one daughter for him, left permanently. It was not until some years after that he remarried, and then to a young widow who left her children behind to come to him. Parle's old mother looked after his daughter, who did not take to his second wife.

The years 1977–9 saw a re-enactment of the dramas of 1964–5 in Nikint's case. Every lineament of his initial attitudes showed once more in his renewed conflict with Mepil. By this time, however, he had married a second wife, Kopil, from a Minembi group (the same clan as that of his brother Pangk's senior wife, also called Kopil), and he had built a new house away from his father's old settlement, Mina, much closer to the houses of Wömndi and Parle. Here Kopil stayed, raising a separate herd of pigs and bearing a son for Nikint. For at least five years, she and her small boy were clearly his favourites. Nikint rarely visited Mina, and did not regularly garden for Mepil or provide her with firewood. Instead, she was cared for by Onombe, Ndamba's worker. Onombe lived at Mina, sleeping in the men's house which Ndamba at first built for all his sons to use when they were grown up but unmarried. As the sons moved out to found settlements or part-settlements of their own, Onombe stayed. He received his food either from Ndamba's second wife, Kuklnga, or from Mepil. Ndamba himself slept in an older men's house of his own, where he kept his possessions. Onombe was at hand to help both Kuklnga and Mepil with firewood and gardening work, and he also planted a good deal of coffee of his own, which was harvested regularly from 1970 onwards. Nikint looked after Kopil and planted coffee with her in a garden site belonging to a matrilateral parallel cousin of his from within his own clan. Both wives were supposed to share in the work of picking and processing the coffee beans and he to divide the cash proceeds between them. Both he and Ndamba tended to favour Kopil, however, on the grounds that she was hard-working, quiet, and obedient, and that she did not go to stay at her natal home as Mepil did. Nevertheless, Mepil bore three children, a girl and two boys, while Kopil was unable successfully to conceive a second child, a problem which caused tension between herself and her husband.

The new phase of conflict coincided with the purchase by Ndamba's supporters of a Toyota Land Cruiser truck, financed from coffee sales. The truck was obtained on 11 July 1977. Nikint made a very large contribution to it (K 1,200) as did Onombe (K 1,000) and Ndamba (K 650). The sons of Ndamba, plus Onombe, together accounted for K 4,070 out of the total purchase price of K 6,410.[6] Nikint planned to learn how to drive the truck himself, but at first a licensed driver from a neighbouring Kawelka clan was called in: he had to be paid occasionally and fed regularly. The whole enterprise of saving the money to buy the car had itself placed a strain on relationships between husbands and wives in particular, and because Nikint saw himself as in charge of the vehicle's management and running, he was less and less often at home. At the same time he claimed more and more cash from coffee production in order to buy petrol for the car and to pay its driver and himself to use in town. He also began to collect money in fares from passengers and to spend it on beer; allegedly, also on girls.

Even before the car was actually bought, Kopil became upset with Nikint. One of her brothers brought a contribution of K 64, but the collection was already over. Nikint asked him to take it back and to repay a much larger sum owed as a part of *moka* exchanges later. Kopil, thinking that perhaps her brother's money would have strengthened her own claims to ride in the car, took this as an insult, but Nikint stubbornly claimed that his action had been straightforward. Wömndi commented to me that Nikint should have taken both Kopil and her brother to one side and talked about the matter quietly. 'Nikint does not listen to what women say', he added. The next moment of conflict I recorded between them was 27 November 1977. The Kundmbo clan as a whole was by this time deeply involved in collecting money for a *moka* gift to another neighbouring group, the Minembi Mimke. Men were busy criticizing each other for failing to do their best. In one sub-clan, two new small groups began to crystallize out for the reason that its men were finding it difficult to pull together as one. As well as money for the main gift, Ndamba and the big-men of the other sub-clans had decreed that extra money be gathered to purchase huge pigs, these to be slaughtered by the Mimke recipients and the pork distributed to their helpers, especially their own women. It was another time, then, of exceptional effort and tension. At a division of money received in *moka* from Ndamba's maternal clansmen, in-married wives of the group had received only K 240 out of the total of K 3,200. Thirty-six men and boys accounted for K 2,960, an average of *c*. K 82 each (the range was between K 10 and K 200); for women, the average was K 8. 57, older women in practice being given K 2 and the younger ones K 10 – this followed by an exhortatory speech from Pepa on the need for the women to work hard and contribute to the men's next *moka*. That was on 23 September, and the pressure to augment what was received in order to make a larger gift to the Mimke (and thus 're-invest' the money) began almost at once. On the occasion in late November when the money of the Kiklpuklimbo men was brought out and counted, Nikint found himself short of a few kina and told Kopil to bring out some cash she had saved from the sale of lengths of sugar-cane at market. She went into the house, returned with a bundle, and scattered coins and notes on the grass, clearly indicating her anger that he should requisition what she had worked to accumulate. Nevertheless, he took it.

Kopil was angered further by the fact that she had been ousted as favourite wife by an interloper whom Nikint had discovered on one of his journeys to town, a hard-faced and experienced woman who was reputed to have been through several marriages and who kept a tight hold on Nikint, especially on what he had at any given time in his wallet. Mepil seemed less concerned; she had for long been relegated to the background and was possibly even amused to see Kopil fall from favour and Nikint, usually so ebullient, thoroughly under the thumb of the new wife. Nikint fell sick, first with a raging toothache, then with pneumonia. He claimed he was upset with the constant demands made by senior men that he make a prominent contribution to the *moka*, and he threatened he would not give the K 400 he was asked to raise but only K 200 instead. His uncle, Moka, was called in to bespell him, since Ndamba privately considered that, aside from any other cause, the sickness might be due to menstrual pollution from the new wife. None of the Kiklpuklimbo men liked her, and all wished that she would go. Ndamba was particularly hurt by her presence, since she had ousted his own favourite, Kopil, and he was particularly sensitive to the problems of pollution, since he had in 1973 sponsored a performance of the Female Spirit Cult, in which all his sons had participated. Those who have been through this cult are supposed to gain protection against pollution, but they must be meticulous in observing sexual taboos, for otherwise it is thought that the jealous Spirit will withdraw her protection. Nikint's close attachment to his new wife, and her own past history, convinced Ndamba that she posed a threat to the health of the whole settlement, as well as to that of Nikint himself. Everyone began to speak about the problem, other than in earshot of the wife herself. Her own insistence on shares of pork at distributions increased the men's dislike of her and the fear that she might be a witch. Moreover, it was pointed out that she had come to Nikint seeing that he had a car and that she was likely to leave if it broke down, and, being rather old, was unlikely to bear him any children. The criticisms reached a crescendo when Nikint abandoned supervision of the truck on 28 December 1977, in favour of drinking beer with his new wife near to the local mission station. The driver proceeded to crash it at high speed only a few miles away, while on his way to pick up clanspeople at a ceremonial dance near to Mount Hagen town. It was widely said that the wife had made a kind of sorcery, *wulya wulya*, on Nikint so that he could not think straight. The car was out of action for many months, and the wife duly left Nikint during this time.

Senior sub-clansmen then began to urge on him that if he must have a third wife, he should at least marry a young woman from a well-known and nearby group, through whom useful new exchange links could be set up. There were, indeed, other girlfriends from such groups who looked on him with favour, and some visited him to see if he was interested, but he was not. I interpret this as his refusal to place himself too firmly into exchange networks decided for him by his senior kinsmen. He had gained his driving licence and was also in 1978 managing the construction of a store, in which he planned to have a share. It seems evident that he sensed his father's growing wish that the mantle of leadership should fall on him and was torn between his adherence to the value of publicly achieved prestige and the growing necessity to support this with time-consuming private work and negotiation. 'Business' began to emerge more as an alternative aim. His growing impatience with both of his established wives and his apparent lack of concern that they and their children should stay with him seem to reflect his ambivalence about taking on responsibility in general. On one occasion, in August 1978, he told Kopil she was not to go to the settlement Mina and pick coffee there, for it was Mepil's plot, and she would be like a dog or a pig if she took from it. But Mepil, in turn, was told not to harvest his other garden, although she argued that her daughter, Peni, needed some money for her school fees and the coffee in her plot was not ripe for picking. For months, Kopil had been asking Nikint to build her a new woman's house: the old one, put up in the early 1970s was now rotting and no longer kept out the rain. She offered that her brothers could come and build it and Nikint reward them with a meal and some money. Finally, she kept some cash (supposedly K 12) from sales of coffee as a first step towards saving money for this end. Nikint demanded it, she refused; he hit her, and she thereupon left for her own natal place, taking their son with her. She remained for many months before returning.

Many times Kopil had spoken to me quietly about her need for a new house. It was an elementary recognition of her marital rights in general that she required, and Nikint's violation of these rights, coupled with his insistence that he control all the money coming in and his failure to support Kopil when she was once sick and had to stay at the mission hospital, finally turned her against him. She pointed out that when he was sick, she had killed one of their pigs to help him get better, but when she was in hospital, he never once visited her or sent any money.

She came back at a feast held to celebrate the construction of a new ceremonial ground by Ndamba in April 1979, but returned without staying, having seen that her house was quite uninhabitable. In June, Nikint married a new wife again and thus began conflict with Mepil, who had been left briefly by herself when Kopil earlier departed. There was in addition a source of financial unease about the further marriage. A father and brothers, and also sub-clansmen and other close kin and affines, will all help a young man with his first and also his second marriage, if he contributes to group activities. But marriages contracted in early middle age, after the initial period of 'setting-up', are regarded as largely the individual's own responsibility. In this case Ndamba had not been consulted, and he contributed only about K 10 in money. Other senior men also held back. Nikint was therefore forced to dip heavily into his own resources again, and it was said that he did so by taking out of the store profits K 500 or so, when others considered that they had a claim on these because they had helped him previously. So conflict over the wife became deeply involved with conflict over the store.

The wife herself was from a group which was notorious to the Kundmbo as expert in sorcery and hostile to the Kawelka as a whole. Again, Nikint found her in town, though she was actually related to Kopil, and Kopil returned to make friends with her at first until driven away by Nikint himself. Mepil decided to take a more aggressive stand. To keep the peace, Ndamba and Pepa tried continually to forbid Mepil to enter the settlement at Kiltkayake where Nikint had set up house with Parle. She asked why such a rule should hold and frequently came by. The new store was back in operation by this time, and from his share of it Nikint was rumoured frequently to bring rice, fish, and meat for secret consumption at night in Parle's house. When Mepil passed by, the newest wife called out, 'come to me and smell the rice and meat on my mouth! I'm eating "double fives" [ten kina notes] as well.' Mepil fought with her and then twice with Nikint. He told her to go back forever to her own kin and take her children with her as well. In order to obtain the new wife, he had actually taken two of Mepil's pigs, yet he made no returns for this and also grumbled when her father came to request help with the marriage of her younger brother. He refused to meet his father-in-law, whom he regarded as greedy and demanding, and went off to town instead. His children by Mepil now spent much of their time with their mother's people. Peni would not stay with Nikint at all after he had refused access to his coffee garden. Mepil herself remained, partly because she was expecting another child. Up to 20 September 1979, there was no solution to the conflict. Pepa and others freely voiced their criticisms of Nikint's untoward conduct. He himself simply said that he had married the wife 'in order to be a captain in such a new venture': again, I see this as his second act of rebellion against parental choice. Indeed, since he was at odds with Mepil very soon after his first marriage in 1964, and his father definitely chose Mepil for him, there seems to have been an element of rebelliousness involved from the beginning. (By September 1980, Mepil had actually returned again, staying at Mina and keeping out of the new wife's way.)

V

These actions by Nikint would remain very hard to understand, unless seen against the background of the general developmental cycle of political events within the Kiklpuklimbo sub-clan, and it is on this process that I now concentrate.

While Kondi and Kuperi were alive, Ndamba stayed at Mina. When Kondi died, and the rites for his funeral were completed, Ndamba began his plan to make a new ceremonial ground at Kiltkayake very close to Kondi's old settlement. In conjunction with this, Ndamba planned also a whole sequence of *moka* events, which he saw quite explicitly as his last big activities and the means whereby he would attempt to consolidate the exchange partnerships of his immediate sons and secure the continuing support of others in the same network of exchanges. Basically, he wanted to make this last big *moka* to his mother's people, of Tipuka Kengeke clan. This would be a prelude to the extensive death-feast which would be due to him and the maternal kin, when he died. To this end, he organized the reception of a *moka* from Kengeke partners and the transmission of most of this, plus much more, to other friends among the Minembi Mimke. A little later, on completing his ceremonial ground and men's house, he organised a *moka* to Kiklpukla men on the official basis of his sub-clan's link with these through its name. His idea was that if both Mimke and Kiklpukla partners made returns quickly, a hugely augmented *moka* could then be made back to the Kengeke – who might then even make returns again before his own death, since they live in a fertile area at a lower altitude than the Kundmbo and plant much coffee. By making sure that his sons received and gave prominently in all these events, he hoped to keep them at the forefront of the clan's affairs. The car purchase was for the same end. And, of his sons, he had decided that Nikint was best to succeed him. Indeed, Pangk, the eldest son, fell into disgrace during 1978–9 through following his senior wife to her own place, when she left him after Pepa had supposedly insulted her for trailing around the countryside looking for men. Pangk, clearly very upset, went to retrieve her, but instead she retained him. It is curious that Ndamba did not then turn to Pepa, the youngest son, who was also favoured by their big-man in-law Ongka, for Pepa had none of the severe domestic troubles that afflicted Nikint, and he worked at home with his two wives, as well as speaking up at exchanges. Yet Pepa had the drawback of a hasty tongue: Wömndi claimed to me, in fact, that Pepa had got him too into serious trouble.

The background to this allegation was as follows: At Kondi's funeral feast, many guests came, as is normal, including several Kombukla tribesmen, related through the marriages of Wömndi and his sisters. Unfortunately, one of these guests died the day after visiting Wömndi's place, and suspicion of sorcery arose. Some declared that Wömndi had listened to his own father-in-law and administered poison to the deceased, since there was an issue between the father-in-law's and the deceased's clan. Pepa, for whatever reason, was said to have blurted out some remark implying as much. Consequently, Wömndi's affines were upset also at this talk, and his children kept getting sick. Wömndi therefore blamed his predicament on Pepa and called on him to help put on a small feast to restore his in-law's feelings, but Pepa would not. From that time, Wömndi began to hold himself a little apart. He took a full share (K 100) from the money from the Kengeke, but on the occasion he announced that he did so only for Ndamba's sake and that from then on the Kiklpuklimbo would not be united; they would do things separately. The burden of his speech was that he had already found, when they tried to do things together, that some men let them down and they found it difficult to fill the gaps. Men received in distributions, but ran away at the next *moka*. Those left in charge were embarrassed. Let them not then, make promises on behalf of the Kiklpuklimbo as a whole, instead, let each man and his sons pursue exchanges separately.

Wömndi's remarks here were strongly prophetic: Kuri, who insisted on receiving the large share of K 200, subsequently vanished every time the discussion of how to organize returns was broached during 1979; Kowa, Ndamba's stepson, spent most of his time visiting elsewhere, as did Ndat, Kuri's brother: the Kiklpuklimbo were angry because he had taken with him the badge of his office as a 'Komiti', in which capacity he ought to be central in group affairs – Ndamba said it should go to Pepa instead. Pangk was embroiled in difficulties at his wife's place, where he was later accused falsely of poisoning a Minembi man and placed in some danger. Finally, Nikint's two senior wives had both effectively left him, and his latest wife was more interested in consumption than production. Ndamba tried very hard throughout the latter part of 1979 to get his followers to repay the Kengeke gift, using a *moka* he and Nikint had received from men of Minembe Papeka (male in-laws who still wished to exchange with Ndamba even though Nikint's marriage was in trouble). Ndamba promised to distribute this sum in order to stimulate his men to collect for the Kengeke. Yet everyone else dragged their feet, and Wömndi especially announced that he simply did not 'understand what Ndamba was saying', since it was obvious no-one was ready.

Ndamba's lack of success here indicated three things:
(1) he was right to be thinking of 'retiring', however informally, from his central role, since he was finding it very hard to maintain this;
(2) none of his sons was able to step into his own position of influence, and this had at least partly to do with the switch from pigs and shells into money as a major medium for *moka*-making. Since money has so many potential uses, it is harder to persuade people to put it together for *moka* gifts;
(3) Wömndi now felt separate enough to declare that he no longer listened to or understood Ndamba's plans. Although he had never directly opposed Nikint and Pepa in the past, he now also began to do so. Like many others, he was upset that Nikint and his own younger brother Parle dominated the use of the Toyota truck and used it almost entirely to bring in their own store goods for sale, cutting others out.

Wömndi had an interest in a part of the store, and he now began to point out that the land on which the store and ceremonial ground were built was not Ndamba's but his, through his father's claims, and that he could, if necessary, tell Nikint to leave; second, he began to sound out possible supporters, including myself, who might help him to fund the purchase of an alternative vehicle to fetch goods and carry people. The only other vehicle, belonging to the rival sub-clan in his clan-section, had broken down, and Wömndi judged that his own coffee trees would soon begin bearing heavy crops and bring him in a flush of money. The snag for him was that his brother Parle had stepped away from him in the direction of Nikint. While Nikint and Pepa were to some extent at odds over the vehicle, then, so were Wömndi and Parle: lineage 'brothers' joined up at the expense of their immediate sibling ties. The focus of conflict was control over new 'business' resources, plus a certain refusal to play the leading role in exchanges which Ndamba was trying to engineer for Nikint. Nikint's and Parle's new wives were rather similar in their ways: determined to travel with their husbands in the car, relatively uninterested in bearing children or rearing pigs, and sharply malicious about older women. While Wömndi was convinced that Parle's wife kept him exhausted and was gradually killing him by menstrual poisoning, Parle himself opposed his elder brother on the running of the store and sided with his wife in stirring up the animosity of Wömndi's own junior wife against the senior one. Such cross-cutting animosities and unresolved issues certainly made concerted social action very hard, and it was apparent that Ndamba's influence was not sufficient to hold everyone together. Rather than succession to his leadership position, then, it appeared by the end of 1979 much more likely that disintegration was about to occur, or would at any rate ensue after his death.

When one is dealing with close kin relationships, however, one can expect that such disintegration will be staved off for as long as possible. By mid-1980 the tide of events had turned in Ndamba's favour again. Wömndi prepared his cash contribution for the *moka* to the Kengeke, and from then on in fact vigorously supported Ndamba in his wish to complete the gift, seizing on the occasion to criticize Nikint and Parle for their heavy cash losses in gambling, the lack of goods for sale in the store, and the now decrepit state of the truck. His assistance to Ndamba, then, was in fact just another way of expressing his resistance to the notion that Nikint could become Ndamba's successor. The *moka* was finished in early September 1980, with a huge money component, exceeding K 10,000. Nikint retrieved some of his honour by providing K 300 in cash (to Wömndi's K 600) and several pigs; his wife Kopil also returned to her role as pig-keeper and enjoyed a brief limelight in bringing up pigs to the ceremonial ground and discussing them publicly with spectators. After the *moka* was over, relationships in general became more relaxed, but rivalry undoubtedly remained between Wömndi and Nikint. Ndamba continued to express the wish that we could simply return to the old pattern of unity under his influence. He evidently realized that without such unity, it was unlikely that any single successor to himself would emerge. What he did not, perhaps, see was that the conditions for the emergence of a successor were rather different from those which held when he first made his own mark.

What do we learn from this extended case history about family relations among the Melpa? It is abundantly apparent that succession to big-manship is a hazardous and contingent matter, and that the hazards are compounded now by the divisive effects of social and economic change. Yet this is not simply because of rivalry between brothers for supremacy or for material inheritance. For example, land claims are not an issue between Pangk, Nikint, Pepa, their stepbrothers, and others in their lineage. Nor does any one of the younger men appear inordinately ambitious: rather, the big-man's own favourite son appears keen to blot his record and maintain independence. It is equally plain, and instructive, to see that Ndamba has made a plan for the final stage of his own leadership and its conversion into a position of strength for his sons. Wömndi is aware of this and is correspondingly intent on making it clear that he will not be party to such a programme for hegemony. At a wider level, Ndamba is also trying to consolidate the leading role of his whole sub-clan vis-à-vis others in the clan, and to pull in energetic members of the other sub-clans to be with the Kiklpuklimbo in exchanges. Wömndi again doubts that this process will survive Ndamba's own lifetime, and does not truly see himself as able to step into the big-man's shoes. Rather, he too is looking for some further 'business' opportunity to take up. Interestingly, it is mostly those men who are less central in the sub-clan's affairs who sometimes stress its strength and unity. Ndat and Kuri, for example, who are of a different lineage set from Ndamba, often talk about 'the name of the Kiklpuklimbo' as a whole. And Pangk, who is the eldest but least forceful of Ndamba's adult sons, speaks often of the importance of 'brotherhood', using the archaic phrase *öngin mel eimb*, 'a brother is a creative thing'. Whether that sentiment can influence events in the future remains to be seen, and the test will surely come after Ndamba's death, a death which he, far-seeing and profoundly identified with his sub-clan, spoke of already in 1977 at the division of the money from his mother's kin. Then he told the sons that in taking this money they must pledge themselves to show unity and honour at least in giving him a proper funeral feast, placing him on a trestle above the ground for mourners to see and cry over and killing pigs for his ghost at the proper time. Regardless of whether one of his sons becomes a big-man, it is certain that the memory of Ndamba will remain strong in his group and will influence people's attitudes and actions for long after his death.

VI

The case history discussed here has centred on one family within a sub-clan of the Kawelka people. But interwoven with this family history, there are matters which for their explanation depend on understanding the wider context of change: particularly coffee growing, the running of stores and the purchase of vehicles, and the use of money as a new valuable in ceremonial exchanges. It is very hard to be sure whether these crucial new events and practices have actually altered the patterns of succession and rivalry over succession to leadership in any fundamental way. In my view, patterns of rivalry have always been complex, and this is predicated on the fact that while there is a definite feeling that someone should emerge as a big-man in each small group, there is yet no definite rule specifying how this should occur, nor indeed any practical guarantee that it will occur. However, there are certain ways in which the process has been modified by economic change, as follows: first, and most significantly, alternative aims have been created, and sons may claim that they wish to take up 'business' rather than traditional-style big-manship. Second, as women gain and desire more access to money, conflicts between husbands and wives are becoming severe. Since men depend on women for much essential labour, such conflict prejudices their chances of success in *moka*. Third, as money has many different uses, ordinary lineage kinsmen, not particularly fired with ambition, are likely to use it for their private patterns of consumption rather than primarily for ceremonial exchange. These three factors together make the process of succession perhaps even more indeterminate than it was in the past.

To characterize the present phase of change is not easy, then. It is not possible to argue either that the social system is simply reproducing itself or that its main frameworks have broken down. The key to the situation clearly lies in the exchange system as such. Conflict does not centre directly on land or on the possession of money but on who does or does not take part in *moka*. Status is evaluated in terms of *moka* performance, just as it was in 1964. But the conditions on which the *moka* depends are now deeply implicated with the commercial use of land, since money used in *moka* is obtained from the sale of coffee grown on the most fertile parts of clan territory. And *moka* alliances are pursued with groups whose men have good coffee gardens. If commitment to *moka* continues (and it has strong ideological underpinnings), one can envisage a stage at which conflict over access to land would become overt, since only those with adequate good land could stay in the *moka* system as a whole and expect to maintain high status in it. But this point has not been reached, nor will it necessarily be reached, since there is always a percentage of people who drop out of the competition in any case, and thus pressures within the system are reduced.

Another matter which is very hard to assess is whether the quality of feelings between kin has been altered significantly by the penetration of money into the life of the clan. In some senses, it obviously has been altered: people now ask for money before they will part with thatching grass for their fallow gardens, for instance; Ndamba had to pay Wömndi's Kombukla wife over K 500 for a pig to use in the September 1980 *moka* (though she in turn said it was actually worth K 800, and they were doing this to 'help' him); those who help with gardening work expect a meal of purchased store foods rather than home-grown vegetables. Relationships are, then, more and more mediated through cash. However, it is wrong to suppose that there was not calculation and rivalry prior to the advent of cash: that there certainly was. The pearl shell economy, run by big-men as financiers, had already produced this circumstance, albeit without capitalist relations of production. At the same time, there was, and remains, a strong ethic of sharing, and deep shame attaches to those who exhibit selfishness and greed, for these characteristics are indicative of witchcraft. It seems, therefore, that an answer to the problem of exactly how the social system as a whole, and the feelings of people within it, will be affected by and respond to the process of monetization and commodity production must wait for some further years of observation before it can be clearly formulated.

NOTES

1 For a general survey of arguments on 'succession' in Highland societies, see W. Standish, *The 'Big-Man' Model Reconsidered: Power and Stratification in Chimbu, Port Moresby*. Institute of Applied Social and Economic Research, Discussion Paper 22 (1978).
2 A. J. Strathern, *Ongka* (London, 1979), 11ff.
3 Cf. A. J. Strathern, 'Gender, Ideology and Money in Mount Hagen', *Man*, new series, 14 (1979), 543, where a list of pigs purchased for this event appears.
4 K = Papua New Guinea Kina. K 1 = £ stg 0.7.
5 On the cult's history, see A. J. Strathern, 'The Red-Box Money Cult in Mount Hagen, 1968–71', *Oceania*, 50 (2) (1979–80), 88–102, and 50 (3), 161–75.
6 For more details, see Strathern, 'Gender', 539–47.

9. The Aragonese royal family around 1300

ROGER SABLONIER

'Provisional fragments of an experiment initially undertaken with a great deal of scepticism.' This should be the sub-title of this study on the relationships, ways of acting, and forms of experiencing in the Aragonese royal family around 1300. The materials available arose in a very special social and cultural context,[1] and serious methodological problems posed themselves from the outset. The social construct of a royal family is to be seen both by its structure and by its function as an 'open-lineage family'.[2] Nevertheless, this chapter is concentrated on and directed towards the cluster of relationships in the nuclear family. It deals chiefly with relations between spouses, between parents and children, and between siblings, which does not mean that this 'nucleus' should *a priori* be seen as the central zone, the axial region of the whole system. The restrictions on method imply a limitation but not a fundamental objection to attempting to understand and describe as concretely as possible the forms, the shape, and intensity of relationships in this narrow circle.

In the relationships between royal spouses, between parents and children, and between siblings in the royal house, an understanding of the complex combined effects of material and emotional interests is an important consideration. It is of course immediately apparent that the 'real' elements, so to speak, directed towards perpetuating and transmitting property and positions of power, are clearly visible. It is not simply a question here of ensuring succession by biological means, rights of inheritance, and of marriage strategies. Beyond all this, the royal house stands in a particular relationship to the State. With the children – sons and daughters who will have careers and marry – not only are chances of power and domination in an analogous sense 'produced' but also, one might at least suggest, from their function and position so is the State. Its operation was still linked very closely to the personal presence of its holder, above all the royal family. It is precisely this pronounced real/functional relationship that marks out in obverse a framework within which emotional ties, affective experiences, and feelings must be examined with particular care. The real and material claims, which are to be understood against a background of

210

quasi-objective assumptions and structural conditions of the royal exercise of power, have to be transformed into familial strategies of action and norms of living. This does not happen independently and cannot be separated from the way in which these claims and norms are respectively conceived, experienced, and reflected on by the specific individuals directly concerned with them. Solidarity and harmony, psychological tension, and conflicts arise both within the dynamics of the internal family and in the sphere of public activity, which in turn have reciprocal effect on each other. It is therefore axiomatic that emotional factors and material bases cannot be seen as simply in juxtaposition or as alternatives.

The relatively limited original and historiographical material available for the study of medieval royal families presents significant problems of interpretation. We shall have to be content with clues and approximations. Taking the case of James II of Aragon (1267–1327) arises primarily from practical grounds, since we have in this instance a documentation which for the period is unusually full, and this makes the exercise rather more promising. In addition, James II's biography has already been very well researched.[3] Most of this chapter is based on documentary material already in print. In the early years of this century, Heinrich Finke made many of these sources available for further research and studied them from the standpoint of his own times.[4] 'King Jaime was a family man, a pater-familias'.[5] His judgement, which in every respect is an interesting one, was also accepted by Martinez Ferrando, who recently published a very detailed and reliable, if chiefly biographical and culturally historical, description of the family of James II, which includes an extensive appendix of sources.[6] Contemporary royal chronicles also provide interesting information.[7]

I

First, a few relevant facts. James II was born in 1267, succeeded his elder brother Alfonso as king of Aragon in 1291, and was married four times. A contract of marriage concluded in 1291 with Princess Elisabeth of Castile, who was apparently only eight years of age at the time, was dissolved in 1295, although the young lady held the title of Queen of Aragon during the four years. At the end of October 1295, he married the twelve-year-old Blanche of Anjou–Naples, who died giving birth to her tenth child in 1310. After protracted negotiations, James II then married Maria of Cyprus–Lusignan, who was over thirty, in 1315. She died in 1322, without having produced any descendants. Immediately after her death, he married Elisenda of Moncada, a daughter of the high aristocracy of his own region, who survived him by fully thirty-seven years.

Except in the case of the last marriage, political reasons behind the choice of consorts are easy to find. In 1295, the Pope had not only decisively promoted the planned marriage with Blanche, but had also provided the formal legal reason – that of too close a blood relationship – for the separation from his first wife. The aim was to settle the political differences between the Pope and Anjou-Naples on the one hand and between the former and the Aragonese on the other. The political factors involved in the later marriage with Maria of Cyprus–Lusignan are equally clear. The initiative seems to have originated in Cyprus, but James was seeking further ways of exerting an influence in the eastern Mediterranean. Behind this desire were not only the ideas of the Crusade but also interests involving trading policies. He even had certain hopes, which turned out to be without foundation, of inheriting from the Lusignans. In addition, Maria's brother, who was reigning jointly with his mother, was known to be a rich man and thought to be obliged to give a large dowry in view of the fall in prestige involved. The awareness of the importance of marriage ties as a means of initiating or strengthening political relations can be clearly seen in the marriage plans for the children, a point to which we will return later. What needs no further argument here is the fact that in these matters the Papacy and the Church exerted a more or less great influence, since they had at their disposal a dispensation from the impediment of consanguinity and also means of exerting political and financial pressure.

How were the marriages arranged? They were the result of negotiations and agreements and not complete until *copula carnalis* had occurred, of course.[8] Special emissaries, who for reasons of discretion and reliability were usually clerics, negotiated the conditions. In Maria's case the sources give great detail about the proceedings to be followed.[9] The negotiations extended over more than three years, and there were various reasons for this delay. The main problem was the age of the young lady in question, a criterion that along with the dowry and her beauty (*pulcritudo*) formed a major part of the brief for the negotiations. Right from the start, James had given strict instructions that the bride must not be over twenty-five years of age. This was only relevant for Heloise, however, Maria's younger sister. Their brother Henry did not want to release the younger girl until her elder sister was married. Moreover, possible claims of inheritance would have had to be made over to Heloise. In order to hide Maria's real age – she must have been over thirty in 1311–12 – he also refused to let the envoys see her until he had received firm assent from them. Compromise suggestions that two of James's children should marry Henry and Heloise on the same occasion were rejected because of the disparity in age. In the initial stages, it was also impossible to come to any agreement about the size of the dowry.

In the early part of these negotiations, there was very probably some discussion on the possibility of a marriage between James and the young Clementia of Hungary. However, Robert of Anjou–Naples, the brother of Blanche (who had died in 1310) and James's brother-in-law as a result of his earlier marriage with the latter's sister Violante (d. 1302), objected violently to this.[10]. He invoked the memory of Blanche, expressed his fears for the rights of the children of her marriage, and also reminded James that it was well known that *regine multum possunt* and thus that the widows of kings could ruin much, at least while sons were still minors. This is not only interesting evidence of the constant fear of an untimely death amongst these people. Quite independently of the question of reasons of a political nature – which were undoubtedly present – a real function of kinship relations can be seen in it. Robert was presenting himself as an uncle on the maternal side for the rights of the children after their mother's death. Moreover, in doing so he addressed his brother-in-law as *frater*, as a real brother. The assumption that by using the appropriate terminology higher family obligations and values are brought into being seems a fairly obvious one.

It is no longer possible to determine what weight this objection had in real terms. However, despite all the twists and turns, a marriage agreement with Maria finally came about. Right up until the last moment it was not certain whether the envoys might not bring her younger sister back to Catalonia. Nevertheless, James did not behave like one of his ancestors, who concluded another marriage while the Byzantine princess whom he had agreed to marry was on her way to him and had to provide a replacement when they met.[11] When Maria finally arrived in Catalonia at the end of November 1315, she was received with both due ceremony and great warmth. The marriage took place in December, followed by valuable gifts and appropriate written undertakings specifying presents from the bridegroom to the bride and his provisions for her widowhood. The Cypriots who had accompanied her on her journey also made thorough enquiries as to whether the values of these gifts matched what he had undertaken for Blanche in her lifetime. On their departure, James was annoyed to find that he had to give them the money they needed for their return journey.[12]

The question of age, so difficult in this case, points to a general problem: the age of readiness for marriage, which was a major point in all such discussions, arose not just from legal considerations. The *copula carnalis* was the consummation of marriage, and the prospect of offspring was a decisive factor. James I, the grandfather of James II, tells with very great perspicuity in his auto-biographical chronicle how he was hurried into marriage as young as possible, as he was expected to produce an heir as soon as he could because of his poor health. He adds almost apologetically that for a year he and his wife 'had not been able to do what man and woman should do, as we were still too young.'[13]

Judging age and sexual maturity and with them potential fertility was one of the uses of inspecting the bride, and exhibiting her before the ambassadors plenipotentiary was an important part of all negotiations. The instruction to envoys to judge both the *qualitas figurae* and the *quantitas staturae* should be understood quite literally. In the case of the planned marriage between his daughter Violante and the son of a French king, for example, James II had the inspection of the bride organized down to the last detail. *Inter alia*, her naked breast was to be shown to the ambassadors.[14] The bride had to be *apta ad prolem*, or, in the even clearer wording used in other instructions, *utilis ad prolem*, fitted for producing children.[15] Even if, in the actual case of Violante, there were specific circumstances helping matters along, with the argument of sexual maturity playing a central role in relation to women in competition with her, this practice of examining the bride must have been a general phenomenon. There appears to be no indication that the purposes of the ceremony went beyond this to the establishing of virginity and were perhaps of a more symbolic nature. Incidentally, it is worth noting that the problem of male infertility was known. In the same circles, for example, a widow was recommended as a suitable choice for remarriage on the grounds of her virginity, which she was said probably never to have lost, as her husband had been impotent as a result of his illness.[16]

When the bride was being inspected and chosen, the *covinent belea*, the 'appropriate beauty' was also considered, whatever was understood by the expression.[17] This is particularly crudely expressed in the scornful remarks of Aragonese envoys that a certain Bohemian competitor at the French court should not be taken seriously, since she had a squint, an ugly face, and was already twenty-two and not eighteen as the king had been told.[18] Nothing escaped the keen eye of the inspection envoy: when the time came for Elisabeth to be prepared for inspection by the Austrian envoys, the father not only gave precise instructions on how she was to dress but also sent for a surgeon to put her teeth to rights.[19]

The insistence that the king's wife should be beautiful – and Maria was described to James as *molt bela*, 'very beautiful' – is explicable in many ways, including the fact that she was obliged to be on public show as part of her duties. Nevertheless, the problem of physical attraction, and hence of securing heirs, must also be considered. And for this the Aragonese royal house had a traumatic example retained in the royal chronicle. It seems that the founder of the Catalonian dynasty, Pedro I, had in his day only once, and that with difficulty and from necessity, been moved to share his bed with his wife, Marie de Montpellier, in order to perform his duty and get her with child.[20] And yet he was not exactly sexually inactive, for the royal chronicle of James I says that on the morning of the decisive battle of the Albigensian Crusade (1213) he could not (or was allowed not to) stand up at Mass 'as he had earlier lain with a woman'. In the same place we have a description of the methods used by the barons of Provence to gain his political support: they let him see their wives, daughters, and most attractive kinswomen, as they knew that he was an *hom de femnes*, a great ladies' man.[21]

Questions of fertility and the duty of procreation played a major part in bringing about these marriages and should also be kept in mind when certain phenomena connected with the situation of the spouses in marriage are described later in this chapter. One thing is clear: Blanche more than came up to expectations as far as offspring were concerned. She had her first son by 1296, and from then on with almost clockwork regularity produced another four sons and five daughters, all of whom reached marriageable age. In 1308, she had made her will, explicitly because she was afraid of the imminent next birth.[22] In 1310 she did in fact die at the age of twenty-seven, immediately after a birth. There could scarcely be a more vivid expression of the function and destiny of the consort of a king. There is, comparatively speaking, much to be said about the activities and position of Blanche.[23] For most of the time, she lived in Tortosa with her retinue, her *casa*, in the geographic centre of the kingdom and in the largest of the many royal residences. The king was constantly travelling around the kingdom, occupied with the exercise of royal rule. His wife often accompanied him, in 1298 and 1309 on campaigns, and clearly often on hunting expeditions. It also seems certain that until they were five or six years of age the children remained chiefly in her care or that of her senior court official. At this stage of their lives at least, James allowed her to exercise great influence on the care and education they received. Her own documentary activity – she had her own chancellery – was limited to marriage business amongst the king's kinfolk and in court circles, which was a political activity in itself, and an animated correspondence with her own Angevin relations. Fostering relationships with her own kin cannot be analysed in more depth here, but one allusion will serve as an example. Blanche very probably had an important part in James's consistent support of the Angevins in Naples, even to the extent of engaging in open war with his own brother, Frederick III of Sicily, although in the view of many of his contemporaries this was against the interests of his own dynasty.

There is no doubt that to some extent links of affection developed between Blanche and James. The forms of address that James used in his letters were passionate enough to stand out from the usual run of formal phrases.[24] Occasionally they reveal quite strong feeling and respect. It can be shown that he tried to keep the news of her father's death from her for almost six months, probably from concern for her health.[25] The significance of the fact that Blanche was particularly attached to the little provincial church where their marriage had taken place should also not be underestimated.[26] In this respect, James's grief after her death was extremely revealing. He sent news of the sad event expressed with real feeling to a whole series of European princes, which in itself was unusual, and expressed to the Pope his decision not to remarry.[27] It is also rather strange that, even though intending to build her a special tomb of Greek porphyry, he did not have her body transferred to the royal family vault in the monastery of Santas Creus until five years later, immediately after the arrival of his new wife, Maria, in Spain.[28] Remarriage and final physical separation, wedding ceremonies, and the ceremonial interment all interlock here, and surely not fortuitously. In addition, Blanche was remembered to a particularly high degree, both in public and within the family.[29]

James's relationship with Maria was in the sharpest contrast to that with Blanche. Once she had been received with all due ceremony and the wedding had been celebrated with lavish presents, difficulties soon began to arise. Contrary to what had been agreed, Maria brought only a part of her dowry with her, and this led to a constant to-ing and fro-ing which dragged on until June 1319 without James ever getting everything. That in itself was not unusual, but James was increasingly annoyed by it as his letters of remonstrance show. This correspondence also seems to have been almost the only contact he had with his new brother-in-law, and was quite different from what had earlier been the case with Robert of Anjou. As a means of exerting pressure, James set in hand in 1318 a massive reorganization and reduction of queen's court, a very significant action in view of the importance of the latter's symbolic value. Either the delay was much greater than usual or James was simply particularly determined to collect the dowry.[30]

Apart from the limited political and financial advantage, there was another quite different problem. It was perhaps not merely by chance that soon after the wedding James commanded baths to be installed in the palace in Valencia which was to be the queen's residence.[31] Was that a way of furthering hopes of fertility? In fact, Maria had no children, and that was a hidden but heavy strain on their relationship. For example, James gave to the monastery of Montserrat a picture of the Mother of God, to which the queen had to kneel in supplication in the course of a ceremonial procession imploring fertility.[32] Later, on one occasion, James had to take steps against poisoners in Maria's entourage.[33] Perhaps behind that lay Maria's desperate anxiety about her fertility. Symbolically, Maria's fear of never having children is almost the opposite of Blanche's fear of the next birth.

The sources give only indirect indications of Maria's activities and position. In contrast to Blanche, whose entourage she had also partly taken over, she seems hardly ever to have appeared publicly after 1317 or scarcely even to have seen the king. After 1320 in particular, she seems to have led an isolated life, one beset increasingly with sickness since 1318. She had virtually no contact with the rest of the royal family, the one exception being her stepdaughter Violante, who occasionally stayed with her. She is very infrequently even mentioned in the family correspondence. The initially friendly tone of James's letters to her grew increasingly cooler, even though he always treated her correctly and with due politeness, bordering on brutal objectivity, particularly in comparison with his manner with Blanche. Even when she was seriously ill around 1318, he only sent her a few relatively formal and insipid words of sympathy. At the same time, he was taking far greater pains with the arrangements for her possible death. A further example: when informing her of the (presumed) death of her brother in 1320, he did not write to her personally but gave the task to her confessor.[34]

After her death on 10 September 1322, at which he was clearly relieved, he became more than explicit. Only three weeks later, he wrote secret instructions for an envoy who was to seek a dispensation from the Pope (consanguinity and the date, fixed for the following advent) for his marriage to Elisenda of Moncada.[35] He did indeed mention in it the dead woman's *probitas* (worthiness) and *honestas* (honesty), but also bitterly stressed her *vetustam inaptitudinem*, her 'unfittedness due to age'. On account of this, he said, he had long had to live in despair and without the consolation of a wife and had been severely plagued by the lusts of the flesh. In order to be able to enjoy some of the pleasures of life, he begged to be allowed to marry, so as not to fall into uncleanliness (*immundiciae*), all the more so as no further harm could come to his kingdom or his children as a result of it. Even externally, Maria's memory was so to speak cancelled, for the news of her death was sent in a rather cool and formal manner to her brother Henry and the remaining Cypriot servants sent home without delay.[36]

The moralizing parts of the letter to the Pope will be noted with a certain scepticism. The extent to which ecclesiastical ideas on the morality of marriage had been interiorized is an open question, for in the aristocracy in particular there were opportunities outside marriage for the immediate satisfaction of sexual and emotional needs. And yet it is noteworthy that in the period after 1295 there is no knowledge of any further illegitimate children of James II. Given the many sources, this fact seems fairly certain. On the possibility that there were such children, it would be all the more eloquent if a particularly stringent secrecy lay behind it.[37] There had been claims of this nature dating from his stay in Sicily before 1295. Indicative of his suspicious thoroughness is a notarial document that he had drawn up concerning one of these claims.[38] It sets the circumstances of the lapse out in detail, even to the colour of the clothes and a convincing and realistic explanation of why the result had been twins – he had had intercourse twice with the woman, once in the evening and again the following morning. On another occasion, he admits that he probably had several women when he was young, but maintains that he cannot be more certain with regard to specific cases.

On the whole, James II seems to have been a great deal more reticent in such matters than his ancestors. Once again, transmitted experiences from his family history may also have had an influence. His grandfather had left a motley crew of illegitimate children behind him. One of them stirred up the opposition of the nobles after 1270 and plunged the kingdom into a profound internal crisis. Apart from that, order in the royal house meant ultimately order in the State. In 1324, James II forbade, *res perniciosa*, under the threat of the severest penalties, men to seek entry to the public baths in Valencia at hours reserved for women. And just as he proceeded against people in the queen's court who indulged in indecent talk with women, he created a public office to control prostitution.[39]

In the final analysis, how are the differences in the marital relationships of Blanche and Maria to be understood? In the case of Blanche, one could speak of a markedly positive convergence of exchange. She brought not only her dowry and the prestige of her high ancestry, for the union also ensured considerable political advantages, whilst ostensibly at least allowing the opposition of the Papacy and the Anjous to be neutralized. At the same time, she also made an outstanding contribution to perpetuating the succession and power of the house by means of her abundant fertility and health. There was also an undeniable personal inclination, a positive emotional tie between husband and wife. The relationship with Maria was the precise opposite. Its political benefit was small, the hopes of an inheritance came to nothing, the dowry was a long time coming, and she had no children. Linked to that, there was a striking frostiness in the emotional climate. It is impossible to say which of these two levels was ultimately more important, but it is clear that the question of fertility was a central one. There is no doubt – and this should be noted in passing – that for Maria marriage was linked to great suffering and deep humiliation, even though there is no direct reference to this in the sources.

II

What form did the relationship between parents and children take? Blanche, as has already been mentioned, bore ten children who survived: James (1296), Maria (1297 or 98), Alfonso (1299), Constance (1300), John (*c.* 1301), twin girls Blanche and Elisabeth (*c.* 1302), and then, with a greater distance between them, Peter (1305), and Ramón Barengar (1308); the birth of Violante (1310) caused her mother's death. The turning points in the lives of the children between the ages of six and eight and twelve and fourteen can be seen, particularly clearly in the case of the daughters, in the available material. Constance's marriage treaty was concluded when she was only six, and in 1305 Maria, who was seven at the time, had to draw up formally and in her own name the instructions for the envoys who were to deal with the project of a later marriage with someone from the French royal family. From the age of twelve, the children assumed the tasks of adults quite completely. At that age, the daughters were ready for marriage. The sons admittedly married rather later, but by the time they were twelve at the latest, the king had appointed and completed the multitude of educators and attendants, making them into their own *casa*, or court. John, who from birth had been destined for a clerical vocation, was appointed Chancellor when he was twelve, and the firstborn, James, for whom the three-year-old Leonora of Castile was brought to the Aragonese court as a bride in 1312, was appointed Procurator-General by his father in 1313 at the latest, at which time he was about sixteen.

The external circumstances of royal life were of major importance with regard to the way the children grew up.[40] The family was always on the move, and there was no joint household. In the first stage of their lives, the children were most often with their mother. On one occasion, James expressly referred to a mother's responsibility for nurturing the children, and on another he said explicitly that their health was also part of that same charge.[41] However, from their birth onwards a multitude of nurses, tutors, male and female attendants was active on behalf of each one of them. At this stage of their lives they frequently did not stay long in the same place, and later it was indeed rare for them to do so. As far as we can see from the sources, there was a certain division between the daughters, who also commonly appeared more frequently together, and the sons. The elder sons, James and Alfonso in particular, are often seen after 1310 in their father's entourage.[42]

The great feast days of the Church, and in particular Christmas, were very important occasions when the family came together.[43] Such times not only served as a means of expressing feelings of solidarity (we shall return to this aspect of personal contacts in another context), but were also used as an opportunity to settle important political matters, which also included family business. The great Christmas festivities also served as a demonstration of royal power and of the unity of the king's household and therefore had a clear public function. The feasts were just as important as a means of settling family conflicts. This is never as clearly seen as in the dealings between father and firstborn son: as a result of disagreements, the father, in 1318, sharply rejected 'certain excuses' with which his son had sought to justify his absence at Christmas and demanded in no uncertain terms that he be present.[44]

These family feasts were exceptional situations. For the growing children, it was everyday life that was important, marked as it was by constant movement, the alternating separation from parents and siblings and the permanent and close proximity of a retinue of their own male and female attendants. From the very start these children lived in a much wider field of relationships than that of the nuclear family. The multitude of attendants and the entourage were partly recruited from the more distant kin of the royal house, but it was the most important men from the royal circle of counsellors who had the most important tasks. Some of them were occasionally sent out to other 'courts'.[45]

The importance of choosing and supervising these attendants was not only recognized in the Aragonese court. Henri de Lusignan made enquiries during the marriage negotiations for Maria as to who would be responsible for the upbringing of her children.[46] James's awareness of this question was of course acute as was to be expected in a man of such striking thoroughness. He issued very many instructions about his children's attendants and entourage. This sometimes went to almost ridiculous lengths. On one occasion he is known to have asked for information about a certain nurse, only to be told by the lady in charge of her that she was quite reliable apart from a certain propensity to gossip.[47] The greatest and most circumspect care was taken with the court of the eldest son.[48] On the whole, the ties of kinship and entourage seem to have ensured that, with regard to the more important responsibilities of the court of the Infantes, the royal descendants were socialized in the desired way. Political and family responsibilities coincided, and the whole formed a complex system composed, so to speak, of interdependent satellites instead of a royal household.

In a case like this, where other authorities have replaced parental ones with regard to education and care, it is probable that the children and young people involved will have developed closer and more intense relationships with the members of their court. Unfortunately, this can only be seen very occasionally in the available sources. Thus Elisabeth, who had married into the Austrian royal family, found it hard to send her own entourage home as her husband and father had demanded.[49] Relations with the confessor were naturally particularly close, given his special function, and Elisabeth, despite her husband's reluctance, was given a Catalan-speaking priest.[50] As for the eldest son, his confessor was suspected of being behind the wish to enter a religious order – we shall return to this matter later – and was immediately replaced by the father.[51] In the case of the firstborn, James, his hatred and fear of the high officials of his court appointed by his father became clearly visible, and this too was a particular relationship.[52] No doubt it would be possible to reach significantly more conclusions in this whole area of problems if we had the help of more source materials.

This overall situation should be borne in mind if we now proceed to reflect on the relationship between parents and children. With regard to the mother, there is little that can be added from the sources to what has already been said. We shall, however, have to accept that her influence during childhood was considerable. She was certainly involved in the early (and abortive) plans to marry her daughter into the French royal family, and no doubt she was also involved in the decision of her son John and her daughter Blanche to enter the Church. Both their Christian names were decided by her. When she lay on her deathbed, her husband called all her children round her with the exception of Constance. (The omission of the latter is of interest in connection with later quarrels between them.) For years afterwards they were presented with objects from her personal treasure. There is also considerable symbolic significance in the fact that the journey of the Infante John to receive the tonsure at Avignon was financed by the Pope from the sale of objects from her strictly private possessions specified in her will.[53] John was later to play an outstanding part as an intermediary between some of his brothers and sisters and his father. Was he perhaps taking on one of the functions of the mother, for which he too was particularly suited, as he was not in competition for an inheritance?

Blanche's early death brought with it a new situation but no basic changes in the way the royal household was organized, even though the father was now obliged to take decisions for the younger children alone. He flatly refused the offer of his sister, the queen of Portugal, to take one of his daughters – there was no question of it being one of his sons – into her protection, giving as his reasons the marriage plans of one, the ill-health of another, the intention of entering a convent for a third, and, in the case of his youngest daughter, Violante, the fact that she was still too small.[54] Violante was the only one of the children to have any close contact with their stepmother, Maria. At first she was brought up with Eleanor of Castile, who was of more or less the same age, but in 1315 or 1316 she was handed over to Maria. He explicitly mentions the latter's request to take the child into her protection *pro solacio et consolacione*, 'for her solace and consolation'. Violante later stayed with the widowed Infanta Maria. She was also the only one of the children to be remembered by Queen Maria with presents from her own personal property.[55] All the others had had minimal contact with their stepmother or none at all as a result of the tension between her and James II.

In the sources, the king's activities on behalf of his children can naturally be seen more clearly. In his own way, he was most solicitous about them. The sources contain a vast number of written instructions, not only in connection with the creation, supervision, and payment of their entourage, but also with regard to journeys and accommodation and, not least, concerning the provision and type of food and clothing.[56] In particular, his concern for their health was constant. He sometimes seems to have demanded daily reports on it and often summoned physicians to their sickbeds with great haste.[57] All the children, like the king himself, were in fact very often ill.

This incessant concern for the children's health had as its prime cause the real-life conditions they lived in. This was true of other activities: the residences and quarters used were not always kept ready for immediate habitation and sometimes had to be fitted out before they could be lived in. Stopping-places, routes, and retinues all raised problems of security. The appearances of kin of the royal family were always a public occasion, and not only had a worthy ceremonial to be maintained – clothes were particularly important also – but all possible dangers had to be avoided.[58] In larger towns, there was the problem of uncontrollable crowds, and one possible cause of disorder was the provision of food for the whole train of the royal family. The royal chronicles offered the constant reminder that in the thirteenth century the royal couple had been held prisoners by rebellious nobles.[59] The very real fear of poison and the dagger should not be underestimated. It is expressed in an exaggerated form in the court order of Peter, the grandson of James II, who was ruling in 1336, in which it was decreed that at Holy Communion, the abbot of the domestic monastery and his scholars should partake of the host and the wine before the king.[60] As late as the middle of the thirteenth century at least, the chances that offspring would survive were rated rather low: James I anticipated, in his will of 1248, the possibility that the male line would become extinct, although five of his sons were alive at the time.[61]

Ultimately, this preoccupation with the health and security of the children was directly based on maintaining 'capital'. But in a different sense, there was something else behind this activity. The constant requests for information and the constant stipulations about accommodation, routes, and entourages imply at once a strict supervision by means of paternal authority and to a certain extent a constant claim on availability. Activity relating to the family is clearly paralleled by efforts in the administration of state power. The concern about health has a similar significance: a sick king is unfit to travel and hence to govern. For that reason, there is as little mention of illnesses as possible in the self-portrait painted by James I in his autobiographical chronicle.[62] What was true of the king also applied to the royal house: the health of all the members of it is not only a sign of blessing but also an external and visible sign of the vitality and power of the dynasty. Consequently, the two elements of strict supervision and paternal concern for health remained a major example of behaviour in relationships for the sons and daughters once they had grown up. It is at that point that it becomes clear that this paternal concern had at one and the same time the character of a mutual obligation and (to no lesser degree) an affective content. We shall return to this point later.

We can now examine a major area of paternal concern, the question of arranging marriages for children or placing them in a clerical career. In this area, James II claimed a total right to direct his children and take decisions on their behalf, although the influence of their mother during her lifetime and that of the court entourage should not be underestimated. It is possible to follow in detail his almost endless planning and negotiating in the field of the politics of marriage.

Decisions about clerical careers were made particularly early. The third son, John, who was destined for the priesthood from birth, was already in possession of numerous benefices from his sixth year and was consecrated Archbishop of Toledo at the age of nineteen. The third daughter, Blanche, who was partly brought up in the convent at Sijena by the time she was five, entered finally when she was twelve. The father was in almost as great a hurry with the older daughters. There were negotiations about a French marriage around 1303–4 and then again in the case of Maria around 1305–6. Constance had been promised to the Castilian grandee Juan Manuel since 1304. In 1306, a mutual agreement to marry was negotiated, and the six-year-old Constance was sent into the protection of her future husband in Castile immediately afterwards. Juan Manuel had had to promise solemnly not to seek intercourse with her before she was of age; as the language of the sources has it, 'not to marry (casar) her, except to beget children'.[63] The marriage did not take place until 1313. To a certain extent, Constance was a pledge in political agreements, a guarantee that political relationships would be stabilized. In the meantime, Frederick the Handsome, the Duke of Austria, had begun negotiations in connection with his projected marriage with Elisabeth in 1311. When the marriage treaty was concluded in October 1313, Elisabeth travelled with a large entourage to Vienna by way of Avignon.[64] Negotiations concerning the youngest daughter were not started until 1322, when she was twelve. Once again, these were with the French royal family. They lasted for almost three years, but finally petered out. There were further negotiations with England and Castile, but no marriage was achieved during her father's lifetime.

Things did not proceed quite so quickly with the sons. The firstborn, James, was of course the trump card. In his case, the decision was taken in 1312 when, following the political agreement with Castile, the three-year-old Infanta Eleonore was delivered to the Aragonese court to be brought up, with a view to a later marriage with James. She too was a kind of pledge as Constance had been earlier. In both their cases, the entourage they brought with them played a major role in court espionage and in channelling information.[65] James stubbornly refused to give the promise of marriage that had been demanded of him after

1316 or 1317, and the serious conflict that arose from this will be discussed later. As part of the same set of moves, the second daughter, Maria, was married to the Castilian Infante Pedro in 1312, the main aim here being to complete the system of mutual ties. In 1314 the second son, Alfonso, married a rich heiress from the nobility of his own country. Most of the available correspondence concerning proposed marriages deals with the second-youngest son, Peter. At first some approaches were made to France on his behalf, but he later presented his father with a list of five nubile female relatives of the king of England, indicating the age and dowry of each of the candidates.[66] He clearly enjoyed greater freedom than his brothers. He too was not married while his father was still alive. Even less important was the marriage of Ramón Barengar, about whom the sources have significantly little to say. In 1327 he married his maternal first cousin and later, after becoming a widower, a daughter of the Aragonese peerage.

The changing political motivation is very noticeable in the case of the eldest children in particular. What does 'marriage policy' mean when, as in most of the cases so far examined, the prospects of inheritance were barely or not at all mentionable? The creation of ties by means of marriage was sometimes explicitly described as 'making friends'. In 1307 the French king almost mockingly told James II not to rush into anything with his eldest children. The envoy is said to have answered that all kings wanted to make an early start, and he was in haste *pour avoir plus damis*, 'to gain more friends'.[67] In 1312 Frederick the Handsome also sent his ambassador to request Elisabeth's hand because he wanted to enter into a *mutuam amicitiam specialem*, a 'mutual and particular friendship' with James.[68] The expression *federari amicitiam*, 'to embark upon a friendship' is also used in connection with the ending of political hostilities.[69] The role the children played as objects is particularly striking in the case of Castile, but on both sides daughters of tender years were handed over into the protection of the other side and regularly exchanged with a view to marriage.

Both sides, Aragon and Castile, hoped that political relations would become more stable as a result of closer relations through marriage. In the competitive situation they were in, the ties – as is often the case – served less to create any kind of solidarity than to create limitations of claims and mutual checks. As a result of confusion within Castile, it was James II who temporarily gained by far the most in the way of political influence. Who was the stronger partner can to some extent be seen in the fact that the Castilian sons-in-law were integrated into the house as 'sons', in a manner of speaking, whilst both Pedro and Juan Manuel occasionally received large gifts from James but were continually fobbed off with promises about the payment of the dowry.[70] That such politically inspired *amicitia* in the field of alliances by marriage could also have a concrete function when there were no such immediate interests involved is shown by a further detail. Frederick the Handsome, a son-in-law of James II, asked in 1314 whether the latter was perhaps annoyed about a marriage agreement between his sister Catherine and Duke Charles of Calabria, the eldest son of Robert of Naples and James's nephew, on account of his Sicilian policy.[71] It is also interesting in the same context to note that James II never, despite all his efforts, managed to conclude a connection with the French royal family. Rules and strategies, the levels of political planning and the real duration, costs, and gains of these 'friendly' relationships in the example we have chosen would be well worth a special and systematic study.

James II has often been accused of being an unscrupulous marriage broker. It is interesting that there are one or two faint suggestions that he – or his contemporaries – were occasionally slightly uneasy about the violence done (by today's standards) to his children. He seems to some extent to have been aware that his daughters were not fully grown up when they married. This is probably why he scolded Elisabeth, who had been married into German royalty, for her childish and silly letters.[72] There was some point in giving her a very large entourage and (despite Frederick's protest) a Catalan-speaking confessor. In 1311 James's brother Frederick of Sicily refused to agree to a marriage project suggested by the Pope for his daughter, who at that time was about thirteen, on the grounds that she was still too young and that he wanted to let his children make a free choice between the religious life and marriage when they were older.[73] Although this occurred in a context capable of political interpretation, his declaration nevertheless shows a remarkable awareness of the relevant problems. It is also not purely fortuitous that James II kept the preparations for the bridal inspection most carefully secret from his twelve-year-old daughter Violante, given the uncertainty attached to the project.[74]

But the accusation of unscrupulosity misses the heart of the matter for quite different reasons. It misses the fact that 'family' action is simply synonymous with sober political action (in a form no longer entrusted to us). By acting in this way he not only discharged what in his view were important state and political duties but also, and equally conscientiously, ones connected with his immediate family. He was perhaps the means to marriage and had the absolute power of decision in this respect, but there was also the fact that his children had the right to expect him to concern himself with their marriages or ecclesiastical careers. In this sense, too, his younger sons could claim his help – and after his death, that of their eldest brother – in connection with their plans for marriage. It could also be said that the start of marriage negotiations for the daughters was perhaps just as much a recognition of their personal value for the dynasty and of their claim to be regarded as adults. To this extent there was a connection between the life-cycle of the family and the range of ways and means available at that time for political initiatives and dealings.

In the case of the eldest son, James, who was to succeed his father on the throne, the question of marriage led to a quite acute conflict, which in a sense was a typical father/son conflict but nevertheless quite unusual in the course it took.[75] Since approximately 1311–12, the king had gradually given his son many of the tasks of a ruler. At first he was full of praise for his skill and the way he acquitted himself. After a short time, however, there were complaints about his unnecessary severity and arrogance. The situation became rapidly worse around 1317–18, and James began to accuse him of incompetence and unsociability. In 1318 a monk's cowl was discovered in his quarters, and at the same time he broke off all personal contact with his father. At the heart of the disagreement was the fact that he continually found new pretexts for refusing his consent to the proposed marriage with the Castilian Infanta, Eleonore. It was not until 1319, when he at last met his father, that he finally consented to it. It is clear from various sources that during the discussions between father and son *muy fuertes paraulas*, 'very hard words', were spoken and that, quite literally, the fur sometimes flew.[76] But that was not the end of the matter. On the wedding day appointed by the father, there was an almost incredible scandal. Before the assembled wedding guests, the prince ran away and cast himself on the protection of the Church. He later declared in writing that he had only consented to the marriage from fear of his father and did not want to marry, to conclude the *copula carnalis* with Eleonore, and that during his whole life he had never touched a woman. He stubbornly opposed a further meeting with his father, and despite his renunciation of the throne and entry into an order, his *viae perversae* often produced agitation. In 1323 it became known that he was going about Valencia with a *quadam pessima mulier*, clearly a prostitute. Shortly after that, his father had him secretly (he was not to travel through towns) and indeed forcibly brought to the royal domestic monastery of Santa Creus and confined there. From that time on there is no further mention of him in royal documents.[77]

The most noteworthy aspect of this story is probably the fact that the final break was a result not of differences of opinion about the way he carried out his duties as a ruler but of his flight from marriage. His partly contradictory behaviour is not so easy to explain. His letters – in his desperation he wrote both to the Pope and to his uncle Robert of Naples – indicate acute inner conflicts. After 1317, there are several clear expressions of his bent for the monastic life and of his fear of his father and the burden of ruling.[78] There is the possibility of the influence of Franciscan spiritual teaching at the court in this connection. On the other hand, as Procurator-General, his regime had initially been a harsh one, and his father had given him advisors whose main task was to ensure that 'he did not do more than was necessary'.[79] Behind his refusal there was perhaps disappointment at the unsuccessful attempt to drive his father from the throne.[80] The fact that Eleonore was still not fully sexually mature when the wedding was due to take place and that James was not prepared to take the biological risk that this entailed might also have played a part in the matter. Some support is offered to this view by the strange fact that he later made secret preparations to seek out his disdained bride.[81] Perhaps he simply did not want to meet the political commitments to Castile that were entailed by the agreement that his father had entered into.

The behaviour of his father lends itself more readily to analysis. His letters connected with this matter sometimes show a mixture of confused indecision and resignation – he too wrote to the Pope – and at others a total determination to impose his own will. Towards his son he vacillated between reproaches, conciliatory understanding, unyielding severity, and naked threats. The unsuccessful marriage celebrations meant final failure in his eyes. In his own words he was 'in utter despair' and saw in it 'great danger for the kingdom'.[82] His first political preoccupation was political equilibrium with Castile. The failure meant not only the collapse of a carefully created network of mutual restraints and commitments, for his failure to meet his promise could, he immediately feared, entail reprisals against his two daughters, Maria and Constance, who had married into the Castilian house. Indeed, from this time on he decisively lost influence in Castile, all the more so as in addition Maria's husband was killed in battle against the Moors in 1319, and she returned to Catalonia in 1320. Eleonore, the rejected bride, was sent home. The marriage subsequently planned for her with the Infante Peter never materialized, although she did finally marry Alfonso in 1329 after the death of his first wife. This was clearly a form of restitution, based not on modern moral criteria but on a sense of personal virtue within the system of *amicitia*.[83]

However, the main reasons why James II behaved in such a precipitate way are to be found on another level. If one reflects, their real importance illustrates the fact that similar difficulties were not so infrequent in royal families. This was so at the end of the thirteenth century not only amongst the Angevins and in Majorca, but also in the Aragonese dynasty itself: James's elder brother, Alfonso, king from 1285–91, had also not entered into the marriage his father had arranged for him, and in 1285 James himself declared in writing before a notary his refusal ever to enter into the one arranged for him.[84] The promise that he made in 1291 to marry Elisabeth of Castile was also never finally kept. At the same time, however, he was a staunch defender of the indivisibility of the kingdom and primogeniture. The decisive measures in connection with the institutionalization of this dynastic law date from this period, after the way had been prepared for them by James's father Peter.[85] On the other hand, James I, between 1235 and 1262, had made fresh provisions for his estate on no fewer than six consecutive occasions, with divisions of property each time and continual changes of content.[86] One of the consequences of this had been the appearance of the kingdom of Majorca, which had subsequently aligned itself against Aragon on several occasions. There had been several disputes about reincorporating it which had led to military struggles within the dynasty. There is no doubt that events of this kind contributed towards changes in the domestic law and the constitution of the State.

It must have been all the more intolerable in such circumstances for James to realize that he would leave behind him an unresolved succession. A proper arrangement, definitively made, could only be the result of the marriage of the firstborn and the potential reproduction of the line it entailed. The increasing violence with which he urged marriage can be understood, for in the winter of 1318/19 he was very ill – at death's door, as he himself said[87] – and totally incapable of political activity. This came on top of his permanent fear of an untimely death and the awareness that he was already an old man, and made it even more urgent to ensure the succession. The withdrawal of his eldest son made him fear that the younger ones, none of whom had so far been named as a substitute, might put forward claims which, as past experience had shown, could very easily lead to conflicts and divisions. His reactions to the marriage scandal of October 1319 were suitably energetic. Barely two months later, James was required to make a formal renouncement of all his rights and enter a religious order the very same day. The second son, Alfonso, was immediately declared *primogenitus* (firstborn) and hence heir to the throne.[88]

But the area of insecurity was even wider than this. Behind the extreme severity shown to James was a concern for the dignity of the royal house and, just as strongly evident, a struggle to remove once and for all the ever-present risk that he might renew his old claims. By 1325 the son of Alfonso, and heir apparent, had been designated as his father's successor. Once again, the fear of an untimely death played a part in this, for Alfonso had always been weak and sickly, and his father's reflections on his capacity to rule can be clearly seen. This meant that it was even more important to counter all possible claims from the younger brothers as consistently as possible. Indeed, Peter seems initially to have made his own claims to the succession, which meant the risk of severe conflicts and real dangers for the unity of the kingdom should Alfonso or his father die suddenly.[89]

The conflict between the father and his eldest son also lead us to reflect on the relationship between the former and his grown-up children. Here we must make a distinction between those who had left their home and those who were still under his influence. The married daughters were, so to speak, released from home or at least from paternal authority. James II admonished his son-in-law, Frederick the Handsome, to look after Elisabeth not only as a husband, but also as a father (*vices gerens patris*).[90] He instructed Maria to treat her mother-in-law, the widowed Queen Maria de Molina, 'as her own mother'.[91] Written communication between them, however, remained very frequent. The daughters informed their father of political events and conditions at the court (a very important function of 'friendship'). News of pregnancies, births, and deaths, was followed by James's congratulations or condolences, as appropriate. In particular, there was a regular exchange of news *de statu*, about health and welfare.[92] The mutual exchange of reports and questions on this matter, which was also considerable amongst sons and daughters still within James's direct sphere of influence, was not merely a formality. It would be truer to say that such news was desired on both sides and indeed regularly demanded, and no doubt an affective content over and above any functional significance can be assumed.[93]

The latter is seen very clearly when James 'orders' his often sick daughters to get well again.[94] But the father always feels that it is his duty to help, and medical advice, salves, and physicians were sent not only to neighbouring Castile but also to distant Austria. Elisabeth, who was losing her sight increasingly quickly after 1324, described her painful fate in a letter to her father written in 1326 with the telling quotation that *fortuna* (fate) had been her stepmother (*noverca*) in her last years.[95] James's particular concern was for Constance, who became increasingly ill after 1315. He was unable to turn her wish to return to Valencia, where she had been born, into reality.[96]

Maria, however, who had been widowed during the past year, was brought back to her homeland together with her small daughter in 1320. There were very quickly serious difficulties with her, however. Her character was perhaps obstinate and restless; James was in any case obliged to take repeated action against her intrigues. In particular, she openly opposed her father's arrangements for the protection of her interests at the Castilian court, and here and in other areas she proposed her own highly individual policies.[97] Her sister Blanche was just as independent. She had been prioress of Sijena since 1321, and had caused her father a number of problems. Quite unconventionally, for example, she sided with persecuted and ill-treated women from the high aristocracy; her father was strong in his condemnation of actions that he saw as incursions into State business.[98] In 1322 Blanche accepted her sister Maria into the convent. It is noteworthy that after 1335, when their father and elder brothers were dead, both sisters left the convent and returned to Barcelona and Valencia.[99].

Interestingly enough the sons on the other hand, with the exception of the eldest, seem to have given less cause for open disagreement. As an ecclesiastic, John was of course in a particular position. He was given important political tasks by his father and also acted as an intermediary between him and his daughters. Apparently in 1326 he accepted without protest his father's instructions to abandon certain fasts and penitential practices to which he was drawn but which caused the latter concern for his health.[100] The second son, Alfonso, had in no way refused his father's very strict guardianship, and indeed owed his succession to the throne to it. In his instructions for the Sardinian campaign of 1323, he was not only forbidden the usual intercourse with mercenaries but also any political action without his father's knowledge and any personal initiative.[101] In addition, James prescribed exactly where he was to stay with his wife and even the attendants the little son of the Infante should have.[102] We can only glean a little about Peter's initial demands that he rather than his brother Alfonso should be heir to the throne. He was made a count in 1322 and given a high court office in 1323, which seems to have made the situation more stable.[103] As can be seen from the negotiations concerning their respective marriages, Peter and Ramón Barengar seem to have enjoyed a great deal more freedom as younger sons. Their father was not as actively concerned for them in the same way as he had been for their elder brothers.

In this connection, there is a final and very important phenomenon to describe. There is regularly in letters from his children the complaint, or even the bitter reproach, that their father has clearly forgotten them, and that they did not hear from him in enough detail.[104] There is a frequent wish for an actual meeting in the near future, a 'getting-together'. This was particularly the case with Constance. Even before her marriage, she was writing that her father showed no concern for her and had clearly forgotten her.[105] She had been almost permanently ill since 1315.[106] From her brother John, who had visited her at his father's bidding, we have a graphic report of her condition in her last years. She sometimes refused to eat, had uncontrollable fits of weeping, and was tormented by *imaginacions*, or hallucinations. John urged his father to act at once and feared permanent damage to her mental health. Her wish to return to her birthplace, Valencia, became a tearful plea, and she believed that only a meeting with her father could cure her: 'if I could see you, I should immediately be healed'.[107] In a letter to his son Peter, who was ill, James also mentions the latter's urgent wish to see him, 'so that he might recover all the more quickly in his presence'.[108] The above are merely particularly striking examples, and there are other occasions when the desire for 'consolation', 'encouragement', and 'joy' arising from personal contact with James are expressed. The exchange of letters, and through them reports on health, was to some extent a substitute for such meetings, which was all that was possible given the distances involved, and this is occasionally overtly stated.[109].

In each case, these requests for physical proximity and the desire for healing must be taken very seriously. The lack of actual contact can be seen as one of the basic psychological characteristics of the whole family, which also gives an insight into individual mental tensions and conflicts, even if it does not mean that we should assume that there were deprivation syndromes in the modern sense of the term. It is not possible to separate affective contents and objective material reasons. The closeness of the relationship with the king, shown by personal contact, was also a source of prestige for his children. His presents to them, and to his sons-in-law, had a similar dual function. When they reproached him for 'forgetting them', it was also a demand, for it reminded James of his obligations.

Rather than give a summary at this stage, one fact should be pointed out. The central line of the whole parents/children cluster of relationships is in the last analysis the relationship between father and eldest son, and hence the assuring of the succession. In relation to this, every other level is not actually unimportant, but is at least of priority in terms of it. The extreme clarity of this objective and material factor in no way implies that the real experiences of those involved were not marked to a fairly high degree by emotions and feelings. Not, of course, only in forms that we would consider 'positive' ones. And those involved? Even if their sense of values is hard to grasp, the letters of both the firstborn, James, and those of Constance and Elisabeth seem to show explicitly that what the children were compelled to do brought them great suffering and pain and cost each of them a great deal. With the firstborn, taking the measures that were considered objectively to be the correct ones was by no means easy. The opposite was the case.

III

A third and final field of relationships is that of those between the siblings. This is a very broad topic, in connection with which only a few remarks concentrated on one or two reflections on the relationships of the children of James II can be made. In this restricted framework there were also certain rather special factors. On the one hand there were no stepbrothers and stepsisters as there usually were in cases of successive marriages, when very frequently there would be a whole range of them in royal houses. On the other, almost none of James's illegitimate children appeared in the context of the royal house or the royal court, and the problem of the relationships between legitimate and illegitimate children can sometimes be quite an important one. Thus the father of James II, Peter II, is said to have ordered his half-brother to be drowned to leave the way clear for a single heir.[110] Interestingly enough, one of the illegitimate brothers of James II was a member of the inner circle of court advisors.[111]

What would be particularly rewarding, but cannot be attempted here, would be a closer analysis of the relations between James II and his younger brother Frederick.[112] Only brief details can be given here. Against his brother's wishes, Frederick had had himself crowned King of Sicily in 1296, and in the years up to 1302 James had engaged in open war against him on the side of the Pope and the Angevins. Politically, James later remained uncompromisingly severe towards him but nevertheless made serious attempts from time to time to make peace between Frederick and Robert of Anjou, the brother of his wife Blanche and husband of his sister Violante until her death in 1302. To Robert, he wrote, he was 'so bound by kinship (*affinitas*) that he saw him as a brother (*frater*)', and elsewhere that Frederick was 'tied to him fraternally by nature' (*natura fraterna colligacione*) and Robert 'by kinship (*affinitas*) and inclination (*dilectio*)'.[113] The brother-in-law was seen as equal in value to the brother, and yet there was a certain shading. And in particular in the detailed correspondence between the brothers, the considerable scruples that James indulged in his activities are clearly expressed. In 1302, at the end of hostilities, he also sent him as a gesture of reconciliation of the highest symbolic value, a gift of the favourite sword of his father Peter II.[114] For his part, both before and after the war, Frederick repeatedly addressed his brother as 'father' or 'brother and father' and took great pains to keep the contacts alive.[115]

There is nothing unusual about open enmity between royal brothers, and in the Aragonese royal family there was a rich and bloody tradition of conflicts between brothers or blood relations of various lines. What is much more worthy of note is that James II clearly suffered as a result of the dispute and often tried to effect a reconciliation. That can be seen as an expression of his changed understanding of the State and an attempt to represent, as father of the dynasty, a closed and stable domestic power. Nevertheless, a higher tie, based on that of fraternal affection and operating not least in the affective field, seems to come into play. The contemporary chronicler Ramón Muntaner could not easily deal with 'family' realities, and in his royal chronicles the conflicts between brothers is suppressed as far as possible and the unity and solidarity of the dynasty evoked.[116] Propagating dynastic ideologies to political ends can hide the fact that such unity had to be manufactured precisely because it was in danger.

Now to the children of James II. Here as everywhere, a key fact in the relationships of siblings is that of inheritance. James's dynastic measures and his conflicts with his eldest son have already been described above. From them it is clear how strongly in this area relationships between siblings, or at least between sons, are shaped by the father. With the support of his father's authority, Alfonso, the second son, finally prevailed, with an astonishing degree of success, against his younger brothers. Nor did the latter emerge without any benefits,[117] for at an early stage they were recompensed at the material level by means of a firm transfer of specific incomes. In addition, Peter took at Alfonso's behest a decisive part in government affairs and later became one of the most important political advisors of his nephew Peter, who ruled from 1336, and whose staff of officials and advisors Ramón Barengar also joined. That mere details were important to James II when it was a question of an heir is shown by the fact that in 1321 he scolded Elisabeth for calling her brother Alfonso by name and using the familiar pronoun for him in one of her letters.[118] Direct and massively conflictual repercussions of the problem of inheritance on the sibling relationship, which in general were by no means unusual, did not occur.

A systematic analysis of the sibling relationships would have to begin with the circumstances of the royal family during the childhood and youth of the offspring as described above. A particularly well-established pattern – which can only be touched on here – can be seen in the grown-up children. As far as can be seen from the sources, relationships were not determined with direct reference to the succession but usually very strongly by the father himself. At many points in the sources – and the scolding letter to Elisabeth referred to above is also an example of this – it can be seen how the father tried to retain a strict supervision of the relationships between his grown-up children. It was he, at least according to his claim, who decided when and where one or more of his sons and daughters were to meet.[119] He clearly had a deep distrust of direct contacts. His favourite son John, the cleric, had to report in detail on his visits to Constance, and occasionally he specifically tried to hinder or limit the meetings of his wilful daughter Blanche and her brother John.[120] The particularly close relationship between Blanche and Maria – the latter had followed her sister to Sijena in 1322 –

was clearly a reason for keeping a close watch on their activities. He perhaps thought that closer contacts between the brothers and sisters were a threat to his authority and a danger to the stability he had achieved with such effort.

There is much to indicate that affective ties amongst the siblings were often to some extent weak, or at least that their strength varied from individual to individual, and that often there was even a considerable distance between them. Here is one example of such a weakness. In 1324, James II was able to induce Peter, the youngest but one of his sons, to seize his eldest brother in Valencia and forcibly take him to Santa Creus, even going so far as to declare, in the relevant written instruction, that he need have no scruples about using force.[121] Nor is there any indication that any of the brothers or sisters took their eldest brother's part. On the other hand, there are examples which would indicate the opposite, and these are largely, and certainly not fortuitously, connected with John, the cleric. He did a great deal for his sick sister, Constance, just as for her part Constance was deeply concerned about him and his influence with their father. Blanche too kept trying to establish contact with John, to her father's displeasure, as has already been mentioned.[122]

It was also Blanche who expressed her feelings for her brother John in a singular way and in doing so perhaps took her revenge for the oppression she had suffered as a result of her father's bid for power. Shortly after her brother's death in 1334, she had herself and a very close circle of followers locked in Tarragona Cathedral at night, broke into her brother's grave and took the corpse, 'from which the flesh had not yet fallen from the bones', back to Sijena in secret, where he was re-interred with great simplicity.[123] Perhaps not the least of her intentions was to have her dead brother near her while she prayed and thus strengthen considerably her position in the royal house. What she did can also be related to the fact that – as Martinez Ferrando has very plausibly suggested[124] – in Tarragona Cathedral the body of the highly respected 'holy' brother had covered that of the firstborn, the 'sinner', who had died two months earlier, in an attempt to redeem symbolically the shame of the house.

In one way or another, Alfonso acted immediately.[125] He was horrified by the dreadful deed and ordered the body to be returned to Tarragona at once. This was again the task of Peter, to be carried out in great secrecy as had been the seizure of the eldest son. Such conflicts had to be kept or settled within the family, mainly for the sake of the good name and honour of the royal house but also and chiefly because the hierarchy of power within the family legitimized such action by allowing it. In acting thus, Alfonso assumed, in the eyes of his brothers and sisters (parallel to his political position as heir to the throne), the role of father. This is also shown in other ways: he played a decisive part in the marriage negotiations concerning his younger brothers and sisters and, replacing his father, concerned himself continuously with the health of Elisabeth in distant Austria.[126] With Violante, who in 1330 became a widow after only two years of marriage, there was soon a major conflict, for it was a long time before he did anything about her return from Romania. She wrote to him sarcastically, saying that she would no longer be put off by letters full of empty promises, even if she had grown 'quite corpulent as a result of all this writing'.[127] Even from his own people, Alfonso had to endure the reproach that he did not treat her like 'her brother and father'.[128]

This last example also shows more clearly than any other how the rights the father claimed were counterpoised by the claims the children made for care. In the same sense, there was also a claim involved when Frederick of Sicily called his eldest living brother, i.e. James II, his 'father and brother'.

These few references must suffice to illustrate the relationships between the siblings. On the whole, the role of the father seems to have been the absolutely dominant one as far as shaping them is concerned. After the father's death, the eldest son took his place for his brothers and sisters. Between him and his siblings, the same hierarchically structured reciprocity, as it were, that had been so evident between father and children in questions relating to marriage and contacts came into play.[129] It was that same relationship which ultimately could temper or make bearable the claims to domination and the right to power appropriate to the person at the highest point of the family hierarchy. Structural situations, in such cases, determine the space in which individual behaviour can operate, but that is not to say that the space in question is not significantly different in extent or used or occupied in various ways. In addition, the almost literary quality of the story of the theft of the corpse, with its echoes of Antigone, provides a very impressive confirmation of the fact that the sibling relationship did not only include objective and functional connections.

IV

What remains to be said at the end of the 'great family drama'[130] of James II? Neither the method of enquiry nor the limitations of the topic allow of far-ranging conclusions, and what will be said now takes the form of suggestions for possible further development rather than that of definitive results.

One thing seems certain. With regard to the duration, intensity, and value of relationships in the nuclear family, the problem of ensuring the handing-on of possessions and power is of primordial importance. The emphasis obviously changes as the course of lives moves on. Initially, the relationship between husband and wife occupies the centre of the stage, to be replaced, as the sons grow up, by that between the father and his eldest son.

The dominant position is always the father's, even allowing for the fact that the relative quantity and nature of the written material must strengthen such an impression. With the material at our disposal here, it is impossible to define exactly the significance of the nuclear family within the overall system of the 'royal family'. Nevertheless, the father's activities in all spheres of relationships clearly indicate a certain concentration on this nucleus. It was not by chance that

Heinrich Finke rediscovered the bourgeois *paterfamilias* in James II![131] What Finke meant of course was an interiorization of emotional ties that were to some extent positive, at least of 'paternal feelings'.

It is not only in the conflict between James and his eldest son but indeed everywhere that emotional factors and affective contents are unambiguously present. They are of course quite differentially intense and extremely multi-directional. They are certainly not simply 'positive' and creative of solidarity, particularly when we do not confuse, in the parent/children relationship, the attitudes of the father and mother with the real experiences of the children. The supposition that some of the children were subject to very great, and perhaps excessively great, demands in their individual psychic domain is justified, even though the sources only indicate this obliquely.

The activity of the father is also linked to structural conditions and particularly to a certain reciprocity with regard to the maintenance of hierarchy and stability. What is more, it is to a high degree externally determined or orientated, in so far as one can differentiate between the external and the internal in this context. At what was a critical time and an important sphere of influence for James, the marriage with Blanche harmonized political relationships. The number of viable children she brought into the world was a major factor in determining the extent of the available means of political activity, and the concentration on the eldest son served James's very energetically pursued political aim of defending the unity of the kingdom.

This last remark leads to a further aspect of the problem of the royal family and the State which is of particular interest to the historian. James's family correspondence is part of the documents dealing with his general activities as a ruler, and this external circumstance is of quasi-symbolic significance. His ways of acting in relation to his family were basically parallel to those related to his activities as a statesman, to his public and political practices as a ruler. His energetically pursued and more or less successful centralizing and concentrating of State administration and the exercise of power into the hands of the king not only raised the value of the public significance of events within the nucleus of the royal family.[132] It also led to a stricter centralization and a marked interior and hierarchical concentration of his exercise of family office, i.e. of his control within the family. The king was at once the centre of State and family relationships, and the efforts to achieve order and stability, morality and well-being, to see that moral duties and expectations were fulfilled in both domains, were mutually complementary. And the struggle against the independent nobility in the domain of State matters was complemented by the achievement of primogeniture and the control of adult children in the family. The rebellion of the eldest son likewise was a rebellion of his subjects.

On the whole, it is not only a condition but also a transformation, an important process in the history of Aragon around 1300, that is dealt with here. This was a decisive period for the political power and internal consolidation of the Catalan–Aragonese State. Underyling this centralization and consolidation of the 'State' system were changes in the political, economic, social, and mental context which called for new forms of organization and control of the means of power. At the same time, these processes were also at work within the royal family. Admittedly, earlier sources only offer limited means of comparison, but indirectly at least the change is evident at two levels. The first is that of dynastic law, where James II was the first to achieve non-divisibility and primogeniture. The second is that of the form in which family history is reflected. James I, the grandfather of James II, reports in his autobiographical chronicle, when he deals with family matters at all, quite unashamedly on the complicated mixture of concubines and wives prevailing in his father's and his own time. In Chronicle of Pedro III, that of the grandson of James II who reigned after 1336, there is on the other hand an important place allotted to family history, related almost exclusively to linear succession, giving marriages, numbers of children, length of life, transition from father to son.[133]

NOTES

1 Without the criticism, comments, and encouragement of many friends and colleagues – and particularly those of David Sabean – this chapter would never have been more than a series of unsatisfactory sketches. Nor does the author claim that in its present form it is any more then a provisional outline needing further reflection. A more thorough treatment of the subject is in hand.

2 See L. Stone, *The Family, Sex and Marriage in England, 1500–1800* (London, 1977), 4f, and 23ff; J. L. Flandrin, *Familles, parenté, maison, sexualité dans l'ancienne société* (Paris, 1976), 18ff.

3 Mainly used here: J. E. Martinez Ferrando, *Jaume II o el seny catalana, Alfons el Benigne*, 2nd edn (Barcelona, 1963); and the work by the same author quoted in n6 below; and F. Soldevila, *Historia de Catalunya*, 2nd edn (Barcelona, 1963).General data on the policy of James II are not indicated individually in the notes. For further reading, J. E. Martinez Ferrando, S. Sobreques, and E. Bague, *Els descendents de Pere el Gran* (Barcelona, 1954). On the Angevins, see E. G. Leonard, *Les Angevins de Naples* (Paris, 1954).

4 H. Finke (ed.), *Acta Aragonensia, Urkunden aus der diplomatischen Korrespondenz Jaimes II*, 3 vols. (Berlin and Leipzig, 1908–22); and supplements (*Nachträge*) in *Spanische Forschungen der Görres-Gesellschaft*, series 1, 4 (1933), 355-536 (reprinted with the supplements, Aalen, 1966–8); the introductions are also important. Referred to below as Finke, *AA*, vols. 1–3 or *Nachträge* by number, introductions by page).

5 Finke, *AA, Nachträge*, 628; see also Finke, *AA*, vol. 1, 182 (*der sorgsamste Familienvater*).

6 J. E. Martinez Ferrando, *Jaime II de Aragón. Su vida familiar*, vol. 1 (Texto – referred to below as Martinez, 'Texto', with page), and vol. 2 (Documentos – referred to below as Martinez, 'Documentos', with number) (Barcelona, 1948). The biographical data are all from this source, without individual references in the notes.

7 The four major royal chronicles (Crónica de Jaume I (= *Llibre dels feits*), Crónica de Bernat Desclot (hereafter Desclot), Crónica de Ramón Muntaner (hereafter

Muntaner), Crónica de Pere el Cerimoniós) are quoted from the best available edition with extensive commentaries: F. Soldevila, *Les quatre grans Croniques* (Barcelona, 1971).

8 On marriage problems see particularly G. Duby, 'Le Mariage dans la société du Haut Moyen Age', *Il matrimonio nella società altomedievale*, vol. 1, Settimane di studi sull'alto medievo, vol. 24, 1, (Spoleto, 1976), 15–39. The legal aspects are treated in various essays by J. Gaudemet, *Sociétés et mariage*, G. Duby (ed.), (Strasbourg, 1980), see also the bibliography. On the significance of the *copula carnalis*, see Martinez, 'Documentos', no. 305.

9 Martinez, 'Texto', 199ff; particularly Martinez, 'Documentos', nos.70, 117, 122, 136, 137, 153.

10 Finke, *AA*, vol. 1, no.202.

11 *Llibre dels feits*, chap. 2.

12 On the reception etc. Martinez, 'Texto', 222ff; on the beginnings, see *ibid.*, 23ff.

13 *Llibre dels feits*, chaps. 18 and 19.

14 Finke, *AA*, vol. 1, 318, 319 (and 320); he also arranged for a bridal inspection in the case of Blanche. See Finke, *AA.*, vol. 3, no.21 (1295).

15 Finke, *AA*, vol. 1, no.319, vol. 3, no.238.

16 Finke, *AA*, vol. 1, no.30, vol. 3, no.60; Blanche was pronounced *non seducta in aliquo* (Martinez, 'Texto', 3 n3).

17 Martinez, 'Documentos', no.117.

18 Finke, *AA*, vol. 1, no.323.

19 Finke, *AA*, vol. 1, no.233, postscript.

20 *Llibre dels feits*, chaps. 5 and 48; Desclot, chap. 4; and Muntaner, chaps. 3 and 4. On the significance of the stories as legends of the origin of the dynasty, see R. Sablonier, *Krieg und Kriegertum in der Crónica des Ramón Muntaner* (Bern, 1971), 23; also J. Vincke, 'Der Eheprozess Peters II. von Aragon (1206–1213)', *Spanische Forschungen der Görres-Gesellschaft*, 5 (1935), 108–89.

21 *Llibre dels feits*, chaps. 8 and 9.

22 Martinez, 'Documentos', no.57.

23 Martinez, 'Texto', 5ff.

24 Martinez, 'Texto', 4 n6.

25 Finke, *AA*, vol. 3, no.94.

26 Martinez, 'Texto', 15f; Martinez, 'Documentos', no.57.

27 Martinez, 'Documentos', no.61, 399; Finke, *AA*, vol. 1, 180.

28 Martinez, 'Texto', 18ff; Martinez, 'Documentos', nos.62, 202.

29 Finke, *AA*, vol. 1, 180; see also the praise of Ramón Muntaner: Muntaner, chap. 182; and below, p. 217.

30 On dowries see Martinez, 'Texto', 219, 230, 234ff; and Martinez, 'Documentos', no.230, 233; on court organization, Martinez, 'Texto', 244ff; Martinez, 'Documentos', nos.256, 261, 265.

31 Martinez, 'Documentos', nos.201, 209.

32 Martinez, 'Texto', 240f.

33 Martinez, 'Texto', 261; Martinez, 'Documentos', no.325.

34 The examples referred to are in Martinez, 'Documentos', nos.263, 264, 234; for further letters see, for example, Martinez, 'Documentos', nos.236, 266, 272, 274, 323, 388.

35 Martinez, 'Documentos', nos.399 and 400.

36 Martinez, 'Documentos', no.396.

37 On the whole matter, see Martinez, 'Texto', 189ff; on James's relationship with his own illegitimate siblings, see Martinez, 'Texto', 196 n24.

38 Martinez, 'Documentos', no.281; Finke, *AA*, vol. 3, no.171; further sources are, for example, Martinez, 'Documentos', nos.429, 450, 453; Finke, *AA*, vol. 1, 189 n3.
39 On James's illegitimate son, see Desclot, chap. 69. The examples quoted are Martinez, 'Documentos', no.414; Finke, *AA*, vol. 3, no.37; Martinez, 'Documentos', no.259; see also Martinez, 'Texto', 298f.
40 On this point generally, see Martinez, 'Texto', 25ff, 36ff.
41 Martinez, 'Documentos', nos.46, 31.
42 On the latter see, for example, Martinez, 'Documentos', nos.93, 98, 101, 102, 104.
43 See Martinez, 'Texto', 35f; Martinez Ferrando, *Jaume II*, 168.
44 Martinez, 'Documentos', no.273.
45 For a detailed treatment of the whole question, see Martinez, 'Texto', 36ff, 42ff.
46 Martinez, 'Texto', 215.
47 Martinez, 'Documentos', no.58.
48 Martinez, 'Texto', 44.
49 Finke, *AA*, vol. 1, no.244, see also nos.243, 245, and vol. 3, no.128.
50 Finke, *AA*, vol. 1, no.236.
51 Martinez, 'Texto', 49 (also on the rejected bride!).
52 Martinez, 'Texto', 85f, 88; Finke, *AA*, vol. 1, 188.
53 Martinez, 'Texto', 15 (Blanche's deathbed), and 143; Martinez, 'Documentos', no.80 (sale for John).
54 Martinez, 'Documentos', no.68, see also no.67 (instructions for the education of Ramón Barengar, who was still a small child).
55 On Maria and Violante: quotation from Martinez, 'Documentos', no.207, no.373 (will), no.208; Martinez, 'Texto', 39f.
56 For example Martinez, 'Documentos', nos.55, 59; Finke, *AA*, vol. 3, no.68, in particular 1311ff; Martinez, 'Documentos', nos.89–105, 108–12, 132, 151.
57 For example Martinez, 'Documentos', nos.36, 45, 50, 51, 142, 154, 163, 467; see also Martinez, 'Texto', 22, 60.
58 On this point see Martinez, 'Texto', 63ff; also, for example, Martinez, 'Documentos', nos.87, 470.
59 *Llibre dels feits*, chaps. 22–3.
60 Martinez, 'Texto', 37 nl.
61 Soldevila, *Historia*, 285 n59, 301, 335.
62 On this silence in the chronicle, see *Llibre dels feits*, chap. 213, 292 n2. On the illnesses of James II, see Martinez, 'Texto', 58ff. As a source, see for example Martinez, 'Documentos', no.295. See also his reproach to his son for his lack of travel and public activities, see Martinez, 'Documentos', no.253.
63 Martinez, 'Texto', 135.
64 On the fate of Elisabeth see H. R. v. Zeissberg, *Elisabeth von Aragonien, Gemahlin Friedrichs des Schönen von Oesterreich (1314–1330)*, Sbb. Akad. Wien, phil. hist. Klasse, vol.137, (Vienna, 1898); and the same author's, *Das Register Nr. 318 des Archivs der aragonesischen Krone in Barcelona*, Sbb. Akad. Wien, phil. hist. Klasse, vol. 140, (Vienna, 1898), with many extracts from the sources.
65 See Martinez, 'Texto', 50f; Martinez, 'Documentos', nos.107, 116, 127.
66 Finke, *AA*, vol. 1, no.333.
67 Finke, *AA*, vol. 1, no.306.
68 Zeissberg, *Elisabeth von Aragonien*, nos.2–3, 134.
69 Martinez, 'Texto', 149.
70 See, for example, Martinez, 'Texto', 77, 108 n4.
71 Zeissberg, *Register*, nos.43–44, 46ff.
72 Finke, *AA*, vol. 3, no.143; in 1319 Maria was still described by her father as *ninna e*

joven (Martinez, 'Documentos', no.322).

73 Finke, *AA*, vol. 2, no.441.
74 Martinez, 'Texto', 185.
75 This is fully covered in Martinez, 'Texto', 83–106. See also Finke, *AA*, vol. 1, 186ff. On the inherent nature of the father/son conflict in agnatic systems, see J. Goody, 'Introduction', in J. Goody (ed.), *Succession to High Office*, (Cambridge, 1966), especially p. 45.
76 Quotation from Martinez, 'Documentos', no.299. On this, see also no.295; and for comparison Finke, *AA*, vol. 3, no.59.
77 On the whole section see in particular the following sources: Martinez, 'Documentos', nos.299, 305, 306, 409, 410; Finke, *AA*, vol. 3, no.170/1; see also, for example, Martinez, 'Documentos', nos.139, 184, 253, 273 (before 1319), then 276, 279, 295, 296, 326–9, 337, 338; Finke, *AA*, vol. 3, nos.170/2–10.
78 Particularly expressively in Martinez, 'Documentos', no.279, see also no.299.
79 Martinez, 'Documentos', no.234.
80 This indirectly indicates the chronicle of Peter IV. See Martinez, 'Texto', 86.
81 Martinez, 'Texto', 96.
82 Martinez, 'Documentos', no.299; and Martinez, 'Texto', 91.
83 Martinez, 'Texto', 106 n2, quotes an interesting parallel example.
84 Finke, *AA*, *Nachträge*, 624 (notarial text 1285).
85 See Martinez Ferrando, Sobreques and Bague, *Els descendents*, 135; F. Soldevila, *Historia*, 407, also 384, 389f and 445; also P. E. Schramm, 'Der König von Aragon. Seine Stellung im Staatsrecht (1276–1410)', *Historisches Jahrbuch*, 74 (1955), 99–123.
86 Soldevila, *Historia*, 262f, 282–6, 306f, 316f.
87 Martinez, 'Texto', 255ff; and, for example, Martinez, 'Documentos', no.299; on consciousness of age, see Martinez, 'Documentos', no.322 (*somos vieio*).
88 Martinez, 'Documentos', nos.305, 306; see, for example, communication to Elisabeth, Zeissberg, *Register*, no.64, p.68.
89 On the facts concerning Peter, See Martinez, 'Texto', 160–2; on Alfonso, *ibid.*, 129, 132; and Finke, *AA*, vol. 3, no.197.
90 Zeissberg, *Elisabeth von Aragonien*, no.63, p.188.
91 Martinez, 'Documentos', nos.149, 150.
92 For example, Zeissberg, *Register*, no.2, pp.10f, no.78, pp.86f; Finke, *AA*, vol. 1, nos.244, 246, vol. 3, nos.143, 161; Martinez, 'Documentos', nos.120, 131, 141, 168, 238, 240, 245, 286, 317, 331, 366.
93 On the significance of health, see above, p.221. On the demand of news, see Martinez, 'Documentos', no.331; Zeissberg, *Register*, no.66, p.69, no.78, pp.86f.
94 Martinez, 'Documentos', no.322, writing to Maria, who was ill, telling her to make an effort and take her father as an example; see also *ibid.*, no.245.
95 Finke, *AA*, vol. 1., no.256.
96 On efforts on behalf of Constance, see Martinez, 'Texto', 136ff; Martinez, 'Documentos', nos.170, 436–8, 448, 452.
97 Martinez, 'Texto', 115ff, 119ff; and, for example, Martinez, 'Documentos', nos.301–4, 370, 416–22, 426–8, 449.
98 Martinez, 'Documentos'. nos.359, 360, also 390, 449.
99 Martinez, 'Texto', 177.
100 Martinez, 'Documentos', no.440.
101 Finke, *AA*., vol. 3, no.197; the document is anonymous but probably based on James's instructions.
102 Martinez, 'Documentos', nos.314, 347.
103 See Martinez, 'Texto', 160f.

104 See, for example, Martinez, 'Documentos', nos.65, 88 (here expressly as honour), 317 (the importance of seeing people in judging their health; see, on this, also no.441), 331, 402, 444, 445; also Martinez, 'Texto', 57f.
105 Martinez, 'Documentos', no.65, see also no.170.
106 Martinez, 'Documentos', no.436 (here, *inter alia,* 'dubito de ea . . . de diutina intellectus lesione').
107 Martinez, 'Documentos', no.444.
108 Martinez, 'Documentos', no.402.
109 Finke, *AA*, vol. 1, no.164 ('vesitar nos per vostres letres!'); Martinez, 'Texto', 17 n47; Finke, *AA*, vol. 3, no.136 are also relevant.
110 Desclot's chronicle, chap. 70; *Llibre dels feits*, chap. 550.
111 Martinez, 'Texto', 196 n4; on James's general contribution, see above p.217.
112 On this see, generally, Finke, *AA*, vol. 1, 178f, vol. 3, 59, *Nachträge*, 625ff; Martinez, 'Texto', 287f; Soldevila, *Historia*, 399f.
113 Zeissberg, *Register*, no.44, pp.47f; and Finke, *AA*, *Nachträge*, 626.
114 Finke, *AA*, vol. 1, 178.
115 See Finke, *AA*, vol. 1, 178; and Martinez, 'Texto', 201.
116 See Sablonier, *Krieg und Kriegertum*, 28f; for example, Muntaner, chap. 84.
117 See Martinez, 'Texto', 52f, 159ff, 179ff.
118 Martinez, 'Documentos', no.469.
119 See Martinez, 'Texto', 53 and 176; for example, Martinez, 'Documentos', nos.443, 339, 361.
120 Martinez, 'Documentos', nos.436, 443; Martinez, 'Texto', 176.
121 Martinez, 'Documentos', nos.409, 410, 412.
122 See Martinez, 'Texto', 147ff (John/Constance).
123 Martinez, 'Documentos', no.459; see also Martinez, 'Texto', 176f.
124 Martinez, 'Texto', 101.
125 Martinez, 'Documentos', no.459.
126 Finke, *AA*, vol. 3, nos.217, 258 (contact with Elisabeth, as early as 1325); on the marriage negotiations, see *AA*, *Nachträge*, 640 (in connection with Peter).
127 Finke, *AA*, *Nachträge*, 651.
128 Finke, *AA*, *Nachträge*, 650.
129 See above, p.222.
130 Martinez, 'Texto', 293.
131 See above, p.211 and n5.
132 See, for example, the general review in Martinez Ferrando, Sobreques, and Bague, *Els descendents*, 135ff; also Finke, *AA*, vol. 1, 30ff; Martinez, 'Texto', 293ff; and Soldevila, *Historia*, 375f.
133 On dynastic law, see above p.226 and n86 and 87. Examples from the chronicle of James I, above p.226 and n22; from that of Peter III, chap. 1, 1 (1006ff) and 1, 42 (1017ff). At least, the *Llibre dels feits* was part of the reading of the Infantes James and Alfonso, see Martinez, 'Texto', 46.

Part V. Passageways: family values and survival strategies

10. Afro-American kinship before and after emancipation in North America

HERBERT G. GUTMAN

I

It was only in the 1960s and the 1970s that historians began seriously to question the legacy bequeathed them by E. Franklin Frazier's influential social history of the Afro-American family.[1] Before the 1960s, of course, a generation of historians explicitly rejected the racial assumptions common in pre-1940 historical scholarship and significantly rewrote the history of Afro-American slavery. Their pathbreaking works shared Frazier's anti-racist and harsh environmentalist assumptions. Exceptional (or privileged) slave men and women were shown to have triumphed over *the system*, but the *system's* exploitative severity molded most ordinary slaves into classic lumpenproletarians, a powerless aggregate of displaced African and Afro-American men, women, and children. Before the 1960s, others than historians, the novelist Ralph Ellison prominent among them, disputed Frazier's environmental determinism and its underlying reactive assumption that interpreted slave belief and behaviour as little more than an imperfect imitation of the dominant culture and as evidence of adaptation to a crude 'opportunity' model.[2] Ellison asked whether enslaved Africans and their Afro-American descendants could 'live and develop over three hundred years simply by reacting'. Few North American historians in the 1940s and the 1950s were examining historical evidence to answer such questions, much less even asking them.

The shift among students of Afro-American history in the 1960s and the 1970s to the 'Ellison question' did not occur in a vacuum. In these same years, historians studying other subordinate social classes grew increasingly dissatisfied with the prevailing reactive models used to explain their belief and behaviour. The so-called 'Ellison question' therefore was quite similar to the questions that increasingly concerned those European and American labor and social historians who had gone beyond reactive models in seeking to understand lower-class formation and development, patterns of lower-class belief and behaviour and the changing relations between subordinate and dominant social classes.[3]

241

But no group's history had been more completely twisted than that of slaves and poor ex-slaves.

Such misunderstanding rested, in good part, upon a profound misperception of the historical development of the slave family and especially the enlarged slave kin group in the century-and-a-half preceding the general emancipation. With notable exceptions, a vast and often useful historical scholarship prior to 1960 studied either what was done for slaves or what was done to them because it was assumed as a given that most slaves could do little more than react to diverse external stimuli. It followed that the study of slaves became mostly the study of what owners did to and for them. The assumptions historians made about either slavery or slaves (not the availability of evidence) dictated the questions that deserved study.

The assumption controlling much pre-1960 research was that a *discontinuous* family experience *over time* made it nearly impossible for slaves to retain, to accumulate, and to transform and then transmit distinctive but changing slave (or class) experiences and beliefs from one generation to another. Unlike other but far less constrained subordinate social classes, slaves could not sustain cumulative traditions – rules, social norms, and cultural beliefs essential for organizing their everyday work and life – interpreting and then dealing with their oppression, socializing and then protecting their children, interacting with owners, overseers, and other non-slaves, and developing enlarged social networks called institutions. The absence of such traditions severely limited choices slaves could make, and, not surprisingly, the choices slaves regularly made (clues to their beliefs) went unstudied.

The major legacy this generation of scholars bequeathed to historians had far less to do with such 'controversial' subjects as the stability of slave marriages, 'matrifocality', and 'African survivals' than with the assertion that an incapacity rooted in recurrent family fragmentation made it impossible for ordinary slave field hands and laborers to interact with mainstream cultural practices and beliefs and simultaneously develop and sustain historically derived values and behaviour patterns of their own. That incapacity – whatever its cause – isolated the slaves from the mainstream of historical analysis. 'Class', E. P. Thompson reminds us, 'is (or ought to be) a historical category, describing people in relationship over time, and the ways in which they become conscious of their relationships, separate, unite, enter into struggle, form institutions, and transmit values in class ways.'[4] The generational fragmentation of slave families made it unnecessary for historians of slavery to study process and to probe how slaves transmitted 'values in class ways'. The historian asked different questions about slaves than about other exploited social classes. Such groups managed to accumulate new historical experiences and transform them into institutional arrangements and alternative belief systems through which they interpreted their oppression and interacted with their oppressors. Enslaved Afro-Americans could not do so.

II

We now know that this entire view of the enslaved Afro-American is mistaken.[5] Studying some of the common *choices* slave men and women made has uncovered cumulative Afro-American traditions that developed over time and spread over space. Studying slave domestic arrangements and household formation on six developing and very different plantations in the century preceding the emancipation uncovers two important uniformities in these settings. First, at all times and on all six plantations the typical slave household was double-headed. Over the full family cycle, most slave children (including those sold or separated from their families of origin for other involuntary reasons) grew up in such households. Second, and equally important, at all times and on all six plantations, households headed by a single parent (the mother) existed over the full family cycle. These households had not been broken by the sale or death of a father: a male parent had never resided in them. The relative importance of these different domestic arrangements varied on the plantations studied, but these variations are far less significant than the coexistence of different (possibly competing) types of slave households in all plantation settings. Such diversity suggests that the fact that most slaves settled into doubled-headed arrangements is evidence of owner indifference and of slave preference. Owners surely did not sponsor competing types of slave domestic arrangements. No evidence exists, moreover, indicating that slave owners either prevented slave women from heading 'single parent' households over the full family cycle or punished them for doing so. Slaves often chose between alternate types of domestic arrangements. The choices they made are clues – nothing more – to their beliefs.

Some of the common practices associated with slave family life differed from those found in the mainstream culture. Although white marriage rules in general await detailed study, it seems clear that blood cousin marriages were sanctioned among large plantation owners. Slave exogamy contrasted sharply with planter endogamy. Slave sexual beliefs and practices also differed from those of their owners. No evidence shows that slaves internalized the so-called 'Victorian ideal', which subordinated sexual intercourse to marriage, although slaves scorned marital infidelity as did mainstream cultural norms. By the second quarter of the nineteenth century (if not earlier), Anglo-American cultural norms no longer sanctioned pre-nuptial intercourse among white women, much less childbirth prior to marriage. But contemporaries – slaves and ex-slaves among them – observed the prevalence of pre-nuptial intercourse among slaves. Evidence of childbirth prior to marriage, moreover, is found in all plantation slave birth registers. Its relative importance remains unclear, but perhaps as many as three in ten married slave women had one or more children prior to marriage.

Slaves and their owners differed in their attitudes toward women who had all their children outside of marriage. The dominant culture rejected such women. Slaves did not. Some slave mothers everywhere never married, and many had as many as eight children. Their families of origin did not reject such women. Children born to these women regularly had the names of maternal kin. During the Civil War, moreover, such women (who described themselves as 'single' mothers) regularly accompanied their parents and grown siblings to federal refugee camps.

The ways in which slaves and their owners named newborn children for members of immediate families differed. Owners and other whites regularly named a son for his father and a daughter for her mother. A slave father often had a son named for him, but a daughter seldom received her slave mother's name. Sometimes a daughter had her father's given name and might be called Josephine or Georgeanna. A slave child's legal status followed that of its mother, and slave owners rarely recorded a father's name in plantation birth lists. Fathers were more likely to be separated from children than mothers. Naming a child for its father, therefore, confirmed that dyadic tie and gave it an assured continuity that complemented the close contact that bound the slave child to its mother.

The common choices so far reported come almost entirely from studying six plantation communities over time. Each of these developing 'plantation' settings differed from the other in significant ways, including location, type of ownership, size, economic function, the age of a slave community ('time'), and slave sale, purchase, and gift transfer. The slaves in these settings differed in many ways from each other, but similar domestic arrangements, kin networks, sexual behavior, marriage rules, and naming practices existed in all six settings. Such evidence in no way means that the slave family was – as some have suggested – 'autonomous'.[6] These distinctive practices in diverse settings in which enslaved men and women experienced their oppression differently do no more than reveal the limitations of even the most sophisticated reactive 'models'.

Even more is known than these important (and incomplete) details about slave domestic arrangements and about certain distinctive slave family beliefs and practices. The slaves as a developing social class (made up mostly of field hands and common laborers) forged a widespread, adaptive, and distinctive kinship system out of their African and American experiences, processes that began well before the invention of the cotton gin and even before the American War for Independence. Uncovering the enlarged slave kin group – not the isolated slave 'nuclear family' but the relations between slave families of the same and especially of different generations – tells us something new about Afro-American slaves and something of paramount importance about the Afro-American historical experience.[7]

That slave men and women attached great importance to relations between families of different generations and to extended kin is revealed in historical sources other than reconstructed plantation birth lists. Three letters indicate these attachments and cast grave doubt on the arguments of those historians who identify affection with affluence. The first, written in 1807, was sent by the Virginia slave Gooley to her former owner who had moved to Kentucky and taken some of Gooley's children and other blood kin with her:

you will please to tell my Sister Clary not to Let my poor children Suffer & tell her she must allso write & inform me how she & my children are . . . Mr Miller is now on the brink of death, & is about to sell 40 of his Negroes and it is likely Joshua may be one. I wish to stay with him as long as possible as you must know its very bad to part man and wife. I should be glad to no what sort of life Clary leads . . . be pleased to inform me how my little daughter Judith is & if she is now injoying health . . . P.S. . . . old Granny Judy goes about and that is all.

The second letter was written fifty years later (in 1857). The Georgia rice planter Charles C. Jones sold Cash, Phoebe, and some of their children. A letter arrived from them postmarked New Orleans:

please tell my daughter Clarissa and Nancy a heap how a doo for me Pheaby and Cash and Cashes son James . . . Please tell them that their sister Jane died the first of Feby . . . Clarissa your affectionate Mother and Father send a heap of Love to you and your husband and my Grand-Children Phebea. Mag. & Cloe. John. Judy. Sue. My aunt Aufy sinena and Minton and Little Plaska . . . Give our love to Cashes Brother Porter and his wife Patience. Victoria gives her love to her Cousin Beck and Miley.

An ex-slave wrote the third letter a year and a half after the general emancipation. His sister had written seeking funds to return to their home in Maryland.

My dear Sister

I take my pen in hand to write a few lines to inform you i received your leter and was so glad to hear from you. This is the third leter i have wrote to you since i heard that i had a sister in the land of of [sic] the living; and i dont know wheather you got my letters or not. i am living in Maryland at *Miss Nancy Cores* with my relatives. your Father is living and well. all your cousins send love to you. i am sory that your husband has left you in distress. you must write to me and tell me the news, how all is getting on out where you are and what you are doing, and when i get a letter from you i will try [to] help you to get here with me. and tell me who you are living with. i have been sole too to virginia and to North Caryline for E[i]g[h]teen years. u have been Back three years to Maryland. i am well at this time. i shall close by saying write as soon as you can and believe me

Yours loving Brother
John Rone[8]

That slaves attached such importance to the enlarged kin group (as contrasted to the immediate family) escaped the attention of most owners. No record survives indicating that owners noticed that slaves did not marry blood cousins. Indeed, no record survives indicating an awareness of general slave marriage rules. A single birth list – that recorded in 1773–4 by Charles Carroll – indicates kin ties beyond the immediate slave family.[9] Owners rarely if ever recorded the naming of a slave child for its slave aunt, uncle, or grandparent, but such naming occurred frequently. A single source records the concern of an overseer for the extended slave family. The slave James Williams fled Alabama in the year 1830. He had been a driver on a cotton plantation and reported:

it was the object of the overseer to separate me in feeling and interest as widely as possible from my suffering brethren and sisters. I had relations among the field-hands, and used to call them my cousins. He forbid me doing so, and told me that if I acknowledged relationship with any of the hands I should be flogged for it.

III

The enlarged slave kin network served the slaves in two distinct ways. We now know that inter-generational slave kin and quasi-kin linkages served as slave passageways through time, connecting up changing structures. Changing but nevertheless historical slave notions of right and wrong as well as slave notions of legitimate slave social and cultural practices were taught to children by immediate and distant older kin. Such an enlarged perspective allows us to see the slave family as far more than an owner-sponsored device to reproduce the labor force and maintain 'social control'. If owners encouraged family formation either to reproduce the labor force or discipline the adult male worker (and these two processes are not necessarily similar), that decision had profound, if unanticipated, social and cultural consequences among the slaves. Inter-generational linkages developed. Passageways for a developing slave culture shaped the beliefs of the new subordinate class. 'I suspect', Frederick Olmsted said of slaves and their owners in the 1850s, 'that the great trouble and anxiety of Southern gentlemen is – how, without quite destroying the capabilities of the negro for any work at all, to prevent him from learning to take care of himself'. Most slaves were learning to 'take care' of themselves from kin and quasi-kin.

The kin network served other functions than that of passageway. Obligations rooted in kin ties developed over time into obligations between slaves unconnected to one another by blood or marital ties. It is well known that slaves and their owners often addressed adult slaves by kin titles ('aunt' and 'uncle'). No evidence has been found indicating that whites used such terms of address prior to 1800. Slaves (and I mean Africans, not Afro-Americans) did so before that time. On slave ships, according to Orlando Patterson, 'it was customary for children to call parents' shipmates "uncle" and "aunt"', and even for middle-passage adults to 'look upon each other's children mutually as their own'. Later in time, kin terms of address toward non-kin-related slaves were used frequently by slaves and their owners. Owners used such non-reciprocal terms of address to show personal attachment toward favored slaves and to define essential status differences between slaves and non-slaves. Slaves did so for very different reasons. They had real aunts and uncles and had reason to address such men and women by appropriate kin titles. But parents and other adult slaves also socialized slave children to address all older slaves as aunt and uncle.

Making children do that socialized them into the enlarged slave community, not the 'family'. 'They show great respect for age as is manifest from one custom of theirs', said a Yankee teacher in wartime Virginia. 'They always call an older person Aunt or Uncle. We had two servants living with us. One was a boy and the other a girl. The boy who was younger always called the girl Aunt.' Years before, a northern white met an elderly Mississippi plantation slave whose owner said that 'Uncle Jacob was the regulator on the plantation; . . . a *word* or *look* from him, addressed to younger slaves, had more efficiency than a *blow* from the overseer.' Kin terms of address taught young slaves to respect older ones, kin and non-kin alike. Such persons had authority within the slave community and were given status by investing them with symbolic, or fictive, kin titles. Socializing children in this way, moreover, also bound them to fictive kinsmen and kinswomen, preparing them in the event that death or sale separated them from parents and other blood kin.

Fictive, or quasi-, kin played yet other roles in developing slave communities, binding unrelated slave adults to one another and thereby infusing these groups with conceptions of reciprocity and obligation that had initially flowed from kin obligations. Over time, obligations toward a brother or a niece became obligations toward a fellow slave or that slave's children. Fictive aunts and uncles bound children to quasi-kin outside the immediate slave family, and the ties between a slave child and its fictive aunts and uncles bound that child's parents to such persons. That much is suggested by Sidney Mintz's and Eric Wolf's study of ritual co-parenthood and Esther Goody's study of pro-parenthood.[10] In modern Western societies, Goody observes, 'all parental roles are concentrated within the nuclear family', but such roles 'are potentially available for sharing among kin or even with unrelated neighbors or friends'. Such sharing often serves other purposes than caring for deprived children. It is also a way of 'forging links between adults', a way in which 'many societies make use of bonds between parent and child'. Mintz and Wolf suggest that ritual co-parentage creates quasi-kin ties between a child's parents and that child's ceremonial sponsors, ties that make 'the immediate social environment more stable'. According to them, the type of class and social structure affects the choice of quasi-kin. A relatively uniform social and class structure means that co-parenthood was 'prevailingly horizontal (intra-class) in character', but the presence of 'several interacting classes' structures co-parentage 'vertically (inter-class)'.

Afro-American slaves were never a self-contained social class, a fact affecting how individual slaves sought protection for themselves and especially for their children. Some, usually privileged slaves and especially those belonging to a family over more than one generation, found such protection in modified reciprocal co-parental relationships with owners. But not all slaves could (or wanted to) have the protection resulting from such cross-class linkages. And most owners felt no such obligation toward their slaves. Slaves developed alternative (if fragile) means for protecting themselves and their children. Fictive kinsmen and kinswomen – the generalized slave uncle and aunt – served as very important instrumentalities in furthering group solidarities and in ordering a daily life regularly disordered by the choices slave owners made. Fictive kinship complemented exogamous marital rules in distancing slaves from their owners and thereby weakening dependence based upon ownership.

Initial enslavement shattered kin ties for all but a few Africans. The conversion of kin relationships into symbolic (or quasi-) kin ties on slave ships is evidence of active survival strategy and culture change. The 'old' was used to deal with the 'new' and, in turn, the 'old' was transformed. Let us shift from the slave ship to the slave plantation, from the enslaved African to the Afro-American slave, and from the mid-eighteenth to the mid-nineteenth century. The sale of children from immediate families as well as the breakup of marriages increased the importance of quasi-kin obligations. A young slave sold from the Upper to the Lower South between 1800 and 1860 (and between 700,000 and 1,000,000 men, women, and children were moved in that migration, the largest internal forced migration in the nineteenth-century Western world) was cut off from his or her immediate Upper South family but found many 'fictive' aunts and uncles in the Lower South. During the Civil War, the consequences of quasi-kin obligations also revealed themselves dramatically. Despite the wartime devastation, the disruption of the plantation system, and the emancipation, northern soldiers and missionaries found very few orphan children among the slaves and ex-slaves. Children cut off from their parents and other older kin were being cared for by neighbors.[11]

An overall historical process associated with class formation and development has been suggested in these few pages. It can be broadly sketched, covers the entire era of enslavement, and involves four closely related but nevertheless distinct 'stages':

1 Family and kinship patterns of belief and behavior associated with diverse West African societies.
2 The destruction of settled kinship and family patterns following the slave trade and initial enslavement (first in Africa and then in the New World) but accompanied by the slaves non-kin relations with symbolic kin functions.
3 The emergence of settled Afro-American slave family and kin groups following the initial disruption associated with enslavement and the early creation of symbolic kin networks.
4 The development of inter- and intra-generational linkages between slave families accompanied by the transformation of conceptions of family and kin obligation rooted in blood and marriage into conceptions of quasi-kin and non-kin social obligation.

Fictive kin are not distinctive to slave cultures. But because slave society so constricted general associational life, fictive kin probably served as more important devices for enlarging social networks among slaves than among dependent social classes with relatively wider choices.

Obligations rooted in beliefs about ties between adult brothers and sisters and other kin served as 'models' for affective obligations binding together larger groups of slaves, a development that involved a special tension distinctive to slave society. That tension changed over time and varied from place to place. But it was always present. The choice between forming a reciprocal relationship with an owner ('massa') or with a fellow slave ('aunt' or 'uncle') caused this tension. It was a tension that had its roots in the conflict between duties based upon ownership and obligations based upon kinship and quasi-kinship.

IV

The enlarged kin group accompanied ordinary Afro-American slaves into legal freedom. It – not the isolated 'nuclear' family – formed the core of all poor Afro-American communities in the full century-and-a-quarter that separate us from Afro-American enslavement. Anthropologists studying the contemporary black poor – Carol B. Stack and Demetri B. Shimkin and his associates, among others – have demonstrated that the kinship system forged under slavery retains unusually positive functions among poor rural and urban blacks living in the last quarter of the twentieth century. These outstanding works, however, lack an historical dimension and are too functional in their emphasis, although they make it clear that the poor black family cannot be understood in isolation from the enlarged kin group. And they demonstrate how exchanges between kin and quasi-kin based upon principles of reciprocity and obligation allow the poor to deal with severe deprivation. Shimkin and his associates describe the extensive 'gamut of rights and obligations' associated with membership in a rural Mississippi black extended family: 'it runs, in general, from pressures for solidarity in public decisions . . . to cooperation in work, aid in job hunting, co-residence privileges, child fosterage, care in old age, . . . and gifts and inheritance'. The social scientist Raymond T. Smith finds similar patterns among the urban poor: 'the dominant impression is of people helping other people, whether it be by lending, by looking after children, by giving gifts of various practical kinds, or by transfers of money'.[12]

V

The impressive work by Stack and Shimkin (and his associates) on the positive functions of the extended family among late twentieth-century poor blacks is not matched by detailed historical analysis of the poor black urban and especially black rural extended family between 1865 and 1960. Gutman's work, for example, neglects the post-emancipation extended black family and focuses instead excessively on the composition of poor black households in the rural and urban South in 1880 and 1900 and in the urban North in 1905 and 1925. Except for Elizabeth Raul Bethel's and Elizabeth Hafkin Pleck's studies, little useful historical work exists on the black extended family after emancipation.[13]

Studying the behavior of ex-slaves between 1861 and 1867 begins to fill in that gap. It enlarges our understanding of the slaves as a social class upon their emancipation by revealing something about slave beliefs that had been transmitted from generation to generation prior to the emancipation. Neither the American Civil War nor the general emancipation had transformed Afro-American slaves into a new race of men and women. These external events enlarged the arena in which they could make choices. But too little time had passed by 1867 to think that underlying slave cultural beliefs had yet been radically transformed. Studying what ex-slaves did between 1861 and 1867 allows the historian to reexamine two separate but related questions. First, what in their experiences as slaves explains common patterns of behavior among them as ex-slaves. And, second, what does their behavior as ex-slaves reveal about the relationship between inward slave beliefs and outward slave behavior?

VI

How slave passageways sustained an ethic of self-help as well as an ethic of mutuality and generalized obligation is revealed in the behavior of wartime 'contraband' men and women in and near Alexandria, Virginia.[14] Their early condition was deplorable. Between mid-June and early December of 1862, 3354 contrabands passed through the Alexandria camp. A visit among them by New York Quakers in October 1862 revealed that sometimes as many as ten or twelve persons were quartered in rooms no more than twelve feet square. The runaway North Carolina ex-slave Harriet Jacobs noticed that the 'little children pine like prison birds for their native element'. Smallpox ravaged the refugees that first winter. D. B. Nichols, the Superintendent of Contrabands, distressed the refugees. He allowed several dead blacks to be buried in a 'box', angering resident runaways who had a 'great respect for the dead'. A District of Columbia black said the contrabands believed Nichols 'better suited to be an overseer of a Southern plantation'.

But the condition of the Alexandria refugees improved, largely because of their own individual and collective efforts. In the 1863–4 fall and winter months, they built several hundred one and two room cabins (ranging in value from $40 to $100) for themselves. They paid an annual ground rent. Government teamsters among them had $5 taken from each monthly wage payment for 'public' support of disabled refugees and helpless women and children. About 7000 refugees lived there in August 1864; twenty-five received public assistance. 'Hundreds . . . in the last twelve months', said an army physician among them, 'built houses of their own, and paid every dollar for them, besides supporting their families.' About 1000 houses had been built by the refugees. 'All they need', the physician concluded, 'is protection, plenty of work at a fair price, and punctual payment.'

Schools started quickly among the Alexandria refugees. 'The first demand of these fugitives when they come into a place,' observed a reporter, 'is that their children may go to school. Another surprising fact is that the poor negro women had rather toil, earn, and pay one dollar a month for their children's education than permit them to enter a charity school.' A white teacher did not work with the Alexandria contrabands until October 1862. By that time, blacks managed three other schools. Before the war's end, at least sixteen other blacks taught in or ran Alexandria schools. In April 1863, about 400 children attended such schools. The total contraband population then numbered about 2000. One school started in a former 'slave pen'. Another (a 'self-sustaining' school with about 150 pupils) was housed in a building put up as a Lancastrian school at the bequest of George Washington and meant to be 'forever free to the poor of the city'.

Harriet Jacobs and her daughter Linda started Alexandria's most important contraband school. New York Quakers had sent the two former North Carolina slaves there in 1862 to conduct relief work. When she left in the fall of 1863, Alexandria contrabands had agreed to build a school house, but on her return a few weeks later they had not yet finished it. 'Their funds got exhausted', Jacobs reported, 'and the work was at a standstill'. But she and her daughter (later aided by the daughter of a prominent Boston black caterer) started a school. Jacobs reported: 'one of the freedmen whose cabin consisted of two rooms, gave it to us for our school'. The place proved too small. Jacobs held 'a little Fair' and raised $150 in building funds. By October 1864, Alexandria blacks had spent $700 from their earnings to support the school. Jacobs raised another $300 in donations from friends. The contrabands did more than give money. Their voluntary labor built a school house worth about $500.

Sometime in 1864, the blacks enlarged the building. It was now 60 feet long and 28 feet wide and 'well-lathed and plastered'. At its start, a bitter dispute threatened the school's future. Jacobs described it:

a question arose whether the white teachers or the colored teachers should be the superintendents. The freedmen had built this schoolhouse for the children, and were Trustees of the school. So after some discussion it was decided that it would be best for them to hold a meeting, and settle the question for themselves. I wish you could have been at that meeting. Most of the people were slaves, until quite recently, but they talked sensibly, and I assure you they put the question to a vote in quite parliamentary style. The result was that the colored teachers should have charge of the school.

The school opened in January, 1864, with seventy-five pupils; two months later it had 225 pupils. By August, 1864, it was 'the largest school and schoolhouse in the city'.

That the Alexandria contrabands were not unusual in their beliefs and behavior is learned by comparing them to rural ex-slaves living in northwestern South Carolina, a rich cotton-producing region that was home to about 100,000 blacks, nearly a third of the state's former slave population.[15] Benjamin Franklin Whittemore, a Massachusetts resident, an Amherst College graduate, a Methodist clergyman, and a former Union army chaplain, supervised education there for the Freedmen's Bureau between 1865 and 1867 before entering Republican state politics. After he toured the region in January 1866, he pleaded for outside help: 'the negroes are willing to deny themselves and do all they can to obtain knowledge, but they can not do much'. The Freedmen's Bureau, moreover, was powerless, 'in many particulars, inoperative because of its poverty', and very much in need of Congressional monies. A year later, Whittemore remembered the region in early 1866 as 'a wilderness in every particular'. Nearly all blacks there farmed, and on 1 January 1866, they celebrated Emancipation Day by 'besieging' Bureau headquarters to complain about poorly drawn contracts that defrauded them and about inadequate food supplies. Such behavior spread fear of insurrection, and Bureau officers worked hard to arrange settlements with white employers. 'Mutual dependence', Whittemore worried, had to be 'taught, felt, and acknowledged.' Afterwards, store orders remained common and cash payments few. A crop failure in 1866 – just one third of the normal crop was harvested – caused even worse troubles. In June, 1867, Darlington ex-slaves addressed Boston's Mayor: 'we are on the eve of Starvation. We have no way in God's world to get provisions. Only through our Friends North . . . If there is any chance in the world to get anything to eat in your city, do for Heavens Sake Send us some and save us from Perishing.'

Despite their increasingly difficult economic circumstance and some local white opposition to schooling for their children (' "philanthropic or puritanic" institutions for "niggers" '), ex-slaves over the entire region contributed significantly to their children's education. An ethic of mutuality similar to that among the Alexandria blacks shaped their behavior. They moved an old 'Confederate building' ten miles from Florence to Darlington to start the district's first school. By April 1866, six schools existed and a month later eleven. Northern soldiers had burned a Marion school house, so its teacher met classes in the woods where blacks had put together a makeshift school. In Sumter, blacks first built 'a rude shelter in the yard of a Mr. Williams, one of the most enterprising of its colored citizens'. Summerville got its school some time before July. Two white women offered two acres of land for $200 as school property. Local blacks, many among them poor and destitute, crowded an army barracks used as their church to agree that if the northern societies paid for the land and the government supplied lumber, they would build a school to open in October. Dan Meyers, 'a good carpenter', spoke first: 'I is a plain man and alers does what I agree, and I say that I will stan' by the good work till it's done finished.' The next speaker added: 'I is called a good carpenter; I has no children of my own to send to the school; but I want to see the house built, and I gives two weeks for it.' Others offered labor, and some, including young boys, gave small sums of money. In all, the blacks raised $60 and pledged twelve weeks of labor. 'The women', said the school teacher Esther Hawkes, did 'their part', too, 'offering to board or lodge the workmen as they best could'. 'These destitute people', Hawkes mused, 'living, some of them, in rude huts made of mud and palmetto, one might suppose that all their interest was necessary [just] to keep them from starving.'

Schooling made significant progress among these upcountry South Carolina blacks by the fall of 1866. Whittemore pleaded with the American Freedmen's Union Commission in late September: 'I am at present wanting eight teachers, where schools of over sixty pupils each are awaiting them . . . The parents are begging me to send them the "school teacher".' The demand for teachers had outrun the supply for good reason. The burned Marion school had been rebuilt ($200); Darlington blacks gave their labor and money for a school ($500); Simmonsville ex-slaves ditched and fenced and then built a home for the teacher ($150); Sumter blacks moved a building forty miles and then reconstructed it ($250). Lynchburg ex-slaves also moved and fixed up a building ($150). So did Florence blacks ($350). In Camden, ex-slave muscle and money meant a new school house ($800) and the rental of an old building for $30 a month. School houses also went up on the Mulberry plantation ($100) and in Springville ($100). Kingstree blacks spent $600, and in Snow Hill they fashioned a log house and then a separate abode for the teacher. Boykin plantation blacks lacked ready cash, but ninety-four formed an association to sustain their school. Society Hill blacks constructed 'a fine commodious school house' valued at between $500 and $600. Cheraw freedmen, who had permission from local whites to use the town hall for educational meetings, promised to pay rent regularly, and in Bennetts-ville they agreed to move and reconstruct a distant building for their children. Overall, Whittemore figured that each community had expended an average of $320 by October, 1866.

More than cash sustained the new schools. In Camden, for example, most Negroes worked crops on contract and saw no cash until they had gathered the full crop. Teachers there did not suffer discomfort. 'They furnish us with beds, bedding, and furniture for our rooms free, though they do not pay the rent', said a male teacher. 'They sell articles to teachers at under price, and bring in gratuitously articles of food. The girls at the night school have made me some presents.' 'There is no lack of a disposition to do all in their power now', said Whittemore of these people in October, 1866. 'Indeed I think they *have* done it.' Between 1 September 1866, and 31 January 1867, Camden Negroes raised $120 to pay school rent, heat the school building, and furnish the dwellings of school teachers. 'They have performed *all they have promised*', reported Jane Smith from Sumter. 'They were to pay a certain sum toward the erection of their church, which they have done. They were to whitewash it, to buy a bell, build a belfrey, furnish lamps, lumber for the pulpit, and several comforts for the teacher. All this, *they have done*.' 'They half supply our table now', Smith went on, adding, 'they are very poor this winter'. Whittemore summed up the year's work in January, 1867. Twenty-two schools had been set up, and over 4000 children instructed. The blacks owned, unencumbered, more than $12,000 worth of church and school properties, 'two-thirds of which' had been 'secured by their own industry, skill, and collections'.

Much more than either Yankee benevolence or federal largesse made the school house a reality among former north-eastern South Carolina slaves in 1866 and 1867. Communal values and sanctions shaped the activities of ex-slaves there. 'He who makes himself prominent in opposing the establishment of a school', noticed Whittemore, 'is looked upon as an enemy to the *race*, and worthy of suspicion, or "to be let alone" when contracting is called for.' The success of such community sanctions depended on shared values. Nevertheless collective effort required work by individual persons. We have the example of Julia Bird, the sole supporter of her eight children. The Snow Hill school house had been built without a chimney. One was added, but inferior labor had made it useless without repairs. Others declined to repair it; then Julia Bird volunteered. She and four of her children spent a full Saturday fixing the chimney. 'She dug the clay', said a teacher, 'and with her own hands mixed the mortar, and repaired the chimney so perfectly that it had worked like a charm ever since . . . Said she didn't want the school to stop a day.'

This evidence from Virginia and South Carolina tells us much about the ex-slaves. But what in their experiences as slaves had prepared them for such behavior? And what does their behavior reveal about their inward beliefs as slaves? Attitudes toward work, religion, and family and kin that developed during slavery and were difficult if not impossible to act upon then sustained notions of obligation and mutuality among many ex-slaves. Ex-slaves on the Georgia plantation Henry Lee Higginson leased in 1866 confused their Yankee employer: 'they help each other in picking the different patches of cotton, as it opens. If they receive help for it, they return help, not money.' Davis Tillison, who headed the Georgia Freedmen's Bureau that same year, reported, 'I know of colored men who work hard all day and into the night, and who give one third of all they earn to the support of the poor of their own race. This I learn, not from their own lips, but from those of white neighbors.' A perfectionist Afro-Christianity encouraged benevolence among such men and women. About 1800 destitute former North Carolina slaves lived at the Camp Trent refuge. Crop failures in 1867 meant that many picked cotton for between a quarter and a half a cent per pound. It was hard for individuals to make 25 cents a day. That fall between 300 and 400 children attended a Camp Trent school. Adult refugees formed an educational society and paid 10 cents to join it. The clergyman Amos York headed the group and quickly collected $8. The following letter to a private northern relief agency accompanied the money:

DEAR SIR we THE members of the Educational Society auginized in Trent Settlement NC Do Forward to the Sociation Eight Dollars $8 to aide in Serporting our teacher Rev J W Burghduff. The amount is small But is the Best we can Do under the Present Circumstancis we are a Poore and Destitute People and the times are wary harde But we feel willing to try to help our selves as we Can of such we hope the small amount will Be accepted.

> Respectfully yous
> AMOS YORK *President*
> SOUTHEY HUNTER *Sect*

'Please ancer this as sunde as it comes to hand Direct Box 121.' 'The amount is small, I know', admitted a missionary school teacher, 'but we are very much like the widow spoken of in Luke xxi. 1–4. It is all we had.'

Ex-slaves over the entire South shared beliefs with men like Amos York. That happened because class obligation built upon kin obligation as well as Afro-Christian perfectionism. A meeting about their schools among St Helena's Island, South Carolina, ex-slaves in 1868 indicated how some of these separate strands had come together. Hastings Garret spoke first and according to the Yankee teacher, Laura Towne, urged that 'rich and poor . . . come forward at once and assist in support of the schools, each putting in according to his means'. He asked Towne to speak, and she and another white teacher advised the blacks to rely less on outside financial aid and more on their own resources. The 'elders and principal men' spoke, too, and promised to raise money and 'contribute themselves as soon as they could'. But cash was short then so Garret advised that they 'set aside a piece of land, work it fruitfully, and devote all its produce to schools'. Others spoke:

Uncle Liah, who had previously spoken . . . said that they were all poor, and each could do but little, but this was a work for many. It may be as it was at Indian Hill, where the great burial-ground was raised by each Indian throwing just one handful of earth upon it every time he passed. Uncle Aleck said, Should each man regard only his own children, and forget all the others? Should they leave that poor neighbor widow with her whole gang of children, and give them no chance for a free schooling?

Such beliefs – 'each putting in according to his means', setting aside a piece of land for a communal purpose and all working it, and considering free schooling for the 'poor neighbor widow's children' – had nothing to do with the moral paternalism of their former owners or of the Yankee missionaries and school teachers.[16]

Reactive models cannot explain the beliefs and behavior of ex-slaves like Julia Bird, Hastings Garret, and Amos York. The alternative is not a romantic one. We are instead directed to reexamining the relationships between class formation, class development, and changing patterns of class belief and behavior. By the 1860s, most Afro-American slaves were descended from a four-or-five-generation class experience. Emancipation transformed an established and developed subordinate class, allowing ex-slave men and women to act on a variety of class beliefs that had developed but been constrained during several generations of enslavement. Static conceptions of either social class or the relationship between dominant and subordinate social classes prevent us from studying this historical process.

VII

It might be argued that these Virginia and South Carolina ex-slaves were unusual in their behavior because they came from relatively stable settlements in which kin and social obligation had a better chance of surviving than in more turbulent places. We shift therefore to northern Mississippi and, in particular, to Yalobusha County. Except for the few who lived in the town of Grenada, nearly all Yalobusha ex-slaves worked the land. Slaves had made up more than half of the country's population of 17,000 residents in 1860. Only six free blacks had lived among them. About one in four slaves lived on the county's thirty plantations that each employed at least fifty slaves. About two in three had been owned in units of twenty or more slaves. The Yalobusha slave men and women experienced their enslavement very differently from their Virginia and South Carolina brothers and sisters. The county they lived in had developed very rapidly prior to the Civil War, and neither its slaves nor its non-slaves lived in a settled condition. Most significantly, these blacks had been detached physically from the settled slave passageways that had developed among Upper South slaves prior to 1800. They were among the survivors of the single most important external social and economic process affecting nineteenth-century Afro-American slaves: the involuntary transfer of hundreds of thousands of men, women, and children from the Upper to the Lower South.

A single document – the 'Freedmen's Complaint Register for Yalobusha County'[17] – draws us to this remote place and its ex-slaves. So does the larger local setting. The document details grievances by ex-slaves and is filled with accusations of abuse and mistreatment by former owners and other whites. Even by southern white standards Grenada was a conspicuously dangerous place for ex-slaves to assert themselves. Violence flared in the fall of 1865 when state-sanctioned white militia disarmed some ex-slaves. A train carrying the families of black Union Army soldiers was derailed, too. The next year armed whites drove off ex-slaves laboring as railroad section-hands. Federal soldiers restored the blacks. Local whites beat a northern white missionary sent to work among the Grenada blacks. A few days later whites shot and killed a federal official who had defended the missionary. They drove off some Yankee teachers and beat a protesting local white banker. Such behavior convinced the *New York Times* that a 'perfect reign of terror' existed in Grenada.

But it did not deter grieved ex-slaves from making accusations against local whites and demanding satisfaction from the few resident federal authorities. Their verbatim complaints between mid-July and the end of November in 1866 are printed below:

July 17   Billy Martin a freedman under contract with J. W. Marshall who lives 12 miles west of this place complains that the above named man whipped his son 16 years of age severely and told him to take his boy (from) the place. Says the party will not pay him.

July 19   Lizzie – colored – states that she is employed on contract by John Richardson . . . that yesterday her employer beat her with a club also beat her boy.

July 20	Malvinia – col'd – complains that her employer, Allen Aden res. about four miles from Grenada beat her with a club because she objected to having her child abused.
July 22	Mary Smith (colored) living with Eli D. Neil Carroll Co. complains her daughter 8 years old is held by Hardin Smith, he claiming to have her apprenticed to him. Mary says she never gave her consent.
July 22	Sally Saunders makes the same complaint in regard to her son about 17 years of age. Boys name is Lewis Washington.
July 22	Amanda Bryant (col'd) living with Geo Townsend Carroll Co. complains that her daughter 12 years of age was apprenticed to Stephen Thompson without her consent.
July 22 cont'd.	Henry Bryant her husband is in jail in Carrollton charged with enticing the above named girl (his daughter) away from Thompson.
July 24	John (freedman) states that he for himself and family agreed with Mr. Alexander to work this year for $250 and that they worked until about three weeks since when John left there and as he abides by the advice of Mr. Alexander to avoid danger of being killed by a man with whom his son has been working. He wants assistance in getting his family from Alexanders but tells an equivocal story.
July 25	Hannah (col) complains that James Howell living three miles on the Carrollton road holds her child a girl of four years of age and refuses to give her the custody of or to allow her (the mother) to come on his place. Hannah is now living with J. Paine.
July 29	Eli – (col) lives with Jefferson Crickery about 9 miles this side of Pittsboro Calhoun Co. states that a bunch of men disguised beat a cold woman 'Rinda' with switches; also beat 'Ben Cottwin' (cold) 500 lashes. He also states that three col'd men have been killed within the last three weeks; one of them was skinned alive. He does not know the names of the last victims but is positive that these murders have been committed.
July 30	Eliza Avant (col'd) living at Wim Bakers Coffeville complains that her four children have been apprenticed to Wm. Avant without the consent of the mother. (The names of the children are Leah 14 Hagar 9 Tom 8 & Pink about 7 years old) Eliza has made application to have the children given to her, Avant refuses – claiming his right under the apprentices law.
Aug. 1	Charles (freedman) . . . says his employer drove him and his family off his place – and threatened to shoot him if he returned. His contract was for half the crop.
Aug. 6	Jacob Campbell states that his wife was tied up to a tree and whipped and lashed. She being heavy with child at the time he interfered and they beat him with fist and club. John Jordan and Geo Jordan were the men who done the whipping they live in

Choctaw (?) Co. 5 miles from Duck Hill.

Aug. 9   Anderson (freedman) has been at work for Mr. Robertson 8 miles east of Bob Williams place. Last night Robertson beat Anderson seriously also whipped his daughter.

Aug. 15   Natt Pittman and his wife Norah appear and state that they bargained with A H Branch of Carroll County near Winona to cultivate 20 acres of land in cotton & corn and receive all he can raise over 75 Bus Corn & 500 pounds of lint cotton. Nat & his wife worked until about the 7th of August when Branch drove Norah (Nat's wife) away from his place with violence and threats, five or six days later Nat left of his own accord. Branch keeps Norah's goods and refuses to give them up.

Aug. 16   Wm Cooly & Sarah Donaway his wife complain that Sarah's daughter Harrier was bound to Mrs. Powell of Carrollton without consent of either parent and wish her return to their custody.

Aug. 18   James Allen (freedman) claims the guardianship of Jane aged about 15, a daughter by his former wife, also two children by his present wife Harriet viz Ritts age about 11 and Calvin about 9 and Andy a grandson of his first wife aged about 8 years. These children were all apprenticed to Mrs. Melinda Allen (a former owner) without due notice to or consent of either party, being obtained. James Allen and Harriet his wife are able and willing to support the above named children.

Aug. 18   Caroline (cold) claims the custody of her children viz John aged 16 Lucy 14 Jack 10. She states that these children were apprenticed to Winifred Metcalf of Carroll Co. 6 miles this side of Carollton without her consent and that she is able and willing to support them. She states that she has made application for the custody of the above children which was refused. The applicant now lives at Dr. Rosemans near Greysport 8 miles from here.

Aug. 20   Lydia asks that she have the custody of her children who are apprenticed to James Grey . . . against her will . . . Moses 12 Rachel 10 – Lydia lives with Mrs. Ely.

Sept. 4   Harriet Inman now living (at) Rev. Mr. Richardson complains that her two children Willie aged about 12 and Payton aged about 8 years are claimed by Mr. Ned Ingham of Tallahatchie Co. as apprenticed to him and that they were not bound to him in accordance with law. Inman lives about three miles below Tuscoma Ferry.

Sept. 12   Cudjoe freedman works for H. Talbert Carroll Co. – complains that he hired his mother in law and her daughter to Henry Cole – no contract was made and that they mother & daughter left Coles employ on account of ill treatment and that Cole called on Cudjoe to have them returned to his employ, that he did so and the mother left again, that Cole overtook him on the road and asked him where he was going, he told him to carry the Water Melons to his house – Cole told him not to go to his house. Cudjoe replied he would not if Cole objected. Cole then told him he must keep along until he told him to stop and drew his pistol and drove him about one quarter of a mile when Cudjoe stopped and Cole fired on him twice the shot going through his sleeve. A magistrate . . . imposed a fine of $100 – Cole refuses to pay and the magistrate cannot collect the fine or arrest the party.

Oct. 5 [Name missing] freedman complains he has been discharged by Mr. Bob Davidson without pay – and that his wife Martha is still on the place and that they will not let her off.

Nov. 15 Hannah a freedwoman states that Mr. Jim Howall living three miles from this place on the Carrollton road has a child of hers 4 years not apprenticed and will not let her have it. Threatens her life if she comes for it.

Nov. 26 Isaac freedman in the employ of Benjamin Sanders . . . complains that on the 24th inst he was beaten by Mr. Burt the father in law of Sanders and that his son was whipped by Sanders.

Date ? Lizzie Horsford or Horston (cold) lives with Mr. Houston near Coffeville complains that her employer beat her for going to church. Witness Dr. Means Mrs. Horford mother & sister & the colored people on the place.

Date ? Amanda Miles (cold) lives in Grenada desposeth as follows that on the morning of the 19th inst. she was assaulted and beaten on the premises of her husband by Thomas Sherman of Grenada.

Date ? Henry Jones freedman works for Mr. Ballard . . . Henry was shot by Mr. Ballard for not working on the road when ordered to – These parties live 12 miles on the road to Coffeville. Henry was badly wounded but not killed – Reported by Rhody sister to Henry.

Date ? Susan Johnson freedwoman under contract with Frank Johnson . . . makes complaint that her husband Henry Johnson was shot . . . by one John Evans the overseer. The wound is supposed to be fatal being through the head . . . witnesses in the case are the wife and sister of Evans and all the freed people on the place.

There is much for the historian to learn from this record of ex-slave behavior in rural Mississippi in the summer and fall of 1866. (Records detailing similar complaints by ex-slaves, incidentally, are found over the entire immediate postwar South.) It is probable that some of these ex-slaves exaggerated their complaints and that some even lied to the federal authorities. The record nevertheless reveals much about inward slave beliefs on such diverse matters as family responsibility, conceptions of obligation, and notions of right and wrong. What matters is that these clues describing inward slave beliefs come from Yalobusha County, Mississippi, ex-slaves. That is a critical fact because the Yalobusha ex-slaves were mostly first- and second-generation Mississippi black residents. Their immediate forbears had been Upper South Afro-American slaves. The inter-regional slave trade populated places like this one with men and women drawn violently from the Upper South. Some of the 1866 complainants may have been involved in the vast inter-regional transfer of labor that shattered so many slave families, others surely were the children of such men and women. What the Yalobusha ex-slaves revealed in their behavior in 1866 tells us much of importance about the slave passageways through which their immediate forbears had traveled. First- and second-generation Mississippi blacks carried Upper South Afro-American slave beliefs and values with them into the Lower South. Those victimized by this process were cut off abruptly from the slave passageways – the enlarged kin and quasi-kin networks – that then existed among their parents, siblings, and other relations. But the brutal and involuntary process that cut them loose also spread Afro-American (or slave) rules for living (an alternative culture that had developed among earlier slave generations) from the Upper to the Lower South. Those involved in the involuntary dispersal of an enslaved labouring population were not transformed by the inter-regional slave trade. Instead, that older and established slave culture served them as they shaped new slave passageways to sustain generations of Lower South slaves and ex-slaves.

VIII

Much more is known now (in 1980) about that older and established slave culture than in 1976 when *The Black Family in Slavery and Freedom* was published. That is because of important new research and publication dealing with eighteenth-century North American slaves. Among the plantation slaves studied by Gutman, only one group – those growing tobacco in Piedmont North Carolina – could be studied in detail during the late eighteenth century. The arguments in that work about the enlarged slave kin group and its functions rested primarily on nineteenth-century records and especially on records for the 1830 to 1860 era. In his brilliant critique of Gutman's work, the Latin American historian A. J. R. Russell-Wood wrote, 'the formative period of Afro-American culture preceded by several decades the War of Independence. And yet it is precisely for this pivotal period that Gutman is weak'.[18] Russell-Wood poses important questions about the relationship between the enlarged kin network and class formation and class development and suggests, 'by the 1760s, Afro-American culture was already in what might be referred to as the late formative period . . . It could well be argued that Afro-American culture had evolved through to the full manifestation of its major characteristics and by 1760 had reached the stage of development which was no longer formative.' Critical questions about culture formation require study of the 'origins of the African experience in the Americas, not in a later stage of creolization'.

It is possible to respond to Russell-Wood's suggestion and thereby enlarge our understanding of the relationship between the enlarged kin network and slave class formation and development. Eighteenth-century Afro-American kinship networks and domestic arrangements can be seen clearly in the records of planters who periodically inventoried their holdings, kept birth lists of their bondsmen and bondswomen, or indicated slave family connections in ration rolls, estate censuses, and wills. In 1773, Charles Carroll of Annapolis listed his several hundred slaves and noted their familial relations, age, residence by quarter, and occupation. The heirs of his only son compiled a similar, though less detailed, list after the latter's death nearly a half century later. There are also Carroll inventories dating back into the seventeenth century. Similarly, Thomas Jefferson enumerated the slaves on his Piedmont Virginia plantations at least once each decade from the 1770s until his death a half century later. Richard Bennehan, an ambitious clerk on his way to establishing North Carolina's largest tobacco plantation, began his slave birth register in 1776. And C. C. Pinckney pieced together a South Carolina estate between 1808 and 1812 that included records about bondsmen and women he inherited and acquired through marriage reaching back into the 1750s.

Taken together, the domestic arrangements revealed in these diverse eighteenth-century sources indicate that the practices common among slaves between 1830 and 1860 existed already prior to 1770. The data on marital rules remain unclear, but the domestic arrangements, kin networks, sexual behavior, and naming practices among these eighteenth-century African and mostly Afro-American North American slaves are unambiguous. These findings are revealed in the joint research and forthcoming publications of Mary Beth Norton, Herbert Gutman, and Ira Berlin.[19]

The most significant fact about this new evidence is the moment in time for which it exists – the 1770s. That moment in time is important for reasons indirectly associated with the American War for Independence. It is the relationship of this evidence and especially the pervasive presence of multi-generational family connections among Chesapeake (Virginia and Maryland) slaves to the social transformation of the Chesapeake slave population between 1720 and 1750 so ably analyzed by the historical demographers Russell Menard and Allan Kulikoff that give this date its importance. Menard and Kulikoff have demonstrated that prior to 1710, the Chesapeake slave population hardly reproduced itself and that its growth depended heavily upon the importation of African slaves. Significant social, cultural, and demographic changes altered this pattern so that the labor force began reproducing itself. The details of this analysis need not detain us except to note that prior to 1720 inventory records listed one slave child under the age of sixteen for every two slaves aged sixteen to fifty. Three decades later more slave children than slave adults were listed in similar records. The reproduction of the slave labor force meant a declining need for African slaves. (In fact, the largest number of African slaves – 210,000 or fully half of those imported into North America – arrived in the decades in which the native-born slave labor force began to reproduce itself.) The reproduction of the slave labor force so early in time had a cultural, social, and even political importance that paralleled its obvious economic significance. Inter-generational kin linkages – central to the development of all social classes and to the historical relationship between structure and process – could only develop and become important in a population that reproduced itself.

The preconditions for the development, sustenance, and transmission of a distinctive Afro-American culture rested first on the reproduction of the slave labor force and then on the development of kin networks – not mere 'families' – that connected generations of slaves in space and over time. The awareness among these mid-eighteenth-century slaves of third and even fourth generation ancestors tells much more than that they retained a consciousness of their 'roots'. That fact allows us to relate class formation to class development, to examine changing class beliefs and practices over time, to study how old slave beliefs became new slave beliefs, and to interpret the ways in which slaves regularly borrowed from the changing mainstream culture (itself class divided), often redefining what became a part of the new cultural patterns they were developing. The Scottish SPG (Society for the Propagation of the Gospel) missionary, Alexander Garden, who settled in Charleston, South Carolina, in 1726 described the process in 1740:

they are as 'twere a Nation within a Nation. In all Country Settlements, they live in contiguous Houses and often 2, 3, or 4 Famillys of them in one House, Slightly partitioned into So many Apartments. They labour together and converse almost wholly among themselves, so that if once their children could but read the Bible to them . . . this would bring in at least a Dawning of the blessed Light amongst them; and which as a Sett or two of those children grew up to Men and Women, would gradually diffuse and increase into open Day. – Parents and Grand Parents, Husbands, Wives, Brothers, Sisters, and other Relatives would be daily Teaching and learning of one another.

In two decades, Garden predicted, such slaves 'would not be much inferior to that of the lower order of white People, Servants & Day Labourers (Specially in the Country) either in England or elsewhere'.

The new eighteenth-century data about slave family and kinship affect more than our understanding of the relationship between class formation and development.[20] The Pinckney records, for example, include information about sale, death, transfer, and gift as well as birth, and a full study of these records strongly suggests that slave blood ties (especially those between grown siblings) were more lasting and more significant than marital ties. The Bennehan birth list and related documents, moreover, allow us to make an equally important if different point. The slaves belonging to Jefferson and Carroll were owned by Chesapeake planters of great wealth, men untypical of eighteenth-century slave owners outside of South Carolina. It might be argued that the familial arrangements among these slaves depended upon their status as plantation slaves. Most Chesapeake slaves and many lowcountry ones lived in small, farm-size units. Their circumstances doubtless necessitated distinctive strategies for survival. But by the 1770s, they shared the same kin-related values as plantation slaves. Evidence of this is drawn from the experience of the slaves owned by Richard Bennehan.[21] Bennehan acquired his bondspeople in small numbers and in a non-plantation setting, Orange County, North Carolina. Farms dominated the region, and, in 1780, when Bennehan began his climb into the planter class, only 3% of the county's slave holders held more than twenty bondspeople. Most of his slaves were newly arrived in the area, and there is no evidence that any had previous plantation experience. No nearby estates existed that might house complex kin networks similar to those in the Chesapeake. By the turn of the century, Bennehan's slaves had established patterns of marriage, child bearing, and naming common to slaves long accustomed to the plantation setting. Two in five of the 103 slave children born between 1803 and 1830 had the name of either a father or another blood relative. What young Bennehan slaves learned from older kin was not the mere product of 'plantation culture'. That fact is what gives the Bennehan slaves so much importance. The generation born after 1795 matured enmeshed in kin relations and were plantation slaves. But their immediate forbears had not been plantation slaves. They acted on beliefs that antedated their experiences as plantation slaves. Those beliefs – particularly the attachment of such great importance to the enlarged kin group – accompanied the first group of Bennehan slaves into the plantation experience and shaped the ways in which these men and women interpreted and interacted with it.

IX

Afro-American slaves emerged as a distinctive social class between 1720 and 1750. That class developed over the next century and was transformed during the American Civil War. It is now clear that the enlarged kin network played a central role in this long and painful process. But the changing role of the enlarged kin group awaits careful study as do such subjects as sex-role segregation, the relationship between consanguinity and affinity, the relationship between kinship and co-residence, and slave kin strategies in diverse settings including small farms, villages, and cities. More significantly, what is now known about slave kinship needs to be related to changing patterns of production and to changing patterns of subordination implicit in the master–slave relationship. 'Systems of kinship', the anthropologist Stephen Gudeman points out, '. . . both incorporate and mediate impulses emanating from other domains. Abstracting a family system from its context has the merit of underlining its patterned normative basis but the demerit of diminishing our understanding of its functions and meaning.'[22]

The restoration of what Gudeman calls 'context' promises to do more than enlarge our understanding of the changing ways in which slaves and their poor descendants used kin networks to deal with their oppressive circumstance. That enlarged context deepens our understanding of the Ellison question. It enriches our understanding of the communal ethic that led so many ex-slaves to sacrifice for literacy and to endanger their lives by filing complaints against abusive former owners and other whites. We shall comprehend why vast numbers of married and older ex-slave women everywhere withdrew from the labor force following emancipation and even why ex-slave husbands and wives apparently frequently disputed over to whom the wage belonged. It should become clear why wartime South Carolina Sea Island slaves (then supervised by the Federal army) refused to grow cotton, wanted to plant corn, broke the cotton gins, hid the iron work used for repair, and finally agreed to grow cotton but planted corn between the rows of cotton and then refused to pay the military rent on the land on which the corn grew. Such behavior rested on beliefs embedded in slave kin and quasi-kin networks. So did this petition submitted to the federal authorities in 1866 by Liberty County, Georgia, ex-slaves. They had worked on rice plantations, and the italicized portions of their petition were underlined in the original document:

We the People of Liberty County . . . appeal to you asking aid and counsel in this our *distressed condition*. We learned from the Address of *general Howard* that We Were to *Return* to the *Plantations* and *Work for our Former owners* at a *Reasonable contract as Freemen*, and find a *Home* and *Labor, Provided We can agree. But these owners of Plantations . . . Says they only will hire or* [document illegible] *the Prime Hands* and our *old and infirm Mothers and Fathers* and *our Children Will not be Provided for* and this Will See Sir Put us in *confusion . . . We cannot Labor for the Land owners . . .* [while] *our Infirm and children are not provided for, and are not allowed to educate or learn . . . We are Destitute of Religious Worship, having no Home or Place to Live When We Leave the Plantation, Returned to our Former owners; We are a Working Class of People* and We are *Willing* and *Anxious* to worke for a *Fair Compensation*; But to *return to work upon the Terms that are at Present offered to us, Would Be We Think going Backe into the state of slavery that We have just to some extent Been Delivered from.*

We *Appeal* to *you Sir and through you* to the *Rulers* of the *Country* in our *Distressed State* and [document illegible] *that We feel, unsettled as Sheep Without a Shepard, and beg your advice and Assistance*, and *Believe that this is an Earnest Appeal from A Poor But Loyal Earnest People.*[23]

E. P. Thompson may have had the Georgia ex-slaves in mind when he wrote that 'feeling might be more, rather than less, tender or intense because relations are "economic" and critical to mutual survival'.[24]

NOTES

1 E. Franklin Frazier, *The Negro Family in the United States* (New York, 1940, and revised edition, 1948).

2 Ralph Ellison, *Shadow and Act* (New York, 1964), especially the essay dealing with Gunnar Myrdal's work.
3 The classic work, of course, is E. P. Thompson, *The Making of the English Working Class* (London, 1963).
4 E. P. Thompson, 'Folklore, Anthropology, and Social History', *Indian Historical Review*, 3 (1978), 247–66.
5 The evidence in this and the five succeeding paragraphs is found in Herbert G. Gutman, *The Black Family in Slavery and Freedom 1750–1925* (New York, 1976), chaps. 1–4.
6 See, for example, the review of Gutman, *The Black Family* by Eugene D. Genovese, *Times Literary Supplement* (25 Feb. 1977), 198–9.
7 Gutman, *Black Family*, ch. 5.
8 These letters are found in Gutman, *Black Family*, 103, 184, 207.
9 The Carroll birth list is discussed in Mary Beth Norton, Herbert G. Gutman, and Ira Berlin, 'The Afro-American Family in the Age of Revolution', forthcoming.
10 Sidney W. Mintz and Eric R. Wolf, 'An Analysis of Ritual Co-Parenthood', *Southwestern Journal of Anthropology*, 6 (1950), 341–68; Esther N. Goody, 'Forms of Pro-Parenthood, the Sharing and Substitution of Parental Roles', in Jack Goody (ed.), *Kinship, Selected Readings* (London, 1971), 321–45.
11 Gutman, *Black Family*, 228–9.
12 Carol B. Stack, *All Our Kin: Strategies for Survival in a Black Community* (New York, 1974); Demetri B. Shimkin and associates, *The Extended Family in Black Society* (New York, 1978); Raymond T. Smith, 'The Nuclear Family in Afro-American Kinship', *Journal of Comparative Family Studies*, 1 (1970), 55–70.
13 Elizabeth Hafkin Pleck, *Hunting for a City, Black Migration and Poverty in Boston, 1865–1900* (New York, 1979); and Elizabeth Raul Bethel, *Promisedland, A Century of Life in a Negro Community* (Philadelphia, 1981).
14 The evidence in this and the five succeeding paragraphs is from an unpublished manuscript, Gutman, 'Emancipation and the Ethic of Mutuality'.
15 The evidence in this and the five succeeding paragraphs is from *ibid.*
16 Gutman, *Black Family*, 229.
17 This important document is found in Record Group 5, Freedmen's Bureau Manuscripts, National Archives, Washington, DC.
18 A. J. R. Russell-Wood, 'The Black Family in the Americas', *Societas, A Review of Social History*, 8 (1978), 1–38.
19 Norton, Gutman, and Berlin, 'The Afro-American Family', begins the reexamination of these eighteenth-century records.
20 Gutman, *Black Family*, ch. 8, discusses preliminary ways in which the work of the historical demographers Menard and Kulikoff can be integrated into an understanding of slave class formation and development.
21 Gutman, *Black Family*, 169–84.
22 Stephen Gudeman, 'An Anthropologist's View of The Black Family in Slavery and Freedom', *Social Science History*, 3 (1979), 56–65.
23 Herbert G. Gutman, *Slavery and The Numbers Game: A Critique of Time on the Cross* (Urbana, 1975), 171–3.
24 E. P. Thompson, 'Happy Families' (Review of Lawrence Stone, *The Family, Sex and Marriage in England, 1500–1800*), *New Society*, 41 (8 Sep. 1977), 499–501.

11. Parental strategies : calculation or sentiment? : fostering practices among West Africans

ESTHER GOODY

The link between parents' love for their children and arrangements made for their rearing is forcibly put in an oft-quoted account by an Italian nobleman of English family life at the end of the fifteenth century:

> the want of affection in the English is strongly manifested towards their children; for after having kept them at home till they arrive at the age of 7 or 9 years at the utmost, they put them out, both males and females, to hard service in the houses of other people, binding them generally for another 7 to 9 years. And these are called apprentices, and during that time they perform all the most menial offices; and few are born who are exempted from this fate, for every one, however rich he may be, sends away his children into the houses of others; whilst he, in return, receives those of strangers into his own. And on enquiring the reason for this severity, they answered that they did it in order that their children might learn better manners.[1]

The Italian traveller is scornful of this explanation and comments:

> but I, for my part, believe that they do it because they like to enjoy all their comforts themselves [i.e. they won't have to feed and clothe other people's children as well as they would their own] and that they are better served by strangers than they would be by their own children.[2]

Nearly 500 years later the English themselves pass very similar judgments on the practice of West African families living in England of placing their children with English foster parents:

> Ann [not her real name], aged nine, a Ghanaian girl fostered nearly all her life by a white professional English couple in suburban Surrey, can stay in their care, Sir George Baker, President of the High Court Family Division, decided yesterday. He said that he could not bring himself to send her back to Africa, where the real parents wanted to take her . . . 'My answer in the best interests, present and future, of this girl – despite the blood tie, the race, despite colour, is that I cannot bring myself to send this child to Ghana, and I, as well as the girl, would feel a rankling sense of injustice were I to do so,' he said.[3]

Judge Baker had begun his summing up by saying:

The reason why I am giving this judgment in open court is that I think the public, and particularly potential foster parents ought to know of the practice, indeed custom, of West Africans and other coloured people who come to this country, which is that the husband is a student, often a perennial student, the wife works and the children, particularly those born here, are fostered out privately, often for many years, and often as a result of newspaper advertisements or cards in shop windows or by the introduction of friends. The children are brought up in and learn our British ways of life. When a strong bond of attachment and love has been forged between the children and the foster parents, the natural parents take them away, even tear them away, to go with them to West Africa or elsewhere. There is overwhelming evidence before me of this practice, and there have been two other cases before Judges of the Family Division in the last few weeks.[4]

Like the High Court Judge, social workers have assumed that West African parents in England 'for one reason or another are either unwilling or unable to provide a home for their children'.[5] As these children are placed in English homes by private arrangements – making contact with foster parents through local advertisements, advertisements in national magazines or through friends – it is impossible to estimate how often this occurs. Some indication is given, however, in Holman's findings that 60% of the children in a sample of 144 private foster homes in the Birmingham area were West African.[6] Since, according to the 1971 census, there were then only 880 people in Birmingham who had been born in West Africa (in a total population of over one million), the proportion of West African children is clearly very high. In the group of 296 West African families we interviewed in London, exactly half had placed one or more children with English foster parents or were currently doing so. It would seem that fostering of young children with English families is 'normal' for West Africans in England.

It is curious to find such close parallels between dark ages Wales and Ireland, where the placing of children with foster parents was common, England of the middle ages, and modern West African families in England. It is all the more striking when compared with the way other immigrant groups in England manage their responsibilities for children. For none of these other groups use English foster parents at all.[7]

These cases of contested custody over West African children, and the frequency with which they are placed with English families, raises questions very similar to those posed by the fifteenth-century account of 'apprenticeship' in England. Why are parents willing to let other people rear their children? Is the conception of parenthood different from our own? Can such parents really 'love' their children?

The advantage of having a contemporary example of this pattern is that it is possible to investigate the meaning to the parents of fostering their children, to see it in the round, rather than reflected in such observers' comments as happen to survive in historical records. In fact the sending of children to grow up with others is very widespread in traditional West African societies and is still current today – indeed has taken on new forms appropriate to the modern conditions, of which the placing of children with English foster parents is only one example.

The 'meaning' of West African fostering

At the manifest level there are very nearly as many 'meanings' of fostering as there are forms specific to different West African societies.

Dagomba princes were sent to a senior official, a eunuch, who lived outside the capital town. There they grew up in austere surroundings under strict discipline so as, the Dagomba say, not to become soft with life at court. It was also hoped in this way to keep them safe from attacks by jealous rivals. One son of each woman of the *lunsi* drummer families had to be sent to grow up with his maternal kin and learn to play the drums and sing the praise songs which helped to establish the chiefs' political authority. It is the right of the mother's family to claim a son, and their ancestors could punish any father who sought to prevent it. Girls of both ruling and commoner families were sent to live with fathers' sisters to provide domestic assistance and companionship.

Mossi girls, daughters of both chiefs and commoners, were liable to be sent to the court of senior chiefs to serve royal wives and later to be bestowed as wives, perhaps given to a court page who had shown his loyalty, or to a minor chief, or even to a stranger who wished to settle in Mossiland. A child of this sort of marriage was sent in turn, as a serving girl or as a page, to grow up at court and so continue the cycle. Mossi children were claimed for service at court because the chief had the force to seize them (should the parents refuse), because it is useful to the chiefs to have their services and to be able to establish alliances through arranging their marriages, and indeed because it is useful to their parents to have contacts at court.

Mossi and *Hausa* first-born sons are sent to grow up with kin in another household because it avoids the tensions which arise from parents living in close proximity to their first child. Otherwise strict avoidance must be observed between them: parents feel awkward speaking directly to the child, in eating with him, in being alone in a room with him, etc. It is much easier if this first-born is living in another household. In towns, married Hausa women are virtually always Muslim, and are expected to live in semi-seclusion, neither going outside the house during the day, nor receiving any but close women friends and kin within the household. Yet practically all Hausa women engage actively in trade of some kind, whether the selling of cooked food, retailing of small items, or production of soap, oil, embroidered caps, etc. for sale. This is only possible if there is an intermediary through whom they can buy in the market, send messages, and arrange commercial transactions. Where a woman has no child of the right age, she looks for a foster child to rear. Hausa merchants send their sons to one another to rear, to learn trading, to avoid direct business competition between father and son, and to create the basis for commercial trust between families who would otherwise be open competitors.

Kanuri boys often themselves seek out craftsmen and traders to work for, so as to learn skills their fathers cannot teach them. Others are placed by their parents with officials in order to serve them and to establish the basis for a clientship relationship, at first between the parent and foster parent, and later between the grown child and his foster parent.

In *Gonja* parents expect to send one or more children to grow up with kin: boys to a parent's father or brother (real or classificatory); girls to a parent's mother or sister. Gonja say that the children are 'owned' by all the siblings of both parents. This means that these people have responsibilities towards their children, and that they may claim a child to live with them, often in a village many miles from the parents' home. The Gonja explain these rights over children as part of the rights over people and property which go with kinship authority and the inheritance of that authority. Such claims are ignored at the risk of supernatural punishment from the ancestors. Although the Gonja do not discuss fostering in terms of training in specific skills, they firmly believe that a child will develop a stronger character if reared away from its parents.

All these forms, and there are others which could be cited, developed in pre-colonial times, and most survive at least in part today. Other forms have emerged in the coastal societies which evolved in response to the many centuries of European trade in cloth, guns, and metal for gold and slaves. They tend to be easier to 'explain' because they are more functionally specific. Thus 'pawning' of both adults and older children to creditors seems to have occurred widely on the coast, though it was also well known inland, and probably was indigenous prior to the mercantile period. The 'pawned' individual worked for the creditor until the original debt was paid, serving both as collateral on the debt, and his or her work providing the interest. If the pawn ran away, the debtor began to pay interest on his loan. However, pawning a child to a trader or craftsman was recognized as a way of teaching him adult skills. Various forms of apprenticeship appeared on the coast when new occupations were introduced. Thus Ga boys were traditionally taught their father's craft, or, if they wished to learn another, it was the father's duty to seek a teacher from among the kin of his own and his wife's parents. The son was then entrusted to this man in a ceremony which called the gods to witness both parties' goodwill. Quartey-Papafio writes of an early Ga apprenticeship, in which the master retained rights over the services and earnings of his apprentice as long as he lived.[8] This was modified in the late nineteenth century by the payment of a very large lump sum when training was completed and the apprentice was 'freed' to work for himself. Today in coastal societies, apprentices come from villages and small towns as well as from the cities to learn modern crafts (like radio repair, printing, and dry cleaning) which offer an entrée into the world market economy not available in rural areas. Masters take apprentices both for the labour they contribute, and because a busy workshop is a sign of success which brings in business. Perhaps the most extraordinary modern example comes from urban Lagos. Poor parents have been found to bring a child to the police, complaining that he is beyond control in order that he be sent to a correctional school, where modern trades are taught in an effort to redeem wayward youth by giving them a secure way to make an honest living. The parents apparently care little about the temporary reputation of a son, if he can secure a good training that will establish him in a profitable trade in adulthood. More ordinary forms of apprenticeship abound in cities and the larger towns. It has recently been estimated that in Nigeria there were 2 million apprentices (nearly all aged between twelve and thirty) in comparison to about half a million in all forms of wage and salary employment.[9]

In Liberia and Sierra Leone the settling of freed slaves created a rigidly hierarchical system of Creole elite and subordinate tribal peoples. There very quickly grew up a system of Creole families taking tribal children as 'wards'. These children worked in the household, which supplied them with food and clothing, and the opportunity to learn Creole English and Creole culture. Later they sometimes were sent to school, though not to the same schools as the family's own children. It is widely accepted that by this route many tribal children 'passed' into Creole society. Today the elite contains both tribal and Creole elements and well-off tribal households also take in wards from the rural areas. In West African countries lacking such an explicit Creole element, children are sent in much the same way to professional and business people who live within the modern world of the towns. School teachers are especially likely to be asked to take children, even unrelated ones, for they are seen as able to understand and manage the complex educational system through which access to elite positions is largely controlled. A recent variation on this theme in Ghana is the sending of their sons by successful Accra market women to a particular village outside the capital which has a reputation for Christian piety and a good secondary school.[10] The child pays to board with a local family which takes responsibility not only for his food and shelter but also agrees to supervise his homework and train him to be a good Christian. Professional families are beginning to seek to avoid responsibility for schooling relatives' children, except for close kin, although such school children contribute substantial labour in cooking, child care, washing, and gardening.[11]

The explanation of the meaning of these several institutions for rearing children apart from their own parents has taken the form of setting out the gains (and costs where evident) to parents, pro-parents, and child. But in making explicit the transactional balance which 'accounts' in each case for the institutionalization of placing children in other families, does it necessarily follow that calculation of relative advantages is *antithetical* to parental love and affection? There seem to me to be two stages to this argument. First, we must establish whether these various transactions are in the interests of the parents only, with the child a hapless pawn, or whether the child's own interests are also being served. Then there arises the question of whether arrangements made on the basis of 'interest' are necessarily in contradiction with sentiments of affection.

In whose interest?

In order to answer this question it is necessary to bring some order to the array of instances already cited. I have shown elsewhere that West African societies can be roughly sorted into three sets: those which do not systematically practise the rearing of children outside the parental family; those which regularly send children to kin; and those which send children both to kin and also to non-relatives. These three sets of societies can also be grouped in terms of political structure into unlineal descent polities, simple states, and complex hierarchical states. The resulting pattern is as shown in the table.

Delegation of parent roles[12]

None	*To kin*	*To kin and to non-kin*
Unilineal descent	Simple states	Complex hierarchical states

The problem then becomes the identification of the factors which account for this relationship between political structure and arrangements for rearing of children. A preliminary step remains. It is clearly not the case that these West African children are being completely adopted by their foster parents (any more than this was so for England in the middle ages.) Rather, it is older children who are sent off, and it is their training and sponsorship into adult roles which is being delegated to others. Training is taken to be the imparting of skills, and sponsorship to be the transfer of such resources as are necessary in a given society for entry into recognized adult roles.

Our problem then becomes why should unilineal descent group (UDG) polities retain the training and sponsorship of children and adolescents within the natal family when other West African societies institutionalise the delegation of these roles? It is empirically the case that in the UDG polities of West Africa there are few if any alternative economic roles to that of farmer/herdsman. Thus the imparting of skills necessary for adult economic roles can be as readily carried out by parents as by anyone else. When it comes to resources for sponsorship, the same answer holds. For rights to economic resources are vested in the local descent group, as is full citizenship and ritual status. To enter fully into adult roles a youth must farm, herd, and sacrifice with his local descent group. Fortes for the Tallensi[13] and the Bohannans for the Tiv[14] have shown the kinds of handicaps which are sustained by men who settle with maternal kin. Although the mother's descent group is obliged to offer hospitality, it cannot provide the same full complement of rights and resources as one's own agnates (in these patrilineal societies). In this situation, to place boys with families outside the local descent group would carry no advantage for the parents (who would lose the services of the youths) or for the boys (who would gain no training or resources additional to those available at home).

What does such an approach contribute to understanding why delegation of training and sponsorship to kin is so common in the simple states? Taking the Gonja and the Dagomba as paradigmatic cases, it is clear that adult role skills are somewhat differentiated in comparison to the UDG polities. In these simple states there are blacksmiths, drummers, fiddlers, butchers, diviners, barbers, and chiefs. These occupations do not form endogamous groups; rather there is frequent marriage between them. Further, linked in various ways to the introduction of political office is a relatively high rate of spatial mobility. People marry and settle in villages different from those in which they were born. The consequence of this differentiation and mobility is that resources are no longer localized. And it must be understood that among the resources shared by these (bilateral, rather than unilineal) kin groups are rights in one another. These include rights to service from junior kinsmen and rights of support in time of trouble. In both Gonja and Dagomba the paradigm for fostering involves relatives pressing claims on children of close kin. And given the spatial mobility of these systems, such claims result in the sending of children to live in other villages. The Gonja state claims in terms of the rights of siblings over one anothers' children. The Dagomba tend in addition to phrase them in terms of the rights of a woman's kin to train one of her sons in the profession of the mother's people. Often, but not always, these claims are supernaturally sanctioned. That is, the failure to acknowledge and act on them may result in illness, madness, or death.

If we ask whose interests are being served in these kin-delegating systems, the culturally meaningful reply might be 'the ancestors' since they are believed to seek the preservation of the links between their descendants, the links between their corporate-but-cognatic kin group and its members. At the same time a transaction model would show that successful claims to children meant that the foster parents gain rights to their work, that overburdened parents could in this way share the responsibility of supporting a large family, that lonely widows rely on foster daughters for companionship as much as for domestic help, that children thus escape from difficult home situations; it is a balanced equation. Indeed the Gonja consider it a sufficient explanation to say simply that 'a child should know the people of both the father and the mother, those of the father's village and the mother's village'. That is, it is seen as of great importance to a child to know who all its kin are, for it can then, in its turn, press claims on them – for labour, assistance, and a share in any jointly held property. In many ways these simple states look like the UDG polities in their emphasis on the joint resources held by kin groups. The differences lie, first, in the fact that overlapping rights are held by two sets of kin in the child and that the child in turn holds rights in both maternal and paternal relatives and their resources. And second, these kin are physically dispersed so that to claim rights effectively a positive effort must be made to keep in touch across the generations. By placing a child with a particular kinsman or kinswoman, the latent kin links between them are reinforced by what I have called the reciprocities of rearing, that is the rights and obligations and affections which are built up in the course of socialization.

While such a model may be satisfying in accounting for the willingness of families in simple states to allow others to rear their children, it has little direct power in explaining the new patterns or delegation of training and sponsorship to non-relatives which appear in the more complex hierarchical states, such as the Hausa emirates of northern Nigeria, Bornu, and Songhoi.[15] In these states there emerge, in addition to the continued sending of children to kin, several functionally specific institutions for the delegation of training and sponsorship. These can be seen as responses to two processes which occur in differing degrees in these complex systems. First, the division of labour is far more complicated, with the result that occupational skills are very diverse, and there is a wide range of choice for youths who do not wish to follow their fathers' work. This choice becomes almost an imperative in the more complex states where few men are only farmers. The complex division of labour results in a situation in which many goods and services must be obtained from others, and in order to do so a man must himself have some way of entering the market, either by producing goods and services for others to buy or by selling his labour. Quite often youths respond to this situation by learning a series of simple skills, perhaps petty trading, simple carpentry, and then tailoring, until one is found which is both congenial and sufficiently lucrative.

The second process is an increasing elaboration of patron/client relations in response to increasing political hierarchy. Bqth M. G. Smith and R. Cohen have written at length (on Hausa emirates and Bornu respectively) about the nesting political offices which extend from the local hamlet to the paramountcy, and both describe a second set of unofficial officials who counterbalance the first. In order to succeed in political office or economic enterprise and avoid punitive taxation, individuals must establish special relationships of clientship with particular officials. One way of doing this is to place a son in the official's household as a page. If all goes well, the official will feel obligated to look after the interests of both father and son (and will in return have loyal supporters for his own concerns).

Apprentice fosterage is a response to occupational differentiation – i.e. a more advanced division of labour. The labour of the child is exchanged for training in adult occupational role skills. The craftsman has no prior claim to the child, and the child and his parents no claim on the craftsman. Accounts of placing of children with craftsmen in traditional complex states do not mention money payments, although the craftsman is usually expected to provide food and shelter as well as imparting his skill. The training of such an apprentice creates obligations on him to continue to assist his master even after he becomes an independent craftsman in his own right. Indeed an account of nineteenth-century apprenticeship on the coast of Ghana speaks of the apprentice as continuing under the master's authority and turning over to him all proceeds of his work so long as the master lived.[16] It may be significant that this occurred in a society (Ga) in which descent groups were still at that time of political importance. However, even in the absence of descent groups, Hausa fathers seek to retain control over their adult sons' labour in Gandu farming.[17] Where the master retained such a control over the labour of an ex-apprentice, it is probably best seen as the transfer of reciprocities normally owed the father for training and sponsorship to the man who actually trained and established the apprentice.

A regular response to the proliferation of officials in complex hierarchical states is alliance fosterage. This is the only form of fosterage clearly reported for East Africa[18] and appears also in medieval England and Ireland. However, it would be a mistake to see this as entirely different from apprentice fosterage. It still serves as training and sponsorship for adult roles, where these are political or a blend of political and economic. For instance, it is probable that the personal followers who act as unofficial lieutenants for powerful Hausa chiefs include men who are trusted in part because they have grown up at court. Similarly ambiguous is the position of sons of merchants reared by other merchants.[19] This is clearly training for an economic role but at the same time forms the basis for an alliance between the two merchant households. In transactional terms the political officials or merchants gain service and loyalty in exchange for patronage and often for a job as 'one of the firm'.

The new division of labour which has emerged from the progressive incorporation of West African states into the modern world economy has produced a great proliferation of forms of apprenticeship, as well as educational fosterage and service fosterage, as ways of getting into the modern occupational system. Some of these (particularly wardship and educational fosterage) also serve to establish modern patron–client relationships, which provide followers for those who would be influential and opportunities for those who are upwardly mobile. It is striking, but hardly surprising, that these modern forms of parental role delegation echo those which emerged in traditional complex hierarchical states, for they fulfil the same underlying function of providing youths with the training and sponsorship necessary to enter adult roles to which their own parents and kin have no direct access. The particular roles are different, as are the particular transactional balances which motivate the individual participants. But the function in relation to social reproduction is the same in both traditional and modern complex hierarchical states.

If we return to the question of 'in whose interests?' in relation to the three models of parent role allocation, we must conclude that the parents benefit directly only in the UDG polities where they retain the labour of their adolescent children. In simple states where children are sent to kin, the parents benefit indirectly from the maintenance of the joint rights to support and resources held by the dispersed kin group, but they lose the immediate help of their children, and some of those who were reared by kin settle permanently in their foster homes. In the more complex hierarchical states, not only do parents lose the direct labour of adolescent children, but they also receive no delayed benefit from the realization of rights held jointly by kin. In some cases the parents will benefit from alliances established through the placing of their children with important people. Skills learned in apprenticeship may provide support in the parents' old age.

Indeed, the one formulation which applies equally to the pattern of allocation of parent roles in each of the three types of polity is that parents arrange for their children's training and sponsorship in the way which will place the children in the best possible position as adults with respect to those skills and resources which are required to 'succeed' in that particular economic and political structure. In short, parents appear to be denying themselves immediate benefit from their children's assistance in order that the children shall have the most advantageous position possible in the social system as adults.

Material interest and emotion

If this formulation is accepted, what can we conclude about the 'reasons' for parents' behaviour? Do they act this way because they 'love' their children? Or because they hope that their children will succeed and thus be better able to care for them in their old age? At this level of abstraction such a question cannot be answered. But on the basis of observations in Gonja it is clear that parents are often reluctant to part with their children and only do so because they feel they must. And where children are ill-treated, or where they pine for their parents, they are usually taken home again. Despite the 'customary' nature of fostering in Gonja, it is carried out within the constraints of sentimental attachment between parents and children and indeed is often a response to the sentimental attachment between an adult child and elderly parent or between siblings forced to live apart.

What does seem to emerge clearly from this overview of West African parental role allocation is that it is highly responsive to changes in the real distribution of economic and political resources but that the clearest predictor of the nature of this response is the successful placement of children in adult roles and not the immediate self-interest of the parents. Parents' motives in seeking to make their children successful adults are as complex in West Africa as in our own society. Hopes for a comfortable old age, ambition for one's children (and indirectly for oneself?), anxiety over a problem child, a sense of obligation to close kin – but these are the very stuff of emotional involvement.

Wider implications

It is of course a large jump from West Africa to England in the fifteenth century, or indeed to contemporary West African immigrants in London. An extension of the argument based on the West Africa material must be at best tentative. However, it is not entirely arbitrary. The Italian traveller goes on to say, of the English way of rearing children in the fifteenth century:

if the English sent their children away from home to learn virtue and good manners, and took them back again when their apprenticeship was over, they might, perhaps, be excused; but they never return, for the girls are settled [i.e. married off] by their patrons, and the boys make the best marriages they can, and, assisted by their patrons, not by their fathers, they also open a house and strive diligently by this means to make some fortune for themselves . . . the apprentices for the most part make good fortunes, some by one means and some by another.[20]

It thus appears that the English fifteenth-century practice was also aimed at placing children in the society through the intervention of patrons in exchange for the children's services while growing up and on the basis of training in the patron's household.

It may seem unlikely that the same model can be applied to the very young children of West African immigrants in London, since training and sponsorship are usually effective in adolescence. However, it is clear from our interview material that what West African parents are seeking for their children is the modern equivalent. For they want them to grow up at ease in Western culture, to speak English without an accent, and to move easily through the modern school system. Since the family is temporarily living in England in order that the parents may secure qualifications for elite employment on their return to West Africa, it seems an obvious advantage to be able to place the children in English families and so secure them easy entrée to the culture and language of modern West African elite society. British authorities have indeed assumed that parents placing their children in English families 'for one reason or another are either unwilling or unable to provide a home for their children'. Yet the background to the court case over Ann's custody makes it clear that the parents at no time intended to give up their rights in their daughter and that they remained throughout deeply attached to her:

Ann was placed with English foster parents when she was three months old. Two months later, when it became clear that the foster parents assumed they would adopt her, Ann's parents took her home. After reassurances they allowed her to return again to the foster parents, but when she was four the foster parents again pressed for adoption, and Ann was again removed by her parents. Her father then wrote to the foster parents: 'I must make it clear to you that [Ann] belongs to us and nothing can separate us and the baby, not all the riches in the world. The child is ours, and will be ours forever and take it from me that you will never see her again.'[21]

Later an agreement was reached and the foster parents understood that Ann was to stay with them until she was 18 and finish her education. When Ann's parents later were ready to return to Ghana and wanted to take her with them, the foster parents took action to retain custody over the child (then nine years old). On hearing in court that Ann must remain in England, her parents were very upset, her father saying that since they were Akans (a matrilineal people), his wife's relative would hold him responsible for returning without the child; he dared not return without Ann. (Her mother became hysterical).[22]

At the most conservative, it would seem clear that there is no simple association between arrangements of family roles and the emotional commitment to them. Constraints of the wider society set the conditions for optimal management of family roles. Emotions are generated in the playing out of these roles within the limits set. Because the interests of close family members are so intricately linked, it is very difficult to demonstrate either altruism or exploitation. Emotional commitment itself is the more constant factor.

NOTES

1 Anon., *A Relation or rather a True Account of the Island of England . . . . about the Year 1500*, Camden Society, vol. 37 (London, 1847), 24–5.
2 *Ibid.*, 25.
3 *The Times*, 5 Dec. 1972.
4 *The Times*, 5 Dec. 1972.
5 C. Hill, *Immigration and Integration* (Oxford, 1970), 87.
6 R. Holman, *Trading in Children: A Study of Private Fostering* (London, 1973).
7 For negative cases, see J. Watson (ed.), *Between Two Cultures* (London, 1977). In family crises social services personnel may arrange the placement of any child with temporary foster parents. This may happen to immigrant families as well as to English families.
8 A. B. Quartey-Papafio, 'Apprenticeship among the Gas', *Journal of the African Society*, 12 (1913–14), 415–22.
9 A. Callaway, *Nigerian Enterprise and the Employment of Youth*, Nigerian Institute of Social and Economic Research, Monograph 2 (Ibadan, 1973).
10 D. K. Fiawoo, 'Some Fertility Patterns of Foster Care in Ghana', in C. Oppong, *et al.* (eds.), *Marriage, Fertility and Parenthood in West Africa* (Canberra, 1978).
11 C. Oppong, 'Education of Relatives' Children by Senior Civil Servants in Accra', *Ghana Journal of Child Development*, 2 (1969).
12 E. Goody, *Parenthood and Social Reproduction* (Cambridge, 1982).
13 M. F. Fortes, *The Web of Kinship among the Tallensi* (London, 1949).
14 P. and L. Bohannan, *The Tiv of Central Nigeria*, Ethnographic Survey of Africa, Western Africa, vol. 8 (London, 1953).
15 In fact we must also retain the kin-delegation model, for kin continue to make claims on children, and the same kinds of factors seem to be operating here as in the simple states.
16 Quartey-Papafio, 'Apprenticeship'.
17 M. G. Smith, *The Economy of the Hausa Communities of Zaria*, Colonial Research Studies, vol. 16 (London, 1955); P. Hill, *Rural Hausa: A Village and a Setting* (Cambridge, 1972).
18 A. I. Richards, 'Authority Patterns in Traditional Buganda', in L. A. Fallers (ed.), *The King's Men* (London, 1964).
19 I. Tahir, 'Scholars, Sufis, Saints and Capitalists in Kano', PhD Thesis (University of Cambridge, 1976).
20 Anon., *A Relation*.
21 Transcript: Re 'O' (a minor), High Court, Family Division, before the President, Sir George Baker (4 Dec. 1972). Transcribed from tape by the Mechanical Recording Department.
22 *Ibid.* and transcript: Appeal in the Court of Appeal (CA), before Davis and Megaw (Lord Justices) and Sir Seymour Karminiski (26 Mar. 1973).

Part VI. Family values and class practice

12. Kinship and class consciousness : family values and work experience among hospital workers in an American southern town[1]

KAREN SACKS

This paper is about how one group of hospital workers – ward secretaries – view themselves and their work. It considers the role working class family socialization plays in generating their views and the organizations which sustain and express them in collective action. It explores the hypotheses that in the working class there are continuities between family and workplace when it comes to values, recruitment, and organization and that both places reinforce each other in developing class conscious ways of seeing and acting.

The first section describes how the ward secretary experiences her job. The informal rules and practices generated and taught by ward secretaries diverge considerably from management notions of hierarchy and bureaucracy. The second section deals with some of the family sources of ward secretaries' views of themselves and their job. The third part discusses a walkout organized by ward secretaries, which attempted to force management to recognize their central role in coordinating in-patient medical care. It deals with how they came to share a particular view of their work and how their informal social networks allowed them to act effectively. The final section discusses the development of these networks since the walkout.

In the hospital studied, there are slightly more than 200 ward secretaries: 75% black women, 15% white women, 8% black men, and 2% white men. They work all shifts at all places in the medical center with in-patients. Their job is to coordinate all patient care on a ward, each ward being assigned to a particular service, such as Medicine, Surgery, Obstetrics and Gynecology, Pediatrics, and Psychiatry. Services are subdivided into units, each with a supervisor who can set variable work schedules. Each unit includes several wards, whose secretaries thus have a supervisor in common. In general they have much more work contact with the ward secretaries of their own unit than with those outside.

I

The job

A hospital is a bureaucracy, and as in any other bureaucracy, face-to-face human service can only be delivered if the proper paperwork is filled out. Without a record of what has been done by a variety of people, who may seldom or never see each other, there can be no planning for treatment. Every real act in the health care bureaucracy has its paper or computer image. Ward secretaries keep and organize these records for all patients on their ward. They coordinate ward personnel and schedule their services. They often say that they manage the ward or that they 'make the hospital run'.

When patient records were put into a computer system, ward secretaries continued coordinating and organizing information, orders, and tests but with different tools. Instead of writing requisitions by hand and waiting for messengers to deliver them, they typed them onto video data terminals or 'scopes', which electronically registered them at their proper destinations, while a teletype printed out a paper record of each scope entry. The job essentially stayed the same, or so it seemed to hospital management. Many of the secretaries involved in the changeover disagreed and have been trying more or less vigorously to get management to see it their way.

Though ward secretaries do not put it this way, I see two aspects to the job. One has to do with the coordination of medical care records. The other has to do with the coordination of the people involved in care. These two aspects require different kinds of skills, and successful ward secretaries need to use both kinds. The hospital administration does not recognize the second at all and only recognizes part of the first.

Management is most concerned with the record-keeping aspect of the job. A quasi-official and widespread management view of ward secretaries is expressed in *Job Descriptions and Organizational Analysis for Hospitals and Related Health Services*, a 1971 (reissued 1978) joint venture of the US Department of Labor and the American Hospital Association. It describes the job of ward secretary as requiring a high school education but no previous experience. Under 'worker traits' it stresses the abilities to understand procedural routines and verbal instructions, to do arithmetic manipulations, and to maintain clerical detail. This description focuses on the relationship of ward secretaries to charts and requisitions and says nothing about their relationship to people. While coordinating records is more complex than management is willing to grant, I will not discuss this aspect of the job here, for it is not the major point of conflict for ward secretaries.

Almost all secretaries I spoke with said the same two things about their job. They see themselves as the nerve center of the ward. 'Everything that's done has to go through us. We just about run the hospital.' They also maintain that the job is hectic and 'a real mental strain'. The stress comes from having to coordinate people at very different points on the hospital hierarchy, many of whom are as harassed as they are: 'that's the scariest part of the whole thing. That's why I say you have to have your stuff together – to be organized.' One woman summed up the job as a 'lot of tension; ten people talking to you at once, the phone ringing, and the teletype is jammed, doctors talking to you like you're supposed to know everything'. The most frequent statement about what they liked about the job was along the lines of, 'being around people. You're never lonely.' 'I really like being a ward secretary; I love it. You get to meet a lot of people.' A few secretaries have been offered or contemplated jobs which pay more and have decided against them because they would be in touch with fewer people. One woman said she could think of nothing worse than being cooped up and isolated in an office, having to sit and type all day. However, many ward secretaries *have* applied for, and taken, higher paying jobs.

It is no surprise that people cause the biggest headaches and at the same time are the greatest pleasure and reward of the job. In this respect, the ward secretary's job is an administrative job but in a very peculiar way, one that is set up for stress and conflicts. Secretaries point out that they deal with the public and consequently need to 'mind their p's and q's'. They also need to orchestrate the activities of specialists at all points on the medical center hierarchy. Administrators, with their high pay, status, and formal authority, have an easier time telling people what needs to be done than do ward secretaries, who also have a significant amount of such work to do. However, they have no formal authority and have to carry out their tasks despite their low status in the hospital pecking order. There is plenty of talk about teamwork and 'the hospital family' by hospital administrators, but there is no recognition that health care teamwork encompassing many departments needs on-the-spot coordinating. That job falls to ward secretaries, who have to do it without bossing or ordering because they lack any authority and because some personnel, particularly doctors, do not take it well.

Just what evidence is there that secretaries are health care coordinators? One woman put her goals succinctly: 'our main job is seeing that patients get their tests in the least amount of time possible'. The picture is clearer if we look at what ward secretaries coordinate. They convey the care plans and doctors' orders to the nurses, lab personnel, and dieticians who carry them out. They link the wards where patients 'live' to the departmental people who deal with a particular facet of their care. Obviously, the schedules of many people have to be meshed, sometimes with diplomacy, sometimes with firmness.

One ward secretary pointed out that they were the main people to consider the patient's needs as a person in scheduling tests. In doing so the secretary has several things to consider. First, she needs to know how long each test is likely to take. A liver scan, for example, can take three hours. Some departments will cancel patients' tests if they are not on the floor when called. While diplomacy may help in stalling for time, it is better not to schedule too closely. Second, and more important, doctors seldom consider whether or how much a particular test or series of tests can fatigue a sick person. While secretaries theoretically have no direct patient contact, they do in practice. One woman told me she did not like to schedule anyone for more than two or three things in a day because most patients easily became exhausted. Ward secretaries need to exercise their judgment to mesh doctors' plans for treating an illness with the state of a sick person's constitution at any given time.

Routine work is also about directly coordinating people. The phones ring fairly constantly. 'Mostly it's people wanting to know where a patient is and what he or she has done. Some things can't be done before others. If a patient needs four tests in one day, I'm on the phone for fifteen minutes getting each department to tell me when they're through so I can have a messenger pick them up and take them to the next place.'

Teaching is another invisible and unrewarded job. As in any large teaching hospital, primary care and responsibility for each patient is given to first year interns – if the patient has no private physician. The work load of ward secretaries increases each July when new interns come on because interns do not know many of the hospital's procedures, nor do they know their way around. One secretary commented matter-of-factly, 'new interns are indoctrinated to get all they can from the ward secretaries'. Some interns leave blood specimens on the ward desk. 'We are not supposed to handle specimens, but someone has to make sure they get to the lab and that the results get back.' Other interns expect ward secretaries to schedule tests which hospital procedures require the physician to schedule. Teaching people who are overworked, high up on the hospital's pecking order, and not told that they are being taught is a difficult assignment. Because it is unofficial teaching – not part of their job description – ward secretaries get no support from hospital administration. Housestaff do not recognize it as a necessary part of their training and seldom appreciate it either. Indeed, ward secretaries often complain about the abusive way doctors treat them and about how the whole burden of resisting and 'straightening them out' falls on their shoulders.

Ward secretaries also help coordinate nursing. Nurses, as they come on duty, get a care plan for each of their patients. In the past they came to the desk to find out what the orders were. 'Now (on some units) they expect to be called and told.' One secretary does this even though she really does not have the time and resents the extra work because 'it's a pain to have the doctor asking if the test is done and to have to say you don't know. I'd rather initiate the procedure by calling the nurse and telling her.' I have often observed nurses, housestaff, and medical students ask a ward secretary to phone someone for information for them when they were standing next to the phone. They continued to stand there during the conversation, to clarify their question to the secretary in response to a query she relayed from the party on the line, and to wait for the answer from the secretary when she got off the phone. Ward secretaries are often irritated by this behavior and regard it as something of a status display or pulling of rank.

Coordinating people requires a range of interpersonal skills. When it dawned on me that ward secretaries were orchestrating people's work, I began to wonder what kind of skills *were* needed to do this. Many of them described in detail the interpersonal skills for dealing with people in a hierarchical system that they had learned from senior ward secretaries and from experience. There is a widely shared understanding of what it takes to maintain cooperation from people whose jobs often put them in conflict. Their stories described interpersonal conflicts with higher-ups – supervisors, nurses, administrators, and doctors – and the rules each has developed to handle and resolve them.

Offensive behavior from higher-ups included criticism in public, blowing up at the wrong person, and being loud and abusive without provocation. Some supervisors were said to act this way – until stopped by each ward secretary independently. On some services, it was said of doctors that loud abuse was their automatic behavior, that they acted as though they had a *right* to yell without regard for anyone's feelings, and that they felt no obligation to apologize when wrong. In addition, some doctors were racially prejudiced, and some ward secretaries felt that this underlay the disregard for their feelings and capabilities. One secretary described doctors as 'a *lot* of trouble. They'll curse you.' 'The new ones come in; we break them in. We have to. We have a couple that are prejudiced. We have a couple who are real nice. I tell the girls, "you have to stand your ground or they'll walk over you".'

No one likes abusive behavior; but there are many ways people can dislike something and yet reinforce what they don't like, for example by accepting it publicly and grumbling privately. Ward secretaries do grumble, don't always confront abuse, and some take more than others, but they do not systematically play out any of these abuse-reinforcing patterns. 'You can't be but one person. If you let a person know from the beginning who you are and where you stand, you won't have much trouble.' Ward secretaries are willing to be understanding only if doctors give them the same consideration. 'We're all people, we're not children; we are all grown and we are here to help one another. I don't think your MD or PhD should be such an influence.' Systematic flare-ups and lack of apologies indicate that doctors (or supervisors, etc.) regard such behavior as a prerogative of their status. Some secretaries felt they were being treated like children: 'a lot of people forget that everybody is an adult'.

Ward secretaries are trying to socialize people trained for hierarchy to behave as members of a team. In the managers' rule it is acceptable for a superior to criticize a subordinate publicly (and not visa versa); it lets everyone know their relative statuses. But according to the informal rules of workers, such behavior demeans the superior as an adult and embarrasses the subordinate, also as an adult. One ward secretary mentioned having trouble with a nurse who spoke to her 'like dirt' when she first arrived. This secretary responded to her supervisor's public criticism by insisting on discussing it with her in the back room together with another ward secretary. She emphasized that a public fight, or criticism, was embarrassing and demeaning.

Another ward secretary analyzed several situations in which she learned the difference between the right and the wrong way to speak up. When she was new, there was a doctor with whom she could not get along. The daily arguments upset her and resolved nothing. Looking back she realized that the doctor was wrong to pick a fight in public, but that instead of challenging him by yelling back, she should have taught him how to behave. To do that, you 'take them in the back room and argue it out one on one'. She stressed how important it was to insist, calmly, on correct and considerate behavior even in small things and to have a sense of humor. One doctor was in the habit of dumping a mixture of charts with and without written orders in the ward secretary's box. This created added work for her because she had to search all the charts for orders. She told him this, and he grudgingly separated them, saying, 'you want anything else?' She answered, 'yes, I'd like a cup of coffee'. In this case she explained the consequences of the doctor's actions for her work load and did so without anger. The doctor's response was ambivalent: he accepted the correction but resisted being criticized by someone below him. The ward secretary then used humor to upset the status relationship and to reinforce the positive, co-worker aspect of the doctor's response. It gave him both reason and reinforcement to act as a co-worker: he got the coffee.

Ward secretaries need to teach those they coordinate how to deal as adults and members of a team, with the inevitable conflicts and confusions that arise. 'I'm an adult; I'm grown. If you can't speak to me without yelling, don't speak to me at all.' This approach cuts through hierarchy and authority. Holding fast to a status pecking order can make it almost impossible to solve problems and resolve conflicts such that people can continue working together. Almost all ward secretaries indicated that they had to set rules and that they were successful in doing so. Just about everyone had one or another variation on, 'when I first came I really had trouble with these doctors (or supervisors or administrators), and I had to set them straight. Now they know their limits and we get along fine.'

II

Family and work continuities

Ward secretaries discussed the good hospital worker in many of the same ways that they discussed the good adult in a family. Their rules of behavior at work were expressed in family terms and concepts. This suggests that family relationships are an important source for practical meanings of adulthood, autonomy, hierarchy, and equality. In talking about their families with ward secretaries and other workers, three things emerged 1) a concept of work; 2) the intrinsic value of specific interpersonal skills; 3) a relationship of hierarchy, equality, and adulthood.

Work

Pride in doing a good job is expressed in many family interviews. Women discuss the household, child care, and part-time wage jobs they performed while still in school as qualitatively similar. But they focus less on the tasks themselves than on the responsibility and initiative they took for knowing what needed doing. The mental and organizational aspect of work was central. It was rewarded by praise but by being given more responsibility as well. One woman's father told her that she released him from having to worry about whether the house was clean: 'if you're around I know everything's taken care of'. She described how she arranged her part-time job, school, and housework and how she threw her brothers and sisters out of the house on Saturday mornings so she could get the cleaning done when she had time. These women were taught in their families that housework and work for wages are not qualitatively different and that the mental organization – coordinating things, setting priorities of time and effort – of both is a most significant source of pride and a sign of adulthood. An adult is someone who can take responsibility for making decisions, arranging and accomplishing things autonomously. The rub comes when parents are reluctant to yield that autonomy in non-work aspects of their children's lives, when parents feel they retain responsibility for their children's decisions. All the women who described this conflict resolved it by moving out. They all said that there was no bitterness about the move, no break in the relationship. Moving out was a sort of rite of passage to exercising the range of autonomy they had learned.

Interpersonal skills

Probably the most important family rooted workers' values are the interpersonal skills that families value and teach. Mediating, resolving conflicts by reconciliation, and providing emotional supportiveness and advice are things people bring up frequently. I asked Alice, a ward secretary, who she saw as the center of her family. It is clearly her grandmother. She lives in town, and everyone visits her on Sundays and holidays. 'She loves to cook. If you want to find out something you call her.' She keeps up with what everyone's doing 'and what you shouldn't do'. For the most part people listen to her advice. She is also likely to enlist the help of her children in helping one another.

Alice is the center of a workplace network that joins pairs and small groups of very close friends. She sees herself as closer to a few real friends than to her family at this point in her life. 'A real friend is willing to help whenever you're in need.' She distinguishes real friends from 'the others I just be with'. There is a certain 'fit' between her value on a few close people and on the way she's organizing a birthday club – on linking good friends to other good friends – a chain of small, strong links of trust. But as I will try to show below, it is a group at the same time and also part of a larger community. At least that is part of their hope for the club.

What about Alice's family in all this? Did she learn to bring people together, to seek and give aid in her family? And what about people in her network? Do they share Alice's values; have they laid their expectations on her? Alice was raised by her mother's mother and father. Her grandparents had twelve children and Alice was raised with her aunts and uncles – they were really more like brothers and sisters – on a farm near a small town to the north. Recently one of her aunts, Jody, who is about Alice's age has been coming to Alice for advice and has been sending other cousins to talk about their personal, health, and marital problems. Not long ago, Alice's baby half-sister stayed with her when she was having problems with her husband. Alice says that she is having responsibility put on her and that she feels good about it. People seek her out for personal advice because they know that she had a hard time with her first husband, knows what personal adversity is about, and has come through it stronger and wiser. Other people reinforce her own sense that she has grown from the experience. Alice is a center in a large family. But, as with her friendships from work, Alice's family relations are two-way, and she goes mainly to Jody for advice.

Beverly, the center of the other network described below, stresses mediation and initiative in smoothing interpersonal family and work relations and in collective action. While she doesn't see any person as having taught her, she does see the critical events as having been in the context of her family relations: keeping peace is the central relation to her family. That came from Beverly's initiatives as a teenager. 'Respecting parents is the utmost. That was my God.' But when she graduated from high school, Beverly decided that she had to move into her own apartment if she was going to grow independently and without argument. From Beverly's description, it appears that her move created a family role that was needed but not really there so long as she stayed at home – and therefore as a child in her parents' eyes. The role was that of adult mediator: Beverly's mother calls on her for advice. Her parents' expectations and treatment of her have been taken up by her brothers and sisters, who also call on Beverly for advice, mediation, and help with interpersonal problems, even though she lives a long distance from them.

Acceptance and reinforcement of her personal initiative transformed her 'personal God' into a social role of family center. Beverly's personal discomfort and her attempts to deal with it apparently helped others in the family to see a need for a mediator. As long as she lived at home, her parents were responsible for resolving conflicts. Beverly resolved part of the family's contradiction as well as her own by moving out. She created a new and needed role – non-parent mediator – and the family reinforced and helped to give the role shape. Even though Beverly seems to have modelled her own role, she is now a role model for her baby (nineteen-year-old) sister.

It is possible that Beverly learned how to mediate and learned ways to take initiative in non-family contexts. She described herself throughout high school as 'a sheltered kid', quiet, not allowed to go out after school, and therefore not into high school socializing. But her mother was secretary of the church for twenty-five years, and Beverly went to church every Sunday until she moved out. Also, in high school she began working as a messenger in a hospital on her work-study program. After graduation, independent adulthood, and full-time hospital, then post office work, Beverly gave in to her mother's urging to go to college. But it was just not what she wanted, and she left after a year and a half. In 1971 she became active in the black liberation movement and spent some three years working at her hospital job and recruiting and speaking on college campuses. She moved to town to continue political work in the unionization campaign at the hospital.

Hierarchy, equality, and adulthood

Black and white women alike described their families as simultaneously egalitarian and hierarchical. On the one hand, respect for parents was central: 'I never talked back to my father. I did disagree and brought my point up but not to the point of impudence.' 'Part of black family teaching is to give respect to elders in your behavior.' 'I would never walk into my mother's house with so much as a beer.' Because of their *social relationship*, parents and elders have certain rights to establish ground rules, to command some deference and services from children. It has nothing to do with their personal abilities. But prerogatives of and respect for social position are of a very different order *and do not take away from* the respect due to all individuals regardless of position, simply because they are adults (or children on the way to adulthood) and because this presumes some autonomous and self-motivated development. 'Children are expected to make decisions, rather than parents imposing them.' One woman explained how yelling at a child was not good (though hard to avoid). Her son says, 'it's part of child abuse'. He is 'disappointed more than scared. It makes him mad – maybe the same way as being yelled at on the job – it's demeaning.' At work, ward secretaries were prepared to work for and grant people prerogatives they felt were due to their place in the job hierarchy, but they were equally insistent on their rights as autonomous adults. Part of this is the right and expectation that they will organize their work on their own, will 'assign their own priorities' (a phrase that crops up often), and will not be watched and directed.

III

The walkout

In April 1974, the ward secretaries organized a walkout by calling in sick. 'We got everything we wanted; that's how I know if we stick together we can get it.' This walkout was also one of the sparks to the union campaigns of the next four years. A newspaper story at the time and interviews with more than a dozen participants five years later stressed pay, working schedules, and treatment by hospital administrators, doctors, and nurses. But underneath this, ward secretaries walked out because management also belittled their job and their intelligence.

Issues

The computers triggered it. 'The majority of us felt with all this new training they should offer us more money. Any time you work with a computer they should give you more. If you're lucky enough to get in research, you could make much more out there than here.' Introducing computers helped to bring out deeper issues of respect and recognition. In subsequent actions more than in words ward secretaries were saying 1) that their medical and computer skills made them employable at a variety of places; 2) that these skills combined with those that had always been part of the job should command more pay; 3) that they should be recognized as coordinators of patient care on the wards and be given due respect from doctors, administrators, and nurses. From management they wanted higher pay and status forms of respect. From co-workers they wanted adult/family forms of respect. I think that they are not the same and that the distinction is important.

The group of ward secretaries who went through the changeover to the computer in the early 1970s were at the center of the walkout. Pay and certification of their competence in using the computer system were linked concerns. One ward secretary found that her counterparts in a hospital in another city – mainly white women – started at $5 per hour in 1974. Several ward secretaries told me they started at $2 per hour in 1970. In 1979, there were some with ten years seniority who had just started to get $5 per hour. The hospital changed their original job title – data processing technicians – when it was thought that technical classification would mandate more pay than a clerical one. Ward secretaries also wanted certification, which was particularly valuable for getting better jobs elsewhere. Job mobility was seen as the reason management did not certify them. 'Without certification, you cannot move, and if you can't move, they can pay you what they choose.'

Ward secretaries described different paths that brought them together. Those on the cardiac intensive care unit (CICU) were angry at having to watch the heart monitors. Monitor attendants were paid 3–13¢ per hour extra, but this did not compensate for the skill required or the stress involved. When the monitor attendant/secretaries quit, the hospital replaced them with nurses – at a higher rate of pay.

On Surgery, Obstetrics and Gynecology, and Pediatrics, scheduling was a problem, with ward secretaries working eight to ten days at a stretch without a day off. Different units had different patterns of abuse to contend with. On pediatrics, 'a lot of ward secretaries were mad because they weren't getting the respect they deserved from the doctors' – especially senior doctors. On surgery, supervisors came in for the most consistent criticism – in rejecting ward secretaries' efforts to improve the work schedules, in leaving them with full responsibility for trainees, in always checking up but never helping out, and in not standing behind the secretaries when they were right. On some of the medical wards there were problems with RNs (registered nurses), particularly where nurses in charge gave orders to ward secretaries to do things that were not part of the job. One woman was disciplined when she refused to take a specimen to a part of the hospital that was dark and empty at night. Since there was no medical urgency, she asked that it wait until morning when a messenger could take it. Finally, among some ward secretaries there was resistance to the administration's choosing their uniforms. One saw this as the spark that got some of them to call a ward secretary meeting to discuss the situation.

Not all ward secretaries shared all these grievances. Some of the more active had few complaints beside pay. 'We just about run the hospital, but we're being cheated out of the money.' Because money is a measure of respect as well as a means to buy bread, those with few daily problems also got involved.

Most ward secretaries are black, and this is one of the better paying jobs black workers can get in significant numbers at this hospital. The systematic underrating of a complex job by hospital administration could only reinforce racist ideas about the abilities of black women. The town had an active black movement from the late 1960s to the mid-1970s, and many ward secretaries were involved in some facet of it while in high school, when the town's schools were segregated. 'At the hospital was the first time I *saw* what they were talking about – whites on top and blacks on the bottom. Ward secretaries were considered dumb even though we were running things. Even if I hadn't been to Freedom School, I couldn't take not being treated like a human being.'

Community and work networks

Many of the secretaries who were at the center of the walkout knew each other from high school. 'All of us (some dozen women) came out of high school together – the class of '68 or '67 or '69 – it's not clear how we all landed together.' While they were in high school, many of them had some experience with the movement in the town's black community – teaching summer freedom schools, picketing for housing improvements, or registering people to vote. 'Back in the '60s, that was the thing. You got your work-study program and worked for Operation Anti-Poverty. There was always a social struggle for years and years. I worked for Anti-Poverty when picketing was the thing and the emphasis was on sticking together.'

Many black and white ward secretaries are from the town and have ties of kinship, school, church, and neighborhood all interwoven such that there are many hospital workers with whom they share some relationship. By the same token, work organization influences which of the many kinds of ties they have to each other. The hospital is where many have made their closest friends, most of whom are other ward secretaries and LPNs (licensed practical nurses). People tend to tell friends and relatives about job openings and to recommend them, so ties of kinship, work, and friendship reinforce each other. Kin, in-laws, and prior acquaintances become friends when they work together. Most ward secretaries agreed that friendships came from or were deepened at work. In short, one brings family and family values *to* work; one creates family and re-creates family values *at* work.

There seem to be certain workers who are key in forming interpersonal networks. I call them centerpeople. Such women exemplify family values and reinforce them by their actions. Their initiative in setting up social groups and activities is an important part of the process by which co-workers 'become family' and are able to enforce familistic values in the workplace. Centerpeople are structurally important for sustaining perspectives and behaviors that are simultaneously working class and familistic in contrast to managerial notions and norms.

The organization of work 'from above' established close contact between ward secretaries within a unit or between paired wards, so that those on all shifts within a unit were in daily communication. Informal social networks reinforced these lines of communication, with ward secretaries and nurses (mainly LPNs but also RNs) on a ward or pair of wards getting together for holiday parties, informal cookouts, picnics, and dinners throughout the year. Unit lines seem more important than physical proximity in the hospital. Indeed secretaries on a ward of one service next to a ward on another could not think of any secretaries they knew there. Likewise, adjacent wards of the same service under different unit supervision have little day-to-day contact. 'You tend to get together with people under the same supervisor.'

Organization 'from below', among ward secretaries who knew each other from high school – ties of neighborhood, kinship, and friendship – brought together different units and services. The core network in 1974 seemed to be the group hired between 1968 and 1971. Most of them were concentrated in Medicine, but a fair number were in Surgery. This network included almost weekly out-of-hospital socializing among mainly single ward secretaries and nurses on several wards of both services.

Each of these ward secretaries was also part of some kind of network on their unit. Thus two surgery ward secretaries from this core group, together with several other secretaries on their unit, acted as centerpeople for holding meetings and informing those on their wards of events. Those who missed meetings checked in with the two 'core network' secretaries. Another ward secretary from the core network who worked nights tried to bring the news to people on that shift.

Services other than the two largest were less involved in the walkout. To the extent that people from these services stayed out, it seems that they were connected to people in the core by ties of kinship, friendship, or neighborhood. Some from one small service stayed out not only because of the general issues but also because their friends from the core group expected them to. There has been a major turnover on the other small services in the last five years, and I did not learn much about networks five years ago. However, on these services, ward secretaries who were close to participants elsewhere did join despite the fact that there was much fear of retribution and not much in-service support for doing so. The service where friendship and social networks were densest, the bases of trust and communication were most secure, participation in the walkout was highest, and fear of retribution was lowest.

Until recently most ward secretary training took place on the wards and was the responsibility of senior secretaries. In teaching attitudes, they also teach their definition of the job. By insisting on egalitarian respect from 'higher-up' co-workers, they are communicating a message to new ward secretaries that the job is one of coordinating and administering. By telling them that those at the top of the hierarchy have less understanding and need more teaching, they stress the idea of a team of complementary specialists. This is the most important aspect of on-the-job training by ward secretaries. They are generalizing, sharing, and passing on a working class/familistic 'head set', a consciousness of themselves as responsible adults, of their right to insist on adult treatment and to stress cooperation over domination and subordination.

Events

Three ward secretaries organized a meeting of those on all the units. 'We compared our salaries, which the hospital doesn't want you to do.' They talked about management piling more work on and about having no say in choosing their uniforms. Calling other ward secretaries led to a meeting at one person's home. About thirty ward secretaries showed up, two or three from each area. 'It was surprising how angry people were.' The lone male secretary present was chosen to be spokesperson. 'He was the only male, so he was our spokesman.'

The major issues were 1) pay; 2) two free weekends each month and long stretches of work without a day off; 3) abuse from doctors, nurses, and administrators; 4) more help at the desk. 'You worked a ward by yourself then.' Several ward secretaries mentioned the attitude of a specific administrator who was reported to have said that you could pull a ward secretary off the street anytime, that they were a dime a dozen. 'That was supposed to stop us from walking out, but it had the opposite effect.' Management's initial answer to the ward secretaries' demands was that it would 'work on it'. Considering this an inadequate response, those present in the meeting with management called a second meeting at the home of the spokesman. Though the sequence of meetings is not too clear, this meeting was attended by about seventy-five ward secretaries, a very impressive showing considering that there were between 125 and 150 ward secretaries at the time. They felt a strike would show clearly how important ward secretaries were, that the hospital could not run without them. 'We felt we had a jump on them.' Someone pointed out that they would be in danger of being fired if they went on strike without a union. The resolution was for everyone to call in sick.

The whole process took only a few days. 'We knew if we gave the administration time to get to people they'd chicken. On the third night we called people to stay out the next day – so by the time the snitches got to it we were on strike.' People have different memories of the length (two to four days) and time (weekend, midweek) of the walkout. Two women resolved some of the discrepancies when they pointed out that their major problem was knowing when to stay out. They would hear two different days from two different people. 'It was raggedy getting started.' They felt most people stayed out four days, and then a 'group here and there began going back'.

During the walkout there were also meetings – those called by the hospital and strategy meetings called by ward secretaries. One of the more active secretaries commented that the administration had them 'in one meeting after another' to try to pry out of them 'how we got together after they been trying so hard to keep us apart. It was *fun* – to see them sweat.'

Almost all ward secretaries agreed that the walkout was effective, particularly on the largest services. Supervisors and nurses attempted to cover the wards, and some secretaries came to work. Those working had to cover several wards, and many worked double, or even three shifts. The biggest effect was felt on the day shift, which handles most of the work. Only secretaries knew how to work the computer. Under the system in use at the time, every order had to be processed through a code number which was listed in a manual. If a person did not know how to use the manual, it was impossible to use the computer. Ward secretaries agreed that the hospital – and the patients – suffered from having untrained people working. One commented, 'they use patients as an excuse to kill you – and they're robbing the patients blind.' Another said that the place was 'a mess' when they returned and that it took a lot of work to put it back together.

One service provided the backbone with the most active leadership and the highest participation rate. There was also a significant turnout from the largest. But from the smaller services there was little participation, though for different reasons. One of the few ward secretaries who participated from her service told me that her service had very good working conditions. 'On the other side they bottle up their problems; here we talk about it right then.' On the other service there was harassment from supervisors. Some ward secretaries were called at home and told not to stay out.

Supervisors knew through the grapevine that a walkout was in the wind. Reports differ on the prevalence of 'snitches', but most people thought they were insignificant, because the supervisors did not know when or how the walkout would take place. Some supervisors told secretaries they would need a doctor's note to get paid for a sick day. On at least some wards this was no problem because 'the doctors were glad to write excuses'. But on the small services: 'it was real shaky. You didn't know if you were going to have your job when you got back.' Sympathy was high, but those I spoke to were not sure of the actual participation rate. 'Some ward secretaries acted later like they participated, but they didn't. Some came in and broke the picket lines, and some secretaries were mad at them.' Many from this service came to meetings outside the hospital, but few showed up for those with the administration. From what little I could gather, in the outlying buildings no one stayed out or attended meetings. One woman said they heard something was going on, but did not feel that it was about them.

Victories

The walkout brought some real changes. 'We said the only way we'll come back is if you don't fire anybody'; management hedged, 'and we said we'd still be sick – so they gave in. We got uniforms the color we wanted. They wanted us to pay for it. They paid. We got respect. You know how doctors throw charts? Now they can't.' Ward secretaries received an immediate 20¢ increase and pay was raised from level 3 to level 4 the following January (and has since been raised to level 5, that of non-ward, predominantly white secretaries). An unpopular administrator somehow disappeared. Secretaries on the largest service received alternate weekends off. Lines of authority were clarified between nursing administration and ward secretary administration, so that secretaries were no longer in the middle.

The number of ward secretaries increased – ultimately by about 60%, or 40%. But this seems to have been gradual and uneven over time and by unit. On the day shift, mainly, there are supposed to be two secretaries working a ward. 'It's bearable with two; with one you worked your ass off.' Whether the number of ward secretaries in the largest service increased is not as clear. One secretary there thinks it has held constant since the walkout. Another points out that they have had a high turnover and constant vacancies. When she began working there in 1976 there were two secretaries on most wards. 'Now it's rare to have two on a ward at once. Now they just have the second as needed – a floater.' The other big service has two secretaries per ward.

About eight months after the walkout, the hospital presented ward secretaries with a computer certificate. 'They just gave it to keep us quiet.' But even this seems to have required some additional meetings and organizing. One woman said that they got the certificates by having a meeting of their unit with supervisors and unit administration. The initiators were senior ward secretaries central in the walkout. 'If they complained, others would follow suit.'

Though there has not been any major confrontation, the battle between the hospital and the ward secretaries has not stopped by any means. Points of conflict became more apparent during union campaigns, but they are still visible in the midst of what people describe as 'quiet times', when 'everybody's content' or 'apathetic'. Ward secretaries, especially those active in the walkout, were very active in the union campaigns. One secretary noted, 'All of a sudden someone realized our job was important. Any time you have a walkout, it does tell somebody that . . . you do have the ability to organize.' The walkout gave them all a 'sense of accomplishment'. Their walkout taught other workers that unity can pay off. For their part many ward secretaries saw unionization as a way of extending their own improvements and extending them to other hospital workers. The hospital is working indirectly to erode the solidarity, pay, and staffing gains, and the main issue of conflict remains today what it was five years ago: ward secretaries' insistence that they be paid at the level of skill that the job actually requires and management's insistence that the job is not skilled.

IV

New networks and centerpeople

Social networks as well as job events have changed somewhat in the five years since the walkout. After 1974 the core high school network began to disintegrate as people transferred or quit. In the last three years, three centerpeople have left the largest service, leaving few personal ties between the two major services. For the remaining people ward-based, out-of-hospital social networks 'from below' have become more central. Yet ward secretaries still look to some of the remaining centerpeople from the old core for initiative in dealing with job issues. The centers of two networks, Alice and Beverly, both commented that when something was happening that had to be dealt with, one of the core ward secretaries would get in touch with them, and they in turn would discuss it in their network. These two networks have grown up since the walkout. They are lines of communicating familistic/class values and resistance but in a muted form.

The first network has developed over the years largely from people's close personal ties to Alice. Recently she has begun a social club that seems to be joining several smaller networks together. Alice has worked on her unit for about eleven years and has helped train many ward secretaries. In the course of training Yvonne, they became friends. When the house next door to her came up for sale, Alice bought it. In turn, Yvonne has kept up with Willa and Violet, whom she knows from high school. Willa is a ward secretary on another service and Violet's co-worker is Alice. Yvonne has become 'best of friends' with her co-secretary on the ward where she now works. This ward has no ward secretaries at night, is far away from the main wards, and, as a new research ward, is in a kind of unpleasant administrative limbo for ward secretaries. Though neither leaves the ward on her break, Yvonne usually takes her lunch with some of the secretaries or nurses on the two paired wards of Alice's unit. She and her co-worker look to 'the other side' of the hospital for social relations. Violet and Alice both join these wards with a ward under a different administration.

The distant Medical Specialty ward, also relatively new, became part of this network in a similar way. Alice helped train Tanya, most of whose immediate family is out of state. In 1975 Tanya's closest friend and roommate, who was also a ward secretary, left town, whereupon Alice invited Tanya to stay with her until she could get back on her feet financially. Tanya usually takes her breakfast on Alice's ward. Though it is technically against the rule for ward secretaries to visit on other wards, the supervisors here do not enforce it. Secretaries say that this is because their supervisors know that they are accomplishing the purpose of the rule, making sure the ward is covered at all times, in their own way. Tanya works closely with her co-secretary Sylvia. Sylvia started working evenings on Alice's unit and socializes with the secretaries and nurses there whenever she works an evening shift. For her part Sylvia is something of a centerperson on her ward. 'Some people say I'm the "Dear Abby" of the ward.' But at the present time she spends most of her non-work time with her small son. Tanya is a bowler and has met many of her friends through bowling. Among them is Rose, a ward secretary who works all wards. Together with Alice, she is her closest friend.

Alice and her co-worker, Violet, are also very close friends. Violet knows Tanya and Rose from the hospital Ladies Bowling League. She knows Yvonne from high school. Because Alice is not from town, she does not have high school ties. Both she and Yvonne are centers of the network of nurses and ward secretaries on the two wards they work.

Last January Alice suggested to Tanya, Rose, and Violet that they form a birthday club. The idea was for each person to invite one or two people whom they liked to be with and whom they thought others would also enjoy. They hope to get fifteen members, each of whom would pay a $25 membership fee. That treasury would then be used to give each member a birthday party – or whatever the person wanted – on her birthday. Other members would also give gifts. They also discussed sponsoring a needy family each Christmas and fund raising projects for this to be held during the year. 'And at Christmas time we'll give a big Christmas party; that's for everybody.' When the club gets going, they hope to be able to take a trip together. So far, the sure and possible members are ward secretaries and nurses from this medical unit network. Alice sees the club as creating a social group for women who are in similar situations. 'At least it gives you something to do besides go to church and work. It's something to look forward to,' and, she adds, 'especially for single girls from out of town.' Most women in this network are single parents.

Sometimes more comes from having a good time than just having a good time. Even when a group's purpose is social, its activity can become one of the many ways working class communities create themselves by defining a larger group that they 'do for' or 'do with'.

The second social network joins ward secretaries on the four wards of General Medicine. This network has more formal qualities in that secretaries hold regular dinners once a month. They also organized for a year in advance to rent a hall and give a public dance last Christmas. They agreed to contribute $1 each pay period (every two weeks) to a fund for rental, decorations, and refreshments. Virtually all of the secretaries on the unit participated. They also cooked food and sold some 200 tickets. Tickets were sold mainly to friends who worked in the hospital, and flyers advertising it were put up through the hospital. Ward secretaries were again taking the initiative in bringing hospital workers together. Five years ago they had spurred the union campaign and had been at its center. Now, with no political activity, their form was social.

The center of this network, Beverly, is from out of state. She started work during the union organizing drive, several months after the walkout, and was an activist on the organizing committee. She is the centerperson – as treasurer for the Christmas party, as a person to whom ward secretaries go for work problems, and as a person active in unionization efforts. In a holiday season conversation, a ward secretary on another unit was praising the togetherness of those on Beverly's unit and bemoaning the lack of it on her own, where there were no good parties.

I asked her what started all the social activity. At one level, she said being a political person and an organizer encourages a person to think in group terms. When Beverly finished her probationary period as a ward secretary, she publicly identified herself to management as well as to workers as a union organizer. Her job was to concentrate on signing people up for the union. 'I talked to everybody. That was fun work.' As an activist, she gravitated toward the group of militant ward secretaries from the local community who had been at the center of the walkout. Even today, some of this group in listing their high school cohort include Beverly as part of it for all practical purposes. But Beverly's network activities also came from more traditional hospital beginnings: she gave a goodbye party at her house for a ward secretary who was leaving. From that point on, secretaries began getting together regularly for dinners every two weeks, and Beverly has been active in keeping them going. That, together with other social events, has been going on for five years. These join ward secretaries of all four wards of the unit. Beverly's initiative with the Christmas party built a more public and formal level onto an on-going network.

The close personal friendships and family-like relations I have described are among black women. As ward secretaries and LPNs, they are also the main builders of ward and unit networks. Whites and men are not excluded, but the hospital's segregated hiring patterns together with those of the medical hierarchy reinforce color and sex lines. Ward secretaries are mainly black women; so are LPNs. RNs are overwhelmingly white. Like ward secretaries, LPNs have a fairly low turnover. In the words of one secretary, they are 'more stable people'. RNs here, as elsewhere, stay on average between six months and a year. Also, RNs tend to associate more with doctors, and LPNs with ward secretaries, attendants, and messengers. 'You'll see interns eating with RNs but never with LPNs or a ward secretary' – this from a white ward secretary. Most of the secretaries I spoke with stressed that color did not separate secretaries and nurses at work. Some emphasized that both black and white workers on the ward – including RNs – were part of the dinners, picnics, and other events that were held at people's homes.

On one ward all the ward secretaries were black, and all the nurses were white. The nurses took the initiative in organizing out-of-hospital parties and dinners. While the secretaries I spoke with praised the good relations that existed regardless of color at work, they also said that the black workers did not go to the parties outside of the hospital, even though 'they (MDs and nurses) all get after us the next day for not coming'. Every year the ward secretaries and messengers (also black) talked among themselves and declared, 'if you go, I'll go', but they never did. One woman said that they were all afraid that they would not fit in outside the hospital – and that discovering it might hurt and jeopardize the good work relations they had. Another contrasted it with parties and showers in the hospital – where everyone goes and brings gifts 'because everyone's here' – they belong and do not have to explain themselves. She pointed out that people do not 'feel at ease' going to a party with white people with whom they have only a work relationship – however pleasant it may be. That is, a ward network 'from above' is an inadequate basis for black–white socializing. But both women also indicated that the root of this lay in the hospital's segregated hiring pattern. One said that if there were more black nurses, ward secretaries would be more comfortable about going, for they would not have to hurdle both barriers of race and hierarchy at once. They pointed that there had once been a black nurse on the ward, and she attended the parties.

Denise and Evelyn, ward secretaries who were centerpeople in the walkout, stress the disintegration of the core high school network. They note that there are fewer organized parties and dinners on their unit, that their wards no longer socialize with others on the unit, and that there is also less militance among ward secretaries. Evelyn pointed out that five years ago most secretaries were younger and single and that single people mainly take responsibility for organizing social activities. Denise pointed to a single nurse who initiated such picnics and parties as there were and to a few single RNs and LPNs who were involved in socializing. But this view downplays the close relations both these women have with their sister- and cousin-in-law who are secretaries on the same service. In one sense, the core group has disintegrated; in another sense, it has been reconstituted in different networks and includes additional ward secretaries.

These two centerpeople have themselves helped bring about these changes. In different ways they have both indicated a desire to opt out of the responsibilities of being a center – even though they wish someone else would take up the initiative for continuing the social and political activity. Denise pointed out that ward secretaries of the unit used to have a Christmas party but that they did not have one last year. She explained that she and another secretary (no longer there) had organized it, but, 'we didn't want one last year'. The other centerperson, Evelyn, describes her current preference for socializing with different groups of people. 'This way I don't need to entertain, to see that no one's feathers get ruffled, to keep the relationship going.' She sees this as a way of resolving the strain of having to be responsible for creating smooth interpersonal relations within a group: 'I find myself always in the middle of ten thousand different people who don't like one another, pulling at me.'

At one level their descriptions sound like 'burnout', a common enough thing among organizers and activists. I suspect that an important part of when one 'burns out' – in social or political life – has to do with periods of change in family life. Both women, close friends, describe themselves as in the midst of change. Denise married young and is rethinking and perhaps reshaping her decision; Evelyn is single and contemplating settling down and/or going to school. Both describe themselves as exploring new possibilities – various social circles, school, marriage, separation. 'Trying on' life possibilities is not really compatible with the commitment to taking responsibility for bringing people together in a single context, which is precisely what is required of a centerperson.

These women as well stressed marriage and children as influencing their involvement in work-based socializing. Some women, single parents, said they got out less with small children and more as their children got older; married women said they spent most free time with their families. But single parents also said they liked to be with their children, that they liked to be with other single parents, and that because they were single, they took extra effort to seek out family-like relations with both men and women at work – especially when their children were small. In one network, married women and their children made up most of the people at dinners and picnics. 'The husbands and boyfriends usually don't show.' Having – or not having – husbands, boyfriends, or children does not really stop women from getting together *when there is a context for doing so without being put in a bind.*

Centerpeople help create such contexts. To do this I think requires a certain amount of life stability on the part of the centerpeople. The centerpeople of the post-walkout networks describe their lives as stable, though their family circumstances differ greatly. Alice is divorced with children. Beverly is single without children. Alice began building a network only after she had resolved a long-standing unstable marital situation. The centerpeople of the third network, Evelyn and Denise, stress the (different) changes they are going through.

Conclusion

At this point I simply suggest that working class families place high value on interpersonal skills in dealing with conflicts such that relationships can be maintained in spite of friction. They also have a high regard for the organization, responsibility, and autonomy upon which being a good worker is based. Development of these skills is recognized as important for becoming an adult. Centerpeople are crucial to forming the work-based social networks within which this perspective is reinforced. I had had a tendency to see this as a creator role and to forget that leaders and initiators cannot create what people do not already want. After all, no one has to 'join' a network, much less be active in it. To paraphrase an old slogan, what if a centerperson called a network and nobody came? These women see initiative as having two sides – the one which comes from an individual and the one that is laid on her by others. As Beverly put it, 'I'm usually the one to initiate anything. People say, "Jones, why don't we do this?" – and they wait for me to do it.' If you take initiatives, people check in with you, and part of checking in involves suggestions and expectations. Cathy described the same process in her family. She took the initiative as a child in many household tasks and was reinforced by both praise and expectations of other family members. 'They added yeast to it [her initiative].' Centerpeople, then, exemplify more general working class values and are important parts of a more general process by which workers bring family members to the workplace, turn relatives into co-workers and friends, and make friends like sisters or godparents. From this vantage point I see a continuity between family and work – in how work, both wage and non-wage, is defined – which is absent from a management perspective and which underwrites workers' militance.

NOTES

1 This is actually a paper-in-progress based on current fieldwork. At this point, my analysis of family and social network is just beginning and is *extremely* tentative. I am somewhat more confident of the workplace discussion, in part because I have had more direct contact with it, and in part because almost all the workers I observed and interviewed have read, commented on, and in some sense 'verified' it. Some of them trenchantly criticized and unambiguously torpedoed the first draft. The second draft and its analysis is much improved thanks to them. I plan to submit the family analysis to the same treatment. I would also like to thank Carol Stack and Dorothy Remy for their comments, Kay Day for her very important insights into how family socialization provides bases for workplace values, and Connie Rayborn for typing this paper. The third draft has benefitted from the comments and discussion at the Round Table and from subsequent comments by David Sabean. The paper is based on fieldwork supported by a post-doctoral fellowship at the Center for the Study of the Family and the State at Duke University, NIMH Grant No.5 T32 MH15188-03.

13. Linen was their life : family survival strategies and parent–child relations in nineteenth-century France

LOUISE A. TILLY

Nineteenth-century followers of Frederic Le Play regretted the modifications in family organization which they attributed to industrialization and urbanization and to changes in inheritance law. These early social scientists observed peasants and workers and their families, first in France, then in other countries. They produced a series of monographic accounts, each focused on a family 'type', which followed Le Play's evolutionary scheme, rejecting the liberal view that industrial capitalism and individualism brought with it prosperity and the potential for human self-actualization and happiness. For Le Play and his school, the farther away a family stood from the traditional agricultural society – conceived as a family-centered world where true happiness came from loyalty to the family and acceptance of rules of behavior which would strengthen family – the more 'disorganization' threatened, the closer at hand were social and moral pathology. One consequence of this world view is an attachment to what to others seemed anachronistic family forms and praise for those who continued the old ways.

Thus Charles Blaise, writing in 1899 about the handloom weavers of the Cambrésis region in the department of the Nord, commented,

in general, the attitude of the Cambrésis weaver is excellent. Gentle to his own, quick to help his unfortunate neighbors, the worker welcomes the visitor openly, with kindness. He possesses a wealth of native loyalty which manifests itself in all his public acts and in friendly relations with his merchant/manufacturer boss. He also has plenty of self respect.[1]

Compare this deeply conservative interpretation to Michael Anderson's evolutionary view of family and industrialization. His study of Preston, Lancashire, in the mid-nineteenth century argues that the uprooting effect of migration and urban life led to a short-run, calculative, instrumental orientation towards kin. He notes that there are 'scraps of evidence' that there were similar attitudes in pre-industrial England. This he explains by suggesting 'that the critical life situations faced by these populations were almost as great as, while their resources in general considerably less than, those of Lancashire operatives'. He concludes, however, 'that a really strong affective and non-calculative commitment to the kinship net could develop and "traditional" community solidarity became possible' only with industrial prosperity and the welfare state.[2]

This paper examines the development of work organization and kin relations in families of the Cambrésis handloom weavers in historical context up to about 1920 to see which interpretation – the Le Play 'Golden Age' view that the old way of life went along with warm kin relations based on mutual obligation, or the Anderson view that property and uncertainty promoted calculative kin relations, presumably fragile and tense – is correct. Is there indeed a 'climate' of kin relations associated with poverty and uncertainty? Are kin relations likely to be close and warm, or close and instrumental in a situation where family members are resources in household economic calculations? In order to establish the context, the economic history of the handloom linen weaving industry of the Cambrésis is first traced, focusing on the town of Avesneses-Aubert and asking how and why handloom weaving lingered there for so long. The quality of the weavers' work life is also examined in this section. Second, the demography of the town is reviewed within the economic context and for its implications for family relations. Finally, the autobiographical account of a woman born in 1891 in Avesnes is the source for descriptions of the emotional climate in families there.

The history of linen weaving in the Cambrésis

Avesnes-les-Aubert is a small city near Cambrai where the weaving of linen on handlooms continued well into the twentieth century. This seemingly anomalous survival existed alongside large-scale industrial capitalist mechanized linen spinning and weaving in factories in the same region.

Domestic linen weaving in the countryside around Cambrai was already well established in the eighteenth century as shown by a contemporary report that linen manufacture 'is located most often in the countryside, very seldom in the cities'.[3] During the revolutionary period (An III) a report of Paul-Joseph Nicodéme to Citizen Pérès, representative of the people with the army fighting in the Low Countries, described the way the weavers lived: 'on an arpent of land a linen manufacturer could have his home, his workshop, stalls for several cows, a horse or mule, a soup garden, and enough space to grow all the linen needed for a large family to spin and six or eight weavers to weave'. As Guignet notes, this description suggests that the weaver was an independent master, not necessarily dependent on a capitalist entrepreneur.[4] He appeared to own his land and his tools, and to be a worker himself as well as a master. There was a division of labor within the family: women and girls did the spinning and the master weaver and his assistants (some of them doubtless his sons) wove. The family was not totally detached from the land, but it was no longer primarily agricultural. One of the villages of the Erclin valley with perhaps 300 looms at work in this period was Avesnes-les-Aubert.

In the early-nineteenth century, the linen industry fell upon hard times. Although domestic weaving continued in some villages, they specialized instead in wool or cotton. At the 1844 Exposition, the linen production of the Cambrésis was reported to be 10,000 bolts annually, a steep decline from 35,000 around 1815. In 1855, the president of the Chamber of Commerce of nearby Valenciennes noted that the industry was 'in such a state of decay that one can consider it no more than a remnant of the past'.[5] These pronouncements of the demise of linen handloom weaving were premature.

The report on the arrondissement of Cambrai prepared for the Enquête Industrielle of 1873 noted that in many communes, weavers owned their own looms and worked in their cottages, supplementing this work with agricultural labor. This stage was a reversal of patterns of 'protoindustrialization' in which industrial work was a supplement to agricultural activity which was inadequate to support families on their holdings. Domestic manufacturing was the primary activity of the Camberlots, as these people were called after the chief city of their region, some of whom owned cottages and looms; seasonal day labor in agriculture was the supplement.[6] The statistical summary for the town of Avesnes-les-Aubert produced for the 1873 Enquête shows that 1300 persons were employed in linen weaving: 700 adult men weavers, 350 women, 250 children (under sixteen years of age) and 50 owners and managers of the 'fabrique'.[7]

In the spring of 1878, another survey was conducted, because the mayors of communes of the Cambrésis had pressed their representatives in the Chamber of Deputies in Paris for aid. Orders to report were sent from the Minister of Commerce and Industry to the Prefect of the Nord and, finally, to the Subprefect of Cambrai. He acknowledged bad economic conditions but noted that the problem was not unemployment properly speaking. Those who wished to work as weavers in the Cambrésis could find work but at ridiculously low wages. Many were leaving the arrondissement, heading for nearby industrial areas where factory jobs were plentiful. Some years later, when Blaise reported on this migration, he noted that residents of the larger towns were most likely to leave, and hand weaving became more concentrated in smaller places.[8] The official inquiry in 1878 found that though there was substantial outmigration, those workers who remained 'received barely $\frac{2}{3}$ of what was necessary to buy food not to mention housing or clothing'.[9]

Matters did not improve. Some Camberlots worked on sugar beet farms close by, the 1878 report noted. After 1880, however, inefficient sugar beet cultivation in the Nord was driven out by competition of new farming areas to the west and south, with larger, better capitalized, and more technologically advanced farms. Chicory cultivation was introduced in the Nord in place of sugar beets, and Belgian farm workers migrated to work these fields. The Camberlots, Abel

Châtelain writes, switched to a longer, seasonal migration to follow sugar beet agribusiness. They spent six months out of the year living and working on sugar beet farms in the Paris region and Normandy. He concludes that sugar beet cultivation, labor intensive as it was, kept these people working in rural industry even as urban industrial concentration was ruining it.[10]

Although many Camberlots left and others divided their year as weavers and farm laborers, a core of year-round weavers stuck it out. In February, 1889, official reports on the occasion of a strike describe Avesnes-les-Aubert and its workers, who were still primarily weavers of heavy linen (*toile*) and handkerchief linen. The weavers' wages were 0.85 to 1 franc per day, based on piece work for six fourteen-hour days weekly. With such low wages (urban industrial wages for adult males in nearby Roubaix were at minimum around 3 francs a day), they subsisted on bread and root vegetables. Their misery had caused the strike, the police reported.[11] Again in June, 1895, hundreds of weavers struck in Avesnes and nearby towns in another struggle for a living wage.[12] Interestingly, this strike took place in the summer, when the seasonal farm workers were absent on their yearly migration. The year-round weavers, refusing to adapt by seeking supplemental income, apparently chose instead to press their employers for better wages. This fact stands to remind us that the weavers were divided into at least two groups, one which adapted by supplementing low wages by seasonal migration, the other which tried to make a go with weaving alone. It was the latter who were ready, in 1895 and, as we shall see below, in 1906, to mobilize to promote their interests in collective action. There are suggestions that this division into two groups was partly a matter of age and marital status; young, single men and women were most often those who migrated to do farm labor.[13] Nevertheless, whole families also joined the migration.[14]

Ways of work and life in the Cambrésis around 1900

By the last decade of the nineteenth century, the weavers were wage-earning proletarians except for the anomaly that they owned their own looms. Le Play described this organization of work, which he called the *fabrique collective*, as a step in his evolutionary scheme of changing work structure. The *fabrique collective*, he argued, had emerged as a consequence of increasing demand based on distant markets. A merchant entrepreneur was the intermediary between the workers and their markets. But, as Charles Blaise, whose law thesis used Le Play's model for its framework, noted, 'the entrepreneur denied the artisan the sale of his product and reduced him to a worker, whose only right was to a wage agreed upon beforehand. Even if the wage were high, the artisan paid for task work has no direct connection with the market; he works for a merchant capitalist instead'.[15] The economic rationality for the preservation of this seemingly outmoded organization of production in the industrial age was twofold, according to Blaise. First, finer linen was produced by hand rather than machine weaving, so some hand woven linen was a high priced luxury good. Second, handlooms could respond more rapidly to changes in fashion and taste than could factories with fixed plant and large investment. There, economies of scale were necessary for efficiency. The tiny units of hand weaving could more easily change over to a new style.[16] The fact that the weavers absorbed the cost of rapid and small-scale changeovers was surely one of the attractions to merchant entrepreneurs dealing with them. Nevertheless, Blaise believed that the system was for the good of both workers and capitalists, for the weavers had no capital with which to buy raw material, no knowledge of the market for which they produced.[17]

This apologist for the domestic organization of work noted that the 'collective form' of manufacturing had not caused any of the disasters sometimes attributed to it.[18] Le Play and his followers believed that a combination of agriculture and small-scale industry was the best social organization.[19] The main problem of the handloom weaver was not his disadvantaged structural position but the fact that he no longer owned his own house or baked his own bread! (Blaise's language here makes these changes appear a matter of personal choice and, further, a choice arising from poor judgment on the part of the weavers.)

The weaver's work force was his family. The mother was charged with the cooking, sewing, and care of the rest of the cottage, but the weaving room (usually in the cellar, lighted by half moon windows which admitted daylight) was the male weaver's territory. He swept it daily and whitewashed its walls regularly. The shop was deliberately kept damp and cool. The loom, *l'outille*, was simple, often very old, and 'always the property of the weaver'. The weaver sat on a board tilted so that his or her body was pushed forward, thus providing extra leverage for the arms and legs that manipulated the loom.[20]

The family and its occupation, linen weaving, were inextricably linked:

the father of the family groups the community of workers, of whom he is the natural head, in the workshop at the looms. He himself works too, giving each of his family members the joint responsibility of working in the enterprise. All the family members collaborate to varying degrees, without exception, in the production of cloth.

From an early age, the children of both sexes help their father do his job by producing the *trames*. This task consists of winding the linen thread on a bobbin, which is then placed in the hollow of the weaver's shuttle. Once they are 13, the children are rapidly taught how to weave by their own family and assigned to their own loom.[21]

Compare Blaise's description with the firsthand account of Marie Catherine Gardez, *femme* Santerre, born in Avesnes-les-Aubert in 1891:

there in the big, half-dark room [the cellar], lit only by several high windows, were the looms on which everyone in the village wove during the winter months for eighteen hours each day.

After my time at school – being the youngest, I was given the chance to go . . . I too had 'my loom'. I was still so tiny when I first began to weave that I had to have wooden 'skates' attached to my feet so I could reach the pedals. My legs were too short to reach them.

At four a.m. we awoke. Dressing quickly, with water from the court fifty meters away, where a well served all the families in our *coron* [an attached row of houses],[22] and hop, we

went down to the cellar with two coal-oil lamps. During this time, my mother lit the round
stove that heated the main room . . . she called us, at around 10, to come upstairs and get
our 'coffee'. It was a long time to wait after waking before we got this hot drink [chicory]
that seemed delicious to us . . . My sisters and I, we made handkerchiefs that we wove into
big rolls of linen. My father, who was more skillful, made the wider pieces of linen . . .
himself.

Every Saturday, one after another, running, because we wished to waste as little time as
possible, we would take our cloth to the agent, an inhabitant of the *coron* like us, who
collected the work, and got the money for it.

. . . I would return home and give the money to my mother. Then my sisters would go,
then papa, to take their work.

We couldn't make ends meet with these earnings. We had to live all winter on credit. We
paid up on our return from the season in the country.[23]

The Gardez family were seasonal migrants to a large sugar beet farm in
Normandy. Continuing Blaise's account: 'the mother is concerned above all with
house work, aided in her many tasks by her daughters. The rest of the time she
also prepares, often rising before dawn, the bobbins for the weavers' shuttles; if
there is an idle loom, she hastens to replace a sick or absent worker'. Marie
Catherine also testifies to her mother's vital role: 'Mama tended to the
housecleaning, scoured the floor, scraped the table with a shard of glass, threw
fresh sawdust on the tiles, and boiled potatoes and at the same time prepared the
shuttle bobbins that we would use the next day.'[24] Blaise concludes: 'as one can
see, everyone works in the family workshop. There, each person finds the task
appropriate for his or her strength and intelligence. The children, far from being
a burden for their parents, become very real resources for the family. Raised to be
weavers, they become weavers.'[25]

Without the unpaid help of his wife and children, it would have been
impossible for the weaver to support a family. Even so, there were sharp cycles in
the trade, and in any ordinary year there were likely to be several periods of
unemployment.[26] Like other followers of Le Play, Blaise believed that the
Napoleonic family law code, which called for division of inheritance among all
the children, had caused the fragmentation of land holdings and the proletarianization of the weavers. Yet despite the consequent poverty, the loss of
home ownership, the abandonment of independent family-based baking of
bread, the family workshop was morally superior to the factory. Although the
family workshop was, regrettably, no longer a pure patriarchal unit or a stem
family as was the peasant household, it was very solid and noteworthy. This was
so because of the mediation of family and family relations between family
members and the economic system.[27]

Another report about the linen hand weaving industry comes from the news
accounts of the strike of September, 1906. The 13 September front page editorial
in the *Progrès du Nord* summed it up with its headline: 'One Franc 75'. That was
the average daily wage of weavers at that time.[28] The striking weavers demanded
an average increase of 15% on their piece rates (which varied according to the
article produced) and an arbitration board for employer/worker disputes.
L'Echo du Nord, another local newspaper, published a series of background

articles during the strike. E. Şimonet, the author of the series, like Blaise, presented a sentimental picture of an old way of life, foreign enough to his readers to appear quaint. Simonet sees urban migration and factory work as 'one of the worst blights of recent years'.[29]

The old weaver interviewed for the newspaper articles showed the reporter his *étile* – a corruption of *outil* – the local word for loom. He explained how the work was done by family groups, although by his account both *trames* and warps were prepared outside the weaver's cottage in centralized shops owned by merchant capitalists. One of the issues of the strike was the establishment and preservation of a standard length for the warp (and thus of the finished bolt of cloth). Of course, the issue at bottom was adequate pay, but the way it was expressed emphasized the artisanal aspects of the weaver's work, in which he produced a piece of work of standard quality from start to finish without supervision. The measuring standard for the length of the warps was kept in the city hall, as had been the measures of guild weavers in the old regime. (Rural weavers, however, had not been guild members at that time.) The wages the old weaver cited were quite variable: for fine cloth, up to 3–3.5 francs a day; for ordinary cloth, 1.75–2. The bosses, claiming to suspect pilferage of thread and other cheating by unsupervised workers, resisted increasing the *tarif*. The workers insisted it was the bosses who were cheating on the *tarif*. 'Weavers are demanding better wages, because even in the countryside, it costs money to live.'[30] The linen weavers evidently had some leverage against their employers still, for the strike ended with a partial victory.

Poverty dogged the weavers of the Cambrésis until the First World War; during the first weeks of war, the German invasion swept their region. Cambrai and other towns were burned. Since the war broke out in the first days of August, the seasonal farm laborers were away. Most were unable to return for the entire war period. The region became occupied territory. In 1918, the retreating German army forced all men out of villages; they were followed by the women and children, unwilling to be separated from their husbands and fathers. For the town of Avesnes-les-Aubert, the evacuation was an enormous disaster; 1600 people were lost. The inscription on the Monument aux Morts for the War of 1914–18 in the town square shows that civilian casualties outnumbered military ones by 10 to 1. Some 36% of the inhabitants died in the war.

Paradoxically, the destruction of machinery and the death of so many workers offered a reprieve to hand weaving. As Pierre Hamp, a novelist and sociological journalist of the Nord put it:

the war both destroyed the new factory and burned the old wooden loom. The two ages of labor were demolished together. Everything had to be rebuilt. An *Outil* of wood can be built in two weeks; a factory takes two years. The old skill was resurrected. The better paid workers rediscovered the joy of using their hands again. Long before a single factory smoke stack reappeared in the Cambrésis, the shuttles rattled in the cellars of the villages.[31]

An accident of fate gave new life to this extraordinary way of working. It also gave Hamp the chance to rewrite his salute to the linen weavers (his completed manuscript was lost in a fire in 1914) in these evocative lines:

what joy in the linen thread! What more beautiful for a man than to throw the shuttle rhythmically, sixty times a minute . . . [the weaver] had but one friend: the cloth. He left not a single bit of fluff on the finished fabric to disturb its smoothness . . . The rhythmic sound of the loom was like the beating of his heart; he lived inside the sound and rejoiced in its regularity . . . Fine cloth, long-practiced skill, a man happy in his ancient craft, working the loom of his ancestors . . . [the weaver] talked to his loom. How many things he had told it in the years he had worked with it. He didn't see the loom as a tool made of wood and string to fashion the cloth, but as a kinsman . . . He declared, 'In order to weave well, your loom must be your partner.'[32]

Nevertheless, by the time Hamp published his novel, he could see the future: 'the good times had at last returned [after the war], but the weaver soon found his ancient misery, poor pay, all over again'.[33]

The handloom weavers of the Cambrésis were survivors. Those who stayed in the trade adopted strategies of behavior which would facilitate that survival. The pattern of seasonal migration was one adaptation. Strong family orientation and demands for loyalty to family interest was another. The household unit of production and the integration of learning the craft and growing up promoted family orientation. Blaise returns again and again to this familial orientation of the weavers. In reference to family formation and parent/child relations he notes;

a new household is established each time a child marries. Because the new household is set up in the same locality, because it is a weaver's work shop, and because of reciprocal affection and respect between old parents and their children, the new household is closely linked to that of the parents. The newly married couple are aided by the division of the inheritance when the elders die, but they can subsist even before as a distinct unit . . . The work of the domestic unit is a source of gain because of the conditions of work.

The child performs his apprenticeship under the affectionate direction of his father or his elder siblings. The first thing he sees consciously is the loom. Understanding work is his first intellectual effort. One can truly say he is born a weaver.

. . . [The mother] is loved and respected by this community of workers because of her important contribution. Because of the charm with which she surrounds herself, the men do not wander . . . the cabarets are empty, there is no alcoholism, girls are raised properly. In this way, happy and durable marriages are built.

Children stay near their parents and help them in their old age.[34]

Demography of a handloom weaving town

Strong occupational homogeneity and family/community orientation are reflected also in the demography of Avesnes-les-Aubert. Guignet's family reconstitution of the village shows that it was growing rapidly in population at the end of the eighteenth century.[35] 'What were the components of this growth? The study of marriage shows that the *mulquiniers*, linen weavers, were extremely immobile, forming practically a demographic isolate.' For the entire period, 1757–1906, only two bridegrooms were from a parish more than 10 kilometres away, and only in one decade, 1790–99, did the proportion of grooms born inside the *parish* itself fall below 81%. (The brides were even more likely to be born in the parish, but this reflects the Catholic practice of marrying in the bride's parish as much as lack of geographic mobility.)[36] Migration was certainly not a major factor in population growth.

On the other hand, a pattern of younger marriage among Avesnes brides over the period 1757–99 contrasts quite sharply with the urban pattern of nearby Valenciennes, where the age of marriage was rising. Fertility was high in Avesnes (although evidently somewhat lower than in Valenciennes, perhaps because Avesnes women were wet nurses for Valenciennes infants and thus benefited from the temporary sterility of heavy nursing). Despite very high infant mortality, it was natural increase that was the major component of the rapid population growth in Avesnes-les-Aubert in this period.[37]

Similar patterns obtained one hundred years later. In 1886, the town had a population of 4301, of which 3861 had been born in the commune. Less than 2% were born elsewhere! The average size of the households was 4.6 persons and 13.9% of the population was under the age of five. The overall child/woman ratio (children under five per ever-married women aged twenty to forty-nine) was 1.0, extremely high. Although the child/woman ratio is a very approximate indicator of fertility, everything points to continuing high fertility in Avesnes.

Analysis of census material (a 50% sample) from the 1906 nominal lists of Avesnes shows household size considerably smaller, 3.9, but with many familiar characteristics.[38] First was the overwhelming importance of the textile industry as employer: 67% of males and 71% of women who listed occupations had textile occupations. The textile industry was equally important as an employer at all ages, with the exception that married women seldom reported occupations. If they were members of weaver families, they were doubtless helpers even though they were not formally so designated. Interestingly, and providing a curious echo of the Old Regime, all domestic weavers were called *patrons tisserands* (master weavers.) There was an extremely high proportion of children aged ten to fourteen with occupations (24% for boys, 22.6% for girls), and of these, almost all (97% for boys, 91% for girls) worked in textiles.

The census also shows clear patterns of links among family names, trade, and community. Hand tabulation of the census sample population shows that 15% of households, containing 22% of the population, were headed by persons with six names: Santer, Herbin, Chopin, Waxin, Guidez, and Coupez. Herbin was the most common name, with 187 persons in 25 households, 7.5 per household. The vast majority of the households with these names were headed by weavers, and the mean number of persons per household greatly exceeded that of the mean for the sample as a whole. Evidently survival strategies of weavers had brought about considerable intermarriage among those who stayed in the town.

The population as a whole was young: 32.9% under the age of fifteen; 10.4%

under five; 58.9% under thirty. Young persons under twenty-five were very likely to live with their parents, much more likely than in nearby Roubaix, a factory industrial town. The characteristics of households with children in Avesnes, 1906, strongly resembled those of rural England and of an English industrial town, Preston (as described by Anderson), in 1851, or of Roubaix, in 1872, and differed quite markedly from the patterns in contemporary French cities (See Table 1). Extremely high child/woman ratios for young women, and particularly for the wives of weavers, are unlike those for other French cities in 1906, and are higher even than child/woman ratios forty-five years earlier for other French cities.[39]

Table 1. *Children* in the population of various communities*[40]

	Rural England 1851	Preston 1851	Roubaix 1872	Roubaix 1906	Amiens 1906	Avesnes-les-Aubert 1906
Children as percentage of population	47.0	49.0	48.6	42.7	34.7	47.5
Percentage of households with children	74.0	81.0	77.0	60.7	56.2	74.5
Mean size of groups of children	3.0	2.9	2.8	2.5	2.0	3.0
Mean number of children per household	2.6	2.7	2.2	1.5	1.1	2.2

Thus quantitative evidence based on census bears out contemporary accounts of the overwhelming importance of the linen textile industry in this Cambrésis town and of the characteristic family organization of such work, especially child labor. Two demographic patterns which accompanied the economic homogeneity and household mode of production are also clearly visible: high fertility and extended co-residence of children with their parents. The household organization of production and division of labor within the household made many children an integral goal of family child-bearing strategy. As the economic underpinnings of the linen hand weaving industry became weaker and weaker in the course of the nineteenth century, some families migrated from the Cambrésis; in other households, some of the children migrated to find other jobs. The seasonal migration to do agricultural field labor was another adaptation, whether practiced by young people alone or by entire families. Both families who persisted in full-time weaving and those who divided their time between weaving

* Children defined by relationship to household head, not age.

and seasonal field labor continued high fertility strategies. To them, many children offered a possible solution to their poverty, for children could work with their parents and contribute to the family wage pot. This strategy is consistent with the observed behaviors of high fertility and high labor force participation of children. Another consistent behavior is low school attendance, also characteristic of Avesnes-les-Aubert.[41] The situation resembled that described for eighteenth-century France: 'the obstacle to schooling lay first of all in the loss of earning power that schooling represented by its immobilization of potential child labor. Investment in schooling in an old regime type of society was more than a cash investment for families, it was a time investment.'[42] Among these hand loom weavers, the work community and family coincided; families pursued strategies which counted heavily on children to work with parents and contribute to family welfare.

Interpersonal relations within the family

Economic distress and severe constraints on individual choice accompanied the economic importance of family or household. What did this imply for personal relations? How did the families of Avesnes behave within these brutal work regimes? The oral history of Marie Catherine Gardez shows that despite brutalizing work and poor living conditions, families did lead lives of dignity in which they enjoyed and bestowed love and respect. Other families were torn by anger and contention. The community, her account suggests, disapproved of contention and ill-will. In order to illustrate these points, let us follow her description of her parents, who were born in the late 1840s, their interrelations as a couple and with their children, and then look at the parents of her husband, Auguste Santerre, and their struggle with their oldest son. We close this section by putting the two families into the context of community opinion suggested by the autobiography.

Marie Catherine tells us that her father and mother spoke little between themselves. ('That's probably what I still find most surprising: the few words they uttered each day.') Nevertheless, her father was always courteous to his wife, whom he 'adored'. She repeats later that they were always happy because they adored each other. They were both illiterate and had no knowledge of the world, but they had good sense and intelligence. The couple worked together and shared opinions. The wife accepted her household responsibility and performed it efficiently. When they migrated to Normandy, for example, her daughter tells us that once assigned the family quarters, the mother quickly went to the cook stove, 'her' post. The father dealt with the world outside. His opinion was dominant in public decisions, such as that which sent their thirteenth child to school. He also did some tasks which seem to be more domestic than not: he baked the bread in the communal oven and arranged for credit at the baker and grocer. It was her father who scolded Marie Catherine for her first flirtation: she was too young at sixteen to marry; the young man in question was too short; what's more, he was the son of the merchant's agent and hence responsible for the exploitation of the weavers. This latter opinion was one of the very few political views he expressed, according to his daughter's account. The other moment when he entered the political sphere was when he supported the religious orders as teachers in a demonstration which led to his arrest; he also sent her to Catholic school rather than the communal school. Her mother left the scolding of their daughter to the father, as she left the formulation of opinion to him also. The father, in turn, spoke in the plural, for himself and the mother, when serious matters were at hand. Their daughter thought it seemed natural that they have but one opinion. And, indeed, sometimes it didn't even take words to establish, as when their eyes caught each other in recognition of her feeling towards Auguste, the man she would marry.

Marie Catherine felt that her childhood, deprived as it was in material aspects, was a happy one; her chief joy was the company of her parents. As the youngest of the large family, she was privileged to call her mother 'maman' rather than the more formal, respectful 'ma mère' expected of her elder siblings. She praises her parents for their firmness and kindness. They disciplined not through violence and shouts but respect. Nevertheless, the children were not permitted to speak at meals; of course they never questioned their parents. The father taught the children to weave and how to do field work. He always urged them to do the job right: 'whatever you do, do it well'. He pressed them to work hard and steadily but never spoke in anger to force such behavior. He criticized other parents for exploiting their children as workers at too tender an age. 'Too young' is relative, of course; his children all started work at the age of ten at the latest, even Marie Catherine who went to school. The father made miniature loaves of bread as treats for his daughters; he was solicitous enough of them to see that they got fresh air and exercise during the long weaving days. He sang for them when they worked in the fields, finished their rows and carried them to bed when they were exhausted. Marie Catherine's only conflict with her parents was about the tentative courtship by young Haguet. Her father's irritation gave her pause, but she concluded that it was best to accept his judgment, since he had more experience with life and was himself married. Nevertheless, her parents accepted her marriage two years later, when she was eighteen, as they seem to have accepted similar young marriages of several of their other daughters. (I was able to identify three daughters in the 1906 census listing and estimate their age of marriage by the age of their oldest child.) Perhaps the fact that two of her older sisters were unmarried still and working at home when Marie Catherine married made this acceptance easier.

Auguste Santerre's parents were younger than Marie Catherine's; he was the oldest child. In the 1906 census, he (then eighteen) and two sisters, aged sixteen and fourteen, were listed as weavers alongside their father. There were eight younger children in the family, the youngest born the very year of the census. The

Santerres claimed all of their son's earnings; they denied him any personal allowance even when he was twenty years old. This was the cause of contention which led Auguste to leave home and board with Marie Catherine's married sister. The elder Santerre attacked his son when he heard that he was leaving, beating him with his fists, his sabot, his belt. Marie Catherine exclaimed that Auguste should have defended himself, but he stated simply, 'one doesn't strike back at one's father'. Although her parents allowed the courtship (this was 1908, when she was seventeen and he twenty), the Santerres violently opposed it. Even when the wedding took place they dragged their feet. Their approval was needed, for Auguste was a minor. They came very late to the ceremony at the city hall; the mayor had to send the *garde champêtre* to rout them out. They came in work clothes to symbolize the fact that they had been pulled, unwillingly, from their looms, the father in a rage, the mother resigned. After the wedding, the Santerres walked with the wedding party toward their houses but turned off the path to their house without a word.

Parent/child relations after marriage of the young couple reflected those before. Marie Catherine's family let them weave in their cellar; she used her old loom, and Auguste was loaned a loom by a son-in-law of his wife's family. The mother prepared (for pay) the *trames* of Auguste and Marie Catherine as well as those of her husband and daughters still at home. When the young couple moved to a larger cottage with a weaving cellar, Marie Catherine's father gave her the loom. The young couple were reconciled with his parents when they had a child. The grandparents came, awkwardly, to see the baby and, without words, relations were restored. The father gave Auguste his loom at that time. Later still, Marie Catherine tried to build happier ties with her in-laws, carrying her son to visit his grandparents, bringing small gifts to them. As poor as all the families were, the Santerres, she notes, were even poorer, for the father was not a good weaver. His gruffness and bad temper was borne by his wife who was resigned and passive. Nevertheless, in the end they cared for their grandchild when Auguste and Marie Catherine went to work for the season in Normandy, and in 1914 they succeeded in traveling to the west with the child to join his parents, who were unable to return to Avesnes.

Most of the social moments mentioned in Marie Catherine's account were family celebrations of religious feasts, Christmas, first communion, marriage. The only persons present who were not members of the nuclear families involved were in-laws, except for her godparents, who seem not to have been kin. The only visitor mentioned in the whole book is the brother of her mother. People did not visit casually, especially at meal time. Yet, there were connections among the residents of the *coron*. The women neighbors gossiped about the events of their lives, passing the word of births and deaths. They went together to get meat when a farmer butchered cattle. The families who went to Normandy on the seasonal migration traveled together and consulted on procedure. As Marie Catherine grew up, the institution of the noon promenade became an occasion for courting.

The teenage girls walked and the young men watched them. The mothers, hastening between their tasks, 'walked', too, to supervise the exchange of glances and words.

The behavior of the Santerres toward their son was the subject of gossip and criticism by Lucie, Marie Catherine's married sister, who eventually took him in as a boarder. Her parents did not speak about it but looked disapproving and dismayed. The mayor of the town was irritated over their reluctance at the wedding. He criticized 'that damned good-for-nothing Santerre who always has to act different from the others' but was relieved when they finally turned up, for he disliked seeing 'the harmony of the village' disturbed. In his irritation, however, he refused to shake their hands in congratulation on the marriage of their son.

Conclusion

The examples from real life show variability of the emotional climate of kin relations in families whose lives were constrained by poverty, patterned by limited economic adaptation, and characterized by strong family orientation and little chance for individuality. Neither Charles Blaise's Le Play-style interpretation of the family economy as producing warm family relations nor Michael Anderson's interpretation of their calculative nature is borne out. Nevertheless, these examples also suggest that within the developmental cycle of the family, there could be a cyclical pattern of parent/child relations based on birth order.

First born and early parity children (especially sons) were those whose labor and wages were most eagerly awaited by parents. Their sense of family loyalty and acceptance of obligation had to be strongly developed, for their parents' claims on them would come early and last long. Their marriages would be delayed and family help for a marriage (such as providing a loom), limited, for their siblings could take their place at a family loom. This was the case of Auguste Santerre, the oldest of eleven. His hope to be able to save to set himself up in a new household was denied by his father. Despite his sense of the injustice of this decision (a sense shared by others in the community), he refused to strike his father or deny his authority. He chose instead to submit to his abuse and then to leave the family production unit. He received no encouragement or even acceptance of his marriage. Under similar circumstances, older children, particularly males, may have been late to marry or likely to move out of the weaving trade because they were unable to save the capital needed to buy a loom. Either behavior represents a hard choice and occasion for contention.

Middle children were most likely to be allowed to marry young, to leave home and enter other occupations than weaving. Youngest children could possibly be kept at home longer, but they could take their looms as they left. Another possibility, however, is that youngest children were allowed to marry young, were given their looms, and lived close to their parents, to help them in their old age. This is the pattern followed by Marie Catherine and the Gardez family. The other two younger sisters who married after Marie Catherine did not marry weavers, and they left the community. The three sisters and the brother who lived in Avesnes in 1906 were all weavers.

If the experience of Avesnes-les-Aubert was like that of other French rural and urban areas, the late-nineteenth and early-twentieth centuries were a time of declining infant and child mortality. This would have meant more children surviving to adulthood than expected, hence more children to establish in adult occupations. With the characteristic large families, a certain proportion had to be sent away to make their own fortunes and to liberate their looms for their younger siblings. Those who became weavers carried on the old way of life and reproduced the old strategies and customs. They received the looms from their parents to start new households and owed their parents care in their old age. Relations between these children and their parents were likely to be informed by different expectations than those of the children who left. The latter got nothing, did not continue the old way, emigrated, and are lost to the historian. A child's birth order was an important determinant of which behavior he or she followed. Birth order also could be a factor shaping parent/child relations such as degree of socialization and, possibly, affection. Focusing on the survivors, the adaptors, the persistors provides a partial picture of family relations, and it is that part which was more likely to be cordial.

NOTES

Research for this paper was supported by a Rackham Faculty Research Grant, University of Michigan.

1 Charles Blaise, *Le Tissage à la main du Cambrésis. Etude d'industrie à domicile* (Lille, 1899), 78.
2 Michael Anderson, *Family Structure in Nineteenth-Century Lancashire* (Cambridge, 1971), 177–8.
3 Archives Nationales de la France (AN) F 12 652, No. 92, cited by Philippe Guignet, *Mines, manufacturers et ouvriers du Valenciennois au XVIIIe siècle* (New York, 1977), 199.
4 Guignet, *Mines, manufacturers*, 212.
5 *Ibid.*, 225.
6 Archives Départementales du Nord (ADN) M 605/4: Enquête Industrielle, 1873. Report on arrondissement of Cambrai to Prefect of the Nord.
7 The 'fabrique' was the putting-out system, consisting at this time of fifteen independent merchant entrepreneurs.
8 Blaise, *Le Tissage*, 28.
9 ADN M 581/141: Enquête sur la situation des ouvriers tisseurs du département, 1878.
10 Abel Châtelain, *Les Migrants temporaires en France de 1800 à 1914*, Publications de l'Université de Lille, vol. 3 (Villeneuve d'Ascq, 1976), 688–90.

11 AN F 12 4665. February, 1889, reports on strike in Avesnes-les-Aubert.
12 ADN M 625/67. Weavers' strike, Avesnes-les-Aubert (1895).
13 Blaise, *Le Tissage*, 70; E. Simonet, 'Chez les tisserands du Cambrésis. II. Un example de travail à domicile. Préparation et tissage. Le tarif de 1905', *L'Echo du Nord*, 13 Sept. 1906.
14 Serge Grafteaux, *Mémé Santerre. Une vie* (Verviers, 1975), *passim*; Blaise, *Le Tissage*, 70.
15 Blaise, *Le Tissage*, 13.
16 *Ibid.*, 17.
17 *Ibid.*, 40.
18 *Ibid.*, 16.
19 *Ibid.*, 29.
20 *Ibid.*, 35.
21 *Ibid.*, 36.
22 *Coron* is the word commonly used for the brick row housing in French coal mining towns. There was no coal in Avesnes-les-Aubert, but it is the word used by Marie Catherine Gardez for the row housing in her natal town.
23 Grafteaux, *Mémé Santerre*, 10–11.
24 *Ibid.*, 11.
25 Blaise, *Le Tissage*, 36–7.
26 *Ibid.*, 53–4, 55–6.
27 *Ibid.*, 65–6.
28 Newspaper clipping in ADN M 625/79. Weavers' strike, Cambrésis and arrondissement of Valenciennes (1889).
29 Simonet, 'Chez les tisserands du Cambrésis. II.'
30 Simonet, 'Chez les tisserands du Cambrésis. III. Les bases du conflit. Le livret de compte. L'augmentation demandé', *L'Echo du Nord*, 15 Sept. 1906.
31 Pierre Hamp, *Le Lin* (Paris, 1924), 118.
32 *Ibid.*, 130.
33 Hamp, *Le Lin*, 128.
34 Blaise, *Le Tissage*, 66–8.
35 Guignet, *Mines, manufacturers*, 339–42, 622–33.
36 *Ibid.*, 620.
37 Guignet, *Mines, manufacturers*, 626–38.
38 This computer analysis was performed on a sample of half the households in the town listed in the 1906 census. The nominal list for that year notes each individual resident's name, address, place and date of birth, occupation or condition. It frequently includes mention of marital status, but marital status is not provided by check off and must be deduced from name, position on list of household, age, if there is no explicit mention of relationship to head of household. The list also provides a notation of where people are employed, which includes whether they are workers or '*patrons*'. In Avesnes-les-Aubert, the word *patron* designated self-employed workers as well as true entrepreneurs.
39 Louise A. Tilly, 'Structure de l'emploi, travail des femmes et changement démographique dans deux villes industrielles: Anzin et Roubaix, 1872–1906', *Le Mouvement social*, 105 (1978), 33–58.
40 Source: Rural England and Preston, Michael Anderson, 'Household Structure and the Industrial Revolution: Mid-Nineteenth Century Preston in Comparative Perspective', in Peter Laslett and Richard Wall (eds.), *Household and Family in Past Time*

(Cambridge, 1972), 232; Roubaix, 1872 and 1906, and Amiens, 1906, a 10% sample of census nominative list; Avesnes-les-Aubert, see n38.

41 Louise A. Tilly, 'Individual Lives and Family Strategies in the French Proletariat', *Journal of Family History*, 4 (1979), 143–4.

42 Roger Chartier, Marie-Madeleine Compère, and Dominique Julia, *L'Education en France du XVIe au XVIIIe siècle* (Paris, 1976), 42; see also Mary Jo Maynes, 'Schooling the Masses: A Comparative Social History of Education in France and Germany, 1750–1850', PhD Dissertation (Michigan, 1977).

Part VII. The idioms of family in work, domination, and custom

14. Village spinning bees: sexual culture and free time among rural youth in early modern Germany

HANS MEDICK

Few 'customs' allow the close connection between work, sociability, and free time in the rural-village plebeian culture of early modern Europe to be seen so clearly as the winter-evening *Spinnstube* (spinning bee).[1] In the Spinnstube it was not a question of spinning flax and wool inside the peasant or cottage industrial family. Such was, without question, before the advent of the mechanical spinning machine, a widespread everyday work routine. The Spinnstube on the other hand presented a form of work sociability. It was precisely characterized by the fact that it went beyond the boundaries of household and family. Its typical supporters were the age and friendship group of the youth and the neighbourhood. Its productive basis was overwhelmingly rooted in the working processes of women, especially spinning, but also knitting, lace-making, sewing, and 'feather-splicing'. At the same time, the function of the Spinnstube was not exhausted by the labour carried on in it. Sociability ranked at least equally with work and often surpassed it.

The Spinnstube was a typical practice associated with evening free time and started when the daily routine was finished. Its work processes – such as spinning and knitting – were relatively simple. It took place also in the period of the year when work was not so heavy. It was limited to the winter months, that is during the period of the peasant annual routine when agricultural intensity clearly dropped off and left a greater area of play for sociable pleasures, celebration, and 'expenditures' of all kinds.

In this manner, at the evening social gathering of the unmarried rural population, especially of the unmarried girls, one encounters the Spinnstube in numerous variations in the folklore literature. With a few exceptions, it has not yet been the subject of a very intensive consideration. Most studies of the Spinnstube have been by folklorists, who have been interested in its caretaking function – as a treasure trove of popular musical, poetic, story-telling, and also magic survivals.

The tendency of these older folkloristic studies was a rather idyllic glorification.[2] At the period when the custom was perceived to be disappearing, one believed it important to rescue it as a rural 'institution of nature' against the depravity of city life and also – as one source had it – against the 'war of destruction' carried on by the police and priests.

On the other hand, the East German folklorist Musiat has suggested that one should undertake an exact investigation of the social and economic function of the custom for the everyday life of village (class) society.[3] This is not sufficiently accomplished only by an analysis of the social structure of the Spinnstube, as Musiat has attempted quite helpfully for the case of the Sorbian Spinnstube. Rather, it appears necessary to take in the total dimension of 'material culture' in which the custom was located. This demands on the one side, of course, the analysis of the economic function of the custom, but on the other equally the investigation of the mediation of the social-cultural experiences, practices, and patterns of values with the reproduction of the village mode of life.

In my opinion the central function of the custom in precapitalist peasant society is to be found in the relationship of the Spinnstube to the youth-sexual culture and the rural customs of courtship.[4]

Repeatedly one finds in the literature indications of the widespread distribution of the Spinnstube beyond Central Europe, 'from Brittany to the Himalayas'.[5] However, here it is a question of being concrete and going beyond a surface concern with the geography of words and concepts. It seems crucial that in the notion of 'Spinnstube' itself a particular location of community life is equated with a specific kind of work and sociability. Even where the word was not known, the institution could exist in fact. Under diverse names such as *Kunkelstube*, *Lichtstube*, *Lichtkarz*, *Liechtstubeten*, *Rockenstube*, *Vorsitz*, *Kaiserloß*, *Heimgarten*, *Maistube*, *Spillstube*, *Spinntrupp*, *Stoberta*, and so forth, it was a strongly defended custom, which in some places existed well into the twentieth century. During the early modern period, it was under strong attack from state and police and subject to regulation by church and moral authorities. I myself have encountered the very concrete and positive memories of the Spinnstuben – or as it was synonymously called, *Lichtstuben*, *Kunkelstuben*, or *Rockenstuben* – in the reports of the inhabitants of a weavers' and peasant village in the Swabian Alp in Southwest Germany, whose history I am writing. Here, in Laichingen, the custom, despite strong opposition, especially from church officials, was still very much alive up to the years before the First World War (in a neighbouring village indeed up to the 1950s). At the beginning of this century, a village observer well acquainted with the *Lichtstuben* described them in the following way:

while the older people spend the evening with the family or with acquaintances, the youth gather in the 'Lichtstube'. Right after confirmation the boys and girls are concerned to found their own [separate] *Lichtstube* or 'Ebahihaus' [the 'anyplace' house]. The owner of the house concerned, the *Liachtmo* or the *Liachtweib* [i.e. *Lichtstube* father or mother], receives a certain compensation in money or foodstuffs. Generally it is pleasant and merry in the *Lichtstuben*, especially on the first or last evening, *Pfeffertag, Lichtmeß und Fastnacht*, when it is celebrated with beer, white bread, sausage, and cakes. On such nights there is no question of work, although normally great attention was paid to knitting, sewing, or crocheting. Along with the work, one deals passionately with the news of the day and everyone gets his 'kick' – as the Laichingen inhabitants say quite rightly. When one is tired of talking, a few folksongs are sung. Perhaps also a few boys will visit. Around 10 o'clock everyone goes home. Often then both sexes meet up, which naturally does not occur without disturbing the peace. But it is very difficult to fight against the bad consequences of the institution. The whole thing is too deeply rooted.[6]

The earliest pictorial description of a Spinnstube I have found comes from the time of the Reformation. The one page print, meant for popular distribution, was by the Nürnberg wood-cut artist and copper etcher, Hans Sebald Beham, from 1524.[7] It treats in an ironic manner from the perspective of the city-dweller the crudity, corporeality, and earthiness of the rural-peasant Spinnstuben activities. The common sociability of both sexes in a room, which approximated an overlarge peasant living room, quite clearly outweighed the purely female work of spinning. Men and women carry on in such a way that dancing, drinking, and above all bodily-sexual contact set the tone. Every attempt – from outside through the door – to bring in light and the correct morality of work to the Spinnstuben activities appears from the outset to be condemned to failure. Female Spinnstuben work is only carried on by a single figure in the background. She is the centre of the picture but in no way is the centre of the action.

One cannot decide from pictorial evidence alone how far this description stems from the fantasy of the author alone, or how far the exaggeration of the urban literary-satirical tradition of peasant mockery plays a role, or how far in fact the reality of the Spinnstuben activity is indeed captured. Noteworthy is that the description demonstrates a pattern of behaviour which approaches historical authenticity and reality. Otherwise, the practice of suppression would not be understandable, which, since the period of the Reformation, in Catholic and Protestant areas alike, up to the nineteenth century, was carried on against the institution of the Spinnstube. The suppression is contained in the numerous state and church warnings, ordinances, and prohibitions.[8]

Certainly, such testimonies of Spinnstuben customs, to which we are limited for the sixteenth and seventeenth centuries, are not from the participants themselves. They are only of an indirect nature and arise from perceptions from outside or from 'above'. Still, even though they are written from the point of view of the rulers, they are in no way worthless as social-historical sources for the investigation of popular culture. Indeed what becomes clear in them in the first place is the attempts of the local and state, civil as well as church, authorities to control and regulate the Spinnstuben rather than to forbid them. (Similarly, in the reverse-image against which the suppression was directed, can be traced the 'real' elements of the Spinnstuben culture.)

Above all it is apparent that the regulations drawn up by the authorities almost

A Spinnstube (Hans Sebald Beham, 1524)

without exception were aimed at the Spinnstube as a form of autonomous and communal sociability of unmarried youth of both sexes. If the institution could not be stopped, it should at least be controlled. In the place of 'furtive assemblies' and 'suspicious conventicles', such events were to take place only with 'gracious permission' of the 'gracious authorities'. This is the sense of the village ordinance of Herrlingen in Württemberg (near Blaubeuren) from 1587 under the title 'Gunggelhäuser [= Kunkelhäuser, Lichtstuben] und heimbliche conventicula': the

Gunggelhäuser, where namely the young fellows of both sexes run together and where much wanton frivolousness creeps in, should be forbidden for ever, unless the gracious authorities give their gracious permission for them to be held. If a house father holds a *Gunggelhaus*, he should be punished with 1 *rh.fl.* [*Gulden*] and 30 *kr.* [*Kreutzer*]. The young men, however, will receive two days in the tower with bread and water, and the girls the stock. There shall never be secret meetings, suspicious conventicles, and mobs in the houses of the subjects. Offenders will be treated as rioters and rebels and fined or subjected to corporal punishment.[9]

The goal of the numerous ordinances was not only a general, but a very concrete regulation and control of the institution of the Spinnstuben. Above all the unmarried men, and also the married, were to be excluded. The goal was to accomplish a desexualized 'Spinnstube' which would be limited to purely female work and sociability. 'Item no unmarried son or servant could go to the *Kunkel* or *Hofstube*, nor commit a violation with yelling, singing, or throwing stones by fine of 10 shillings. The wives and daughters who gather to spin should be allowed to do so unhindered if they keep still and behave honourably.'[10] The demand for the exclusion of the male population, especially the young men (sons and servants), included not just the visiting of the Spinnstube itself. Often meeting on the way to or from the Spinnstube was also interdicted. In consequence it was also forbidden for the 'unmarried fellows' to hang around in front of the Spinnstube: 'item, the unmarried fellows shall also not stand in front of the *Gunggelhaus* as has happened so often with such excess before'.[11] The demands for the separation of the sexes and the exclusion of the male youth from access to the Spinnstube are central motifs in the regulations and ordinances and demonstrate thereby the frequent contrary practice. It appears that the ordinances are not in the first place concerned with economic interests – namely an interest in increased work discipline and achievement (although this is in no way neglected) – but rather in moral policing or control. At least for the period of the sixteenth and seventeenth centuries, the stress of the rulers' vigilance was less on the work in the Spinnstuben than on the sociability that was specific to them. In the foreground was the concern to prevent immorality and fornication, which were seen as practically necessary consequences of the uncontrolled association of the sexes, especially the 'sneaking around' together of the unmarried youth:

similarly we wish to do away with and forbid the *Kunckelstuben*, in which all kinds of immorality and fornication are carried on, so that if one or the other person in order to save on light wants to hold a *Kunckelstube*, he must inform the magistrates accordingly and if he receives permission must not allow any men, let alone servants or boys, entrance. No house father or mother shall tolerate or allow servants or maids, even their sons, during the day or night to have special secret meeting places or haunts, from which nothing good can come, by strict punishment from the authorities.[12]

What did the sociability of the Spinnstuben look like in detail in the – relatively abstract – perspective of the magisterial regulations and directives concerning moral behaviour? Next to general indications about 'immoral speech', 'unuseful gossip', or 'disorder with annoying discourse, singing of shameful songs, or with drinking and playing games', one finds in detail an exact consideration of the specialities of Spinnstuben sociability. Above all, dancing as a Spinnstuben activity was often criticized, as were, emphasizing the connection with shameless corporeality, such matters as 'touching' and 'holding', 'shameful exposure', and 'shameful tearing about', which accompanied this form of sociability.[13] If one side of the Spinnstuben sociability was the sensual-physical pleasure in dance and play, then the other side – inexorably tied up with it – was the oral–verbal communication through story-telling, song, and joke. It was a question above all of criticism and control of village community life, of the material life of adults, of the passing on of magic and irreligious customs and the holding up of official religion to ridicule and irony. Especially, the sexual culture of the youth received expression in play and merriment, in the form of sexual allusion, suggestion, and crude amusements, above all in jokes, songs, and poems:

nothing else happens but exposing people and destroying their honour. Whatever annoying happens in the community will be gossiped about in the *Kunkelstube*. One sings wanton and immodest songs. One talks immodestly and tears annoyingly about. One dances freshly. One sins: 1. by destroying honour; 2. ridiculing spiritual things, the sermons; 3. singing and discussing immodest things, – playing love pranks, making crude immodest jokes in front of the opposite sex, telling immodest stories about married people. They cook, eat, and drink what they have stolen at home.[14]

Excessive eating and drinking of the youth in the Spinnstube, above all at the cost of the peasant or artisan families from which they came, is another typical point of criticism, whenever it was a question of '*Gunggelhäuser*', 'in which one cooked or otherwise consumed dainties with drinking or in any other manner, by which things are stolen or taken from the masters by the servants'.[15]

Noteworthy here is the all-inclusive, total character of the sociability, which specified the activity of the Spinnstuben and which becomes even clearer in the regulations and directives of the magistrates. 'Pigging' and 'petting' are the categories under which the activities can be grasped, that is in modern German – 'Schmausen und Schmusen'. But also here 'Schmusen' in the older sense of the term – if I may be allowed an excursion into the history of concepts – namely in the sense of 'discussing and talking', played an essential role.[16]

With the often noted and criticized joking–ridiculing communication form of the Spinnstube, whether 'coarse and immodest jokes about the other sex', 'love pranks', or 'ridiculing of spiritual things', the Spinnstube emerges as a central place of the rural plebeian culture of laughter. The playful, often obscene reversal of the everyday to an imagined 'world turned upside down' was a living element of the Spinnstube. The physical-sensual culture of laughter and ridicule of the early modern 'common people', which Mikhail Bakhtin,[17] Natalie Davis,[18] and others[19] have described, with the example of carnival as an extraordinary counter-world, had in the Spinnstube its everyday location. An essential side of this 'world turned upside down' of Spinnstuben sociability was caught by Grimmelshausen when he described in his book, the *Adventures of Simplicissimus*, a dream which the hero had after visiting a Spinnstube:

it appeared to me, so the story went, as if the ox slaughtered the butcher, the deer trapped the hunter, the fish ate the fisherman, the donkey rode the man, the layman preached to the priest, the horse galloped on the rider, the poor laughed at the rich, the peasant made war and the soldier ploughed.

At the same time as quintessence of the experience of the Spinnstube a so-called *Wockenbrief* is cited by Grimmelshausen, i.e. a love pledge from a man to a woman typical of the Spinnstube. It contained the verse: 'Oh, how fine, when the man spins and the wife carries weapons.'[20] Such playfulness in and with the 'upside down world' describes one of the most continuous and stubborn elements of Spinnstuben culture. Still in the eighteenth century, it was present in the villages on the Swabian Alp, that I am studying, in numerous mask and mummery rituals, for example where women dressed as men in the Spinnstuben and then went to dance, or men – in ironic violation of the ordinances – went along to the Spinnstuben dressed as women.

Of course these 'joking relationships' of the Spinnstube can be seen in the first place as a means for the youth to distance themselves from the earnestness of living in the adult world and as a possibility to free themselves for a short time from the burden of everyday-life in an imaginary counter-world. Still this game, especially in its distinction as ritual of ridicule, contains at the same time its earnest, often bitter side. The playful, joking, temporary reversal of the norms of the adult world meant in no way its denial or indeed questioning of everyday relations. To the contrary, exactly in the rituals of ridicule, the role of the Spinnstube as guardian of public morality was displayed. If one emphasizes as in the above citations the 'gossiping about people', 'destroying reputations', 'gossiping about what happens in the community', especially the 'relating of immodest stories about married people' – all as essential elements of the sociability of the Spinnstube – then this points to one central social function of the Spinnstube. With its results of laughter, story-telling, and ridicule, it was not unimportant as a critical forum of the village public and an organ of local, unofficial popular justice.

Of central importance was the role of the Spinnstube above all as one of the places around which the sexual culture of youth concentrated. To this point more will be said later on the basis of sources from the eighteenth century. Still, already in the distorted image of the ordinances of the sixteenth and seventeenth centuries, the Spinnstuben were clearly places for the unfolding of sexuality, sensuality, and emotionality anchored outside the family, whose supporters were above all the age group of the unmarried in the villages. The exclusion from the Spinnstuben of unmarried 'sons and male servants', which was so often repeated, aimed at the suppression of this side of the carrying-on in the Spinnstuben. It attempted to break through the uniquely collective 'regulation of the selection of mates' by the age group of the youth itself, as it was so frequently encountered in the rural-village sphere of European societies from the sixteenth to the nineteenth centuries.[21]

The social kernel of the criticism of the institution of the Spinnstube was oriented not only towards the internal activities of the Spinnstube itself but above all towards its function inside the more inclusive customs of courtship and the choosing of partners. The relatively autonomous Spinnstuben, which were subject to little family control, put the whole village marriage system in question – a marriage system which was tied to inheritance and landholding and the maintenance of homogeneous classes. This is clear in the following citation: 'often in such gatherings the daughters are led astray from their parents and talked into unfitting marriages behind their fathers, sometimes even seduced and brought to shame.'[22] Such a custom posed, therefore, a 'moral danger' in so far as the control of the family and kinship system through the village marriage market was put into danger. Thereby the class-endogamy of the village upper class was put into question – and therefore the basis of its domination. These relationships are to be seen above all in the reversed image of the moralized Spinnstuben, licensed and reformed by the rulers, which the regulations outlined and thought to establish, which set the activities of the younger generation under a double control: 1) the occasional observation of the church or civil village magistrates, 2) the permanent management of the 'honourable' house father, house mother, or neighbour.

Simply excluding the unmarried men was not considered sufficient. Even the purely female gathering was believed to be sinful to excess, although the girls themselves could discover no sins:

the immodest wantonness which the girls carry on among themselves, they do not consider to be sinful, although they are much more dreadful sins because they occur among a single sex . . .

Therefore the magistrates should destroy the *Gunkel-Häuser*, even those of one sex, for they are often the most annoying, because the sin which cries to heaven is greater than other sins. Such places are a destruction of the youth, especially of the female sex, a plague of immodesty, destroyer of good morality, a school of coquetry, an enemy of honour, a den of vice, the favourite dwelling place of the devil . . . Because a house father or house mother is responsible in his or her conscience to keep the children and servants from wicked occasions and to keep them as much as possible under the eye, I cannot see how they can let their charges run around in the *Gunkel-Häuser* without committing a sin, especially as the children are in quite apparent danger of seduction, as experience teaches.

Many a house mother should ponder what she saw and heard in such assemblies when she was young.[23]

This radical pastoral suggestion is not the normal case, although it clarifies the attitude which most often determines the regulation of the institution: the Spinnstube and its social activities were to be, so to speak, moralized and domesticated, and thereby embedded in the family. At best it was to take place in a form which went beyond the family if it was kept in bounds by neighbourhood and always under the rule of the house fathers and mothers:

when honourable people and their children or servants, especially to save on wood and light, or otherwise out of good friendship, wish to go to their neighbours or good friends with their spinning and other work, then they should not be prevented, but they remain responsible to see that all frivolous games, obscene words, and unprofitable songs, and the like are avoided.[24]

In a particularly pure form, this tendency towards 'familiarizing' the Spinnstube under the impetus of the magistrates, which goes right through the ordinances of the sixteenth and seventeeth centuries, appears in a later edict of the Würzburg bishop in the eighteenth century:

from the general ordinance [against Spinnstuben] we exclude only assemblies of such close blood relations, where unmarried sisters and sisters-in-law, sister's or brother's children, in the houses of their father's or mother's brother or father's or mother's sister come together with their work. With such an assembly, the form and disadvantages of a Spinnstube would be missing. However, we trust that when parents – either out of negligence or because they are hindered in some way – cannot accompany their children there and back, then some other close relatives will do so.[25]

Thus, as viewed from above, the Spinnstube and its social activity was above all to be moralized and domesticated by becoming familial.

The chief direction of the criticism of the institution of the Spinnstube during the sixteenth and seventeenth centuries dealt with the 'free time' of the evening after work was done and was concerned in the first place with the socio-cultural reproduction of village life. On the one hand, one can see in it a magisterial, moral police concept which was concerned above all with the premarital 'intercourse' of the sexes, and its integration into the framework of family, kinship, and neighbourhood. In close connection with this there was the desire to tame the sensual and physical popular cultural forms and expressions of this 'intercourse'. On the other hand, the frequent mention of practices which were in contradiction to these notions shows how deeply they were rooted in youth culture and how tough the resistance to state attempts to control them. This led in the eighteenth century to 'enlightened' compromises, which will be discussed below. It is important to understand that the moral police perspective was not the only point of reference of the criticism of the Spinnstuben. There seems also to be in the early phase during the sixteenth and seventeenth centuries a direct economic interest in work discipline and productivity. This had great importance even if it was not the crucial point.

But here it is also important to be specific about region. In the Southwest German regulations since the sixteenth century, there are only very general warnings about work discipline, for example in the form, 'that one [in the Spinnstube] should devote oneself only to work and avoid all dancing, playing, and cheeky songs'.[26] On the contrary, there are no standards or proposals about concrete work performance in a particular unit of time (as so much spun thread in an evening or week). Totally different is the situation for the East Elbian territories based on *Gutsherrschaft*. Here feudal work obligations up to the seventeenth and eighteenth centuries continued to affect the Spinnstube. Above all members of the servant class who stood in unfree relationship of forced labour were obligated to carry out specific work in the Spinnstube. In a milder form this was valid also for the youth who were not obligated for services, at least in the eighteenth century. This is to be seen clearly in a contemporary report from Upper Lusatia around 1700, 'On Amusements, Delights, and Games amongst the Wends':

thereby the children and servants both have their certain times to spin, since they have to spin during the evenings. They begin on St Burckhard's Day [11 October] and continue on to Wednesday before Maundy Thursday. On both sides special customs are usual . . . On the last Wednesday, the spinners all bring a little brandy for a farewell party. Some of them take a broom and knock out the lights by which they are supposed to spin. The amount that the maids are supposed to spin from St Burckhard's to St Martin's are 10 skeins fine yarn, or 8 of medium quality or 6 of coarse. During one winter day and evening together, they spin 2 haspels fine or medium all measured according to the long reel. Since the servants and others who join together think that they can accomplish their portion with more pleasure if they are together in good society, they go at times to the neighbours or other houses. There are also 'Rockenstuben' where many young people assemble. Because quite often wicked and wanton things take place, such Spinnstuben and *Rockenstuben* were forbidden in the year 1677.[27]

These obligations to spin – and this is important – were not bound to participation in the Spinnstube. It was not the Spinnstube as such that brought the obligations. These resulted rather from the relations of dependence and force inside the households of the 'Gutsherren' or peasants.

In the rural territories of Northwest Germany, the custom of the Spinnstube also appears to have been bound up more with work obligations than was the case in the German Southwest. The obligations of servants to spin a certain amount for their masters (*Zahlspinnen*) were to a large extent fulfilled in the Spinnstuben. How far the non-familial 'great Spinnstuben' predominated over a form strongly integrated into the large peasant household, whose idyllic ideal Justus Möser pictured in his essay, 'Die Spinnstube. Eine Osnabrückische Geschichte',[28] must be more closely investigated. In any event in the North German area, and not only there, there was a clear connection of Spinnstuben work and sociability with the intensification of rural commodity production in textiles since the seventeenth century. This can be explained by the fact that the work-intensive hand-spinning of flax increasingly became the crucial bottleneck for the expansion of proto-industrial commodity production of textiles in the face of the great rise in overseas demand for linen cloth. Along with the increased cost of the spinning work of the youth age groups, there went an expansion of the 'free' area of Spinnstuben sociability and a correspondingly increased intensity of this sociability.[29]

That this development was not restricted to the Northwest German area can be seen from a Spinnstuben ordinance from Württemberg at the beginning of the eighteenth century (1727),[30] according to which 'unmarried males', although in general to be excluded from the Spinnstube, 'were excepted from the ordinance in such places where males also spin'. There, in places of proto-industrial spinning, the male youth were to be conceded their own Spinnstube, still to be kept separate from that of the women.

In what direction did the Spinnstuben develop in the eighteenth century, the period of mercantilist policy, of manufacturers and enlightenment? First a short description of the change of the magisterial discourse over the Spinnstube will be given. The picture of the Spinnstube here (1727),[31] which belonged to the wool manufactory of the count of Waldstein at Oberleutensdorf in Bohemia, demonstrates certainly an extreme case, which cannot be generalized. It is not a question of a 'domesticated' or 'familiarized' Spinnstube. Certainly it is not one of the eighteenth-century ones which were indeed under control but still relatively autonomous, in which the youth themselves set the tone. Noticeable is the complete separation of work from sociability, as was enforced by a Bohemian feudal lord and great land owner on the basis of supervised production processes

of a model manufactory. Such a separation of working processes from sociability in the context of manufactures remained a great exception even in the period of proto-industrial expansion as experienced in textile production during the eighteenth century, especially in spinning. Before the invention of mechanical spinning machines, household-industrial activity predominated and was at least in many regions supplemented to a considerable extent by the work of the Spinnstube. Although the picture is neither representative for the working processes of spinning nor for the development of the Spinnstube itself, it remains interesting for a social-iconographic and social-historical perspective. It demonstrates in the use of the word 'Spinnstuben' for the productive relationship of the new manufactures a generally changed view and interest by which the authorities now perceived the Spinnstube in the village. This was especially so because it was apparent to the interested observer that in fact the collective forms of intercourse of both sexes in the Spinnstube brought with it a kind of social self-control and self-censure, which perhaps was more effective than open police control from above: 'the larger social grouping has everywhere the same effect; in the Spinnstuben as in the large balls in the city, it opposes immorality.'[32] In contrast to the finer norms of city taste and city morality, the pleasures of the Spinnstuben of the rural population might appear indeed as 'rude'. Still what was earlier considered as immoral appeared now only as mere 'inconveniences' and had some claim for understanding. For its enlightened and economically thinking supporters, the Spinnstuben pleasures of the rural young seemed a compensation for a hard and arduous life of work and was therefore in a certain way a necessary 'gift':

the pleasures of the rural people must be ruder, to a certain degree, just as the rural people themselves are ruder than other classes of people. Otherwise the pleasures would have no attraction for them, would be no pleasure at all. And certainly no one would wish that the few remaining pleasures be legally taken away or limited . . . One could maintain that innocence is like the stomach; certainly not the best one is brought into disorder by the smallest excess.[33]

In most German regions during the eighteenth century, the church criticism of the institution of the Spinnstuben continued unabated. The practice of civil as well as church authorities in the control, regulation, and supervision remained. However, the Spinnstube now found its 'enlightened' advocates in the officials and publicists.[34] These defenders of mercantile performance discovered the economic usefulness and productivity of the specific forms of sociability and 'merriment' of the Spinnstube. The special connection between work and 'free time' appeared to offer advantages especially as over against the tiring work inside household and family. What was earlier seen as immoral was not now unconditionally moral. Still it was seen as a custom which the ancestors wisely established, because it was useful for national industry:

I could show from the oldest spinning songs and traditions most convincingly that the merriments [of the Spinnstube] rooted in the tastes of the rural folk were originally connected by our wise forefathers with this kind of spinning, and that it chiefly caused the spinning of thread to become the most widespread and continuous manufacture, indeed a real national industry.[35]

The defenders of the institution of Spinnstuben did not content themselves with such global evaluations. Their interests and sharp glance went right into the Spinnstube and valued exactly what had been traditionally disvalued by the magistrates, namely the gathering of both sexes in the Spinnstube and the competition of the women in terms of the village marriage market as a motive which could be used for the national economy:

further, the following grounds appear to counsel the maintenance of the Spinnstuben. It encourages work in a large society of compeers, especially when many young males are there to cast a watchful eye on the industry and quickness of the girls, who would be their future wives. This is much better than when a girl spins alone with her mother or sister.[36]

Always under the supposition that the Spinnstube stood under the sensible leadership of a house father or mother, the traditional moral scruples in comparison to the economic advantages, at least for a minority of observers, no longer weighed so heavily in the scale. What seems especially noteworthy is that the majority of moral police critics of the institution of the Spinnstube also went over increasingly to economic arguments.[37] For them, however, the Spinnstube appeared not so much as an economically useful pastime but rather as a loser of time, which instead of spurring on work only led to unuseful expenditures such as developed from a tendency for 'nosh'. For these critics such activities could only be controlled by getting rid of public work sociability of the youth and by concentrating the work from the Spinnstuben in household and family.

In the face of such efforts at domestication and familiarization, the question about the effectiveness of magisterial control of the institution of Spinnstube must be raised. Above all one should ask about the internal life, the capability of opposition, and the changes in the practice of sociability, work and merriment, as they were bound together with the village Spinnstube. An answer here is only possible through intensive local and regional studies. Two regional examples from the eighteenth century which I want to go into show how limited the attempt to regulate on the part of the magistrates was, how little enlightened economic discourse affected the events in the Spinnstube.

In Southwest Germany in the territory of the Duchy of Württemberg, there existed strict ordinances and regulations over the Spinnstuben which were repeatedly renewed in the eighteenth century.[38] Still they did not correspond completely to the practice at the level of the village. There, separate Spinnstuben for the youth of both sexes alongside forms of familial and neighbourhood Spinnstuben were allowed. The overwhelmingly largest part of the village participants was composed of unmarried youth of the female sex. In places of intensive rural textile production, the corresponding form of male gatherings existed, but were never so important in terms of numbers. All Spinnstuben or *Lichtstuben* were under the supervision of a respectable 'Licht' man (*Lichtherr*)

A Spinnstube in the eighteenth century[39]

and he was responsible to the village morals-court (the church consistory). For all participants of the Spinnstuben and *Lichtstuben* as well as for the *Lichtherr*, a strict obligation of registration existed. This regulation of the institution of the Spinnstuben, however, did not get in the way of the traditional, customary association of both sexes with each other, as the many fines levied by the courts show. The appearance of the male village youth at the Spinnstube of the women, at least for a short time during the evening (usually between 9 and 10 at night) was a usual practice. Here the rules of the 'game of the sexes' were determined very strongly by the women present, and not, as is often supposed, exclusively or even to a large extent by the men of the village.

A case such as that of the weaver journeyman, Conrad Hügel, from the village mentioned at the beginning, Laichingen, throws a distinguishing light on the social rules of play in Spinnstuben activities. On 28 November 1759 at 11.30 p.m., at a visit of one of the numerous Spinnstuben, Hügel was beaten so badly that he was only out of danger of dying after twenty-one days. He was beaten by all of the women present with their distaffs. What happened was that Hügel transgressed the 'honour' of the assembled female company. He reported in the village over the custom of dancing of some of the women in the Spinnstube. The violence occurred when he attempted to 'sit by' one of the women against her will – i.e. in the meaning of the term 'sit by' (*vorzusitzen*): by custom to joke – and physically flirt with her. The contemptuous reaction of the young man to his rejection by the girl and his refusal to pay for a spindle broken in the exchange, provoked the collective female counter-violence. It was claimed by the women that their reaction was their 'good right', and in the face of the painful consequences they simply noted: 'they should have injured him even more'.[40]

A relatively autonomous development of the institution of the Spinnstube in the course of the eighteenth century can be seen above all in those regions and localities of Württemberg in which a labour-intensive mode of production with a correspondingly high demand for the labour of unmarried youth took a central place in the village social economy. This was the case in areas with partible inheritance. One increased area for the labour of the youth could be rural household industries (for example, weaving) but also certain forms of labour-intensive agriculture, as, for example, viniculture, as well. In such situations the 'marriage system of parental authority' was not the rule as in single son inheritance areas, nor were the lines of class so sharply drawn between the different strata of the village. Especially in periods of a rising demand for labour as took place in household industries and agriculture since the second half of the eighteenth century, the youth enjoyed an increased autonomy in the everyday life of the village.[41]

The second example comes from the territory of the bishop of Würzburg. Here Spinnstuben since 1783 – with the exception of a remnant form reduced to family and relatives – were completely forbidden.[42] The ordinance, labelled by such enlightenment publicists as the Göttingen professor Schlözer as 'Industrieverbot', provoked a call on the part of these publicists several years later for an investigation – a kind of *enquête*.[43] It demonstrated not only the complete lack of effect of the magistrates' measures, but also showed a surprising multiplicity of regional Spinnstuben institutions, this especially in the economically backward areas of the Rhön-mountains in Franconia. Written from the perspective of participant observation, the reports offer interesting insights into the life of the

Spinnstube itself. Beyond they allow clarity over the practical goals of the
enlightened 'doctors of the popular mind' and publicists. The latter were actively
engaged in the observation of the life of rural society, coupling this, however, with
new interests in domination. They wished to use the old forms of sociability as
instruments for establishing their own 'enlightened' notions of education: 'I see the
Lichtstube as the most wonderful institution for leading the rustic out of the animal
kingdom into the realm of rational being and by which he can be reformed into the
most lovely class of all mankind.'[44] To return to the empirical side of the investigations, what is apparent is the diversity in social composition and ways of passing
time of the 'winter socials of the rural people'. Alongside the Spinnstuben of the
unmarried girls and boys, corresponding social 'customs' of the married, adult
males and females were described:

> it [the *Lichtstube*] is there where it was established, and so far as I know it, was almost
> always composed this way: young men, girls, mostly of the same age, married men, seldom
> wives, gather together in groups of six, eight, twelve or more every evening, especially in
> the winter at the home of a third neighbour or neighbour woman, whom they have
> selected as their friend. Right after supper the gatherings begin and last until 10
> p.m.[45]

Also afternoon meetings of unmarried and married women (with a preponder-
ance of unmarried) were mentioned, as well as similar meetings of men. They
were then continued into the evening. This indication of differential composition
of *Lichtstuben* according to age classes does not give any information about their
specific activities and forms of sociability or about their everyday social and
economic functions. However, these were described in quite some detail.

Alongside other customs and practices, the 'social economy' of work in female
Spinnstuben was closely observed. Clear is the astonishment of one of the
enlightened observers who had hoped for a market-oriented, commodity-
producing industriousness of the Spinnstuben, but who made, however, a
notable discovery. For in the peasant villages of this region of Germany, which
were not yet characterized by capitalist market relationships – and where the
investigation concentrated – neither the demands of the market nor the demands
of the rulers gave form or impetus to the rhythm of production of linen thread.
What specified production in the Spinnstube was the nature of the village
marriage market. It provided the necessary coercion to gather a trousseau or
Brautschatz, which at least in part was not the result of individual personal work
of the members of the Spinnstube but came through social exchange of bridal
gifts among themselves at the occasion of a marriage:

> most busy are the people in these gatherings [i.e. Spinnstuben] when a girl in the village
> plans to marry. Here the girls arrange among themselves how much flax each will
> contribute in order to make a gift called the *Brautrocken*, to the bride. If the girl married
> outside the village, then the *Brautrocken* is to be seen at the top of the bridal wagon with
> ribbons streaming from it. Everyone watches when such a wagon passes by. From the size

of the *Brautrocken* everyone can conclude how much the bride is esteemed by the corps of girls.[46]

This example demonstrates more than it seems at first glance: the reputation which the unmarried girl won in the circle of her comrades in the Spinnstube had an influence on her future life, even after the marriage. It was translated into the material contribution of spun thread which the Spinnstube made to her trousseau (*Brautschatz*). This contribution was not only material but to a high degree also of a symbolic-moral character. It established a mutual exchange relationship among the members of the Spinnstube. It was produced at every marriage. That, which at least for actual use any individual could have produced, increased by its detour over the 'social division of labour' the solidarity of the Spinnstuben community of women. In each *Brautrocken* the competence of the Spinnstube as a collective morals court was brought to expression and given renewed force. Towards the outside the collective contribution of work which was incorporated in the *Brautrocken* described a kind of 'symbolic capital' (Bourdieu), over which the respective members of the Spinnstube disposed in the village public. The greater or smaller the *Brautrocken*, the greater or smaller the honour of the bride. Accordingly, the size of the *Brautrocken* determined her social esteem inside the village public.

The work contribution of different male age groups in the Spinnstube was not subject to the same social constraints and is correspondingly estimated as small. For the married men non-work was tacitly acknowledged. Only for them was the evening clearly free and recognized as free from work. Contrariwise non-work of the young men in the Spinnstuben was not so self-evident. It is mentioned – although from outside observers – and at the same time disapproved. In this, there was a clear distinction between the occasional afternoon Spinnstuben, in which the lads could clearly be seen with the knitting needles in their hands, and the evening gatherings, which for them – corresponding to the example of the adult males – were not the occasion for work but always the 'occasion for idleness'.[47]

It was only for the married women that the evening sociability of the Spinnstube was frequently – though not in principle – put into question due to the drudgery of work: the lack of time because of work in the house even in the evenings is given as one reason which hindered their regular participation in the *Lichtstube*. The other was the power relations in the family:

the *Lichstuben* of the married women are more seldom, because the time is just not enough for them, and during the evenings they still have many tasks in the house, the care of the children, etc. When these tasks are finished, they then take their rest in order to build up new energy for the next day. Also the jealousy of the men when their faithful partners leave the four walls, causes them to look askance at the possibility.[48]

The central point of free evening sociability of married men and women is the exchange of information and the discussion over problems and objects of daily life, although with clear differences according to sex. Among the women the exchange over everyday problems of the household economy and the censuring and settling of village conflicts were in the forefront. In addition the acknowledgement of fear and superstition, which worked on the individual with anxiety and distress, played a role, but through common 'consultation' such matters were relativized, alleviated, and endured:

one talked intimately of one's babies, of a cousin, of a neighbour, of flax, spinning; of geese, ducks, chickens, and eggs; of making cheese and butter, and probably had a word about blue milk, a dried up cow, caused by a wicked neighbour.

Many a stone, which lay heavy and long on the heart, would be lifted at the discussion of this topic, and unexpected freedom would enter the good heart through comforting, through reliable experience, interpretation, explanation, and expertise of the many women present, and the assembly would be closed in rapture.[49]

With the men, alongside discussion over agriculture and experiences of village everyday life, the centre of discussion was composed of reasoning, especially when politics came under consideration and the interest extended out from the village:

if a stranger comes travelling through, he will generally show up to the Spinnstube in order to share his store of novelties, and if a newspaper reader came from the village into the room, he was hardly allowed to catch his breath. Even if he did not bring the newspaper with him to read out loud, he had to describe the latest events in exact details. If one or the other neighbour knew something, he brought it up as well and now began the glossating, reasoning, and prognosticating over the latest marvels. Indeed the most wonderful things were to be heard there. With not a little pleasure, I used to listen to these disputations, and I must say, clearly, that I was often astonished over much of the reasoning of the simple peasant, and often profited more from such disputations of the unlearned than from those of academics.[50]

According to the impression which comes from these exact descriptions of contemporaries, the evening gathering in Spinnstuben of adults took place in a strictly isolated, sex-specific sociability. Dramatic high points came by chance, especially from reports over the outside world which were brought in by the stranger or the newspaper. The meetings were always ended early because of the exhaustion of the participants.

The youth met in a completely different style. Their meetings drew their tension right from the beginning from the 'play between the two sexes'. Already in the early part of the evening in those Spinnstuben, in which girls and boys gathered separately, the expectation and the knowledge of the later coming together determined the contents and the rhythm of the sociability. Here there were specific differences between both sexes. The social forms of the female Spinnstube were not hierarchical. 'In these assemblies there is simply no order of rank.'[51] The sociability is determined at the beginning by the work of spinning and the exchange over 'matters of family and village'. Later, songs and traditional stories take over. Always the conversation is stamped by the expectation of the coming gathering. The social activity of the boys in the course of the evening involved two quite distinct phases. It began with a so-called

'Gunckel', the meeting of a set group of male youth, which would be held with the 'greatest regularity'. In contrast to the female equivalent, the forms of intercourse here were distinctly hierarchical and determined by the rigorous subjection of the younger to the older: 'the strictest subordination takès place'. The important function of the preparation and organization of festivals and parades of the village was only occasionally the chief activity of the *Gunckel*. Their everyday sociability can be described at least in the early phase of the evening as an attempt at a collective copying of the modes of behaviour of the married adults, from smoking and playing cards to reasoning, politicking, and reading aloud the newspaper. Relatively early in the evening the *Gunckel* breaks up into smaller groups. With considerable detour one ends up 'after a great deal of mischief' at the female Spinnstube. The written and unwritten laws of the 'Gunckel' forbid male youth the individual penetration into the female Spinnstube. As with the girls, so with the boys, a strong collective morality prevailed. This has been passed down allegorically in a Spinnstuben ordinance,[52] not written by the authorities, in which the female Spinnstuben was spoken of as the 'common pasture', to which it was forbidden to go secretly and individually. The rights and obligations to the 'common pasture' could indeed be exercised individually – the going together of pairs – but had to be arranged collectively beforehand: 'no one should hanker after going to the common pasture ... They [the youth] should not go secretly to the Spinnstuben and lurk around but go publicly and talk with people and carry the spindles of the maidens.'[53] Given this arrangement of male access to the family Spinnstuben from one of the infrequent ordinances of the youth collectivity, the question arises over the concrete course of events: how did the high point of the evening Spinnstube look from both sides – male and female? Here only the perspective of contemporary observers can help us, not that of the participants themselves:

the girls bring their work to the lord of the Spinnstube, their spinning wheels, knitting needles as well as their news, love stories, anecdotes about dances and other matters. There will be knitting, spinning, laughing, teasing, and telling stories, all waiting longingly for the appearance of the courtiers, and then the game will begin all over again.

The young boys take care not to forget their store of jokes, their cards, and their smoking pipes. When these fellows find themselves together in their own company, they smoke and play cards and pack out their store of jokes, drollities, and satires for a while according to their abilities. After a time one or the other or a couple of close friends gets the desire to get something tasty to eat. They wander away without particularly saying good-bye from what has become a rather boring, monotonous group, stroll up and down the streets getting into mischief, and make their visit finally to the fair sex. Above all they make the rounds, i.e. they go on shanks's mare to every *Lichtstuben* of the girls, or make a small visit of state, or for a change just drop in for a minute. Finally they end up at the place where their Dulcinea longs impatiently for them. Now they stay until the end of the assembly, using up the rest of their bag of tricks, completely ready for conversation. By chance the rogue lifts the distaff of the merry, familiar beauty, who answers him for his craftiness with a loud smacking kiss.

Probably there are several dirty *double entendres* or one allows himself a few other liberties – for a change. Finally each gallant accompanies his beauty to her father's house, at times also a step further – in all stillness and honour – and thus the lively society breaks up.[54]

If this testimony of enlightened observations in comparison to the moral police prejudice of the pastoral or magisterial critique – as we have met them – brings us more knowledge, still these observations did not take place without hidden meaning. The interest of enlightened figures in the events of the Spinnstube was in no way that of unprejudiced participants or that of an encounter with 'otherness'. The social, sensual, and emotional coherence of the Spinnstube was first and foremost considered as 'the great fulcrum . . . the broad military road . . . the most wonderful institution, whereby the rustic could be reformed and brought out of the animal kingdom into the realm of rational being'. The observer hoped – as he stressed – 'without force' to be able to exploit the curiosity of the rustics for the book. With help of the magic qualities, which were still imputed to the book as to its reader in a milieu predominantly composed of illiterates, he wanted to lure the Spinnstuben participants into travelling the same path which was already marked by the moral and industrial police of the mercantilist state and by the 'morality' of developing bourgeois society. At the end of this 'morality', however, stood – as was admitted – 'the pure source of the economy'.[55]

First one speaks to him in his own language and then one initiates him into the learned language of writing. At the very beginning one brings books into the *Lichtstuben* of the girls and boys for pure entertainment, for fun and satire. One would give them, for example, a comedy, for they compose and play comedies worse than any – or something similar. Even if it just brings a belly laugh, if it will only entertain and contain nothing too destructive, it can act as a bait to cause them to develop a taste for the exquisite riches of ideas which they do not know about and to bring them without noticing away from purely sentient views. If the beginning succeeds and their curiosity is raised, then one can bring in morality. They will then seek the useful for themselves – and find it by themselves.[56]

These examples go beyond a mere answer to the question of the efficacy or inefficacy of magisterial control of Spinnstuben customs in the eighteenth century. They afford us a look into the strange world of the social-moral economy of the rural-village society of the eighteenth century. Just as work, free time, and sociability were so little divided one from another, so were culture, morality, and economy. Still it would be false, I think, to see in the all-inclusive character of this mode of life the historical utopia of a unity now lost of reason, emotion, and action. This slice out of the world of early modern popular culture as it can be seen in the custom of the Spinnstube should not be considered with a hasty and uncritical longing for a healthier world. Instead of a romanticization and idealization of the past, one should pause to consider that sensuality, boisterousness, and serenity in popular cultural life always went together with a rigorous and violent social-moral control and – what is perhaps more important – with permanent insecurity of life and with want.

NOTES

1 The older German literature: K. A. Barrack, 'Die Spinnstube nach Geschichte und Sage', *Zeitschrift für deutsche Kulturgeschichte*, 4 (1859), 36–69; C. Wendeler's Section on 'Kunkel-oder Rockenstuben', in his 'Zu Fischarts Bildergeschichten', *Archiv für Literaturgeschichte*, 7 (1878), 332–60; more recent works: A. Nägele, 'Schwäbische Kunkelstuben. Ihr Brauchtum und ihre Bekämpfung. Ein Beitrag zur Geschichte des Bauerntums', *Volk und Volkstum. Jahrbuch für Volkskunde*, 3 (1938), 92–120; H. Sonrey and H. Schröder, *Der Spinntrupp im deutschen Volkstum* (Berlin, 1939); an interesting ethnographic description of the comparable custom of *Stickhütten* and *Spinnhütten* in the Balkans and in Hungary is B. Genda, 'Arbeitshütten auf der Balkanhalbinsel', in B. Genda, *Ethnographica Carpatho-Balcanica* (Budapest, 1979), 269–87; the most interesting recent analysis of a regional Spinnstuben custom is to be found in Rudolf Braun's classic: *Industrialisierung und Volksleben. Veränderungen der Lebensformen unter Einwirkung der verlagsindustriellen Heimarbeit in einem ländlichen Industriegebiet (Zürcher Oberland) vor 1800*, 2nd edn (Göttingen, 1979), 119ff, 128ff. A short but good synthesis is to be found in E. Shorter, *The Making of the Modern Family* (New York, 1975), 124ff.

2 A good example is O. Böckel, *Psychologie der Volksdichtung*, 2nd edn (Leipzig, 1913), 126ff, but also Sonrey and Schröder, *Der Spinntrupp im deutschen Volkstum*.

3 S. Musiat, 'Zur sozialen Struktur der obersorbischen Spinnstube', *Zeitschrift für Slawistik*, 8 (1963), 259–68.

4 The rooting of the Spinnstube in youth-sexual culture and customs of courtship is analysed in the pioneer study: K. R. V. Wikman, *Die Einleitung der Ehe. Eine vergleichende ethno-soziologische Untersuchung über die Vorstufe der Ehe in den Sitten des schwedischen Volkstums*, Acta Academiae Abonensis, vol. 11, 1 (Abo, 1937).

5 K. Bücher, *Arbeit und Rythmus*, 6th edn (Leipzig, 1924), 92.

6 M. Schurr, *Konferenzaufsatz Laichingen 1909*, Archiv der Württembergischen Landesstelle für Volkskunde, Stuttgart.

7 Reprinted with the kind permission of the Germanisches Nationalmuseum, Nuremberg.

8 Sonrey and Schröder, *Der Spinntrupp im deutschen Volkstum*, 127ff; Nägele, 'Schwäbische Kunkelstuben', 101ff. A very rich source, not only on Spinnstuben, but also for other fields of rural everyday life in the small territories and principalities of South West Germany during the early modern period up to the eighteenth century is: W. Wintterlin (ed.), *Württembergische ländliche Rechtsquellen*, 3 vols. (Stuttgart, 1910–41).

9 Wintterlin, *Württembergische ländliche Rechtsquellen*, vol. 2, 918.

10 *Ibid.*, vol. 3, 154.

11 *Ibid.*, vol. 3, 36.

12 *Ibid.*, vol. 1, 525.

13 *Ibid.*, vol. 3, 36, 366, vol. 1, 444, vol. 3, 303, vol. 2, 917, vol. 3, 210.

14 'Aus einem alten alemannischen Gebets- und Erbauungsbüchlein' (seventeenth and eighteenth centuries), as quoted in A. Birlinger, *Aus Schwaben. Sagen Legenden, Aberglaube, Sitten, Rechtsbräuche*, vol. 2 (Wiesbaden, 1874), 360f.

15 Wintterlin, *Württembergische ländliche Rechtsquellen*, vol. 3, 296.

16 See J. and W. Grimm (eds.) *Deutsches Wörterbuch*, vol. 9 under 'Schmus, Schmusen'; H. Fischer, *Schwäbisches Wörterbuch*, vol. 5 (Tubingen, 1920) under 'Schmuse'.

17 M. Bakhtin, *Rabelais and his World* (Cambridge, Mass, London, 1968).

18 N. Davis, 'The Reasons of Misrule', in N. Davis, *Society and Culture in Early Modern France* (London, 1975), 97–123.

19 One of the most recent studies: B. Scribner, 'Reformation, Carnival and the World Turned Upside Down', *Social History*, 3 (1978), 303–31.

20 Quoted from the *Adventures of Simplicissimus* in Sonrey and Schröder, *Der Spinntrupp im deutschen Volkstum*, 82f.

21 On this see Wikman, *Die Einleitung der Ehe*, esp. chap. 12, 369ff.

22 *Vernewte Policeyordnung* (Rath der Stadt Nürnberg), 1572, as quoted in Barrack, 'Die Spinnstube', 65.

23 'Aus einem alten alemannischen Gebets- und Erbauungsbüchlein', as quoted in Birlinger, *Aus Schwaben*, vol. 2, 360f.

24 *Policey Ordnung Christian Marggraffens zu Brandenburg. Zu dero Land und Fürstenthum Burggraffthums Nürmberg 1622*, art. 12 as quoted in Barrack, 'Die Spinnstube', 67.

25 *Verbot der 'Nächtlichen Spinn- und Rockenstuben' durch Franz Ludwig, Bischof zu Bamberg und Würzburg v. 13.11.1783*, reprinted in A. L. Schlözer, *Stats-Anzeigen*, 4, 14 (Göttingen, 1783), 215–17, here 217.

26 Wintterlin, *Württembergische ländliche Rechtsquellen*, vol. 3, 331, 608.

27 A. Frenzel, 'Von der Wenden Lustbarkeit, Ergötzung und Spielen', MS. quoted in Musiat, 'Zur sozialen Struktur der obersorbischen Spinnstube', 260f.

28 J. Möser, 'Die Spinnstube. Eine osnabrückische Geschichte', in J. Moser, *Sämtliche Werke*, vol. 4 (Oldenburg-Berlin 1943), 42–52.

29 On this see the essays from the *Hannoverisches Magazin* quoted below.

30 *Württembergisches Spinnstubenreskript* from 1727, Hauptstaatsarchiv Stuttgart.

31 Reprinted with the kind permission of the Deutsches Museum, Munich. On the historical and economic context see H. Freudenberger, *The Waldstein Woolen Mill: Noble Entrepreneurship in Eighteenth Century Bohemia*, The Kress Library of Business and Economics, vol. 18 (Boston, Mass., 1963), 24f.

32 Anon., 'Über die Spinnstuben auf den Dörfern in hiesigen Landen', *Hannoverisches Magazin*, 96 (Nov. 1790), 1522–6, here 1524.

33 *Ibid.*, 1523f.

34 Most interesting on this is a controversy in the *Hannoverisches Magazin* since 1790: Anon., 'Über die Spinnstuben' (as quoted in n32); A. E. Münchmeyer (Pastor), 'Gegen die Spinnstuben', *ibid.*, 96 (Dec. 1793), 1522–32; Anon., 'Noch etwas gegen die Spinnstuben', *Neues Hannöverisches Magazin*, 29 (Apr. 1794), 460–4; H. Goldmann (*Oberverwalter*), 'Über die Spinnstuben', *ibid.*, 61 (Aug. 1794), 962–84.

35 Anon., 'Über die Spinnstuben auf den Dörfern', 1522f.

36 *Ibid.*, 1525f.

37 Cf. Münchmeyer (Pastor), 'Gegen die Spinnstuben', 1525ff.

38 See Nägele, 'Schwäbische Kunkelstuben', *passim*.

39 Reprinted by kind permission of the Germanisches Nationalmuseum Nuremberg. 1759, 18 Dec. 1759, 2 Jan. 1760, 48–57.

40 *Amstprotokolle Laichingen*, vol. 1756–1968, under the dates 29 Nov. 1959, 17 Dec.

41 See the related arguments by David Sabean in his two articles: 'Intensivierung der Arbeit und Alltagserfahrung auf dem Lande – ein Beispiel aus Württemberg', *Sozialwissenschaftliche Informationen für Unterricht und Studium*, 6 (Oct. 1977), 148–52; 'Unehelichkeit: ein Aspekt sozialer Reproduktion kleinbäuerlicher Produzenten. Zu einer Analyse dörflicher Quellen um 1800', in R. Berdahl *et al.* (eds.), *Klassen und Kultur. Sozialanthropologische Perspektiven in der Geschichtsschreibung* (Frankfurt, 1982), 54–73.

42 See above n25.

43 Anon., 'Über die Spinnstuben im Wirzburgischen', *Der Fränkische Merkur*, 2 (1795), 598f; Anon., 'Das gesellschaftliche Leben der Landleute in den Rhön-Gegenden die

Wintermonate hindurch', *ibid.*, 5 (1798), 958–75; Anon., 'Die Lichtstube', *ibid.*, 6 (1799), 1583–95, 1617–26.
44 Anon., 'Die Lichtstube', 1620.
45 *Ibid.*, 1585.
46 Anon., 'Das gesellschaftliche Leben der Landleute', 963f.
47 *Ibid.*, 966.
48 Anon., 'Die Lichtstube', 1587.
49 *Ibid.*, 1588.
50 Anon., 'Das gesellschaftliche Leben der Landleute', 966.
51 *Ibid.*, 962.
52 Reprinted, *ibid.*, 971ff.
53 *Ibid.*, 973.
54 Anon., 'Die Lichtstube', 1585f.
55 *Ibid.*, 1627.
56 *Ibid.*, 1625f.

15. Family fun in Starve Harbour : custom, history, and confrontation in village Newfoundland

GERALD M. SIDER

There was a proverb more often used than any other, of which I must either believe it spoilt by misquotation or else confess myself too dull to perceive its force: 'We must live in hopes, supposing we die in despair.'

> Reverend Julian Moreton, *Church of England Missionary to Greenspond, Bonavista Bay, Newfoundland, 1850–63*[1]

I

Central to the marxist perspective are the antagonisms around which production is organized and which the organization of production continually regenerates. 'The very moment civilization begins', Marx wrote, 'production begins to be founded on the antagonism of orders, estates, classes, and finally on the antagonism of accumulated labour and immediate labour.'[2]

For all those who work under direct supervision – slaves, some agricultural estate-workers, industrial wage laborers, etc. – the fundamental and characteristic antagonisms take shape between those who produce and those who direct production and appropriate the surplus. The lines of antagonism are clarified by the continual experience of domination within the day-to-day processes of production: those who direct these processes are the explicit agents of those who appropriate the surplus. Such continual domination may be evaded or resisted by informal work groups or by individuals, through varied and continually changing means, but the experience of direct domination remains ever-present in the work process and thus contributes to the enormous chasm between 'work' and other activities. Antagonisms generated within the work process may be 'carried' out of the workplace – the idiom is precise – just as sentiments and relations of kin, community, and friendship may be 'carried' in: but the separateness of work from other social domains simplifies, as well as clarifies, not just the lines of antagonism but the foci of unity.

Within the framework of merchant capital there exist peoples who, while generating a product that will be appropriated, organize and direct the work processes themselves.[3] Constrained to produce by the force of imposed

340

circumstances, they organize themselves along lines of family, kin, community or collectivity not only to produce what they must but (perhaps in conjunction with resistance) to continue to do so. This self-direction (by groups, not individuals) of the work process and the extended duration of this self-direction, which entails more than simple repetition over time and includes the reproduction of the local social preconditions for production, makes it impossible for the producers clearly to separate work from other social activities. Work groups are always more than work groups, and they express their multifaceted form in the work process as elsewhere. Similarly, the social connections through which the preconditions for work are reproduced over time are not specific to any one social process.

In such situations the lines of antagonism and unity – even those directly generated by external domination, and even those that take their shape upon or within the work process – being pervasive, rather than compartmented, possess a particular historical dynamic. The core feature of this dynamic is the merging of work and non-work within the context of appropriation,[4] so that the contradictions between the community's self-generation of value for its own use and purposes and the community's generation of exchange value (for a miniscule, but essential return) permeates, and develops through, all the social institutions of the community. What we call the class struggle in developed capitalism takes shape in merchant capitalism not only through the formation of modern classes but also through the deformation and reformation of family, kin, and community.

When merchant-capital-producing communities are subsequently transformed by the reorganization and increasingly direct domination of production, the patterns of unity and antagonism that had developed within families, kin groups, and the community itself can persist into at least the early development of wage labor relations and the early formation of wage laboring classes.[5] In Newfoundland, and perhaps elsewhere, one of the more significant vehicles for this persistence has been local custom. Developing in the context of merchant capital, and not 'archaic'; specific to the precise forms that patterns of conflict and alliance take in particular communities, rather than expressing an abstract and timeless human symbolism; replicated throughout regions but 'special' to the communities that enact them, custom can create social knowledge for its participants, and through the continuity of certain kinds of custom[6] can convey this knowledge and the attendant social relations into historically new situations. This mixture of unity and antagonism in work and non-work, the expression of contradiction within custom, and the role of custom in reshaping social contradictions raises questions about the role of custom in history, particularly in the history of merchant capital. It is to this set of questions that the following analysis of a Newfoundland custom is addressed.

In the tiny fishing villages along the coast of Newfoundland there are customs so undramatic, so ordinary, that they have attracted almost no mention by early generations of visitors, commentators, or diarists; they enter the written record primarily as they are mentioned by anthropologists and folklorists describing what they see during the time they were present. These minor customs have left almost no mark on the historical record, yet they are so widespread and so similar not just in their details but in how they are situated in the social life of each community that these customs must have a history. By this I mean more than simple duration over time, with change; I mean that such customs must have been part of the historical development of the present situation in these fishing villages.

One such custom is called, by Newfoundland fisher-families, a 'scoff'.[7] A scoff, in one meaning of the word, is a party, but a party for which the food is stolen, or, as the Newfoundlanders say, meaning something slightly different from simple stealing, the food for a scoff is 'bucked'. To generalize, from a variety of forms, the food is not usually taken from a person who is actively disliked, nor is it usually taken from a close kinsman, nor from the one relatively prosperous person in the community, the fish merchant: it is taken from another fisher-family living in the same community. The people from whom the food is taken are, with an occasional local exception, not invited to the scoff; each couple that is invited brings some food that they have bucked for the occasion. The three, four, or five couples invited to a scoff soon learn from whom the food has been taken, and there is much merriment among them – a lot of sexual teasing, both verbal and physical, a lot of drinking, and a very fine meal of vegetables and meat, at someone else's expense: all rather unusual forms of behavior in these usually quiet villages of rather reticent people.

We can, and shortly will, examine the 'simple structure' of this custom: separate it into its components and show how each of these components interlocks with other components of the same custom and with other customs. The sort of structure that is revealed by such methods is neither 'true' nor 'false' – it is flat, and so misleading.

We can go further, and connect the structure of this custom to the social relations between people. We can fit the custom into a round of social life and by so doing tie custom to history – show custom emerging in the context of new forms of social relations, declining as these social relations decline, and while it endures we can show how custom is a part of the existing social relations. We can, in other words, make custom *responsive* to history, see how custom functions *within* history, but this is not enough.

What we need to do is to see how custom *participates* in history: how it not only responds to but also shapes the process of events. It seems strange to attempt this task with a custom for which we have so sparse an historical record, but despite the obvious disadvantages, the absence of historical documentation points our task in a potentially fruitful direction: we must look within the structure of custom, with new ways of conceptualizing what the structure of custom is, and find in this perspective a structural dynamic – the expression of historical change within custom and the participation of custom in change.

II

In the summer of 1972 by far the most popular song in Newfoundland was called 'Aunt Martha's Sheep'.[8] It was played over the provincial radio networks at least ten times a day; it was sung by children playing in yards and roads and by adults at late evening social gatherings around the kitchen table, soup kettle, and whiskey bottle. People sing a lot in rural Newfoundland, making up new songs and demonstrating an extraordinary repertoire of old songs. But this song was special – it was the same song sung over and over. I have heard nothing like the popularity that this song had, with one exception, and that was in the coastal swamps of North Carolina, among Blacks and Indians, at the height of the civil rights struggles in the winter of 1967, when Aretha Franklyn – a Black woman with a magnificently powerful voice – came out with the song 'Respect'. 'Respect' at that time was described to me by Black folks as 'the Negro National Anthem'. Let us look a little more closely at the Newfoundland equivalent.

'Aunt Martha's Sheep' is a ballad about a small bunch of men who help themselves to one of 'Aunt' Martha's sheep. 'Aunt' does not mean a relative; the term is used to refer with respect to any older woman. Aunt Martha calls the Royal Canadian Mounted Police (a new possibility in the isolated villages of Newfoundland, based on their recent acquisition of radio-telephones). A 'Mountie' arrives, knocking on the door as the men sit down to their feast of sheep stew. They invite the Mountie in, telling him they are having 'a bit of moose', and asking him to join them. Moose, in Newfoundland, are ordinarily reserved for tourists to kill, with licenses selling at $500 each. A small number of licenses are given out locally, by lottery, and there is a lot of easily understandable local resentment over this. When moose is eaten in Newfoundland, it is often illegal – but by one of those laws not systematically enforced. The Mountie joins them for the 'moose' stew and perhaps some ale and then, when the meal is done, he leaves to try to catch the culprits who stole Aunt Martha's sheep, with the men wishing him all good luck in his endeavor. The last verse states: 'we might have taken Aunt Martha's sheep, but the Mountie ate the most'.

The meal was a scoff, except for the Mountie, who was a new feature. What gives the song such force is not simply 'putting one over' on the Mountie but doing it in good humour and in the context of a scoff, the traditional vehicle for ambiguous and hostile social relations.

The richest description of scoffs in the anthropological and historical literature on Newfoundland comes from Professor James Faris's study of the north coast Newfoundland fishing village he calls 'Cat Harbour', in which he lived from January 1964 to March 1965. A brief history of Cat Harbour will provide an introduction to the social context in which scoffs occur.[9]

The first settlers came to Cat Harbour in the late eighteenth century. They chose to settle on a rocky headland between two large bays, and built their houses in an area of shallow seas and rough and treacherous coastline, which had no fresh water, avoiding uninhabited and nearby good harbors with plentiful fresh water. They were not only trying to settle within rowing distance of the codfish, for fish were plentiful near the good harbors as well, but they were also trying to settle out of range of the British naval patrol boats. Year-round settlement on the coast of Newfoundland was illegal until the nineteenth century, as British Crown policy sought to reserve the Newfoundland cod-fishery for the boats that sailed from England every spring and returned each fall. Newfoundland settlers interfered with this seasonal, migratory fishery, and from time to time they were burnt out or forced out. Settlers were perhaps more likely to be allowed to remain if they chose a site that could not be used by the migratory fishery.

By the end of the eighteenth century, the law against settlement was only sporadically enforced, as the merchants who sponsored the migratory fishery wanted some people to stay during the winter to guard the fishing equipment and to catch bait for them. Moreover, in the winter and spring settlers could trap fur-bearing animals and obtain seal pelts, all of which would be exchanged with the merchants upon whom the settlers were dependent for supplies. The policy against settlement and the use of British naval patrol boats to 'enforce' this policy is thus best understood as increasingly being as much a form of dominance over necessary settlement as a constraint against settlement.

From the inhabitants' point of view, their settlements began in ambiguity. By gardening and by pursuing a range of commodity-generating economic activities in addition to cod-fishing, they could 'afford' to produce cod for a low price,[10] and could also provide the merchants with important services, but their presence could also interfere with the merchants' fishery. One major outcome of the domination of the settlers embedded in this contradiction was their continued impoverishment, and the difficulty they had in developing a more capital-intensive, and more autonomous, fishery.

These settlers fished for cod – their major economic activity – from small, open row and sail boats, at first with handlines and by the mid- or late nineteenth century with different types of nets or with long lines with multiple hooks. Handlines could be used by one person; nets and long lines required crews of two to five. The crews were usually composed of male agnatic kinsmen: fathers and sons, brothers, occasionally cousins. These kinsmen constituted the core of the crew, and as will be discussed in section IV, below, they were held together by the structure of inheritance. To this core crew were occasionally attached 'sharemen' who worked for a portion of the catch, who did not own any of the equipment, and who were excluded from inheritance. As the fish were caught, the wives, daughters, sisters, and mothers of the crew – plus an occasional 'servant girl' and sometimes with the help of men – 'made' the fish, a difficult and complex process of splitting, cleaning, salting, washing, and resalting the fish, turning it in the cool sun to dry.[11]

In the early years of Cat Harbour, merchant schooners came once a year – in the fall – when they picked up the dried and salted cod and gave, in exchange, consumption and production supplies: corn meal, salt pork and salt beef, twine, axes, nails, and so forth. A little later the merchant schooners came twice a year: in the spring to give supplies on credit and to arrange to pick up the fish in the fall. In the fall when the merchants received the fish, they would give more supplies for the winter. These were cashless transactions, and in the early years of the twentieth century, when Cat Harbour got a resident merchant who lived year-round in the community, these transactions were still conducted through credit accounts on the merchants 'books' and not for cash.

In the mid-nineteenth century, the population of Cat Harbour was a little over 100, and it rose slowly through the twentieth century, reaching a peak, in 1960, of 290.[12] The size of Cat Harbour is typical. In 1961, the census of Newfoundland listed approximately 1000 communities, towns, and cities: 970 had fewer than 500 people; 800 had fewer than 300 people. Almost all are coastal villages that now or previously were based on the inshore cod-fishery.

Typical also is the slow rate throughout the twentieth century by which the usual material comforts of western societies have come to Cat Harbour. It has been only since the last decade of the nineteenth century that, gradually, frame houses replaced log cabins, that kerosene lamps replaced cod-liver-oil torches, that cast-iron stoves replaced fireplaces – an important change, for when Cat Harbour had only the less efficient fireplaces, the inhabitants had to abandon their houses every winter and move to sod shanties in the woods to be near their fuel. In 1961 Cat Harbour got its first road out of the village; before that the only access to Cat Harbour was by sea – as it still remains on most of the south coast. The villages in Newfoundland are thus known as 'outports'.[13] Cat Harbour got its first electricity in 1963, a not unusual date in outport Newfoundland, and in 1967, under pressure from the government, the village was abandoned and the population relocated: a fate that has befallen hundreds of Newfoundland outports since the early 1960s.[14]

From its beginning until its end, Cat Harbour was a fishing village, and the annual round of activities centered, here as elsewhere, on an intense period of about three months, from the time the ice went out in early June until the storms and fogs of early September. During this period men fished for cod with 'traps' (large box nets), and women worked daily at preserving the fish. A crew of three men in a small boat, now with a diesel engine, and three or four women working ashore, salting and turning the fish by hand, might put away, in ten to twelve weeks, between 30 and 60 tons of fish.[15]

The whole year turned on this endeavor. After Epiphany ('Old Christmas Day', 6 January) nets were knit and mended by men and by families, boats were built or rebuilt, engines overhauled. By March the exciting and dreaded seal-fishery started as men went out on the ice-floes after pelts, and after one of only two sources of cash income that, until the Second World War, most families ever saw. But in the twentieth century every family line in Cat Harbour has lost at least one man to the ice in this spring seal hunt.[16]

By May sealing ends, the small boats go in the water, and the cod-fishing starts.

346 Gerald M. Sider

People joke wryly about the intensity of the cod-fishery: husbands and wives say they sleep 'back on' (back-to-back) for the duration and that old people don't die during the season: 'sure, no one would have time to come to the funeral'. Indeed, Professor Faris found statistically fewer deaths.[17]

In the fall, after the cod nets are spread to dry, the festivities start: first the weddings, then the scoffs, and then the Christmas 'times'.[18] During this season, less intense productive activities are pursued. In September and October there is a small-scale handline fishery; men go out alone in boats, or in twos, and 'jig' (handline) for cod. By the beginning of October the wooden piers and fish drying racks are taken down and stored away from the force of the winter storms. Women pick and bottle berries, some men go into the woods to cut pulp for the paper companies – the other opportunity for a cash income. In November, when the woods are snow-covered and the ground ice-hard, men go for a week or so into the woods to cut and haul out their winter supply of firewood. Women may paint their kitchens. There is a rest from the fishery in this period; nets will not be mended until the new year.

'We all', Cat Harbour people say, 'attend each other's weddings',[19] and indeed, a wedding may have over 200 people, a funeral half the village or more, and during the Christmas 'times' of parties and of mummers, people visit back and forth across the entire village. But the scoffs, which come between the weddings and the Christmas 'times' are much smaller affairs – three, four, perhaps five couples are present. In a few places, for example on the north coast, scoffs are larger; up to eight or even ten couples.

The word 'scoff' has two distinct referents. In the first sense, a scoff refers to a dinner – almost always a family dinner – which the family makes from its own food and which is a particularly fine meal. In the second sense, it refers to a party for people from several different families, and all the food is 'bucked'. In this second, party, sense, 'scoff' can refer to the whole evening that the couples or friends spend together, drinking, dancing, playing cards, singing songs, teasing each other, telling tall stories and jokes, and eating, off and on, throughout the evening. The word 'scoff' also, more specifically, refers to one particular event during this party – the late-night supper which comes towards the end of the evening. This supper is a meal of fresh meat, not the salt beef or salt pork which is gotten from the merchant in exchange for fish. The meat is either wild – game that is hunted or even sea-birds – or domestic: sheep, cows, geese, or even chicken. The meat is typically served in the usual stew, with potatoes and vegetables.

All the food for a scoff – the meat and the vegetables – *has* to be 'bucked'. The vegetables are taken from someone's storage bin, root cellar, or right out of their garden; the meat is cut off a carcass hanging in someone's fishing shed, or if it is a small animal, like rabbits, or birds, like geese, the whole animal may be taken. In some places, for example Fogo Island on the north coast, where most of the meat comes from the merchant, the scoff can be mostly vegetables. In the one recorded instance that I have found of an outport with scoffs that are exclusively by and for women, only vegetables are bucked.[20] This scoff occurs only near the end of the harvest, during the time that women sometimes help each other take in and preserve the food from their family gardens.

A lot of food is taken. Harold Squire, in the history of the village of Eastport, comments that the people at a scoff all ate their fill and often a substantial amount was left over for the people who gave the scoff.[21] Usually everyone who comes to the scoff brings some bucked food, while the couple who hosts the party provides the meat for the main meal. Sometimes the host gives a scoff to celebrate his birthday; sometimes there is no special event that the scoff marks. The people who come to a scoff are friends, almost always of the same general age-grouping and often brothers-in-law. Brothers, particularly married brothers, seem (on sparse evidence) very rarely to scoff together (and perhaps also not to buck food from each other); the tensions of family production, as will be seen in section IV, are too great. Sisters apparently do scoff together, though the references are always to brothers-in-law (and their wives), perhaps indicating the importance of meat (which men usually provide) at the meal, and perhaps indicating a male ethnographic bias.

Scoffs are special, and the people in the outports make a careful distinction between stealing food for a meal, which is universally regarded as wrong and condemned, and bucking food for a scoff, which is regarded as legitimate – except by the people from whom it is taken.

Professor Faris lists four criteria that distinguish bucking food from stealing it.[22] First, and a point which all the authors who mention scoffs also note, the food is not taken from those in dire need. Second, there must be more than one couple at the meal. Third, the meal must be what is locally called a 'time' – by which is meant that the usual bounds of reserve and decorum are transgressed or broken. Fourth, everyone at the scoff, or from whom the food is taken for a scoff, must be people in good moral standing in the community – not strangers, not the merchant, and not people who are regarded, for whatever reason, as having gone against the local code of moral behavior. Professor Rex Clark (himself from a Newfoundland outport) suggested to me that on Random Island local opinion would not allow poor people to buck for a scoff – it would likely be defined as stealing.

The people from whom the food is taken must not be invited to the party.[23] What the victims try to do is to get it all back, either by what they call 'second plundering', which means taking the food back after it has been cooked, or at later time. 'Second plunder', the people say, 'is the sweetest.'[24] The term plunder is also used for shipwrecks, which are stripped of their goods, and which people second plunder from each other.

'Scoffs', writes Harold Squire, 'were not as widely known in the early days as [they were] in the late 1800s and in the early part of the twentieth century.' In that period, Squire notes, they were 'taken part in chiefly by the younger men. The older people frowned on it, especially the name.'[25] This indicates that people were conscious of the more usual meaning of 'scoff' in English – to mock aggressively or to act with contempt (as in 'scofflaw'). The first recorded use of 'scoff' in reference to the pilferage of food is at the turn of the twentieth century. In this early usage, it referred to pilfering for a party by the crew of schooners from other outports, with the party taking place on board the schooner[26] (a form of reverse plunder?). Such schooners, it is important to note, were invariably welcomed when they put into harbor at another outport, and they were also resented as competitors for the fish.

Scoffs still occur in the outports, and although evidence indicates they are declining, the song 'Aunt Martha's Sheep' suggests that they are still very much a part of the popular imagination. But some features have changed. Professor Ellen Antler, who did field research on the north coast in the early 1970s, wrote me that one woman, then in her forties, said that as a young woman they would, at the end of a scoff, buck someone's sled for a ride, but now that there are roads and cars instead of sleds, no one would think of taking a car: for that would be theft, whatever the circumstances.[27] Before examining the social relations within which scoffs occur and the social relations that scoffs generate, a few remarks should be made on the simple structure of the scoff.

First, the food that is taken is produced by the people themselves, who raise it or hunt it. One might take some salt meat, which comes from outside, through the merchant, but the main meal has to centre around fresh meat. Sleds that people bucked were also made by themselves; cars come from outside. People in scoffs deal directly with each other in terms of what they have directly produced. This point can be underscored by contrasting scoffs to the treatment of witches.

People in Cat Harbour, as in other Protestant outports, believe in witches. They are usually women, sometimes men, but always outsiders. The major ways that witches are dealt with is through a practice called 'shooting the witch's heart out'. To do this one takes a silver coin, cuts it into pieces, loads it into a gun, goes into the woods, draws a heart on a piece of paper or a board, shoots it with the gun, and then waits for the witch to fall down, or the jinx on one's boat to be lifted.[28] Witches, in other words, are shot with the core symbol of the external world – a coin – and even though people have a very good idea of who is witching them, they do nothing directly to the witch but only to a heart drawn on a piece of paper. Witches are outsiders (for example, midwives, who come from other communities) and are opposed through a symbol of the outside world. But people who scoff are insiders, and they primarily buck food: food is the core symbol of hospitality, and the kitchen is the one room in every outport house open to any person and which any resident of the outport feels free to enter without knocking.

Bucking occurs at only one other occasion in addition to scoffs. On 5 November, towards the end of the season for scoffing, most outports have 'bonfire night' (the English origins of this custom are usually unknown). On bonfire night people buck barrels, casks, net floats, any wooden container not locked up, old hen houses, or any old wooden object, and they burn them. All these objects are home-made. Some are prized, others are old and worn. People try to hide their best barrels; it is the one night in the year when the fishing sheds are locked. Sometimes these locked sheds are broken into, although this is considered only marginally legitimate.[29] In recent years, bonfire night is changing. More emphasis is placed on taking natural objects, such as trees or branches, which do not belong to anyone, and in scavenging old tires and debris. There are several fairly recent reports of people being asked for 'donations' for the bonfire and having the desired item bucked if they refuse to give it. Bonfire night is primarily for those too young to scoff (early teenagers) and is also participated in by outsiders, such as the school teacher (traditionally, in the outports, a recent high-school graduate). Lastly, bonfire night will frequently victimize the merchant, who is ignored in the scoff. To the young may be given a large part of the task of confronting the agents of the outside world – and bonfire night, more than scoffing, contains obvious symbolic connections to the outside world. In one instance, as part of the pranks associated with bonfire night, a group of young men, led by the school teacher, dumped an outhouse (an outdoor pit toilet) into the harbor – with an old man in it, who waded to shore. As the outhouse drifted in and out of the harbor over the next week, the residents called it 'the mail boat'.[30]

As adolescents grow up, they become observers at bonfire night and participants at scoffs. They will continue to scoff, with diminishing intensity, until their children are grown. This shift from bonfires to scoffs occurs in the context of the increasing focus of young adults on community social relations and on the directly and indirectly helpful, hostile, and competitive connections between the people of an outport. The combination of direct and indirect connections between people, expressed in the scoff, can be illuminated by contrasting scoffs with weddings and Christmas parties. At both those occasions the host provides the food and – focusing for the moment on one kind of Christmas party (as reported for Cat Harbour) – the village Santa Claus; everyone is welcome to come. (This party will be discussed in section V.) The Christmas mummers, too, cover the entire village, visiting or being visited by nearly everyone. The scoff includes only a few people and it has, as it were, two sorts of hosts – the one who gives the party and the ones, not present, at whose expense the scoff is given. Note the dual connotation of 'expense': the unwitting hosts paid for the food through their labor, and, by having the food taken from them, they have been mocked and indirectly assaulted as well.

The issue of indirect assault can be underlined again by comparison with weddings and mumming. Men get drunk at weddings, and weddings are the major occasions for men to fight with each other. These fistfights do not occur at the wedding itself; men go out of the reception hall in small groups to drink, and in going back and forth to a celebration which can last eight to ten hours, on the roads away from the wedding party, they sometimes fight, with the later excuse that they were drunk.[31] Mummers, under their masks, sometimes assault people in disfavor with the community – in olden days actually beating the person, more recently by mock assault. At weddings and in mumming the victim is directly struck, albeit under the disguise of alcohol or of masking; in scoffs the victim may only gradually, through rumor or through his own observation, realize that he has been taken.

To understand the logic and the historical dynamic of scoffing, it must first be situated within the context of merchant domination of the village fishery and then within the context of family and village organization. One of the significant linkages between these different social domains turns out to be food.

III

Until the 1830s the seasonal fishery which came out from England every spring employed labor under servant contract. This meant that the servant signed on to fish or preserve fish for the duration of the season in return for a wage fixed in advance – say £20 for the season. In order to get servants, their wages were legally given first claim on the local merchants' subsequent sale of the catch. As the fishermen, who came from England or Ireland, had an approximate idea of what fish could be sold for in Europe, the problem was to make them keep fishing as intensively as possible after they had caught enough to cover their wages. The merchant sponsors also faced the problem of varying size of the catch due to natural causes: the weather and the availability of cod in the spot they stayed for the summer. The fishermen were due the same wage regardless of the size of the catch.

To resolve this problem a share system was developed in the early nineteenth century, where the laborers fished for a fixed share of the catch. The merchants found this also not to their liking, for some years when the storms were few and the fish ran in large numbers, the catch was enormous – and the proceeds had to be shared with the fishermen.[32]

In the late eighteenth and early nineteenth centuries, as the number of Newfoundland settlers grew, a new arrangement slowly developed. In 1841, with the end of the legally guaranteed servants' lien on the fish for their wages, this new system became nearly universal in Newfoundland outports. It was known as the 'truck' system, and it lasted almost unchanged until after the Second World War.

The truck system matched the destitute settlers' need for provisions with the merchants' hunger for fish, and it did so without cash. In the spring families received their fishing supplies and food on credit from the merchant in return for a binding agreement to give the merchant their total catch in the fall. When they turned the fish over, the account was balanced in the merchant's books and the fisher-family could draw any balance in supplies for the winter. If there was no balance due them, they could hope the merchant would 'carry them on the books' until spring.

So the relationship continued from year to year. Merchants met together once a year in August in the capital city of St John's. There they did what is called 'breaking the price' – they decided what price they would charge for the provisions they had given on credit in the previous spring and what price they would pay for the different grades of fish in the coming fall. The fisher-families thus made their contracts in the spring without knowing what they were being charged for goods or what they would receive for the fish in the fall. This system of 'breaking prices', which seems to have been done primarily by the larger merchant houses, who had their agents and dealers along wide areas of the coast, established minimum prices for provisions and maximum prices for fish. From place to place these prices varied, with some merchants charging more for provisions and allowing less for fish. In any one village the prices charged and paid to the fisher-families were uniform, although a merchant could alter the 'income' of fisher-families by applying different standards of grading for the fish he took.

What is absolutely crucial here is *not* the point that would occur to all of *us*, that the system set the merchant against the fisher-family and permitted the merchant to exploit and to gouge the fisher-families, but rather the point that was obvious to the fisher-families: that this system set fisher-family against fisher-family. One of the early Newfoundland historians, Reverend Charles Pedley, wrote in 1863:

as . . . the voyage depended [in part] on causes beyond human control . . . a proportionate margin of profit had to be laid on the goods given out so as in case of success to compensate for the risk of failure; and also to make the gain from the man who did succeed cover the loss arising from the want of success in another man indebted to the same merchant.[33]

The system redirected the rage of the fishermen from the merchant to each other. I again quote Pedley:

the fisherman . . . knew that for the supplies for which he was indebted he had been charged an exhorbitant rate, on the chance that he might not be able to pay, and therefore [he] scarcely felt the responsibility of the debt . . . But the worst effect of this system fell on the man who, more industrious than the others, was therefore as a rule more successful . . . He knew that it fell on him to make good to the supplying merchant the failure arising from his less diligent neighbor.[34]

As this system continued and became increasingly consolidated, it brought in not only the men who caught the fish but the women who cured them. In the First World War, with a sharp rise in price and in demand for cod, the merchants stopped grading the codfish they took but took all the fish in one community at one average price, a system locally called 'tal qual' (as is). John Szwed, studying the east coast outport 'Ross', points out that this penalized people (specifically the women) who put in the effort to cure their fish well, as the average price lumped together their good work, at much effort, with their neighbor's easier and poorer cure.[35] The 'tal qual' form of payment was not restricted to the First

World War but came and went at different times in different places in Newfoundland. Professor McCay, who has done extensive fieldwork in northern Newfoundland, said that the bitterness over this issue was overt and explicit and, perhaps, more enduring than the form of payment itself.

Grading fish (and also producing fish of different grades) is a complex process, in which the size of the fish, the amount of salt used, and the quality of the cure all enter into the evaluation. The better grades of fish are not only larger but require much more labor and skill to cure properly and a certain amount of luck in having the necessary dry, cool, and sunny weather. Skill and extra work can sometimes, but not always, compensate for poor weather. Thus the quality of the fish will vary for reasons that are both within, and outside, people's control.

Throughout the late summer and early fall, the merchant receives from the families in the outport fish that differs substantially in grade. While fisher-families would have some idea about what quality fish is being produced in the village, and by whom, they would have no way of knowing exactly what the 'average' cure in the village is or whether some fish differed from the average due to weather or work. When the merchant bought fish from the community at one average price, he had a substantial amount of room for deceit – and none of the reasons advanced in the literature (e.g. the fish was being rushed to market) contribute as much to explaining 'tal qual' purchasing as does this potential for deceit – for the fish almost always had to be graded before being shipped to market, as purchase contracts were written for specific grades of fish.[36] Fisher-families might suspect that they were being cheated by the merchant, but they would have no way of knowing exactly, as they would have no way of knowing who was producing what quality of fish, or why.

People coped with this situation by reducing their own curing efforts. Merchant associations, their representatives in parliament, and the export brokers complained constantly that tal qual buying lowered the quality of fish produced. Yet it was never outlawed, never regulated, even when the fish-merchants dominated the government. Even though the village merchant exercised some control over quality by occasionally refusing to continue to deal with a few people who did extremely bad cures, the pattern was set – a pattern of complex competitiveness: being sure that you are not doing more than your neighbor and that your neighbor is not doing less than you.

The competitiveness and the concern for who is doing what quality cure was compounded by the merchants' 'averaging' prices, whether or not when buying tal qual, making the more successful fisher-family cover his losses from the less successful. This averaging meant that the merchant lowered the community-wide prices paid for fish and raised the community-wide prices charged for provisions, until there was enough profit from the good fisher-families to cover all the losses – which lowered the income of all the families in the community. It was a double 'average' – in grade and price – imposed on families that did not have any social or cultural forms to collectivize the catch or the curing process but kept both the affairs of separate and distinct families.

In addition to the antagonistic relations between families generated by this double 'averaging', outport families were in direct competition with each other for certain crucial resources: particularly the few best places to moor nets for the season and for waterfrontage that was most suitable for unloading boats and, especially, for curing fish (which took a substantial area). The competition for these scarce resources was unmediated by the merchant; families were pitted directly against each other. In some communities the first crew to put down their cod-trap for the season kept that berth for the entire season but ran the risk of having their trap destroyed by the early spring ice. In some places people raced out on a certain day; there are stories of men dying in this race, leaving the harbor at night in fog. In other places berths were chosen by lot, and in other places they were quasi-hereditary.[37] Merchants not only did not mediate this competition, but they also rarely intervened to diminish it by encouraging the less risky lottery: that shift was accomplished by the community itself. Good waterfront sites were allocated within the community by patrilineal inheritance and division of the parental site: a matter of some tension within and between families, as the complexities of inheritance, orphanage, and rearing of some children by non-nuclear kin created competing claims between families and as the large size of outport families created tensions of preferential inheritance within families.

It is likely that the intra-community tensions did not emerge with the rise of the family-fishery in the early nineteenth century, but rather that they intensified dramatically toward the end of the century. First, cod-traps, which make fishing location especially important, were introduced near the end of the century. At least of equal importance and of more comparative relevance, the late nineteenth century saw the collapse, in most outports, of the more capital-intensive forms of fishing and the reduction of schooner fishermen to small-boat, inshore fishermen.

The mechanism of this collapse is intricate and can only be briefly indicated here. Along with the family-based, small-boat inshore fishery that began in the early nineteenth century, more capital-intensive forms of fishing developed. This was the schooner fishery, which went from south, west, and southeast coast outports to fish the ocean banks. The boats were owned by outport residents, and the crews were largely drawn from the outport. On the north coast, schooners went to 'the Labrador', carrying whole families for the summer. These same north coast schooners engaged in the seal-fishery during the spring. The replacement of sail by more efficient, but much more expensive, steam transferred much of this seal-fishery to the capital city, St John's, which had greater financial resources.[38]

Several of the largest fish-merchant houses, to which the outport schooner fishery was often connected, collapsed in the depressions of 1873 and 1893, further contributing to the demise of this form of fishing. The building of railroads in Europe, which facilitated the transport of north European fish to the traditional Newfoundland Mediterranean market, lowered the price for Newfoundland salt fish (which took months to get to market and had a higher spoilage rate), and thus pressured the Newfoundland fishery back toward the least developed, and the least costly, form of fishing.[39] Lastly, the increasingly tight hold of merchants over the inshore fishery left less and less surplus for local development. Whatever the causes, the demise of the schooner fishery (which lasted, in a few places, until the 1950s) was also the demise of forms of fishing that were more autonomous from local merchant domination, and its passing left behind families who were increasingly unable to resist this domination – expressed most directly in the merchant's control over food.

The connection between food and domination has a long history in Newfoundland. Fish servants, who worked for a fixed wage plus room and board, were called 'dieters' (as were those sharemen in the early family fishery that the family fed).[40] 'Diet' is an early Newfoundland term for a meal, and a dieter is someone who is fed by his or her master. Becoming a dieter was called 'going into collar'; 10 May, the traditional day for dieters' contracts to begin, was called 'Collar Day'. 'Collar' is used, in Newfoundland, for the rope to tie up boats and also for the rope around a dog's neck: the relevance of the second meaning is indicated by the Newfoundland idiom for Collar Day: 'out dogs and in dieters' – dogs being kept inside or in pens for the winter.

Merchants used their control of food – trading food (and supplies) for fish – to control the family-fishery. To begin, families that did not fish well enough were not given food for the winter. People were paid on credit accounts that were exchangeable only for food and supplies at the merchant's establishment. One man, now in his early fifties, told me that as a young man, if he wanted cash from his own account instead of food (for example, a quarter for a dance), he had to go to the merchant's office and 'beg' for it: state his case, and if the merchant concurred, sign for it. Adults faced this also, if for example they needed cash for a visit to the doctor. Professor Chiaramonte told me of one instance, on the south coast, where a community 'struck' for higher fish prices, and the merchant broke the strike in one day by withholding food.

This system continues to the present. Merchants take welfare checks, which families receive from the state, and give food in return – and sometimes cash. One merchant on the south coast bought a movie projector and showed movies a few times a month. The price of admission was five pounds of margarine or the equivalent – food gotten from the merchant and turned back to him to be resold.

The Newfoundland idiom for merchants supplying families is 'the merchant "carries" fisher-families on his books'. For all the antagonism of this relationship, the dependence indicated by this metaphor is explicit: in one instance, the fisher-families of a south coast outport rejected a higher price offered for their fish by a Nova Scotian firm, as they could not be sure that the firm would 'carry them' in bad times.[41]

But families often used the merchant and their family account with the merchant to mediate significant cooperative activities. Professor Firestone, for example, in his study of the outport 'Savage Cove', notes that two families, linked by married brothers who fish together, will keep a common account for food as well as fishing supplies with the merchant. The phrase they use to describe this is 'we all eat out of one barrel'[42] – not 'one pot'. Pots are part of a family's equipment; barrels, other than water barrels, belong to the merchant.

I am arguing that the form of trade imposed by the merchant – the truck and tal qual system – set family against family in the outports. But the fragmentation was not total, for the village still maintained several forms of cohesion as a community. Consider the following: outport people in Newfoundland scoff, and it is fairly clear that through the scoff they recreate or reproduce in their midst the same kind of competitive and antagonistic social relations that the merchant introduced among them. But the scoff is still the custom of a community. If you were to relocate a group of Newfoundlanders from an outport and move them into a housing project in a factory town, it would be unthinkable for them to buck for a scoff in that new context. People in housing projects experience appropriation as individuals and react accordingly, while the fish merchant's appropriation, however severe, is community wide and community focused.[43]

IV

Socially patterned forms of closeness and antagonism occur within, as well as between, outport fisher-families. To understand the tensions within families, it is necessary to see families in two different ways: as a unit for the transmission of property and as a unit for work, and then to see how these two domains are connected.

Several major kinds of property are necessary for the family fishery: a house, usually with a garden, usable waterfrontage, a boat, an engine, and cod-traps or fleets of gill nets. While brothers seek to acquire their own house when they get married, they may continue to fish with their father or, more often, with a brother, in order to share equipment. When fathers retire or die, each piece of major equipment is inherited seperately by the sons. Two points characterize this situation: brothers must fish together in order to pool equipment and they must stop fishing with their brother and start fishing with their sons as their sons grow older in order to retain the sons' earning within the nuclear family and so accumulate a full set of fishing equipment.[44]

The kin links between men, sustained by inheritance, decidedly do not constitute a corporate kin group.[45] The crew not only splits – often as soon as it can – but it sometimes does so before it is economically logical. Women, gardening together as sisters, also often split before the logic of the development cycle of families requires it.[46] Working together is clearly often a trying matter, and the origin of family splits in the tensions of fishing, rather than in other aspects of family life, is best indicated by the local idiom for such splits: 'rowing out'.

But work not only drives families apart, it also, of course, holds them together. Divorce in outport Newfoundland, to take the most salient example, hardly ever occurs. Relations between spouses may become cold and formal, but the price of not catching and preserving fish as a family unit is becoming a shareman, rather than a fisherman, or the woman becoming a helper in the 'shore crowd' that cures the fish and so being excluded from relations of transmission, and formation, of property.

Families are held together by caring and intimate feelings perhaps more than by institutional constraints. Children are desired, and much fuss is made over them. Boys take pride in working with their father; girls are actively involved in a wide range of both domestic and economically productive activities – social occasions and occasions for the display of skill. Centering on the kitchen – the largest, warmest, and most lively room in an outport house, the family can be, and often is, the context for the expression of closeness.

But the closeness is mixed with tension. Protected by the privacy of its dwelling place, by the isolation of separate families in the work-process, and by the absence of public rituals that would express either family antagonisms or closeness, tensions within families are harder to see than are tensions within communities. Some clues to the processual structure of these family tensions may be given by the scoff itself and particularly by the double usage of the term 'scoff' referred to above: as a party – a community ritual – and as a family meal, where the whole family sits down together for a particularly fine and plentiful meal from its own supplies of food.

Eating together contributes to making this family meal special. In a large family people often eat in 'shifts', and in and around the fishing season, when family members have different work schedules, they often help themselves from a standing pot of soup or stew on the stove, or to bread and tea. Visitors may be served along with whoever happens to be eating. For the special meal the whole family living in the house eats together, and usually just the family. This special meal, however, is not called a family dinner but a 'scoff'.

Like the scoff-as-party, the food is fine and plentiful. The scoff-as-party is based on exclusion – not just of those who are not invited, but also, and with particular symbolic force, of those whose food is being eaten, those at whose expense the party is being held. And this too has an analog within the family scoff.

The tensions within the family are based not only on the practical impossibility of divorce and on differential inheritance and work opportunities, but also on the fact that some of the children will have to leave the community, and the well-being of those who remain depends on this. Inheritance is a source of tension insofar as some of the critical factors of production, such as shore facilities or net berths (in places where net berths are hereditable), are indivisible and in the longer-settled communities not easily duplicated. On the rocky coastline there are often only a limited number of places close to the good sources of fish to moor boats and to dry fish. Some work in fishing and in curing fish is easier and pleasanter than other tasks, and children are often favored with the better tasks – and, in large families, with the opportunity to fish with the family, which has important implications for inheritance.

More poignantly, some children – especially in the longer and more densely settled eastern coasts of Newfoundland and particularly those from large families – will simply have to leave, moving westward in Newfoundland to more desolate places, or going 'to the mainland': Canada or New England. Without expansion in the community-based fishery into large-boat, open-ocean fishing and without alternatives to fishing, there is often no room in the family or the community for all the children without a marked decline in catch for those who remain.[47]

The unity and warmth of the family scoff thus occurs, as it does in the party scoff, but more subtly, in a context of exclusion and of tension. These tensions within the family perhaps have contributed to keeping the family from being a well-spring of social or cultural resistance to merchant domination. Kin terms, drawn from the nuclear family and used as metaphors of *egalitarian* closeness, are absent in Newfoundland. Adult men address each other, when feeling particularly friendly, as 'my dear', 'my love', and more often, as 'my son' – which women also use to address adult men; women and men call adult women 'maid' – men say 'my maid', and men and women frequently call men 'bye' (boy) or 'my bye'. 'Uncle' and 'aunt' are common terms of respect for elders – as is 'skipper' – and are used by adults and youngsters alike to refer to people who are not related to them. But 'brother' and 'sister' – crucial terms in the Black and poor White churches in many parts of the United States and Canada and spreading from there to urban Black political movements and to a lesser extent to labor unions – are not used as metaphors in Newfoundland.

Two incidents will introduce the intermixture of mutual aid and tense distrust of involvement with each other that characterizes outport social interaction between families. In the south coast outport of 'Deep Harbour' Professor Louis Chiaramonte observed

a man [who] was attempting to unload a dory (boat) engine onto a wharf. While he was struggling with it, two passing men stopped to watch. He worked for 30 minutes, while the onlookers stood by. They would not offer to help, nor did he expect it, for he first had to see if he could unload the engine himself. After he had worked hard at it and failed, then he asked them to give him a hand.[48]

The situation is, once again, complex: there is a recognition of need and quiet offers of help and also subtle maintenance of an egalitarian distance. The two observers did not just stay to watch the man struggle with the engine in order silently to witness the futility of his efforts; one imagines they also stayed because they knew they might be needed. Nor do those that offer help maintain a simple superiority. For example: in every outport there are people who can perform certain crucial tasks much better than others – the craftsmen who can repair or build a boat, carve a water-tight net float, repair or rebuild a house or an engine. All these craftsmen are also full-time fishermen. When they help another member of the community, they are almost always paid less than they could have earned had they spent the time fishing. When Chiaramonte asked three boat-builders in Deep Harbour why they do it, they all said: 'because you can't refuse a man in need; you have to do what needs to be done'.[49] And while they are paid less than they could have made by fishing, the craftsmen always ask for less than they are paid: the person being helped restores a part of the balance by paying more than the price set.

The second example comes again from Professor Faris's observations in Cat Harbour. It concerns a fishing crew composed of two cousins who jointly owned the equipment and a helper who worked for a smaller share of the catch. This crew

was always getting caught in heavy stormy seas, causing their wives and the community . . . anxiety over their safety. On two occasions the most seaworthy boat in the community had to be sent out in raging storms to make sure they were not in distress . . . In another instance the church bell was rung to guide them in through thick fog. Both of [them] were successful and experienced fishermen, but neither wanted to make decisions about when to come in. The crew was . . . by no means unusual.[50]

We might note, to begin our comment, that the crew had no reported difficulty in deciding when to go out – the problem was not starting to fish, but stopping: that is, making a decision that would have lessened or limited another crew-member's income.

Despite all this cautiousness there is a great deal of closeness and demonstrative affection. The closeness that does exist is not just verbal but also physical. Adult men will sit on the kitchen sofa sprawled out over each other, and people growing up in the small outport houses often sleep two or more to a bed until they are married. Infants sometimes spend their first year, or even two, sleeping between their parents. One young man – aged about twenty-two – whom I knew in an outport, and who was about to leave for a job in the capital city, admitted to me that he was frightened: he had, he said, never slept alone in a bed at night in his entire life.

The 'separateness' and 'individualism' that Chiaramonte, Faris, Firestone, and Szwed all find as characteristic features of the outports they studied must also be seen in this context of closeness – neither aspect, by itself, is wholly true, neither aspect is wholly false. The complex line between truth and falsity brings us to another characteristic form of outport culture: a type of story they tell each other that they call a 'cuffer'.

V

A 'cuffer' is a special kind of story that is told at informal social gatherings, which pretends to be a straightforward recounting of significant events in the past but which is, in fact, untrue from beginning to end. A cuffer would begin, 'remember the summer of 1948 when Sam Jones lost his [cod] trap to the ice?' – only in fact it was 1949, and it was Sam's cousin Jack that lost, not his net trap but his boat. As a cuffer is being told, some men will be agreeing 'Yes, bye' – as people often do with any statement, whether they think it true or not, and others will be starting to disagree, to 'correct' the story and the storyteller, perhaps because they didn't realize at first that a cuffer was being told, or perhaps because they just wanted the fun of a sham argument.

Cuffers are told for amusement and to provoke argument. And they provoke some fairly intense arguments. Men shout, occasionally shove, make bets, and even threats to each other: but they are not supposed to get really angry. 'Any real quarrel between persons', Faris notes, 'is labelled "black" (the symbol for strangers) and is to be avoided at all costs.'[51]

A cuffer is, as I see it, a lie about history: more precisely, a lie about a part of the people's past that everyone knows, or almost knows, and so everyone knows, or almost knows it is a lie. But they fight about it anyhow, or they pretend to fight.

Cuffers are told by adult men to other adult men. As with scoffs, and as Professor Faris points out, not every man in the village is permitted to tell cuffers but only full members of the local moral community.[52] Cuffers are told in the small shops and in the fishing sheds where men gather in the evenings. When men go into the woods to gather firewood, they tell each other cuffers about sexual affairs and exploits – also matters of common knowledge in these small villages.

For all the tensions cuffers cause, they are encouraged: 'tell us a cuffer, George',[53] one man asked another. This ambiguous mixture of assault and affection, of closeness and distance, is also evident in the personage of the village Santa Claus.

Santa Claus is, as a symbol, an object of fear: parents threaten misbehaving children that Santa will take them away – as they also say about the visiting nurse and doctor. At Christmas time a member of the community is chosen to be Santa Claus for one night. People who give presents to each other – spouses, parents to children, adults to each other – do not give the presents directly but bring it to the community hall and have Santa give it. Santa calls the recipient's name, and people, even adults, show a marked reluctance to go up and get the gift. The audience calls out encouragement, and Santa calls out insulting remarks, shrewd observations, and for adults, sexual innuendos. Why do people give gifts to each other this way? As they say: 'if you're going to give someone something, its easier if you get Santa to do it, isn't it?'.[54]

What is being given is not just a present but a whole package, to a recipient who is both victim and equal. And as with the scoff and the cuffer (and Christmas mumming as well), it is easier on the culprits if people cannot quite identify them, at least at first, and cannot quite figure out if they should be really angry. The situation here is startlingly similar to the impact of tal qual buying on the village – a situation where it is impossible to evaluate the average price because it is impossible to know what grades of fish are being produced or why. The truck system of purchasing fish itself has the same effect: it averages the returns of the good and the poor fisherman without the people of the village being able fully to know, except in a few cases, if the differences in catch are due to luck or intensity of effort.

Scoffs, along with these other village customs, seem to recreate, in the midst of the village, the antagonistic social relations that are structured into both the merchants' and the families' organization of the production of salted and dried codfish. Scoffs also depend on, and recreate, the alliances and co-involvements of the outport. The question now before us is: do such customs as scoffs simply reflect a structure that has its origins elsewhere, or do such customs create their own social dynamic? The answer begins in the contrast between scoffs and gifts.

VI

Three incidents will serve to open the question of the logic of the gift in Newfoundland outports and in contemporary anthropological theory – and the relation of scoffs to gifts.

The first incident occurred in a Conception Bay outport town in the 1930s:

my uncle, who was a merchant, had an odd sense of humor. In the depression days he would play the meanest tricks on the poorest people. I was always one of his gang after I became an acceptable age. The town had the usual two or three beggars who were supposedly sick or crippled. One night during the Christmas holidays he was in the mood for mischief. He looked me up and we decided that we would play some sort of trick on Bobby Smith. Bobby had been on government relief for a lifetime. On the day of the night in question my uncle, through the Orangemen, had collected two horseloads of firewood for Bobby along with some food and Xmas gifts. When we arrived at the Smith place that night the first thing we noticed was the firewood piled against a wall which was about four feet outside the house. We decided to founder the works against the side of the house facing the cemetery. This would block the doorway. However, having many tricks played on them, Mrs. Smith was upstairs looking out for any such event. We did not know this. As we were about to founder the wood, the contents of a kettle of boiling water came at us from above. Our little plan failed. We went back to his store, and packaged a week's groceries which we had Mr. Smith pick up the next day and haul home on his slide. The Smiths never knew who tried to play the trick on them.[55]

The second incident was reported by Professor Szwed for the village of 'Ross' on the west coast, and it occurred in the early 1960s:

Jack Angus was having trouble hauling his winter's cut of wood out from his camp, several miles in the woods from the road. He had no tractor, and had recently lost his horse in an accident. Tom, a financially better-off wood cutter, offered to haul his wood out with his tractor. No bargain was struck in advance, and once the wood was out, Jack offered to pay for the work. Tom rejected the offer, however, accepting only a few bottles of home-brew in exchange for his efforts. There was no doubt that Jack still felt indebted to Tom, for he told of the kindness of the act at every opportunity he had. Similarly, he sought to do a number of small favors for Tom, such as offering first to help him cut some of his wood, and later to sell him some sheep at a very low price. Yet this did not discharge the debt, for as Jack Angus put it: 'I'd like to do him a good turn like he done me, but he don't need anything I could do for him. He's after making a pile [going to make a lot of money] this winter, so his worries are over. Still, I feel as I'd ought to do something for him . . . I owes him a lot.'[56]

The third incident was told to me directly by the person it happened to – a resident of Placentia Bay. Toward the end of the Great Depression (1939), this man, as a child of ten, was working packing salt fish for the merchant for 4¢ an hour. After working steadily for several hours on the first day, bending over the entire time, he straightened up to rub his sore back. The merchant, watching, told him, 'go on home if your back is sore, and send your mom or grandma in your place'. Forty years later, the man still remembered this with considerable bitterness. The year before this incident, as a child of nine, he lived at the merchant's – lighting the fires before dawn each morning, running errands, doing small jobs – in return for his room and board, a sack of flour for his family, and a new pair of canvas pants, which was not part of the contract but which the merchant gave him 'extra'.

Each story is immensely complex; each worth a paper in its own right. A few specific comments must suffice as a prelude to discussing the general themes that emerge from this set of stories. In the first story, it is important that the Smiths seemed to know that along with the gift – of wood and food – would come an attack: Mrs Smith was specifically on the lookout for this. While the prank was played by the merchant and his 'gang', I suspect it must have had more general approval – Newfoundland outport houses are always so close together that had the neighbors been outraged at the action, they would have intervened. And after the prank failed there was a second gift, as if becoming a victim were a form of reciprocity for the original gift, for which a further gift is due.[57] The reciprocities of this transaction, in which the victim becomes an equal, are clearly indicated by the subtle changes in naming in the original text: the story starts out with '*Bobby* Smith' – the name has been changed here but the diminutive form is equivalent – being on government relief, and ends, via Mrs Smith's counter-attack, with *Mr* Smith coming to collect his groceries.

In the second and third stories, no form of reciprocity was possible – neither in the positive sense, for Jack Angus felt he could not repay a gift in the context of inequality, nor in the negative sense, for the child could not protect himself, via a counter-attack, against having his own values and sense of self-worth turned against him.

Marcel Mauss dissolves the process of giving gifts into three component actions, and in so doing provides the basis for an analysis of reciprocal interaction that characterizes the whole twentieth-century anthropological understanding of egalitarian social relations. The gift, Mauss argues, can be understood as the socially engendered obligation to give, to receive, and to repay.[58] In one of the most important of the recent elaborations on this process, Bourdieu points out that between the gift and the repayment there must always be an interval and a difference. To return immediately the same thing that was given is to mock the gift and to reject the social relationship implicit in the act of giving.[59] The importance of Bourdieu's observation is that it provides one way of seeing how temporality is structured into the culture of a people.

The gift has a long-term temporal structure: it creates potentially enduring relations of gift and counter-gift. The scoff is short-term: a one-night party, food taken, perhaps an act of revenge, of counter-theft, and there the matter ends. The gift creates ties not only between the giver and receiver but within the community as well, as people both contribute to their representative gift-givers and give moral support and prestige to those who give and receive well – with style, flair, and a sense of the fully appropriate. The scoff creates some ties of good feeling and mutual support between those who enjoy the party, while simultaneously creating ill-will with the victims. The gift, however, beneath the surface structure of good-will and close and equal ties, contains a deeper structure which has the constant potential for inequality: gifts that cannot be repaid, obligations that cannot be discharged. The gift can thus be the basis for the formation of long-lasting relations of obligation and of service – ultimately labor service – that crystalize in the domain of symbolic action and carry over into the social relations of production. The scoff, to the contrary, has beneath its surface of antagonism no potential for creating ties of inequality, no potential for the fundamental antagonisms created by such unequality. The scoff creates pleasure and anger and social distance and isolation but no ties of future service or obligation. The social fragmentation engendered and reinforced by the scoff might well contribute to merchant domination over the community; I will discuss that possibility below.

The analytical problem we now face is this: Bourdieu's analysis of the gift, emphasizing the fact that repayment must occur after an interval of time and must be different from the original gift (thus perhaps calling forth a counter-gift from the original giver), suggests one important way time is structured into the process of exchange. With scoffs this is not the case, or not as powerfully so. Further, we noted that the equality characteristic of gift-exchanges contains the potential for inequality, and this is also not the case with scoffs – the initial inequality of scoffs contains no potential for creating further, or long-term, inequality within the community. The scoff reinforces a competitive egalitarian-ism of similarly isolated, similarly situated families that establishes no effective claims either on each other or between the people and the merchant. The scoff is not a basis for effective defense against merchant domination but, rather, indirectly supports this domination. The scoff encourages people to think, wrongly, that they are the authors of their antagonisms toward each other,[60] a belief that coexists with their knowledge of the merchant's impositions. By further undermining village unity and by partially mystifying the source of disunity, the scoff contributes to a political passivity that defuses the class struggle within the community and shifts the locus of action outside the community – between merchant and industrial capital or between competing merchant capitals (e.g. the competition with the Norwegian or Icelandic cod-fishery).

Effective social transformations can no longer originate within these villages, but village customs are not irrelevant. Such customs as scoffs recreate and reinterpret, within the village and within one class, the history of that village and those people as social knowledge. Custom, as a form of shared knowledge, can constitute either one basis for class consciousness or self-created mystification of real class antagonisms. At this point we cannot say which, but we can say how.

VII

Custom, I suggest, can be defined by three characteristic features and three revealing contradictions. First, customs are specific clusters of practices that people recognize as special – different from ordinary life and ordinary ways of interacting, often because they mark special events: holidays, life-cycle rites, or special kinds of get-togethers. Customs also are self-consciously traditional – that is, the people who engage in them, even when they are doing something fairly new, ordinarily maintain that the practice originated in the past and often the distant past. Further, custom is recognized by its participants as particularistic – as something they do as co-members of a village, or a region, as co-religionists, or as sharers of a common ethnic identity. To sum up this first point so far: custom is self-consciously traditional, self-consciously particular, and self-consciously special. Yet these customary occasions – weddings, funerals, saints days, and so forth – are also ordinarily and usually where people try out new relationships; where under the color of tradition, the protection of a particularistic audience, and the specialness of the occasion, new social relations are formed and old ones abandoned. These new relations are, of course, a specific focus of life-cycle customs, but if we look closely at such customs, including, for illustration, our own participation in them in our own lives, we will see that for the audience, as well as the central actors and for many different kinds of customs, people often learn new things about each other and alter their social relations accordingly. Custom is thus the self-conscious point of articulation between the old and the new.

Second, despite the fact that customs are characteristically local and particular – to a village, a neighborhood, a sect, a religion, or whatever – customs in fact are the at least partly self-conscious point of articulation between the local area or group and the wider social world in which that group exists. Newfoundlanders may not fully realize the extent to which the scoff and the cuffer recreate the antagonistic ties between families that were created by merchant domination of the trade, but they know full well that all their customs – weddings, funerals, church teas, and scoffs – are theaters of subtle inequality subtly expressed in dress, household furnishings, gifts, and perhaps even in body language;

inequality that has its origins both in local circumstances and in the magnification of local economic differentiation through differential connections to the outside world. Customs are something that local people or particular groupings of people do with each other and to each other, mixing and merging the external with the internal, and recreating in their midst the social forces of the larger world. Custom creates social boundaries – 'we do this our way' – but these boundaries are, in the modern world, more illusion than reality.

Third, we must both confront and use the historical specificity of the conceptual category 'custom'. In thirteenth- and fourteenth-century England, the word custom meant three things: 1) a common and usual way of acting; 2) the service or rent due from tenants to their lord; and 3) the tribute or toll levied by a lord or by local authorities on commodities coming within a border.[61] All three senses of the term define or delineate boundaries and do so by marking local differences in the social, ritual, or economic transactions that occur within these boundaries.

The word 'costume', which in the early 1800s came into the English language from Italian, through French, is derived from the same word as custom. Costume was used in 1802 to mean 'a mode or fashion of personal attire or dress, belonging to a particular nation, class, or period'. In 1881 it was used to mean 'a fashion or style of dress appropriate to any occasion or season'.[62] This linguistic change suggests that custom – real local differences – had, by the 1800s, become reduced to surface form, a variable cover over a similar underlying reality. And indeed, by the beginning of the nineteenth century, throughout Europe and the European-dominated world, it had probably become obvious to almost everyone that the fundamental social forces operating in local areas did not originate within these local areas.

There is thus a disjunction – a gap – at the heart of custom, a gap between local practice and local action, rich and meaningful, and the forces that trivialize local practices. In this gap reside both the limits and the potential of custom in the modern world – the participation of custom in history.

I am arguing that custom merges and includes the contradictions of the old and the new, the local and the external, the reality and the illusion. Lest it be thought that I invented this argument and am imposing it upon the Newfoundland people, I ask you to listen closely to the words of a Newfoundland folk ballad, sung in the 1960s about a state road-building project ten years earlier. It is called the Ballad of the Five Boss Highway:

> If the work it is hard boys
> These men you can't blame
> But there is just one rule no man can deny
> No man has a right for another to drive [to drive another]
> On that was the rule in days of yore
> Of all we [our] grandfathers that have gone before
> But its not the custom of me or you
> So we'll just drop the old rule and follow the new.[63]

Custom is far from being as anthropologists typically regard it – thoughtless and routine practices, left over from the past, perhaps containing some hidden, timeless symbolism. Such customs as scoffs are best understood as a form of *knowledge* by the people who engage in and continue or change them. Not just knowledge of each other or of the 'right' way to enact the custom but, in the deepest sense, a form of critical knowledge of their history.

By this I do not mean history as we understand it in the schools – such and such happened on this day in this place. That kind of abstract history is only one form in which the past can be understood. I mean that custom teaches people about their history as it is lived – as it has shaped their social interactions. Custom in this sense, is history *become* knowledge – social, not private knowledge – which is one reason why customary traditions are always being changed by the participants: they are always learning new things about themselves in changing circumstances which call their social existence and their traditions into question.

Such customs as scoffs are ambiguous. This ambiguity originates not just because the social relations expressed by such customs as scoffs are ambiguous – a mixture of closeness and antagonism within the community – but for far more basic reasons. The fundamental ambiguity of scoffing is that it, like other salient customs, *is at one and the same time penetrated by outside forces* (in this case the forces of merchant capitalism) *and also created and enacted by the community* – something of their own, something that expresses and defines their own experience and their feelings about what might happen or has happened.

It is precisely this deeper and more profound ambiguity of custom that enables custom not only to convey history but to shape it – to start with what is given, to start from a crystalization and an expression of the past and to become, from this base, one of the crucial loci for claims on the future.

This dynamic potential of culture is not universal, not timeless, not placeless, but is itself historically specific. Artisans, for example, often ritualized interactions *within the workplace* in the early days of manufacturing and used these rituals as a locus of struggles with their employers. Newfoundland fisherfamilies, fragmented rather than combined in their working relations, ritualized their relations not in the workplace but in the community.[64] They have created the potential, as the song 'Aunt Martha's Sheep' shows, for using these rituals to contest not exploitation in the workplace but the intrusive presence of the state in their community. I am not suggesting that these rituals could have a decisive impact – to the contrary they contain as well the potential for self-mockery and thus, ultimately, for political passivity. But that too is as significant as the active role of custom in history.

Were customs simply derivative from social or political–economic organization, such customs as scoffs would likely address the social organization of appropriation. But customs also both express and shape the understandings and the claims of those who enact them – the community of participants as it defines and knows itself. Those who participate in enacting customs are rarely, if ever, all the members of a social system: thus the 'belonging' of custom to its participants

366 Gerald M. Sider

is one of the main factors partially separating particular customs from, and partially articulating these same customs with, the larger social system in which they occur. On the basis of this partial separation and articulation, custom can play a partly independent role in history, a role which sometimes contributes to active involvement in change and sometimes is a force for quiescence.

The Newfoundland data suggests four major factors which distinguish what sort of role custom will play in history: the content of the knowledge custom conveys, the ties custom creates, the social composition of the participants, and the diversity of customs present.

The knowledge conveyed by outport customs is of the victim as an equal – a way of knowing the identity of the family and the community and of knowing the family and the community as the author of its bonds and its antagonisms. The political and economic quiescence this knowledge engenders is reinforced within the domain of custom by the symbolic and social exclusion of the merchant from the community of participants in Newfoundland village customs, by the transitory nature of the social ties custom here creates, and especially by the social isolation of the outports, based in part on the similarity of adjacent outports, which keeps the whole set of village customs from being inter-penetrated by divergent customs with divergent meanings (a situation *not* ordinarily found in 'tribal' societies nor in the socially more diverse agrarian regions of industrializing nations). When the social ties custom creates are more enduring, and in situations where the knowledge custom conveys is made more explicit and more focused on the social organization of appropriation, custom may have a more active role in forming claims against domination and exploitation.

NOTES

The first draft of this chapter was written for discussion at the Max-Planck-Institut für Geschichte, Göttingen. Professor Dr Rudolph Vierhaus graciously extended the support and hospitality of the Institute for the summer of 1979 and provided the framework for extended productive discussion. Drs Hans Medick, Alf Lüdtke, and David Sabean of the Institute contributed rigorous and stimulating critiques of the entire project, as well as of specific points. The second draft benefited from the critical remarks of Bernard Vernier.

The Institute of Social and Economic Research, Memorial University of Newfoundland, provided a much-appreciated grant for field research on 'scoffs' in January 1980, and the Folklore and Language Archive of Memorial University, Professor Neil V. Rosenberg, Director, and Philip Hiscock, Archivist, gave me access to their indispensable materials and much good and helpful advice. Anne Hart, Head Librarian of the Newfoundland Collection at Memorial University, was also particularly helpful. Professor Ellen Antler, Steven Antler, Rex Clark, Louis Chiaramonte, Keith Matthews, Bonnie McCay, Tom Nemec, Rosemary Ommer, Robert Paine, and George Story shared with me their extensive knowledge of Newfoundland and their concern for good explanation, as did William and Mary Norman, Rita Barry, Patrick Barry, William and Shirley Martin, and Eric Shave of Dunnville, Placentia Bay. Lina Brock, Christine Gailey, William Reddy, and Eric Wolf made important contributions to the final form of the analysis.

'Starve Harbour' was a beautiful settlement of New World Island, just off the north coast of Newfoundland, which no longer exists. It is depicted in Prowse's *History of Newfoundland.* (My thanks to Professor E. Seary for help in locating this settlement.)

Abbreviations used in notes

MUN   Memorial University of Newfoundland
ISER   The Institute for Social and Economic Research, MUN (including their publications series)
MUNFLA   Memorial University Folklore and Language Archives

1 (Rev.) Julian Moreton, *Life and Work in Newfoundland: Reminiscences of Thirteen Years Spent There* (London, 1863).
2 Karl Marx, *The Poverty of Philosophy*, Collected Works, vol. 6, (New York, 1963), 132.
3 Merchant capital can coexist with a wide variety of productive forms, including slavery and different kinds of tribute-paying formations (cf. Samir Amin, *Unequal Development* (New York, 1977), chap. 1), extracting 'tribute' through traditional elites, who may be directly involved in the productive process. In other situations, such as Native North Americans in the fur and skin trades, Newfoundland fisher-families, and certain forms of family production in 'proto-industrial' Europe, there were few or no intermediaries within the work process, and the producing group articulated directly with the agents of merchant capital.
4 Several hunting and gathering people have no separate linguistic category for 'work', and thus, we assume, do not separate work from non-work. What is special about the Newfoundland case and similar situations is the tendency to merge work and non-work in the context of appropriation.
5 This perspective on the dynamics of capitalist development being partly rooted in the resilience of family and community production – the capacity of developing capital to increase its extraction of surplus based in part on the capacity of families to retain traditional forms of orientation to production – derives from the analysis of proto-industrialization developed by Hans Medick in 'The Proto-Industrial Family Economy: The Structural Function of Household and Family during the Transition from Peasant Society to Industrial Capitalism', *Social History*, 1 (Oct. 1976), 291–315.
6 In an earlier analysis, 'Christmas Mumming and the New Year in Outport Newfoundland', *Past and Present*, 71 (1976), I emphasized the historical unity of custom and the existing social relations of production. Mumming was shown to have emerged and declined with the emergence and decline of the family fishery (1840s–1950s). This chapter examines another Newfoundland custom, the 'scoff', which emerged well after the family fishery developed and which persists. Mumming primarily expressed the unity of the community of producers; scoffing, as will be seen, expresses both unity and antagonism. The analysis of mumming and scoffing is not contradictory; the customs have different historical dynamics. A comparison of scoffing with certain Native American customs, such as the potlatch (suggested by David Sabean, personal communication) suggests a general point: customs that convey both unity and antagonism may be more likely to endure beyond the specific social situation in which they take form.
7 Quotation marks are used to indicate Newfoundland idioms.

8 The song, by Dick Nolan, is available on a record entitled *Fisherman's Boy* (RCA, CAS2576, St John's, Newfoundland, 1972). Robert Taft, 'Of Scoffs, Mounties and Mainlanders: The Popularity of a Sheep-Stealing Ballad in Newfoundland', forthcoming, has uncovered and reviewed the folk antecedents of this ballad, and he gives the full text.

9 This historical and social-organizational description of Cat Harbour is excerpted from James Faris, *Cat Harbour*, ISER, Newfoundland Social and Economical Papers, vol. 3 (St John's 1972) and his 'Validation in Ethnographical Description: The Lexicon of "Occasions" in Cat Harbour', *Man*, 3 (1968), 112–23. The points where I have incorporated his analysis of the cultural themes and the points where I diverge substantially will be brought out subsequently. Even where I diverge most sharply, my debt to the richness of his data, his sense of the significant, and his analytical clarity is very large.

10 Faris, *Cat Harbour*, chap. 2.

11 An analysis of the role of women in this process of production is given in Ellen Antler and James Faris, 'Adaptation to Changes in Technology and Government Policy: A Newfoundland Example', in Raoul Andersen (ed.), *North Atlantic Maritime Cultures* (Ninth International Conference of Anthropological and Ethnological Sciences (1973)) (The Hague, 1979).

12 The demographic history of Cat Harbour, along with the necessary cautions about its accuracy, is presented in Faris, *Cat Harbour*, chap. 4 and Appendix A, chart 2.

13 The common term for these fishing villages – 'outports' – conveys a multiple set of meanings. Most directly, it refers to any fishing village or town outside of the capital, St John's, especially to places where access was, until recently, primarily or only by sea. Also, as Professor Bonnie McCay pointed out, it conveys a sense of dependency: one village can be spoken of as an 'outport' of a regional market town or of a fish-merchant firm.

14 Parzival Copes, *The Resettlement of Fishing Communities in Newfoundland*, Canadian Council on Rural Development (Ottawa, 1972), présents the statistics on relocation and the government's rationale. A critical analysis of relocation, emphasizing the political and economic processes leading up to the forced abandonment of several hundred fishing villages and the social and cultural basis for the difficulties people experienced resisting relocation is presented in my 'The Ties that Bind: Culture and Agriculture, Property and Propriety in the Newfoundland Village Fishery', *Social History*, 5 (1980), 1–39.

15 This is my very rough estimate, based on aggregate statistical data of the crudest sort, collected by the government.

16 Faris, *Cat Harbour*, 40.

17 *Ibid.*, 157.

18 Professor Faris's concept of 'occasions' and 'times' is presented in *Cat Harbour*, chap. 12, and developed into an analytical typology in 'Validation'.

19 Faris, *Cat Harbour*, 156. The reference here is to the fact that people will cross (Protestant) denominational lines, otherwise rather sharply drawn, for these occasions.

20 The woman's scoff is briefly described in Ms Bonnie Bennett, Collector, 'Winter Months in Blackhead, Conception Bay, during the 1930s', MUNFLA, MS., 79–199. My thanks to Philip Hiscock for this reference.

21 Harold Squire, *A Newfoundland Outport in the Making: The Early History of Eastport*, (n.d. privately published), 40–1.

22 Faris, 'Validation', 117–18.

23 Some informants mentioned that they had heard of places or occasions where the

victim was invited and gradually led to realize that the food was 'his'. If this occurred, it was probably not frequent.

24 Faris, *Cat Harbour*, 162.
25 Squire, *Eastport*, 40.
26 I owe this reference to Professors George Story and William Kirwin. See their forthcoming dictionary of Newfoundland English, University of Toronto Press. Also see the *English Dialect Dictionary* (Edinburgh, 1906) for the associations of the related word, 'scoff', with plentiful eating and with social disorderliness.
27 Professor Ellen Antler, personal communication. The place referred to is an outport on Fogo Island in the same general region as Cat Harbour. Professor Bonnie McCay provides a thorough and useful description of changes in social relations and technology on Fogo Island in her '"Appropriate Technology" and Coastal Fishermen in Newfoundland', PhD Dissertation (Colombia University, 1976).
28 Faris, *Cat Harbour*, 135–41.
29 *Ibid.*, 162.
30 The description of this incident courtesy of Mr Boyd Trask, Collector, 'Mischief Nights', MUNFLA, MS., 68–24, 132–3.
31 Faris, *Cat Harbour*, 157–61.
32 Steven Antler, 'Colonial Exploitation and Economic Stagnation in Nineteenth-Century Newfoundland', PhD Dissertation (University of Connecticut, 1975), provides one of the best economic analyses of the early nineteenth-century organization of the fishery. His distinction between a truck and a lien system, used to clarify matters in the early nineteenth century, is not relevant here.
33 Rev. Charles Pedley, *The History of Newfoundland from the Earliest Times to the Year 1860* (London, 1863), 205.
34 *Ibid.*, 206.
35 John Szwed, *Private Cultures and Public Imagery: Interpersonal Relations in a Newfoundland Peasant Society*, MUN, ISER, Newfoundland Social and Economic Studies, vol. 2 (St John's, 1966), 52. Here he is speaking in particular of the village of 'Ross', however he cites the Amulree Commission's report (Gt Britain, Nfld Royal Commission, 1933, *Report*, cmd 4488, 105–6) to the effect that the problem was general: '[merchants] know that in a number of cases, formerly a minority, now a majority, the advances made [in the spring] will not be fully recovered, partly from causes outside the fisherman's control, such as the low price of fish or the failure of the fishery in some localities, and partly because, as the result of the combined operations of the tal qual and credit systems, the less energetic fisherman can no longer be trusted to make a good cure. The merchants therefore fix their prices at a level which will ensure them against possible loss on their supplies. This means that the good fisherman, who may be relied on to do his best, is paying for the shortcomings of his fellows. The lower the price of the fish, the greater the margin required to safeguard the merchants against loss, and the greater the burden borne by the good fishermen.'
36 On the marketing of fish, and the impact of village tal qual purchasing on marketing, see David Alexander, *The Decay of Trade: An Economic History of the Newfoundland Saltfish Trade, 1935–1965*, MUN, ISER, Newfoundland Social and Economic Studies, vol. 19 (St John's, 1977).
37 They passed from father to son, but possession was challenged from time to time.
38 Peter Neary. '"Wabana You're a Corker": Two Ballards with some Notes Towards an Understanding of the Social History of Bell Island and Conception Bay', paper presented to the Canadian Historical Association, 1973, 27–8.
39 The impact of European railroads on the Newfoundland fishery was pointed out by Professor Keith Matthews, who also alerted me to the reduction of socio-economic

differentiation in many outports over the course of the nineteenth and early twentieth centuries.

40 I am indebted to Professor George Story for the history of the word 'dieter' and for the related linguistic forms and idioms. The term dieter perhaps also contains the modern sense of 'controlled feeding', but here the control is not voluntary.

41 I owe these last three examples to Professor Louis Chiaramonte.

42 Melvin Firestone, *Brothers and Rivals: Patrilocality in Savage Cove*, MUN, ISER (St John's, 1967).

43 I am indebted to Professor David Sabean for this observation.

44 A more complete analysis of the logic of work and inheritance is given in my 'Christmas Mumming'.

45 Ronald Schwartz, 'The Crowd: Friendship Groups in a Newfoundland Outport', in Elliott Leyton (ed.), *The Compact: Selected Dimensions of Friendship*, MUN, ISER (St John's 1978).

46 Faris, *Cat Harbour*, 93.

47 This is, of course, not to imply that the village population is 'adjusted' by emigration to an optimum *ecological* point, for the ecological environment that the fishery uses, including the shoreline, is defined by their socially caused poverty and not given in nature.

48 Louis Chiaramonte, *Craftsman–Client Contracts: Interpersonal Relations in a Newfoundland Fishing Community*, MUN, ISER, Newfoundland Social and Economic Studies, vol. 10 (St John's 1970), 10.

49 *Ibid.*, 28–9.

50 Faris, *Cat Harbour*, 104. See also 103 on work-songs being used to coordinate heavy labor without direction from a leader.

51 *Ibid.*, 149.

52 *Ibid.*. 149. See also 'Validation', *passim.*

53 *Ibid.*, 148.

54 *Ibid.*, 160–1.

55 The description of this incident again courtesy of Mr Boyd Trask, Collector, whose reporting of Newfoundland customs provides some of the most sensitive and nuanced documents in the Folklore Archives. (MUNFLA, MS, 68–24, 130).

56 Szwed, *Private Cultures*, 93–4.

57 I am indebted to Professor Christine Gailey for this observation.

58 Marcel Mauss, *The Gift* (New York, 1967).

59 Pierre Bourdieu, *Outline of a Theory of Practice* (Cambridge, 1977), 4–6.

60 Dr Ellen Antler suggested this point to me.

61 *The Oxford English Dictionary.*

62 *Ibid.*

63 Szwed, *Private Cultures*, 53.

64 Dr Alf Lüdtke suggested this point.

16. Mothers, sons, and the sale of symbols and goods : the 'German Mother's Day' 1923–33

KARIN HAUSEN

Preliminary observations

The idea of investigating and illustrating the history of Mother's Day was initially motivated by purely didactic considerations. I wanted to include busy housewives and mothers in an anthology of essays on the social history of leisure aimed at a broad public. Mother's Day, which is a rather peculiar institution, seemed a possible topic. Tracing its apparently unproblematic history, however, involved me quite unexpectedly in an exciting tangle of circumstances that it was tempting, fascinating, and foolhardy to explore. Mother's Day festivities in Germany were not a Nazi invention. The yearly event had been celebrated since 1923 and staged with increasing success. In attempting to work out the logic of this process, I discovered that all the complex and multi-faceted social reality of Germany in the inter-war years was involved in a study of the banal little phenomenon that we call Mother's Day.

It became fashionable as a result of stage-management by economic, social, and political pressure groups. All the resources of modern mass media systems and advertising were used to stage it everywhere in Germany in as uniform a way as possible. The propaganda campaign was successful. By 1932, Mother's Day seems to have been generally recognized and readily accepted as a newly created festival.[1] The success of the publicity suggests that those choreographing the event had a public that was very ready to accept both the form and the content of this new addition to the holiday calendar. Indeed, on closer examination it becomes evident that current ideologies, pictures, and symbolic treatments used in connection with Mother's Day were not new creations but simply a convenient drawing-together of previously diffuse ideas. In the Weimar era, mothers, motherhood, and maternity seem to have been inescapable themes conveying widely inclusive individual and collective experiences, conflicts, fears, and longings.[2]

The general theme of motherhood was elaborated at many different levels. One was public concern for the relative and perhaps even absolute deterioration in the circumstances in which mothers lived and worked. The training and convales-

371

cence of mothers and the aim of making them functional again if they were overburdened became new welfare priorities. Mothers were also the pivot of all publicly discussed and speedily institutionalized health and population policies. Since the end of the nineteenth century, the bearing, raising, and upbringing of children had been ever more vigorously claimed, provided for, and controlled by society, but at the same time the emphasis was still on mothers carrying out their social function in private households and 'autonomous' families. This consciously contradictory social provision for maternal functions was, with broad social and political agreement, adapted to women. But there was violent political argument about whether, with reference to 'the natural vocation of motherhood', the social emancipation of women should be rejected, tolerated, or desired. In discussions about paid employment and professional training for women, and about legal and political equality of men and women, there was more mention of the social necessity of the maternal function than of women's rights to self-determination.

Characteristically in these discussions on social utility and in the debate on the reform of the abortion law, concrete, individual experiences of one's own mother and acquired social and psychic norms of masculinity and femininity were directly and positively felt. Since the eighteenth century, there has been a systematic attempt[3] to depict the supposed privacy and intimacy of the family as a refuge and extend their possibilities further to new population groups in what has been seen as the inhuman world of socially organized work. This meant such a profound rooting of the opposition of family/home and work in the sexual division of labour that only women in their 'vocation as housekeepers, wives, and mothers' were supposed to be able to ensure that the family would endure, and endure as a refuge for humanity. The merging of home–family–wife into a hoped-for creative unity seems to have survived into the twentieth century with a shift of emphasis in which 'woman' is seen overwhelmingly as 'mother' and scarcely any longer as 'wife'. There are many indications that it is not only the general trend towards a biological interpretation of social relations that has led to a determination of the social position of women in terms of their function of giving birth and feeding. It is clear that at the beginning of the twentieth century there was also a generation of adults who, as children, had had very different experiences of their fathers and mothers, seeing one as distinctly masculine and the other as distinctly maternal.

These relationships became apparent to me beyond the immediate history of Mother's Day. Penetrating further into the tangle of presumed circumstances would have meant no longer being able to utilize solely scientific distance and the social historian's professional equipment as a basis for investigation. In my first interpretation of the German Mother's Day, I paused at this boundary, but I now want to go on.[4] The fact that in offering this paper even my extremely cautious presentation of the material has provoked a discussion in which 'emotion and interest' overlapped as both a topic and as a subjective concern encouraged me to develop my own experiences with the historical material connected with Mother's Day and my observations, ideas, and speculative interpretations during the research. I should like to thank David Sabean for challenging these interpretations in his long critical commentary on my first essay and for pointing out possible links.

My second attempt at a study of the German Mother's Day still shows clear traces of clumsy work. I had considerable difficulty in finding a suitable way of expressing my ideas on the complexity of the subject. By complexity, I mean that economic, social, and political factors as an interdependent whole constitute both the structure and dynamics of historical change and that this objective cohesive entity can only become reality through the medium of persons. Persons, however, live, act, think, and feel as individual and collective interests, intentions, wishes, hopes, and fears brought into being not only by the present but also by individual and collective life-histories and by general history. The relevance of these overall statements to the Mother's Day material discussed here is indicated by Hans Medick and David Sabean in their reflections on the theme of 'interest and emotion in family and kinship'.[5] In the private family, emotion and interest are experienced as a single unity in the interaction of its members. The cohesive whole of family life and experience is by no means exclusively private and intra-family in structure: it is always at the same time publicly and socially constructed. Using the Mother's Day material as an example, I intend to show how in the conditions of social production and reproduction prevailing at the beginning of the twentieth century, emotions, modes of behaviour, and interests based in the family were sold and utilized on the market-place of economic, social, and political interests and, conversely, how collectively produced images and interpretations of social reality, created *inter alia* by advertising, penetrated and stamped family life.

In order to separate these interwoven chains of argument into a clear pattern, I shall use a sleight-of-hand to falsify historical reality and thus make it subject to analysis, proceeding as if the individual levels of investigation corresponded to one of several superimposed layers of reality. My first task will be to give a short account of the most striking features of the history of Mother's Day. This has already been done in detail elsewhere. I shall then indicate and describe as accurately as possible individual arrangements and requisites for the fashioning of the festival. For this more narrowly historical section, I shall then introduce two more developed schemes for interpreting the phenomenon. One scheme relates Mother's Day to the actual conditions of life and work of mothers in the 1920s and to the social and political attempts to secure their desired performance for the future. The second places Mother's Day in an ideological and socio-psychological context that was clearly of great value, especially for men. Here, Mother's Day is seen as a convenient manifestation of latent guilt feelings about mothers and of simultaneous expectations from them. The cult of the mother propagated by Mother's Day could have acted as a kind of promise to transmute historical experiences which had deeply shaken confidence in a patriarchal society in order to recapture the old security. The phenomenon of Mother's Day will be examined in the light of each of these schemes in turn. It would be more suitable and satisfactory to pursue both investigations simultaneously. I nevertheless hope to be able to make clear, using the procedures I have chosen, how intensely the image of the mother was part of the reality and pathology of the Weimar Republic.

The German Mother's Day, flower-sellers, and *Volk* educators

Mother's Day was always given the epithet 'German' to separate it from its American origin, for like many twentieth-century innovations this enrichment of German customs was also borrowed from the USA. There, in 1907, Ann Jarvis came forward with the suggestion of celebrating a special day for mothers. Her incessant propaganda on its behalf over the following years undoubtedly owed both its impact and its success to the highly developed 'cult of motherhood' there.[6] The fact that the cult was outstandingly profitable for economic and political interests was of course in her favour. President Wilson declared Mother's Day an official day of celebration in 1914. German imitators sometimes preferred to think of it as originating in Nordic Scandinavia, where it had been naturalized since 1918.[7]

In Germany, the Verband Deutscher Blumengeschäftsinhaber (VDB) (League of German Florists) seized the initiative with regard to Mother's Day in 1922.[8] Their colleagues in America, who had made the carnation the Mother's Day flower, showed them the way to a flower festival that would stimulate business. After the committee of the League had decided, in 1922, to propagate the idea of a Mother's Day in Germany too, it gained a year later in its new managing director, Dr Rolf Knauer, an eloquent and dynamic propagandist. He travelled in connection with the idea, advocating with great fervour the creation of a 'Mother's Day movement'. From 1922, the constant advertising tactics of the florists' trade was to conceal any commercial interest 'and to stress only the ideal side of the cult of the mother'.[9]

This strategy was realized as local branches of the League, with Knauer's support (his talks to invited guests seem to have aroused public enthusiasm), set up 'neutral committees' to prepare the Mother's Day festivities.[10] These non-party and non-denominational committees included representatives of local authorities, churches, schools, and welfare unions, and the fact that such people were participating insured both idealism and publicity. Other targets for the idea of Mother's Day were youth organizations and women's associations. Lured by advertisements, the press was willing to print articles on Mother's Day in its news and features sections. Florists contributed free bouquets and decorations for presentation in hospitals, old people's homes, and at public Mother's Day celebrations, and also distributed publicity items such as brochures, signs, and labels to customers and schoolchildren and provided 'neutral' posters and slogans both in their own windows and for advertising pillars and cinemas. Even the radio network helped the cause. Knauer gave his first radio talk on Mother's Day as early as 1924.[11]

In the whole advertising process, it is particularly surprising to note the extent to which the florists' trade paper was used to provide an ideological preparation for its readers in the matter of honouring mother. There were occasional criticisms that this or that individual florist had acted rather too commercially and against the agreed policy of the League.[12] At the end of the twenties there were regularly brief analyses of Mother's Day trade. In general, however, articles on Mother's Day spoke of the highly intrinsic value of honouring mother and the 'neutral' nature of the festivities. The florists appear clearly to have benefited from this ideological unanimity in more fields than that of training in customer relations. They themselves appear to have acquired from this general attitude their own incomparably higher qualification with regard to Mother's Day trade than that of their competitors in the field such as confectioners, parfumiers, stationers, and shopkeepers selling textiles and domestic goods. Only flowers, of course, were non-materialistic enough to symbolize the deeper inner values of Mother's Day.[13]

Despite unmistakable progress in the dissemination of the idea of Mother's Day, the campaign did not at first lead to the hoped-for rapid breakthrough. It was not until Knauer succeeded in creating a more convincing institutional basis for an advertising policy directed towards ideal aims that German society wholeheartedly adopted the new occasion. This aim had been achieved in 1925, when the Arbeitsgemeinschaft für Volksgesundung (Study Group for *Volk* Recovery) committed itself to the idea of Mother's Day, and the central committee Knauer set up to prepare for Mother's Day went on to become a committee of the Arbeitsgemeinschaft in 1926.[14] That meant that the main organizing body for Mother's Day publicity was now in the hands of apparently disinterested '*Volk* educators'. Knauer himself first became a member of the board of the Arbeitsgemeinschaft in 1926. By April 1927, he resigned, declaring that in view of his position as director of the VDB the work that the Arbeitsgemeinschaft was doing for Mother's Day 'should not appear to be linked to the furtherance of material interests'.[15] The business aspects of Mother's Day were consequently that much less explicit. The florists styled themselves further as the selfless servants of a lofty idea and offered their customers not only flowers but also their own and, until 1929, Arbeitsgemeinschaft-produced materials for Mother's Day. The impresarios of the celebration in order to express their high ideals and lofty concepts willingly put up with the commercial and market relationships linked to such effective advertising. This union of dissimilar partners helped Mother's Day, an amalgam of commercial interests, 'moral' ideas, and social policy, to achieve from 1925 onward its now incontestable position of overwhelming strength.

When Knauer came into contact with Arbeitsgemeinschaft circles, that body was in process of reorganization.[16] Its predecessor, the Volksgemeinschaft zur Wahrung von Anstand und Sitte (*Volk* Association for the Defence of Decency and Morality), which had been founded early in 1920, had virtually abandoned its activities in the inflationary years. A new beginning was planned for 1925 with the transformation into the Arbeitsgemeinschaft. According to Article 1 of its constitution, the aims of the Arbeitsgemeinschaft were:

> by means of a union of sections of the German people conscious of their moral duty and responsibility, to stress publicly the bases of German virtue and good morality, to engage actively in spiritual renewal and corporal improvement with particular attention to population policy and to serve as an influence on legislation and administration concerning the internal and external recovery of the people.[17]

The Arbeitsgemeinschaft was set up as a linking organization between the major welfare associations with the aim of systematically discussing 'on neutral grounds' matters of common interest 'in the border area between social and ethical problems' with representatives of government and various authorities. In 1926 the Deutsche Gesellschaft für Bevölkerungspolitik (German Society for Population Policy) merged with the Arbeitsgemeinschaft. By the end of 1927, the latter had 171 individual and 349 corporate members, of which 26 were public authorities of one kind or another. The closest contacts of the Arbeitsgemeinschaft were those with the co-ordinating committees of the Protestant, Catholic, and Jewish welfare organizations. Other principal participants were representatives of women's leagues from the various denominations, of movements to encourage morality, anti-drink societies, the Reichsbund der Kinderreichen (National Association for Large Families), and the Gesellschaft zur Bekämpfung der Geschlechtskrankheiten (Association to Combat Venereal Diseases). By 1928, six specialist committees had gradually emerged, which covered the whole programme of 'popular recovery'. These were: 1) population policy, 2) health care, physical training, and alcohol, 3) sexual ethics and questions of sex education, 4) cinema, theatre, and press, 5) pornography and objectionable matter, the protection of young people in the entertainment field, 6) preparation for Mother's Day.

The practical contribution the Arbeitsgemeinschaft made in achieving these aims was mainly that of producing material, information, and publicity. All their work was informed by the conviction that extensive popular education and legislation were necessary to halt the threat of a decline resulting from the collapse of morality and a falling birthrate.[18] The '*Volk* educators', who ranged ideologically from religious-conservative to *voelkisch*, attacked Weimar society, which they saw as entirely afflicted by moral weakness, crisis, and collapse. Their particular concern was for the situation of the family, which they saw as severely damaged by war and revolution and endangered by harmful ideologies originating in the USA and the USSR. Their day was said to be severely afflicted by bad marriages, divorce, the 'degradation of the whole sexual life', by free love, open marriage, and nudism, and the 'immoral sexual ethics' of the young resulting from 'obscene' theatre and cinema shows and their destructive effects, such as the misuse of alcohol, venereal disease, abortion, and a low birth-rate.

It was on the basis of this ideological consensus that the Arbeitsgemeinschaft provided help and distribution facilities for members. The leading figure was a twenty-six-year-old doctor of medicine (and from 1926 also a doctor of philosophy), Hans Harmsen.[19] He was appointed as secretary in the first instance only for a year and without a fixed salary. Before the official founding of the Arbeitsgemeinschaft, he had already worked successfully to have Knauer's Mother's Day taken up by that organization. This was because he saw in the 'Mother's Day project', as it was put forward to the Arbeitsgemeinschaft by Knauer:

a particularly favourable means of influencing the greatest number of people . . . It will immediately be possible to acquaint many circles not yet associated with our work more closely with questions of population policy and social ethics, to put the importance of the family fairly and squarely on the agenda, and to create links transcending the boundaries of denominations and the state.[20]

Propaganda was organized centrally by the 'Vorbereitenden Ausschuß für den Deutschen Muttertag' (Preparatory Committee for the German Mother's Day). Apart from Harmsen and Knauer, its members included a representative each from the Reichsbund der Kinderreichen (National Association for Large Families), the Evangelisches Wohlfahrtsamt (Protestant Principal Welfare Office), the Evangelische Frauenhilfe (Protestant Women's Aid Group), the Verband zur Bekämpfung der öffentlichen Unsittlichkeit (Association for Public Morality) and, from 1930, from Caritas.[21] The office of the Arbeitsgemeinschaft took on the clerical work. Advertising costs were covered by donations and the sale of Mother's Day literature. In 1928, for example, 4,800 advertising items, 18,450 pamphlets, 8,500 prospectuses of publicity material, 3,800 postcards, 40 sets of slides, and 550 other communications were sent out.[22] Press and radio material was also established. The little 'Mother's Day Writings'[23] published in the *Schriften zur Volksgesundung*, introduced an understanding of its deeper meaning, gave reports of exemplary festivities, provided suggestions and inspiration for ways of organizing the celebrations, and inspired reporting of the tempestuous forward march of the Mother's Day movement at home and abroad. Its chief function was to publicize the guidelines drawn up by the Preparatory Committee,[24] with details of methods tried out between 1923 and 1925, as a means of giving the movement a single norm for Mother's Day.

The associations represented on the Preparatory Committee offered oppor-tunities for encouraging local initiatives. Following the florists, local groups of the Reichsbund der Kinderreichen had declared right from the start that a general Mother's Day would be ideal for their aims.[25] Even before 1926, their specialty was the organization of official celebrations of fruitful motherhood, at which well-known local politicians would present a savings-book, an inscribed plate or similar gifts as signs of recognition to mothers with many children. The Evangelische Frauenhilfe[26] believed in early 1928 that as the largest mass organization (it had some 600,000 members), it should accept the *fait accompli* and participate in the arrangements for Mother's Day, which was now established. At first, it referred its members to material produced by the Arbeitsgemeinschaft but from 1930 produced its own. This organization, which since 1897 had co-operated with the clergy in organizing and carrying out the professional and voluntary community work of women members of the Protestant churches, had, since the middle 1920s, been increasingly concerned with the education, care, and convalescence of mothers. From 1930, it used Mother's Day as an opportunity for its own 'mother service' branch to organize street collections. Presumably, like this group, the other major associations of the Protestant church took decisions in their central committees and called for the celebration of Mother's Day. On the other hand, the Catholic church[27] and its associations maintained a watching brief until around 1930, although this did not of course exclude participation at local levels. The tradition of devotion to Mary was probably a decisive factor in this striking distancing from the secular cult of Mother's Day.

Although I have not examined in detail which associations and organizations joined in the Mother's Day movement and when, or which places and regions in Germany became part of the movement at a particular time, there are many indications that the 'German Mother's Day' emerged victorious from its publicity campaign around 1930.[28] Despite their differing interests and aims, the innovative stage-managers succeeded in ten short years in establishing Mother's Day as a special day. In doing so, they invented scenarios, images, and varying activities to express and impress what they maintained was the rich depth of that festival for the honouring of the mother. These will form the subject matter of the next section of my chapter.

The cult of the mother as image, ceremony, and ideology

These differing interests of the stage-managers were in accord in that their aim was to set a sign, which would put the seal of universal social approval on certain formative images and be effective, with mutual support, in explaining the significance of situations, providing norms of behaviour, and encouraging buying. In the management of Mother's Day, something which in societies with a capitalist system of production is normally concealed by a mystifying economic rationality becomes at one point astonishingly evident. Here, what I have to say is based on the ideas of the anthropologist Marshall Sahlins. He sees as the specific characteristic of that system the fact that symbolic production is an integral part of the production of goods: 'rational production for gain is in one and the same motion the production of symbols. And its acceleration, as in opening up new consumer markets, is exactly the same as opening up the symbolic set by permutation of its logic.'[29] To understand capitalist economies as cultural systems, we must see in the production and distribution of goods also a dialectically mediated production and distribution of culture. Objects of value incorporate not only their value expressed in terms of money but also symbolic value. Sahlins points out that advertising men are specialists in the cultural meaning of these connections. I should like to point out that in addition advertising also works with those interpretations, once they are discovered, as a shaping force on the social production of culture and goods. This alternative relationship could probably easily be seen in advertising for cleansing materials.

The publicity for Mother's Day in Germany was also an inseparable mixture of interpretations and intentions to shape an event. In order to separate the individual elements of the Mother's Day celebrations, I shall first use publicity material from the period 1923–33 issued by the VDB, the Arbeitsgemeinschaft, and the Evangelische Frauenhilfe. I shall then move on to arrangements for the festivities in individual towns, and how these were communicated to the central organizations and published by them.[30] This material does not of course enable us to decide whether or how Mother's Day was celebrated in individual families, but it probably does provide a key to the logic behind the choreography of the festivities.

The first point of interest about Mother's Day is that it is celebrated on the second Sunday in May. A decision about the month was disputed at first.[31] May was finally decided on chiefly so as to have a single date for the whole of Germany and because if a festival involving flowers was to take place between Easter and Whitsuntide, florists would be in a better position to meet the great demand. It was also the month when Catholics traditionally honoured Mary. There was never any argument about the choice of day. Sunday was the day when the dead were remembered, and it should also be the day for Mother's Day. There were differences between Mother's Day and 1 May, which the workers had made their own day of struggle and celebration, at first by refusing to work on it, and the International Women's Day on 8 March, which was first claimed by women socialists in 1911 by means of demonstrations supporting women's demands. As distinct from these militant secular celebrations and their battle for demands, Mother's Day was to be as a Sunday celebration a day of harmony and peaceful contemplation.

It was also typical of Mother's Day and its future development that it was introduced in Germany in 1923 with the imperative slogan 'Honour your mother',[32] reminiscent of the Fourth Commandment 'Thou shalt honour thy father and thy mother', but with a significant alteration. Only the mother (the only mother) was to be honoured. The father was not included. In addition, the command was addressed collectively and not individually, the plural pronoun in German indicating this. At that period, however, honouring someone collectively was chiefly connected with memorial services for heroes and the dead.[33] The popular alternative title for Mother's Day at the time was 'Der deutschen Mutter Ehrentag' or 'Der Mutter Gedenktag', and the German wording suggests this kind of significance. The phrase 'Honour your Mother' also provided the basic note for the next few years. Occasional variations were 'Honour your mother with flowers' or 'Remember your mother on her day'.[34]

In Berlin in 1923 posters with the inscription 'Honour your mother' appeared in shops, on advertising pillars, in the 'better' inns, in banks, post-offices, tramcars, underground and railway stations.[35] The inscription was explained by an appeal composed by Knauer,[36] *Der deutsche Mutter Ehrentag*, which was displayed and in schools, churches, and in newspapers sometimes personally distributed. This appeal orchestrated the theme of the slogan and supported 'honour' with a 'why' and 'how'. At this point, however, it seems best first to describe the form that Mother's Day took before going on to examine what the phenomenon was meant to symbolize and convey.

The stage-managers did not mean Mother's Day to be a 'noisy, public occasion' but 'an intimate family and domestic festival'.[37] The Mother's Day committee of the Arbeitsgemeinschaft therefore established this intention in 1927 and maintained it subsequently. Guideline no. 1 declared that 'Mother's Day shall be primarily a quiet family and domestic occasion.'[38] As early as 1923 it was established, following the first Mother's Day, that the occasion should not include 'an outward honouring' of the mother by means of flowers pinned to her dress, as had become usual in the USA and as had been suggested for trial in Germany, since that would not 'correspond to the more inward inspiration of the German Mother's Day'.[39]

In his appeal in connection with the first Mother's Day, Knauer had already urged that the festivities should be conducted 'in the German home'. His plan for the occasion was as follows:

on that day we should decorate our home in a festive way. The place of honour belongs to the mother. Let it be decorated. Gifts of flowers should tell her of our love and gratitude . . . In the close circle of our loved ones, let us tell our mother the feelings we have in our hearts for her. Let us praise her again in loyalty and devotion, offering our day's work for her joy and honour. From the depths of her soul our better selves shall create new power and courage.

If, Knauer says, things are done in this way, 'everything in our souls that is living in love, honour, and gratitude towards our mother . . . will become really visible'.[40]

It is worth analysing these stage directions. It is striking that the mother is not seen as an active subject, and indeed the celebrations could take place in her absence, with simply an idea of mother being honoured. The relationships of those conducting the occasion with the object of it, prescribed in the three formulaic words 'love', 'honour', and 'gratitude', are 'living' in their souls and seek revelation. The 'place of honour' decorated with wreaths and flowers and like an altar is provided as a place of revelation and solemn vow. The celebrants are then supposed to acquire the strength and courage they need from 'the depths of her soul' in order to fulfil their vow and to offer their daily work in fidelity and devotion for her joy and honour. The obvious sacralization imposed (the raising of the mother to the status of a stylized mother-goddess) persisted in later years, but to a lesser extent. The *Arbeitsgemeinschaft* version[41] recommended that 'on this day, everything should be centred around the mother in love, gratitude, and honour. This will mean that she has the opportunity of blessing her little community from the treasure-house of her inner life'. The decorated 'place of honour' and the assembled family community remained lasting components of the occasion. The children were also recommended to free her from all her normal duties on that day, so that she could become 'the still centre' of the family.[42] Further requisites for the 'intimate' family occasion were bouquets, small gifts, and artistically written or recited poems. It is striking that only the mother and children were brought together. It was the latter who were to decorate, do the housework, and give presents. At most, the father had a role in the wings, as a kind of prompt for the children on stage.[43] As a husband, he was superfluous, but as a son he could perform all the more intensely his duty of remembering an old, distant, or dead mother.

This way of staging a family celebration that was at once both national and intimate seems to owe something to the Christmas celebrations and their wealth of traditions. In the last third of the nineteenth century, they had become closely related to the supply of presents on the market and developed into a general popular custom. Its focus was the candle-lit tree, in Weber-Kellermann's words 'the ceremonial centre of an almost liturgically appealing programme of festivities'.[44] The parallels between the two occasions are clear. Their appreciable differences are due to their differing social functions. Christmas, with the figure of Father Christmas/*Ruprecht*, who can both give and withhold presents and is thus a major influence on children, is centred upon an active father-figure. Mother's Day, however, involves a mythically idealized, stylized, and completely passive mother-figure. Even the rituals of giving characteristic of each occasion in our day, which are not based on reciprocity, are arranged so that giving and accepting have opposite directions. At Christmas, children receive gifts for good behaviour from a mythically distant and anonymous donor. On Mother's Day, children give symbolic gifts as an expression of gratitude for her 'motherliness' to a mother who is indeed known but is temporarily by the celebration remote and alien.

This extremely dissimilar relationship to the gifts for mother and children was certainly deliberately and consciously built into the ceremonies by the florists. Children not yet able to express verbally the particular mother/child relationship implied in Mother's Day were to use instead flowers as their 'language'. The florists claimed that they dealt in goods generally accepted as universal symbols for the relationships between human beings. They maintained that 'we communicate many meanings and suggestions, particularly when it is a question of expressing warmth, thanks, joy, and sympathy without any obligation to reciprocate these emotions', and insisted that the flowers in question 'become in the hands of the true giver magicians spreading happiness, joy, and peace into people's minds and hearts'.[45]

If thousands of Mother's Day celebrations in isolated families were to be uniformly orchestrated to conform to this formula, the distribution network of efficient agencies existing in twentieth-century societies was an essential factor in linking private families into the wider social context. Children and young people were called upon to take the Mother's Day message to their own families. Schools, churches, youth organizations, and women's associations willingly took on the task of explaining the spirit and form of Mother's Day to children and young people. Amongst the things that had to be taught were the following detailed instructions for the occasion, the majestic and pious 'Ten Command-ments for Mother's Day' circulated by the Mother's Day committee of the *Arbeitsgemeinschaft*:[46]

1 Free your mother from all work on the Sunday, so that she can have a holiday.
2 Early in the morning, put flowers on the bed or the table.
3 If you are away from home, send her a letter or a card with a little present.
4 Go to the cemetery, if your mother is dead, or if another mother from your circle of relatives is there, and decorate the grave with spring flowers, as mourning wreaths are laid there on *Totensonntag*.
5 Try to find out if any mother in your neighbourhood is in need or worried, say consoling words to her, take her hand and give her a small gift.
6 If you know of a mother in hospital, in an infirmary, or an old people's home, remember her. Do not ask whether it is someone else's duty.
7 If you see an old mother on the street, go up to her and be friendly to her or give her a small gift if necessary.
8 Take away burdens from a mother, whether she be young or old, accompany her and help her if necessary.
9 Now and on Mother's Day itself be thoughtful, translate the thought into a deed, and see that others do the same.
10 Resolve that now and in the future you will respect, honour, and support your own mother and all German mothers on every day and always as well as on Mother's Day. Make sure that others do the same. Then Mother's Day will be a blessing for the whole German people!

These 'commandments' clearly show that there was a smooth transition from a private celebration for one's own mother to a completely public cult of motherhood in general. Indeed, public celebrations had been foreseen from the start when planning Mother's Day, since that was the only way to motivate social agencies as intermediaries for contacting children and young people. It was therefore desired that the various associations and arrangements used in the service of Mother's Day should also be creatively and generally enlighteningly active. In so far as possible, 'neutral' committees should co-ordinate such activities, uniting people at a higher level than those of party or denominations. The initiators of Mother's Day also gave the necessary help.[47] Publishing exhaustive reports of the occasion in individual places was not simply a means of strengthening the movement by giving details of its success. It was also done to inspire the 'neutral committees' for the next Mother's Day. In addition, increasingly comprehensive information about publicity material was being produced by the central committee of the *Arbeitsgemeinschaft*. Apart from postcards and slides which could be either purchased or borrowed, it could offer in particular details of suitable literature. Suitably produced collections of poems, songs, sayings, prose, and playlets on the maternal theme were its province just as much as literature on educational problems and social, medical, and population questions.

From the beginning it was usual to 'create the underlying feeling for Mother's Day celebrations by means of a special publicity evening'.[48] That might be in the form of a lecture, as was the case in Liegnitz in 1926 when the chairman of the 'neutral committee' opened the evening and was followed by a representative of the Catholic church, a doctor, an Evangelical minister, and a headmaster, who all gave a talk on the theme of 'mother', or that of preliminary celebration in which the lecture was preceded and followed by appropriate songs and poems about mother.

The public celebrations on Mother's Day itself were very varied in kind. The small town of Moers, near Duisburg, had organized a kind of popular festival since 1924. Its programme for 1926 was as follows:

Saturday 7 May, *7.30 p.m.*: Slide show for youth who had finished school, but for everyone else too, 'Mother and Child', lecture with living tableaux from art. Celebration with music, address, and poems. The Moers School of Music and others will play for us.

Sunday 8 May *evening* [more probably morning] 7.30 Remembrance at mother's grave in the Moers cemetery, trombones, poems, and addresses. Church choir. *From 9 o'clock*: Music and songs in the hospitals, orphanage, and in the parks of the town. Festival services: *11 a.m.*: Morning service in the Castle yard. Address by representative of local administration. *4 p.m.*: Main service in municipal park: address by the mayor, music, songs, recitations, gymnastic displays, addresses. *8 p.m.*: Closing ceremony by Evangelical town mission in the Evangelical church.[49]

In Kiel,[50] where the town council and, in particular, the Arbeitsgemeinschaft für öffentliche und freie Wohlfahrtspflege (Association for Public and Free Welfare Care) had been organizing Mother's Day celebrations since 1924, philanthropic associations decided the public programme. The 'morning events' took place in the municipal theatre. There was 'an artistic and ethical framework', and 'good mothers with large families' who were poor were presented with a savings-bank book bound into a bouquet. Children also sold donated flowers and postcards on the streets. The proceeds went to children in need of convalescence in 1924 and to mothers in the same position in 1927. The municipal health department, in addition to all this, arranged a ceremony together with women welfare workers in the mother's advice centres. This involved not only coffee and cakes but also musical items and, as the main event, an 'instructive talk by a paediatrician'.

However, public events in the *Festsaal*, with singing, recitations, *tableaux vivants* and playlets, and a lecture of an appropriate nature were probably more common, since they were less demanding.[51] It was certainly not rare for clergymen to take part in the programme and to speak of the honour of motherhood in their Sunday sermons and celebrate 'Mother's Day as a religious occasion'.[52]

Whether the occasion was celebrated publicly or privately, however, for those ultimately shaping it a particular quality had to govern the multiplicity of forms it could take. The celebrations had to serve 'the representation of the lofty idea of honouring motherhood',[53] sometimes also referred to as 'worshipping of the mother',[54] and this 'idea of Mother's Day [should] take shape in its moral dimension without any subsidiary matter.'[55]

This quality was described in clichés such as 'high moral idea', 'pure moral idea', 'beautiful thought', and 'purity and beauty of the thought of Mother's Day'. Two elements of meaning mingled when there was talk of 'the lofty, sublime thought within the day on which we honour mothers'.[56] There was an appeal on the one hand to the 'morally lofty value of honouring mothers'[57] and on the other to the conviction that Mother's Day had 'a deep social significance'.[58] The occasion lay claim to 'great significance' and would have 'fulfilled its purpose' if, 'whether the occasion be celebrated quietly or noisily, the cultural mission of Mother's Day was not forgotten'.[59] In his appeal in connection with the first German Mother's Day in 1923, Knauer had suggested that it should become 'a great dedication and celebration of the Fatherland'.[60] This aim was not to be achieved during the lifetime of the Weimar Republic. That the occasion was a 'beautiful custom' with its own particular atmosphere was, however, stressed very vigorously by all those stage-managers. In order to study this particular quality in greater depth, I shall first examine the central ideological cohesion of the cult of motherhood contained in the Mother's Day propaganda and then the emphasized or intended social effect of the uniformly celebrated occasion.

The question as to the ideological framework in which the cult of the mother could be propagated as a moral idea can be divided into two component questions: what makes the mother worthy of being honoured; and by whom and for what reason should she be honoured? The multiplicity of writings explaining anew each year the 'deep' meaning of Mother's Day provides precise answers to this list of questions. The propagandists were not addressing their public on the question of mothers as individuals in particular social and economic circumstances. What they wanted to create – and it was the only thing they wanted to create – was an understanding of the *idea* of the mother and hence the mother as an embodiment of idealized qualities and ways of behaving. They talked about mothers without saying anything about what a 'wife and mother' was, what skills she had or what work she did. In these writings, women are reduced to the symbolic parts of the body: hearts, or, much less frequently, hands. The 'mother's heart' stood for love, the 'tireless hands' or 'hard-working hands of a mother' stood for work. Work and love underwent a symbolic transmutation into physical parts of the body. Mother = heart = love. The cluster of qualities embodied by 'the' mother and called 'motherliness' was the 'sum of all that is sweet and high and holy in this world.'[61] 'Motherliness' can be more accurately paraphrased on the one hand as fidelity, goodness, understanding, warmth, concern, and on the other as devotion, sacrifice, self-denial. Those writing on Mother's Day were wont to strengthen these nouns by means of adjectives such as unwearying, inexhaustible, immeasurable, and boundless. The following is a quotation from the florists' trade paper in 1924: 'Oh, mother's heart, how bottomlessly deep is your love! No word can express for us how measureless is your devotion, your self-sacrifice, your fidelity.'[62] Honour or worship declared worthy became a mother stylized into an idea removed from all earthly dimensions. This idealized mother had no needs of her own;[63] not even weariness could overcome her, and her doing was all spontaneous and uncomplaining self-sacrifice.

The following poems and advertising jingles are taken from the *Verbandszeitung Deutscher Blumengeschäftsinhaber* (*VDB*). They illustrate some of the themes discussed in the text: the inexhaustible nature of mother's care, mother as refuge, mother as a symbol of social unity, Mother's Day and flower-selling.

Eternal Flame
Oh you, Holy Saint, born never to expire,
Oh you, Comfort in distress,
Oh you, Abator of sorrows,
Oh eternal One!
Your white throne of granite stairs
Already stood when God to the first humans called
In the dream garden of his paradise.
There his 'let there be' also called you to life:
That you the living creature
Should escort on earth's pilgrimage
So long a breathing being goes his rounds,
So long a new one blossoms from the old,
An infant soul begins its course:
You follow the track which marks its way,
Unconquerable, profound,
Oh you, Eternal One: Mother Love!

VDB, 3 May 1929, p. 345

Is there one day in the German Reich,
When old and young can be alike,
Where no party, hate and envy
Destroy our love of unity?
Oh yes, my heart, do not despair,

I know of such a day, where
We are free from ill-will and decay,
The second German Mother's Day,
Coming on the 11th May.

VDB, 25 April 1924, p. 279

Mother's Day
The mother's care does not abate,
She toils for children both early and late.
Thus thank her for her drudgery
On the Second German Mother's Day.

VDB, 9 May 1924, p. 311

German child!
Your mother's goodness thank today,
Bring her blossoms fresh in May!

Today as love's most tender spoken,
Fresh flowers in her hand's the token!

A word of thanks to mother say,
Through flowers your thoughts to her convey!

Today your thoughts on mother set,
And give fresh flowers at her fête.

VDB, 13 April 1928, p. 352

The image of the mother thus proposed was clearly intended to acquire credibility and conviction from the rich store of childhood experiences. The 'longing look backwards' to the 'mother figure' was just as clearly assumed as the 'happy childhood' in which the mother gave of her consolation, love, and 'brought back self-confidence'.[64] In a particularly extreme image, the recollected mother/child tie was stylized in the expression 'true mothers bear the torch of our longing'.[65] A close examination of these turgid texts, so exaggeratedly sentimental as to be unbearable today, shows clearly that the stage-managers of Mother's Day were firmly establishing the desired cult of the mother as a cult of the mother-image. 'Gratitude, love, and honour' were to provide the longed-for smooth return to the mother. The call to honour the mother on her special day clearly contained the promise, or even the commandment, that it would lead back to the mother. In one place, for example, we read that 'motherliness' is 'our salvation' and that it alone 'has given grace to our souls'.[66]

The propaganda was not content simply to give concrete expression to individual longings for mother. Its first aim was to mobilize its public for the collective goal of establishing a better future for the German people. 'In the day which is dedicated to the cult of the mother, creative powers in the life of the German *Volk* are hidden.'[67] The intended social function of Mother's Day would be achieved simultaneously in three directions. The cult of the mother would once again reunite the divided nation, re-establish the family as the embryonic cell of the State, and educate young people for their future responsibilities. Seen in this way, the Mother's Day movement was a kind of revival movement, which aimed to shake awake new forces capable of drawing the *Volk* back from the brink of a precipice. The contemporary situation was seen as gloomy. In the general 'political and economic distress' of the time, the much-discussed 'destruction of family life' was seen as the most dangerous threat that would produce 'moral decline' and 'failure of communal feeling and readiness to make sacrifices'.[68]

In this situation, Mother's Day was intended to be a useful contribution to 'a real moral rebirth of our people'.[69] A simple conjunction of ideas lay at the origin of this phrase. 'The mother is the guardian of family life'[70] was a notion that had long been part of the general stock of ideas. The 'collapse' of the family that was so often asserted could therefore be ascribed to a failing of the mother. Propagandists for Mother's Day consequently also criticized the 'decline of femininity and motherliness amongst our people'.[71] As a result of materialism, individualism, and an unlimited search for pleasure, women were said to have become indifferent to their vocation as wives and mothers. The cure the propagandists proposed was: 'Send us good mothers, and things will be better for Germany.'[72] Here, Mother's Day had its part to play. The cult of the mother, as a force for education, was to subject women, and more particularly growing girls, to the idea of motherhood and thus to make it incumbent on them to choose their 'natural' vocation. Men and boys were to be brought up to honour their mothers and value the family. The organizers of Mother's Day also ardently expected to enlighten them about the 'great questions of our existence as a *Volk*', the meaning of 'motherhood', 'racial hygiene', and 'sexual education'. As a long-term *Volk* pedagogical aim', Mother's Day meant hope for 'a sense of the importance of the family' with 'families rejoicing in their children as the fount of all the power and virtue of the people'.[73]

The exemplar of the mother lovingly sacrificing herself had the overridingly great advantage of being valid irrespective of wealth, poverty, or membership of any particular class or social stratum. The managers of Mother's Day were clearly correct in their assessment of circumstances in Germany and their assumption that all sections of the population would welcome a cult of this kind. Their introduction of Mother's Day as an occasion to integrate the whole nation was a logical next step. Their premises, that 'the common love and honour for the mother binds all members of our people together with new bonds',[74] were constantly expressed in new variations. To these were added the injunction to bridge all gaps between parties and denominations on Mother's Day and to celebrate the occasion as one of harmony and reconciliation. Hopes for a *Volksgemeinschaft* were expressed whenever the general idealism of 'the love of the home, of the fatherland, and of the mother' were stressed as unifying power.[75]

The suggested 'moral' idea of Mother's Day was at first simply an ideological, social, and political pretension which the stage-managers intended to use as a means of establishing their new 'people's custom'. It became a reality, however,

Mother's Day store decoration from Blumenhaus Emmrich, Breslau 10, Mathiasstr. 74
Source: Verbandszeitung Deutscher Blumengeschäftsinhaber, 17 (1933), p. 1.

when it was incorporated into the directions for staging. Local publicity agents united behind it and transmitted it to children and young people as the message of Mother's Day. The written and the spoken word, in so far as they are available to the author in the form of the texts of poems, songs, speeches, sermons, and newspaper articles, were combined to turn the pretension into coin of the realm. Now and again, pictures showing the mother resembling the Madonna, dressed in old German costume, and in close communion with the child were circulated. From the late 1920s, florists received precise instructions on how to use the idea of Mother's Day in window decorations as an effective means of advertising. It was recommended that Mother's Day texts, pictures of mothers, or plastic figurines of women 'showing all the characteristics of a mother in their features or posture' should be incorporated into floral displays to catch the eye.[76] The illustrated example shows a shop window as a kind of altar of Our Lady with a children's procession.

The uniformity and constant repetition of such statements cannot but have had some effect in the long run on a public willing to read, hear, and see. This kind of propaganda was probably capable of bringing more sharply into focus all the potentially available ideas of the mother and transforming them into a guiding image to be used as the occasion arose.[77] If that is so, Mother's Day could be interpreted as a collective attempt to establish and prescriptively propose patterns of behaviour within the family for the whole of German society. That means that two impulses in the sacralization and stylization of the Mother's Day mother are of central importance. First, it must seem in order, and hence appropriate, that *the* mother is effective in the family through sacrifice. The effort of the mother should not be measured by any human criteria. An annual thank offering is to express this situation and to help women to accept in future the burden of this superhuman maternal service to humanity. Those, however, who year in and year out claim the sacrifice of the mother should discharge their debt of gratitude on Mother's Day in order to be able to continue to demand and accept that sacrifice. The cult of the mother was to be a social recognition of a firm basis for future care and self-denial on her part and blameless acceptance on that of children demanding care and of grown-up sons. This monstrous logic reveals the central aim of the staging of Mother's Day, to which all those staging it were committed, despite minor variations.

So far, Mother's Day has been considered as a production which became a historical reality as a staged event in more and more places in Germany every year.[78] The individual mixture of private and public ways of seeing the figures in family interaction, of popular education and popular celebration, of a simultaneous strengthening of community and family cohesion, of business and symbol-laden communication, and of ideal values and the political interests of the day that can be observed in it also indicate that Mother's Day was almost certainly more than merely a successful piece of stage-management. In the following paragraphs I shall consequently try to widen the range of the analysis and consider Mother's Day as both a part and an interpretation of the social reality of the Weimar Republic. My concern will no longer be to show why the occasion came into being and what guiding images it helped convey, but rather to use the insights gained from an analysis of the Mother's Day phenomenon to bring together and interpret certain other social phenomena of the Weimar era.

Mothers in the Weimar era

What were the social circumstances producing the intense publicity for a 'German Mother's Day'? Such a question cannot be exhaustively answered by merely referring to the particular interests of specific branches of consumer industry. Nor can the mere existence of social and political pressure groups and major social agencies in the twentieth century explain why they were committed to Mother's Day. Clearly, a fairly major section of social reality must be considered. I shall therefore proceed from the supposition, which is perhaps more than merely plausible, that there was a connection between the Mother's Day propaganda and the social situation and status allotted to mothers. The predominant image of the self-sacrificing mother and the clearly formulated aim of Mother's Day – educating young girls for motherhood – are the first indications of this.

The following investigations are based on the hypothesis that the wide acceptance of the suggestion for a day of public recognition of mothers indicates that 'motherhood' was taken seriously as a social problem.[79] A publicity campaign in this form is to say the least difficult to imagine if being a mother is seen as being primarily a natural phenomenon and a private occasion. A prerequisite for understanding motherhood as a social problem is that society should attempt to prescribe and establish which maternal functions women have to carry out and that they should not be willing or able to do what is expected of them.

Those living at the time saw this as the major threatening situation in the 1920s. On the one hand, the declining birthrate was seen as a regrettable deficiency in maternal achievement.[80] And on the other the fact that mothers were overburdened by their responsibilities to the point of physical and mental collapse and that they were therefore unable to function was seen as a social and political scandal.[81] The first aim of social and political attempts to remedy this was to increase the ability and willingness of women to function as mothers. The Mother's Day propaganda was ideally suited for inclusion in a programme of this kind. The deeper structural causes of the problem were not, however, affected by such an approach. It was still widely accepted that the inevitable course of things was for mothers to have totally insufficient resources for the tasks which society expected of them.[82] The first drafts in a comprehensive family policy[83] provided for extensive economic support for large families. In the twenties, however, the means for providing for families even in extreme poverty, and in particular mothers with small children, simply were not available.

It was apparently socially inconceivable in the inter-war years that mothers should try to lessen their responsibilities. Such a course could have led to a fall in standards of achievement, and against it was the fact that since the end of the nineteenth century the generally rapid rise in standards of housekeeping and the care of children were seen purely as social progress and not as involving a greater burden of work for women. On the other hand, mothers could have been relieved of some of their burdens by providing them with help either from within the family (i.e. from the husband) or from outside by means of social institutions. It was held to be better in principle for the family to attempt to concentrate all the work in the private household on the mother. Taking care of the children outside the home was largely viewed as an undesirable emergency solution. It was indeed demanded by the socialists and communists, but at the institutional level it developed only slowly and hesitantly. Probably even fewer households than before the First World War could afford professional domestic servants.[84] Abolishing the sex-specific division of labour within the family was quite clearly outside the tolerated thought-patterns of the time.[85] In its place, consistent birth control was practised as a private form of adaptation to a changed situation. Parents, and particularly mothers, were prepared to increase expenditure per child to meet social standards. However, they also saw it as their right to decide how many children they would spend for. Since the beginning of the twentieth century, birth control had been increasingly practised in all sections of the population.[86] For these very reasons natalist politicians campaigned against this form of protection against excessive burdens adopted in the privacy of the family and drew sombre pictures of the threatening 'national death', the gloomy consequence of the refusal of potential mothers to meet their responsibilities.[87]

There have so far been no extensive investigations of the actual living and working conditions of mothers in the 1920s. There were as few statistics about mothers at this time as about families. Whether and at what age married and unmarried women lived together in one household with their children and how many children there were and of what age cannot be exactly discovered. Purely indirect data concerning family situation, size of households, employment and birth trends mean that only crude trends can be discerned. It is possible that contemporary research by individuals contains more detailed information.[88] Any evaluation of such material, however, is beyond the scope of the present study. I have made use of readily available and hence less informative sources.

It was probably of considerable importance to the actual conditions of life for women that even in the Weimar era they were seen in the powerful leading image of the time as standing beside their husband and 'breadwinner' principally in their major, indeed 'natural', role as housewives and mothers. Women brought up to motherliness were expected to function primarily in private families and only vicariously in the public through 'organized' or 'spiritual motherhood'.[89] This major image interpreted the actual social situation of women in an extremely ambiguous way. Their position was undergoing profound changes under the pressure of the enormously accelerated economic and political developments following in the wake of the First World War. Economic pressure and recently created opportunities brought about by improved education caused women of all ranks of society to seek more vigorously for work outside the home. But women who followed this general trend still saw themselves as typecast in the image of the wife and mother and directed towards an increasingly more precisely defined maternal role.

This norm, however, was affected by the reality of an enormous surplus of women in the Weimar Republic. Around 2 million servicemen had been killed in the Great War. Of these, almost 70% were unmarried, and almost half died between the ages of eighteen and twenty-five.[90] Accordingly there were 2 million more women than men in Germany in 1925 and 1.8 million in 1933. In the twenty to sixty-five age-group the number of women was respectively 1.8 million and 1.7 million greater than that of men.[91] As the population expert F. Burgdörfer formulated it in 1929, that meant 'a more or less unused child-bearing capacity of 1.1 million women arising from the loss of men in the war'.[92] This unequal division of the sexes meant that women had less chance of marrying.

Table 1. *Population by sex and marital status*[93]

		Percentage married	Percentage widowed	Percentage divorced
1925	Women	39.4	8.7	0.6
	Men	42.2	2.9	0.3
1933	Women	42.7	9.0	0.9
	Men	45.1	3.1	0.6

Table 2. *Unmarried age 35 and above*

	Born between 1881 and 1885				Born between 1886 and 1890			
	1925 Number in 000s	%	1933 Number in 000s	%	1925 Number in 000s	%	1933 Number in 000s	%
Women	369	16	293	13	259	12	221	11
Men	219	11	124	6	148	7.5	102	6

The majority of the approximately 15.8 million (1925) and 17.7 million (1933) married, widowed, and divorced women have been mothers. But there was a striking difference between the lives of those who had married long before the war and those who married at its end. A survey conducted in 1939[94] showed that in the case of women married before 1905 with husbands engaged in agriculture, there was still an average of 5.5 births; in those marriages contracted between 1915 and 1919, the figure was 3.6. In the case of wives of workers whose husbands were not engaged in agriculture, the figures were 4.7 and 2.8 respectively. With wives of officials and of salaried employees outside agriculture the figure fell from 3.4 to 2. In large towns the overall average of all births per marriage fell from between 3 and 4 to between 1 and 2. It should be added that it seems probable that not only contraceptive devices were responsible for this successful family planning. Indeed, it is likely that it was chiefly due to abortion. In the middle

1920s there were estimates of some 500,000 abortions a year.[95] In the world depression, very many more women had recourse to this illegal and consequently particularly harmful form of birth control.

Housewives were thus most often working in households which were distinctly smaller because there were both fewer children and fewer domestic servants than in 1910.

Table 3. *Percentage of households of more than one person in Germany*[96]

	2–4 persons	5–7 persons	More than 8 persons
1910	54.6	34.8	10.6
1925	64.2	29.4	6.4
1933	71.8	24.1	4.1

Households in the inter-war years were not only smaller. In large towns at least, they occupied houses and flats equipped with gas, water, and electricity and hence were easier to run.[97] The problem of sufficient living space was of course as acute as ever. The government housing figures for 1927, showing a shortage of 750,000 houses and flats and a further 300,000 unfit for habitation or overcrowded, give an indication of how acute the housing shortage was.[98]

It is quite certain that on the one hand working conditions for women with children had improved. But this observation is deceptive, for on the other hand a glance at the economic suppositions about the work of women and mothers reveals a considerable extent of poverty and need. Mothers with children to care for lived in extremely poor economic conditions if the father left them before the children were capable of earning. In most cases, they had to have an income in addition to their alimony or pension or perhaps even to provide for the whole family. Wages for women were still very low, so that they were seldom able, even by working more than eight hours a day, to keep several people. In order to ensure the survival of their families, they sought help from welfare agencies.[99] Not only very many mothers, but also even mothers who had been brought up to a future as wife and mother in comfortable economic circumstances, found themselves in this precarious position. Unmarried mothers in particular had long had to rely to a very large extent on their own earning power to provide for themselves and their children. In the twenties, the percentage of live-born children of single mothers rose from between 8 and 10 from 1900 to 1914 to between 11 and 12. The absolute number of illegitimate children fell from around 170,000 yearly between 1900 and 1924 to around 150,000 after 1920.[100] It is also very likely that these women lived with the father of their children more frequently than before the war.[101] In each case the group of abandoned and divorced mothers was more numerous. As in earlier years, they experienced great hardship and very often had to rely on relief assistance.[102] But the chief addition to the ranks of these women with no 'breadwinner' was the rapidly increased number of widows from various social strata as a result of the war.[103] In October 1924, there were 366,140 war widows who had not remarried and were entitled to relief. Their total number of children was 963,040. Almost all of them had such a tiny pension that they could not keep their families without a supplementary income. An idea of the size of this group, living in extremely difficult conditions, can be obtained from the 1933 census.[104] There were 2.4 million households whose head was a widowed or divorced woman, and 468,000 of such households included children under sixteen years of age.

Even in 'complete' families, the family income was not provided by the husband's job in almost a third of the cases. In 1925, which was an economically 'good' year, 3.7 million of the 12.7 million married women in the country had full-time non-household occupations. The job figures for 1925 and 1933 showed 29% of married women as being in employment. The proportion of married women amongst female wage-earners as a whole was 32% in 1925 and 36% in 1933.[105] More than half the married women in employment were over forty years of age.[106] These figures include wives working in the small commerical and agricultural concerns of their husbands. The advantage for them was that there was no great distance between their homes and their place of work. For those working for their husbands, the disadvantage was that they were doing so without pay. Of the approximately 850,000 married women working for an outside employer in 1925, around half were employed as industrial workers.[107] Amongst them were some 100,000 women who worked at home or in a small workshop.[108] It can safely be assumed that the 1925 and 1933 statistics do not show all the married women who more or less regularly supplemented their household budgets by their own paid employment.[109]

Married women, and more particularly mothers, who were in paid employment as well as performing their household duties took on the extra burden mostly from necessity and not from inclination.[110] First amongst these were the mothers of the 950,000 children registered in 1924 as of some 721,000 fathers injured in the war and still entitled to a pension and in particular the approximately 235,000 wives of severely-disabled men.[111] These latter could hardly have been in a position to maintain their normal standard of living merely with the pension and wage of the man of the family. The wives of unskilled, semi-skilled, or seasonal workers with more than two children to provide for were also still obliged to take on extra paid work. High unemployment, short-time working, and a level of real wages below that of pre-war years also affected the families of other manual and non-manual workers, however. In times of crisis in the Weimar Republic, families of commercial and agricultural workers were threatened with economic decline, as well as those of officials, whose steady incomes were shrinking both as a result of inflation and of compulsory saving. Inflation wiped out savings and in particular worsened the economic situation of the middle classes. Unemployment, which had been high even before the Great Depression, also largely destroyed the hope that grown-up children would be able to contribute to the family budget. The opposite was the case. Straitened family finances had the additional burden of providing for the needs of such grown-up children.

Wives and mothers had the main responsibility for looking after the family properly with reduced means. Women reacted to this situation by reducing their own consumption in order to maintain that of husbands and children and by working to the limits of endurance and beyond in the attempt to cut costs in the home, to do what was necessary for the children, and to earn more money from their own work whenever the opportunity arose.

In the educated middle classes, conditions in the 1920s meant that more and more wives had to give up the services of domestic and daily staff because of their cost. They now had to do themselves the jobs which previously had been considered degrading and dirty for women of their class. Electrical and other household appliances enabled them to manage these chores. I am not convinced that the introduction of technology into the household was enough of a psychological compensation to make women who since the turn of the century had been better educated more suited to the role of presiding domestic genius. The fact that in the twenties the role of the mother was seen as weightier than that of the housewife and that her responsibility assumed an impressively precise form was probably of considerable help in furthering this aim. For just such families, the notion of the intimacy of the modern family, which had been ideologically propagated for over 150 years, became a broad social reality after the Great War.[112]

In direct opposition to the bourgeois ideal of the family, however, was the fact that in many families the wife was obliged to take paid work to support or replace the husband in his role as breadwinner. For women in the Weimar Republic too, paid employment meant that for wages approaching those of men, a woman had to perform a great deal more. The greatest chances of employment were found in sectors where wages were low, and even there women's pay was at least a third lower than that of men. Married women were even more disadvantaged on the labour market than single adult women, since they were practically and ideologically hampered by what was seen as their natural role of caring for their families.[113] The massive discrimination against married women as 'double earners' used as fuel in the campaign of dismissal during the years of demobilization and the Great Depression did not of course succeed in driving them from the labour market. The campaign was, however, an effective means of ensuring that henceforth married women got the very worst jobs.[114]

The information from readily available statistics is perhaps meagre, but the picture emerging from it is unambiguous. Statistically, just under a third of all married women, and probably even a larger proportion of all women, were totally unable to devote themselves to the elevated role ascribed to them in the Weimar era despite socialist attempts at change, that is, the fulfilment of their obligations as housewives and mothers. Conversely, however, it is just as clear that all of them, including wage-earning mothers and housewives, had made great efforts to attain the standards in their work obligatory since the end of the nineteenth century and to avoid arousing, both within and outside the family, the criticism that they were 'sluts' or 'neglectful mothers'.[115]

The attempts of the social reformers eventually to restore working-class families by means of compulsory domestic training for girls who had left school as soon as they could began in the 1880s but were never entirely implemented. And indeed their practical use for a working-class woman who had learnt to keep a thorough account of all income and expenditure was very limited when she was married and had to manage with a small and varying income.[116] On the other hand, the general spread of hygiene that was encouraged by health policies and eagerly promoted by the soap industry seems to have been generally effective. Fastidious order and cleanliness were the declared means of combating all the carriers of disease that lay unseen in dirt and dust to attack health. This constrained housewives to spend a great deal of time and energy cleaning and washing. Thorough cleaning and wash-days became tyrannous tasks taking several days. The fight against everyday dirt and constant untidiness was all the harder when the number of persons living together was high and the flat or house and its fittings and equipment poor. It is quite clear that the alleviation of housework by technical means followed rather than preceded an increase in the amount of work judged to be appropriate.[117] A further range of jobs that made ever-greater demands on working-class wives was a result of higher standards of clothing and the teaching of needlework in schools. Wives had to make some of the clothes for all members of the family and above all to keep them clean and serviceable. Mothers of economically deprived families were subject, in so far as they made use of them, to the massive social control of the creches and kindergartens and particularly of course of schools with respect ot the care of the bodies and clothes of their children.

The campaign against infant mortality that really began only around the turn of the century brought into focus and increased the further innovation of life-supporting care for infants.[118] Initially aimed chiefly at unmarried mothers and working-class women, infant and child care was quickly institutionalized and directed with ever-increasing vigour towards women from every social stratum. Its aim was to provide education in 'bringing up children on rational principles' and to recruit between 60% and 80% of all infants and mothers shortly after birth by means of advice centres under the supervision of a doctor.[119] The first infant advice centre was opened in Berlin in 1905. There were 73 in 1907, and in 1920 and 1921 alone a further 1,600 were set up.[120] In 1927 specialists in infant care set out as their basic premise that the less care and attention was devoted to mothers, the higher the level of infant mortality would be.[121] Associated regulations for post-natal care provided for the first time facilities for a great number of women to devote themselves to breast feeding and child care immediately after the birth of the baby.[122] The campaign against infant mortality was extremely successful, as Table 4 shows.

Table 4. *Infant mortality in Germany (per 1000 live births)*[123]

	1896–1900	1901–5	1906–10	1911–14	1915–26	1932–4
No. of infant deaths	213	199	174	164	102	75

In the Weimar Republic maternal education was not restricted to child care.[124] Courses and classes for mothers were started in various towns. In one of the announcements sent out by the *Arbeitsgemeinschaft für Volksgesundung* in 1926,[125] it is stated that on these courses 'mothers of all levels of education work together, united in the thought of motherhood, to increase their knowledge of the question of the child and its education'. At the end of the Weimar Republic, welfare organizations in particular had begun to institutionalize education and convalescence for mothers. The Nazi *Reichsmütterdienst*, set up on Mother's Day, 1934,[126] was simply the continuation of these potentially very promising beginnings, which the *Evangelische Frauenhilfe* had already supported with street and door-to-door collections on previous Mother's Days. The *Reichsmütterdienst* ran its operations in 1936 with 150 schools for mothers and numerous touring courses.[127] The educational programme for women over the age of eighteen, who were expected to enrol for a course of instruction of twelve double hours (for which fees were payable) in the local branches of the Nazi women's movement, gave instruction in household economy, health education which included infant care, children's illnesses, eugenics and the upbringing of children, and making a home. The 'vocation' of housewife and mother as it had been called since the beginning of the nineteenth century, now had its own form of vocational education.

In the twenties it was a vocation that was exercised in very different conditions from those obtaining in other fields. In households with low but adequate income from the husband, the associated housework and child care took up on average eighty-seven hours per week. Housewives who had to manage without paid help or the support of an older daughter worked seventy or more hours for their families, with virtually no help from their husbands. Any help they did have came from their children and principally from eldest daughters.[128] Time off during the day, relaxation at weekends, and annual holidays are twentieth-century innovations which at first passed this 'natural vocation' by.

A fascinating empirical investigation of the industrial town of Hamborn, written by Li Fischer-Eckert in 1913, documents the frequently hopelessly heavy labour of the wives of relatively well-paid miners and foundry workers.[129] Four-fifths of the 500 women questioned had been brought up in the country and employed either at home or as domestic servants before marriage. Fischer-Eckert attempted to arrange households into categories.[130] There were 103 in the category 'comfortable home, adequate but no luxury'. In 189 households, there were housewives who 'could only keep their families adequately housed, healthy, clothed, and fed with the very greatest effort'. In a further 58 households there was the desire but not the ability to perform properly as a 'good housewife'. In the opinion of the investigator, the remaining 145 households had 'fallen into complete neglect'. Fischer-Eckert commented on this permanent situation in words which later applied critically to the sacrifices made by mothers which were glorified on Mother's Day: in their case it was clear that:

the labours of Hercules fell onto the weak shoulders of women, with inadequate means of providing for child after child, keeping illness, sickness, and death at bay and ensuring order and cleanliness and at the same time devoting themselves conscientiously to the upbringing of their children . . . But it is not only that physical strength is so often sacrificed to this war of attrition . . . it is just as bad that in this constant concern with the physical needs of the children the whole of the personal life of the mother gradually has to suffer, that she has to learn never to think of herself and finishes up by being a mechanical instrument seen only . . . as a piece of property without rights, both by others and by herself.[131]

There was little mention, and then purely in a negative way, of this reality in Mother's Day propaganda. We read in 1929 that 'Mother's Day is to bring to the attention of all governments, administrations, and employers the plight of poor mothers of large families. Their place is not in factories and offices, but at home.'[132] In the same context was criticized the fact that the German 'home and hearth', as the stage-managers of the German Mother's Day liked to express themselves, was normally an inadequate and very expensive dwelling. They were not, on the whole, concerned with social and political help, but with a national cult of the mother. The Mother's Day programme contained no provisions for improving the living conditions of mothers. It simply proposed compensating them for enduring comparatively poor conditions of living and working by honouring them. Implicit in the programme was the assumption that an annual celebration of social recognition of mothers would ensure their selfless contribution for the future.

In fact, mothers did not withdraw their service to their family when it made excessive demands on them both physically and mentally and could only be performed as a sacrifice. Once women had become mothers, they could hardly resort to strikes. Before then it was possible to some extent for women to refuse their labour with some degree of success. This they could do by deciding for or against marriage with a man claiming domestic labour from them and for or against having children, which would force them into the role of socially defined maternal duties. It was an innovation that women in the twentieth century were beginning to make use of this not particularly wide area of possible decisions, and this clearly caused insecurity and fear in quite a few men. There was no provision in the dominant notions of 'masculinity' for individual and social autonomy for women, and such goals could only be seen by men as an attack on that masculinity. It seems to me that in this respect the organization of Mother's Day has more to say about men than about women in Weimar society.

Mother longing, mother order, Mother's Day

Even in the light of the concrete plight of mothers, of the refusal of maternal obligations and general changes in sexual and family behaviour implicit in the decline in the birthrate, the ideological content and symbolic shaping of Mother's Day are only partly disclosed. It certainly becomes clear that the social agencies committed to Mother's Day wanted to halt the social changes, which were feared as a wrong development, and the general 'crisis in the family', which was seen as imminent or indeed acute. This was based on the correct observation that so far there had been no suitable social appreciation and recognition of their work. But why did they decide on a way of honouring the mothers by a periodic ceremony celebrating her self-sacrifice?

Such an open question calls for further explanation. My starting point here is the observation that men arranged an occasion for mothers in which the latter were not subjects, but objects. Boys, girls, and grown-up sons played the active parts, whilst the husband and father had no visible role on stage. Adult males were relegated to children's parts, and the task of adult females in so far as they were mothers was to endure passively the honours offered them by young and adult children. In this form, honouring the mother became the cult of the mother. A comparison with 'Father's Day', which became widespread under that name in 1930, makes the individual nature of Mother's Day clearer.[133] On that occasion, fathers take leave of their families and go off to demonstrate their freedom by singing and drinking in men's associations along with bachelors.

These observations call for interpretations touching upon both the fields of psychology and the investigation of myths. Simone de Beauvoir's broad cultural and historical panorama of the myth of 'woman' offers an inducement to investigate the motives of the production and the social function of the variation on the Christian mother-myth represented by the example of the Mother's Day material historically specific to Germany in the 1920s.[134] Here I will not take up these questions. I readily accept, however, her postulate that mother-myths are produced by men as an interpretation and shaping of their relationships with the 'second sex', nature, and the environment. She stresses the Christian-patriarchal progressive domestication of the woman as a complete handmaiden of the man that is built into the cult of the Virgin Mary. 'As servant, the woman receives a right to the most glorious apotheosis.'[135]

The usual declarations about the image of the mother formulated for Mother's Day were indubitably part of a mythical orientation, but at the same time an expression of current longings and fears. This connection is of interest to me. Peter Loewenberg's essay, 'The Psychological Origins of the Nazi Youth Cohort',[136] shows how collective life history and general history might be transmitted. His demonstration is interesting but not so convincing that I would wish to imitate it in my investigations of Mother's Day. Loewenberg uses theories from psycho-analysis and developmental psychology which claim to be valid for all times, and he accepts these claims. It seems to me, however, necessary to historicize such theories themselves as they are used on historical materials, since the father/mother–child/children cluster and its significance for the growing child is not a natural but a socially and hence a time and class-bound phenomenon.[137] Consequently there is little point in making use of theories from psycho-analytical and developmental psychology simply as yardsticks and premises in historical analysis. In this respect, the much more cautious method of analysis developed by Klaus Theweleit in his elucidation and interpretation of the Freikorps literature of the twenties as 'male fantasies' seems to me more productive.[138]

My own attempt at interpretation will deal with the more limited question of what is conveyed by the fact that in the twenties men were willing, in their capacity as sons, to pay public homage to 'the' mother. My interest in the phenomenon of the family is both as history and in history. In my attempt to elucidate, I assume that relationships between mothers and sons have a great deal to do with the relationships between men and women. The intention of proceeding from an investigation of the stage-management of Mother's Day to a special investigation of the mother/son relationship could be seen as a conscious preliminary decision. This was forced upon me as I made the observation that but for a few exceptions male children formulated the psychologically positive ideas in the Mother's Day prose and rhymes. The small children who appeared most active on Mother's Day were certainly no more than the messengers of homage sent by adults. Admittedly, in my interpretation the grown daughters were at least in theory equally entitled to be included in the events with the adult sons. After reflecting upon the matter, I would maintain that for the daughters, who were actual or potential mothers, it was necessary to remain at a distance from the manner in which the celebration was staged as a mother cult. Still, women quite clearly helped make Mother's Day popular in their activities in women's associations, social work, schools, and kindergartens. Beyond this surprising confirmation, I have not been able to go, despite further research. Certainly it would be important to find more additional information over which women were active in staging Mother's Day, what reason they had for engaging themselves, and what programmes they developed for the celebration. More informative for its meaning would be to find out how women behaved on the day dedicated to them, which women actively engaged themselves, which ones acted indifferently or decidedly rejected it as unreasonable. These questions cannot be answered on the basis of the material I have examined, which allows only a decoding of the logic of the staging, and this points most clearly to the activities and projections of the grown sons.

In patriarchal families and societies, the mother/son relationship assumes outstanding importance. This assumption would seen to be confirmed in relation to the turn of the century by the fact that Freud attempted to explain the development of the male child within a specifically bourgeois family cluster by means of his theory of the Oedipus complex. The price the son has to pay if he is to achieve identification with his father and subsequently the creation of his own ego and super-ego independent of those of his parents is the suppression of the intense and pleasurable link with his mother. Historically this interpretation is based on sharply defined and radical sexual stereotypes and roles which are valid both inside and outside the family. In Imperial times the model for femininity was 'motherliness', elaborated and expressed in social terms.[139] Its corollary and complement was not however 'fatherliness' but 'manliness'. Sexuality and domesticity were ascribed to the sexes in extremely dissimilar degrees. Consciously conceived education and the power of the *de facto* situation adapted human beings to the appropriate model. The struggle to conform to the norms of adult life of this kind exacted a psychological toll which could still be detected.

An impressive illustration of this situation is provided by the respected educationalist and psychologist Eduard Spranger. He was born in 1882, and in the 1950s was still writing on maternal love and 'motherliness' in the style of the twenties, showing the goal of maternal love directed first towards the child, then to the young boy, and then the 'son, already a grown man'.[140] Without any commentary, Spranger simply relates maternal love to the mother/son relationship. As early as the 1921 edition of his *Lebensformen*, he wrote so matter-of-factly about the son/husband experiences with the mother that it appears that he was able to take the reader's agreement for granted. In it he adds to the 'ideal basic types of individuality' the 'social type', whose 'highest form on earth' he sees as being the mother. In addition to being present in the mother, this type is also chiefly represented, he says, in 'wife', since 'woman lives through love, whereas man's deepest love is for creative achievement'. Man, as a 'nature seeking love' turns, says Spranger, to the mother/wife 'whose nature is love':

it is part of . . . the basic spiritual cast of the male principle in the world (which does not always coincide with the man) that his need to be loved is stronger than his ability to love. The unilateral effect and tense differentiation of his inner being longs as it were to be led back into the undivided maternal womb of life by means of a feminine love.[141]

I suspect that the experiences of the First World War and the post-war period were a strain on and a threat to these men who were so disposed to 'manliness', for on the one hand the 'male principle' of society and with it the binding aims offered for men were called into question, and on the other the way of escape towards wife/mother seemed to be barred by the newly opened chances to women for their legal, social, and economic emancipation. This double threat might well be the background against which the longing for the mother was no longer apparently one which appeared individually tied together with a man's adult role and was therefore publicly stereotyped and stylized as a collective cult of the mother.

Before the First World War, the basically patriarchal structure of society had remained stable despite women's and youth movements and despite cultural criticism. The ideal of manliness adapted to a military form was unambiguous, even when it had to be interpreted in terms of the soldier in uniform or the soldier as hero. George L. Mosse has already pointed out the relationships between the frequent war fever amongst men who, before 1914, were bored with their everyday lives and strove for glory and adventure and the cult of the war dead in the Weimar era.[142] This cult created heroes in an unheroic age in order to counter the lack of direction caused by the fact that the war had been both total and lost. The sacrifice of the life and health of men must not seem to be of no avail in the long run, for a sense of pointlessness unleashed violent energies that endangered more than simply the system of political domination.

The war had developed a dynamism directed against the principle of a masculinity hitherto unchallenged as a socially dominant power. Even before the war the sense of optimism and progress that went with male achievements in technology, economics, and social matters had lost ground to cultural criticism with its nostalgia for the natural. Now, however, the male principle was revealed as super-powerful and merciless destruction. With its unprecedented losses of human life and destruction of material and ideal values, the Great War was seen as an excess of male politics, wars, economy, and technology. But it was not only the male world that was brought into question by total warfare and to an even greater extent by defeat. Men themselves paid for 'manliness'. It was not conquering heroes but men wounded in body and mind who discarded their uniforms. Success meant not being one of the 2 million dead, and dragging around the more than 4.2 million war wounds in civilian life was a form of prosaic bravery.[143]

It was almost certainly all the harder for men to be sure of themselves when they could no longer attract the approval of higher authority for their military discipline and loyalty to the Kaiser. Loewenberg has drawn attention to an article by Paul Federn dating from early 1919.[144] Its subject is a psycho-analytic interpretation of the revolution from the 'fatherless society'. Sons united as subjects of the authoritarian paternal state are described as having lost their sense of security with the loss of the ultimately disappointing father who had been unable to protect the 'motherland' or (which amounted to the same thing) the 'mother'. They now wanted, in the 'fraternity' of the Councils (Räte), to use their own plenary powers to 'love and protect their motherland'.

Men also possibly felt that their new insecurity was threatening, since women had actively managed without men in war conditions.[145] They might therefore seem to be superfluous. It had also been shown that women bound to the idea of 'motherliness' and their children could function as representatives of men in the family and in the social work process. The freeing of 'men's jobs' that was carried out with such severity during the demobilization phase should be seen, along with the campaign against double earnings during the depression as a probable indication of men's sense of their own value.[146] Manliness, which in the twentieth century was defined in terms of competitiveness in the world of work, was, however, still without a firm basis even after freeing of men's jobs, for this basis was transformed by rationalization and threatened by unemployment in the Weimar era. Unlike women, men had no opportunity of defining themselves in relation to their family if they lost their job.[147] It was also not without importance that they saw their place in society as being questioned by the 'new woman'.[148] The prototype new woman was no longer condemned to waiting for marriage and motherhood and hence necessarily dependent on what men expected of her. She was concerned with education, had a job, engaged in public activities, and acknowledged and lived her sexuality. There was little trace in her of anything to arouse the male desire for the sacrificial motherhood of the wife.

The cult of the mother promised to exorcise the double threat contained in this situation. What men hoped for in a mother became the object of a celebration. This hope united the longing to be caught up once more in 'unquestioning maternal love'[149] and the acute desire to escape from a doubtful adulthood. Like the cult of the war dead, the cult of the mother was probably also an attempt to exercise some form of control over these socially incalculable fears and longings felt by men, to concentrate them into a collectively binding form, and make them public. In this way, the cult would become an alternative to the repression of the longing for the mother, which had become ineffective.

Wilhelm Reich has stressed the power of the mother cult as a force for social integration in his *The Mass Psychology of Fascism*.[150] In his view, the Nazis clearly understood how to base policies which would be effective in terms of mass-psychology on a fixated link to the mother, and he sees the 'idealization, the apotheosis of motherhood', as a way of making women appear not as sexual beings but merely as 'child-bearers'. Together with illusions about 'purity', such things were, according to Reich, a clear expression of the sexual repression compulsorily operated in families. The sociologist Harold Laswell has also pointed out that with the cult of the Führer the Nazis not only promised to re-establish a superior paternal authority, but also offered to enthrone motherhood once more.[151]

The intensity with which the theme of the mother was elaborated in the Weimar era supports my hypothesis that the 'fatherless society' of the twenties hoped for an escape into the idea of the mother and feared at the same time the loss of the mother. The reception of Bachofen can be seen as an example of this.[152] The 1920s saw a renewal of interest in his work that was remarkably wide-ranging in its effects. Until the end of the nineteenth century, Bachofen's theories on matriarchy only had been of interest to legal theorists for professional, and to socialists for political, reasons. In the twenties, his works were republished in several part-collections and launched with accompanying interpretations of a social scientific and historical–philosophical nature. Adherents and opponents flocked to these new editions. At that time Alfred Bäumler, along with Ludwig Klages, was a leading interpreter of Bachofen.[153] He saw him as more than simply a high figure of romanticism, and related his discovery of the mother to the present-day situation. From Bäumler, he was both 'a mother's son' and 'the son of the mother', and in his interpretation of maternal rights the 'relationship with the son formed the systematic focus'.[154] In his view, the defeat of the dark forces of motherhood and death achieved by partriarchy was never final,[155] and the present time showed all the characteristics 'of an age when the mother would come into her own', with its decline in morality, its mixing and confusion of the sexes, and despair: 'a glance at our present age clearly and immediately shows the meaning of that which is not contained in institutions. It is an open secret that paternal power, the domination by men, has now been broken, that monogamy and paternal rights are mentioned in law books but have disappeared from life.'[156] Bäumler traced Bachofen's effect back to the 'juxtaposition of the two most powerful emotions that stir the human heart: maternal love and the sense of death'.[157] The mother's lap is mother earth. This ambivalence in the mother/son relationship was to find a more pedestrian expression in the Mother's Day promotional material by Dr Rudolf Knauer of the German Florists' Association.[158] In his first appeal, he not only spoke warmly of the maternal sacrifice but also praised the generosity of mothers who had given their sons for the fatherland.

Bäumler, who had written his introduction to the 1926 edition of Bachofen, with evident fascination, later came down clearly on the side of the renewed victory of the son. In 1943, he extolled Rosenberg's *Mythus*.[159] This writer can be seen as, *inter alia*, the prophet of the movement against matriarchy, turning against the Bachofen glorification of woman and accusing men of 'having been incompletely men' and thus of having produced female emancipation.[160] His *Mythus* is a call to self-conscious 'manliness': 'today, in the midst of the collapse of the feminized older world, German thought demands authority, the power to create types, concentration, discipline, autarchy (independence), the protection of the character of the race, a recognition of the eternal polarity of the sexes.'[161] And yet in the twenties the hope of a complementary maternal world to be confirmed by the ideas of matriarchy seems to have been at least as strong as this call to masculinity. In an 'age of technically civilizing brutality that is probably a denial of life', the mother, as a life-affirming principle, was to show the way to a better future.[162]

'Motherliness' had been the slogan adopted by the middle-class women's movement at the end of the nineteenth century to enhance their demand for equal rights with the altruistic promise that the world would be a better place as a result of the public activities of women who were mothers.[163] The extent to which in the late twenties hopes that a positively valued maternal principle were the basic elements of a future society were widespread can be seen in two particularly extreme views. Erich Fromm,[164] who had made an intensive study of Bachofen as early as 1920, took up the theme once again while he was a member of the Institut für Sozialforschung (Institute for Social Research) with a review of Robert Briffault's *The Mothers* and an essay on the meaning, in terms of social psychology, of the theory of maternal rights. He distinguished between matricentral and patricentral complexes and the differently formed psychic structures present in them at a given time. His long-term hope was that socialism would ensure that the matricentral complex would be socially dominant. In his view, this would mean that there would be an optimistic confidence in conditional maternal love, which in the long run would produce a greater aptitude for enjoyment and happiness, and that 'the maternal qualities of pity and love for the weak and those in need of help' would become the new ideal.[165] The opposite political point of view was expressed by Ernst Bergmann, a professor at Leipzig University. In his book *Erkenntnisgeist und Muttergeist*, published in 1932, he ranged far and wide in history and philosophy and finally urged a new society imbued with the idea of 'the maternal spirit' and the 'ideals of racial hygiene and discipline' as opposed to 'masculinized woman', bolshevism, and socialism, and also to monogamy. According to him, there was 'no notion of salvation that was loftier, more truly in keeping with nature, with religion, or modern biology than the spirit of maternity for the cultural remains of a humanity smitten with madness'.[166] Of however varied a nature the theorizing about 'mother' may have been, the examples indicated make it abundantly clear that after the Great War there was obviously a great willingness to indulge in fantasies centred around the mother. In this respect Mother's Day was obviously more than a peripheral phenomenon of Weimar society; it created a particular connection between the daily lives of mothers and the thought patterns of sons.

The investigations arising from the 'German Mother's Day' have taken me over a great deal of ground. It is not my intention here to summarize what was discovered on the way. I should like instead to draw attention to the perceptive observations of Alice Rühle-Gerstel, whose book *Das Frauenproblem der Gegenwart: Eine psychologische Bilanz* was published in 1932 and banned by the Nazis in 1933. This is what she had to say about Mother's Day:

once a year the German nation honours its mothers. On one day in the year they are drawn into the limelight, praised with publicity, decorated with sentimentality, honoured with verses and extolled with moving pathos . . . Then in the evening they gradually creep back into the modest twilight of their everyday lives, there to carry out their many humble tasks until next year. Back to husbands and children, back to the family.[167]

The picture she draws encompasses the opposition between the falsity of the official celebrations and the work of the mother, which was unnoticed by society since it was performed in private. Rühle-Gerstel stresses that in an atmosphere of male dominance motherhood can never free the female sex from its completely subservient status. Yet the dominant were always trying to 'devalue that which did not belong to themselves'. Hence the work of mothers was seen as a 'sexual characteristic' and not as a social performance. The omnipresent domination existing also in the family, she maintained, forced exclusively altruistic functions onto women as wives and mothers. Their role was to exist for others, not for themselves, and to give up both their individual lives and their personality.[168]

To open up a new perspective on my own attempts to interpret Mother's Day in history, I should finally like to quote Rühle-Gerstel's interpretative juxtaposition of the ideology and the conduct of the mother:

the cult of the mother and the high esteem in which maternal love is held originates in men. Women no doubt also have many ties of gratitude to their mothers, but in fact they have received less from them to be grateful for than sons have, nor have they the prerogative of belonging to the other sex. Objectively, sons have a better right to praise the altruism and self-sacrifice of their mothers, since they have benefited more from them. It is highly fitting that women, and particularly mothers, should be praised by the whole male sex for their qualities of selfless and altruistic devotion. For these qualities form the background against which the higher value of those receiving them stands out more sharply. For the sex which is always obliged to take great pains to seem the stronger sex, it is sweet and reposing to be able to be weak in one situation, and it is with the mother that the strong man can feel weak without demeaning himself. That also explains, however, why as a rule mothers accept their allotted role with enthusiasm: in relation to their children they are strong, and that is not only a source of happiness in and for itself, for it is doubly so when the sex of the child increases such strength. To be strong vis-à-vis the son, authoritative, an ideal, means for a woman to have at least one man under her thumb. That he is content to enjoy this either because he is a child or because as an adult he needs one situation in which he can be weak is what makes this role a satisfactory one. Hence the most dedicated mothers are those women who are oppressed, undervalued, and weakened in all other areas, particularly in marriage. Their value in relation to their sons is a compensation for all the other values of which they have been deprived.[169]

NOTES

1 See H. Harmjanz, E. Rohr (eds.), *Atlas der deutschen Volkskunde*, vol. 1, maps 1–120 (Leipzig, 1937–9). The following are relevant here: Mother's Day 1932, map 33 = indications of the date of introduction; map 34 = extent of participation of occupants.

2 The rise in the number of publications with 'mother' as a main element in the title is graphically illustrated in the key-word lists of the *Deutsches Bücherverzeichnis. Eine Zusammenstellung der im deutschen Buchhandel erschienenen Bücher, Zeitschriften und Landkarten* (Leipzig). See also the bibliographical survey by H. Sveistrup and A. von Zahn-Harnack in *Die Frauenfrage in Deutschland* (Burg b.M., 1934).

3 See G. Bock and B. Duden, 'Arbeit aus Liebe – Liebe als Arbeit. Zur Entstehung der Hausarbeit im Kapitalismus', in *Frauen und Wissenschaft. Beiträge zur Berliner Sommeruniversität für Frauen July 1976* (Berlin, 1977), 118–99; U. Gerhard, *Verhältnisse und Verhinderungen. Frauenarbeit, Familie und Recht der Frauen im 19. Jahrhundert* (Frankfurt, 1979); K. Hausen, 'Die Polarisierung der "Geschlechtscharaktere" – Eine Spiegelung der Dissoziation von Erwerbs-und Familienleben', in W.

Conze (ed.), *Sozialgeschichte der Familie in der Neuzeit Europas. Neue Forschungen* (Stuttgart, 1976), 363–93.

4 See K. Hausen, 'Mutter zwischen Geschäftsinteresse und kultischer Verehrung. Der "Deutsche Muttertag" in der Weimarer Republik', in G. Hauck (ed.), *Sozialgeschichte der Freizeit. Untersuchungen zum Wandel der Alltagskultur in Deutschland* (Wuppertal, 1980), 259–80.

5 See above, pp. 9–27.

6 J. P. Johnson in his 'How Mother Got Her Day', *American Heritage*, 31 (Apr./May 1979), 15–21, is insufficiently far-reaching in his psychological interpretation of Ann Jarvis's motives. For the wider context of the mother cult, see A. Douglas, *The Femininization of American Culture* (New York, 1977). There is a reference to Mother's Day on p. 75.

7 See the older studies of J. Meier, 'Muttertag', *Zeitschrift für Volkskunde*, 46, new series 8 (1936/7), 110–12; E. Strübin, 'Muttertag in der Schweiz', *Archiv für Schweizerische Volkskunde*, 52 (1956), 95–121; L. Weiser-Aall, *ibid.*, 203–13. For France, see M. Peyrant, 'La Fête des Mères', *L'Histoire*, 34 (1981), 90ff.

8 I have made use in the following pages of the *Verbandszeitung Deutscher Blumengeschäftsinhaber* (*VDB*). See in particular *VDB*, 20 Mar. 1923, 67–9; 17 Apr. 1923, 88ff. It is clear that Knauer was often presented to his public as 'Director of Studies', as is shown by a newspaper report in *VDB*, 16 May 1924, 324. He later gave himself the title of 'founder of Mother's Day'. (See R. Knauer, 'Entwicklung des Muttertages', *Völkischer Beobachter*, North German edn, 13/14 May 1934, entertainment supplement.)

9 *VDB*, 25 Jan. 1924, 29.

10 All items from *VDB*, 1923–4.

11 See *VDB*, 23 May 1924, 336.

12 See, e.g. *VDB*, 3 May 1929, 343; 18 Apr. 1930, 142; 3 Apr. and 10 Apr. 1931, 108 and 114ff; 1 Apr. 1932, 1.

13 When Mother's Day was introduced in 1922, the committee of the *VDB* had decided to use the slogan, 'Say it with flowers.' See *VDB*, 23 Sept. 1932, 9ff. For the definition in other branches see *VDB*, 13 Apr. 1928, 349f. and 1 Apr. 1932, 1.

14 See *VDB*, 26 Mar. 1926, 262.

15 Minutes of the committee meeting of the Arbeitsgemeinschaft für Volksgesundung of 6 Apr. 1927; on Knauer's entrance, see minutes of the meeting of 19 Apr. 1926, both in ADW CA 928, vols. 3 and 2 respectively. (For abbreviation see n16.)

16 Items from 'Akten betr. die Arbeitsgemeinschaft für Volksgesundung', in the Archiv des Diakonischen Werkes, Berlin, referred to as ADW CA 928, vols. 1–4; *Tätigkeitsbericht der Arbeitsgemeinschaft für Volksgesundung* for the years 1926–32 printed as vols. 4, 6, 10, 14, 16, 18, 20 of the *Schriften zur Volksgesundung* (Berlin), for 1925 in ADW CA 928, vol. 2; more precise references are given in Hausen, 'Mütter'.

17 Quoted from *Tätigkeitsbericht* (1926), 4.

18 The *Schriften zur Volksgesundung* published by the Arbeitsgemeinschaft are very informative about the ideology involved. See also Hausen, 'Mutter', 259–62.

19 According to ADW CA 928, vol. 2, it was decided to re-establish the Arbeitsgemeinschaft on 30 Mar. 1925. This was done on 11 May. Harmsen had been in office since April. On 4 Apr., Knauer sent his Mother's Day memorandum containing an appeal to Harmsen to the director of the home mission, and on 5 Apr. Harmsen sent it to all members of the major and minor committees of the Arbeitsgemeinschaft.

20 ADW CA 928, vol. 2, *Tätigkeitsbericht* (1925), 3.

21 Minutes of the general meeting of 13 May 1930, 5, in ADW CA 928, vol. 4.

22 *Tätigkeitsbericht* (1928), 18.
23 This material will be cited as follows: vol. 3 (1927), 'Der Deutsche Muttertag'; vol. 5 (1928), 'Der Deutsche Muttertag. Grundlegendes und Erfahrungen im Jahre 1927'; vol. 9 (1929), 'Der Tag der Mutter – Muttertag. Rückschau auf 1928 und Ausblick auf 1929'; vol. 13 (1930), 'Wie feiern wir den Muttertag? Anregungen zur Ausgestaltung des Muttertages auf Grund von Programmen und Berichten über Veranstaltungen im Jahre 1928 und 1929'. Three thousand copies of these volumes, each of some forty pages, were printed. After 1930, details of preparation for Mother's Day were sent out, as an economy measure, only by means of information sheets.
24 See the preliminary guidelines in *VDB*, 1 May 1925, 413.
25 On the Reichsbund der Kinderreichen see Hausen, 'Mütter', 268f.
26 On the Evangelischen Frauenhilfe see Hausen, 'Mütter', 269–76.
27 I wish to thank Doris Kaufmann for this information about the Catholic reaction; see also S. Beissel, *Geschichte der Marienverehrung in der katholischen Kirche seit dem Ende des Mittelalters* (Freiburg, 1910).
28 Around this time national daily newspapers were beginning to mention Mother's Day.
29 M. Sahlins, *Culture and Practical Reason* (Chicago, 1976), 215.
30 See nn8 and 23; and *Frauenhilfe, Monatsblatt für kirchliche Frauen-Gemeindearbeit; Muttertagshefte* of the *Arbeitsbücherei der Frauenhilfe*, vol. 17 (1930), vol. 22 (1931), vol. 25 (1932), vol. 27 (1933), vol. 31 (1934), vol. 34 (1935). As I have quoted extensively from Hausen, 'Mutter', textual examples used here are chiefly from *VDB*.
31 See *VDB*, 20 Mar. 1923, 68; 25 June 1923, 147; 28 Aug. 1924, 477.
32 *VDB*, 5 May 1923, 105 recommends sending out publicity bills with the inscription; 'Honour mother. First German Mother's Day Sunday 13 May 1923. Mother thinks of you always. Think of her on Mother's Day!'
33 Remembrance Day also developed into a profitable occasion for florists.
34 See, for example, *VDB*, 27 June 1924, 378 and 15 July 1927, 528.
35 See *VDB*, 25 May 1923, 122ff.
36 Reprinted in *VDB*, 17 Apr. 1923, 88.
37 *VDB*, 9 May 1924, 311.
38 Vol. 3 (1927), 9.
39 *VDB*, 25 June 1923, 147.
40 *VDB*, 17 Apr. 1923, 88.
41 Vol. 9 (1929), 13.
42 *VDB*, 8 May 1925, 423.
43 *VDB*, 6 May 1927, 359.
44 See I. Weber-Kellermann, *Die deutsche Familie. Versuch einer Sozialgeschichte* (Frankfurt, 1974), 226.
45 *VDB*, 11 May 1928, 415 and 7 May 1926, 367. There are many examples of the symbolism of flowers as the basis for publicity material in this periodical.
46 The 'commandments' were reprinted in every Mother's Day volume published by the Arbeitsgemeinschaft.
47 See n23. The supply of appropriate Mother's Day materials increased rapidly.
48 Vol. 3 (1927), 17; and report on Liegnitz.
49 Report in vol. 3 (1927), 21; see also *VDB*, 6 June 1924, 349.
50 Report in vol. 5 (1928), 19; see also *VDB*, 18 Apr. 1924, 271f, *VDB*, 7 May 1926, 367.
51 *VDB*, 2 May 1930, 161.
52 Vol. 5 (1928), 23.
53 *VDB*, 7 May 1926, 378.

54 *VDB*, 18 Apr. 1924, 171f; 2 May 1930, 161.

55 *VDB*, 25 May 1923, 122.

56 *VDB*, 18 Apr. 1924, 271f.

57 *VDB*, 8 Aug. 1930, 276.

58 *VDB*, 8 Apr. 1927, 293.

59 *VDB*, 6 May 1927, 360 and 4 May 1928, 401.

60 *VDB*, 17 Apr. 1923, 88.

61 *VDB*, 25 Apr. 1924, 280.

62 *VDB*, 9 May 1924, 309.

63 *VDB*, 25 April 1924, 280. There seems no fear of the absurd picture of a mother not being too tired for any further demands after twenty-four hours of self-sacrificing work.

64 Quotations from *VDB*, 25 Apr. 1924, 279; 21 Mar. 1924, 177; 9 May 1924, 310.

65 *VDB*, 22 Apr. 1927, 326.

66 *VDB*, 22 Apr. 1927, 326; 20 Apr. 1928, 366.

67 *VDB*, 3 May 1929, 343.

68 *VDB*, 22 Apr. 1927, 326; 6 May 1927, 359.

69 *VDB*, 25 June 1923, 147.

70 *VDB*, 21 Mar. 1924, 177.

71 Vol. 9 (1929), 18. For what follows, see vol. 9 (1929), 3 and 22; vol. 5 (1928), 5 and 15; *VDB*, 18 Apr. 1924, 271; 29 Apr. 1927, 351.

72 *VDB*, 22 Apr. 1927, 326.

73 Vol. 3 (1927), 7 and 12.

74 *VDB*, 25 Apr. 1924, 281.

75 *VDB*, 6 May 1927, 360.

76 *VDB*, 3 May 1929, 344; the first mention of shop window decorations occurs in *VDB*, 27 Apr. 1928, 380.

77 On the function of such images see R. Firth, *Symbols, Public and Private* (London, 1973), esp. 54–91.

78 In the Third Reich Mother's Day was given the higher status of a national festival. This deserves a separate study.

79 See, for example, A Schreiber (ed.), *Mutterschaft. Ein Sammelwerk über die Probleme des Weibes als Mutter* (Munich, 1912).

80 A good overview of discussion in terms of population policy is given in D. Glass, *Population: Policies and Movements in Europe* (London, 1967).

81 Article 119 of the Weimar constitution provides elucidatory comment here. For example: 'Marriage is the basis of family life and the means of maintaining and increasing the nation under the particular protection of the constitution. It depends on the equality of both sexes [para. 1]. The sanctity, well-being, and social promotion of the family is the responsibility of the state and of local authorities. Large families have a claim to compensatory help [para 2]. Motherhood has a claim on the protection and care of the state [para 3].'

82 On the scope of social-democratic demands, see L. Schroeder, 'Die proletarische Frau als Hausfrau und Mutter', in A. Blos (ed.), *Die Frauenfrage im Lichte des Sozialismus* (Dresden, 1930), 148–82.

83 On programmes related to family policy, see F. Zahn, *Familie und Familienpolitik* (Berlin, 1918); G. Bäumer, *Familienpolitik. Probleme, Ziele, Wege* (Berlin, 1933).

84 The number of persons employed in domestic service fell by some 12% between 1907 and 1925. Of the total of 1.36 million women employed in households in 1925, more than 300,000 were daily cleaning women. Almost 72% of living-in employees lived with people with independent businesses and in most cases probably supported the

wives who were also working. See A. Geyer, 'Die Frau im Beruf', in Blos, *Frauenfrage*, 207–9. According to Coyner (see n88), 303ff, only 5.7% of women working for white collar families and 11.2% for officials had a wage from such work amounting to between 600 and 900 marks.

85 Discussion was concentrated instead on the double burden borne by those women who did paid work as well as working in the family home.

86 See J. E. Knodel, *The Decline of Fertility in Germany, 1871–1939* (Princeton, 1974).

87 See F. Burgdörfer, *Der Geburtenrückgang und seine Bekämpfung* (Berlin, 1929); H. Harmsen, *Geburtenregelung. Das Europäische Bevölkerungsproblem* (Berlin, 1927) (=vol. 7 of the *Schriften zur Volksgesundung*).

88 See for example the evaluation of household accounts provided by the Statistisches Reichsamt for the families of 896 manual workers, 546 salaried employees, and 498 officials for 1927–8 carried out by S. J. Coyner, 'Class Patterns of Family Income and Expenditure during the Weimar Republic: German White-Collar Workers as Harbingers of Modern Society', PhD thesis (Rutgers University, 1975). The form of my questions owes much to T. Mason, 'Zur Lage der Frauen in Deutschland 1930 bis 1940. Wohlfahrt, Arbeit und Familie', *Gesellschaft. Beiträge zur Marxischen Theorie*, vol. 6 (Frankfurt, 1976), 118–93, esp. 121–8 and 134–9.

89 These ideas had been an integral part of the middle-class women's movement and clearly too of the denominational women's organizations since the late nineteenth century.

90 See *Wirtschaft und Statistik*, 2 (1922), 386; *Statistisches Jahrbuch*, 44 (1924/5), 24–7.

91 Derived from D. Petzina, *et al.*, *Sozialgeschichtliches Arbeitsbuch*, vol. 3, 'Materialien zur Statistik des Deutschen Reiches 1914–1945' (Munich, 1978), 28.

92 Burgdörfer, *Geburtenrückgang*, 47.

93 Table 1 is based on information from the Statistiches Bundesamt (ed.), *Bevölkerung und Wirtschaft. Langfristige Reihen 1871–1957 für das Deutsche Reich und die Bundesrepublik* (Stuttgart, 1958), 15. Table 2 is based on information from *Statistik des deutschen Reiches*, 401 (Berlin, 1930), 171ff and *Statistisches Jahrbuch für das deutsche Reich*, 54 (Berlin, 1935), 12.

94 See Knodel, *Decline of Fertility*, 121. Coyner, 'Class Patterns of Family Income', 189, found three or more children in only 26% of manual workers' families, 12% of salaried employees' families and 16% of officials' families.

95 Estimates in J. Wolf, *Die neue Sexualmoral und das Geburtenproblem unserer Tage* (Jena, 1928), 70–5. See also Glass, *Population*, 311–13. In 1926 an amendment to para. 218 had reduced the maximum penalty for abortion, previously one of penal servitude, to imprisonment. A broadly based campaign in 1931 for the suppression of para. 218 met with no success. See A. Grossman, 'German Abortion Campaign 1931', *New German Critique* (Autumn 1978).

96 *Statistiches Jahrbuch*, 55 (1936), 34.

97 See Coyner, 'Class Patterns of Family Income', 293ff.

98 See Schroeder, 'Die proletarische Frau', 176; L. Preller, *Sozialpolitik in der Weimarer Republik* (Düsseldorf, 1978), 483.

99 See for example E. Lüdy, *Erwerbstätige Mütter in vaterlosen Familien* (Berlin, 1932), a contemporary investigation of the situation of 184 unsupported mothers in Berlin.

100 *Bevölkerung und Wirtschaft*, 20.

101 Pension claims and job problems were new reasons why in the 1920s women insisted on a formal dissolution of marriage. See, amongst others, H. Harmsen, *Der Einfluß der versorgungsgesetzlichen Regelung auf die wirtschaftliche und soziale Lage der Kriegerwitwen. Eine soziologische und bevölkerungspolitische Beurteilung und Kritik unserer heutigen Versorgungsgesetzgebung* (Berlin, 1926). (=*Veröffentlichungen auf dem Gebiete der Medizinalverwaltung*, vol. 22, no.5.)

102 *Bevölkerung und Wirtschaft*, 23.
103 *Wirtschaft und Statistik*, 5 (1925), 29f. The first official census took place in October 1924. The position of wives drawing a pension from insurance for accidents and illness of their husbands was even worse than that of war widows. See Schroeder, 'Die proletarische Frau', 174. See also H. Hurwitz-Stranz, *Kriegerwitwen gestalten ihr Schicksal. Lebenskämpfe der Kriegerwitwen nach eigenen Darstellungen* (Berlin, 1931).
104 See *Statistisches Jahrbuch*, 55 (1936), 31.
105 On employment, see, in addition to Geyer, 'Die Frau im Beruf', and Mason, 'Zur Lage der Frauen', S. Bajohr, *Die Hälfte der Fabrik. Geschichte der Frauenarbeit in Deutschland 1914 bis 1945* (Marburg, 1979); R. Bridenthal, 'Beyond Kinder, Kirche, Küche: Weimar Women at Work', *Central European History*, 6 (1973), 148–66; see esp. Bajohr, *Hälfte der Fabrik*, 25. Coyner, 'Class Patterns of Family income', 215, establishes that women with their own incomes were to be found in 45.9% of the families of manual workers, in 14.7% of the families of salaried employees and officials. There were none in the latter category when there were children, whereas in the families of manual workers with children the figure was 32%.
106 *Bevölkerung und Wirtschaft*, 33.
107 Calculated by Geyer, 'Die Frau im Beruf', 214; see also 214–27.
108 See Bajohr, *Hälfte der Fabrik*, 214ff.
109 I have in mind modest work at home, casual work, and particularly sub-letting. On this last item, see Coyner, 'Class Patterns of Family Income', 238: 13.2% of families of manual workers, 10.6% of those of salaried employees and 9.6% of those of officials in her sample had sub-tenants.
110 According to Geyer, 'Die Frau im Beruf', 213. She bases her ideas on a questionnaire used in the industrial survey of 1927 and on pp.190–5 interprets the results of her own enquiries in late autumn 1928. See also Deutscher Textilarbeiterverband (ed.), *Mein Arbeitstag. Mein Wochenende* (150 reports by women textile workers) (Berlin, 1930).
111 *Wirtschaft und Statistik*, 5 (1925), 29ff.
112 By this is meant the reduction of households to the nuclear family and the increasingly common assumption of personal responsibility of the wife for household and children.
113 According to Bajohr, *Hälfte der Fabrik*, 46 and 56, in industry women's wages were around 25–40% less than those of men. In agriculture they were some 20–55% lower. For individual branches see pp. 28–70.
114 On 'double-earner' discrimination during the demobilization period and during the world slump, see Bajohr, *Hälfte der Fabrik*, 158–67 and 180–8. On the discrimination against married women in unemployment benefits, see pp.174–7. On the ideological context, see also Mason, 'Zur Lage der Frauen', 136–9. Geyer, 'Die Frau im Beruf', 213, calculates that at most only 200,000 of the jobs held by married women would have been worth taking by men.
115 This is impressively documented in Deutscher Textilarbeiterverband, *Mein Arbeitstag*.
116 On instruction in domestic science, see G. Tornieporth, *Studien zur Frauenbildung* (Weinheim, 1979).
117 The history of the provision of running water, gas, and electricity, like that of the introduction of technical household appliances into most homes, has still to be written.
118 See for example G. Tugendreich, *Die Mutter- und Säuglingsfürsorge* (Stuttgart, 1910).
119 See S. Engel and H. Behrendt, in A. Gottstein, *et al.* (eds.), *Handbuch der sozialen Hygiene und Gesundheitsfürsorge*, 4 (Berlin, 1927), 90.

120 *Ibid.*, 33 and F. Rott, *Handbuch der Mutter-, Säuglings-und Kleinkinderfürsorge*, vol. 2, *Verzeichnis der Einrichtungen der Mutter-, Säuglings- und Kleinkinderfürsorge im Deutschen Reich* (Berlin, 1925), iv.
121 Engel and Behrendt, in *Handbuch*, 42f.
122 See for example Schroeder, 'Die proletarische Frau', 168–70.
123 Knodel, *Decline of Fertility*, 289.
124 It would be interesting to investigate travelling exhibitions on popular health, which were obviously quite frequent events. See, for example, *Mutter und Kind. Wanderausstellung mit einer Abteilung Erbkunde des Deutschen Guttemplerordens Berlin. Führer durch die Ausstellung* (Berlin, 1927).
125 ADW CA 928, vol. 2, 8/1.
126 See C. Kirpatrick, *Nazi Germany: Its Women and Family Life* (New York, 1938), 73–8; informative too are E. Trode and E. Liebetruth, *Die Mutterschaftshilfe in Deutschland* (Berlin, 1937); J. Stephenson, *Women in Nazi Society* (London, 1975), 37–56; Mason, 'Zur Lage der Frauen', 139–49.
127 See, for example, K. Schloßmann-Lönnies, *Von den gesetzlichen Grundlagen für die Muttererholungsfürsorge und Mutterschulung* (Potsdam, 1930) (= *Arbeitsbücherei der Frauenhilfe*, vol. 18.); Hausen, 'Mutter', 270.
128 See M. Baum and A. Westerkamp, *Rhythmus des Familienlebens. Das von einer Familie täglich zu leistende Arbeitspensum* (Berlin, 1931).
129 L. Fischer-Eckert, *Die wirtschaftliche und soziale Lage der Frauen in dem modernen Industrieort Hamborn im Rheinland* (Hagen, 1913).
130 *Ibid.*, 78f.
131 *Ibid.*, 68 and 90.
132 *Schriften zur Volksgesundung*, 9 (1929), 17.
133 There is a discussion of Father's Day in *VDB*, 1 May 1931, 141 and 25 May 1934, 3; see also *Tätigkeitsbericht* (1932), 5.
134 S. de Beauvoir, *Das andere Geschlecht* (Reinbek, 1968), 152–205.
135 *Ibid.*, 182.
136 P. Loewenberg, 'The Psychological Origins of the Nazi Youth Cohort', in *The American Historical Review*, 76 (1971), 1457–1502.
137 For this, see M. Poster, *Critical Theory of the Family* (New York, 1978).
138 K. Theweleit, *Männerphantasien*, 2 vols. (Reinbek, 1980).
139 See, for example, E. Key, 'Mütterlichkeit', in Schreiber, *Mutterschaft*, 587–601, who sketches in the 'modern' cultural programme for 'motherliness' and leaves the reader with this promise: 'Motherliness will teach the mother how to remain a Madonna, the mother with her own child safe in her arms as shown by charity and art: the mother whose full breasts are also there for the lips of the child who is not her own'.
140 E. Spranger, 'Mutterliebe' (lecture), and also his 'Mütterlichkeit', in A. Fechner-Mahn (ed.), *Eduard Spranger. Stufen der Liebe. Über Wesen und Kulturaufgabe der Frau. Aufsätze und Vorträge* (Tübingen, 1960), 113–47 and 177–82, here p.129.
141 Quotation from third edition (Halle, 1932), 182. This quotation does not appear in the abridged edition of the *Lebensformen* which appeared in 1914 in the *Festschrift für Alois Riehl*.
142 G. L. Mosse, 'Soldatenfriedhöfe und nationale Wiedergeburt. Der Gefallenenkult in Deutschland', in K. Vondung (ed.), *Kriegserlebnis. Der Erste Weltkrieg in der literarischen Gestaltung und symbolischen Deutung der Nationen* (Göttingen, 1980), 241–61; see also K. Vondung, 'Einleitung. Propaganda und Sinndeutung', *ibid.*, 11–37.
143 See *Statistisches Jahrbuch*, 44 (1924/5), 24–7.
144 P. Federn, *Zur Psychologie der Revolution. Die vaterlose Gesellschaft* (Nach

Vorträgen in der Wiener Psychoanalytischen Vereinigung und im Monistenbund) (Leipzig, Vienna, 1919), p. 29.

145 See Ch. Lorenz, 'Die gewerbliche Frauenarbeit während des Krieges', in J. T. Shotwell (ed.), *Der Krieg und die Arbeitsverhältnisse* (Stuttgart, 1928), 319–89; and Bajohr, *Hälfte der Fabrik*, 101–58.

146 See Mason, 'Zur Lage der Frauen', 130–9.

147 This is impressively covered in M. Johada, P. F. Lazarsfeld, and H. Zeisel, *Die Arbeitslosen von Marienthal. Ein soziographischer Versuch* (1933) (Frankfurt, 1975).

148 See, for example, the account given by Wolf, *Die neue Sexualmoral*, 66f, of women in the modern United States who risked the happiness of marriage, husband, and children for the sake of their own aims. There is an excessively systematic anti-feminism in E. F. Eberhard, *Feminismus und Kulturuntergang. Die erotischen Grundlagen der Frauenemanzipation*, 1st edn (Vienna, 1924).

149 The concept comes from E. Fromm, *Die Kunst des Liebens* (1956) (Berlin, 1965), 64; for further differentiation between paternal and maternal love, see pp. 64–7 and 72–7.

150 W. Reich, *Massenpsychologie des Faschismus. Zur Sexualökonomie der politischen Reaktion und zur Proletarischen Sexualpolitik* (Copenhagen, Prague, Zürich, 1933), 156.

151 H. D. Laswell, *The Psychology of Hitlerism as a Response of the Lower Middle Classes to Continuing Insecurity* (1933), quoted in Loewenberg, 'Psychological Origins', 1485. An impressive example of the Nazi cult of the mother is *Mutter. Ein Buch der Liebe und der Heimat für alle* (Berlin, 1934; Verlag Mutter und Volk).

152 For a good overview see H. J. Heinrichs (ed.), *Materialien zu Bachofens 'Das Mutterrecht'* (Frankfurt, 1975). It contains an introduction and a selection of essays on Bachofen.

153 A. Bäumler, 'Bachofen. Der Mythologe der Romantik', the introduction to M. Schroeter (ed.), *Der Mythos von Orient und Occident. Eine Metaphysik der Alten Welt. Aus den Werken von J. J. Bachofen* (Munich, 1926), i–cclxxxiv.

154 *Ibid.*, cclxxxviii.

155 *Ibid.*, ccxciv.

156 *Ibid.*, ccxci and ccxcii.

157 *Ibid.*, ccxiif.

158 *VDB*, 17 Apr. 1923, 88, and 8 May 1925, 423.

159 A. Bäumler, *Alfred Rosenberg und der Mythus des 20. Jahrhunderts* (Munich, 1943).

160 A. Rosenberg, *der Mythus des 20. Jahrhunderts*, 8th edn (Munich, 1933), 507.

161 *Ibid.*, 504; see also 38ff. for his disagreement with Bachofen.

162 W. Deubel, 'Der Kampf um Johann Jakob Bachofen', *Preußische Jahrbücher*, 209 (1927), 66–75, esp. 66.

163 See, for example, G. Bäumer, *Die Frau in der Krisis der Kultur*, 2nd edn (Berlin, 1927), esp. 37–9; similar to this Mina Weber, *Aufstieg durch die Frau* (Freiburg, 1933).

164 E. Fromm, *Gesamtausgabe*, vol. 1, *Analytische Sozialpsychologie* (Stuttgart, 1980). 'Einleitung', xiii, 'Robert Briffaults Werk über das Mutterrecht (1933) 79–84, and 'Die sozialpsychologische Bedeutung der Mutterrechtstheorie (1934)', 85–109.

165 Fromm, 'Sozialpsychologische Bedeutung', 104.

166 E. Bergmann, *Erkenntnisgeist und Muttergeist. Zur Soziosophie der Geschlechter* (Breslau, 1932), 448.

167 The book was republished with a new title, *Die Frau und der Kapitalismus* (Frankfurt, 1972), p. 28.

168 Bergmann, *Erkenntnisgeist*, 31, 32, 140, 184, 243.

169 *Ibid.*, 243f.

Index

415